FIELDING'S Benelux

HOLLAND
BELGIUM
LUXEMBOURG

1993

Current Fielding Titles

FIELDING'S ALPINE EUROPE 1993
FIELDING'S AUSTRALIA 1993
FIELDING'S BENELUX 1993
FIELDING'S BERMUDA AND THE BAHAMAS 1993
FIELDING'S BRAZIL 1993
FIELDING'S BRITAIN 1993
FIELDING'S BUDGET EUROPE 1993
FIELDING'S CARIBBEAN 1993
FIELDING'S EUROPE 1993
FIELDING'S FRANCE 1993
FIELDING'S HAWAII 1993
FIELDING'S ITALY 1993
FIELDING'S MEXICO 1993
FIELDING'S NEW ZEALAND 1993
FIELDING'S PEOPLE'S REPUBLIC OF CHINA 1993
FIELDING'S SCANDINAVIA 1993
FIELDING'S SELECTIVE SHOPPING GUIDE TO EUROPE

FIELDING'S THE GREAT SIGHTS OF EUROPE
FIELDING'S WORLDWIDE CRUISES 6th revised edition
FIELDING'S ALASKA AND THE YUKON
FIELDING'S BUDGET ASIA Southeast Asia and the Far East
FIELDING'S CALIFORNIA
FIELDING'S FAMILY VACATIONS USA
FIELDING'S FAR EAST 2nd revised edition
FIELDING'S HAVENS AND HIDEAWAYS USA
FIELDING'S LEWIS AND CLARK TRAIL
FIELDING'S LITERARY AFRICA
FIELDING'S SPANISH TRAILS IN THE SOUTHWEST
FIELDING'S TRAVELER'S MEDICAL COMPANION

FIELDING'S

Benelux

HOLLAND
BELGIUM
LUXEMBOURG

1 9 9 3

by
H. CONSTANCE **HILL**

FIELDING TRAVEL BOOKS
℅ WILLIAM MORROW & COMPANY, INC.
1350 Avenue of the Americas, New York, N.Y. 10019

For my mother and my father

Every perfect traveler creates the country where he travels.
．．．．Nikos Kazantzakis

Copyright © 1992, 1993 by H. Constance Hill

All rights reserved. No part of this book may be reproduced or utilized in any form or by any means, electronic or mechanical, including photocopying, recording or by any information storage and retrieval system, without permission in writing from the Publisher. Inquiries should be addressed to William Morrow and Company, Inc., 1350 Avenue of the Americas, New York, N.Y. 10019.

Recognizing the importance of what has been written, it is the policy of William Morrow and Company Inc., and its imprints and affiliates to have the books we publish printed on acid-free paper, and we exert our best efforts to that end.

ISBN: 0-688-11878-X

Printed in the United States of America

Second Edition

1 2 3 4 5 6 7 8 9 10

Text design by Marsha Cohen/Parallelogram

All maps by Mark Stein Studios

ZEELAND
Western Schelde
Zeebrugge
Ostend
Bruges
EAST FLANDERS
WEST FLANDERS
Ghent
Schelde R.
Antwerp
ANTWERP
Mechelen
Eindhoven
LIMBURG
Maas River
Dusseldorf
GERMANY
Cologne
BELGIUM
Ieper
Brussels
BRABANT
Waterloo
LIMBURG
Hasselt
Maastricht
Aachen
Lille
Tournai
HAINAUT
Mons
Liege
LIEGE
Meuse River
Namur
Spa
NAMUR
Dinant
Ourthe River
ARDENNES
Clervaux
Bastogne
Meuse R.
Wiltz
Vianden
Mosel R.
LUXEMBOURG
FRANCE
Echternach
Bouillon
LUXEMBOURG
Trier
Semois River
Luxembourg
Moselle R.

ABOUT THE AUTHOR

H. Constance Hill is a freelance writer whose work has taken her to six continents, of which *the* Continent is a favorite. She has lived in Holland and brings experiences from twenty-five years of travel to and through the Benelux to this book. Her articles appear in a variety of newspapers and periodicals in the United States and Canada. When not in the Benelux, or on another travel beat, she lives in Boston.

CONTENTS

INTRODUCTION · · · **1**
  A Visitor's Overview of the Benelux / **2**
  How to Use This Guide / **4**
  Prices / **6**
    Restaurant Price Categories / **7**
    Hotel Price Categories / **7**
  Hotel Ratings / **8**

PRACTICAL TRAVEL INFORMATION · · · **10**
Planning Your Trip / **10**
  When to Travel / **10**
  Weather / **11**
  Time / **13**
  Seasons, Celebrations, and Ceremonies / **14**
  What To Bring / **17**
  Planning Aids / **19**
  Documents / **21**
  Health Tips / **22**
  Money / **23**
  Hotels / **25**
  Restaurants / **25**
  Film / **26**
  Language / **26**
  Personal Security / **28**
  Emergencies / **28**
  Embassies/Consulates / **28**
  Postal/Telephone/Telegram/Fax / **29**
  Duty Free / **30**
  Customs / **30**
Transportation / **31**
  Air / **31**
  Rail / **32**
  Ferry / **33**
  Bicycle / **33**
  Bus / **34**
  Car Driving Aids / **34**
Travelling in the Benelux / **37**
  Nightseeing or Illuminations / **37**
  Museums / **38**
  Metric Weights and Measures / **38**
  Electric Current / **39**
  Smoking / **40**
  Tipping, VAT / **40**
  News and Newspapers / **41**
  Business/Shopping Hours / **41**
  Miscellaneous / **41**

THE BENELUX CULTURAL LEGACY · · · **43**
  Art / **43**
  Architecture / **56**
  Decorative Arts and Traditional Crafts / **64**
  Music / **71**
  The Muse / **77**

FOOD AND DRINK · · · **84**
Food / **84**
  Indonesian Food / **87**
Drink / **89**
  Belgian Beer / **89**
  Luxembourg Wine / **92**
  Dutch Spirits / **94**

THE BULB FIELD BUSINESS · · · **95**

THE BELL EPOCH: CENTURIES OF CARILLONS · · · 102

HOLLAND · · · 112
Introduction / 112
- The Dutch Landscape / 112
- Map / 114
- The Dutch People / 117
- An Historical Perspective / 119
- Keys to the Kingdom / 122

Randstad Holland: An Introduction / 126

Amsterdam / 128
- Guidelines / 128
- Map / 130
- Amsterdam in Context / 133
- What to See and Do / 139
- Shopping / 150
- Accommodations / 152
- Restaurants / 160
- Entertainment and Events / 165
- In the Area / 166
  - Aalsmeer / 166
  - Zaanse Schans / 167
  - Alkmaar Cheese Market / 167

Haarlem / 169
- Guidelines / 169
- Haarlem in Context / 170
- What to See and Do / 175
- Accommodations / 178
- Restaurants / 178
- In the Area / 179
  - Spaarndam / 179
  - Cruquius Museum / 180
  - IJmuiden / 180
  - Franz Roozen Bulb Growers / 181
  - Zandvoort / 181

Leiden / 182
- Guidelines / 182
- Leiden in Context / 183
- What to See and Do / 191
- Accommodations / 193
- Restaurants / 194

The Hague / 195
- Guidelines / 195
- Map / 198
- The Hague in Context / 198
- What to See and Do / 203
- Shopping / 210
- Accommodations / 211
- Restaurants / 214
- Entertainment and Events / 216

Delft / 217
- Guidelines / 217
- Delft in Context / 218
- What to See and Do / 225
- Shopping / 228
- Accommodations / 229
- Restaurants / 230

Rotterdam / 231
- Guidelines / 231
- Rotterdam in Context / 234
- What to See and Do / 238
- Accommodations / 243
- Restaurants / 245
- In the Area / 247
  - Kinderdijk / 247
  - Dordrecht / 247

Gouda / 248
- Guidelines / 248
- Gouda in Context / 250
- What to See and Do / 251
- Shopping / 253
- In the Area / 254
  - Oudewater / 254
  - Schoonhoven / 257

Utrecht / 258
- Guidelines / 258
- Utrecht in Context / 260
- What to See and Do / 262
- Accommodations / 266
- Restaurants / 267
- In the Area / 268
  - Slot Zuylen / 268
  - Kasteel De Haar / 268
  - River Vecht / 269

Northern Holland / 270
Old Zuiderzee Villages and the New Polder Province / 272
  Guidelines / 273
  The Route / 274
  On the Road / 275
Central Holland / 293
  Guidelines / 294
Arnhem / 296
Apeldoorn / 300
Amersfoort / 304
Southern Holland / 309
Zeeland / 310
  Guidelines / 312
  On the Road / 314
North Brabant / 322
  Guidelines / 323
  On the Road / 325
Limburg Province / 331
Maastricht / 332
  Guidelines / 332
  Maastricht in Context / 335
  Accommodations / 342
  Restaurants / 343
  In the Area / 345
    Southern Limburg Province / 345

BELGIUM · · · 356
Introduction / 356
  The Belgian Landscape / 356
  Map / 357
  The Belgian People / 358
  Map: Belgium's Language Frontier / 359
  An Historical Perspective / 364
  Keys to the Kingdom / 375
Brussels / 380
  Guidelines / 380
  Map / 382
  Brussels in Context / 384
  What to See and Do / 392
  Shopping / 408
  Accommodations / 409
  Restaurants / 416
  Entertainment and Events / 420
  In the Area / 422
    Waterloo / 422
Flanders: An Introduction / 426
Antwerp / 434
  Guidelines / 434
  Map / 435
  Antwerp in Context / 437
  What to See and Do / 445
  Accommodations / 458
  Restaurants / 461
  Entertainment and Events / 463
  In the Area / 465
    Middelheim Open-Air Sculpture Museum / 465
    Cogels-Oyslei / 465
    Mechelen / 466
Bruges / 467
  Guidelines / 467
  Map / 469
  Bruges in Context / 471
  What to See and Do / 479
  Shopping / 488
  Accommodations / 489
  Restaurants / 493
  Entertainment and Events / 495
  In the Area / 496
    Damme / 496
Ghent / 496
  Guidelines / 496
  Ghent in Context / 498
  What to See and Do / 503
  Accommodations / 511
  Restaurants / 511
Belgian Coast / 514
  Guidelines / 514
  On the Road / 516
  In the Area / 522
    Ypres / 522
Wallonia: An Introduction / 525
Tournai / 529
  Guidelines / 529
  Tournai in Context / 531
  What to See and Do / 536
  Accommodations / 539

Restaurants / **540**
In the Area / **541**
Beloeil Castle / **541**
Liège / 544
Guidelines / **544**
Liège in Context / **544**
What to See and Do / **549**
Accommodations / **554**
Restaurants / **555**
The Meuse Valley / 556
Guidelines / **557**
On the Road / **558**
The Ardennes / 566
Guidelines / **567**
On the Road / **568**

THE GRAND DUCHY OF LUXEMBOURG · · · 588
Introduction / 588
The Luxembourg Landscape / **588**
Map / **589**
The Luxembourg People / **591**
An Historical Perspective / **593**
Keys to the Grand Duchy / **602**
Luxembourg City / 607
Guidelines / **607**
Map / **609**
Luxembourg City in Context / **611**
What to See and Do / **615**
Shopping / **621**
Accommodations / **621**
Restaurants / **624**
Entertainment and Events / **626**
In the Area / **626**
Luxembourg American Cemetery at Hamm / **626**
Grand Tour of the Grand Duchy / 628
Guidelines / **628**
The Route / **630**
On the Road / **630**

BENELUX BIBLIOGRAPHY · · · 641

BENELUX LEXICON · · · 644

HOTEL QUICK-REFERENCE TABLES · · · 649

INDEX · · · 657

INTRODUCTION

Though little used beyond the borders of its member countries anymore, the name BENELUX—an acronym for *BE*lgium, the *NE*therlands, and *LUX*embourg—remains a convenient cognomen to refer to the three small but significant European constitutional kingdoms about which this book is written. In size, the Netherlands (Holland) about equals that of the U.S. states of Massachusetts, Connecticut, and Rhode Island combined. Belgium is the same minus Rhode Island, and the Grand Duchy of Luxembourg is smaller than Rhode Island. Put in Canadian terms, the Benelux trio together is between the provinces of Nova Scotia and New Brunswick in size. Undoubtedly, the slightness of their geographic stature has contributed to the fact that Holland, Belgium, and Luxembourg are less well known to foreigners than some other European entities. But, although counted among the Continent's smallest countries, the Benelux, in many spheres, and over many centuries including the present, have exerted an influence within the world well out of proportion to their size.

For fully two millenia, since Roman days, the region that today comprises the physically petite political states of Holland, Belgium, and Luxembourg, has been in the mainstream of European culture and history. History could hardly have produced a different result: The flat barrier-less landscape in Holland and Belgium's Flanders, and the continental crossroads location of all three Benelux countries, virtually invited vying empire builders from Spain, France, Austria, and Germany. Politically, self-definition was—and in some regions remains—difficult for Holland, Belgium, and Luxembourg. The name *Nederland* (Netherlands, or Low Countries), which first appeared in the 11th century, until the end of the 18th century included present-day Belgium as well as Holland. (Today, the Netherlands is the formal, technically-correct name for Holland alone.) During different periods, Luxembourg has been annexed by both Holland and Belgium. With their complicated interconnected history and inter-related rulers and royal families past and present, there are many reasons why it is appropriate that these three countries should be covered together in this book, and why they are well served under the name Benelux.

The term BENELUX came into being in 1948, when Belgium, the Netherlands, and Luxembourg, a trio of troubled economies that had been despoiled during Nazi occupation in World War II, devised a formal association to simplify and stimulate trade amongst themselves. Building on a bilateral agreement begun between Belgium and Luxembourg in 1921, the Benelux was established "with the objective of bringing about total economic integration by ensuring free circulation of persons, goods, capital, and services, and by following a coordinated policy in the cconomic, financial, and social fields; and by pursuing a common policy with regard to foreign trade." If that mandate sounds more than a little like the European Community (EC) "single market" economic initiative, it's not surprising. The Benelux union served as a forerunner of the Common Market and, since the EC's founding (1967), Benelux countries have hosted its headquarters in the Belgian capital of Brussels, and other important EC institutions in the Grand Duchy's Luxembourg City. The implementation of the legacy of law established by the end of 1992 to ensure the complete economic integration of the 12 member nations of the European Community is expected to bring about a new standard of stability and prosperity for Europe. And this remarkable undertaking is simply an enlarged view of the vision that gave birth to the BENELUX.

A Visitor's Overview of the Benelux

The pint-size proportions of the Benelux tourism triumverate offer the advantage of short distances to trek. Due to the particular pattern of Europe's early economic and cultural development, the Benelux boasts an array of remarkable and significant sights situated conveniently close to one another. As well as being packed with appealing people, the Benelux also boasts a concentration of transportation connections: Holland has the world's densest rail network, Belgium the densest road network. The majority of destinations of major interest to travelers in Holland are within an hour of each other by train, and many can be reached in 15 minutes. A similar rail situation exists within Belgium. All three Benelux countries have excellent roads and signage, and plenty of rural landscape to explore.

The small sizes of Holland, Belgium, and Luxembourg have been instrumental in accommodating travelers in another way. Centuries of seafaring and cross-continental trade led citizens (especially those who spoke Dutch, which has never been spoken as a first language by more than a limited number of people worldwide) to learn other languages, in the belief that it was they from the small Benelux countries who needed to reach out to foreign trading partners and travelers. It's a skill they practice still, and we visitors with less-than-proficient foreign languages benefit enormously from it. In the Benelux, most citizens seem to enjoy, rather than resent, the opportunity to use their English. The barrier to the knowledge of other cultures that foreign language can create for travelers has been broken down; because of the widespread local use of English in the Benelux, a cross-cultural exchange of information is fostered. Since one of the primary pleasures of travel is meeting and speaking with people locally, we can be grateful to those in Holland, Belgium, and Luxembourg for making it possible for us—through *their* command of English—to reach beneath the facade of foreignness and learn about their history, humor, and humanity.

Essentially, two languages make do for the three countries, but one of the three needs both of the two to make sense of itself. That one is Belgium, which has a legally defined language "frontier" that cuts the country right through the middle west to east (Dutch/Flemish to the north, French Walloon to the south). Although the important rivers of the region don't form the most significant political boundaries, those that converge at Rotterdam—the Maas (Meuse), Rhine and Waal—referred to in the expression "below the Moerdijk," delineate a distinct difference in "mentality" between the Dutch in the north and the Dutch in the south of the Netherlands.

Benelux countries are comfortable to travel in because of their universal cleanliness (Dutch shopkeepers even wash their sidewalks), and similar living standards. And there really is something for every traveler in the Benelux countries, including some of the most impressive sights and experiences in Europe. There's an exceptional wealth of fine art (particularly paintings, beginning with the 15th-century Flemish period), and traditional decorative arts (Delftware, tapestries, lace). Wonderful examples of architecture include feudal fortresses, Gothic and Romanesque churches, Renaissance stadhuizen (town halls), Baroque palaces, up to 20th-century Art Nouveau homes and Art Deco hotels. Pleasures to be pursued range from folklore to royalty, sophisticated shopping to satisfying a sweet tooth, fields of flowers that stretch for miles and music that fills the air.

Scenery is distinctive and varied, though you won't find Alpine altitudes. Luxembourg does, however, have a region that Dutch tourists in the last century designated "Little Switzerland," and the name stuck. The North Sea presses against the coast ever so persistently seeking to reclaim the below-sea-level polder land set just beyond its reach behind dikes. (Holland's hydro-engineering, as can be seen at the Delta Works Expo in Zeeland, is recognized around the world.) More recreational experiences take place on North Sea resort piers and promenades, and in the coastal dunes with their walking and biking paths. While human hands have cut Holland's flat, brilliantly green grazing fields into geometric shapes by canals (reflections from which help produce the luminous atmosphere that inspired the region's famous landscape painters), raging rivers in Belgium and Luxembourg have cut deep valleys for quaint towns in the Ardennes.

Holland, Belgium, and Luxembourg can hardly be considered off the beaten track; indeed, as their tourist offices have promoted for years, they lie near the very heart of continental Europe, well-situated on all air, sea, river, rail, and highway routes. Yet, somehow, the Benelux countries too often are shortchanged in travel guides, and inadequately informed travelers short-shrift sights there that are worthy of a much more lingering look. After London, Paris, and Rome, Amsterdam is the most visited city in Europe, but even that city's compelling appeal of 17th-century charm and contemporary cosmopolitan polish often is seen in short order. Perhaps the information in this book will help correct such short-sighted sightseeing.

During the decade of Europe's passage from the 20th century into the 21st, we'll be hearing more about the small, stable, self-confident Benelux countries—not *despite* their size, but *because* of it. In matters politic, small is usefully non-threatening: The Benelux countries don't bruise big country egos, are less narrowly nationalistic in their outlook, have fewer areas of ardent interest to defend, and, overall, are more able than some other members to encourage flexibility in the European Community. How contemporary the great Rotterdam-born humanist Erasmus (1466–1536) sounds in these 16th century words: "That you are patriotic will be praised by some and easily forgotten by everyone; but in my opinion, it is wiser to treat men and things as though we held this world the common fatherland of all."

Regardless of a strengthening EC and the greater progress towards a single European market that begins on January 1, 1993, do not fear that there will be a diminishment of the distinctive features that attract travelers to the Benelux. Although "Euro-culture" and multinationals seem to thrive in the Benelux, the unique qualities of Holland, Belgium, and Luxembourg have not disappeared. While it's true that today you may have to seek out the *truly* quaint—women in traditional costumes, men wearing wooden shoes, working windmills, fishermen on horseback drawing their nets from the sea—you'll find charmingly characteristic aspects of the Benelux cultures all around you.

How to Use this Guide

Sadly, too many travelers use the small sizes of the Benelux countries as a rationale to "do" destinations within them on day trips, leaving too little time to appreciate the unexpectedly rich rewards that await. As you plan your trip, you'll often hear it proposed: Base yourself in Amsterdam and Brussels, and head out on day trips by train to Leiden, The Hague, and Delft, or Bruges, Antwerp, and Ghent. Of course, Benelux trains are terrific, so it's entirely possible to travel that way. However, Holland's and Belgium's capital cities are the most expensive overnight places to park yourself (not to mention a car) if control of your purse strings is a point of consideration. And, apart from price, if you don't spend a night in a destination that truly warrants being seen after dark as much as by day, you may miss out on what could have been a milestone on your trip. I love Amsterdam, find much to admire in Brussels and, as much as any traveler, am glad not to have to move luggage and change hotels too often. But this book will suggest that you do just that occasionally, in order to experience the best in Benelux travel.

One purpose of this book is to provide sufficient information to enable you to take stock of the travel options, to plan and prioritize a trip according to *your* preferred style, tastes, and interests. Both first-time and repeat travelers to the Benelux should find sufficient coverage to enrich their exploration. For the many "vacation-poor" Americans, getting one's travel time's worth is particularly important—whether the dollar is weak or strong—and I hope this book will help them do so.

This single-volume travel companion provides both Benelux background essays (see *Culture, Bulb Fields, Carillons*) for arm-chair reading, and comprehensive on-the-road resources for when you're traveling. Under *Transportation* in *Practical Travel Information* at the front of the book, you'll find information on getting to and around the Benelux on public transportation (also covered under individual destinations). If you're literally taking to the road, there are details under *Driving*. Information that refers to the Benelux as a whole, or that spills across borders, has been included in the forward chapters of the book, while that covering a single country (for instance, landscape, people, history) appears in the opening section of the individual country.

While this volume provides overall coverage of the Benelux countries, it seeks to offer readers an appropriate sense of selection, since travel time and money usually are limited. Although no star rating for sights and cities has been given *per se*—your opinions might differ from mine, in any case—you will be able to assess the relative importance of a museum, town, or region based upon the amount of space allocated to it. Foremost attention is focused on those Benelux destinations that have delighted travelers over the decades, since places, like works of literature or music, come to be considered "classics" for a reason. Facts have been rounded out with flavorful details that put the place in context. Driving excursions to attractive, interesting areas off the more tourist-trampled track are included in *On the Road* chapters. Benelux regions of more limited interest to foreign visitors are presented in overview.

In general, the focus of this book is on the cultural aspects and attractions that make the three small countries of Holland, Belgium, and Luxembourg delightfully distinctive within Europe. (Do not expect to find here sightseeing suggestions such as safari or fantasy theme parks; regional tourist offices will have details if you desire them.) In local tourism literature, you may come across small regional museums that read *on paper* like interesting choices that are not included in this guide. In most instances, the omission is deliberate, and means either that I have found the museum to be of limited interest for foreign travelers, to have no English description of exhibits, or to be in an excessively remote location. Such decisions are meant to save you frustration and wasted touring time, energy, and money. In cases where museums or attractions, even without much English-language documentation, nevertheless warrant a visit, I have included them.

Food for thought (see *The Benelux Cultural Legacy: Art, Architecture, Music and the Muse,* etc.) usually leads to thoughts of food (see *Food and Drink*). While no one will be surprised to hear you're going to Holland to view the artworks of the 17th-century Dutch masters, many won't know that Belgium is widely considered one of the gastronomic gathering spots of Europe. The chapter on food and drink covers cuisine style, regional specialties for all three countries, and background on the region's indigenous drinks: Belgian beer; Luxembourg wine; and Dutch liqueurs. For specific restaurant suggestions, see *Restaurants* under individual cities and towns. As to where to rest your head, for ideas, star-rated, in a range of prices, consult *Accommodations* in the appropriate city or town. The *Hotel Quick Reference Table,* with specific prices, appears at the back of the book. Look for entertainment suggestions under *Events and Entertainment.* *Shopping* is noted under individual destinations, but you might want to read *Decorative Arts and Traditional Crafts* under *The Benelux Cultural Legacy* for additional ideas about what to buy.

Prices

The value of the dollar against the Dutch guilder and the Belgium and Luxembourg francs varies. And there's inflation to contend with, too. Prices for accommodations are raised periodically; Amsterdam hotels tend to review/raise prices each Nov. 1, Belgian hotels the 1st of Jan. Thus, even if you are using this book hot off the press, prices listed in the *Hotel Quick-Reference Table* at the back of this guide, and price categories used throughout it, may have changed. As a result, you are cautioned to use them as a comparative guideline rather than hard fact. Prices quoted are usually the maximum for a property, so you may find a room to your liking at a lower price, for such variables as a room with shower (rather than bathtub), a back room (no view but possibly quieter). Hotel room prices may change with the season, more likely so in resort regions, or in cities, where the disappearance of commercial clients on weekends can mean discounts for pleasure travelers then.

When you wisely select the preselected set course choices of a *prix fixe, tourist menu,* or *dagschotel* (day menu), you may already have lowered the price category of the restaurant you selected, since the restaurant price categories are based on a la carte courses. The word *menu* itself implies such a preselected meal option in the Benelux, rather than *carte* or *kaart,* which is the correct term for the printed listing of dishes available. The elimination of a course—servings are substantial in the Benelux—can also make a meal in a given restaurant less expensive than the price category indicated.

RESTAURANT PRICE CATEGORIES The following price categories are based on a three-course dinner for one, without drinks, but *inclusive* of VAT tax and service. Prices quoted are for major cities (Amsterdam, The Hague, Brussels), and prices, except at renowned restaurants, will be lower, often considerably so, in towns and the countryside. Luxembourg City is somewhat less expensive than Brussels, although it is still a Eurocrat expense-account town; prices in the Grand Duchy countryside are much lower.

	Belgium/Luxembourg	Holland
Very Expensive	BF 3000 or more	Dfl. 100 or more
Expensive	BF 2000–3000	Dfl. 75–100
Moderate	BF 1000–2000	Dfl. 50–75
Inexpensive	BF 1000 or less	Dfl. 50 or less

HOTEL PRICE CATEGORIES Prices are based on double occupancy, with private toilet and shower and/or bath. Breakfast, included at most moderate, all inexpensive, but rarely at expensive hotels, is continental style. It often includes yogurt, cheese, bread, and fruit in Belgium and Luxembourg and, in Holland, breads, sliced cheeses and meats, yogurt, fruit, and cereal. In the Benelux, *deluxe* standard is comparable to North American *first class;* first class to second class, etc. All grades of accommodations throughout the Benelux are thoroughly clean. Some properties charge the same price for all rooms, regardless of the sometimes considerable variations in size and view that can exist in old buildings; speak up when reserving, or, if there's a choice of rooms when you check-in, compare them in person to get one you like. Prices are quoted for major cities, so prices in towns and in the country will be considerably less.

	Holland	Belgium	Luxembourg
Deluxe	Dfl. 450–600	BF 8000+	FLux 4000+
First Class	250–450	5000–8000	3000–4000
Moderate	150–250	3000–5000	2000–3000
Inexpensive	150 or less	3000 or less	2000 or less

Hotel Ratings

I have used a star (★) rating system to assist you in selecting hotels. Within a star category, properties have been listed with the most recommended appearing first. The standard of living in most areas of Holland, Belgium, and Luxembourg is similar enough so that the rating system applies more or less consistently across all three Benelux countries. The hotel selection in this guide is not meant to be comprehensive, particularly in major cities; rather, it includes properties in a range of prices chosen subjectively for various tangible and intangible factors. Among these are atmosphere, visual appeal and view, furnishings, size of bed and bathrooms, friendliness of the staff, and—as for real estate decisions anywhere—location. An emphasis has been placed on properties which are central or close to districts with sights of interest, convenient to public transportation, and, when available, in scenic settings.

★★★★★ A Deluxe hotel, with excellent standards of service and cuisine, and outstanding quality in amenities and atmosphere. The property will have special features, location, or view that raises it above the four-star rating, 24-hour room service, a specialty *a la carte* restaurant as well as a less formal eatery, and often some in-house recreational facilities.

★★★★ A First Class hotel, with superior standards of comfort, cuisine, service, and setting. All rooms with private bath and shower, and all accessible by elevator. A wide range of amenities, including restaurant and room service.

★★★ A Recommended hotel, comfortable, with many amenities, including a breakfast room, bar, and sometimes a restaurant with limited choice menu. Most rooms have private toilet, plus shower and/or bathtub; those without private facilities will have an in-room sink. Some rooms may be accessible by elevator.

★★ A Reasonable hotel, with simple standards but considered above the minimum by virtue of some feature that places it above a one-star property. Lobby or other public room used for breakfast service. Some rooms have private facilities. No elevator.

★ A Budget hotel that meets minimal acceptable standards for plain but decent accommodation. Private facilities unlikely. Breakfast may be available only in one's room due to the lack of a lobby lounge/breakfast room.

Updates

Considerable care has been taken to ensure that the information included in this volume is correct, but change is a constant in the world, even in the small, stable corner of it covered here. While the facts presented are the most up-to-date possible at press time, changes could occur by the time of your visit. Therefore, when travel arrangement particulars are important to you, it's wise to confirm them in order to save yourself inconvenience and expense. Although I cannot be responsible for inaccuracies that result from changes in the travel environment, I will make every effort to keep informed of such developments. Your comments and suggestions for or about the guide are welcome. Write to me c/o Fielding Travel Books, William Morrow & Company, Inc., 1350 Avenue of the Americas, New York, NY 10019.

PRACTICAL TRAVEL INFORMATION

The Benelux countries are exceptionally well-organized for travelers, with information offices located virtually anywhere you would want to find one. The great degree to which English is spoken (and written, in brochures and other travel documentation) thoughout the region will be reassuring. Nevertheless, even though you can rely on almost always finding someone to answer your questions in English, there may be times when you welcome having the information included in this chapter at your fingertips. While the details contained here should be useful to all, they will be of particular help to those traveling independently.

PLANNING YOUR TRIP ....

WHEN TO TRAVEL In Holland, in numbers of travelers, the bulb season (April–late May) rivals July and August as the busiest tourist season. Tourism is especially tied to tulips, which, with early and late blooming varieties, can flower from early April, if the weather is unseasonably warm, to late May, if it's unusually cool, and motorcoach loads of viewers from countries around the world can make the region feel tourist-trampled. Nevertheless, if you enjoy flowers, the spectacle of the bulb fields in bloom and Keukenhof garden are well worth the crowds (see separate chapter *The Bulb Field Business*). On average, April and May are the driest months of the year in Holland. Easter, which may or may not occur during tulip time, is a three- or four-day holiday weekend throughout the Benelux and Europe that results in mass travel movements. Reserve well ahead if your travels are going to span that weekend. Many tourist attractions use Easter as the occasion to open to the public for the tourist season, though some shut again after Easter until early June.

As in much of northern Europe, summer and an eternal hope for sun and warmth keep many Benelux citizens at home to enjoy it. The daylight hours in summer are dramatically longer than many readers (other than those from Great Britain and Ireland) will be used to, due to the high northern latitude of the Benelux; even Luxembourg, the southernmost country, lies north of any part of the U.S./Canada border. The Dutch, with their water-logged below-sea-level land, are avid sailors and many spend summer holidays aboard their craft in the small picturesque harbors of Zeeland, or historic Zuider Zee ports around what today is the IJsselmeer. Should you be heading toward these delightful destinations in summer, when family travel is in full swing due to school holidays, make sure of reservations since hotels are small and limited in number.

Hotels at coastal resorts along the North Sea in Holland and Belgium, especially those with a beach view, can be expected to be fully booked if the summer weather is inviting. Camping, caravaning, and rented bungalows or apartments all are common ways for Europeans to have affordable family vacations in the coastal and resort areas in the Benelux. Travelers interested in such forms of accommodation should book well ahead, as they would for summer holidays at popular destinations at home. Most North Americans, however, will be seeking hotel rooms, often in towns. Because business travel is slower in summer, city hotels may offer bargain prices then, especially if overseas tourism is faltering due to reduced dollar value and recession worries.

In September, there's competition for beds at the best hotels in Amsterdam, Brussels, Luxembourg City, and other business centers in the Benelux, due to start-up sessions of the European Community, the post-summer renewal of corporate travel, and a new autumn season of trade and professional congresses (conventions). The busiest business months are Sept. and Oct., and May and June. Away from cities, September can be a lovely and less busy time for travel. In the Belgian Ardennes, lingering midday warmth and misty early mornings in valley villages are a backdrop for all-inclusive gastronomic weekends specializing in game dishes during the fall hunting season. Much of Luxembourg's tourism, especially outside Luxembourg City, shuts down by mid-Sept., but by then the grape harvest and related festivities take over.

The word for winter in the Benelux is dark. Daylight lasts only from 8 or 8:30 a.m. until 3:30 or 4 p.m. in Dec. and Jan. But the Benelux is at its coziest in winter, with candelit restaurants and pubs, gala events on the cultural calendar, and a festive celebration of the holiday season.

WEATHER An old joke, that may have originated in England, about having *weather,* not *climate,* applies to parts of the Benelux. The weather in Belgium and, especially, Holland can, indeed, be remarkably changeable, with conditions within the Benelux varying considerably, depending primarily on geography. Holland's weather in the more touristic western half of the country can change astoundingly in a short space of time, due to the proximity of the North Sea. At times (more commonly in winter), dreary, drizzily, windy days can linger on, but sustained rain for lengthy periods is not the rule. Despite the high northern latitude of Holland (on a par with southern Labrador in Canada), the sea keeps the climate temperate—not unlike the UK—with the extremes of cold and hot much less than in many areas of North America. While you must always be prepared for sudden shifts in the weather, summers can produce superb sunny days, and clear cheerful days come around the calendar. Countrywide in Holland, average summer temperatures range from 50°–61° Fahrenheit (10°–16°C.), 35° to 46° in winter (2°–8°C.). Year 'round, temperatures in inland eastern Holland average about 4° Fahrenheit / 2° Celsius higher than those on the coast.

Coastal Belgium has the same temperate maritime climate as western Holland, with Brussels generally being warmer by a few degrees than Amsterdam (122 mi./198 km. to the north) in every season. The forested Ardennes area in southeast Belgium, with its greater altitude and less influence from the sea, has a greater extreme between daily high and low temperatures. Countrywide, average temperatures in summer vary between 54° to 72° Fahrenheit (12°–23°C.), and from 32° to 43° (0°–6°C.) in winter.

The Ardennes is inclined to keep the moisture from the sea to its Belgian side, which means that the Grand Duchy of Luxembourg escapes much of the seasonal uncertainty and changeability of weather found elsewhere in the Benelux. Summers are predictably warm and sunny, as the largely outdoor countryside tourism then reflects. Luxembourg's 24-hour average temperature for July and Aug. is about 60°F (16°C.), and in Jan. 37°F. (3°C.).

Average daily high and low temperatures by month will be given for the capital cities in their chapters in degrees Fahrenheit but, locally, Benelux temperatures are given exclusively in Centigrade (Celsius). The standard conversion formulas are: To turn Centigrade into Fahrenheit, multiply by 9, divide by 5, and add 32; to convert Fahrenheit to Centigrade, subtract 32, multiply by 5, and divide by 9. The chart that follows has done the conversion for you. However, if you don't have it handy, and want to know what outside temperature to dress for, this decidedly unscientific method will provide you with a quick answer within a degree or so. First, remember that 16 (C) is equal to its inverted number 61 (F); the same holds true for 28 (C) = 82 (F). Using those as baselines, one Celsius degree is roughly equivalent to two Fahrenheit for temperatures in between.

CONVERSION CHART: CELSIUS/CENTIGRADE/FAHRENHEIT

Celsius/Centigrade	Fahrenheit	Celsius/Centigrade	Fahrenheit	Celsius/Centigrade	Fahrenheit
35	95.0	19	66.2	4	39.2
34	93.2	18	64.4	3	37.4
33	91.4	17	62.6	2	35.6
32	89.6	16	60.8	1	33.8
31	87.8	15	59.0	0	32.0
30	86.0	14	57.2	−1	30.2
29	84.2	13	55.4	−2	28.4
28	82.4	12	53.6	−3	26.6
27	80.6	11	51.8	−4	24.8
26	78.8	10	50.0	−5	23.0
25	77.0	9	48.2	−6	21.2
24	75.2	8	46.4	−7	19.4
23	73.4	7	44.6	−8	17.6
22	71.6	6	42.8	−9	15.8
21	69.8	5	41.0	−10	14.0
20	68.0				

TIME The Benelux countries are in the Central European time zone, which puts them six hours ahead of North America's Eastern Standard Time (nine hours ahead of the West Coast). The Benelux is one hour ahead of Great Britain and Ireland time. Clocks are put ahead one hour on the last Sunday in March, and back an hour on the last Sunday in Sept. (These dates may differ somewhat from "summer time" changes in the United Kingdom and Ireland). Generally, plane, train, and ferry schedules reflect these time changes, but if you are traveling just after one it's worth double checking departure times.

Since the 24-hour system often is used to indicate times on transportation schedules, and opening hours for museums and restaurants, it's a good idea to understand that clock concept. The hours after 12:00 noon continue in numerical order from 13.00 through 24.00 hours. To translate a time past noon from or to the 24-hour clock, simply add or subtract 12 from the time shown. For a rendezvous at 20.00 hours, *subtract* 12 from 20 and you arrive at an arrival time of 8 p.m.; if you wish to take a train at 3 p.m., *add* 12 to 3 and then look on the schedule for a 15:00 hours departure.

SEASONS, CELEBRATIONS, AND CEREMONIES ....

SPRING Carnival is celebrated in the southern Benelux in such a big way not only for its fancy dress fun and kicking up of heels before the beginning of Lent, but also to throw off the winter blahs. More merry-making takes place in the Netherlands south of Rotterdam "below the moerdijk" (in the part of the country that has a considerably higher percentage of Roman Catholics than the Calvinist Protestant north) and in predominantly Catholic Belgium and Luxembourg. In **Aalst** on Shrove Sunday (three days before Ash Wednesday) there's a traditional cortege. Belgium's **Binche** has the biggest Carnival binge on Shrove Tuesday (Mardi Gras) with the famous **Gilles** in full costume. Belgium's other best known pre-Lenten carnivals take place in **Eupen,** in the Germanic eastern part of the country, and in **Malmedy,** in the Ardennes, where there's a particularly spirited affair that starts on the Saturday before the start of Lent, with the town remaining *en fete* for four days. **Maastricht,** in southeast Holland, offers that country's largest Carnival celebration. Unusual, compared to other countries, are Belgium's colorful processions and fetes that take place *during* Lent on Sundays (considered feast days). Many attractions and activities in the Benelux open for the tourist season (til Sept. or Oct.) on the long **Easter** weekend.

The **bulb fields,** and glorious 70-acre **Keukenhof** garden (showplace for Holland's local bulb growers) with its million of tulips and other bulb flowers, burst into bloom from late March until mid-to-late May. In late April, a parade with flower floats winds through the villages of the bulb-growing district.

The annual **Procession of the Holy Blood** in Bruges on Ascension Day (a national holiday) comes replete with costumes and a ceremony that recounts the return from the Second Crusade with a relic of the Holy Blood. Holland observes its national holiday on April 30, the **Queen's Birthday** (it's actually the birthday of former Queen, now Princess, Juliana, but her daughter Queen Beatrix has kept the date for the happy occasion). There's singing and selling in the streets (thousands take advantage of the one-day license-free occasion to hold personal "garage sales" in the streets of central Amsterdam). The month-long **Queen Elizabeth Music Competition** (in violin, piano, or voice) comes each May to Brussels. And the May opening of the fresh **asparagus** ("white gold") **season** gives everyone in the Benelux a gastronomic cause to celebrate. At the end of May, on **Vlaggetjesdag** in Scheveningen, ships are decked in festive flags as the Dutch herring fleet puts out to the North Sea for the start of the herring season. Skippers vie to bring in the first barrel of *groene* (fresh) *haring,* a beloved Dutch treat, which traditionally is delivered to Queen Beatrix. **The Blessing of the Sea at Blankenberge** is probably Belgium's best known fishing-fleet ceremony.

SUMMER Throughout the Benelux, the northern latitude brings late-light nights (until 10:30 or 11 p.m. at midsummer) for lingering sightseeing, followed by nightseeing, viewing the marvelously **illuminated building facades,** bridges, towers, and other monuments whose architectural details are tastefully highlighted with spotlights, producing scenic (not to mention romantic) settings. During the June **Shrimp Pageant,** fishermen in **Oostduinkerke,** on the southern Belgian coast, pull their full nets from the sea on horseback, in an event that now exists virtually only for tourists. June brings the seasonal start up of Monday night **carillon concerts** in Mechelen and Antwerp; many other carillons throughout the Benelux also ring in the summer season. Music of many kinds, and other performing arts, fill the stages set for the June **Holland Festival,** held mostly in Amsterdam, the July **North Sea Jazz Festival** in The Hague, and Belgium's **Festivals of Flanders and Wallonia,** which last through September. In Haarlem, the renowned organ of *St. Bavo's Church* is used for the **International Organists Competition** each July. The **Ommegang,** an impressive medieval-costumed procession recalling the era of the Dukes of Burgundy, takes place on Brussels' Grand Place the first Thursday evening each July. Other nights in summer the Grand Place is the magnificent setting for free *son et lumière* (sound and light) shows, best enjoyed with a Belgian beer from one of the square's many outdoor cafes. The **Flower Carpet** on the Grand Place (every other year in August) is a wondrous work. Luxembourg City lets loose in late August with its annual **Schobermesse Fun Fair,** which keeps alive a several-centuries trade fair tradition.

FALL When in September it returns to one time for taking **mussels** from their sea beds (during months with an "R"), mouths begin to water. **Wine festivals in Luxembourg** in mid-September celebrate the ripening on the vine of the good white grapes that produce the country's fine Moselle wines. The weekend **Wieze Beer Festivals** stand as testaments to Belgium's nearly 600 beers brewed, a tradition that produces some unique tastes. **Fall flowers** are the products paraded in the area around Holland's Aalsmeer, the world's largest flower auction house, on colorful floats in September. **Prinsjesdag** is the mid-September annual opening of the Dutch Parliament in The Hague, where Queen Beatrix and royal family members ride in a horse-drawn golden carriage from the "office palace" of Noordeinde to the *Binnenhof.* October's **Delft Old Art and Antique Fair,** one of Europe's most prestigious, offering museum quality art and furnishings, takes place in Delft's *Prin-*

senhof, the former palace and site of the assassination (1584) of Prince Willem the Silent of Orange. On **October 3** in 1574 Willem went to **Leiden** to congratulate the town for successfully withstanding a devastating seige by the Spanish, an occasion the city has marked ever since. It was in Leiden that certain English separatists lived (1608–1620), before leaving for the New World aboard the *Mayflower* and founding Plymouth Colony in Massachusetts. A **Thanksgiving Day Service** at Leiden's *St. Pieterskerk,* which these pilgrims attended, is held each year to commemorate the connection.

WINTER Winter in the Benelux brings a cultural glut of goodies: opera, ballet, symphony, and dance from fine residential and guest performing arts companies. In Holland, late November features the arrival by ship of **Sinterklaas** (St. Nicholas) in Amsterdam. From then until the December 5th evening family celebration, shops, especially bakeries, take on a holiday look with such traditional treats as large pink marzipan pigs and chocolate name-initial letters from 2 to 12″ high. Many towns string white lights over streets and along canals. Sinterklaas serves as a warm-up for the rest of the Christmas season specialties, such as the **Christmas markets** in Brussels, Eupen, and Luxembourg City. The Dutch cheese town celebrates **Gouda By Candlelight,** with the lighting of a Christmas tree and carol singing in its lovely market square, lit only by candles in all the windows of the buildings that surround it; there's carillon playing, and an organ concert in Gouda's St. Jan's church. **New Year's** in Holland is observed with masses of fireworks set off at midnight.

One always hopes for skating in winter in Holland, none more than the Dutch. *If* (a big "if") the weather gets cold enough, for long enough, the **Elfstedentocht** (11 cities tour) is held. When it's held, beginning well before dawn and lasting until well after dark, hundreds of qualified Dutch competitors and thousands of others undertake a grueling marathon-on-ice-skates across a windswept frozen canal "track" that connects the 11 cities of northern Holland's Friesland province. The event, which was held in both 1985 and in 1986 after a 20-year hiatus due to too-warm weather, is a sort of winter rite of passage for the Dutch, some 90% of whom are reckoned to watch at least some of the event on television (even members of Parliament take a TV break when winners get close to the finish line). To the delight of Dutch everywhere, Crown Prince Willem-Alexander completed the Elfstedentocht in 1986, with his mother Queen Beatrix there to welcome him at the finish line.

WHAT TO BRING..............................

In addition to prescription medicines, extra prescription eyeglasses, and copies of actual prescriptions, you know best what personal items are essential to your well-being, at home or away: a small pair of scissors, a sewing kit, double-sided Scotch tape to secure a hem you don't have time to sew, several sizes of safety pins. A lightweight cork screw is handy if you plan on picnics, either outdoors or in your hotel room when you're too tired to go out for dinner, or want, perhaps, a glass of wine before you walk out on a summer evening after 10 p.m. to see a Benelux city once its night light illuminations are on. Clothespins with hanger-shaped tops that fit over a shower curtain rod or other hook come in handy for hand laundry, for which you should bring a small plastic bottle filled with liquid detergent. A pocket calculator can be useful if you don't like converting the prices of things in your head.

If sound and light are liable to affect your sleep, it's wise to make earplugs and an eyeshade regular travel companions. With earplugs, you can get your beauty sleep while avoiding the wrenching necessity of having to turn down that wonderful front hotel room with a fabulous view because of evening and early morning noise from a nearby tram, or on-the-hour and half-hour carillon bells, for the quiet but boring room at the back. If you wake with the dawn's early light, be aware that it comes as early as 4 a.m. in summer in far-to-the-north Holland, and *pack an eye mask,* however unglamorous that may seem. Once you've worked out how to get a good night's sleep, to make sure you wake up, bring a small travel alarm clock, a reassuring backup, even if you're staying at hotels with wake-up service.

Then, there's the trusty collap^b, M▓▓▓rella. In Holland, especially, and much of Belgium, it s▓▓▓▓▓ ▓f your basic wardrobe when you head out each morning, ▓▓▓ ▓re's not a cloud in the sky. Bring one small enough to fit in y Gate, ▓e ▓r carry-all, two if there are two of you traveling. Once you've ▓▓▓▓▓ ▓urself from the threat of a little rain (and it can pass as ▓▓▓▓▓y as it pours), you can take pleasure if you should see dark clouds doing a furious dance in the high skies above Holland, a sight that often compelled Dutch landscapists to paint it.

If you're a shop-til-you-drop sort, pack especially lightly and include in your suitcase an *empty* durable nylon, hand-luggage-size foldable bag for your acquisitions. Should you forget an item, or run into weather that runs contrary to all the climate "averages" you've prepared for, never mind: The Benelux countries have well-stocked, sophisticated stores where you will find what you need, and may even discover a better-designed version of the item you left at home.

CLOTHES Experienced wanderers will follow the layered, color-coordinated separates, wash-and-wear wardrobe ideas that enable one to travel lightly, be prepared for a variety of social situations, and look well. In the Benelux capital cities, business dress is best for fine restaurants (and top ones in the countryside) and major cultural events, although you'll see everything from student casual to evening wear. In the touristic summer season, dress, even in cities, is somewhat less formal at night, and can be very casual during the day. A raincoat, or rain and windproof jacket, is a suggested outer covering any time of year, and a zip-in liner for warmth could prove useful even in summer; wind and damp can be factors even when actual rain isn't.

Don't skimp on packing sturdy shoes. You may even consider bringing more than one pair of walking shoes; a second could come in handy if the weather turns wet, or when those charming cobblestone streets exact their toll on your soles. You'll be able to buy shoes in the Benelux, but that's hardly the best use of your travel time, and it can be perilous breaking in a new pair during heavy-duty touring. Bring practical evening shoes (low, wide heels and, perhaps, insole cushions); the cobblestones in historic city centers don't disappear with the daylight.

PACKING AND LUGGAGE When considering what to pack, it's useful to mentally "walk through" your trip, keeping in mind planned activities and possible temperature variations. Anticipating the likely range of weather conditions is vital. Remember that Holland rarely comes even close to 90°, and instead, *can be* windy and gray on days during the summer. It's important to include that sweater, windproof jacket, and extra turtleneck lay———

In addition to ke——————t of things you want to take, a good way to remember ite————s get overlooked during last-minute packing is to put ou— London y suitcase a week or so before departure and, when————— .o you, put it in the case *then and there*.

It's not possible to overemphasize the importance of packing lightly. The flexibility afforded when you free yourself from excess baggage is a major physical and mental lift. My personal packing goal is not to lug around a single item I don't use—except an umbrella! If you're using one city as a base but spending some nights in other places, or will be returning to a city for your flight home, you might consider leaving a bag of items you won't need for the next segment of your trip either as checked luggage at the hotel you're leaving (for which there usually is no fee, just a tip to the porter), or leaving unnecessary luggage at a conveniently located (in terms of later travel) train station or airport locker or baggage office.

PRACTICAL TRAVEL INFORMATION · · · 19

Airports in the Benelux are civilized enough to have those lovely free luggage carts, but it's best not to count on porters. Amsterdam's *Schiphol* is superbly planned for getting around with luggage carts; there are large elevators, an underground passageway to the airport's connecting train station, and "stepless" escalators that take you and your luggage cart safely up and down. But when packing for your trip, try always to keep in mind that during it there probably will be occasions when you must be able to manage all of your luggage by yourself.

PLANNING AIDS The Benelux countries' tourist offices, both overseas and locally, are among the best organized and most helpful in the world, and can provide an enormous selection of tourism literature in English, much of it free. Contact the nearest office for travel information before you go.

In the United States:
Netherlands Board of Tourism (NBT), 355 Lexington Ave., 21st. Fl., New York, NY 10017, (212) 370–7367, Fax (212) 370–9507; NBT, 225 N. Michigan Ave., Suite 326, Chicago, IL 60601; (312) 819–0300, Fax (312) 819–1740; NBT, 90 New Montgomery St., Suite 305, San Francisco, CA 94105; (415) 543–6772, Fax (415) 495–4925.
Belgian Tourist Office, 745 Fifth Ave., New York, NY 10151, (212) 758–8130, Fax (212) 355–7675.
Luxembourg National Tourist Office, 801 Second Ave., New York, NY 10017, (212) 370–9850.
In Canada:
Netherlands Board of Tourism, 25 Adelaide St. East, Suite 710, Toronto, Ontario, Canada M5C 1Y2, (416) 363–1577, Fax (416) 363–1470.
Belgian Tourist Office, P.O. Box 760, Succursale N.D.G., Montreal, Quebec, 44A 352 (514) 845–7500.
In the United Kingdom:
Netherlands Board of Tourism, 25–28 Buckingham, SW1E 6LD, (071) 630–0451, Fax (071) 828–7941.
Belgian Tourist Office, Premier House, 2 Gayton Rd., Harrow, Middlesex, HA1 2XU (081) 861–3300), Fax (081) 427–6760.
Luxembourg Tourist Office, 36–37 Picadilly, London W1V 9PA (071) 434–2800).

LOCAL TOURIST OFFICES In Holland, local tourist offices go by the initials *VVV* and usually are located in or close to the central railway station or town center. VVVs in larger towns and cities that also display a sign with a large lower-case *i* (for "Information") and the word *Nederland* can supply information on places thoroughly Holland. Tourist offices in Belgium and Luxembourg identify themselves with the lower-case *i* for information. Brussels has both a Tourist Information Brussels

(T.I.B.) city tourism office in the Hotel de Ville on the Grand Place and an all-Belgium tourist office at 61, rue du Marche-aux-Herbes. Local tourist offices in larger towns in Belgium carry some information on destinations in other regions of the country. The tourist office on the Place d'Armes in Luxembourg City has full information on the city and all the Grand Duchy. In all three countries, look for tourist office directional signs from the railway station if you are arriving by train, or prominently posted street signs as you approach town center (Centrum) if you are driving.

Local tourist offices usually are the best sources for city and regional walking, bike, and driving route maps. Some maps are published by the ANWB (Royal Dutch Touring Club), which charges a moderate amount. Opening times for most tourist offices throughout the Benelux follow local office hours at a minimum, but many are open longer (until 8 p.m. or later weekdays) and on Sat. and Sun. in summer and during other periods of heavy travel, such as Easter weekend. Major tourist offices will also book hotels and other accommodations, particularly in private homes, for which local tourist offices in the Benelux are the best source of information. Tourist offices in cities may book tickets for cultural events and entertainment for a minimal fee.

SENIOR CITIZENS Senior citizens who have flexibility of schedule by virtue of being retired are in a position to take advantage of last-minute travel bargain tours and reduced overseas airfares with restrictions they can live with. Some organizations specifically for senior citizens offer discount travel options. The one with the largest membership, and therefore potentially the most negotiating clout, is the **American Association of Retired Persons** (AARP, 1909 K St. N.W., Washington, D.C. 20049; toll-free in U.S. (800) 227–7737). It is open to anyone 50 and older willing to pay a small membership fee. The **National Council of Senior Citizens** (925 15th St. N.W., Washington, D.C.) also makes available travel and discount information. Among tour operators that specialize in travel for senior citizens are **Elderhostel** (80 Boylston St., Boston, MA 02116, (617) 426–8056), with interesting cultural and educational tours among its offerings, and **Saga Holidays,** 120 Boylston St., Boston, MA 02116, toll-free (800) 343–0273), which offers a selection of value-conscious tours worldwide, including the Benelux, and single destination extended-stay accommodations for travelers 60 and over.

STUDENTS The *Student Travel Catalog* available from the **Council for International Education Exchange** (CIEE, 205 E. 42nd St., New York, NY 10017) is a basic source for discount and tour travel information and services for people under 26, students, and teachers. If you qualify for one, make sure to get an **International Student Identity**

Card, available from CIEE, before you head for the Benelux. It opens the door to many discounted rates and fares.

TRAVEL FOR THE DISABLED Disabled travelers will find certain accommodations to accessibility at tourist attractions, hotels, restaurants, and public transportation in socially-conscious Holland, in particular, and the other Benelux countries. **Mobility International Nederland,** the Dutch member of the international organization (based in London) that arranges individual and group travel programs, can be contacted at Postbus 165, 6560 AD Groesbeek, Nederland. The Netherlands Board of Tourism produces a brochure (cost Dfl. 1) with general travel information. Also available is a listing of the country's accessible hotel and recreation sites, and wheelchair access rental camper vans. There is a special telephone number (030) 331252 staffed Mon.–Fri. 8 a.m.– 4 p.m., through which you can arrange assistance for train travel nationally; call at least one day in advance, by Fri. midday for weekends. Amsterdam's Schiphol Airport and its Metro are accessible to wheelchair users with normal arm function. For more travel specifics, a book by Louise Weiss, *Access to the World: A Travel Guide for the Handicapped* (published by Facts on File, (212) 683–2244), contains useful advice and hotel listings. **Mobility International** (Box 3551, Eugene, OR 97403) and **Whole Person Tours** (Box 1084, Bayonne, NJ 07002) each publish newsletters and magazines for members, and organizes trips. The **Information Center for Individuals with Disabilities** (ICID, Fort Point Place, 1st Fl., 27–43 Wormwood St., Boston, MA 02210) will, for a small fee, provide a list of specialized travel agencies, tour operators, and publications. And the **Travel Information Center** (Moss Rehabilitation Hospital, Tabor & 12th, Philadelphia, PA 19141), will send, also for a small fee, travel information for up to three cities.

DOCUMENTS A passport is required to enter Holland, Belgium, or Luxembourg, but visitors from the U.S., Canada, members of the EC, and most of the British Commonwealth countries, do not need a visa for stays up to three months. No immunization certificates are required to enter the Benelux countries, and no certificate of vaccination is required by U.S. or Canadian authorities from returning residents.
U.S. Passports: Major post offices throughout the country now are able to process passport applications; if your local office doesn't have the forms, it can direct you to the nearest one that does. Federal office buildings also have passport offices. For your initial passport, or if your previous one was issued more than 12 years ago, you need to apply in person (not required for children under 13), with a completed application, proof of U.S. citizenship (a certified copy of birth certificate or naturalization papers), a photo ID, and 2 recent identical passport photos (full-face, 2 × 2 inches, plain background), and $42 (exact cur-

rency, check made out to Passport Services, or money order). If you have a passport not more than 12 years old, you can mail or take it, together with an application and $35 payment, to the nearest passport office. Passports are good for ten years. In an emergency it's possible to get a passport in short order (you can indicate your departure date on the application), but one normally should allow at least six weeks, and try to avoid the spring rush for summer travel. Your passport is returned by mail. If an applicant is under 18, there are some exceptions to the above; check with the Washington Passport Agency, Dept. of State, 1425 K St., Washington, D.C. 20522; (202) 326–6060.

Canadian Passports: Take a completed passport application form, obtainable from a passport office, travel agency, or post office, to one of the regional passport offices, or mail it (Passport Office, Dept. of External Affairs, Ottawa, Ont. K1A 0G3) with proof of Canadian citizenship, two identical passport photos signed by you and co-signed by a professional who has known you at least two years, and $25 Canadian. Application in winter is suggested. The document is valid for five years.

United Kingdom Passports: Passport forms are available at most travel agencies and local post offices. Apply in person at a local passport office, with a certification of birth, two recent identical photos signed and countersigned, 15 pounds sterling, and, if appropriate, a copy of your marriage certificate. Passports are valid for ten years, except for those under 16, and take about a month for processing.

HEALTH TIPS The standard of health care in all three Benelux countries is among the highest in the world—infant mortality is lower, life expectancy higher, than in the U.S. Rest assured that if anything untoward should occur during your travels there, you'll be wonderfully looked after. All Dutch doctors and nurses understand English well, especially since many of their medical courses are taught from English-language textbooks. Most health care professionals in Belgium and Luxembourg also have a mastery of English.

Water: You can safely drink the water almost everywhere in the Benelux. On the rare occasion when this is not the case—such as from a sink in the toilet on a train or one in a rural restaurant—there will be international signage and the words *non-potable* (non-drinkable) clearly posted. Bottled water or other liquids usually are available on a train, from a refreshment car or cart. At restaurants, one normally is expected to buy bottled mineral water, but if you've ordered something else to drink and want water too, ask the waiter for a glass of ordinary tap water. It is unlikely to come with ice. Bottled water is available at all grocery stores and many snack stands. It comes in *gaz* or *sin gaz* (carbonated or non-carbonated) varieties.

Insurance: Travelers covered by medical insurance are entitled to medical treatment in Holland, so it behooves you to check your policy about coverage abroad and the special procedures to follow for reimbursement. Carry your insurance I.D. with you while traveling, and keep all medical receipts for your insurance company back home. It's an excellent idea to carry photocopies of your insurance policy so that you can hand one over immediately if you require treatment, thereby possibly preventing the need for direct payment. In Holland, the Health Service-Foreign Affairs Department in Utrecht can be contacted during business office hours at (030) 618881. As EC citizens, UK citizens carrying a National Health Service certificate are covered for the same medical benefits Benelux citizens have. Your hotel staff should have the names of English-speaking doctors to recommend, and can inform you as to which of the *apotheek* (chemist/pharmacist) shops that open, in rotation, to cover nights and weekends is on duty.

Within Luxembourg, dial 012 for emergency medical assistance, and to locate doctors and pharmacists on duty Sundays and nights. In Belgium, dial 100 in the case of an accident for which emergency medical help is needed.

MONEY

Holland: The official monetary units in Holland are Dutch guilders *(gulden)*, abbreviated Dfl., sometimes Hfl., or simply fl. (short for *florin*, a former name for the coin of the realm). There are 1, 2.5, and 5 guilder coins. The 100-cent guilder is broken down into 5-cent, 10-cent *(dubbeltje)*, and 25-cent *(kwartje)* pieces. The 1-cent piece has been dropped as legal tender; prices are rounded up, or down, to the nearest five cents. Bank notes come in brightly colored 10, 25, 50, 100, 250, and 1000-guilder denominations. The guilder is a consistently strong European currency. At press time, the U.S.$ was trading at approximately 1.85 guilders.

Belgium and Luxembourg: Although these two countries mint and print separate currency, the Belgium Franc (BF) and the Luxembourg Franc (FLux) have the same value and demoninations. In Luxembourg, the Belgium franc is accepted everywhere, though the reverse is not the case. (When leaving Luxembourg, whether or not you are returning to Belgium, make sure your remaining francs are Belgian since for currency transactions the Luxembourg franc doesn't carry the same international recognition as the Belgium franc.) Both Belgian and Luxembourg francs come in 1, 5, 20, and 50 francs pieces, and a 50 centime piece (100 centimes = 1 Franc). Bank notes exist for 100, 500, 1000, and 5000 francs. At press time, the U.S.$ was equal to approximately 30 BF or FLux.

Exchanging Money: Currency exchange rates change daily, so check the financial pages of a newspaper for the most current before you leave. The newspaper figures will be slightly higher than those posted at the *change* (or *bureau de change*) desk at banks in the Benelux. Traveler's checks usually have a slightly more advantageous exchange rate than currency.

No doubt you know the adage: exchange money *only* at banks. Like much advice that's been around for years, it's basically sound. However, bank service charges—a standard Dfl. 5 (over $3 at current rates) per exchange transaction in Holland—are enough to warrant thinking about *how often* you exchange travelers checks or cash, as well as *where*. The **GWK** *(De Grenswisselkantoren),* a nationwide network of Dutch government-regulated currency exchange offices, has locations at airports, major train stations, and border crossing points; most are open evenings and weekends. GWK rates are equivalent to bank rates, but commission charges are slightly higher, though not, in *my* opinion, so much higher that it's worth the inconvenience and waste of time trying to save a basis point—1/100th of a percentage point—or three, on a transaction; and I like the efficiency of exchanging money at Amsterdam's Schiphol GWK counter, from which I can see the luggage arriving. American Express pays rates somewhat less than banks, but doesn't make a service charge on its traveler's checks (of course, they may already have collected 1% of the face value when you bought them).

Unless you get free traveler's checks, as you can from the Automobile Association of America (AAA) if you are a member, you'll be paying coming and going with traveler's checks and you might as well accept the fact, since, in terms of their replaceability when lost or stolen (*if* you can supply the check numbers), they are worth it. No matter how many larger traveler's checks you buy, always take plenty in the useful $20 denomination. You will need your passport to exchange traveler's checks.

Credit cards are widely accepted in the Benelux, although by no means does every hotel, restaurant, and shop do so. Inquire specifically if/which cards are accepted when making reservations at hotels and restaurants. As at home, fewer places take *American Express* than *Visa,* probably the most widely accepted credit card internationally, and *MasterCard*. When you use a credit card abroad, you are charged the exchange rate in effect the day the sale is processed (*not* the day of purchase). Obviously, a lag in transaction processing (which by no means always happens) can work either to the buyer's or the supplier's advantage, depending upon whether your currency is strengthening against the guilder or franc, or falling, but it's worth remembering, exchange rates from one day to another rarely amount to a significant percentage. In my experience, foreign charges have been processed fairly, and using a credit card while traveling abroad certainly can be a considerable convenience. With a major credit card, you can get a cash advance at certain banks in the Benelux. Check with your card-issuing institution at home for specific details and locations. With a major credit card you can also get cash (in any currency) at Holland's GWK offices. And, just in case, you always should travel with the appropriate local telephone numbers and instructions for reporting lost or stolen credit cards.

HOTELS   Cleanliness *is* next to godliness in the Benelux, in every category of hotel and other accommodations. Most hotels in Holland, Belgium, and Luxembourg have far fewer rooms than North American travelers might expect. Since hotels are smaller, especially in tourist seasons (see *When to Travel*), atmospheric, well-located reasonably-priced properties are liable to be fully booked (although it's always worth inquiring at the last minute, in case of a cancellation or "no-show"). VAT (value-added-tax) and service is always included in room rates. Breakfast (some variation on the "continental buffet": breads/rolls, jam, sliced cheese, cold cuts, hard-boiled eggs, fruit, yogurt, cold cereal, and coffee or tea; for an extra charge, you often can order cooked eggs) is usually included in the price at hotels in the three-star and lower category, occasionally at the four-star category. As elsewhere in Europe these days, the more expensive the hotel, the *less* likely you are to have breakfast included in the price.

RESTAURANTS, ETC.   Travelers should be aware that if they use the word *restaurant* when inquiring about where to eat, they may be directed to a more formal, and, therefore, more expensive, dining establishment than they had in mind, since in the local dining lexicon that's what the word "restaurant" implies. In the Benelux, there's a whole range of lower to mid-range-price dining places—designated as *bistro, cafe, restaurant-cafe, brasserie, petit-restaurant, tearoom, eet cafe, traiteur, snackbar, koffieshop, broodjeswinkel* (sandwich shop), *or pannekoekhuisje* (pancake house)—that might fill the bill, and suit your tastes, much better.

It may also be useful to know that the term *menu* most often refers to a dining establishment's preselected daily special (a single dish or three-course meal). It's similar to a *prix fixe, table d'hôte, dagschotel,* or *tourist menu*. Tourist menu (in lower case) is not to be confused with the official **Tourist Menu** program in Holland, another eating bargain plan, in which some 400 restaurants countrywide offer three-courses for the set price of Dfl. 21.50 (1992 price). NBT can supply a booklet that lists all participating establishments. If you really do want to see the menu (whole selection of food available), ask for the *kaart* (Dutch) or *carte* (French).

NOTE · · ·   In the countryside in Belgium, owners may bring their dogs into restaurants (where they generally sit quietly under the table). This is rarely done in towns or cities, and is nowhere near as common a practice as it is in France.

FILM Airport X-ray machines will become ever more evident in today's screened-for-security travel world. Professional photographers know that, at any setting, X-ray machines can cloud your processed and unprocessed film—low ASA is less sensitive—from its first time through the machine. Effects are cumulative, as with each transfer and connecting flight your carry-on belongings are required to make additional passages through X-ray. I *politely* ask a member of the security staff (they are *not* employees of any airline) to hand inspect my rolls of films, and camera if it has film in it; however, he or she is under no obligation and, with security demands tightened, may not have the time nor temperament to do so. If your request for hand inspection is refused, there is virtually nothing you can do about it, hence the wisdom of using a lead-shield pack for both exposed and unexposed rolls of film (although I have heard it said that the X-ray operator then just pushes the setting higher to see through the shield). Film is more expensive in the Benelux than at home, but if you run out there it is readily available at many museums and other shops.

LANGUAGE Because English is so widely spoken within the three countries, you'll find no easier area in continental Europe to travel in than the Benelux. And *that's* the overriding fact to keep in focus, when the subject of language in Belgium and Luxembourg begins to *sound* complicated. The citizens of Holland, who have had an outwardly-oriented commercially-based economy for centuries, have always excelled in mastering other languages, and you'll find their fluency in idiomatic American and English remarkable. From the age of ten until graduation, all Dutch schoolchildren study the language, and the influence of BBC radio and TV from England, as well as American TV programs and films (shown in their original English, only subtitled in Dutch), is so pervasive that learning English is a near-necessity—and fun—for the Dutch. Only in the remotest regions, or among the oldest citizens, will you come across a lack of knowledge of English and, even then, there'll be someone nearby who knows it.

Brussels, capital of the European Community, and Luxembourg City, with its EC institutions, both also the headquarters of multiple multi-national corporations, are multilingual communities. Brussels is officially bilingual in Flemish (Dutch) and French; Luxembourg is trilingual in French, German, and its official *Letzebuergesch*. In both these Common Market countries, English has long been a common-ground language. Again, in rural areas and among older citizens in Luxembourg and Belgium (more so in the southern Belgian region of Wallonia), perhaps not everyone will speak English, but there surely will be someone handy who does.

In terms of native languages, the three Benelux countries basically deal in two. Dutch, a Germanic-rooted tongue, is spoken throughout Holland. Dutch also is the language of the northern part of Belgium known as Flanders; the language is called Flemish, as are the people. A language frontier (see map in *Belgium, Introduction*) divides Belgium roughly in half, north and south, along Romance and Teutonic linguistic and cultural lines that have existed, essentially unchanged, since the 5th century (when the Romans left the region, and Frankish tribes took over). Belgium also has a small German-speaking region in the east, along its shared border with Germany.

Because there are subtle (and sometimes not so subtle) social and political overtones to the language issue both in Brussels and Belgium, you, as a native English speaker, may do best to stick to English in your conversations with Belgians, rather than running the risk of speaking Dutch words to Walloons and French phrases to the Flemish (although, as a foreigner—your accent in either language is likely to reveal you as the English speaker you are—you'll be forgiven your *faux pas*, and won't be accused of trying to force the language issue). This is all just a word to the wise—in English.

After Belgium, life with language in Luxembourg will seem simpler, or at least less political. Luxembourg's official language (since 1984) is *Letzebuergesch*, mostly in use orally. Business is conducted in French (and street signs are in French), while most newspapers are published in German. In addition to that lingual trinity, English is so widely studied and spoken, it's unlikely you'll have any difficulty getting around and meeting people.

Although few residents of the Benelux feel put upon to speak English (most actively enjoy the opportunity to do so), if you show interest in using the occasional Dutch or French phrase, it's bound to please most people. You'll undoubtedly enjoy being able to identify items on menus and signs in stores; at the end of this book, you'll find an English/Dutch/French glossary *(Benelux Lexicon)* with useful general vocabulary and food terms. Under the *Keys to the Kingdom* section for Belgium is a list of respective Belgian place names, so you'll know that signs for *Mechelen* (Dutch), *Malines* (French), and *Mechlin* (English) are all directing you to the same city; road signs normally reflect the language of the Belgian region the town is in, but because the country is small and no place is located very far from its language frontier, you come across all versions.

PERSONAL SECURITY There is considerably less personal violent crime in the Benelux than in the United States, but petty pickpockets and car burglars seem part of the worldwide scene these days. Cities have a greater problem with such random occurrences. Amsterdam is an essentially safe and delightful city to walk in, but be particularly watchful around Central Station and in the neighboring Zeedijk (now much gentrified with five-star hotels, but still carrying on as the colorful Red Light district). Use bags or purses that close tightly, and carry them close to your body. Keep them in your lap (and/or with straps looped through the arms of chairs at outdoor cafes) in public or congested places, and on public transportation.

A good rule of thumb is: If you won't be needing an item, don't take it out on the street with you. Leave passports (you'll only need yours when checking into a hotel, or cashing traveler's checks), extra cash, traveler's checks, airline tickets, rail passes, credit cards, and other valuables in a hotel safe deposit box (available at the front desk if there isn't a safe in your room). There's little inconvenience involved in using one, compared to your increased peace of mind. If two of you are traveling together, make it a habit to split your cash, checks, and credit cards between you, thereby minimizing the risk of losing everything in a single incident, whether through forgetfulness or theft. An individual traveling alone should put money and valuables in several places or pockets, never carrying everything in any single purse, wallet, or carry-all.

It's important to keep important information and photocopies of documents where you can put your hands on them with certainty (perhaps in the bottom of your suitcase in a hotel room, better in a safe). This should include photocopies of passports (the page spread with your picture is sufficient), instructions of what to do in case of lost credit cards, health insurance procedures, and an accurate list of the numbers of unused traveler's checks. Taking such measures ahead of time can save a lot of self-recrimination in the unlikely event that something happens later.

EMERGENCIES To contact the police in Amsterdam during an emergency, telephone 6222222. If you need to report a theft or other loss in the Benelux, go to the nearest police station to file a report, a copy of which will be given to you. If you plan to make a claim back home, your insurance company will want to see a copy of this report as proof of loss. Dial 100 in Belgium in case of an accident for which **medical help** is needed. Dial 012 for **emergency medical assistance** in Luxembourg.

EMBASSIES/CONSULATES
In Holland: U.S. Embassy, Lange Voorhout, The Hague; **U.S. Consulate,** Museumplein 19, Amsterdam, 6790321; **Canadian Embassy,** Sophialaan 7, The Hague, 3614111; **U.K. Consulate,** Koningslaan 44, Amsterdam, 6764343.
In Belgium: U.S. Embassy, Blvd. du Regent 27, 1000 Brussels, 513 38 30; **U.S. Consulate,** Nationalestraat 5, 2000 Antwerp, 232 18 00; **Canadian Embassy,** Ave. de Tervuren 2, 1040 Brussels, 735 60 40;

U.K. Embassy, Rue Joseph II 28, 1040 Brussels, 217 90 00; **U.K. Consulate,** Lange Klarenstraat 24, 2000 Antwerp, 232 69 40.
In Luxembourg: U.S. Embassy 22 Blvd. Emmanuel Servais, 2535 Luxembourg City, 46 01 23; **U.K. Embassy,** 14 Blvd. F. D. Roosevelt, 2018 Luxembourg City, 2 98 64.

POSTAL/TELEPHONE/TELEGRAM/FAX
Post Offices: Hours in Holland are Mon.–Fri. 8:30 a.m.–5 p.m., and in some places Sat. 8:30 a.m.–noon; in Belgium, postal hours are Mon.–Fri. 9 a.m.–12 noon and 2–4 p.m., except for offices located near railway stations in larger towns, which may remain open continuously from 9 a.m.–5 p.m.. In Luxembourg, several post offices have extended opening hours: Place de la Gare (opposite the railway station) is open 24 hours, and Rue Aldringen (at the central city bus terminus) is open Mon.–Sat. 7 a.m.–8:45 p.m. (both accept parcels only during normal office hours). Luxembourg's Findel Airport has a post office open daily 7 a.m.–10 p.m.
Telehouse Amsterdam: This communications hub, centrally located in the city near Dam Square, is open 24 hours a day for telephone calls, telegrams, money orders, and Fax services anywhere in the world.
PTT: In all three Benelux countries, there are government PTT (*post, telefoon,* and *telegraaf*) centers where you can make the lowest cost long-distance and foreign calls. An operator dials the call, and puts it through to you in an assigned booth; when the call is completed, you pay the exact charges (there's no extra service fee such as hotels add, which can make overseas calls exorbitant).

In Holland, to reach an AT&T USA Direct operator, dial 06–0229111; to reach a Bell operator in Canada, or place a collect or Calling Card call to Canada, dial 06–0229116. When phoning Holland from North America, dial 011 + 31 + City Code + local number. When phoning from North America, delete the first zero from the city code; when phoning long-distance *within* Holland, *include* the first zero. For overseas calls from Belgium, dial 11.00.10 for an AT&T USA Direct operator.
Pay Telephones: Instructions for using coin-operated telephones are given in several languages, including English. You can make international calls from telephone boxes that display signs with international flags. Calls from Dutch pay telephones take 25-cent and one guilder coins in marked slots (Belgian and Luxembourg telephones take 5 and 20-franc coins). In Holland, the amount you have unused shows on a screen, and you should drop in more coins during the call when you see the figure nearing zero. Excess coins are returned at the end of a call, but change is not made, so use small coins if calling locally. Rates for calls on all telephones change during the day, being highest until 1 p.m. on business days, lowest in the evening.

Note · · · In the spring of 1991, an extra digit was added to the beginning of all telephone numbers in Amsterdam and The Hague that were not yet seven digits. For Amsterdam add a 6 at the beginning, and for The Hague a 3, if you have an outdated six-digit telephone number.

DUTY FREE Amsterdam's Schiphol Airport duty free shopping is considered among the best in the world. Although it's fair to say that not all purchases can be considered bargains anymore—you'd be wise if you're considering a major electronic or jewelry purchase to check prices *prior* to leaving home so you know what actually constitutes a saving—the extensive selection of shops at Schiphol is, at the very least, a great convenience for certain souvenirs. Instead of lugging Edam cheeses (which can come to feel as heavy as their cannon-ball shape implies) with me to the airport, as I once did, I now buy my food purchases of cheese, chocolate, biscuits, etc. at the Schiphol Dutch "deli" after I've checked most of my other luggage. The best duty-free savings will come on Dutch products: savings on Dutch gin and liqueurs will be more than those on scotch or sherry, for example. There is a fair selection of U.S. Dept. of Agriculture-approved flower bulbs at the airport.

CUSTOMS **U.S. residents** are exempt from duty on the first $400 of combined purchases made abroad, as long as they have not made other such claims with 30 days, and as long as the items are for personal use, not resale. Family members may pool their exemption by filling out a single customs form. Those over 21 may include one liter of alcohol in their exemption. Purchases of documented (keep the papers to show customs officials) antiques (over 100 years old) and original art works are duty exempt. You may send packages to friends that are clearly marked Unsolicited Gift of Value Less than $50, (only one package per address) without paying duty on them. If you're following this procedure to avoid duty—packages sent to your home are not allowed as part of your $400 exemption and separate duty must be paid on them—consider paying the flat 10% of value charged for the first $1000 in purchases over your exemption for the security of carrying your items rather than risking damage or loss in the mail.

Certain items are restricted by U.S. law from entry into the U.S. These include articles made with any part of endangered species (The World Wildlife Fund's brochure *Buyer Beware* is available from (800) 634–4444 if you're considering designer leathers, furs, etc.). Cuban cigars are not permitted, but the fine Dutch ones are. Food products often cause confusion as to what's allowable into the U.S. Cheeses and vaccuum-wrapped smoked fish and other items usually are acceptable, especially coming from such "clean" agricultural countries as the Benelux. Sealed boxed dry items, such as crackers, cookies, and cakes are fine. Fruit, vegetables, and other plants are never allowed, and most meat is not. In Holland, one of the illegal temptations could be bulbs, bought at Amsterdam's Floating Flower Market, or elsewhere, that do not carry the inspection certificate of the U.S. Department of Agriculture. If you do arrive at U.S. Customs carrying bulbs that do not have such inspection labels, be sure to specifically declare them and have them hand-inspected by the agricultural expert on duty. Although Holland has high horticultural health standards, the risks associated with unknown insects and diseases coming into a country should prevent anyone from trying to "sneak" uninspected agricultural items through Customs anywhere. If you take any significant foreign-made articles, such as expensive watches, cameras, binoculars, or designer clothing with you on the trip, it's a good idea to bring the receipts (or other evidence that the items were brought from home) with you for clearing U.S. Customs on return. If you are traveling with prescription drugs, you would be wise to have the prescription with you to avoid possible delays in Customs.

Canadian citizens who remain out of the country for at least seven days may receive an exemption on duty for personal goods up to the value of $300 (Canadian), but only once a year. Allowances of $100 can be claimed once a calendar quarter after being outside the country 48 hours. Families may not pool their exemptions. The first $300 in excess of the exemption is taxed at a flat 20%. Unsolicited gift packages (so marked) with a value of $40 or less can be sent to friends duty free, but you might as well carry all purchases for yourself with you, as they are subject to duty.

TRANSPORTATION..........................

AIR Most North Americans will arrive in Europe by air, and Holland offers one of the most acclaimed airports in the world for organization and efficiency at **Amsterdam's Schiphol.** National carrier **KLM Royal Dutch Airlines** has the majority of flights in and out of Schiphol (on KLM City-Hopper flights within Europe, trans-Atlantic nonstops, and throughout the globe-spanning 146-city KLM system). KLM's U.S. nonstop-to-Amsterdam gateways are Atlanta, Baltimore-Washington Int., Chicago, Los Angeles, Houston, New York, Orlando, and Minn.-St. Paul; KLM offers nonstop flights to Amsterdam from the Canadian cities of Toronto, Montreal, Vancouver, and Calgary (800) 777–5553. Schiphol also offers service and connections on other airlines throughout Europe and worldwide.

The main carrier at **Brussels' Zaventem Airport** is Belgium's **Sabena World Airlines,** which flies nonstop to/from New York, Boston,

Chicago, and Montreal in North America. (800) 955–2000. The Sabena route system includes many major cities in Europe, and beyond.

Luxembourg City's Findel Airport offers service on several airlines to major European cities, including **Luxair** (the national airline) to London's Heathrow. **Icelandair** serves Luxembourg to/from the U.S. (via Reykjavik, Iceland) from New York, Baltimore-Washington Int., and Orlando (800) 223–5500. Intra-European air service remains an expensive way to travel between European cities. What effect "1992" and the anticipated increase in competition between European airlines will have on European routes and rates is still not known.

RAIL Holland has one of the most dense rail networks in the world—and Belgium has the densest. The systems are characterized by frequent service (no place served by train in Holland has less than hourly service), integrated schedules, virtually certain on-time arrivals (particularly in Holland), and international connections that provide efficient rail service from Amsterdam, Brussels, Luxembourg City, and other Benelux cities to all major cities on the continent. Trains are clean, comfortable, fast, and affordable, making them a practical and pleasurable way to tour. Tickets are sold for first and second class; First Class is about 50% more and less crowded, but certainly not essential for comfortable travel. There are smoking and non-smoking cars in both classes. Luxembourg also has a rail network, and train is an excellent way to reach its capital city from elsewhere in the Benelux or Europe; however because of its essentially rural and scenic nature, the country doesn't lend itself as well as Holland and Belgium to touring by rail after arrival.

Rail passes: Several rail passes are available, all representing considerable savings and flexibility, but it's important to analyze your particular travel plans to see if one meets your needs. The three Benelux countries are members of the 23-nation **Eurailpass** network, but Eurail should only be purchased if you plan to make a long-distance sweep of Europe, since if you "buy" more territory than you need on a rail pass, you cut into your savings. The **Benelux Tourrail Pass** provides unlimited train travel in Holland, Belgium, and Luxembourg for any five days (they don't have to be consecutive) in a period of 17 days. A second-class ticket costs Dfl. 154 or BF 3,080; First Class Dfl. 231 or BF 4,620, less for those under 26 years of age.

Perhaps a more limited-area rail pass is all you need. Holland has a seven-day **Rail Rover** (seven consecutive days) for Dfl. 129 (Dfl. 194 First Class). Available only in conjunction with the Rail Rover is the **Public Transport Link Rover** (an additional Dfl. 23.20), covering the same seven-day period. It's good for unlimited travel on *all* Dutch public buses, trams, and subways. As well as offering substantial potentially savings, these passes make travel wonderfully easy by eliminating the need to stand in line to buy tickets. Holland also offers a one-day rail pass for Dfl. 79 (Dfl. 99 First Class). There also are junior (under age 26), child, and family passes at even greater savings. An order form for passes is available from NBT offices in Chicago and Toronto, as well as a booklet, *Touring Holland By Rail*. The information office of Netherlands Railways in the train station at Schiphol Airport is open from 8 a.m.–8 p.m. Mon.–Fri., 9 a.m.–5 p.m. Sat., Sun. and holidays.

For travel solely within Belgium, the **Tourrail Pass** is good for any five days out of 17; prices (1992) are BF 1,800 (BF 2700 First Class), with a Junior Pass (ages 6–25) for BF 1,350. *A Belgian Reduction Card*, for sale (550 BF) only within Belgium and good for one month, entitles the holder to purchase at 50% off any Belgian rail tickets priced over 60 BF. Inquire about reduced rate weekend round-trip rail-tickets. Brochures and prices are available from the Belgian Tourist Office. Sample Belgian rail travel times are: Brussels to Bruges 58 mins.; Brussels to Antwerp 35 mins.; and Brussels to Ghent 37 mins. In Luxembourg, second-class-only **Rover** tickets, good for all buses and trains in the Grand Duchy, are available for a day, a week, or a month.

FERRY: For U.K. citizens and travelers who come to the Benelux via England, a number of ferry routes are in service. The quickest (just under five hours) is on the Jetfoil rail-connected service between London's Victoria Station and Brussels. The same route is served by traditional ferries (nearly nine hours, but minus the Jetfoil supplement). The rail-ship overnight crossing between Hoek of Holland (on the North Sea, west of Rotterdam) and Harwich in East Anglia (northeast of London) is popular, since it takes long enough to get a night's sleep (there's also a daytime crossing). The Dutch ports of Vlissingen (Flushing) and Scheveningen (The Hague) and the Belgian ports of Zeebrugge and Ostend offer various crossings of the North Sea and English Channel to and from England's Dover, Hull, and Yarmouth. *Boat trains* to/from London, Brussels, Amsterdam, and farther afield, are scheduled to connect with respective ferry terminals in time for crossings.

Ferries are the least expensive, most adventuresome means of crossing the North Sea, but also the most time consuming. North Americans need to assess whether the experience and/or savings are worth this means of travel. From 1993 (a completion date that may well need revising yet again), an engineering wonder, the English Channel Tunnel ("Chunnel"), will connect England and France. The beneath-the-channel rail lines will make train travel between London and Brussels considerably shorter, and a great "conversation-piece."

BICYCLE: In many ways, Holland was built around the bicycle. There are some 12 million two-wheelers for a two-legged population of 14 million, and bicycle paths account for as many kilometers as motorways do. An estimated one-third of all transportation in Holland takes place by bike. In a country so geared to bicycles and cyclists, it's great for travelers to know that safe, sturdy, single-gear (more aren't needed since the land's so flat) rental bikes are available everywhere at reasonable prices. Hired bikes cost about Dfl. 8 a day, and must be returned to the original place of hire. You'll probably be asked for a deposit (Dfl. 50–200) and proof of identity (passport or driving license). Some 80 railway stations around Holland have rental bikes and bike parking facilities. Upon presentation of a valid train ticket, you can get a discount on bike hire. In busy travel seasons, it's a good idea to reserve a bike in advance (for more information, request the 16-page publication *Cycling in Holland*).

In Belgium, bikes can be rented at 48 train stations throughout the country. Contact the Belgium Tourist Office for particulars.

BUS: All three Benelux countries have a thorough network of national and local buses. There are few places in any of the countries that you cannot reach by bus—which is almost, but not quite, the case with trains. If you are traveling solely by public transportation, and off the beaten path, you may well find yourself on a bus in the Benelux. Local tourist office information and schedules, helpful drivers and friendly fellow passengers, and the lowest transportation cost-per-kilometer all should benefit your bus travel experience.

CAR DRIVING AIDS: An International Driver's License is *not* necessary. Your current U.S., Canadian, or U.K. operator's license is sufficient. Driving in the Benelux is on the right, the same as in North America and other continental European countries, but not the U.K. Roads in the Benelux are good to excellent and generally well posted. There are plenty of motorways and highways, though those may not be the best roads for you to follow: The Royal Dutch Touring Club (ANWB) puts up six-sided route signs that point to prettier paths, and publishes maps of them. Southern Belgium and Luxembourg have hillier, curvier roads, which will slow you down even if the scenery doesn't. The major rental car companies have offices in the capital cities, but you should book in advance from North America to get the best rates. If you can drive a standard shift (in lieu of an automatic transmission, which are far fewer in Europe), you'll save on the cost of the rental car. Rentals of one week or more may qualify you for a special rate (try for unlimited mileage, at a minimum). Remember to ask for all the charges in advance: insurance and VAT (which adds a hefty 18.5% to your rental bill in Holland right off the bat). Some companies offer leasing arrangements for a minimum period of three weeks, for which rates are tax-free, and include insurance and unlimited mileage. Gasoline (petrol,

BENELUX: PRACTICAL TRAVEL INFORMATION
ROADSIGNS

Danger

No entry

Closed to all vehicles in both directions

End Restriction

Speed limit (in kilometers per hour)

End of speed limit

Parking prohibited or restricted

Standing and parking prohibited or restricted

Priority over oncoming traffic

Oncoming traffic has priority

Yield

Priority crossing

Traffic on roundabouts must give way to traffic entering from the right

Motorway

Expressway: main road with dual carriageway with two-level intersections

Uneven Road

Compulsory path for cyclist and riders of mopeds

Cycle track, forbidden to mopeds with motor switched on

Tourist Information

Local Dutch Tourist Office

In international signage, a round shape indicates restrictions or prohibitions, a square shape provides information, and a triangular one means warnings.

benzine) is pricey, at least twice what it is in the U.S., but distances are short.

When you rent a car, you won't be required to pass any test of Benelux rules of the road. And probably while you'll do fine by following the examples of drivers on the road around you, if you anticipate driving there it's a good idea to know as much about the procedure as possible. Most important is to be aware of the **priorité à droite:** traffic coming from the right *always* has the right of way, even when you're on the main road and a car is entering from an insignificant side street. Generally, Benelux drivers make a point of claiming their priority, so keep the rule very much in mind. Low beams are required when driving between nightfall and dawn, as well as in bad weather. On certain Dutch dikes (such as the Afsluitdijk across the IJsselmeer), large signs warn drivers to turn on their lights (**ontsteekt uw lichten**) in broad daylight to counter the unique shimmer of disorienting light reflecting from the flat land and water. Seat belts must be worn by both driver and front seat passenger. There is usually a minimum speed on motorways of 70 km. per hour; maximum speed limit is 120 km. (75 mph). Benelux countries take a tough stance on drinking and driving. In Holland, highway patrols can stop a driver and administer a breathalyzer test on the spot; blood alcohol limits are lower (.08), fines for abuse higher, than in the U.S. Although foreign travelers are treated politely, ignorance of

CONVERSION CHART: MILES/KILOMETERS

Kilometers		Miles	Kilometers		Miles
1.6	1	0.6	80.4	50	31.0
3.2	2	1.2	88.5	55	34.1
4.8	3	1.8	96.5	60	37.2
6.4	4	2.4	104.6	65	40.3
8.0	5	3.1	112.6	70	43.5
9.6	6	3.7	120.7	75	46.6
11.2	7	4.3	128.7	80	49.7
12.8	8	4.9	136.7	85	52.8
14.4	9	5.5	144.8	90	55.9
16.0	10	6.2	152.8	95	59.0
24.1	15	9.3	160.9	100	62.1
32.1	20	12.4	321.8	200	124.2
40.2	25	15.5	482.7	300	186.4
48.2	30	18.6	643.7	400	248.5
56.3	35	21.7	804.6	500	310.6
64.3	40	24.8	1609.3	1000	621.3
72.4	45	27.9			

If you want to convert from miles to kilometers, read from the center column to the left (1 mile = 1.6 kilometers). When converting kilometers to miles, read from the center column to the right (1 kilometer = 0.6 mile).

CONVERSION CHART: LITERS/U.S GALLONS/IMP. GALLONS

Liters	U.S. Gallons	Imp. Gallons	Liters	U.S. Gallons	Imp. Gallons
1	0.26	0.22	25	6.61	5.50
2	0.53	0.44	30	7.93	6.60
3	0.79	0.66	35	9.25	7.70
4	1.06	0.88	40	10.57	8.80
5	1.32	1.10	45	11.89	9.90
10	2.64	2.20	50	13.21	11.00
15	3.96	3.30	60	15.85	13.20
20	5.28	4.40			

the law will not get you out of such a plight. The **ANWB** in Holland (for roadside assistance, call (06–0888) and Belgium's **Touring Secours** (Wegenhulp), both of which employ distinctive yellow vehicles, are ready, able, and willing to help distressed drivers on principal roads.

PARKING: In cities and many towns in the Benelux, you will encounter the same problems parking your car as you do at home. Some city hotels offer parking (for a fee), but many can't. This is a major reason to consider planning a trip without a rental car, or getting one only when exploring and staying in the countryside. Public parking lots and garages generally are well-indicated on signs showing a **P**.

There are several parking payment methods. The most common for on-street and parking lots is to insert coins (guilder or 25-cent coins in Holland, 5, 10, or 20-franc pieces in Belgium and Luxembourg) in a centrally-located meter in the amount indicated for your estimated length of stay; the machine then issues a ticket, stamped with the date and time, which you should display on the dashboard *inside* your car. Sometimes the space where you are parked has a number painted on it that you must punch into the machine in order to get your ticket. If there is a limitation as to how long you can park, it will be indicated (2 hours = 2 *uur*). If you park at an unattended garage you should take a timed ticket from a machine when you arrive. Although the machine may not have directions in English, the procedure is fairly straightforward and a passing person is sure to be able to help. Last, though scarcely least: Especially in cities, but a good idea everywhere, try not to leave valuables in your vehicle, even in a locked trunk or glove compartment, and *never* leave anything in sight inside your car.

TRAVELING IN THE BENELUX ....

NIGHTSEEING OR ILLUMINATIONS: Some of the most memorable moments during your travels in the Benelux will be seeing public buildings, churches, castles, and monuments illuminated after dark. After dark can be after 10 p.m. in summer in these northern latitudes but the night sights are well worth staying up for. The lighted bridges of Amsterdam romantically reflected in the canals, Brussels' Grand Place glamorously aglow, and the deep Petrusse Valley hauntingly highlighted in the heart of Luxembourg City are scenes you'll not soon forget, nor the many statues, squares, stadhuizen, and steeples that also are artfully floodlit. The summer season, sometimes extended from Easter through September, is when the most monuments are lighted, but an increasing number are spot-lit year round.

MUSEUMS: In Holland, museums generally do not close at lunchtime, but in Belgium they often shut for an hour at noon, sometimes from 12 to 2 p.m. at smaller museums. In Luxembourg you can expect that museums (and shops) will be closed from 12 to 2 p.m. Most, though not all, Benelux museums close one weekday, Monday being the most common in Holland. If you're planning to do much museum meandering, Holland has a *museumjaarkaart* or museum card (Dfl. 45) that provides free entry for a year from purchase date (there is no shorter period pass) at some 375 of Holland's nearly 600 museums, including many of the major ones, which, individually, may charge Dfl. 7 or more per person. The Museum Card does not waive extra fees charged for special exhibits. The card is available at most museums that accept it, and at VVV tourist offices, where you can get publications with information on museums countrywide. The museum card also is sold at NBT in Chicago and Toronto in connection with the Holland Leisure Card.

METRIC WEIGHTS AND MEASURES: Most of the world, including the Benelux, runs by means of the metric system (though not the U.S., which still steadfastly resists its adoption). Whether you need to decipher the temperature in Celsius (see this section under *Weather*) in order to dress for the day, can't wait to buy 250 grams of handmade chocolate pralines or a 1.5 meter length of Belgian lace, want to know how high that handsome town hall tower (given in meters in the town's tourist pamphlet) *really* is, need to fill up the tank of your rental car with liters of petrol, or must know how many kilometers it is to your next destination (see under *Transportation, Driving Aids*), below you

PRACTICAL TRAVEL INFORMATION · · · 39

have the means by which to make sense of metrics, with, perhaps, the help of a hand calculator.

1 ounce = 28.25 grams
100 grams = 3.52 ounces
1 U.S. pound = 0.45 kilogram (kilo)
500 grams = a half kilo (or 1.1 U.S. pounds)
1000 grams = 1 kilo (or 2.2 U.S. pounds)

1 acre = 0.40 hectare
1 hectare = 2.47 acres

1 U.S. pint = 0.47 liter
1 U.S. quart = 0.94 liter
1 liter = 2.12 U.S. pints
1 U.S. gallon = 3.78 liters
1 Imperial gallon = 4.54 liters

1 centimeter = 0.39 inch
1 inch = 2.54 centimeters
1 foot = 30.4 centimeters
1 yard = 0.91 meters

CONVERSION CHART: FEET/METERS

Meters		Feet	Meters		Feet
0.30	1	3.28	13.72	45	147.64
0.61	2	6.56	15.24	50	164.04
0.91	3	9.84	18.29	60	196.85
1.22	4	13.12	21.34	70	229.66
1.52	5	16.40	24.38	80	262.47
1.83	6	19.69	27.43	90	295.28
2.13	7	22.97	30.48	100	328.08
2.44	8	26.25	60.96	200	656.17
2.74	9	29.53	91.44	300	984.25
3.05	10	32.81	121.92	400	1312.34
4.57	15	49.21	152.40	500	1640.42
6.10	20	65.62	182.88	600	1968.51
7.62	25	82.02	213.36	700	2296.59
9.14	30	98.43	243.84	800	2624.67
10.67	35	114.83	274.32	900	2952.76
12.19	40	131.23	304.80	1000	3280.84

If you want to convert from feet to meters, read from the center column to the left (1 foot = .30 meters). When converting meters to feet, read from the center column to the right (1 meter = 3.28 feet).

ELECTRIC CURRENT: Voltage in the Benelux generally is 220 AC, 50 cycles, but in some parts of Belgium it is 110. If you are bringing small electrical appliances, you'll need a transformer and a variety of adapter plugs in order to ensure a match to varying socket shapes. Personally, I'm for *not* taking electrical gadgets on travels, primarily because of luggage weight. If you're planning to stay in First Class properties, you'll often find a hair dryer in the bathroom, frequently a pants-press, perhaps a self-service shoe shine machine in the hall. At many hotels, you can borrow an iron and board or hair dryer by contacting the front desk.

SMOKING: Non-smoking North Americans may be unprepared for the *lack* of designated non-smoking areas in Europe. And, cigar smoking is still a tradition in much of Europe. For years, trains have had non-smoking cars (in second as well as first class), but progress toward non-smoking sections in restaurants and non-smoking rooms in hotels (your best bet is in international chain properties) is slow. Statistics do show that more citizens in the Benelux have stopped smoking than in some other European countries.

PUBLIC TOILETS: The initials *WC* (for water closet) are the most international indication for public facilities, though the term *toilets* is most common. (Don't ask for the "bathroom" unless you want to take a bath; even in hotel rooms, with private facilities, the bathtub and/or shower usually is separate from the toilet.) Americans will find public toilets far more available than at home, and almost always clean. Facilities may be free, though it's a good idea to keep a couple of *qwarties* (25-cent pieces) in Holland and 5-franc pieces in Belgium and Luxembourg handy for coin-operated toilets. Often there are attendants who make change and keep the place clean. Toilets in Holland and in Flemish Belgium are marked *heren* for men, *dames* for women, and *madames* (woman) and *messieurs* (men) in the rest of Belgium and Luxembourg. International signs, with figures in skirts and in pants, often are used.

TIPPING, VAT: Throughout the Benelux, VAT (value-added-tax) and service are included in hotel and restaurant checks, which in Holland will say *inclusief*. In Holland, however, when service has been good, it is customary to add about 10% to restaurant bills, and at cafes to round up the amount by a guilder or so. This is unnecessary in Belgium and Luxembourg. Tips are included in metered taxi fares, which are expensive in all three Benelux countries, and especially so in Belgium and in Luxembourg, where there are extra charges for baggage, Sundays, and night trips.

Refund of VAT on Qualifying Purchases: A resident of a non-EC country who buys an item with a value over Dfl. 300 is entitled to a VAT refund (18.5% in Holland, 19% in Belgium). The procedure is to ask the store *at the time of purchase* for an export certificate (Dutch Form OB90). On leaving Holland with the purchase, have the form endorsed at Dutch customs, and you'll receive the tax refund. If you neglect to get the form at the time of purchase, it's possible to have a Dutch customs official endorse the invoice for the qualifying items, but then you must send the forms back to the store and wait for a refund check. Inquire within Belgium and Luxembourg about the qualifying amount of purchase and procedure for VAT refunds.

NEWS AND NEWSPAPERS: Even certified news junkies will be able to keep up on international events in the Benelux. In addition to the *International Herald Tribune* (with its American sports scores and standings for the addicted), European-printed editions of *The Wall Street Journal* and *USA Today,* and British dailies such as the *Financial Times, Daily Telegraph,* and *The Times* all are available at major hotels and many news shops in the capital cities and commercial centers of the Benelux. The almost-ubiquitous cable channels now available on hotel TVs will, in the western regions of the Benelux nearer to England, pull in the news on the BBC stations from London. CNN International is available at an increasing number of better hotels. Weekly news magazines in English (*The Economist, Time, Newsweek,* Murdoch's *The European*) and plentiful paperbacks are available at airports, major hotels, and in many book stores.

BUSINESS/SHOPPING HOURS: Basic store and business hours in Holland are 9 a.m.–6 p.m. Mon.–Sat., but many department and other stores are closed on Mon. until 1 p.m. Pharmacies (*apotheek* in Holland) are open from 8 a.m. to 5:30 p.m., unless they are designated for longer duty. Small shops, bakeries, and news/tobacco stands, can open as early as 7:30 or 8 a.m. in the Benelux. Certain kinds of shops (butchers, bakers, or drugstores/*drogisterij,* which sell toiletries) may close one weekday afternoon. Hours are posted on shop doors. Department stores usually are open from 9 a.m. to 6 p.m.; there is no closing for lunch in Holland, and only outside of cities in Belgium will stores close at noon for an hour or two (in which case they'll remain open until 7 or 8 p.m.). In season at holidays resorts on the coast or in the Ardennes, family shops and stores may stay open as late as 9 or 10 p.m. In Holland, with the exception of certain resort areas, but including cities and large towns from Rotterdam north, and even Amsterdam, most stores are closed tight on Sundays for the Protestant Sabbath. Sundays in Belgium, bakeries, grocery stores, and flower shops are open 8 a.m.–noon; patisseries are open for your pleasure all day. Many Belgian shops are small family-run businesses that keep long hours; to prevent unfair competition, the Government requires a compulsory closing day—shopowner's choice—once a week.

Many stores in Holland and Luxembourg are closed Monday until 1 p.m. Most museums, offices, and shops in Luxembourg close from 12 noon to 2 p.m. Late night shopping until 8 or 9 p.m. one weeknight (which varies from town to town) is usual throughout the Benelux.

MISCELLANEOUS:

For meetings and greetings in the Benelux, handshakes are the rule with everyone you meet. There's no separate etiquette for women or men, and it doesn't matter who extends the first hand. A person joining a group already assembled should shake hands with everyone. Handshakes also are repeated all around on departure. If relations with a Benelux acquaintance (man or woman) proceed further, handshakes are replaced with kisses, on the cheek. Differences in kissing etiquette— one cheek in Holland, both cheeks in France, and three in Belgium— seem to have become standardized into what a Luxembourg friend calls the "European kiss," which takes Belgium's lead (Brussels, after all, is capital of the EC) of three kisses on alternating cheeks.

- If there are no empty tables at a cafe or casual eatery with self-seating, it is acceptable to ask those sitting at a table that has room for you if you may sit down. While it's not suggested you infringe on the others at the table, the situation can lead to pleasant exchanges.

- As in most of Europe, the story *above* the ground or lobby level is designated the *first floor* in hotels, offices, and apartment buildings.

- In Europe, calendar dates, in events listings, etc., are written *day/month/year:* April 19, 1993, would be indicated 19/04/93. Since mix-ups in days and months could have serious consequences in matters of hotel reservations or appointments, I find it's best to deal with dates by writing out the name of the month, preceded by the numerical day: 19 April 1993.

- However pragmatic the Dutch approach to societal situations may be, it's a misconception that drugs and prostitution are legal in Holland.

- *Queuing,* the civilized practice of waiting in line until one's turn that's been refined by the British, is not much observed in many parts of the Benelux. For buses, trams, and even in shops, it can be everyone for one's self. But do look around in banks, bakeries, etc.—which sometimes have them in effect just during busy times—for machines from which to take a numbered ticket that places you in line for service.

THE BENELUX CULTURAL LEGACY: ART AND ARCHITECTURE, MUSIC AND THE MUSE

ART

The Benelux countries have contributed substantially to the stores of western art and architecture, and have supplied seminal ideas in many areas of artistic endeavor. In Holland and Belgium, geographic location (northern Europe, in contrast to the southern exposure of Italy), the influence of and reaction to ideas introduced by various occupying foreign regimes, and other happenstances of history, all played a hand in the artistic development.

Architectural monuments, under usual circumstances, are bound to the land on which they took form. Thus, save for fire, warfare, and urban updating, visitors to the Benelux in one era and those in the next should be able to see the same visually appealing buildings that have served as both physical and artistic landmarks over the centuries.

Paintings and other smaller fine arts works, on the other hand, are portable, and thus do not remain as dependably on deposit in the countries of their creators. In Holland and Belgium, numerous foreign occupations, as recently as the mid-twentieth century under the Nazis, have greatly affected what art produced there still can be seen there. For example, Dutch painter **Hieronymous Bosch** was a favorite—though his birthplace certainly wasn't—with the region's Spanish Hapsburg ruler King Philip II. Philip had much of the mystical artist's work brought to him in Spain, where today it can be seen in Madrid's **Prado Museum.** When the Austrian Hapsburgs oversaw the Netherlands, a large number of early Flemish paintings, and a particularly impressive collection by **Pieter Bruegel the Elder,** found their way to Vienna, eventually winding up on the walls of that city's **Kunsthistorisches Museum.**

But although many of Holland's and Belgium's artists have long been recognized as masters of such merit that their works hang in galleries around the world, museums in the Benelux remain rich in major and representative pieces by their own most renowned artists from all periods. Some of the most significant and prolific painters, among them **Rubens** and **Rembrandt, Van Gogh** and **Mondriaan,** are extremely well-represented on their home soil, so much so that certain cities and museums are virtual places of pilgrimage.

The distinctive subjects and styles that we associate with Flemish and Dutch art from the 15th through the 17th centuries and more recently first took form in the late 14th century, in the miniature paintings created to adorn the prayer books/diaries of members of the privileged classes. Those small scenes of seasonal daily life, early *genre* works if you will, revealed the realism, however naive, that was to become such a differentiating element in the art of northern Europe from that in Italy. The outstanding example is the *Tres Riches Heures de Duc du Berry*, painted by **Pol de Limbourg** (today's Limburg provinces) and his two brothers between 1410–1416.

The **Master of Flemalle,** today widely thought to be **Robert Campin** (1378/9–1444), the foremost painter of Tournai (Belgium), is the creator of *The Merode Altarpiece* (1425–1428). The center panel of the triptych portrays an annunciation scene, and is one of the earliest instances in which viewers could actually look into a spatial world where everyday reality is represented. The Master of Flemalle used not an aristocratic or court setting, but a Flemish burgher's house as the setting for the Annunciation, an approach that was a significant departure from the Italian Renaissance aim of representing an ideal world. While some medieval religious symbolism survived in paintings in Flanders, the desire to depict the world of everyday articles and life framed a whole new sense of realism. Gradually, the reverential artistic treatment once reserved solely for religious subjects was applied to all aspects of common everyday life, ordinary items thus became "sanctified," and Flemish artists were freed from being restricted to religious subjects in order to portray the physical world.

The work of Robert Campin also marks a divergence between Late Gothic northern art and Italy's concurrent Early Renaissance in its use of *oil* in the paint. The Master of Flemalle was among the first to try the practice, and oil has served as the basic painting medium ever since. Previously, medieval panel painters had employed *tempera,* in which finely ground pigments were "tempered," or mixed, with diluted egg yolk. With the substitution of oil for the water-and-egg-yolk mixture, thicker layers of paints were possible. This enhanced artists' ability to render depth, rich velvety hues, and a variety of textures from thin to thick—all of which greatly increased the possibilities for portraying reality. Campin and his contemporaries are called the "fathers of modern painting" not only for their fresh visions of reality, but also for their means of presenting it.

Late Gothic/Northern Renaissance Period

Jan van Eyck (c.1390–1441), long credited with "inventing" oil painting, did indeed add substantial new dimensions to the effects it could achieve. He worked in Holland and elsewhere before settling in Bruges. Among the signed and dated pieces by Jan van Eyck is the famous Ghent Altarpiece, *The Adoration of the Mystical Lamb* (1432), which had been begun by Jan's brother Hubert. The altarpiece, widely considered the greatest monument of early Flemish painting, was recently restored and repositioned in Ghent's St. Bavo church, to aid the viewing of all 20 panels on both sides of the piece. A fundamental pursued by Jan van Eyck in his painting was "atmospheric perspective," which actually is more important to our realistic perception of deep space than linear perspective, upon which the Italians placed such high priority.

A third great master of early Flemish painting was, like Campin, from Tournai: **Rogier van der Weyden** (1399–1464), sometimes referred to by the French version of his name *Rogier de la Pasture*. Whereas Jan van Eyck explored the reality made visible by light, shadow, and color, Van der Weyden concerned himself more with human feeling. In his portraits, he "interprets" personality, rather than leaving the faces psychologically "neutral." By the time of his death, Rogier had had 30 unbroken years of artistic activity in Brussels (where he was the official town painter), and was considered the most influential European painter north of the Alps.

A generation later, the technically superb works of **Hans Memling** (1435–1494), many of which are in historic St. Jan's Hospital in Bruges, his adopted home, are more idealized than Rogier's. Those of **Hugo**

van der Goes (1445–1482), who also painted primarily in Bruges, evoke a more emotionally intense response from the viewer.

The oldest known engravings date from about 1430, and show the influence of the major Flemish painters of the period. In the mid-15th century came a technical development of surpassing importance in the history of art: the appearance of printed pictures in books. The earliest printed books were produced in the Rhineland about 1450—a landmark event that some historians use to mark the passage from the Middle Ages to the Modern era. Considered second only to the German Martin Schongauer, the first printmaker to gain international fame, is the **Master of the Hausbuch,** who is thought to be Dutch. His prints are intimate and spontaneous, giving the impression of a sketch. The Master of the Hausbuch scratched his designs into a copper plate with a fine steel needle, a technique known as *drypoint,* which permitted fairly free expression. Although the drypoint plates, due to their rather shallow grooves, did not yield many printings, they afforded a wide variety of atmospheric effects. The Master of the Hausbuch was a pioneer in an art form that fellow Dutchman **Rembrandt** would bring to full life a century and a half later in his etchings.

In the 16th century, the Netherlands Low Countries experienced the most turbulent times of any country north of the Alps. When the **Reformation** began, the Netherlands were a part of the far-flung empire of the Hapsburgs under Charles V (who had been born in Ghent), who was also king of Spain. Protestantism quickly became powerful in the northern Netherlands (today's Holland), and attempts by the Catholic rulers to suppress it led to open revolt. After a bloody struggle, Holland emerged independent and widely Protestant, and the southern Netherlands (roughly corresponding to modern-day Belgium) remained in Catholic-Spanish hands. Amazingly, the political and religious strife of the Reformation, which was particularly intense in the Netherlands between 1550 and 1600, did *not* have a devastating effect on art in Flanders and Holland.

The Reformation, which began in earnest about 1520, did place painting in northern Europe in crisis. The question arose as to whether painting could, or should, continue at all, since many Protestants objected to images of saints in churches, regarding them as a sign of popish idolatry. As early as 1526, Humanist **Erasmus** of Rotterdam wrote from Switzerland of northern Europe's artistically troubled situation in a letter commending the German painter Hans Holbein to friends in England: "The arts here are freezing." In fact, only one Protestant region in Europe fully survived the crisis of the Reformation in the art arena: the Netherlands (Holland and Flanders).

During the 16th century, Netherlands' painters struggled—successfully—with two main issues. Even prior to the Reformation, the first had presented itself: how to assimilate the influence of Italian Renaissance art. The second, a direct consequence of the Reformation, was the loss in Protestant regions of painters' single best source of income: altar panels (for Catholic churches). The loss of such traditional commissions led artists to create a repertory of specialized non-religious subject matter to which the Protestant Church could raise no objections. All the secular themes that feature so prominently in Dutch and Flemish painting of the Baroque era—*portraits, still life, landscape, genre* (scenes of everyday life)—had actually been present earlier, as ancillary elements in the works of the brothers Limbourg and Van Eyck, but gradually became better defined between 1500 and 1600. Many artists began to specialize in one particular area.

The idea of specialization was not new in Netherlands art. **Hieronymus Bosch** (1474–1516), a Dutch artist who was born and worked most of his life in the North Brabant provincial town of 's Hertogenbosch (Den Bosch), filled such paintings as *The Garden of Delights* with fantastic figures and imagery; clearly, some symbols are suggestive, some in remarkably Freudian form. Original Sin seems to loom large, but Bosch's own meanings for his images are mostly unknown to us today. Bosch's strange human figures may be almost otherworldly, but there's no question of their connection with the genre tradition that reached rare heights under the genius of **Pieter Bruegel the Elder** (1525?–1569). Though Breugel had traveled to Italy, his paintings of peasant life executed in Antwerp and Brussels were thoroughly Flemish in form and content. Well-educated, a humanist, and patronized by the Hapsburg court, Breugel chose to paint peasants, with a wealth of wit and anecdote that revealed a degree of observation that was far from simple, and served as an example for genre painters in the Netherlands for generations. Though best known for his specialized attention to peasant scenes, Breugel's *Return of the Hunters* is one of the first in which landscape is the main subject of a painting.

Baroque Period

In the Catholic Southern Netherlands (today's Belgium) of the Counter Reformation, **Pieter Paul Rubens** (1577–1640) was the most collected painter of his time, and the dominant figure in Flemish art during his life and well after. As a trained master painter, Rubens went in 1600 to Rome, birthplace of the Baroque style, spending some seven years there. Rubens listened and learned with keen interest in Italy, but does not seemed to have joined any of the "movements" (even though he was certainly influenced by the lighting of Caravaggio's work). While Rubens remained an artist in the Flemish tradition, by absorbing the Italian tradition far more thoroughly than had any previous northern painter, he played a role of unique importance in helping to make the Baroque style international. His influence helped to break down the artistic barriers between southern and northern Europe.

Rubens' exuberant, optimistic style, and his skill in making his works seem intensely alive, counteracted the spiritual crisis caused by the explosion of new knowledge of the world (Copernicus' early 16th-century discovery that the earth was not the center of the solar system had been an unsettling one for many people). The immediacy and dazzling use of color in Rubens' paintings instilled faith and, emotionally, lifted people out of their ordinary life. Particularly in the 1620s, Rubens used his dynamic style in the design of decorative schemes for churches and palaces. While no similar artistic tradition existed in Holland (where pupils of masters were left free to develop their own individual style), Rubens maintained a robust studio with many pupils and guild-member artists who were well-trained in his style, and who would complete paintings after the master had finished making his mark. The differences in talent between Rubens' work and that of pupils who finished his pieces is most noticeable in paintings originally made as altar panels (several remain *in situ* in Antwerp) that have been removed to museums.

Anthonie van Dyck (1599–1641) (a.k.a. Sir Anthony Vandyck), a child prodigy who had become Rubens' most valued assistant before he was 20, was the only other Flemish Baroque artist to achieve international renown. His mature work mainly consists of portraits, especially those executed while he served as court painter to England's Charles I. The aristocrat portrait tradition that Van Dyck created had considerable continental influence until late in the 18th century.

Holland's 17th-Century "Golden Age"

Having achieved *de facto* independence from Spain in 1579, Holland (the seven Protestant northern provinces of the United Netherlands) ushered in the 17th-century set to make the most of a period that promised unprecedented prosperity and growth (both in population and ideas). Dutch 17th-century art is unique not only for its vast quantity of artists who demonstrated superb craftmanship—besides the acknowledged geniuses, there were many "little masters," a non-perjorative term used only to indicate that these painters are less widely known—but for the realism with which it recorded the face of Holland and its people.

Never before the 17th century in Holland had a group of artists looked at the physical world around them with such clarity and set down their observations with such fidelity. Turning away from the religious, mythological, and allegorical subjects that had been the themes of the Renaissance (and remained so, to some extent, in Rubens' Flanders), the Dutch portrayed what they saw around them with great artistry but without affectation. It was no coincidence that this new emphasis on realism in art came when and where it did. The age that produced Rembrandt had *reason* as a guiding principle for its philosophers. One of the foremost was the rationalist Rene Descartes ("I think, therefore I am"), who chose to live most of his adult life in Holland.

The development of certain areas of science paralleled the development of art in Holland. The first important portrait commission that **Rembrandt van Rijn** (1606–1669) received as a trained painter was for the 1632 *Anatomy Lesson of Dr. Tulp* (in the **Mauritshuis** in The Hague). It is an unusual group portrait featuring realistic treatment of a potentially distasteful subject, but its success seems to show that the Dutch were ready to look at the world with realist eyes.

A scientific subject of considerable contemporary interest was optics, and the Dutch were preeminent in the field. The telescope that Galileo adapted for his research had been invented by lens grinders in the Netherlands. Light was of interest to the Dutch artistically as well as scientifically. The light reflected from their flat water-logged land lent a special atmosphere to the increasingly popular landscape paintings. Vermeer flooded his subjects with light, while Rembrandt turned the lamps down low for dramatic effect. One of Rembrandt's teachers, Pieter Lastman, who had traveled to Italy and seen what Caravaggio's work conveyed through *chiaroscuro* (the interplay of light and shadow), passed his impressions on to his pupil, who began to use the device with a skill no other artist has ever surpassed.

Many Dutch towns, like Haarlem, Leiden, and Delft, had artists' guilds in the 17th century that sought to solicit business for members while controlling competition from outsiders. But Amsterdam was an open art market, in which, for the first time in the history of Western art, traditional patronage and guild support were replaced by the interests and tastes of a buying public. The expanding prosperous merchant class was the most common source of commissions, but there also was brisk business at artists' own shops and art dealers, and ordinary citizens could buy paintings at annual fairs and markets. Prices varied, with artists of repute naturally fetching higher prices for their work than more obscure colleagues. The average price for an unsigned picture of a high standard cost about the equivalent of a fisherman's weekly wage, so, while art was relatively expensive, it remained within reach of a large cross-section of the public.

It was a remarkably compact period during which so many outstanding Dutch artists were born, beginning with Frans Hals in 1580. For 75 years in the 17th century, the world was nearly overwhelmed with the output of works of genius and true talent in Holland. Sales of paintings were supported by a broad segment of society, with members of the general public, whether they could afford to or not, developing a nearly insatiable appetite for investing in pictures. Supply kept up with demand, with literally tens of thousands of paintings of a consistent, astonishingly high standard sold. A Frenchman who taught at the University of Leiden in the 17th century wrote, "There can surely be no other country in the world where there are so many, and such excellent, paintings."

For Dutch artists in the 17th century, it was usual to specialize in subject matter. (Rembrandt is one of the few who did not; although most known for his history paintings and portraits as well as etchings and drawings, he was a world of art in himself). A hierarchy in 17th-century Dutch paintings became established. Artistically, history paintings (mostly undertaken by Rembrandt), ranked highest, followed in descending order by portraits, genre pieces, landscapes, and still lifes.

Portraits—Portraits were a plentiful source of commissions for artists in the 17th century, since such paintings were popular as a reflection of the prosperous Dutch people's pride in themselves and their achievements. Because the work was there, many artists practiced portraiture in addition to another specialty. Uniquely Dutch were the large-scale **group portraits** of guilds and civic corporations. The most creative artists used imaginative means to make such group configurations more than static records of status, with **Rembrandt's** *The Night Watch* (at the **Rijksmuseum,** Amsterdam) an outstanding example. Rembrandt's self-portraits (40 paintings, 20 drawings, 10 engravings), are an unprecedented legacy of self-examination in Western art. **Frans Hals** of Haarlem (1580–1666), one of the greatest portrait painters of the 17th or any century, considered avant-garde in his day, portrayed subjects from slightly shabby patrons of local inns to aristocratic couples posing for paired full-length engagement mementos to the famous groupings of the *Regents of Haarlem's Old Men's Almshouse* (at the **Frans Hals Museum,** Haarlem). Vincent van Gogh, who regarded his own work in portraiture as some of his most promising, admired Hals greatly, and wrote of him, "He tried to achieve the painting of the humanity of an entire republic by the simple means of making portraits."

Footnote: The fashion for large, stiff, starched, accordion-like lace collars evident in many a portrait of the late 16th and early 17th centuries led to a fashion for forks in Amsterdam, since the size and shape of the collars made an extension of the fingers necessary for neat eating.

Genre—Genre (scenes from the everyday life of ordinary people) had its roots in earlier Flemish painting, particularly that of Pieter Breugel the Elder. Into the category, which is almost a trademark of Dutch art, falls a full range of subjects: domestic interiors and taverns, servants and skaters, wenches and willful children. **Jan Vermeer** of Delft produced only 32 small paintings in his lifetime, all finely finished studies of a domestic moment frozen in time. **Jan Steen,** one of the most highly ranked genre painters, supplemented his earnings, and his opportunity to observe people, by running an inn. Delightfully peopled skating scenes were painted by **Hendrick Avercamp** (1585–1634), who specialized in winter scenes. Genre paintings can be anecdotal or reportorial, but often are more complex than they seem, since the situations presented often are meant to also show the moral landscape of everyday living. Just in the realm of genre painters, the early 17th century in Holland produced in rapid succession **Adriaen Brouwer** (born 1605), first of the great genre painters; **Adriaen van Ostade** (1610); **Gerard Terborch** (1617); **Jan Steen** (1626); **Gabriel Metsu** (1629); **Pieter de Hooch** (1629), the most popular genre painter of his day; **Vermeer** (1632); and **Nicolaes Maes** (1634).

Landscapes—Our English word *landscape* very probably comes from the Dutch *landschap,* an indication that the Dutch virtually can be credited with "inventing" landscape painting, the art of transforming a simple homely scene into a setting of restful beauty. Dutch landscape painters sketched in nature, but composed in their studio. Gradually, they moved the horizon line lower, and let the open compositions create a unified space pervaded by a new sense of shifting light, atmosphere, and weather—the very components of the Dutch landscape that capture photographers' attention today. Landscapes in 17th-century Holland started out as the least popular form of painting, but, by the end of the century, had proven the most popular, and most numerous. **Jan van Goyen** (1596–1656) was among the Dutch landscapists who discovered the beauty of the sky for the first time in the history of art. **Jacob van Ruisdael** (1628?–1682) was Holland's most outstanding landscapist, while **Aert van der Neer** (1603–1677), who sub-specialized in twilight and nocturnal views, **Aelbert Cuyp** (1620–1691), and **Meindert Hobbema** (1638–1709) are others prominent in the period.

Still Life—Although still life *painters* supposedly stood on the lowest rung of the 17th-century Dutch art ladder, still life *paintings* always were popular with the public. They came into being in the 16th century, carrying the residue of religious symbolism from 15th-century paintings. For all that they could be taken for pure decoration, still lifes, at once the most natural and the most artificial of art work, frequently concealed broader religious and moral ideas of the day. There's great variety in 17th-century still life subject matter, but a common characteristic is carefully arranged, well-recorded objects that almost denote "possession." Still life was a platform for Dutch deftness in realism and technical virtuosity.

Flower still lifes were always well liked. Individual blossoms always were carefully positioned so that they didn't obscure one another. **Jan Breughel** (1568–1625), eldest son of Pieter the Elder, was known as *"Velvet Breughel"* for the texture of the rare flowers and tulips in which he specialized. **Jan van Goyen,** who also did landscapes, specialized in painting tulips (his pictures are virtual "portraits"), as well as speculating in them. It is said that the losses he incurred buying tulip bulbs during the *Tulipmania* era (see chapter *The Bulb Field Business*) took him 30 years to pay/paint off. One of the most distinguished woman painters, **Rachel Ruysch** (1664–1750), who had a famed atelier, also concentrated on flower still lifes. Insects, sometimes shown devouring leaves, in addition to adding realism, can be taken to refer to the transience of life, a recurrent theme in still lifes.

Banquet Pieces—Popular until the 1620s were the so-called *Breakfast Pieces,* which showed the ingredients of an unpretentious Dutch meal of cheese, beer, fish, and bread on a high horizon, tilted table top. Such a painting would have been consistent with the Calvinist exhortation to moderation. The slightly later *banquet pieces* show a chaotic arrangement of half-eaten foods and overturned containers, with utensils resting unbalanced at the corner of the table. Such a scene easily could be a symbol for disharmony in life, or suggestive of the need for restraint in worldly appetites. But critics caution against a temptation to insist on symbolism in still lifes, since such a scene also could just be showing the remnants of a good party.

Pronks are showy still lifes of brilliant colors, rich textures, and complex compositions. They are ostentatious in their display of expensive and exotic objects: Venetian glass; lobsters and tobacco from America; rare shells from around the world. During the period from 1650 to 1675, the Dutch were the richest people in Christendom, and pronk paintings present an exhaustive account of their commercial consumption. In this era, commerce was king in Holland; Dutch merchants' home furnishings rivaled those in other countries' royal palaces. But, tucked somewhere in a pronk painting usually is some indication—perhaps a watch ticking—that points to the passage of time and the impermanence of material objects.

Vanitas—As the Dutch got wealthier, their life style became more open to comment by the still life form known as *vanitas,* which showed little subtlety in its reference to death. The passage-of-time theme is conveyed by snuffed-out candles, hourglasses and other timepieces, rotting fruit among excessive displays of food, and elegant objects of silver and gold that warn of contamination by consumer goods. Without forcing moral judgment, the juxtaposition of objects probably were meant at least to suggest the temptations of the material world, and people's accountability to the spiritual realm.

19th and 20th Centuries

Quite suddenly, the brilliance of the 17th century burned itself out. And, with the French invasion under Louis XIV in 1672–78, the entire artistic atmosphere changed. Mostly lackluster artistic overture ensued until the middle of the 19th century.

Then from Groningen, in the far north of the Netherlands, came the talented painter **Josef Israels** (1824–1911) who, after contact with the Barbizon group of painters in France, introduced the new "open-air" painting in The Hague. (The Barbizon painters themselves had been influenced by the 17th-century Dutch landscapists, and many had traveled from France to Holland to see their works in museums there.) Israels won esteem as a painter of Scheveningen (The Hague) fishermen, and with others founded the **Hague School**. Another notable was **J. B. Jongkind** (1819–1891); whose seascapes, filled with light and misty vapors, are reminiscent of the English painter Turner.

The painters of the Hague School returned the eyes of Dutch painters towards landscape. **Anton Mauve** (1838–1888) so exactly captured the effect of light and representation in his paintings that they seem almost photographic. **Hendrik Willem Mesdag** (1831–1915) was a founding member of the Hague School who also painted seascapes. The three **Maris brothers,** Jacob, Matthijs, and Willem, and **J. H. Weissenbruch** were other members. The quiet, traditional pattern of painting of the Hague School was continued into the 20th century by such painters as **G. H. Breitner** (1857–1923). A fine Hague School collection (as well as the largest Barbizon collection outside France) is displayed in the former home of H. W. Mesdag (the **Mesdag Museum,** The Hague), within walking distance of the great circular **Mesdag Panorama** scenic painting of Scheveningen.

The giant among 19th-century Dutch painters was, of course, **Vincent van Gogh** (1853–1890), a self-taught post-impressionist, whose monumental talent was just on the brink of being widely recognized when he died at the age of 37 from a self-inflicted wound in July 1890. His brother Theo supported Vincent steadfastly both financially and psychologically during the last ten years of his life when Vincent had turned to art to communicate the love of humanity that he had such difficulty expressing in words (except in detailed letters to Theo, which have been preserved). Theo, who was so devastated by the death of Vincent that he lost his health, sanity, and then life all within six months of the death of his brother, had married a Dutch woman, Johanna Bonger, in April 1889, by whom he had a son they named Vincent. It is due to the efforts of Vincent van Gogh's sister-in-law Johanna and namesake nephew that so much of the artist's work (paintings, drawings, and letters with sketches) belongs to museums in Holland, principally the **Rijksmuseum Vincent Van Gogh** in Amsterdam, and the **Kroller-Muller Museum** in Otterlo in the Hoge Veluwe National Park, near Arnhem.

Van Gogh's work, although much of it was realized in France, is deeply rooted in the Dutch art tradition. The first painting that Vincent considered worthy to be called one was *The Potato Eaters,* painted in

Nuenen, a village in the southern Dutch province of North Brabant, where his father was a minister and where potato farming was predominant. The dark palette of earth tones harks back to the 17th century, and a dark interior, lighted only indirectly, shows Van Gogh's familiarity with Rembrandt's use of such effects. It is not surprising to learn that Van Gogh admired Frans Hals, when one compares the energetic quality of the two artists' brush strokes. In his five highly fruitful years of painting, Vincent explored all the aspects of Holland's great artistic traditions: still life (among which are wonderful irises and sunflowers); genre (peasants at their labors); landscapes (some with a low horizon and huge sky that recalls Holland); and portraits (in which he several times in letters to Theo expressed an interest in specializing.)

Apart from his fellow countryman Rembrandt, Van Gogh scrutinized himself more searchingly through the medium of self-portraits than any other artist. Both bring the same honesty, the same realism to their portraits of the artists as representatives of humanity.

Although his earliest works were representational landscapes, Dutch painter **Piet Mondriaan** (1872–1944) is known as one of the chief founders of abstract art. You can see examples of the landscapes in what is the world's largest collection of Mondriaan works in The Hague's **Gemeentemuseum** (itself worth seeing, as the last work by Dutch architect H. P. Berlage, see *Architecture* below). Mondriaan progressed in his paintings through Cubist works clearly influenced by Picasso and Braque until he arrived, about 1920, at the utmost austerity of Abstractism, in which he used only straight lines and primary colors, plus white and black. Mondriaan was a founder of the remarkably influential *De Stijl* group, which sought to exclude decoration and subjectivity from art and architecture. Other members included **Theo van Doesburg** (1883–1935), **J. P. Oud** (1890–1963), and architect **G. Rietveld** (1888–1964), one of whose houses in Utrecht can be visited. One Dutch disciple of De Stijl, **Willem de Kooning,** born in 1904, left Holland in 1926 to continue his creative career in the U.S.

The COBRA group (an acronym for Copenhagen, Brussels, and Amsterdam) includes founding Benelux members **Karel Appel** (born 1921) and **Constant** (born 1920). Interviewed in the group's founding year, 1948 (three years after the end of World War II), Constant said, "We have been stripped of every certainty; no faith remains but this: that we are alive and that it is part of the essence of life to manifest oneself." Their work is characterized by spontaneity, by vivid, warm colors, and by a form and content reminiscent of children's drawing. Constant believed "a painting is not a construction of colors and lines, but an animal, a night, a scream, a human being, or all of them at once."

Belgian art in the 20th century brought several respected names. In the paintings of **James Ensor** (1860–1949) the pessimistic view of the human condition, presented centuries earlier by Hieronymous Bosch, reappears. Nightmarish images of demons and masks fill the works of the reclusive Ensor, Impressionist-turned-Father-of-Surrealism, who lived most of his life inside his house in Ostend. One of the most important Surrealist painters is Belgian **Rene Magritte** (1898–1967), whose juxtaposed motifs have been highly influential. **Paul Delvaux** (b. 1897) played an important role early in the movement of Surrealism. Delvaux's paintings, a significant and well-displayed selection of which are on view in a museum at his house near De Panne on the Belgian coast, shows strong obsessional images of sexuality, travel, and death. Among the Belgian group broadly called the *Brabant Fauvists* because of their use of bold outlines and bright blocks of color are the painters **Jean Brusselmans** (1884–1953), **Rik Wouters** (1882–1916), and **Henri Wolvens** (1896–1977), all represented at Brussels' **Museum of Modern Art.**

Visitors to Brussels interested in contemporary Belgian art can also encounter it in the Metro (see also *What to See and Do, Brussels*). Most stations throughout the system have works, which range from tapestries and tiles to the largest photograph in the world, fantasy landscapes to flights of angels on the ceiling, and sculpture to murals. (One mural by Paul Delvaux is at Bourse Station.) One station (Vandervelde) has the world's largest ceiling fresco after the Sistine Chapel; another (Alma) has been given a complete look of Nature: the pillars are tree stumps, the ceiling is a painted sky with clouds; the walls of Station Stockel are completely lined in the cartoon figures of de Herge.

The Grand Duchy of Luxembourg has produced several artists in the 20th century, though their work is not as widely recognized internationally as perhaps it should be. **Dominque Lang** (1874–1919) and **Joseph Kutter** (1894–1941) are two of the country's best-known painters. All artistic activity in Luxembourg ground to a halt during the Second World War, when the Grand Duchy was "annexed" by Nazi Germany and the fight for survival paralyzed all cultural endeavor. Luxembourg's Prime Minister **Jacques Santer,** who doubles as the Grand Duchy's Minister of Cultural Affairs, believes that the country is still in the process of recovering creatively. Luxembourg artists today receive support both in the form of government grants and commissions from private industry. In many bank offices on Boulevard Royal (Luxembourg City's "Wall Street") hang original paintings, murals, and tapestries by local artists. A recent exhibition of nearly 300 works by 75 Luxembourg painters and sculptors in the EC Commission's main conference center in Brussels was the largest collection of Luxembourg artwork ever assembled outside the Grand Duchy. Luxembourg artists hope that the favorable response to that exhibit will widen their international reputation.

ARCHITECTURE

Celtic tribes, one of which was known by the name *Belgae,* occupied much of what today is the Benelux region until about the 5th century B.C. Dolmens found in the Ourthe Valley (near Liège, Belgium), and earthenworks at Aalburg (outside of Larouchette, Luxembourg) attest to life in these Celtic communities. Julius Caesar came, saw, and conquered the region c. 50 B.C. He founded Tongeren in 57 B.C., and in 15 B.C. *Gallia Belgica* was established as a northern imperial province of the Roman Empire. Tongeren has a provincial museum with Gallo-Roman remains and artifacts, as does nearby Maastricht, over the border in Holland. Luxembourg City has a national museum featuring exhibits from the same period. In Diekirch (Luxembourg), several large Roman mosaics, uncovered intact earlier this century, are on display in a town museum. The Romans remained until the 5th century, after which the region was subjected periodically to vigorous Viking attacks into the 10th century, a fact that could account for the general lack of artifacts from that era.

As the Roman hold weakened during the 3rd century, Germanic Frankish tribes began to penetrate Gallica Belgica. Once the Romans departed, early individualistic artistic influences of the Franks (*Rhineland* or *Rhenish*) began to have an impact on the bordering Meuse (Maas) river region. When the Frankish King Charlemagne—whom the Pope had declared Emperor of the West: Denmark to Italy, and Spain to the Oder—established his court at Aachen/Aix-la-Chapelle, the move conferred increased importance on its neighbors, particularly Liège, which had received an important Bishopric in 721, and Maastricht, which dated from Roman days. In the division of the Carolingian Empire (Charlemagne died in 814), the *Treaty of Verdun* (843) separated what is present-day Belgium both culturally and politically, and led to the development of two distinct *Romanesque* styles. The territory west of the Scheldt River fell to France and became associated with the *Scaldian* style, while from the Meuse River to the east the *Mosan* arose.

Mosan architecture in the 11th century in both construction and decoration was simple, strong, and austere. An impressive example of the style's fortress-like west wall *(westwerk)* can be seen at the **Onze Lieve Vrouwekerk** in Maastricht. The legacy of the Rhine-Meuse style includes two fine arts masterpieces: goldsmith **Nicholas of Verdun's** *Shrine of the Virgin* (1205) at Tournai Cathedral, and the cast bronze font with 12 oxen at the **Church of St. Barthelemy** in Liège by **Renier de Huy** (c. 1113).

The Scaldian style, more elaborate than Mosan and influenced by the French, who controlled the valley of the Scheldt, came into its own in the 12th century, before eventually evolving into the Gothic style. The unusual five-towered **Tournai Cathedral,** whose multi-storied nave dates from 1171, has been called "the cradle of Scaldian-Gothic Art"; two developments of the style visible at Tournai are the exterior decoration, which grows more ornate towards the top, and the addition of an entrance to the westwerk.

A major feature of early Belgian architectural history are the **Flemish burgher** (town aldermen's) **houses** of the late Middle Ages. What are perhaps the earliest (1175–1200) remaining examples in western Europe stand in Tournai, the prototypes of lay architecture in the Scheldt valley. The finest extant examples of early medieval feudal fortresses are Ghent's **Gravensteen** (Castle of the Counts), begun in 1180 although parts visible in the cellar date from the 9th century, and the **Steen** (now the Maritime Museum) in Antwerp, c. 1250, which later became a prison. Ghent's **Koornstapelhuis,** c. 1200, on the **Graslei** is an exceptional example of a Romanesque public grain warehouse.

In Luxembourg City, the oldest building standing is **Um Bock** (13th century), located near the Bock, site of a former Roman fortress that Count Sigfrid, founder of the House of Luxembourg, acquired and rebuilt into a fortified castle (now demolished) in 963. **St. Michael's Church,** some sections of which date from the 11th century, served as Sigfrid's chapel. Turbulent times, and a center-court location for them, dictated that much of Luxembourg's early architecture be in the form of fortresses, then strategically—today, picturesquely—perched upon high points above river valleys. The largest (and best restored) of Luxembourg's medieval strongholds is **Vianden Castle,** whose oldest parts date from the 10th century. In 1417, the castle became the possession of the Nassau branch of what became the Dutch royal family, who much later gave it to Luxembourg's grand ducal family. **Bourscheid Castle,** one of the largest fortress complexes between the Rhine and the Maas, has remains from seven different architectural periods, back to the 11th century. Some sections are restored, including a 14th-century water tower in the wall and 14th-century nobleman's house in the complex; a museum sheds insight into 14th-century building techniques. **Clervaux Castle,** with museums that include a collection of models of some 20 of Luxembourg's finest fortified castles, was the core around which the town was built beginning in the 12th century. It's been gradually aggrandized over succeeding centuries.

The *Gothic* era started more slowly and lingered longer in the Low Countries than elsewhere in Europe. Once embraced, Early Gothic (13th c.) progressed to the more richly-detailed High Gothic (14th c.) and on to Flamboyant Gothic (15th and 16th c.). In Belgium, there were further variations on the theme: Scheldt Gothic, Limburg Gothic, and Brabant Gothic. Many of the Benelux's finest cathedrals took their present shape during Gothic times, including **St. Rombout's** in Mechelen (early 14th– early 16th c.), and similarly-aged **Onze Lieve Vrouwe** Cathedral in Antwerp, the largest Gothic church in Belgium (12th c. Romanesque sections were revealed during recent extensive restoration).

It's been suggested that prior to the second half of the 15th century, architecture in Holland hadn't taken on any specifically Dutch characteristics. But that doesn't detract from the majesty of the country's earlier grote kerks (great churches). **St. Jan's** at 's Hertogenbosch is considered the most important Gothic church (1336–1550) in the Benelux. Utrecht's **Dom Cathedral,** one of the country's most imposing, was begun in 1254, and its detached 14th c. Cathedral Tower is the tallest in Holland at 367 ft. Haarlem's **St. Bavo's** begun c. 1400, is huge enough itself not to be overshadowed by the vast size of the town's Grote Market (main square).

Secular architecture in the form of magnificently ornate municipal buildings may have been the most splendid achievements of the Gothic era in the Benelux. The sense of independence that came with town charters, and increasing commercial confidence (due especially, to the Flemish cloth industry), led burghers in Belgian Flanders and Dutch Zeeland and Holland to build great Gothic flights of fancy—belfries, cloth halls, guild houses, and town halls—to illustrate their successes. Some of the richest examples are the **Ypres Cloth Hall** (a faithful reconstruction of the 13th-c. original which was destroyed in World War I); the **Bruges stadhuis**/town hall (late 14th c.); and **Brussels' Town Hall** (early 15th-c.), the only building on the great Grand Place to survive the 1695 bombardment ordered by French King Louis XIV. Others include the stadhuizen in **Louvain** (1450), **Middleburg** (mid-15th-c.), rebuilt after Nazi bombardment in 1940, **Veere** (late-15th-c.), **Ghent** (1518–35), and **Oudenaarde** (1526–36).

Pride and pleasure in such architectural achievements resulted in a stick-with-tradition spirit that postponed acceptance of Italian Renaissance influence in the region. **Cornelis Floris** (1514–1575) was the first Flemish architect to represent the Renaissance—reinterpreted by local tastes—in **Antwerp's stadhuis** (1561–1565). Though built along Italian lines, it retained traditional late-Gothic Flemish design overlaid with "copy-book" Renaissance details, a combination that added eccentricity to the splendor of guild houses and other buildings on many a Markt (main square). A fine Renaissance house (c.1576), also in Antwerp, is the mansion built for the printer Plantin (today the **Plantin-Moretus Museum**), which made a successful marriage of local building methods and Renaissance forms. The pure Italian Renaissance concept of proportion was not employed in the Benelux until the 17th century, and then sparingly.

Religious upheavals in the 16th century set in motion circumstances that shaped the long-term development of both architecture and art in Belgium and Holland. The **Reformation,** which began about 1520, left men's lives and their families' fortunes in shambles if they couldn't be politic in their ecclesiastical politics. The times took a terrible toll on the artistic past, especially in Holland, where the ravagings of the *Iconoclast* in the 1560s, furthered by the *Alteratie* of 1578 (when Amsterdam, in the northern Netherlands, formally split from Spain, and officially changed from Catholic to Calvinist), were responsible for the destruction of considerable church ornamentation. For example, though few pieces have survived, it is reasonable to assume that sculpture, especially polychrome wood, played a prominent part in church decoration prior to the Reformation. By 1579, the Netherlands had split into the Dutch Protestant northern provinces, while Belgium (the southern Netherlands) remained under the rule of Catholic Spain. In Holland, where all Catholic churches were confiscated by the Protestants, the cavernous, once ornate, ecclesiastical interiors became impressive in their starkness. Altars were done away with, their place taken by pulpits (often beautifully carved), placed mid-church so none could miss the stern Calvinist messages preached from them. The fact that the strict Reform Dutch (Calvinist) Protestants didn't approve of "graven images" contributed to the fact that sculpture did not return to Holland as an art form until modern times (and then was largely secular). Catholics, although technically illegal after 1579, were allowed to continue to practice their religion if they did so inconspicuously, in what became known as Holland's "hidden churches."

An interesting architectural element arose in Dutch society early in the 17th century, when certain wealthy families founded **hofjes** (almshouses) where poor women of advanced age could live independently and with dignity; housing and perhaps food, fuel, and a small allowance were included. Hofjes provided public good while earning donors acceptable public recognition. Donor(s)' names ornamented the entrances and often a richly decorated reception room was maintained as a place to conduct the business of the hofje. These small tranquil self-contained communities were civic undertakings, in contrast to the then still-prevalent religious **begijnhofs.**

The Begijns may have begun when a Liège priest, Lambert le Begue (who died in 1187), encouraged the widows of Crusaders and other women to band together in communities (pious but unbound by vows) for economic and companionship purposes. The movement soon spread throughout Europe, where most towns of any importance had begijnhofs/begijnages, although today only a few in Flanders (see under *Bruges*) survive in their religious form.

Holland's many hofjes *do* continue in their original role as almshouses, in some cases still sustained by the founding families, though most are now maintained by municipalities. Amsterdam alone has about 70 hofjes (there are an estimated 200 throughout Holland), most of which are made up of a limited number of little row houses existing quietly behind a gateway, around a garden, often near the center of town. It's possible for respectful visitors to view the central garden of many of these quaint oases. The best known is Amsterdam's **Begijnhof** (founded in 1346), with one of the city's two remaining timber gables, this from 1460. The Begijnhof lost its religious function as a result of the Reformation, and has since been a municipal hofje. It will change your ideas about "public housing."

Following the separation of the southern Netherlands (Belgium) from the seven united northern provinces of the new Dutch Republic, architecture and art developed differently in the two countries. In Holland, the 17th century took shape in buildings that showed a restrained form of *Classicism*. In Belgium, the *Baroque* style that had begun in Italy and was favored by the Catholic church (at least partially because of its complete contrast to sober Protestant puritanism) found exuberant expression in both the brush and design skills of Pieter Paul Rubens in Antwerp. **Rubens' House** in Antwerp (designed by the artist 1613–1617), although restored, remains full of fine Baroque architectural ornamentation, applied to traditional form. Rubens designed the impressive facade of Antwerp's **St. Carolus Borromeus** (1615–1621) and its rich Baroque interior. Sadly, most of the interior was destroyed by fire when lightning struck the church in 1718, a circumstance that revealed the church to have been Baroque by name only, the actual plan showing a Flemish preference for the traditional. Probably Belgium's most important Baroque church is **St. Pieter**'s in Ghent, in which the unknown architect made interesting use of space and light.

With the occupation of Antwerp by the Spanish in 1585, many architects and artists, and rich burghers who might eventually have patronized their creative efforts, fled north to Holland, newly freed from the Spanish yoke. **Lieven de Key** of Ghent, for instance, became the municipal architect for Haarlem, building that town's **Vleeshuis** (meat hall, 1602–03), and Leiden's magnificent **Stadhuis** (1597), a last flowering of the florid 16th c. gable style.

Hendrik de Keyser of Utrecht (1565–1621) was Holland's last major architect before a French-inspired classical influence took over. He designed Amsterdam's **Zuiderkerk** (1606–14), which was Gothic with Renaissance details, and the later **Westerkerk** (1620), which made the turn toward classicism. De Keyser was fortunate enough to be on hand during the early decades of the 1600s in Amsterdam, by which time the city's growth in prosperity and population necessitated the construction of its still-distinctive concentric canal plan; he designed a number of the canal-front town houses that continue to make the city so visually stimulating.

Jacob van Campen, (1595–1657) from Amersfoort, placed Holland firmly under classical control with his commanding **Amsterdam Town Hall** (1648–55), today the **Royal Palace,** on the Dam at the heart of the city. An enormous structure of stone, with marvelously extensive use of marble in the interior, the building, resting on swampy land, is a terrific tribute to Amsterdam's 17th-century pile-driving people (it rests on 13,600 piles). Van Campen also worked in The Hague, where he designed both the 1633 **Mauritshuis** (Van Campen's pupil **Pieter Post** (1608–1669) took over the actual construction), and **Huis ten Bosch,** today used as a private family residence by Queen Beatrix.

A classical tendency continued through most of the 18th century in Holland. The French invasion of the Benelux in 1672 led to a fascination for all things French. **Daniel Marot** (1663–1752), a French Huguenot refugee employed by William of Orange/William III as an architect in Holland and at the English court, designed the interior, park and gardens for **Het Loo,** a former hunting lodge turned into a royal palace that was recently restored (see *Apeldoorn* under *Central Holland*). Critics called much of Holland's 18th century the *pruikentijd* (age of wigs), and condemned its dandyism and superficiality.

Early in the 19th century, Belgium witnessed an epic European event: the final defeat of Napoleon at Waterloo, just outside Brussels, in 1815. Belgium's own independence in 1830 brought thoughts of a new look for its capital, and several neo-classical plans resulted in Brussels' upper town, including the reconstruction along Louis XVI lines of the **Place Royale.** The monumental (some say monstrous) **Palais de Justice** was built between 1866 and 1883 to the design of **Joseph Poelaert.** Its plateau site is appropriate (the medieval city's gallows stood there), but the 300-foot-high domed building (in overall area larger than St. Peter's in the Vatican) can only have meant much displacement in the still typically working class Brussels' lower town *Quartier des Marolles*. Much more elegant are the arcades of Brussels' **Galeries St. Hubert** by **J. P. Cluysenaer** in 1846.

French influence had departed from the Dutch scene by the time **P. J. H. Cuypers** (1827–1921) arrived with his fanciful historical style. Travelers to Amsterdam are sure to see his two best-known buildings: **Centraal Station** (1885), a monumental building that at first proved too heavy for its 9000-pile foundation and partially subsided during construction, and the renowned **Rijksmuseum** (1885). There was no looking back by the time **H. P. Berlage** (1856–1934) built the **Beurs van Berlage,** Amsterdam's Commodity and Stock Exchange (1899–1903). It severed every connection with historical stylistic principles, and served as a turning point in Dutch architecture with its rational approach amid monumental allure. The **Beurs,** one of the largest buildings in the world at the time of its construction (the facade along the Damrak in the heart of Amsterdam is 460 feet long), has been compared to "a New York skyscraper laid on its side." The ingenious interior design, which reveals the structure of steel, and construction elements of glass, brick, and stone, now serves as headquarters for the *Netherlands Philharmonic Orchestra*. A unique "glass cube" performance hall-within-a-hall, which premiered in 1990, has created great concert acoustics, while leaving Berlage's architectural details intact and in view. Berlage's last building was the **Gemeetemuseum** in The Hague.

The advent of **Art Nouveau** in Belgium—most plentifully in Brussels—came in the 1890s and was very much an artistic accompaniment to the socialist movement. Free thinkers, liberals, and socialists of the period favored Art Nouveau architecture and ornamentation, while the more conservative Catholics favored Gothic and Flemish Renaissance. Certain Brussels neighborhoods and boroughs—Ixelles, Uccle, and on and around Avenue Louise—became steeped in the new style.

Art Nouveau's reign was brief and beauteous, its stylish, sinuous curves abandoned shortly after 1905. The first two revolutionary houses in the style were built in 1893 by **Victor Horta** and **Paul Hankar** who, together with **Henry van de Velde,** were the movement's main proponents in Belgium. In keeping true to the concept, the woodwork, furniture, and all the curvilinear fin-de-siecle fittings were included in a specific project's design. **Victor Horta's House** and studio (so-called even though he did not live there long and sold it before having paid off all who worked on it) was finished in 1898, and became a museum in 1969. It reflects loving attention to Art Nouveau detail; there's hardly a right angle in the house—Horta hated them. Victor Horta also designed the **Musee des Beaux Arts** in Brussels, **Brussels Centrale Station,** as well as the **Musée des Beaux Arts** in Tournai (1928), which shows spatial originality in its concept of exhibit rooms set around a central polygonal entrance hall. Only one of the six Brussels' department stores Horta designed still stands, having been restored and become the **Museum of the Comic.** Little of van de Velde's work remains in Belgium, but one of his most famous buildings is the **Kroller-Muller Museum** in Otterlo, Holland, a 1934 work that reflects the austerity and refinement found in the best early 20th-century Belgian architecture.

Sadly, many of Brussels most significant buildings in the Art-Nouveau style, including Horta's **Maison du Peuple,** headquarters for the Socialists, have been razed. (Brussels continues to practice controversial urban expansion; in the late 1980s, whole residential blocks in the city were leveled to make room for a larger European Community building to seat the expanded European Parliament). For more information on Art Nouveau sites that still exist, see *Brussels, What To See and Do, Victor Horta House.*

Among the outstanding European outcrops of **Art Deco,** a style that began in Paris in the 1910s, are two in Amsterdam. The 1918-21 **Tuschinski Theater,** which opened with the silent Hollywood film *The Old West* accompanied by a full theater orchestra, is an exuberant center-city example (on Reguliersbreestraat, between the Munt Tower and Rembrandtsplein). If you don't fancy a film (today there are five screens, most showing features in English, with Dutch subtitles), ask the usher at the door if you can just take a look at the lobby. There's a lobby bar to lean against as you admire the marvelous wealth of detail, all in excellent repair, since the theater was restored in 1984. Another Art Deco treasure is one of Amsterdam's great meeting places, the deliciously decorated **Café Americain** in the **American Hotel** (which couldn't be more European). Your eyes will have a feast just walking into the cafe, but you'll probably want to sit and sip or sup to give yourself more time to look (located just off the Leidseplein).

Between 1915 and 1925 a style of building flourished in Amsterdam that became known internationally as the **Amsterdam School,** notable for its whimsical and imaginative design, iron and brickwork decorative details, and many different-shaped windows. Examples are especially prevalent as working class housing in Zuid (southern) Amsterdam. The two most acclaimed advocates of the school were **Michel de Klerk** (1884-1923) and **Pieter Kramer** (1881-1961). The Amsterdam VVV has a self-guided walking tour brochure in English on the Amsterdam School.

All three Benelux countries were occupied by the Nazis during World War II (and Belgium and Luxembourg by the Germans in World War I, as well). Devastating damage which changed the architectural face of the region was wrought by invading and Allied battalions both. Nowhere is this more apparent than in Rotterdam, which suffered saturation bombing without warning when the Nazis invaded Holland on May 14, 1940. The city centrum was bombed so badly that you can count on one hand the salvaged buildings. Since the war, city planners have employed many innovative and acclaimed architectural means to recreate a liveable center city for Rotterdam. One of the most imaginative and successful is the "cube-shaped" complex of houses at tree-top level overlooking Rotterdam's lovely cafe-rimmed **Oudehaven** (old harbor). An adventurous project in low-to-moderate priced housing, each three-story sky-lighted "cube" rests on one of its points; until I visited the model "cube" (see *Rotterdam, What To See and Do*), I couldn't imagine from the outside how floors would be flat enough to walk inside.

DECORATIVE ARTS AND TRADITIONAL CRAFTS

Dutch Delftware

Many of us recall that blue-and-white ware—which remains remarkably popular in kitchenware from Woolworth's to delicate place settings of *Vieux Luxembourg* from Luxembourg's prestigious **Villeroy & Boch**—originally came from China: The dragons and pagodas in the enduring "willow pattern" are a helpful hint. In fact, blue and white porcelain existed in China for centuries before finally being brought to Europe. There, it eventually was produced in and became so closely associated with the Dutch town of Delft that the two names have been nearly synonymous ever since.

It was during the early 13th-century reign of Genghis Khan, after Mongol traders returned from their travels with cobalt from Persia—where the metallic dyestuff was used to give a deep lapis lazuli color to pottery—that artisans at the imperial porcelain works in the city of Jingdezhen produced China's first blue-and-white ware. It proved easy to produce in quantity since, while other colors or polychromes required five or more firings, the blue could do with just two. Late that same 13th century, Marco Polo returned home to Italy from his legendary travels to China with a shipload of blue-and-white porcelain of a quality and color never before viewed in the West, and Venetians vied for the treasure.

It wasn't until the 16th century that the first Europeans, the Portuguese, started trading directly with China. Old cargo logs reveal that by mid-century, some 60,000 pieces of porcelain, mostly blue-and-white, were arriving annually in the home harbors of Europe's increasingly conspicuous merchant-class consumers. Toward the end of the 16th century, Holland, being at war with Spain and Portugal, captured several cargos containing Chinese porcelain. In this way the Dutch were brought into contact with the Chinese product, which became highly esteemed. In 1602, the Dutch East India Company was founded in Delft, after which the Dutch dealt directly with China for its blue.

At the same time, efforts were taking place all over Europe to do away with dependence upon the China connection by developing high quality porcelain production at home. A breakthrough came in Holland in the early 17th century, when the Dutch developed *faience,* a refined form of earthenware. The establishment of an enviable blue-and-white ware product couldn't have come at a more fortunate time, with Holland's prosperous 17th-century Golden Age proving a success story for all producers of fine, fashionable objects. The pretty pieces of Delftware quickly proved prestigious. In the 16th century, potters lived all over Holland, but by the 17th century they had concentrated largely in Delft (and Makkum; see below). There, in 1653, *De Porceleyne Fles* (the porcelain jar) factory was founded. Soon, some 30 factories in and around Delft were producing the blue and white ware. In the 18th century, however, a slow but steady decline in demand for Delftware began, due partly to new pottery developments in Germany (*Meissen*) and England (*Wedgewood*) with which the Dutch couldn't seem to compete.

De Porceleyne Fles was Delft's only pottery to survive into the 19th century, and through most of it, it barely managed to keep Delft's once prosperous pottery tradition alive. But, in 1876, the business was bought by Joost Thooft (his initials, a "J" crossed to form a "t" are still put on the bottom of all pieces) and a partner, Abel Labouchere (whose grandson Paul runs the firm today). Together, the men produced a renaissance for Delftware, and in 1919 a "Royal" warrant was conferred on the company. Today, trade in blue-and-white has come full circle: a factory in Taiwan makes Delftware look-alikes.

The delightful town of Delft is filled with shops selling bright blue and white ware and, since the product's so pretty, the commercialism isn't offensive, although the profusion can cause confusion for buyers. While several firms in Holland mass-produce blue and white ware (and put the name Delft on it), *De Porceleyne Fles* is the only one with history behind it. It employs some 150 artisans who produce a wide range of pieces from jugs and ginger jars to decorative dishes and vases for Dutch tulips. Visitors to the factory can see demonstrations by the potters and painters; the showroom with its historical and contemporary collections of pieces has the feel of an art gallery, and an inner court displays the surprising range of outdoor and building ceramic tiles. Predictably, the most popular Delftware design is the pattern with varying shades of blue applied on a white background (in production at De Porceleyne Fles since the 17th century), but the *Delft Polychrome,* with yellow, green, blue, and red-browns on a white background, has been around as long. The *Black Delft* pattern was inspired three centuries ago by Chinese lacquerware, and *Pijnacker* in red, blue, and gold is based on 17th-century Japanese *Imari* porcelain. Those interested in buying Delftware should see the quality (and prices) of handpainted De Porceleyne Fles pieces first, and then decide whether to invest in an original, or purchase a pleasing but less expensive blue-and-white item elsewhere (also see *Shopping* under *Delft, Holland*).

Royal Tichelaar Makkum, still operating under watchful family eyes after ten generations, is the only company in Holland that continues to produce Dutch tiles (and other delftware pieces) following the same tin-glaze process it did when operations began in 1641. Makkum, a picturesque fishing village in the northern Dutch province of Friesland on the shores of what used to be the Zuiderzee (now the IJsselmeer), became the site of a pottery because of the presence of a very suitable chalk-rich clay in the delta area. In 1641, a farmer's son took his mother's inheritance, and a new name, *Tichelaar* (brickmaker), and bought an existing pottery in Makkum. The white tin-glaze coating, a technique introduced into the Netherlands at the end of the 16th century, opened new vistas to Holland's then active ceramic industry (80-odd potteries existed throughout the country between 1600 and 1800), but today Makkum is the only one to continue its use. The mysterious white tin glaze—which originated in the Near East, and was introduced by the Moors to the Spanish, who carried it to the Netherlands—still lends to Makkum ware a glow and brilliance that newer techniques are unable to rival. In addition to the tin glaze, all the blue and polychrome pieces are hand painted; artists use brushes made of hairs from the ears of the famous Frisian cows. There are guided tours and wonderful show/sales rooms. Three and a half centuries after its founding, the factory flourishes, and the Tichelaars have another new name: *Royal* Tichelaar Makkum.

In addition to a broad selection of ornamental pieces, Makkum is particularly well known for its wide selection of tiles, many in the old Dutch designs. Makkum supplies customers throughout the world with tiles from old pattern books; decorators make astonishingly imaginative use of Makkum tiles, and company artists will execute special designs for particular settings or tile panels. Tichelaar is more and more called upon for the restoration of tiled surfaces in historic interiors. (See *Makkum* under *Old Zuiderzee Villages, Holland*).

Tapestries

No one claims it's the oldest, but the 1402 tapestry at Tournai Cathedral is the only one of the period that can be certified as an authentic *Arras*. Belgium's Flanders, which once included Tournai (today in Belgium's Wallonia), was the center of Europe's tapestry making for centuries. Tapestry was in great demand during the Middle Ages, when the great ornamental pieces carpeted the walls of palaces and churches not only with beauty, but warmth as well. Brussels, Bruges, Tournai, Oudennaarde, Antwerp, Grardsbergen, and Edingen were the sources of the finest Flemish tapestries. Much later, when tapestry workshops began in Paris (*Gobelin* and *Aubusson*), they were set up and initially manned by the Flemish.

The Cathedral of Tournai received its Arras (by Pierrot Fere, the

Arras master weaver), which illustrates the lives of St. Piat and St. Eleutherus, as a gift in 1402. Though tapestries from this early period typically lack "depth" in their design and have a limited palette, lively reds and blues highlight the vast area of the Tournai tapestry—Flemish tapestries left hardly any empty spaces—that is filled with figures and buildings that reveal some of the history of Tournai and its renowned church, and shows scenes of the city's second plague. In Tournai's **Museum of History and Archeology** are two large, still remarkably brightly colored 15th-century Tournai-made tapestries.

Bruges was one of the Flemish strongholds of tapestry weaving. Works from Bruges often were smaller than those from other tapestry centers, and distinctive for their pastoral scenes. The **Gruuthuse Museum** has some on display. Many Flemish tapestries incorporated the same subject matter as the master painters of the day; Rembrandt, Teniers, and others often drew "cartoons" (designs) for tapestries. Thus, tapestries reflected *genre* (everyday life), landscapes or nature (*verdures*), and religious, historical, and allegorical scenes. In many cases, Flemish tapestries were made in sets.

Masterpieces among the many tapestries in Brussels' **Royal Museum of Art and History** (it owns 150, of which one third hang on view) are eight of the original ten *History of Jacob* tapestries, considered to be one of the finest tapestry sets from the Flemish Renaissance. Woven in wool and silk in 1534 from cartoons made by Brussels artist **Bernard van Orley,** the massive set was sold to an Italian cardinal in the 1530s, and remained in the same family in Bologna until the end of the 19th century. The Belgian government purchased them in 1950 and had them restored by the **Royal Manufacturers of Tapestry Gaspard de Wit Ltd** in Mechelen.

Guy Delmarcel, head of the tapestry department of the Royal Museum of Art and History, observes, "Tapestry was the movable fresco of the North, and the first art industry." Other historians have referred to tapestries as "mirrors of civilization," noting that one "can read them like books." In fact, nobles are known to have ordered tapestries that illustrated their favorite books. Following the fate of other decorative art forms, tapestries, too, passed out of fashion for a phase. For decades during the 19th century people simply discarded them. But a big exhibition in France late in the century led to their rediscovery as a rich art form.

The De Wit weaving establishment in Mechelen is housed in the former refugee house of the Tongerlo Abbeye, which dates from 1483. De Wit (which celebrated its centenary in 1989) is a family tradition: Present owner Yvan Maes is the great-grandson of the founder. The Mechelen tapestry firm, now an institution in the tapestry world, has survived by being one of the first to expand upon a newly specialized skill, *tapestry conservation,* which is fundamentally different and more affordable than tapestry restoration. Conservation aims to preserve and stabilize the existing fabric of a tapestry rather than attempting to weave in new patches. Maes feels conservation is a "more respectful treatment for a tapestry, more honest to its history."

It is the Gaspard de Wit firm's aim not only to preserve the artistic heritage of tapestry weaving by conserving antique pieces for private customers and museums all over the world, but also to keep the traditional art form alive. Nearly half the current tapestry orders are for modern pieces, so the Flemish craft continues in contemporary times. One of De Wit's modern creations, a tapestry of the space shuttle, hangs in the U.S. headquarters of Northrop Corporation. Another, a work woven from a design produced by Belgian artist Edmond Debrunfaut (and specially treated to repel dust and grime), decorates a Brussels Metro station.

G. De Wit offers visitors a unique setting of workshops and exhibition halls in which to see an exclusive collection of antique and modern tapestries in an historic building. Tours are possible in English, Sat. at 10:30 a.m. Contact the Mechelen Tourist Office about the possibility of visits at other times. Although De Wit is the only tapestry business in Belgium today, there are a number of active self-employed weavers in the Benelux.

Lace

Lacework (*kantwerk* in Dutch, *dentelles* in French) originated in Belgium as a result of the 15th-century fashion for trimming garments with it. Flemish lace was much sought after; both male and female figures in portraits by Netherlands painters of that and later periods wear it prominently. Bruges lace was the most prized of all, since that town's local lacemakers specialized in the popular rose-lace flower pattern and the extremely fine "Fairy Queen" stitch. Bruges has always been home to bobbin-lace, which is executed on a large lap pillow. Mechelen became well known for lace in the 17th and 18th centuries, and Brussels also was a center for the craft. Since the 1970s, Bruges has seen a revival of lacemaking by hand, which has both revitalized the traditional craft and made it competitive as a contemporary art form.

The **Bruges Lace Center** *(Kantcentrum)* has its roots in a lace school founded in 1717, when the Bishop of Bruges decided that lacemaking would ensure a certain income for families in the then povertystricken town. The school served its immediate purpose and proved an ongoing success: in 1860 it had 400 pupils. But by the beginning of the 20th century there had been a sharp drop in attendance and interest. From 1930 onward, there was a general decline in the lace industry, partly because it had gone out of fashion, and partly because what lace was needed could be mechanically-produced abroad and imported for less. By 1960, only an evening division of the 250-year-old school remained open. But because lacemaking was such a traditional handicraft in Bruges that no one wanted to see it disappear entirely, the mayor and the municipality of Bruges arranged for the buildings in Balstraat to be donated for the cause, and the Lace Center was opened in 1972.

The number of women interested in the purely personal enjoyment of lacemaking encouraged the Lace Center to institute a daily group for those already familiar with the craft who could come to the Center when they wanted advice or wished to try their hand at a new pattern in a group setting. Visitors to the center see participants in such groups. Many of the local lace makers have learned to design their own lace creations, and some of their works also are on display. The Center, which gives many courses, annually offers one in designing and making contemporary laces. Also at the center is a museum with many different styles and samples of lace on display; on the walls are copies of 15th–17th century paintings that show clothing richly decorated with similar lace. Bruges' **Gruuthuse Museum** has a wonderful collection of modern and ancient lace, and Brussels' **Royal Museum of Art and History** has its important exhibit of lace on public view.

A number of shops in Bruges and Brussels sell lace. Would-be buyers are cautioned that some items advertised as "real lace" may indeed be handmade, but in the Far East, not Belgium. Machine-made pieces may better suit your pocketbook, so ask questions of shop keepers and compare prices. One way to be sure of what you're buying is to stick to the several official *Quality Control* lace shops in Bruges, which guarantee, by government certificate, that the lace is original local work. The Bruges Tourist Office can supply names (also see *Shopping* under *Bruges*).

Diamond Cutting

Today, 47% of the world's consumption of polished diamonds takes place in Antwerp, where the diamond industry has existed since the second half of the 15th century. By late in the 16th century, a diamond cutters' guild flourished in Antwerp. Sea routes to India introduced the western world to its first major supply of raw diamonds, and produced a highly successful 17th century-trade. But by the 18th century, those fields had been exhausted, and the diamond industry worldwide was in decline. Nevertheless, such was Antwerp's residual reputation in diamonds that in 1787 France's Louis XVI had his crown jewels repolished there. Antwerp's affair with the ancient pure carbon objects—an untempting but accurate description—was rekindled by the South African diamond rush which began in 1869. With a steady supply of top quality goods again assured, Antwerp sparkled anew in the business, and diamond workshops sprang up everywhere. It was Englishman Cecil Rhodes, later Prime Minister of the Cape Colony, who founded the De Beers Mining Company in 1881 (today, De, Beers Consolidated Mining handles 80% of the world's mined diamonds). Beginning in 1913, mines from the Belgian Congo (now Zaire) also began sending diamonds to Antwerp. The hardest substance on earth, diamonds can be used to cut anything. In the 19th century they began to be used industrially; in 1879, the St. Gotthard Tunnel through the Alps was built with the help of diamond-tipped tools. More than 50% of the diamonds mined today are for industrial use.

Of the 20 diamond bourses worldwide, Antwerp has four, including the largest (Amsterdam has the 2nd largest). All told, Antwerp's inner city diamond industry compound of buyers, bankers, brokers, dealers, and craftsmen employs 35,000 people. In Amsterdam you can visit one of several diamond houses for a view of the diamond cutting process, but for background on all the fascinating facets of the diamond business, a trip to Antwerp's **Diamond Museum** (opened in 1988 in Antwerp's diamond district near the Centraal Station) is a brilliant idea. As the museum shows, there's much more to the story of diamonds than carat-color-clarity-cut. Exhibits run the gamut from mining to the materialization of a splendidly polished stone; the "Antwerp cut," which makes stones sparkle more than any other, is universally recognized as the best, and proves that all that glitters is *not* gold. Diamonds get their dazzle from being cut in a way that forms multiple facets (57 create "perfect fire") at carefully calculated angles. Rose "cuts" (the *Antwerp* or fashion rose, and the *Amsterdam* or full rose) date from about 1600, and the *brilliant* cut has been known since 1680, but not until this century were the ideal proportions of diamond cuts scientifically determined. After the First World War, new cuts such as the *baguette* and the *emerald* were created.

The museum has a treasure room where some of the precious gems themselves illustrate the history of fashion's delight with the diamond. Examples from many styles of jewelry are shown, including art nouveau and recent winners of the annual *Antwerp Diamond High Council* competition. A video (in an English version) on Antwerp's historic diamond trade can be viewed (see also, *Diamantmuseum* under *What To See and Do* in *Antwerp*).

MUSIC

You may not immediately think of music when the Benelux countries come to mind, but it's in the air there. Holland and Belgium are carillon countries, with bells in church towers and town belfries that ring out the hours with a song (see chapter *The Bell Epoch: Centuries of Carillons*). More special still, these so-called "singing towers" provide concerts on market days, summer evenings, and other pre-set times, and there's nothing more delightful than settling in with a drink at a sidewalk cafe for a free listen.

Equally exuberant are the sounds that spill from Holland's traditional street organs, with counterpoint offered by the owner as he shakes a container for coins at passersby. Street, or barrel, organs, with their winsome wooden figures and colorful individual designs, appear randomly on shopping streets and squares in Amsterdam and at markets in Dutch towns. Their exuberant player-scroll scripts invariably put a spring in one's step (see also *National Museum for Musical Clocks to Street Organs* under *What To See and Do* in *Utrecht, Holland*).

Alfresco diners indulging at one of the square's numerous cafes enjoy nearly nightly concerts from the bandstand on Luxembourg City's lively Place D'Armes. While Luxembourg may schedule more than most, many cities and towns throughout the Benelux embrace the summer season with musical manifestations in squares and parks.

Organs

Another musical instrument built in to Benelux culture is the organ. Those with a keen interest consider Holland an organ paradise, since, despite its small size, no other country in the world can claim such a treasure of historic instruments. As **James David Christie,** member of the *American Guild of Organists* and organ player with the *Boston Symphony Orchestra,* says, "It's hard to go to a city or even a town in Holland that doesn't have a great, a good, or, at the very least, an interesting organ, and often more than one." He notes that Holland, in particular, but Belgium and Luxembourg, too, have a number of organs that date from the 17th, 18th, and 19th centuries, and some from the 16th.

Christie has the credentials to comment on organs in the Benelux. In 1979, he won **The International Organ Competition** held in Belgium's Bruges, the first American ever to do so, and has returned since to serve on the jury for the competition. In 1990, Christie was invited to Brussels to play the dedication concert for the newly reconstructed organ of the **Eglise du Sablon** on the Grand Sablon. It's indicative of the high honor in which organs are held in Belgium that when the American bank J.P. Morgan wanted to present the city of Brussels with a special gift, the project settled upon was the restoration of this instrument.

The Sablon organ, which is in the Franco-Flemish tradition—a certain style of stop specifications and voicing techniques that affects how the organ speaks—was rebuilt by Georg Westenfelder, a German who now lives and works in Luxembourg. Christie considers the Luxembourg resident preeminent among organ builders in the world today. Westenfelder also restored the classic French-style organ in Luxembourg City's historic 17th-century **St. Michel's church** (founded as a 10th-century castle chapel), which Christie considers the finest instrument of its kind in the Grand Duchy.

In addition to the organ at **St. Gilles,** on which the Bruges International Organ Contest was held, the one in Bruges' **St. Salvator Cathedral,** housed in a beautiful case, has been restored as an electric instrument, designed for an ecclectic range of music. The organ at **St. Annakerk** (near Bruges' Lace School), while not a great musical instrument, is well worth visiting for its lovely case.

The lengthy major restoration (begun in 1965) of **Onze Lieve Vrouwekerk** (the Cathedral) **of Antwerp,** the largest Gothic church in Belgium, is about finished. The organ, too, has been redone, and the combination of music and Rubens' masterpieces specifically painted for the setting provides an experience worth traveling for.

Many of the organs in the Benelux not only make memorable music, but are housed in handsome, historic cases. *The* outstanding example in both categories is the 5000–pipe, 1738 organ by Christiaen Muller in **St. Bavokerk** in Holland's city of **Haarlem.** For a long period this organ was the largest and finest in existence, and is still one of the world's best known. The enormous bulk of St. Bavo, begun about 1400, rises from one end of Haarlem's **Grote Markt** (great market square). The church's cavernous, typically stark, Calvinist interior is dominated at one end by a towering, grand and gilded arrangement of encased pipes adorned with figures—the most photographed organ in the world. From the time of its inaugural concert, the reputation of St. Bavo's organ grew rapidly, and foreign travelers sought out Haarlem to see the instrument. Visiting musicians included Handel and the then 10-year-old Mozart, who played at the keyboard for an hour. His father wrote back to Salzburg of the "excellent beautiful instrument with 68 stops, all pipes being made of tin, as wood is not lasting in this damp country."

Since 1800 the organ has been owned by the town of Haarlem, which employs official organists for the purpose of giving concerts. One of the two present town organists is Albert de Klerk, well-known in Holland for his keyboard compositions for both organ and carillon (St. Bavo's also has bells). A multitude of free municipal organ recitals provides opportunities to hear the remarkable instrument. Every even-numbered year, the city of Haarlem and St. Bavo's host the *International Organ Festival* in July, including a Summer Academy for Organists and an Organ Improvisation Competition—all of which create additional occasions for public concerts.

Though they're off the well-toured track, Christie classifies the organs in **Groningen,** capital city of Holland's northeastern-most province, at the **Martinikerk,** which dates back to 1480 and was most recently restored in 1979, and at the much-restored 15th-century **Akerk,** as "two of the best in the world." The Martinikerk also has a respected carillon of **Hemony bells.** For those with an abiding interest in organs and the time to explore, Christie has discovered that towns throughout the eastern regions of Holland, toward the Germany border, are especially rich in 16th- to 19th-century organs.

If you prefer to integrate organ-seeking with other sightseeing, head for **Alkmaar,** known mostly for its traditional and picturesque Friday morning cheese market. The town's Gothic late-15th, early-16th-century **St. Laurenskerk** (Grote Kerk) holds an historic organ dating from 1643 designed by Jacob van Campen, in a wonderful case painted by Cesar van Everdingen. A small organ in the north ambulatory dates from 1511, and is one of the world's oldest organs still in regular use.

Amsterdam's **Oudekerk** (Old Church), the oldest in that city, dating from about the year 1300, has three organs, the most memorable being the early 18th-century Great Organ by Vater/Muller. This exceptionally interesting old church contains the tombstone of Dutch composer and former Oudekerk organist **Jan Sweelinck** (1562–1621); his works often are included in concerts given by current Oudekerk organist Gustav Leonhardt. (The Oudekerk also has 47 Hemony bells, restored in 1990, and an American carilloneur, Todd Fair.)

Not all of Holland's finest organs are historic. A thoroughly modern four-manual ecclectic instrument adorns Rotterdam's **St. Laurenskerk** (Grote Kerk). A new organ became necessary due to the heavy bomb damage sustained by the great 15th-century Gothic church in May 1940, when Nazis overran Holland and leveled the heart of Rotterdam in a single day.

Those interested in the workings, as well as musical works, can have the inner world of organs opened up to them at Zaandam (located between Alkmaar and Amsterdam), with an appointment at the well-known Dutch firm **Dirk A. Flentrop Organ Builders.**

Major Music Festivals

The largest and most diverse cultural event in the Netherlands is the **Holland Festival,** held annually over several weeks in June. Some performances are scheduled in other cities and towns throughout the country, but the majority of programs are presented in the Amsterdam area. Offerings include a mixture of contemporary Dutch music, drama (some productions in English), and dance (especially the acclaimed **Nederland Dance Theater** company, regarded as one of the best modern groups in Europe). Offerings each year include completely new opera and ballet productions, presented by the **Dutch National Opera** and the **Dutch National Ballet** in the **Muziektheater,** two companies' impressively state-of-the-art, yet intimate, year-round residence which opened in 1986. The Holland Festival, which also features guest performances by companies in neighboring European countries to round out its wide-ranging program, is acclaimed as one of Europe's major cultural events. (Tickets can be ordered by mail; contact your local Netherlands Board of Tourism for schedule information.)

Celebrating its 18th year in 1993, the **North Sea Jazz Festival,** held in The Hague for four days in July, has been proclaimed by an international jury of critics as the best non-American jazz festival. According to W. Royal Stokes, managing editor of *Jazztimes* magazine, the event offers "the most extensive variety of performing artists of any jazz festival in the world." Some 1000 musicians, including such stars as Brubeck, Benson, Blakey, Getz, Gillespie, and Charles, perform in 14 venues, for more than 50,000 attendees.

The Festival of Flanders (*Festival van Vlaanderen*) is a multi-month musical affair held throughout the Flemish-speaking northern region of Belgium. Focused in Kortrijk (reputed for its choral music) in April; Tongeren in May; Bruges in August; Ghent, Brussels, and Leuven in September; and Mechelen and Antwerp in October, the Festival of Flanders brings together leading musicians for events in magnificent historic settings. For information, call Brussels (02) 648 14 84.

Naturally, a sister music festival, the **Festival of Wallonia,** takes place annually in Belgium's French-speaking southern provinces of Wallonia, in various cities, including Tournai and Liège, during the summer and fall. The resident companies, international orchestras, and guest soloists perform in varied venues: opera houses, cathedrals, abbeys, and castles. For information, call Liège (041) 22 32 48.

Centennial Company

Amsterdam's Concertgebouworkest: The caliber of Amsterdam's orchestra, which celebrated a centennial in 1988, combined with the world-renowned acoustics of its recently restored concert hall, make the

Concertgebouw a must for classical music lovers. In September 1988, **Riccardo Chailly** succeeded Dutchman Bernard Haitink (who had held the position since 1960) as principal conductor. Guest orchestras and performers, and chamber music ensembles also present concerts in the Grote and Kleine halls. On Wed. from Sept.–June, there are free lunch concerts at 12:30 p.m.

Celebrated Competition

Belgium's **Queen Elizabeth International Music Competition,** one of the world's most exacting and exciting, has existed for more than 30 years. It was founded by the country's former Queen Elizabeth, herself a violinist, and rotates in the three categories of violin, piano, and voice. The elimination rounds and finals (ticketed public events) are held in Brussels in May at the *Conservatoire* and *Palais des Beaux-Arts,* respectively, with the top prizewinners accompanied by the **Orchestre National de Belgique.** Winners also perform in concerts throughout Belgium in May and June.

Composers

When it comes to composers from the Benelux countries, there is a limited list of names of international stature. In Holland, **Jan Sweelinck** (1562–1621) remains the best known of a host of Dutch composers who had their day and then slipped from sight in succeeding centuries, with only an occasional resurrection at an organ concert. Sweelinck, after studying organ with his father, succeeded him as organist at Oudekerk in Amsterdam in 1580. In that post, his performances made him famous throughout Europe and he attracted to Amsterdam many pupils and disciples. Sweelinck composed pieces for the organ and harpsichord that extended the then-limited aspects of the keyboard style, and helped develop such musical forms as the fantasia, fugue, and toccata.

Another Dutch composer whose works appear in concerts internationally is **Willem Pijper** (1894–1947), who graduated from the Utrecht Music School in 1915, and had his first symphony introduced by the *Concertgebouworkest* in Amsterdam in 1918. It, as well as other pieces of his early work, were influenced by the German post-Romantic school, most of all Mahler, but Pijper soon dropped traditional techniques and structures for a more radical polytonal approach. His most important work in this manner is *Symphony No. 3,* introduced by the Concertgebouw in 1926. As well as being one of Holland's key creative music figures, Pijper was a music critic, taught at the Amsterdam Conservatory and, from 1930 until his death, was director of the Rotterdam Conservatory.

Perhaps the Benelux' best known composer is Belgium's **Cesar**

Franck (1822–1890), born and raised in Liège, where he attended that city's *Conservatoire de Musique*—which has erected a monument to its most famous former student. Franck studied piano, making a concert tour when only 11, and received the Liège Conservatoire's first prize for piano at age 13. With his father's encouragement, and later perhaps exploitation, of his talent, at 14 he entered the Paris Conservatory, where he was a brilliant student, winning prizes for piano, and also for organ, the instrument upon which he eventually concentrated for both composition and performance. Many authorities find Franck's works for the organ the finest since Bach, and his association with that instrument may well have begun during his formative Belgian days of musical training and development. He was principal organist of Sainte Clotilde in Paris for the last 32 years of his life, when, contemporaries reported, much of his greatest music composition was lost simply because it was improvised during organ concerts and never written down. He was appointed professor of organ at the Paris Conservatory in 1872. Cesar Franck is widely played in his native country of Belgium, where his music received a particularly wide hearing in 1990, in observation of the 100th anniversary of his death.

Born in Dinant, Belgium, in 1814, **Adolphe Sax** presented the world with the *saxophone* shortly after 1840. The keyed instrument with a conical tube and single reed made its first appearance in an orchestra in France in 1845. Although the saxophone, and its family members, achieved vogue in America in popular orchestras, jazz bands, and symphonic jazz compositions, it also has been employed in serious music without jazz content, in works by Debussy, Ravel, Prokofiev, Shostakovich, Richard Strauss, and Vaughan Williams. Sax died in Paris in 1894.

Though Belgium's **Maurice Maeterlink's** (see under *The Muse*, following) tragic masterpiece *Pelleas and Melisande* (1893) was a prose play, it inspired many of the period's finest composers to well-known works. Gabriel Fauré adapted the incidental music he composed for the London stage debut (1898) of Maeterlink's play into an orchestra suite that remains one of his most performed works. Debussy's opera (1902) is also based on the Belgian's play, as is Schoenberg's tone poem (1903). Sibelius' similarly-named suite for orchestra is derived from incidental music that the composer wrote for the drama's first presentation in Finland in 1905.

The work of another French-speaking Belgian writer, **Charles de Coster** (1827–1879), best recalled for his *Legend and Adventures of Til Ulenspiegel,* the fateful tale of a Flemish rogue, inspired German composer Richard Strauss's 1895 orchestral tone poem *Till Eulenspiegel's Merry Pranks.*

A more popular and recent composer, **Jacques Brel,** needs no introduction for his songs, which evoke many moods concerning the Belgian people and *le pays plat,* Belgium's flat polder land along the North Sea. There is a Jacques Brel institute in Brussels.

THE MUSE

The Benelux countries have produced their share of scholars, philosophers, and authors over the centuries; several stand out for the vitality of their visions and their long-lasting international influence. Some of the finest early writing to come from the region appeared in times when the *lingua franca* of intellectuals was Latin. Literature in the language of the people became more common after the signing of the *Treaty of Utrecht* (1579), which set the Dutch-speaking northern provinces of the Netherlands apart (beginning a political process that eventually led to the establishment of the separate countries of Holland and Belgium). The use of Dutch by writers proliferated after the people in Holland received independence from Spain under the *Treaty of Munster* (1648). Poetry became a popular form of artistic expression during Holland's 17th-century Golden Age.

In Belgium, where no writers of distinction had appeared since Flemish Antwerp's 16th-century Golden Age, a literary revival began with that country's independence from Holland in 1830. A Flemish language movement began, under the influence of Jan Frans Willems, a poet who generated interest in Flemish folk songs and literature, and Hendrik Conscience (see below under *Belgian Authors* and in *Flanders* under *Belgium*).

More recently, with the few notable exceptions suitably documented further on, literary critics have paid little attention to Benelux writers beyond their own borders. A good deal of the international ignorance about contemporary Benelux literature can be attributed to the ongoing problem of language. Writers from Belgium's French-speaking Wallonia, and those from Luxembourg who have used French, often are considered to *be* French, an understandable impression since many of these writers moved to Paris to achieve success in the larger French-language marketplace of France. Those in Holland and Belgium's Flanders who write in Dutch are rarely translated, the cost too considerable for any but the most successful books. In order to reach a wider audience, some writers in Holland pen prose in English.

Because Luxembourg authors may write original works in French,

German, or *Letzebuergesch* (the West-Frankish dialect—which has many loan words from both the above—that has been the country's official national tongue since 1983), the Grand Duchy's body of literature is trilingual. While this situation would seem suited to attract readers from neighboring European countries, in reality it doesn't in significant numbers.

All this is not to suggest that Holland, Belgium, and Luxembourg do not enjoy lively literary traditions today. New first editions abound in Dutch, and plenty are published in *Frisian* (the centuries-old written and spoken language of Friesland, a northern province of Holland). The active book publishing industry that exists in Luxembourg in *Letzebuergesch* is a deliberate intent to keep the Luxembourg language alive in literature, since the country's newspapers are published only in German and French.

Such publishing priorities show cultural confidence. As Dutch critic Adriaan van der Veen has commented, "A large audience is not a necessary condition for creating a masterpiece."

Dutch Authors

Willem (13th century) was a Flemish poet who translated the stories about *Van den vos Reinarde* (Reynard the Fox)—which date from the 10th-century, when they probably were compiled by monks—into Dutch. Originally told in rhyme, the stories had great appeal to the masses, as they parodied chivalry and satirized the rich, the courts, and the clergy. Reinarde, an outsider, was the small, physically weak, but sly, fox who repeatedly outwitted stronger characters such as the bear, the wolf, and the lion, by turning their contempt for him into traps for them. The heroes and villains in the stories have a mixture of Dutch and French names, reflecting the language split in the Low Countries. The Dutch version of Reinarde is thought to have become the model for many later recountings of the stories, including William Caxton's English translation (1481). Later versions were used as vehicles for making political and social points: Goethe published one in 1794, as did Jacob Grimm (of the Brothers Grimm) in 1834. Perhaps the best known character from the Reinarde tales is Chanticleer the Rooster.

Thomas à Kempis (1380–1471) wrote *The Imitation of Christ,* which is one of the Christian world's most widely-read works of devotional literature. Though German by birth, Thomas was an Augustinian monk who, from the age of 27 until his death at 91, spent a life of meditation and writing in the Mt. St. Agnus monastery in Zwolle, in Holland. Thomas's religious meditation, written c. 1400, reflects the eloquence and ardor of the author, and develops the idea that God is all, man is nothing; that from God flows the eternal truth, which man must seek. As early as 1420, it was in wide circulation; John Wesley was instrumental in having it translated into English.

Everyman, the best known of the English morality plays—an English edition by John Skot was in existence by the year 1521—is thought to be founded on, if not directly translated from, the Dutch *Elckerlijk,* attributed to **Petrus Dorlandus** of Diest about 1495. The 900-line play of dramatic verse describes the search by Everyman for a companion to accompany him to God's judgment seat after Death has fetched him. Everyman is eventually forsaken by all his friends except Good Deeds. With its decidedly explicit criticism of man's behavior on earth, it would have been difficult for medieval audiences to misinterpret the play, and thus performances of it met with Church approval. In the early 20th century, a professional English production of *Everyman* was revived, and toured extensively in England and North America.

Desiderius Erasmus (1466?–1536) was born in Rotterdam and, by the time of his death, had become the most influential and admired writer and scholar of his time. Erasmus is best remembered for *The Praise of Folly,* an immediate and widely-circulated success from its first publication, in secret, in 1511. He wrote the satirical masterpiece, which demonstrated a faith in reason that was remarkable for his times, in seven days, while recovering from an illness at the home of his English friend Sir Thomas More, to whom it was dedicated. In the work, Erasmus offers insight into problems of life that are universal, and also gives an idea of the struggle that he and other early Humanists had in their effort to rid the world of the conventions of the Middle Ages.

An instrumental figure in the Reformation, Erasmus also was the leading figure of a small group of men of the times who, throughout Europe, sponsored the revival of learning that characterized the Renaissance. Throughout his life, Erasmus sought to help people break down the limitations of "the foolish traditions and customs" of the world in his day, and "to help man find the road back to the true God and his true self." One of Erasmus' major works was a translation of the New Testament, which grew out of his conviction that true Christianity was hidden by a thick overlay of dogma and should be purified by a return to the Bible. The more than 3000 letters that Erasmus wrote which have been preserved give a matchless picture of his mind and his times. Located in one of Brussels' inner suburbs is a handsome house museum where Erasmus lived in 1521, during the period that marked the beginning of the Reformation (see *Brussels, What To See and Do*).

Footnote: So admired was Erasmus for his learning, literary ability, and tolerance that the Dutch town of Gouda, where he had his childhood schooling and near which was the monastery he was forced to enter by guardians and at which he was ordained in 1492—the Pope released him from the duties of his order in 1509—has documented an unusual fact to solidify its connection with the great humanist. A plaque outside the *St. Catherine Gasthuis* (now the City Museum) recalls, in Latin, that, though born in Rotterdam, Erasmus was conceived in Gouda. This intriguing detail is known, perhaps, because of contemporary curiosity surrounding the circumstance that his mother gave birth to Erasmus while having an affair with a local priest named Gerard.

Grotius (1583-1645), or Hugo de Groot, a Dutch statesman and jurist who is regarded as the father of international law, was born in Delft of a prominent, learned family. He was educated in Holland at the University of Leyden (Leiden) in the classics, as suited a child of the Renaissance. Grotius, the Latinized version of his name by which he became known, established a law practice in The Hague. Later, he became the city clerk of Rotterdam and, as such, a member of the government of the province of Holland.

Despite that position, for his endorsement of a religious sect that was out of favor with Prince Maurits of Orange, a Calvinist, Grotius received a life sentence in 1618, and was imprisoned in the island-fortress of *Loevestein* (one of Holland's most evocative surviving castles, on the River Waal). Because of his reputation, Grotius was allowed some leniency while under lock and key: he could write, which he did on theological and judicial issues, adding to what became a voluminous lifetime output; and he was allowed a regular supply of books and visits from his wife, both of which contributed to what became one of Holland's favorite historical escape tales.

As the story goes, the books Grotius requested arrived from his home in a large chest and, when they had been read, were returned in the same chest, along with the prisoner's dirty linen. For a while, the prison guard carefully checked the contents each time the chest left the fortress, but, when it seemed that nothing was amiss, he grew lax. Thus, one day in 1621, during a well-planned visit, Grotius' wife Maria had her husband conceal himself beneath the dirty linens, Maria herself taking his place in the cell. By the usual custom, the family servant carried the chest off the prison island to the mainland, but then diverted to a pre-arranged point where a friend of Grotius's awaited him, with clothes to disguise him as a carpenter, whereupon Grotius fled to Antwerp. Maria, though threatened with imprisonment in her husband's stead when the escape was discovered, shortly was released—a heroine.

From Antwerp, Grotius went to Paris, where he became leader of the Remonstrants and, in 1625, published *De Jure Belli et Pacis,* regarded as the first document in the science of international law. Years later, he died in a shipwreck on the way to Sweden, while serving as Swedish ambassador to France. Grotius, buried in Delft, is well-honored by his home town. His tomb is in the 1381 Nieuwe Kerk (where the royal tombs of the House of Orange also rest) on the Markt, in the center of which stands a statue of this illustrious Dutchman.

Rene Descartes, though born in 1596 in France (and dying there in 1650), lived in Holland from 1628–1647, and visited frequently thereafter until his death. The French mathematician and philosopher, considered the father of the modern scientific method, lived much of his productive adult life in self-imposed exile in Holland, which he found to be "an almost ideal place to study." He went to great lengths to protect his privacy, dividing his time between Dutch cities and countryside.

Descartes' major works were written and published while he lived in Holland. He challenged the metaphysical view of the universe in his *Discourse on Method* (1639). Soon after, in one of the most influential works in the history of philosophy, *Principles of Philosophy* (1641), Descartes divided the universe into *spirit,* subject to reason, and *matter,* subject to mechanical laws.

Acknowledged as one of the greatest intellectuals in the history of thought, Descartes freed the 17th-century scientist from medieval dogma. He formulated the oft-quoted principle *Cogito, ergo sum: I think, therefore I am.* Personally, Descartes' life was disrupted by the tensions of the times, torn between old and new ways of thinking. In 1642, Voetius, rector at the University of Utrecht, personalized his enmity for Descartes and his ideas by officially rejecting his "new philosophy" and summoning him to court regarding it. Failing to appear in court to respond to the charges, Descartes was found guilty of libel and sentenced to be burned at the stake, on a pyre—said to be personally requested by Voetius—"high enough to be seen for several miles." Descartes fled to The Hague and put himself under the protection of the French ambassador there. He left Holland for France in 1647, although he returned frequently until his death in 1650.

Baruch Spinoza (1632–1677), famed Dutch philosopher, was born in Amsterdam into a family of Jews that had fled religious persecution in their native Portugal. Regarded as the preeminent expounder of the doctrine of *pantheism,* Spinoza constructed one of the most complete metaphysical systems ever conceived, most notably put forth in *Ethics* (1677). At the base of his complex system is the concept that God exists only in his creations, that Nature *is* God, and that man's highest good is to seek knowledge of Nature, rather than relying on faith. In 1656, Spinoza was excommunicated from Amsterdam's Portuguese Synagogue for "proclaiming dreadful heresy" by asserting that God had to be personified to be understood. His rationalist ideas would have struck contemporaries as heretical, but Spinoza anticipated much of the significant work of 20th-century Existentialists. Spinoza believed that whatever causes people to live in harmony with one another is good. In order to keep free of academic obligations, Spinoza earned his living by grinding optical lenses; glass dust in his lungs killed him at the age of 45.

Less well known on the international scene are the poets of Holland's 17th-century Golden Age, due largely to the lack of translated versions of their work (poetry, with its close connections to original language characteristics, is less successful in translation than other forms of literature). **Joost van den Vondel** (1587–1679) is still considered Holland's greatest poet, honored by Amsterdam's popular Vondel Park, which has a suitably stately statue of the poet centrally located within it. **Pieter Corneliszoon Hooft** (1581–1647) was a metaphysical romantic poet who encouraged contemporary creativity by entertaining a coterie of artists, authors, and musicians at his castle at Muiden (see *Muiden* under *Northern Holland, Old Zuiderzee Villages*). His name adorns what is perhaps Amsterdam's most fashionable shopping street—*P.C. Hooftstraat*—near Vondel Park and in the attractive residential museum district of the city.

Louis Couperus (1863–1923) was the outstanding writer of the Dutch Realism School of fiction. With great talent and ability, Couperus probed the psychological impact of colonialism on Dutch life, writing of the decadence of upper-class life in The Hague with insight and attention to detail. Of his more than 30 novels, *Old People and the Things That Pass* (translated in English) is probably the finest.

Belgian Authors

Hendrik Conscience (1812–1883), born in Antwerp to a French-speaking father and Flemish mother, began to write soon after Belgium had become a nation in 1830. He is regarded as the father of modern Flemish literature, since he was the first to write fiction in Flemish, which had been a dying literary language. Conscience is best known for the historical romance *The Lion of Flanders* (published in 1838), which, set in the period 1298–1305 in the Bruges of medieval guilds and clothworkers, in the era of Philip the Fair and the Battle of the Golden Spurs (still colorfully reenacted), remains a good romantic read. Conscience presents highly accurate and ample period detail and pageant-like descriptions of Flemish history.

Maurice Maeterlinck (1862–1949) was born of old Flemish stock, though both parents were French-speaking, into a conservative, wealthy Roman Catholic family in Ghent. In 1911, he won the *Nobel Prize for Literature,* the only Benelux writer ever to have earned that honor. Maeterlinck's best work was produced in the first half of his life. His *Onirologie,* with a U.S.-born principal character who has strange dreams about his unknown Dutch origin, shows the influence of American authors Poe and Hawthorne. His play *The Blind* caused him to be called the creator of static theater, which Samuel Beckett developed some 60 years later. Maeterlinck's masterpiece, *Pelleas and Melisande,* was first published in 1893. His last book, *Bulles Bleues* (1948), which recaptured happy memories of his youth and young manhood in Flanders, was widely read, as were his essays on Ralph Waldo Emerson.

Ironically, though a writer whose poems, plays, and lyric prose inspired many major composers (see under *Composers* in previous *Music* section), Maeterlinck himself neither understood nor liked music. He lived more than 50 years of his long life in France, but never renounced his Belgian citizenship. Though in midlife a figure of international repute, better appreciated in England and the U.S. than at home, Maeterlinck had fallen into obscurity by the time of his death, and is now best recognized in his native Belgium.

Georges Simenon (1903–1989) is undoubtedly the best-known of all Belgian authors, although he is often thought to be French, since that is the language in which he wrote and it was to Paris he headed in his early 20s, leaving his native Liège to seek a wider market for his works. Simenon is credited with revising the entire approach to the detective story, the literary form for which he is best known. He created the character *Inspector Maigret* in 1934. Many of the 80-odd Maigret stories seem sordid in setting, but at closer glance can be seen as intense psychological studies that deal less with crime than with uneasy, unfulfilled lives. In later years, Simenon produced more ambitious psychological analyses of modern man. The prodigiously prolific Simenon—he wrote more than 200 novels under his own name and another 300 or so under 17 pseudonyms, with total sales well over half a billion—is one of the most widely translated authors in history, with works appearing in more than 50 languages; perhaps a third of his output has been translated into English.

Not an author but a prominent Belgian literary figure nonetheless, created by English mystery writer Agatha Christie, is detective **Hercule Poirot,** who drops information about Belgium as he winds his way through the considerable Christie *oeuvre* in which he is centrally cast. The brilliant, benevolent-despot bachelor character which Christie created in 1916 for her first detective novel, received his Brussels-born Belgian identity because Christie, like many English in the World War I era, had opened her heart to the World War I sufferings of refugees from German-occupied Belgium, some of whom were being sheltered in a parish near her home. Among the many Belgian characteristics displayed by Poirot is his passionate interest in fine food.

So real had Belgian Hercule Poirot become to readers through the pen of Christie, that when he "died" at her hands in 1975, among his many obituaries was a front-pager in *The New York Times* (8/6/75).

Luxembourg Authors

The outstanding work written in the Luxembourgish dialect is **Michel Rodange**'s epic poem *Renert* (1872), which is a picturesque adaptation of the satirical *Reynard* story (see **Willem** under *Dutch Authors*).

FOOD AND DRINK

FOOD

You'll find good food in the Benelux countries—whether you're being served at a cozy Dutch *eet cafe* ("eat cafe"), partaking of a gourmet repast in a superb setting at one of Brussels' stellar-rated restaurants (many an epicurean European considers Brussels second to none as a culinary capital), or sampling street stand specialties such as *frites* (known as French fries, but perfected by *Belgians*) and *haring* (herring) that will redefine your ideas about "fast food." Throughout Holland, Belgium, and Luxembourg, wherever and whenever food is concerned, high standards in ingredients, preparation, and presentation prevail.

Apart from Brussels' most famous and fashionable restaurants, where costs have taken to the stratosphere—Eurocrat and multi-national corporate expense accounts help support high prices—travelers will discover that eateries in the Benelux in every category deliver value for money. The reason this appetizing situation exists has little to do with tourists, and everything to do with the fact that the Belgians, Luxembourgeois, and Dutch themselves like to eat well.

The Belgian kitchen is influenced by the French in the use of sauces, but is generally more substantial, with servings less skimpy in size. Luxembourg more or less follows the Belgian cuisine lead, adding its own regional specialties. A statement that's almost a cliché characterizes both Belgium and Luxembourg cuisine: "It has the quality of the French and the quantity of the German."

Although there are some differences in food tastes across the Benelux, the use of fresh local seasonal fare is shared. Many kitchens pride themselves on regional dishes, some of which have become known far beyond regional boundaries. In the coastal areas of Holland and

Belgium, there's a focus on seafood, while the many rivers throughout the Benelux provide plentiful fresh water fish. Chefs in the Belgium and Luxembourg Ardennes pay particular attention to *paté,* the renowned *jambon d'Ardennes* and, in season, concentrate on game.

The Benelux culinary calendar contains several other select seasons. A six-week period in May and June is much anticipated for the white asparagus from Belgium and Holland's Limburg province. It's known locally as "white gold," not because of export profits—supply can scarcely meet the local demand—but for its delicate taste. The traditional style of serving asparagus is with a sauce of melted butter, chopped hard-boiled egg, and bits of cooked ham. During approximately the same spring period, the much-savored first tender shoots of the hops plants (grown for use in Belgium's intensive beer production) also are served up.

Mussels *(moules/mosselen)* are such favored fare in the Benelux that the coming of a new season (in the months with a letter "R," beginning with September) is eagerly anticipated from the North Sea estuaries where they are harvested all the way to land-locked Luxembourg, where restaurants post signs proclaiming *Les moules sont arrivées* ("The mussels have arrived!"). You'll look like a local while feasting on mussels—waiters will keep bringing bowlsful, served with a side of *frites,* until you beg off—if you hold a full shell in your left hand (if you're right-handed), and use an empty hinged-shell in your right hand as an eating utensil. One of the many popular ways of preparing them is *Moules à la Bruxelloise,* steamed in dry white wine and chopped onions.

Years of encouragement from Dutch friends still have not enabled me to be able to report firsthand on the joys of eating *groene haring,* the first fresh catches of the delicacy brought in by the herring fleet in May. One is supposed to hold a raw young herring, slightly salted and dipped in chopped onion, by the tail and simply drop it "down the hatch," at any one of thousands of street stands in Holland. (You *may* eat it on a bread roll.)

Despite the importance of seasons for some foods, the rich flat polderlands of Holland and Belgium boast an incredible acreage of greenhouses, and the intensive agriculture undertaken in them now makes a healthy variety of hothouse vegetables available year-round. They supply not only shops and family tables in the Benelux and the rest of the EC, but supermarkets across the U.S. and Canada. Thanks to tender packing and air transport from Amsterdam's Schiphol and Brussels' Zaventem (which is located not far from the vegetable auctions at Mechelen, a town so proud of its produce that it puts it on parade each September, in the amusing *Vegetable Corso*), an appealing array finds its way to kitchens worldwide.

Appetizing appetizers, or starters, to a Benelux meal include small

North Sea "grey" shrimp, which the Dutch and Belgians eat on buttered bread, or *tomates aux crevettes* (tomatoes stuffed with the tiny shrimp). Zeeland and Ostend oysters are considered superior in these parts, as is eel, smoked or prepared as *paling in 't groen* (tender eel in a slightly sour green-colored sauce of spinach and multiple herbs). Belgium chicory, or *witloof* (white leaf), endive, and Brussel sprouts duly make their welcome appearance (though sprouts are not offered as often in Brussels as they are in the U.K.).

You only have to see the herds of dairy cows decorating the Dutch countryside to be reminded of Holland's famous full-fat cheeses (which only *begin* with *Edam* and *Gouda*) and other rich products: milk, *milk* chocolate, butter, cream (*slagroom*, in its much-used whipped form), and yogurts, *quarks,* and *vla* (custard) that we never come upon across the Atlantic. If you search, you can find *magere* (skim) milk and yogurt in Dutch grocery stores, but such "slim" products are not so apparent in Belgium and Luxembourg.

In cosmopolitan centers like Amsterdam and Brussels, continental/French cuisine is the rule at many restaurants. But typical Benelux dishes are found on many a menu. *Carbonnades Flamandes,* a beef beer-simmered stew is a popular Belgian dish. Made without beer is the Dutch *Hutspot* beef stew. Dutch beef filet *(biefstuk)* has a different taste, due to Holland's below-sea-level saltwater-fed grazing fields. An order for *filet américain* could come as a surprise; it's not Chicago steak, but steak tartar (raw chopped beef mixed with herbs). Ghent's famous *waterzooi* is a satisfying creamy fish (sometimes made with chicken instead) stew. Holland's *ertwensoep* is a pea soup so substantial that many places serve it only in the cooler months.

Rabbit is a mainstay on menus in Belgium and Holland. Two of the best known dishes are *lapin aux pruneaux* (marinated rabbit fried with prunes) and *lapin de garenne aux griottes* (wild rabbit cooked with vegetables, white wine, and sour cherries). Pork, which is lovely, lean, and plentiful in Holland, is also very popular in the Belgian Ardennes. *Jud mat gardebo'nen* (smoked pork and sauerkraut) is one of Luxembourg's most typical treats. Also a delicacy from the Ardennes in hunting season is *marcassin* (young wild boar). *Boudin de Liège* is a savory, herb-flavored sausage.

Apart from the region's more formally-prepared dishes, informal fare can be fun. First, there are the famed *frites,* potatoes double-fried to what many feel is perfection, and served at stands throughout Belgium and Holland in sturdy paper cones with a dollop of mayonnaise (which you may discover to be a more compatible condiment than catsup). Platter-size Dutch pancakes *(pannekoek),* fully a meal, come in dozens of sweet and savory varieties: cheese, apple, and bacon; crystallized ginger and cheese (my favorite); with fruit, sugar and/or whipped cream. Another reasonably-priced Dutch meal on a plate is an *uits-*

mijter. Available at any cafe or pub, this simple but tasty and filling choice is two slices of buttered bread, each topped with a large slice of roast beef, ham, or cheese, and topped with a fried egg, the whole garnished with a bit of greenery.

Try before you buy at a cheese shop by sampling slices of *Gouda* at its different stages of age: *jonge, jonge belegen, belegen, extra belegen, oude* (young to old, with mature in between). Orchards in Holland and Belgium make fruit pastries popular; in Maastricht, in Holland's southeast province of Limburg, fruit *vlaai* (flans) are a specialty. Belgium waffles *(gaufres),* cooked on the spot in sidewalk shops in cast-iron molds and handed to you warm, come in two kinds: pre-sweetened dough (Liège-style) and unsweetened dough sprinkled with confectioners' sugar (Brussels-style). Dutch *oliebollen* are solid round doughnuts sold at booths at weekly markets. *Gemberkoek* (ginger cake/bread) comes loaded with large chunks of ginger.

Speculaas in Holland (similar to *speculoos* in Belgium) are mixed spice and ginger cookies that can come as big as a baseball mitt at a *bakerij* (bakery), or packaged in more portable sizes. They can be found in many stores all year, but burst upon the scene at Holland's Sinterklaas season from mid-Nov. to Dec. 5th. Then the cookies are baked in molds (popular souvenir items themselves) in the bishop figure of St. Nicholas (Sinterklaas) or other over-size figures.

Although a discussion of rich Belgian handmade filled chocolates *(pralines)* has been left this long, you may be tempted by them much earlier if you have anything of a sweet tooth (heaven help you if you're a chocoholic). *Godiva* is a home-brand in Brussels, but it's still pricey; buy your chocolates at one of the several lower-overhead *Leonidas* street-front shops where the *Bruxelloise* know the quality is the same and the price better. In Holland adults can buy bonbons filled with Dutch liqueurs, and kids (of all ages) can spread chocolate flakes or *hagelslag* (chocolate ''vermicelli'') on buttered bread for breakfast. The Dutch also love *licorice,* sold at candy counters in dozens of shapes and sizes and, for when a sweet tooth needs a rest, in several *salty* varieties.

INDONESIAN FOOD

Its colonial past has given the Dutch what may be Europe's most exotic "national" cuisine: certainly it's no exaggeration to say that Indonesian fare is Holland's most popular food. The 8000-island archipelago of Indonesia (the world's fifth most populous country, reaching between Asia and Australia in a 3000-mile arc) came under the influence of Holland by the 17th century, as a Dutch East India Company colony. The largest islands include Sumatra, Java (with the capital Jakarta), Borneo, and Celebes; Bali is still marketed as an idyllic tourist isle. Indonesia remained part of the Dutch Empire until given its independence after World War II in 1949. Over the centuries, many Dutch worked for companies in Indonesia; when they returned to Holland, they retained their taste for Indonesian fare. After independence, many Indonesians themselves moved to Holland. Thus, with demand created on all sides, Indonesian cuisine became ingrained in Holland.

While in North America there are take-out burger stands on every city block, and in the U.K. omnipresent fish and chip take-aways, in Holland virtually every village has an Indonesian restaurant. The Dutch dine out frequently in their Indonesian eateries, indulging in a *rijsttafel* (rice table) feast if it's an occasion, or picking up a dinner of *loempia* (giant egg roll), *saté met pinda saus* (grilled pork or chicken on skewers with spicy peanut sauce), *kroepoek* (giant shrimp-flavored chips), or *nasi* or *bami goreng* (rice or noodles with meat and vegetables). A Dutch pils or Indonesian brand beer is a usual accompaniment.

The cuisine, even in Indonesia, has been influenced by others over the centuries. The Dutch introduced many vegetables and beer to it, the Chinese contributed various cooking methods and noodle-based dishes, and Indians shared their curry mixtures. Aside from the small side dishes of burning *sambals,* Indonesian food needn't be excessively spicy, and waiters can always counsel you—as they do so well at Amsterdam's much-respected *Sama Sebo* Indonesian restaurant—on appropriate choices. Many dishes are very reasonably priced.

The *rijsttafel* is the grand dining event at Indonesian restaurants, although it is by no means a necessary one in order to sample the pleasures of this tasty cuisine. Among the many rijsttafel dishes—usually at least 16, including spices and "condiments"—such as toasted coconut and peanuts—that are set up on hot plates on your table are a set selection of vegetables and meats in different sauces, some hot, some not, all to be accompanied with steamed white rice mounded in the center of your plate. As the dishes are passed, put small portions of as many as you want around, but not on, the rice. That way you can taste each dish separately. You can go back for favorites until either the serving dishes are empty, or you are full. In Amsterdam restaurants, a rijsttafel usually will be served for a minimum of two persons, with menus ranging from about Dfl. 40 to 75 per person.

About the rijsttafel Aldous Huxley once recounted this incident: "I took the trouble one day to count the number of dishes offered to me. Twenty-six actually appeared before me; but it was a busy day for the waiters, and I do not think I got all the dishes I was entitled to." Perhaps Huxley was reacting to *official* (non-restaurant) rijsttafel ritual, in which the more important the guest, the more dishes served.

DRINK

Benelux food is made more pleasurable by indulging in the indigenous drinks that round out the regional experience. Beer is a common denominator drink for all three Benelux countries, each of which can claim a brewing tradition past and present. Local citizens partake in substantial intake. In a Brewers Association of Canada recent poll of the world's top 14 countries ranked for annual beer consumption *per capita,* the top drinkers were Germans (at 144 liters), but all three Benelux partners appeared. Belgians were 4th at 121 liters, the Luxembourgeois 6th at 116 liters, and the Dutch 13th, between the U.S. and Canada (14th at 84 liters/79 quarts). So, whether production is the horse and consumption the cart, or *vice versa,* the Benelux is beer territory.

Belgian Beer

In Belgium, beer is treated with the respect and good form that usually is reserved for wine. Long a source of pleasure for peasants and working-class people (as can be seen in scenes from 16th- and 17th-century Flemish paintings by Pieter Bruegel the Elder, David Teniers, and others), in the late 20th century, traditional Belgian beers have found acceptance in the gastronomic world as well. Although it's unlikely the *hoi polloi* would care to contrive a beer list, instead of a wine carte, to accompany a six-course repast, interest in beer "culture" certainly is not limited just to Belgium's *haut monde.*

While language can't unite Belgium, devotion to beer does. Even when wine is served with the meal, beer frequently is the Belgian aperitif of choice (one aficionado speaks of Brussels' *queuze* as having the taste of *fino* sherry and the sparkle of champagne). Small Belgian specialty brewers pride themselves on giving their product "bouquet," "palate," and "finish" (aftertaste), so that tasters speak of the "nose" of the brew. When beer isn't served to accompany a dish, it may be used *in* it, in which case regional dishes enter the realm of *cuisine de la bière.* Beers in Belgium may be blended like wines, aged like wines (in wooden casks for two or three years), bottled and corked like wines, presented like wines (in different kinds of stemware: flutes, goblets, snifters), served chilled like white wines or closer to room temperatures like reds, and may even *taste* remarkably like wines, sometimes being referred to as the "Burgundies of Belgium." Of the more than 600 kinds of beer brewed in Belgium, the differences in taste between them can be as substantial as those between a Cabernet and a Chablis.

The alcoholic content of Belgian beer varies considerably from one kind to another. In North America most beers are 3–4%, while in Belgium the evocatively named *Duvel* ("devil" in Flemish) isn't the most potent at 8.2%, nor are "Lucifer" or "Forbidden Fruit," both at 9%. Since beers in Belgium reach 12% alcohol, those setting out on a "pub crawl" there stand warned.

On the large scale, Belgium's modern brewing plants have kept pace with technology, producing classical beers of a high degree of purity for a worldwide population that shows increasing demand. *Stella,* a premium pils from the Artois Brewery, founded in 1366, is the country's best known internationally. At the same time, Belgium maintains tradition with an amazing range of beers from small producers that makes its brewing industry unique in the world.

There are three schools of beer brewing in Belgium: low (bottom) fermentation; high (top) fermentation; and spontaneous fermentation. The high and low distinction refers to fermentation temperatures, and has nothing to do with the percentage of alcohol in the beer. Low fermentation beers are brewed from light malt and ferment for ten days at a temperature between 43°–50° F. (6°–10°C.). During the process, a yeast sediment is formed on the bottom of the vat. All light beers of the *pilsener* type (a method developed in the Czechoslovakian town of Pilzen) are bottom fermented. These beers should be served cold, in clear, tall glasses. Nearly 80% of Belgium's considerable annual beer production is *pils,* primarily produced in large commercial breweries (as it is in Holland and Luxembourg).

High fermentation beers are brewed by infusion from dark malt. The fermentation period lasts a maximum of five days, and takes place at the relatively high temperature of 60°–70° F. (15°–21°C.). At the end of fermentation, the yeast forms a thick scum on the surface of the beer that must be skimmed off. Top fermented beers can be recognized by their dark color, and include most "special" Belgian beers. These beers should be served warmer than pils, in short-stemmed rounded goblets. Somewhat more than 10% of Belgian beer production is in the wide-ranging number of specialty beers produced at relatively small to very small regional breweries throughout the country.

Apart from their specific brewing processes, color is one of the distinguishing features of "specials." **Rodenbach,** a slightly bitter beer matured in wooden barrels by the Roulers Brewery, is red. **Hoegaarden,** a village east of Louvain, is among the few remaining breweries producing "white" (a bittersweet wheat) beer. **Oudenaarde,** in the south of East Flanders province, is known for its dark brown beers, which owe their color partly to an addition of caramel. Even deeper in color is the darkly delicious authentic **trappist beer,** still produced by five abbeys in Belgium (and one in Holland).

The final roughly 10% of Belgium production is in so-called *spontaneous fermentation* beers, which result, literally, from something "in the air" in Brussels. This category, with curious old names such as *lambic, gueuze, kriek, framboise,* and *faro,* covers beers brewed solely in the Senne Valley in and around Brussels. A striking detail of these 70% malt/30% wheat beers is that no yeast is added. Whereas air is the worst enemy of brewers of low and high fermentation beers, it is an indispensable ally to creators of spontaneous fermentation beers, since their fermentation results from a natural microflora existent only in the air of the Senne Valley, which reacts with the boiled malt/wheat/hops mixture while it is cooling in large *open* vats. The beer thus produced, *lambic,* must be stored for between one and two years, after which it is bottled, and undergoes a secondary fermentation in the bottle. A mix of young and older lambic produces *queuze*. Still later, cherries may be added to form *kriek,* raspberries to produce *framboise,* and sugar candy to form *faro* beer.

The Belgian Brewers Association has its headquarters in the gilt-highlighted **Brewers Guildhall,** which dates from 1696, on Brussels' Grand Place. Appropriately, it also serves as a small beer museum. Of the dozens of breweries that have existed in Brussels over the centuries, only one survives as a traditional *brasserier:* century-old *Cantillon.* It opens as a gueuze "museum" during the brewing season (mid-October through April). It's on the roof of Cantillon that the secret to its product is seen: an enormous vat topped with tiles tilted to let in the air, Brussels' atmospheric "yeast," which creates the city's unique brew.

It is said that there are some 200 different tastes of beer in Belgium, and about 600 labels (the number changes somewhat, as new or seasonal beers from small breweries come on to the market, and others disappear). That number requires a lot of learning on the part of bartenders-to-be. Not only do they need to know the *kinds* of beers (and the different labels for each), but *which* goes in *what* glass, and the proper pouring procedure for each. Imagine having to memorize where as many as 300 kinds of beer (that's the approximate number on sale at *De Bruyne* pub in Bruges, where the owner also runs a Beer Academy) are stored, so you could put your hand on any given one when a customer ordered it. Plenty of intriguing conversations with waiters await travelers to Belgian beer pubs.

Belgian brands are among the most popular export brews sold across the border in Holland. There, *Heineken Brewery* is the corporate giant; combined with *Amstel,* which it owns, Holland's Heineken is the world's second largest brewing empire. (Heineken has a brewery conveniently located in Amsterdam that offers tours and free tastings, and sells a wide range of items imprinted with its brand-of-brew logo). Dutch beer today consists largely of the light, thirst-quenching commercially-produced lager (pils). *Oude Bruin* (Old Brown), produced under both the Heineken and Amstel labels, is a tasty, slightly sweet dark beer. As in the U.K., many pubs and cafes in Holland are sponsored by a single brewery and sell only that brand.

Luxembourg has five breweries in its little backyard, all of which produce mainly lager. *Mousel* is the country's largest brewery, and *Clausen* is centered in the capital, in Luxembourg City's "lower" suburb in the Alzette Valley that shares its name. Luxembourg also has the distinction, unique in the Benelux, of producing wine.

Luxembourg Wine

The Dutch *proost,* a perfect toast when raising a glass of beer, is, I've learned, considered too "common" for wine; the French *santé* (or international *cheers*) is the more refined phrase called for when sipping a glass of the grape. Luxembourg is *the* Benelux vintner, having virtually the only vineyards in the tri-country region today (Belgium's vines along the Meuse River were lost in World War I). Luxembourg exports just under half of its finished product; of those exports, nearly 95% go to its Benelux neighbors (80% to Belgium). That figure, combined with the Belgians' reputation for appreciating, and securing, excellent wines to accompany their country's fine cuisine, makes a strong statement about the quality of Luxembourg wines.

Luxembourg's sunny south-facing slopes along a 25-mile (42 km.) stretch of the Moselle River between Wasserbillig and Schengen have been the site of viniculture since before the Romans arrived. The opposite bank of the river is in Germany, and the vineyards there provide the ingredients for the Germanic moselles. For whatever reasons of soil, sun, and other elements, Luxembourg's moselle wines are drier than their German counterparts.

Luxembourg grows seven varieties of white wine grapes on 3,333 acres of vineyards in a band along the Moselle: *Rivaner* (which accounts for 47% of the production); *Elbling* (20%); *Auxerrois* (12%); *Riesling* (10%); followed by *Pinot Blanc, Pinot Gris,* and *Gewurztraminer.* Dry, light, refreshing Elbling is particularly popular among Luxembourgers themselves, while the Rivaner, supple and fruity, is widely exported; tender, tasty Auxerrois often is enjoyed as an aperitif.

In general, it is the spring and summer weather which determines the quantity of wine that will be produced in Luxembourg, and the later season weather that determines its quality. Such was the wonderful weather in much of Europe in the summer and autumn of 1989, that many anticipated a "Year of the Century" vintage. Luxembourg's white wines from that year await your opinion.

Luxembourg wines are carefully quality-controlled by the government organization *Marque Nationale,* which was established in 1935 to ensure consistency, and adapted to new conditions dictated by the European Community in 1971. Grading of the organoleptic qualities—color, clarity, fragrance, and flavor (and effervescence for sparkling wines)—is done by a board of expert tasters appointed by Luxembourg's Minister of Agriculture and Viticulture. Depending upon the average of points awarded by the experts to each wine, bottles carry a control label listing the classification; highest is *Grand Premier Cru,* followed, in descending order, by *Premier Cru, Vin Classe,* and, lowest of the qualifying mentions, *Marque Nationale.*

Luxembourg also bottles a fine sparkling wine produced according to the "champagne method," which, legally, is the only way that word can be used outside of the French district of Champagne. In 1921, Jean Bernard Massard, a winemaker from the Champagne region, discovered that almost identical soil and climatic conditions to those in France's Champagne existed in the Grand-Duchy of Luxembourg on the banks of the Moselle. Today, *Bernard-Massard Cellars* in Grevenmacher annually produces two million bottles of sparkling *Cuvee Brut,* a crisp, dry, delicate blended champagne, which built the reputation of the firm, and an additional 1.6 million bottles of other varieties of sparkling and still wine, of which 75% are exported. From April to November, visitors are welcomed for tours of the cellars and to view an interesting film about wine production in Luxembourg.

More than two thirds of Luxembourg's vineyards are worked by the 1000 members of the large wine-making and marketing cooperative, *Vinmoselle,* which is a combination of the cooperatives formed in the region beginning in 1921. The 300 wine concerns not affiliated with cooperatives are united in the Professional Organization of Independent Wine-Growers.

Luxembourg stages a festival (the second weekend in September at Grevenmacher) featuring a little worship of the Roman god of the grape Bacchus before the late September harvest of the fruit of the vine. Perhaps the most interesting event for visitors is the **Grand Cortage Folklorique,** an impressive parade with floats, marching bands and musicians from several countries, and some fascinating entries, such as the **De Steltenlopers van Merchtem** (Belgium), a group of 25 stilt walkers at astonishing altitudes. There are also many decorated grape-theme carts, from which wine is poured freely into the upraised glasses of viewers, who, as a result, take to more and more dancing and singing in the streets as the parade progresses. If one misses this occasion, it's still possible to feel very much a part of the vineyard scene by driving along paved paths into the very midst of the ripening vines (see under Luxembourg, Moselle Valley), watching the harvesting, and visiting the small Donatus Chapel at Wormeldange situated high on a hill in the midst of the vineyards. From the bench in front of the chapel is an amazing vista over vineyards on both banks of the Moselle.

Dutch Spirits

A particularly Dutch drink is *jenever,* a kind of gin made from juniper that is downed neat. Jenever comes in *jonge* (young), clear-colored with less of a bite, and *oude* (old), with an amber tinge. It's largely a man's drink, though women sometimes take citron (lemon) or other flavored jenever, in liqueur-size servings.

Liqueurs are Holland's other forte on the alcoholic front. *Bols* and *De Kuyper* are the two most widely sold brands. The atmospheric old **Bols Taverne** in Amsterdam serves as a tasting place (and restaurant). A broad selection of Dutch liqueurs at favorable prices is sold at Amsterdam's Schiphol Airport's duty-free shop. The most *fun* you'll probably ever have with a liqueur will be with *Advocaat,* now partaken of mostly by little old Dutch ladies. Still, it's a typical Dutch "drinking" experience that I recommend for its unusualness alone (and, personally, I like the taste). Advocaat is a thick, bright yellow alcoholic eggnog, served in a small juice-size glass with a dollop of slagroom (whipped cream) on top; it comes with a small spoon, since it's so thick that you actually eat rather than drink it. Advocaat also is used as a topping for vanilla ice cream *(Coupe Advocaat).*

THE BULB FIELD BUSINESS: THE DUTCH AFFAIR WITH FLOWERS

You won't be in Holland long before you notice the preeminent position flowers hold in Dutch life. Nowhere else will you see so many people carrying paper cone-wrapped bouquets. There's hardly a happening in Holland that isn't an occasion for giving flowers: neighbors returning from vacation; friends finished redecorating their home; business associates closing a contract; the sun shining after a gray spell or the gray spell itself. Long-standing custom encourages the bringing of flowers when visiting a Dutch home for a first time.

The flower-giving occasion to top all others is a birthday, the high point in the Dutch social calendar (and, often, a holiday from work). The celebrant invites friends and family to his or her home, and most guests—you guessed it!—arrive with bright bouquets. But most Netherlanders need no excuse at all to buy fresh flowers, so it's easy to understand why flower stands and stalls are everywhere in Holland.

'Tis the tulip that's the most favored flower. A colorful history and the sweet scent of commercial success since its introduction into the country centuries ago earned the tulip long-term endearment in Dutch hearts. Today, the flower serves a much more serious role than mere sentimental symbol of Holland.

Unknown to Western Europe until the 1550s—when Ogier Ghislain de Busbecq, an Austrian ambassador to Turkey, is recorded as having first seen the flower being cultivated in Constantinople—the tulip made its way to Holland after Busbecq presented several bulbs to Carolus Clusius, who was returning to Dutch soil from Austria to oversee the *Hortus Medicus* (medicinal garden) at the newly-established (1575) University of Leiden. From the first beautiful blossoms that burst forth from those ugly-duckling bulbs, the Dutch adored tulips. Fortuitously, nowhere else in Europe were better bulbs produced than in the distinctive beneath-sea-level Dutch soil (a mixture of sand and peat, with a touch of clay) found in the North and South Holland provinces.

The almost-immediate Dutch addiction to tulips created an amazing era in horticultural history. In the late 16th and early 17th centuries, Holland became "infected" with a disease known as "Tulipmania." The growing wealth of Amsterdam merchants, who were just coming into their Golden Age of abundance and eager to acquire beautiful and fashionable consumer wares, quickly transformed tulip bulbs into "collectibles." Due to their desirability, tulips frequently played center-stage on still-life canvases created by contemporary Dutch master artists. Reflecting the times, English essayist Joseph Addison wrote in *The Tatler* of his experience at a country inn in Holland. Sitting at dinner he overheard a discussion at the next table about Admiral Such-and-Such, General This, and Captain That. When he finally gave in to curiosity and inquired of his dining room neighbors who these impressive gentlemen might be, the reply was: "Gentlemen? Why, sir, these are no gentlemen. They are tulips of the very rarest and noblest sort."

Much more valuable than the carefully cultivated tulips that served as collectibles, however, were those bulbs that, quite unexpectedly, produced unique flowers through "breaking" (changing) their color and pattern (now known to be the result of a virus). This process produced an active "futures" market for bulbs.

By the 1630s, not only noblemen and merchants, but seamen, servants, and chimney sweeps—anyone with access to even a small patch of soil—were growing and speculating in tulip bulbs. Demand far outran supply, and bulbs were considered as sound an investment as diamonds. Houses and businesses were mortgaged to acquire cash to buy more bulbs. Prices paid at auction for single tulip bulbs soared: to today's equivalent of $750 for an *Admiral Liefkens;* $1825 for a *Viceroy;* $4000 for a *Semper Augustus.* Flemish artist Pieter Paul Rubens was recorded as lamenting that he could only afford to give his wife one bulb for her birthday.

Businessmen bartered for bulbs: A copy of one such transaction records an exchange of "two loads of wheat, four loads of rye, four fat oxen, eight fat pigs, 12 fat sheep, two hogsheads of wine, four barrels of eight-florin beer, two barrels of butter, 1000 pounds of cheese, a complete bed, a suit of clothes, and a silver beaker"—all for one small bulb. Some of the excitement of this period was recreated by Alexandre Dumas in his book *The Black Tulip,* a melodramatic novel about a high-priced competition to breed a bulb that would yield a completely black flower.

Having lost their heads to the esteemed tulip, it was only a matter of time before some of the usually prudent Dutch lost their shirts as well. The "crash" of the tulip market occurred in 1637—and the government stepped in to regulate it. A moderated tulip mania has existed ever since in Holland, however, today taking the form of a billion-guilder bulb business.

Spring's the season to catch Holland's version of the greatest show on *earth*—the bulb fields in bloom—with a finale featuring tulips. Bulb season in Holland begins in late March if the weather is seasonable, and continues through much of May. During the weeks of this natural beauty pageant, the colors in the country's carpet of vivid vegetation change frequently. First, crocuses in yellow, white, and purple patterns predominate. Later, giant stripes in the hyacinth hues of pink, white, and blue stretch to the far, low horizon. Finally, rectangular fields blaze with the brilliance of tulips, whose vast, varied patches of pure color can remind viewers of a vigorous Van Gogh canvas come to life. Tulips come in the widest assortment of colors, and in early and late bulb blooming stages, beginning about late April.

The easiest way to enjoy the bulb fields in bloom—my choice when time is limited—is to see them from the windows of the frequent trains that pass through the heart of the bulb district between Leiden and Haarlem, along the main Amsterdam-The Hague-Rotterdam line. The only drawback to the memorable 15-minute stretch between Haarlem and Leiden is a possible stiff neck from straining to catch every colorful field out both sides of the train. To let the spectacular sight sink in, on occasion, when I've had a Dutch railpass and the bulbs were in a particularly colorful stage, I've traveled back and forth through the fields between Haarlem and Leiden more than once, usually waiting no more than 10 minutes for a train in the return direction. To true fans, a tulip field in full bloom looks as lovely on a fifth view as the first!

If you have your heart set on it, you *can* tiptoe through the tulips, or get close enough to the fields to smell the heady hyacinth scent. When you get a firsthand look at one, you'll notice paths between each row of flowers, so that the field workers can inspect the plants. It's terrifically tempting to head right into a field for a close-up look (and photo), but, remember, it's private property and bulbs are big business, so ask before you act. A rental car gives you the most flexibility. Helpful local tourism staff perform the Dutch rites of spring by signposting the *Bloemen* (flower) *Route* on roads throughout the bulb district. The Route also wends its way through the region's tidy Dutch villages, where public and private gardens provide lots of local color.

If you choose to *doe het zelf* (do-it-yourself) by car, be forewarned that "Tulip Time" is Holland's most crowded tourist season. Coach tours come from all over Europe and Japan, and the Dutch, too, drive out to smell the flowers. Felicitously, in fact, Holland's national holiday, *Koningindag* (Queen's Day) falls on April 30, right in the middle of the bulb season (it is the actual birthday of former Queen, now Princess, Juliana, and was kept as the date for the occasion by her daughter Queen Beatrix, perhaps because it gives the Dutch a day to see their own fields of flowers). Roads in the region during bulb season have heavy traffic. Try to travel early and on weekdays, and have a decent map handy in case traffic on the Bloemen Route makes you want to take to different roads.

Another opportunity to get out among the bulb fields is to take local bus #50 or 51 from in front of the railway station, close to the VVV tourist offices, at either Leiden or Haarlem (going in the direction of the other), and get off when you see a bulb area you'd like to explore by foot. There are some fine bulb fields in and around the village of Hillegom. Dutch bus drivers invariably speak some English, so when disembarking, ask where the return bus stop is, and go and check the posted schedule (there are about two buses an hour) so that you can plan your return to town efficiently.

The bus route goes through the village of Lisse, considered the center of the bulb-growing district, where the relatively-recently-opened **Museum voor de Bloembollenstreek** (Museum of the Bulb District) is located. Exhibits in the small museum (old tools and utensils used in the cultivation of bulbs, technical geologic and soil composition descriptions, etc.) do not have English explanations and did not hold my interest. In this instance, you'll gather more memorable moments if you spend your valuable travel time out with the flowers in the fields and at Keukenhof garden.

The adventurous can take to the bulb fields by hiring a bicycle (deposit and identification required) at either the Leiden or Haarlem train station, having procured a map of the bulb district at the local VVV. This area of Holland is as flat as its stereotype, so the cycling hazard isn't hills, but wind, blowing in from the North Sea.

Despite the 20th-century technology the Dutch bring to their bulb industry, when you get out into the scenic countryside of the bulb fields, it's easy to feel that you've wandered into one of the luminous 17th-century landscapes that amply adorn Holland's art museums. Many of the paintings' earthly elements are still present: restlessly roving cloud formations racing toward the distant low-slung horizon, denoted by a church steeple, windmill, or haystacks. The terrain not planted in bulbs is made up of restful green grazing fields, speckled with cows and sectioned by slim, straight canals. Everywhere, the water-logged land reflects the diffused light that has defined such scenes for centuries.

Whether you get there independently (public trains and buses put you within walking distance), or join one of the local coach tours from nearby Amsterdam, **Keukenhof** garden in Lisse deserves a visit if you're in Holland during its season (approximately mid-March to end of May). One of the world's largest flower gardens, Keukenhof was created in 1949 by a group of prominent Dutch bulb growers as a formal showcase for the local product, which is planted on nearly 34,500 acres radiating out from the village of Lisse. While still serving its original export promotion purpose—orders can be placed on the premises for spring flowering bulbs (which are shipped for planting in the fall) and some summer-blooming bulbs (which require spring planting) can be bought on site—Keukenhof now also has become one of Holland's major tourist attractions.

The 70-acre Keukenhof was designed as a natural lake and woodland setting, within which some seven million bulbs bloom each spring. In addition to ten miles of paths that wind among glorious outdoor plantings of inspirational mixes of color, texture, and form, large greenhouses ensure that visitors can enjoy some 500 varieties of both early and late-blooming tulips even though these may not all be in flower at the same time in the outside beds. At both the outdoor and indoor floral exhibits, visitors can view a full range of bulbs in bloom: crocuses, narcissi, hyacinths, and tulips, as well as freesia, irises, lilies, dahlias, gladioli, and amaryllis.

Although Holland has been exporting bulbs for centuries, mass-market retail sales opened up only after World War II. (In the country's still Nazi-occupied war-torn winter of 1944—Holland's infamous "Hunger Winter," when 20,000 Dutch in Amsterdam alone died as a result of food shortages—the "more fortunate" residents of the bulb-growing district sometimes survived by eating bulbs, though the ever-pragmatic Dutch preserved their best bulb-breeding stock.) When the war was over, the Dutch wanted to show gratitude to their allies, and gift boxes of bulbs seemed a perfect way. In the gift-giving process, new markets were created. Today, approximately 75% of Holland's bulb production is exported, to more than 100 countries. Major importing countries include West Germany, the United States, France, Great Britain, Sweden, and Italy (the Vatican is an excellent customer).

In the Dutch bulb fields, you see men knee-deep in flowers, intent on picking off the blooms. The irony of a bulb's beauty is that, once it reaches full flower, it's best to behead it. This allows the bulb to begin absorbing its stem as food for future flowering power.

Despite the beheadings, there are ample flowering bulbs for visitors to view. With up to five million bulbs blooming on every 10 acres, it takes awhile for the wooden-shoed field hands to get to them all. Furthermore, new bulbs burst into bloom every day, so the broad patterns of color keep constant. And the oranges and pinks of one week are augmented the next by adjoining fields of reds, yellows, and purples so dark they appear to be Dumas' fantasy "black" tulip come to life.

When the stems and leaves die down, the bulbs are harvested. After being disinterred, they are dried, cleaned, and graded into large bulbs (commercially salable) and small bulbs (planting stock). In storage areas for the salable bulbs, temperatures are regulated to coincide with the time of year flowering is desired (for instance, seasons are reversed in the southern hemisphere) and the climate of the country to which they are bound.

The successful hybridization of bulbs demands careful attention and patience. It takes at least six years to grow a first-flowering bulb from seed. It takes another ten years to produce 100 bulbs of the new variety, and yet another 10 before the million-bulb mark—considered the minimum to commercially market a new variety—is reached.

The Dutch mean to ensure their continued prominence in the field, and that means attention to old, as well as new, bulb stock. The **Hortus Bulborum** in Limmen is a bulb research center that displays more than 1100 species, some of them the 17th and 18th-century ancestors of today's crop. Open to the public from mid-April to mid-May, the center collects as many flowering-bulb species as possible. In addition, it seeks to preserve those species that are endangered in order to prevent the loss of valuable genetic material.

There's a festive spirit in Holland's bulb district in springtime. A symbol of the season, and a means by which the color and scent of the bulb fields can be carried away and savored a little longer, are the plump garlands made of fresh-picked flower heads, on sale at roadside stands. Motorists decorate their cars with a cheerful chain, and tour buses often sport several.

Flower heads are not only recycled as garlands, but also used on floats in annual flower parades. For more than 40 years on the last Saturday in April, the **Bulb District Flower Parade** has wound its way like a colorful ribbon from Haarlem to Noordwijk, on a 20-mile procession that passes through a dozen villages to the accompaniment of marching bands. The front gardens of houses along the route also are decked out in blooming bulbs. Millions of florets are imaginatively used on the parade's 20-odd floats, a closer inspection of which is possible in the preparation halls at Lisse the Friday afternoon preceding the parade, and at Noordwijk the Sunday after it.

Blossoms not used for decorative purposes are gathered in baskets by field workers and brought aboard barges that are navigated along the narrow canals that crisscross the bulb fields. Piles of petals are shipped to perfume factories, where attempts are made to preserve their aromatic essence.

Although bulbs may be at their dramatic best in the fields in spring, flowers are not seasonal in Holland, thanks to hothouses and nurseries that produce cut flowers and house-and-garden plants around the calendar. Many are sold at flower and plant stalls that are part of the produce and general wares markets held weekly in many a handsome cobbled main square around Holland. Amsterdam's year-round **Floating Flower Market** on the Singel Canal is special, being open office hours Mon.–Sat. (from April through Oct., you'll also notice it at night, when it's wonderfully outlined in white lights). For more than 200 years, people have boarded its moored barges to browse among cut flowers, bouquets, bulbs, and greenery. Business at Holland's outdoor flower markets is especially brisk in the spring when the Dutch plant their apartment window boxes, small front gardens, or tiny alloted plots in the *volkstuinen* (community gardens) at the edge of towns. The Dutch lavish as much care on these small garden spaces as gardeners elsewhere put into large estates.

Holland grows and exports more cut flowers per capita than any other country. Many are grown in the region around Aalsmeer, site of the world's largest flower auction. Annual Dutch flower transactions—as differentiated from bulb sales—come close to 10 billion guilders, and account for some 70% of all international cut flower trade.

Aalsmeer Flower Auction, located not far south of Amsterdam's Schiphol Airport, is a 75-year-old outfit occupying a 47-acre building in which some seven billion cut flowers and more than 100 million plants are sold each year. Visitors are welcome Mon.–Fri. 7:30 a.m.–11 a.m. The earlier you arrive, the more activity; a public bus from Amsterdam can take you there.

After orientation at the entrance, visitors are free to watch the colorful action from an observation gallery, and follow the proceedings by listening to multilingual audio tapes at key sites. Rarely does commerce create such beauty as that seen on the electronically-controlled carts which daily bring more than five million flowers to market. From a viewer's vantage point in the Aalsmeer gallery, the multicolored flower carts create their own parade across the hall floor.

Each flower variety has its specific location. By 7 a.m., all flowers have been inspected and assigned lot numbers. As the five auction halls fill with as many as 1500 export and wholesale buyers—some 2600 are registered—the auctioneers read aloud pertinent data for each lot and start an auction clock. Ticking backward from 100 towards 1, in a "reverse auction," the clock is stopped when a buyer is willing to pay the price shown.

The efficiency at Aalsmeer is legendary. Buyers can have the flowers they've purchased well-packed and at their disposal within 15 minutes of stopping the auction clock. Many lots are sent directly to Schiphol Airport for same-day delivery to flower shops in cities around the world.

THE BELL EPOCH: CENTURIES OF CARILLONS

Suddenly, a surge of unexpected music spills from a spire, cascades to cobbled streets and squares, rebounds from the fanciful facades of old buildings—resounding everywhere at once. The joyful bursts from carillon bells astonish, and then delight, unsuspecting pedestrians before dispersing in the North Sea breezes above the flat countryside of Belgium and Holland.

It was these smallest of countries that gave the world its largest musical instrument. Fittingly, of the nearly 600 carillons worldwide, fully half are found in Belgium and Holland, where the instrument was developed, refined, and has flourished. Their bells hung high in historic tall towers, carillons send their endearing, unavoidable, voices across the Low Countries.

Carillons carry the fond, flowery epithet of "singing towers," and there's a long-standing local saying: "If you can see the tower, you can hear the carillon." Even though they're the world's loudest musical instruments, rush-hour traffic in the heart of cities, where the centuries-old carillon towers often are located, can make that statement less than true today; but even when I have to strain to hear them, the short carillon pieces that mark the hour invariably make me smile.

True carillon music doesn't come from the automatic mechanism that's programmed to send forth song on the hour, however. The instrument's real voice is released when a *beiaardier* or *carilloneur* personally claims the keyboard, and the tons of bronze bells in the tower boom from a hands-on touch. When a master carilloneur takes command, even the uninitiated can hear the increased character in the chorus of the bells. Carillons in the playing care of professionals can deliver a surprising delicacy of sound, and the room for variations of pace, power, and style in manual performances provide plenty of challenge. As well as massive chords that crash like stormy surf, a carilloneur can coax notes as light as a length of Belgian lace from the instrument, skillfully balancing the voices of bells weighing as few as 16, or as many as 16,000 pounds. And the sounds created by these mighty metallic choirs encased in their carved-stone towers can be as complex as they are compelling.

An important player in Benelux bell lore is the official *stadbeiaardier,* or town carilloneur, who is paid a salary to serve as keeper of the carillon. Job responsibilities, depending upon the size of the town and status of its carillon, include giving public concerts at set times, such as on market days and Saturdays (concerts often are offered more frequently in summer). His lofty playing position high in the town tower can make a stadbeiaardier something of a local celebrity. Included in the job description is the upkeep of the instrument, programming the automated carillon for the tower clock whose tunes are changed periodically, and the general creating of good vibrations as ambassador of the town bells.

Carillon players need strength to make music, for their art form is more physical than many. Few carilloneurs have elevators in their high towers, and hundreds of spiralling steps, up and down, must be negotiated for each practice and performance. A number of towers are open to visitors who are up to the ascent. For the able and interested, there's nothing like a close-up inspection of a bevy of bells, the automated mechanism, and the carilloneur's "cabin" with its keyboard. And, too, there's usually a terrific view, over the town and out across the invariably flat land of Flanders or Holland to the far, low horizon.

To play, a carilloneur sits on a bench before a double-row of polished wood pegs, which serve as the "keys." These console pegs tug on a web of rods and wires (the transmission), which in turn operate metal clappers attached to each fixed-position bell. Weather conditions, particularly wet and cold, affect the metal of the bells, and require the carilloneur to tinker and tune, and tighten the wires that connect the keyboard to the bells. Similarly to the operation of an organ, a row of foot pedals is used to play a carillon's lower notes, the heavy metal sounds of the big bass bells.

The carilloneur plays by striking down on the pegs with the side of his closed fist; protective leather pads are worn on the little fingers of each hand. The force of the blow is adjusted for the weight of the bell—the higher the musical note, the lighter and smaller the bell—and the intensity of sound required. Using both fists and feet, carillon players can work up a sweat. In warm weather, they may strip down to shorts for the workout of an hour-long concert. Nevertheless, playing the carillon shouldn't be too-taxing an effort if the bells are properly balanced.

Though some Benelux carillon bells hang in secular buildings or belfries, most are found in church towers. Nevertheless, even when they're located in a church, the tower and the bells frequently are the property of the civic authorities. This fact lingers from the days during French rule of the region, when Napoleon decreed that a town's bells should be the property of the citizens, in honor of the days when bells served as regulators of community life.

The fact that you can't ignore the bold sound of bells is, historically, the very point of their early use. In the Middle Ages, bells were central to the life of communities. Their use became widespread within the monastic system, in which they were rung to announce the offices, a series of services at set times of the day and night.

The use of bells in secular contexts developed with the rise of towns (which, in northern Europe, began in the Low Countries). Belfries were built to contain the bells that signalled the start and end of the working day, the curfew hour when the town gates were shut and bolted for the night, and warned of the approach of important visitors, or hostile troops. There were separate bells for the different alerting functions, with varying pitches so people could tell the rings apart. Bruges, in Belgium, built one of the earliest town belfries (1299), to house its community bell **Magna Campana.** St. Rombout's church clock tower in Mechelen dates from 1372, and Ghent got its belfry in 1376. Further functions, and additional bells, were added as urban development proceeded; bells began to be used for summoning officials to public executions; publicizing a market or fish auction; raising the alarm in case of fire or a storm; announcing the banishment of felons or the death of a citizen.

Eventually, time in towns needed to be measured more precisely, and bells began to mark the hours. The watchman, whose all-important job it was to ring the bell at the correct times, used a sundial as an aid and, later, a small simple clockwork alarm. This eventually led to the development of mechanisms that could chime the hours automatically, giving rise to tower clocks with bells.

Because the tolling of the hour in the tower tended to come unexpectedly, the idea arose of ringing a few notes of warning a few minutes in advance. Originally, this was always done on four small bells, which were struck with wooden mallets. From the name for that four-bell instrument, the *quadrillon,* came the name for the carillon. From four bells, the number increased to a diatonic series of six or eight tuned bells by the beginning of the 16th century. A simple automatic chime mechanism—the first is thought to have been in Mons, Belgium—came into fairly general use quite quickly thereafter.

The development that marked the true beginning of the carillon as an instrument, according to music historians, was when the procedure of striking the bells with a hand-held hammer was replaced with a rudimentary *clavier,* or keyboard, which enabled the manual playing of the bells. Once the keyboard had been developed, the warning flourishes sounded in advance of the striking of the hour were elaborated into actual music.

According to records, the town of Oudenaard, a thriving medieval textile trading center, put the first carillon keyboard into use in the year 1510, thereby establishing Belgium as the birthplace of the carillon. Oudenaard is in Belgium's Dutch-speaking northern Flemish region where, even today, most of the country's nearly 100 carillons are located. By 1541, Antwerp's Onze Lieve Vrouwekerk (Cathedral of Our Dear Lady) possessed a keyboard for its bells; this was followed by Ghent's acquisition of one in 1553.

Mechelen's St. Rombout's got its first keyboard by 1556, but the church made carillon history in 1583 when it showed off the first instrument fitted out with foot pedals. Since that advancement, substantially little change has taken place in the mechanics of the carillon.

The 15th and 16th centuries were periods of prosperity for Flanders, and led to Holland's glittering 17th-century Golden Age. Successful merchants and shipowners living in Antwerp and Amsterdam, and many places in between, watched their treasure pile up, and wanted something to spend it on that would reflect well on their wealth. Cities and towns, too, became richer, and competed to proclaim their prosperity and prestige. An investment in carillons, the sweet singing bells that had already become closely connected with the character of the Low Countries, became a wonderful way to ring out rank.

The number of carillons increased, and bell foundries multiplied, as each prosperous town mounted a campaign to have more bells than its neighbors. The still-respected Dutch firm **Petit & Fritsen** was founded in 1660 in Aarle-Rixtel, on *Klokkengietersstraat* (bell-casters street). It was in these favorable times that the talented Francois Hemony (born in 1609 in Lorraine, France) and his brother Pierre discovered the secret of perfectly tuning carillon bells.

In this musical metier, Francois made the name **Hemony** synonymous with the finest sounding carillons ever cast. Francois and his brother came to Holland at the request of the city fathers of Amsterdam, to build a carillon for the town hall on Dam Square (the present Royal Palace). Thereafter, they remained in Amsterdam in the main, setting up a casting foundry there, and creating the carefully shaped insides of bells that Francois Hemony—who took more individual care in the casting, while his brother Pierre was more inclined to cast ready-made carillons assembly-line style—knew to be the secret of their musicalness. The shape or "profile" of bells, both inside and out, affect their sound. For example, today's English-cast bells (such as those of *John Taylor & Co.*) have a longer "ringing time," or resonance, than Benelux-made bells; this is because the inside lips of the latter are squared off, while English bells are cast absolutely rounded.

During the period 1646–1667, the Hemonys achieved great fame by producing approximately 50 exceptional carillons, each containing up to three octaves. Three octaves was a state-of-the-art standard in the Hemonys' day, though serious carillons today should have at least four octaves, 47 bells. (Contemporary instruments with fewer than 23 bells/two octaves are chimes.) When master bell-caster Francois Hemony died in 1667, his own bells pealed out at the funeral on Amsterdam's Dam Square for more than 3½ hours.

Some 30 Hemony instruments can still be heard today, almost all in the Benelux. And every town that has one—from Groningen to Gouda, Haarlem to Huy, Antwerp to Utrecht—proclaims that fact loud and clear. Sadly, none of the Hemonys' immediate successors turned out to be capable of producing such high quality bells.

A century later, between 1751–1786, **Andreas Josef Van den Gheyn** of Louvain, near Brussels, rediscovered the tuning method, and the brilliance of his treble bells bested even the sound of the Hemonys. Unfortunately, few of the 23 instruments he made have survived and, with Van den Gheyn's death, history repeated itself and the art of tuning bells again disappeared for more than a century. This, and other factors, led to a decline in interest in carillons.

By the end of the 19th century, many an old singing tower had fallen silent, either because its bells were gone, the instrument was in disrepair, or because there was no one left who could play. At the turning into this century, after some 400 years of musical history, even in the Benelux heartland of carillon culture, the elephantine instrument had become an endangered species.

Fortunately, the pre-First World War *Belle Epoque* period also became a bell epoch, during which fortuitous forces combined to resurrect interest in and restoration of the carillon. Enthusiasm for its native instrument reemerged in the Benelux thanks to Belgian **Jef Denijn**. The son of the then Mechelen carilloneur, Jef, although himself more than proficient on the bells, already had begun a career in engineering when the senior Denijn lost his sight. Fate seems to have stepped in, for at the age of 19 the son was allowed to fill his father's shoes at the keyboard in St. Rombout's. Jef Denijn quickly demonstrated such skills as a carilloneur that he became a star. The series of Monday summer evening carillon concerts that he initiated in the early years of this century became so popular that special trains had to be put on to transport audiences numbering as many as 20,000, who came from Brussels and Antwerp to hear him.

Not only did Denijn have dazzling keyboard skills, but he introduced a new, distinctively Flemish style of playing the carillon called the *tremolo,* which is still popular today. The tremolo, which adds more notes and volume, is produced by the rapid alteration of two notes, a technique meant to simulate resonance. This was a particularly welcome playing aid, since old carillon bells tend to lose resonance, especially in their upper registers.

In comparing the carilloning conditions and styles of Holland and Belgium, **Aimé Lombaert,** stadbeiaardier of Bruges, explains that carillons in Holland usually have smaller bells and are placed lower in their towers. "Because our carillons in Belgium are so high," Lombaert says, "we need more sound." Hence, bigger bells, played more flamboyantly. Dutch carilloneurs classify their bell music as "crisper and cleaner."

It's not just the height of the towers and size of the bells that produce a difference between Dutch and Belgium carillon playing, however. Carillon music, as an integral aspect of local culture, reflects national tastes. Carilloneurs may compose original music for the bells, or transpose or otherwise adapt other keyboard pieces. The Belgian repetoire is romantic, with more trills and ornamental embellishments on the higher bells. There are fewer notes to the "starker" pieces and less complicated harmonies that are preferred in Holland. And North American carillon players tend to favor an even less "notey" style on their home keyboards.

Under Denijn's direction in Mechelen, the carillon became a more popular instrument with the public than it ever had been. He adapted music from folk songs to classics to current hits to suit the instrument, as well as composing an array of original works. He also made some structural refinements, standardizing the keyboard and improving the clapper system. During World War I, Denijn was a refugee in England, where he used his influence to awaken interest in carillons. About this time in England, a clergyman from Sussex, **Arthur Simpson,** rediscovered the necessary knowledge to tune bells successfully, which resulted in the opening of two foundries in England which produced superb new instruments. Many of these carillons found their way on board ship to the U.S. and Canada, where the taste for bells was on a rapid rise.

By the early 1920s, Jef Denijn already had been lifted to legendary status for his keyboard brilliance, but he made a further contribution to the carillon culture of his country that has long outlasted his personal playing prowess. One of his greatest admirers was the U.S. Ambassador to Belgium William Gorham Rice, whose personal dream was to cover his own country with carillons and populate it with well-trained carilloneurs. Rice wrote books to kindle Americans' interest in bell music, and raised money from the Rockefeller Foundation, augmented by funds from the Belgian government and city officials, which enabled Denijn, in his 25th anniversary year as Mechelen's *stadsbeiaardier,* to open the world's first carillon school in 1922. **Mechelen's Royal Carillon School,** flourishing today in its business of educating new generations of players of the bells, has about 40 international students in attendance each year. One among several U.S. graduates of Mechelen is Massachusetts resident Sally Slade Warner, who is especially glad for Ambassador Rice's dream of more carillons for America. A carilloneur for the Phillips Academy, Andover school and St. Stephen's church at Cohasset, Warner benefits professionally from living in the Massachusetts/Connecticut area, where there's a "clump" of nine carillons.

The state of Texas, too, has gathered a congregation of carillons, reaching a baker's dozen in number with the 1988 installation of a new instrument at Baylor University. Many of North America's carillons can be found at colleges, where they add notes of distinction to campuses. In Canada, the province of Ontario has the greatest concentration of carillons, with the 53-bell instrument in the Peace Tower in Ottawa considered by many musicians to be the country's best.

The number of carillons in the U.S. today is approaching 200, the same number as in Holland. However, to put the density of Dutch carillons in perspective, one needs only to point out that Holland is but 1/258th the size of the U.S.

Although its carillon school certainly solidified Mechelen's position as the mecca of bell music, the city's carillon reputation is long standing, as attested to by the fact that the word in the Russian language for carillon is *Mechelen bells*. It's not surprising that back in 1583, Mechelen produced the first carillon with pedals. A town guide told me that, since the 15th century, Mechelen has always sought the newest systems for its bells, and was the first town in Flanders to have a Hemony-cast carillon.

So it was simply a continuation of a long history when Mechelen lowered a new state-of-the-art carillon of 49 bells into St. Rombout's tower in June 1981. Though the old Hemony bells were sentimental favorites, the Mechelen city council voted to replace rather than repair the carillon of which they formed a part. Mechelen's old 49-bell carillon was typical of many, in that its bells had accumulated from several foundries, in this case 12, over nearly five centuries (1460–1947). The old carillon remains housed just beneath the new one in St. Rombout's tower, a delicate masterpiece of Gothic Brabant architecture that now holds 80 tons of bells. Famed bell founder and restorer **Eijsbouts** of Asten, Holland, created a new carillon for Mechelen whose brilliance of sound is breathtaking; many experts consider it the best in the world—for the moment.

Despite superb technology of casting and tuning, over the years, certainly over centuries, bells do wear down, and begin to ring false. Sally Slade Warner shows a carillonneur's soul when saying, "You learn to love the old carillons despite the jarring jangle of their worn-out sound." When the sound does go off a bit, the care of carillons can include grinding out some of the insides of a bell, which, to a limit, can get it to ring true again, though the procedure raises the pitch.

Appropriate to its position as home of the world's *first* carillon school—since 1953 there has been a highly-respected *second* one, **De Nederlandse Beiaardschool,** in Holland, in Amersfoort, near Utrecht (see *Amersfoort,* under *Central Holland*)—Mechelen has more (four) carillons than any other city in the world. In centuries past, however, several Benelux cities had many more than that number. Before the revolution in 1793, for instance, Liège in Belgium's Wallonia boasted 19; Brussels claimed nine carillons in the 17th century, but today has only one (in St. Michel Cathedral, the national church at Belgium), under the care of Paula van de Wiele, one of Belgium's half dozen women carillonneurs and a graduate of Mechelen's Royal Carillon School.

When Mechelen's music students are in residence (Oct. to July) and need to practice, there can't be too many carillons in the city. As it is, visitors to Mechelen may hear carillon music by students at any time. Except, that is, for Silent Week, prior to Easter. Easter Day brings a resounding resurrection.

In summer, when students are away, there's never a lack of talented takers at Mechelen's carillon keyboards. The public can enjoy several regularly scheduled concerts weekly, including Monday nights from 8:30–9:30 p.m., preceeded by an invigorating tour up the 514-step tower for those who haven't worn out their feet during the day. The climb is easier in St. Rombout's than in many a carillon tower because of broad, low steps, a result of the entire tower being restored in the early 1980s to be sure it could shoulder its burden of bells.

There are several stop-off sights as one travels up the tower to the carilloneur's "cabin." One room, 160 steps up, reveals a 17th-century crane, actually a large wooden wheel, in which two men "walked around," using solely foot power to lift bells as heavy as Mechelen's beloved 20,000-pound **Salvator,** Belgium's biggest bell, which dates from the year 1480, to the top of St. Rombout's 300-foot tower.

Although bells can lose their song through a crack or simply wear out with use, as the old carillon of Mechelen did, the material of the bells—metal: 80% brass, 20% tin—historically has made them more vulnerable to war than wear and weather. Over the centuries, many a commander of foreign troops occupying the resistanceless lands of the Low Countries has taken a town's toll literally, by confiscating its carillon bells and sending them home to be melted into mortar. Carillons sometimes survived such ignominious ends through the extraordinary efforts of citizens who somehow managed to lower to the ground, and bury, their bells.

Nazis who occupied Holland and Belgium during World War II followed suit, shipping the insides of many singing towers back to munitions factories in Germany to keep their war machine going against those who had supplied the materials. A 1940 pre-invasion inventory of church and carillon bells in Holland listed about 9000. Stock-taking just after the end of World War II showed that 4660 of these had disappeared, most presumably into the furnaces of Nazi armament factories. While war took a heavy toll on big bells in the Benelux, replacement orders came quickly at the conclusion.

Many who really know bells would argue that the finest carillon in Belgium—some say the world—today is **St. Rombout's** in Mechelen. But despite Mechelen's many merits, it is Bruges that probably can claim to have the most famous of the Flemish instruments, since the bells are heard by the many visitors to the lovely town. One, Henry Wordsworth Longfellow, wrote of that carillon in his 1845 *The Belfry of Bruges:* "I heard a heart of iron beating in that ancient tower." The 47 bells, under the able hands of **Aimé Lombaert** and occasional guest carilloneurs, ring out four concerts a week in summer. Nearly 1000 people a day climb the 366 steps to see the 245-year-old instrument, and, along the way, get to view the equally-aged, world's largest automatic mechanism, a nine-ton brass drum with 30,500 holes set—and reset by hand in new tunes periodically by Lombaert—in careful patterns of pegs, which pull wires to produce the four different melodies that strike the quarter hours on the clock of Bruges' elegant octagonal Belfort.

Not only the people who make and play them, but carillon bells themselves can have personalities and documented histories. Some bells have both names and epitaphs cast around their broad rims. Ghent has such a one, six-ton **Roeland,** the largest in the 53-voice carillon. Around its rim reads an inscription that refers to the historical role of bells in announcing urgent news: "My name is Roeland. When I clap there is fire. When I toll there is a storm in Flanders." Ghent's carillon, the only one remaining of seven that once rang in the city, was restored in the early 1980s. It has a marvelous sound, according to Sally Slade Warner, who has played it and many other carillons in Holland and Belgium but, she notes sadly, can't be heard well because of the poor openings in its tower and noise from vehicular traffic around its base.

There's now a 63-bell, five-octave carillon in Belgium, unique in Europe, in the university city of Louvain, near Brussels. After World War I, a carillon—with one bell for each of the 48 states which then constituted the Union—had been presented to Louvain by American engineering societies to commemorate their colleagues who died in that conflict in Belgium. When that carillon fell into disrepair in recent years, Americans again pledged funds, which were added to by Belgians, and now Louvain has an exciting new instrument. The carillon is used by Louvain University students under instruction from visiting carillon players from nearby Mechelen.

Other notable Benelux carillons can be heard in Antwerp, and across the border of Holland in Breda, Dordrecht, and Delft. Concerts from the singing towers offer superb occasions to sit, sip a drink, and savor the surroundings of the charming old centers of these historic towns.

No city has more charming corners than Amsterdam, and the Oudekerk (Old Church) rests in a cobbled, shady, ancient one. When the May–Sept. 4 p.m. Sat. afternoon concerts commence on its recently restored Hemony-bell carillon, I like knowing that, on this occasion, culture has crossed the Atlantic, since the Oudekerk's carillonneur, **Todd Fair,** comes from the U.S. (Pennsylvania).

Sounds as much as sights impress memories on the mind. The joyful jangle of notes tumbling from a carillon tower could be among the most lasting of your recollections of travels in Holland and Belgium. As Aimé Lombaert notes about playing in the Belfort at Bruges: "Music makes people happy, and a carillon is the instrument which can give this feeling more than any other."

The Belfry at Bruges, with carillon bells. Carillon console is in lighted room behind the face of the clock. *(Photo courtesy of Belgian Tourist Office)*

Aimé Lombaert, stadbeiaardier (town carilloneur) of Bruges at console in the Belfry. *(Photo courtesy of Bruges Tourist Office)*

Pipes and organ case at Cathedral, Antwerp. *(Photo courtesy of Belgian Tourist Office)*

Artist hand painting a blue and white Delftware ginger jar in studio at *De Porceleyne Fles,* Delft. *(Photo courtesy of Netherlands Board of Tourism)*

The Art Room in the Rubens House, Antwerp. *(Photo courtesy of Antwerp Office of Tourism)*

Skylight over stairwell in art nouveau architect Victor Horta's house, Brussels. *(Photo courtesy of OPT, Office of Tourism for the French-speaking Community of Belgium)*

Watching Rembrandt's *Night Watch* at the Rijksmuseum, Amsterdam. *(Photo courtesy of Netherlands Board of Tourism)*

Folklore: the annual *Ommegang* on Brussels' Grand Place. *(Photo courtesy of Belgian Tourist Office)*

Fantasy: Amsterdam illuminated at night *(Photo courtesy of Netherland Board of Tourism)*

Flowers: Dutch bulb fields in bloom *(Photo courtesy of Netherlands Board of Tourism)*

Gravensteen (Castle of the Counts), Ghent. Finest extant example of a 12th century feudal fortress. *(Photo courtesy of Tourist Office for Flanders)*

Domestic architecture in Delft. *(Photo courtesy of Netherlands Board of Tou...*

15th-century Gothic stadhuis, Middelburg, Zeeland. *(Photo courtesy of Zeeland Provincial VVV)*

HOLLAND

INTRODUCTION

The Dutch Landscape

The word Holland comes from the Dutch *hol,* meaning "hollow," and the name Nederland means "low land or country." Thus, whether we call the country by the geographically correct *Netherlands,* or *Holland* (the name of the historically most populous and prosperous province, now used by many foreigners to mean the country as a whole), *by definition,* it's impossible to discuss the Dutch landscape without the subject of water coming to the surface.

Left on its own, the western half of Holland, an area where 60% of the Dutch population lives, would be below the level of the North Sea and the region's rivers. Much of that area is 15 or more feet below the **NAP** (*Normaal Amsterdams Peil*), the world's reference point for sea level, much as Greenwich Mean Time in London is the planet's time standard (see *Amsterdam, What To See and Do, Stadhuis*). No one, including Calvinists, considers the saying "God made the world, but the Dutch made Holland" a sacrilege. It's simply fact that if it weren't for Holland's state-of-the-art hydro-engineering, the Dutch goal, defined by one man as "to possess land where water wants to be," couldn't be realized.

The Netherlands occupies the delta formed over millennia at the mouths of major European rivers, the Maas (Meuse) and the Rhine. A line that runs roughly parallel to the North Sea coast of the continent divides the Dutch land mass into two more or less equal areas: the *low,* at or below sea level in the western, coastal part of the country, and the *high,* the eastern half of the country. The high, formed during the Pleistocene Ice Age, consists mostly of sand and gravel, while the low, clay on which peat has formed, is younger, deposited less than 10,000 years ago. Much of the land was brought downstream by the continental rivers, and some was pushed into ridges by glaciers. The ebb and flow of the marshes and coastal dunes, a more recent element of the formation of Holland, continue uninterrupted today.

A good percentage of Holland today is not natural landscape at all, but the result of shaping over centuries through human intervention. In this century alone, more than 550,000 acres of land were recovered from the bottom of the former Zuiderzee (South Sea). But not until the mid-20th century did the balance sheet in Holland's land-reclamation ledger break into the black. Watery as the land already was, by the 13th century the North Sea was breaching the coastal sand dunes. The job was finished in the great storm of 1287 (which killed 50,000 people in Friesland), when the North Sea reached and flooded a former inland lake, forming the Zuiderzee. That flood, combined with such self-induced inundations to rid the country of enemies as the 1944 Allied bombing of dikes in Zeeland to flush out the Nazis (who occupied the area in order to control the approach to Antwerp harbor) alone gave 40,000 acres back to the sea, and general coastal erosion, have cost the Dutch some 1.4 million acres of land in the last millenium. From the year 1000, by which Friesland was completely diked (barricaded from the sea by earthen embankments), until the Second World War, all the land gained by the Dutch with dams, dikes, windmills, and steam engines amounted to a little less than 1.3 million acres. These figures show that if the Dutch didn't challenge the sea so incessantly, their country wouldn't simply stand still in size: it would shrink—and sink.

The Dutch struggle to contain the sea had begun long before Roman historian **Pliny**, in A.D. 50, described Frisian tribes in the north of the Netherlands as living on ground that "makes one doubt whether the soil belongs to the land or to the sea." He continued: "A miserable people lives there on high hills which they have thrown up with their own hands to a height which they know from experience to be that of the highest tide, and on these spots they have built their huts. They are like seafarers when the water covers the surrounding land, like shipwrecked people when the waves have retreated."

The Frisian mounds *(terpen)* were followed in time by dikes, which eroded all too easily on the side facing the sea, especially in storms. Once the durability of dikes had been improved, builders learned to channel the flow of water by the use of dams. Hydro-control took a significant step with the discovery that surrounding a parcel of land with dikes and installing a system of sluices permitted the discharge of excess water. Gradually, a network of canals that would drain the land in the direction of the North Sea was created. In 1408, the first **windmill** for pumping water was built in Holland. Since the paddle wheel of a single windmill was only capable of raising water about five feet (1.5 meters), for more than that, it was necessary to use several mills in a series, a *molengang*.

Such developments marked the turning point at which the Dutch

HOLLAND
NORTH
SEA
N
Waddenzee
Texel
Afsluitdijk
Den Helder
NOORD
HOLLAND
IJsselmeer
(former Zuiderzee)
FRIESLAND
Franeker
Leeuwarden
Harlingen
Makkum
Sneek
Hindelopen
GRONINGEN
Groningen
DRENTHE
Giethoorn
Blokzijl
Staphorst
Urk
Enkhuizen
Hoorn
Alkmaar
Kampen
Zwolle
OVERIJSSEL
IJssel River
Lelystad
Elburg
FLEVOLAND
Edam
Marken
Zaans
Schans
Amsterdam
IJmuiden
Muiden
Haarlem
Schiphol
Naarden
Spakenburg
De Hoge
Veluwe
Deventer
Enschede
Apeldoorn

Lisse
Loenen
Breukelen
UTRECHT
Amersfoort
Otterlo
GELDERLAND
Leiden
Utrecht
Scheveningen
The Hague
Wijk bij Duurstede
Arnhem
Oudewater
Gouda
Delft
Rhine R.
Schoonhoven
Hoek van Holland
Lek River
Waal River
Rhine River
ferry to Harwich, Eng.
Kinderdijk
Gorinchem
Nijmegen
Rotterdam
Maas River
Dordrecht
ZUID HOLLAND
Goedereede
Maas River
Heusden
Den Bosch
NOORD BRABANT
Brouwershaven
Moerdijk
Breda
Tilburg
Zierikzee
Oirschot
Nuenen
Delta Works
Oosterschelde
Baarle-Nassau/ Baarle-Hertog
Eindhoven
Venlo
Bergen op Zoom
Veere
Middelburg
Vlissingen
ZEELAND
LIMBURG
Westerschelde
Thorn
Roermond
Antwerp
GERMANY
Maas River
Sittard
Valkenburg
BELGIUM
Maastricht
Vaals
miles
0
30
kilometers
0
50

could become offensive, rather than just defensive, in their efforts to control the relationship between the sea and their land. By about 1600, Jan Adriaanszoon had perfected the method of draining large lakes in order to create **polders** (drained land) of a size to support whole towns (in the process, he acquired the nickname *Leeghwater* "empty of water", which he liked so much that he legally adopted it). In a plan to drain the **Haarlemmermeer,** a huge inland lake southeast of Haarlem, Leeghwater, who had successfully drained smaller lakes, advocated the use of dikes and 160 windmills. Although the project caught the imagination of the Dutch public, it was deemed too ambitious by Dutch officials of the day.

In 1774, steam power was used for the first time for polder drainage. When the Haarlemmermeer eventually was drained in 1852, three steam pumping stations (one named for Leeghwater) were used. The three stations pumped nonstop for three years from 1849 to 1852, and pumped 800 million cubic meters of water. (See *Haarlem, In The Area;* **Cruquius,** one of the original steam pumping stations, is now a museum.) Today, Schiphol Airport is located on land (13 feet below sea level) that once was at the bottom of the Haarlemmermeer. Having come from the lake bottom, the soil at Schiphol is so rich that farmers cross its runways—with air traffic controllers' permission—to plant the fields between them.

Another milestone in hydrotechnology was marked in 1932, with the completion of the **Afsluitdijk** (enclosing dike), which sealed the Zuiderzee off from the salt water of the North Sea, and formed the freshwater IJsselmeer lake. The project was envisioned as early as 1667 by Hendrik Stevin, a mathematician, but was realized by **Cornelius Lely,** a single-minded engineer who essentially devoted his life to taming the Zuiderzee. (The capital city of the polder province of Flevoland, which was created from the sea floor, carries his name, Lelystad.) The unfolding of the Zuiderzee Reclamation Act of 1918, which created by stages three large polders, in 1942, 1957, and 1968, is recounted at the **Informatiecentrum Nieuw Land** (see *Lelystad, Flevoland* in chapter *Old Zuiderzee Villages and the New Polder Province*).

In Zeeland, the Dutch have pioneered ways of water control on a grand scale to protect existing land. The **Delta Project,** more than three decades in its realization, was born as a result of a 1953 storm and accompanying tidal surge in Zeeland in which more than 1800 people perished, most livestock vanished, and nearly 500,000 acres were submerged under salt water. The "give and take" with the sea ended in October 1986, when Queen Beatrix threw the switch on a massive storm control system that is a Dutch masterpiece of coastal hydro-engineering unmatched anywhere else in the world. In basic terms, the Project, through a series of giant fixed dams and sluices, reduced the Dutch coastline (and its need for smaller, more vulnerable dikes) by 435 miles, making it more defendable (see under *Zeeland, Delta Project*).

Such was the importance of water management in the region from the earliest days that responsibility for the dikes lay with the Counts of Holland. Later, when land was individually owned (before a central government took over), each man was required to maintain the dikes on his land; when he grew too old to do so, he was obliged to turn his holding over to a younger man who could. Today, Holland has a *Polder Authority,* a *Ministry of Waterworks,* and a *Water Control Board* (one of the country's oldest democratic institutions), all functioning full force. As Amsterdam historian Louis van Gasteren has said: "The sea can never be conquered; the Dutch (just) made a contract with it. We said 'We appreciate you, we respect you, just don't surprise us.' "

The Dutch People

Beyond doubt, the Dutch character has been shaped by Holland's association with the sea. The Dutch never have had the luxury of being spontaneous: it is their deliberateness that keeps claim on the land captured from the sea. The Dutch senses of responsibility and resourcefulness seem almost to have come in on the tide, and their respectability and religiosity (since one never knew when the next "killer" flood might surge across the low-lying land, spiritually, one needed always "to have one's house in order") blown in on a salty breeze.

The necessity of "constructing" the land by damming, diking, and draining the fields wrested from the sea, before building could even begin, and the efforts required to defend it once solid, dry ground was gained, dictated that individual living space be limited. Since land was so precious, qualities such as orderliness and organization, both for individuals and whole towns, were, and are, a virtue. After working so hard for the dry ground on which they rest, it's no wonder the Dutch are home lovers.

The relatively small space in which the Dutch must subsist (with a population of 14.9 million, Holland is one of the most densely-peopled places in the world) makes respect for personal privacy a must. However, the need to reassure the world (or at least the neighbors) of their respectability leads many Dutch to forgo privacy by leaving the curtains of front windows undrawn so all can see how proper (and, perhaps, prosperous) everything is inside.

In fact, the Dutch character is full of seeming contradictions. The people are both parsimonious and generous, tolerant and strict, cosmopolitan and parochial, pragmatic and sentimental. Though the Dutch, quite correctly, pride themselves on their individualism, the social climate of the country strongly supports a collective style of thinking and conformity to conventional behavior. Few Dutch can wholly avoid being concerned about what their neighbors think. Perhaps the essentially bourgeois approach to life in Holland is summed up in this translation of a Dutch saying: "Act normally, and you're conspicuous enough."

Holland's intimacy with the sea led to a Dutch predilection for shipping, which brought its sailors into contact with cultures around the world. Such exposure to many different ideas and attitudes contributed to making Holland a bastion of tolerance. In conjunction with the open-mindedness that they showed to the many displaced persons who found solace over the centuries in their society, the Dutch insisted on personal and commercial freedoms in order to be competitive on the seven seas.

Dutch friends have pointed out to me what they consider one of their national character flaws: always having an opinion on how *other* countries are conducting themselves. (In fact, the Dutch for centuries have exhibited a strong sense of mission; clerical missionary zeal was such that at one time one tenth of all the missionaries in the world came from Holland.) Frankly, I find it refreshing that the Dutch know and care about the rest of the world, and are committed to how well it works. The Dutch people and their government have shown themselves more than willing to put money where their mouths are, a significant stance for a Dutch person, who often is stereotyped as being closefisted to the point of still having the first *dubbeltje* (10-cent piece) he ever earned. In fact, the Dutch population regularly responds with millions of guilders to relief appeals for natural and man-made disasters. The Dutch government, too, is capable of financial commitment to issues: several years ago, it "fell" over a decision not as to *whether* Holland was going to foot a huge bill for environmental clean-up (largely caused upstream on the Rhine River by other countries' factories), but *how* it was going to finance the enormous project.

Water, which both unites and divides Holland, even delineates its religious lines (though the lines have blurred in the recent past). Although there has been a decline in membership in the Dutch Reformed Church (Calvinist) to less than half its former strength (about 28% of the population in 1989, it stood at 49% in 1900), a rise in the number of people who do not belong to any denomination (32%), and a stable percentage of Catholics (36%), the uniquely Dutch socio-political phenomenon of "compartmentalization" still exists. It is the co-existence of organizations (political parties, newspapers, schools, social and sports clubs, hospitals, TV stations, old-age homes) whose members have "similar or identical goals but a different ideological basis"—being either Protestant Calvinist or Roman Catholic.

Very roughly, Protestants in Holland are most numerous in the broad band running across the country from the southwest (Zeeland) to the northeast (Groningen). Most Catholics live *below the Moerdijk* (the region south of the great river estuaries near Rotterdam), in the provinces of North Brabant and Limburg, where the sterner aspects of the Protestant "work-ethic" are much less apparent. Although "compartmentalization" is ebbing somewhat in Holland, nowhere else in Europe—with the exception of Northern Ireland—is such a segmented societal infrastructure in place.

For all the stolid parts of the Dutch character, there's a decidedly sentimental side. The Dutch language is profuse in its use of the diminutive *"je"* (meaning little). It's added to everything from people's names to the most unlikely objects, and also conveys affection. Another characteristic Dutch concept is captured in the word *gezellig* (pronounced rather like *HEH' zelick*), which is literally untranslatable, though "cozy" and "congenial" come closest. *Gezellig* might be used to describe the atmosphere of an historic house, a restaurant made romantic by candlelight, or an appealing "brown" cafe.

The Dutch manage to mix an appreciation for the traditional with modern applications. As much as any traveler in Holland, I love the country's cliches: tulips, dikes, windmills, and wooden shoes. But I'm always intrigued at how the Dutch update ideas. Tulips, no less loved for their beauty, have become an enormously important export business; dikes have been developed by the Dutch into such state-of-the-art hydro-technology as the Delta Works; and today's sleek wind turbines, though mere shadows of the sturdy windmills from former centuries, capture, *and store,* the energy of the wind. And just see what the wooden shoe has evolved to: Still worn for their lightweight, water-resistant features in tulip fields and by farmers throughout Holland, Dutch *klompen*—which perfectly describes the sound one makes in them—were used as the model for astronauts' "moonshoes."

Holland: An Historical Perspective

During the Middle Ages, the area that today is the country called The Netherlands comprised a group of autonomous duchies *(Gelre* and *Brabant)* and counties *(Holland* and *Zeeland),* together with the bishopric of *Utrecht.* Under Emperor **Charles V** (1500–1558), those territories, together with present-day Belgium and Luxembourg (the entire region then being known as The Netherlands, or Low Countries) formed part of the great Burgundian-Hapsburg Empire. The people of the Low Countries had long been accustomed to outside rule, and had no quarrel with Charles, who had been born there (in Ghent) and generally allowed them a degree of autonomy. However, when Charles V abdicated in 1556 (amid the spreading **Reformation**), ceding the Low Countries to his son Spanish King **Philip II,** a dictatorial, fanatical Roman Catholic, the stage was being set for the **Eighty Years' War.**

The harsh policies imposed by Philip inflamed Protestants, who also received anti-Papist preaching from the Calvinists. A wave of religious rebellion swept the Netherlands. The Spanish response to the **Iconoclast** of 1566 (during which Protestant crowds attacked the contents of Catholic churches, slashed paintings, broke sculptures, and burned all objects connected with the hated priesthood, in the process destroying a treasure house of medieval art) was brutal. In 1567, Philip II sent the **Duke of Alva** and 10,000 troops to the Low Countries. Years of *"Spanish Fury"* followed, with town after town beseiged and citizens ravaged.

The first step toward establishing an independent Netherlands state was taken in 1568, when a number of provinces banded together and rebelled under the Dutch Prince **Willem (the Silent) of Orange** (1533–1584), marking the beginning of the Eighty Years' War. Having survived seiges and other attacks, the **Seven United Provinces of the Northern Netherlands** achieved a *de facto* independence from Spain in 1579, although the official *Peace of Munster* under the *Treaty of Westphalia* wasn't signed until 1648 (when the Southern Netherlands—today's Belgium—also became free of Spanish rule).

Following the Dutch republic's freedom from Spain, the 17th-century proved a period of unequaled growth and prosperity in the Northern Netherlands (today's Holland). The people of the Seven United Provinces set out to make the most of their considerable commercial skills, modest terrain, and chief natural resource, the sea. Herring provided both food and a major source of income from export, especially after the Dutch discovered the secret of preserving the fish with salt. Amsterdam became the hub of a far-flung trading and financial empire under the **Dutch East India Company,** which traded with the Far East, and the **Dutch West India Company,** which went to the New World. It was responsible for, among other colonies, the establishment of Nieuw Nederland colony in America in 1623; its settlement **Nieuw Amsterdam** the Dutch later gave to the British (who renamed it New York) in exchange for Suriname (on the northeast coast of South America). Dutch ships from the Seven Provinces sailed the seven seas, carrying spices, exotic goods, and, even more important, grain from eastern Europe.

Dutch farmers, thus freed from growing grain themselves, turned to more specialized and profitable pursuits, such as dairy farming, the cultivation of industrial crops such as hemp and tulip bulbs, employing massive drainage projects that increased the amount of land for the propagation of such products. An extensive system of canals brought city and country closer together, providing farmers with ready markets and city dwellers with abundant and affordable produce. Economic opportunity, and religious and political tolerance, drew immigrants, many of them skilled, from Flanders and elsewhere in Europe.

The mix of these ingredients and the energy of the era created a society in Holland that was unique within 17th-century Europe: urban, mercantile, and democratic in spirit, with a strong sense of pride and achievement. Political power lay less with the princes of the *House of Orange* than with the Protestant mercantile elite, who dominated city councils, provincial assemblies, and the national *States General* at The Hague. There was a great flourishing of culture, particularly painting, to celebrate the increased prosperity. It became known as the Golden Age. Eventually, there arose the need for wars—notably with England over sea-trade interests—to protect it.

The Netherlands remained independent (though the forces of French King Louis XIV invaded Holland in the 1670s) until 1795, when it became a vassal state of the French Empire. **Napoleon Bonaparte** put his brother Louis Napoleon in charge of the country in 1806, but Louis turned out to be too intent on being a decent ruler to the Dutch, and Bonaparte deposed him and annexed Holland to France. French occupation came to an end in 1813, and the 1815 *Treaty of Vienna* established the Kingdom of the Netherlands, comprising Holland, Belgium, and Luxembourg. The ruler of the new country was Dutch **King Willem I** (son of the last *Stadholder,* Willem V) of Orange, who also had the title Grand Duke of Luxembourg, in a union of hereditary roles that lasted until 1890. However, in the more than 300 years that by then had passed since the Southern and Northern Netherlands had been one, Holland and Belgium had grown too far apart in outlook to be able to exist as a single country. Following an uprising by its people in 1830, Belgium was awarded its independence from Holland in 1839.

The Netherlands Constitution of 1814, which had decreed that the king governed and the ministers reported to him, was revised in 1848, and the updated Dutch Constitution created a constitutional monarchy with a parliamentary system, wherein ministers are accountable to an elected parliament rather than the monarch. With the death of King Willem III in 1890, Holland's male succession ended, and Willem's daughter **Wilhelmina** (1880–1962), whose mother Queen Emma acted as regent until she reached 18, became the first of what would be three successive Dutch queens. Queen Wilhelmina served Holland from 1898–1948, seeing her country through two world wars.

During the **First World War,** the Netherlands remained neutral, though not without difficulty, since the Allies maintained the neutrality strictly, not wanting any supplies to fall into the hands of Germans by way of Holland. Holland continued to pursue a policy of strict neutrality right up until the outbreak of the **Second World War,** when, without warning, it was ruthlessly invaded by the Nazis on May 10, 1940, and occupied—for what would be a period just five days short of five years. After the Nazis leveled Rotterdam with a bombing blitzkrieg on May 14, Queen Wilhelmina and her ministers, believing that they could better serve the Dutch people from an unoccupied country, fled Holland across the North Sea to England. Crown Princess **Juliana,** whose husband Prince Bernhard, though a German, served as a member of the

Dutch forces and aide to his mother-in-law Wilhelmina in England, took up residence with her children in Canada for much of the war. When her third daughter, Margriet, was born there in 1943, the Canadians declared the location Dutch soil for the purpose of preserving the baby's royal succession rights.

The southern part of Holland, near Maastricht, was the first region in the country to be freed by the Allies in the fall of 1944. But, due to the disastrous results of the *Market Garden operation* around Arnhem, the northern part of the country remained under Nazi occupation during Holland's long, cold *Hunger Winter* of 1944–45. To the present, *Liberation Day,* May 5, though not a legal holiday, is observed by the Dutch.

The Netherlands was a major colonial power until the Second World War, but after 1945 her colonies began seeking independence. **Indonesia** severed all its constitutional links with the Netherlands in 1949, while **Suriname,** after taking over its domestic affairs in 1954, became a fully independent republic in 1975. The **Netherlands Antilles** (Aruba, Curaçao, Bonaire, St. Eustatius, Saba, and St. Maarten) in the Caribbean are equal partners with the Netherlands under a special charter.

On April 30, 1980, Queen Juliana (who had been queen since her mother Wilhelmina had abdicated in 1948), with a stroke of a pen in the Palace on Dam Square, became Princess Juliana, abdicating in favor of her eldest daughter **Beatrix,** who was installed as Queen in a ceremony in Amsterdam's Nieuwe Kerk.

Keys to the Kingdom

VVVs (TOURIST INFORMATION OFFICES) There are over 400 local VVV offices in Holland, recognized by a triangular VVV emblem; at offices in larger towns, with an additional sign showing an ''i'' and Nederland, all staff members speak English and you can get information on the whole country, and make reservations for lodging and major entertainment events countrywide. The VVV is the source for local maps, public transportation information, bicycle routes, and tourism literature in English. In general, VVVs are open Mon.–Fri. 9 A.M.–5 P.M. at a minimum, and in the spring (in the bulb district) and in summer, hours are longer, and include weekends.

NATIONAL HOLIDAYS New Year's Day; Good Friday; Easter Sunday and Monday; Queen's Birthday (April 30); Ascension Day; Whit Sunday and Monday; Christmas; Boxing Day (Dec. 26). In addition to closings on public holidays, it is well to remember that throughout Holland, the Sabbath (Sundays) is observed quite strictly with store closures (except in resort areas, such as Scheveningen). Many Dutch who live near the border slip over into Belgium, where Sunday shopping isn't impaired by such "blue laws."

WEATHER Average High and Low Temperatures by month in Amsterdam (in Fahrenheit)

WEATHER IN AMSTERDAM—Lat. N52°20′—Alt. 16′

	JAN.	FEB.	MAR.	APR.	MAY	JUNE	JULY	AUG.	SEPT.	OCT.	NOV.	DEC.
Low	31°	31°	35°	39°	45°	51°	54°	54°	49°	43°	37°	33°
High	41°	42°	47°	54°	62°	68°	70°	70°	65°	57°	47°	42°

Days with No Rain	21	20	20	22	22	21	20	20	20	18	19	18

HOLLAND LEISURE CARD/MUSEUMKAART The *Holland Leisure Card* provides independent travelers with discounts of 10%–40% on select transportation, hotel accommodations, admissions to tourist attractions, sightseeing tours, and shopping in Holland. The Holland Leisure Card is valid for one year from its validation, at a cost of US $15, Can. $18 (1992 prices). Sample discounts include 40% off on a one-way or unlimited Day Pass train ticket in First or Second Class, 25% on certain car rentals or sightseeing tours. The Holland Leisure Card-Plus (US $39, Can. $47) includes the *MuseumCard,* which gives free access to 350 of Holland's fine museums. Ordering is through the Netherlands Board of Tourism offices in Chicago (in US) and Toronto (in Canada). The MuseumCard (only) is sold in Holland (Dfl. 45) at the Amsterdam VVV (photo required, can be taken easily and inexpensively at machines at Centraal Station).

HOLLAND WELCOME VOUCHER This program involves 124 hotels (properties with two to five stars) countrywide that have agreed to offer travelers special, pre-paid rates by means of an innovative voucher system. Vouchers sell for US $20, Can. $23 apiece; rooms at participating hotels charge either four, six, or eight vouchers for a standard double room per night, including breakfast (single rooms get a reduction in number of vouchers). Those who order vouchers also receive a 64-page book, which has a picture of each hotel, a description, its location on a map, and general travel information. Unused vouchers are refundable. Contact the Netherlands Board of Tourism for further information.

NETHERLANDS RESERVATION CENTER (NRC) Established by the Netherlands Board of Tourism and the Dutch hotel industry, this no-fee service enables individuals (and travel agents) to get quick, reliable confirmations at some 1700 member hotels in Holland. Concertgebouw and Muziektheater events in Amsterdam can also be booked. Contact

NRC by telephone, fax, or mail (Netherlands Reservation Center; P.O. Box 404; 2260 AK Leidschendam; Holland; Tel: 070–3202500; fax: 070–3202611). Private inquires will be answered by mail.

DUTCH LANGUAGE AND USEFUL VOCABULARY See *Benelux Lexicon* at back of book.

NATIONAL STRIP CARD The key to Holland's public transportation is the National Strip Card *(Nationale Strippenkaart)*, which is valid on all city buses and trams throughout the country. Each city is divided into transport zones, with standard fares payable according to the number of zones traveled through. Each zone costs one strip, plus a basic charge of one strip. So traveling within one zone (within the Centrum in Amsterdam, for example) would cost two strips. Unlimited travel and changes are allowed within each zone until the time stamped on the strip—when you insert it, folded to the proper number for your journey, in the machine at the rear of tram cars, or by the driver at the front of buses (usually an hour from the time you board). The National Strip Card is available at railway stations, post offices, and the GVB (Amsterdam Municipal Transport) information and ticket office opposite Amsterdam's Centraal Station for Dfl. 10.25 for 15 strips, and Dfl. 29 for 45 strips (1992 prices). You can also buy two, three, and ten-strip cards at a slightly higher charge from tram or bus drivers. *Day Tickets* also are available from tram and bus drivers, and in Metro stations in Amsterdam and Rotterdam.

RAIL TRAVEL The modern all-electric Dutch rail network (**Nederlandse Spoorwegen** or **NS**), with its bright yellow carriages, is one of the fastest, most efficient, and easy-to-use systems in the world. Except if you are traveling during business rush hours and want to avoid the crowds, it's hardly necessary to travel First Class (about a 50% surcharge), since Second Class is comfortable and clean. There are no ticket barriers on the platforms; tickets are checked by on-board conductors. At every station, large schedule boards are located in the main hall, and also at most platforms; find the board with the name of the place you wish to travel to at the top, check the current time, and see when the next train goes (schedules use the 24-hour clock). The schedule will indicate whether the train is **Inter-City** (stopping only at major towns) or a **Stoptrein** (which makes all the local stops listed). The **spoor** column shows the track from which the train departs. Trains invariably leave, and arrive, on time. The Netherlands Railways operates more than 75 inclusive day trips by train to major attractions throughout the country, mostly between May and Sept. (information at main rail stations). See *Rail* under *Transportation* in *Practical Travel Information* at front of book for rail pass details.

BICYCLES Everyone—farmers in *klompen* (wooden shoes), well-suited businessmen and women, and the Queen—rides bicycles in Holland: mothers may have child seats fore and aft; people "walk" their dogs by bike; and shoppers manage a week's worth of groceries on two-wheelers. While riders are well taken care of—Holland has over 6000 miles of clearly marked city and countryside paved bicycle paths—pedestrians and drivers need to take heed of them, especially at intersections. Bikes can be rented in practically every city and town across this bike-friendly flat land, and at some 80 railway stations nationally (reservations a day in advance suggested in summer). The going price is about Dfl. 8 per day (less for weekly rental) for the standard, no-gear equipment with back rack for *your* gear. Deposits of from Dfl. 50 to Dfl. 200 usually are required, and one should be prepared to show a passport as identification.

DRIVING Maps are essential companions for independent travelers, and at no time more so than when one is behind the wheel on unfamiliar roads. As a basic, adequately detailed map for countrywide driving, I recommend the *Shell Grote Autokaart Nederland* (approx. Dfl. 2.95, available from the VVV and bookshops). On the reverse side of the large-scale national map are smaller ones for the four largest cities (Amsterdam, The Hague, Rotterdam, and Utrecht), in sufficient detail to get you in, around, and out of town. Signposting on Dutch roads is excellent, usually by town name (rather than route number) in rural areas.

CASSETTE TAPE WALKING TOURS If you've come to appreciate the idea of taped tours, you should know that in Amsterdam, Rotterdam, and Utrecht, self-guided city walking tours on cassette tapes are available at the VVV. In some cases, these can be rented complete with portable cassette player, but in others you need to buy the tapes and supply your own "walkman."

THE ROYAL FAMILY Holland is a constitutional monarchy, with succession to the throne hereditary in both the female and male lines. The Royal House is *Orange-Nassau,* which has historic links with the Netherlands dating back to the 16th century, and its founder, Willem I, Prince of Orange (1533–84), also known as *Father of the Fatherland.* The present head of state is **H. M. Queen Beatrix,** who was installed on April 30, 1980, after the abdication of her mother, now Princess Juliana, who had succeeded to the throne in 1948 when her mother, Wilhelmina, abdicated after 50 years on the throne. Beatrix, born in 1938, is married to Prince Claus, a German, like her father Prince Bernhard. Beatrix and Claus have three sons: Crown Prince Willem-Alexandre (b. 1967), Johan Frisco (b. 1968), and Constantijn (b. 1969), ensuring that Holland eventually will have its first king in four generations. The monarchy is a solidly supported, well-loved institution in Holland. Its informality (somewhat less under Queen Beatrix than when her mother was monarch) amazes the British (whose equally popular monarchy keeps its cachet by keeping at a distance). Beatrix studied at Leiden University (as did her mother) and keeps in touch with her "commoner" roommates from those days. Of the Queen's three younger sisters, Princess Margriet and her businessman husband Peter van Vollenhoven are most involved in sharing with Queen Beatrix and Prince Claus the multitude of openings, dedications, and other engagements that make up the royal calendar.

RANDSTAD HOLLAND: AN INTRODUCTION

Whatever image you have of Holland, its realization is likely to be located in the Randstad. This relatively recently named geo-political entity includes both the oldest and newest in Dutch urban planning, and encompasses Holland's two most distinctive features: **historic towns,** with their tall, narrow, gabled houses, great churches, quaint canals, and museums laden with treasures from the 17th-century Golden Age, and classic **Dutch countryside** of cows, canals, windmills, tulip fields, and, above the far, low horizon, uninterrupted expanses of sky in which clouds create the mountains missing from the water-logged, not-so *terra firma*.

The **Randstad,** best translated as "city along the rim," is the urbanized region of low-lying western Holland. If you imagine **Amsterdam** at the left tip of the open end of a horseshoe, the rest of the Randstad cities fall roughly around its shape counterclockwise: **Haarlem, Leiden, The Hague, Delft, Rotterdam** (including Dordrecht), and **Gouda,** to **Utrecht** at the right tip. The Randstad is 45 miles north to south, and 40 miles across at its widest point, covering an area roughly the size of Greater London. As urbanized as it is, the Randstad is not a megalopolis or continual conurbation. What it is is a chain of highly individual urban entities separated by green spaces. The green fingers of the Randstad (and the many "green thumbs" who live there) provide plenty of photogenic Dutch landscape within it.

Though the relative importance of Randstad cities has changed since the 17th century, all retain their historical significance and serve as major centers today. The term Randstad is an informal one, with no official status or administrative authority. Within the Netherlands, the term is used only to refer to the geographic region in general, and is never meant to minimize the historical, functional, and spatial distinctiveness of each of the component cities.

As early as the 16th century, Holland developed an urban consciousness that has marked Dutch culture ever since. In 1514, some 46% of the people in the province of Holland (the combined area of today's separate provinces of North and South Holland) lived in towns. By the 17th century, an estimated 50% of the Dutch population lived in towns (a statistic not reached in England until that country's 19th-century industrial revolution). Holland's physical environment—the Randstad, with the exception of sand dunes wedged between Haarlem, Leiden, and The Hague and the coast, lies entirely below sea level—which necessited land reclamation to create permanent settlements, doubtless contributed to the development of dense Dutch towns from early on.

Close living conditions, forced upon the Dutch by their water-bound landscape, and the need to congregate in cities in order to be able to defend themselves against invaders of their flat, boggy, and barrier-less countryside, made early town planning a necessity in Holland. That the Dutch today prefer things well-ordered in all aspects of life including their physical environment, is a natural result of their communal history.

In the 16th century, the towns of Leiden and Haarlem were larger than Amsterdam. A 1514 *Enqueste* (census), showed that Amsterdam had 2532 dwellings, while Haarlem had 2741 houses, Delft 2943, and Leiden 3017. Even at their 16th-century size, Holland's towns were not isolated entities, but a network of larger and smaller urban communities, and by 1514, the first form of the Randstad had already emerged. Approximately half of the country's then nearly 300,000 inhabitants lived in towns, while the other half lived close to one. The same situation holds true today, with 90% of the Dutch population considered urban.

Amsterdam became—and remains so, with a population about 750,000 for the city proper, a million in the greater area—Holland's largest city in the 17th century. The inland towns of Haarlem and Leiden, and eventually even Delft, which had harbor rights on the river Schie at Delfshaven (today one of the few remaining historic parts of Rotterdam), lost ground to Amsterdam in the shipping arena. Once "commerce became king" in Holland, Amsterdam, with its connection to the North Sea through the Zuiderzee, and Rotterdam, located near the mouths at the North Sea of major rivers from the interior of continental Europe, became the more prominent cities due to their preeminent shipping lanes.

From a frame of reference *within* the Randstad, the rest of Holland is apt to be thought of as "the provinces." Nevertheless, while residents of the Randstad have an essentially metropolitan mentality, each thinks of him or herself as being from Leiden, or Delft, or Rotterdam, and identifies with his own town's distinct character. (The differences in character for certain Randstad cities has been described this way: One makes one's money in Rotterdam, spends it in Amsterdam, and talks about it in The Hague.) For all new development, the all-important part of the Randstad concept is keeping each major urban center separate from the others by "green" functions, such as agriculture and horticulture (businesses, true, but ones that provide a "green" look), plus natural preserves, and recreational areas.

Within the Randstad is a high percentage of the whole country's infrastructure: significant social-cultural institutions; national government; commercial centers; six universities; and headquarters for the mass media and railroads. The density of population, economic wealth and attractions of all kinds, including tourism, is remarkably different in the Randstad than it is in the rest of the country. Thus, the Randstad is likely to claim much of your Dutch travel time.

AMSTERDAM

Guidelines for Amsterdam

SIGHTS Amsterdam embodies Holland's **17th-century Golden Age,** when it was the richest, most cosmopolitan city in the world (it still can compete for most cosmopolitan). Many of its protected monument buildings (some 7000) date from this period, as does the distinct fan-shaped pattern of **concentric canals** that provide such a visual sense of place and pleasure. Amsterdam art museums hold numerous masterpieces, many by Dutch artists considered among the world's most revered painters (**Rembrandt** and **Van Gogh,** to mention the best known). The broad appeal of this fascinating city comes from clandestine 16th-century Catholic churches to live sex shows, diamond cutters to flower markets, canalside mansion museums to cozy "brown" pub/cafes, and world-renowned performing arts companies to carillon concerts. Amsterdam turns into a veritable fantasyland at night with the tasteful, romantic illumination of canal bridges, gables, and many landmarks.

GETTING AROUND Amsterdam is a walking city (bring comfortable shoes), not only because of its many inviting quiet corners, but because the *Centrum* (center) is compact. A walk from Centraal Station to the Rijksmuseum (which about covers the tourist terrain) would take a strong walker ½ hour (though it's better to allow time for distractions along the way). The VVV (tourist information) sells a two-cassette-tapes package with map for four **self-guided walks** (including *canal houses,* the *Jordaan* district, *old Amsterdam* and the *Jewish quarter*) with background information (you need your own player). Amsterdam has a dense city and regional network of **trams, buses,** and **Metro;** system maps and information are available from the VVV or the GVB (Amsterdam Municipal Transport), both located opposite Centraal Station. A cruise in one of the ubiquitous glass-enclosed boats along its canals remains one of the best introductions to the city. j**Canal Bikes,** with landing stages at several central city locations, provide a pedaling experience on water for up to four. **Water Taxis** are expensive, but **Water Buses** and the **Museum Boat** are more reasonable and provide the same picturesque mode of transportation.

SHOPPING Since the 17th century, when the sailing ships of the *Dutch East India Company* returned laden with exotic items for sale from the Far East, Amsterdam has been an international marketplace. Amsterdam's diamonds, Delftware, and antiques all attract attention from shoppers, as does its full complement of department stores and fashionable boutiques.

ACCOMMODATIONS Accommodations come in a wide range of standards and prices, from luxurious and very expensive down to youth hostels. There's good choice in the "almost" inexpensive and moderate categories, which include a satisfying Dutch breakfast.

RESTAURANTS The linguistically adept Dutch claim you "can dine out in any language" in Amsterdam, and you're unlikely to come across a city where the choices of cuisine are more cosmopolitan in character. While the Dutch "kitchen" isn't overly emphasized, its traditional, fresh, well-prepared, and often hearty fare can be sampled in a number of atmospheric settings in the city. Except for the most casual eateries, a call ahead to book is a good bet, and is essential for the finest restaurants.

ENTERTAINMENT AND EVENTS Amsterdam has a number of prestigious residential performing arts companies, which present full schedules from fall through spring. June's month-long multi-faceted **Holland Festival** is an annual cultural highlight. The **Queen's Birth-**

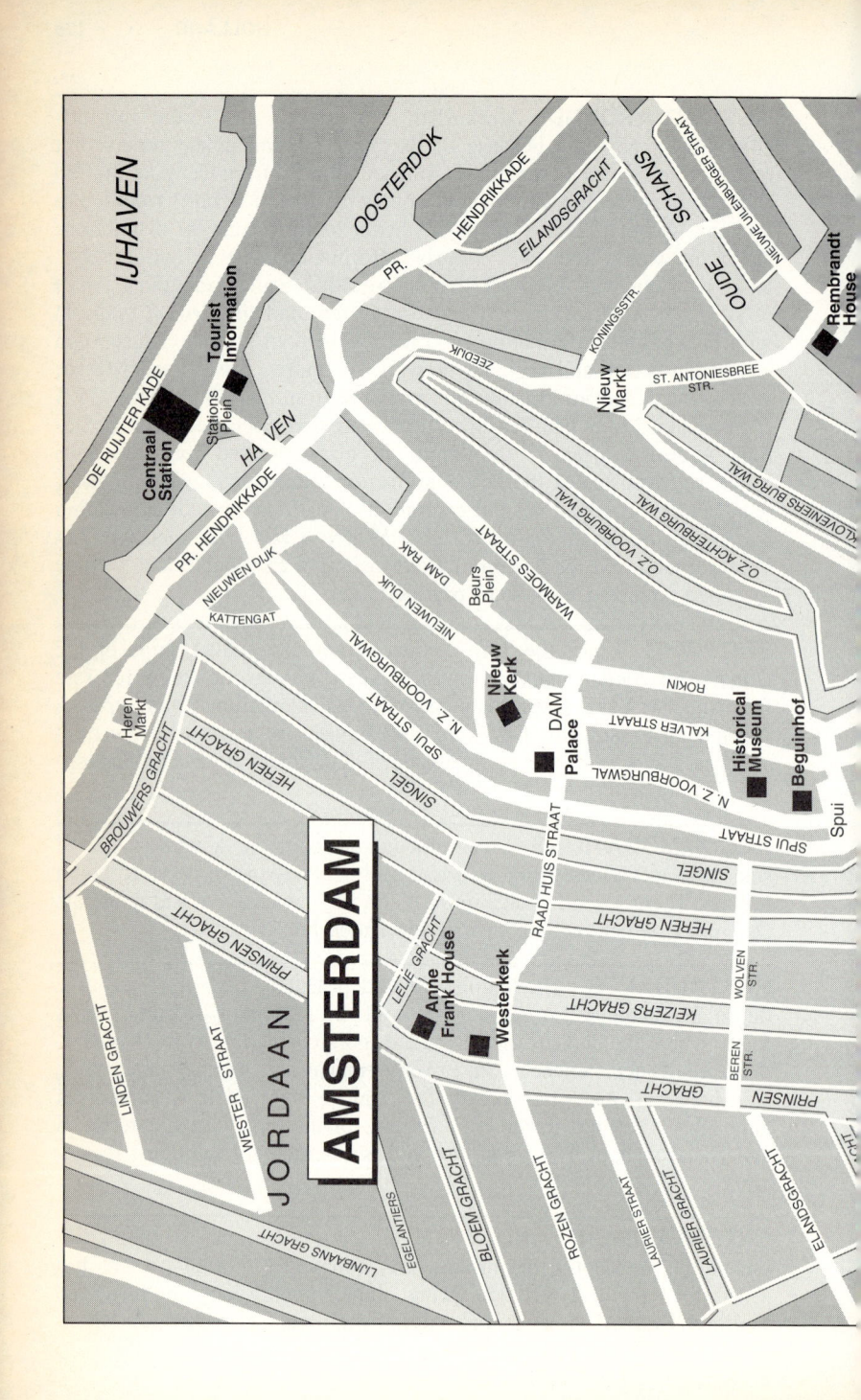

AMSTERDAM

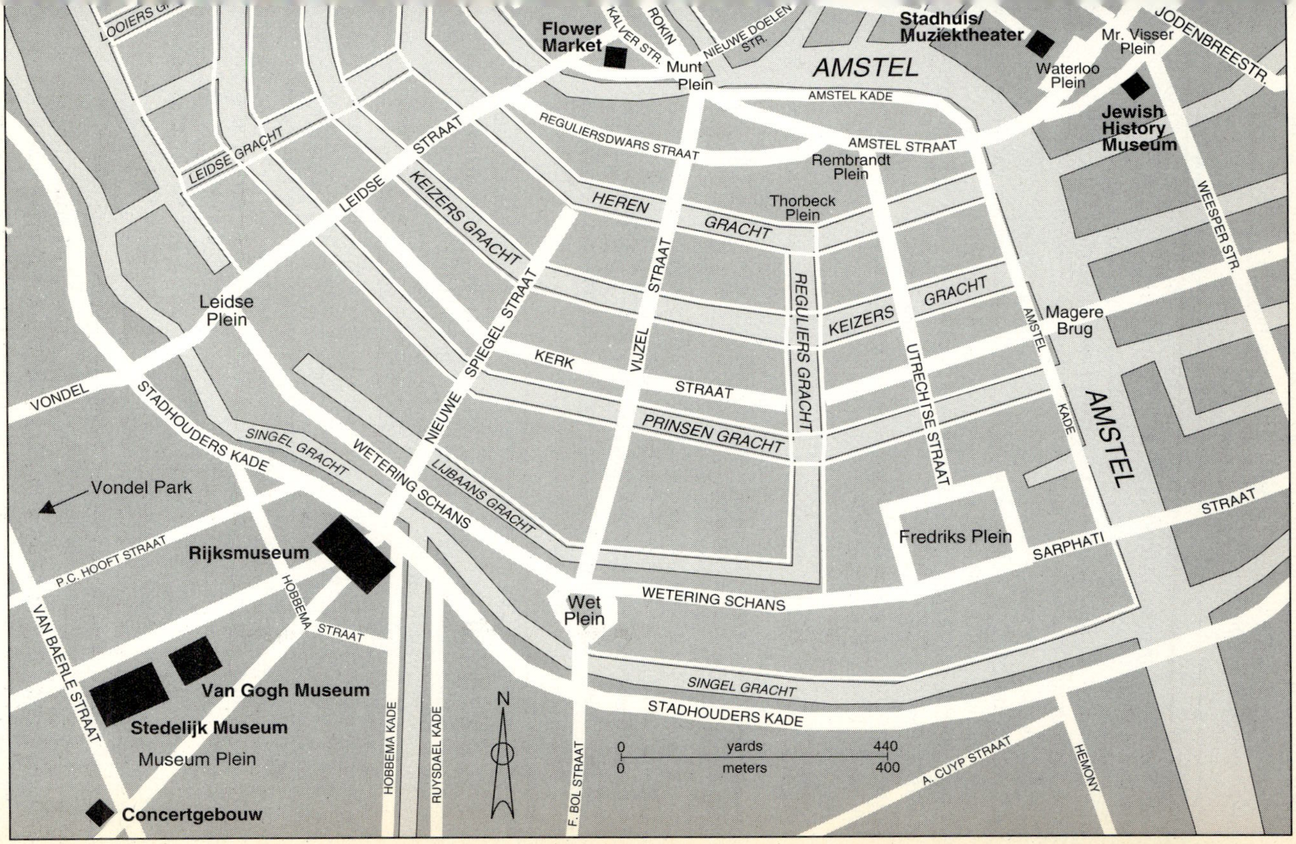
Flower Market
Stadhuis/ Muziektheater
Mr. Visser Plein
JODENBREESTR.
KALVER STR.
ROKIN
NIEUWE DOELEN STR.
Munt Plein
AMSTEL
Waterloo Plein
Jewish History Museum
AMSTEL KADE
REGULIERSDWARS STRAAT
AMSTEL STRAAT
Rembrandt Plein
Thorbeck Plein
LOOIERS GR.
LEIDSE GRACHT
LEIDSE STRAAT
KEIZERS GRACHT
HEREN GRACHT
WEESPER STR.
Leidse Plein
SPIEGEL STRAAT
NIEUWE
VIJZEL STRAAT
REGULIERS GRACHT
KEIZERS GRACHT
UTRECHTSE STRAAT
AMSTEL KADE
Magere Brug
KERK STRAAT
PRINSEN GRACHT
VONDEL
STADHOUDERS KADE
SINGEL GRACHT
WETERING SCHANS
LIJBAANS GRACHT
Vondel Park
Fredriks Plein
SARPHATI STRAAT
P.C. HOOFT STRAAT
Rijksmuseum
HOBBEMA STRAAT
Wet Plein
WETERING SCHANS
VAN BAERLE STRAAT
Van Gogh Museum
Stedelijk Museum
Museum Plein
Concertgebouw
HOBBEMA KADE
RUYSDAEL KADE
F. BOL STRAAT
N
SINGEL GRACHT
STADHOUDERS KADE
0 yards 440
0 meters 400
A. CUYP STRAAT
HEMONY

day (Apr. 30) national holiday has become a crowded city-wide street flea market, and the arrival of **Sinterklaas** by boat in mid-Nov. is enjoyed not just by Dutch children.

ARRIVING Those arriving in Holland by air are likely to do so at Amsterdam's **Schiphol Airport,** which is always rated near the top of frequent international travelers' choices of best organized and operated airports in the world. Through **KLM Royal Dutch Airlines,** Holland's national carrier, and other airlines, Schiphol offers flight connections to points around the globe. A full schedule of intra-European flights operates from Amsterdam's Schiphol on KLM, NLM City Hopper, and other major international carriers. Express trains leave Schiphol for central railway stations in Amsterdam, The Hague, Rotterdam, and Utrecht 24 hours a day. KLM Road Transport operates two shuttle bus services between Schiphol's departure hall and major Amsterdam hotels (approx. Dfl. 15). The half-hourly service is available between 6:30 a.m.–5:15 p.m.

Most **international intra-city trains** from across the European continent (and Great Britain, once the Channel Tunnel is operative) serve Amsterdam, and Holland is a member of the Eurail Pass and Benelux Tourrail Pass networks. Within Holland, Amsterdam is a major link on rail lines throughout the country. Various **ferry services** from English ports in the English Channel and on the North Sea arrive at Hoek van Holland, from which boat trains provide direct service to Amsterdam, via Rotterdam. Amsterdam is reached by Europe's principal motorways from Germany and from France through Belgium.

IN THE AREA With its excellent rail and bus connections, almost anyplace in Holland can be "in the area" for the independent traveler based in Amsterdam. A range of half- and whole-day excursions within Holland are bookable at the VVV or through individual local motorcoach tour companies. Many places located near to Amsterdam have been described in detail in other sections of this book, but **Aalsmeer, Alkmaar,** and **Zaanse Schans** are covered at the end of this section.

TRAVEL TIPS Amsterdam's hippie scenes of the 60s and 70s at the Dam Monument are no longer, though "punks" make an appearance. As in any large city, there are street people (though far fewer than in the U.S., thanks to the Dutch social welfare system). Some are homeless, some are on drugs (hard drug use in Holland has dropped), and since these people are inclined to congregate in front of Amsterdam's Centraal Station, where they are particularly visible to tourists, one could get a distorted impression of the city as a whole. Violent crime in Amsterdam is rare; once you take precautions against pickpockets (see *Personal Security* under *Practical Travel Information* at front of book), which is an intelligent approach anywhere, including one's home town, you'll find Amsterdam refreshingly easy to enjoy. It's safe to stroll at night and to take public transportation anywhere.

NOTE · · · As of spring 1991, Amsterdam converted to seven-digit telephone numbers. Those that did not already have seven digits added a "6" at the beginning, which is what you should do if you come across an outdated six-digit number.

Amsterdam in Context

While being neither the seat of government nor the residence of the Queen, Amsterdam is, nevertheless, the capital and cultural center of the Netherlands. Amsterdam had its beginning when the few inhabitants along the river Amstel built a dam on it in about the year 1270, and gave the town its name. Reclamation of the many lakes around Amsterdam made the thick, marshy layer of peat available for building. A harbor, the Damrak, was built, and an inner harbor, the Rokin, was formed, around which the first trade activities developed. Not many years later (1287), a storm breached the sand dunes to the northwest creating the Zuiderzee (South Sea), giving Amsterdam easy access to the open sea. A finger of land opposite the mouth of the Amstel protected the port against the westerly winds from the North Sea, and the tidal flow of the Zuiderzee prevented the port from silting up.

As early as 1275, Amsterdam was granted exemption from paying tolls on Dutch waterways, and was thus able to focus on trade as well as fishing. In the 14th and 15th centuries, Amsterdam was the most important port between the German Hanseatic League towns (of which it was made a member in 1368) and Bruges, the most important trading town of the time. The favorable situation of Amsterdam led to an increase in trade with the Baltic, and the town became an important stockpiler of grain and other commodities in its many warehouses.

The cargo trade and fishing stimulated industry and attracted many unemployed laborers from the countryside. The original town along the banks of the Amstel (today that stretch of the river is the filled-in **Damrak**) expanded on each side, with the **Nieuwendijk** and **Warmoesstraat,** and then the **Oudezijds Voorburgwal** and the **Nieuwezijds Voorburgwal**. In the 15th century, the town had to be twice enlarged with new moats; the 1425 expansion added the **Singel** and the **Kloveniersburgwal,** and the town was given its first gateways, bastions, and brick fortress.

Amsterdam's buildings, built on soggy soil, at first had foundations of light timber rafts that supported a single-story wooden frame dwelling. Because of its water-confined conditions, land near the center of Amsterdam was, as it remains today, at a premium, with the resulting architectural development of narrow, deep, and increasingly tall houses.

In the 15th century, bricks increasingly replaced timber as building materials due to the risk of fire (and in the early 16th century, thatched roofs were replaced with tiles). The resulting increase in the weight and height of homes required better foundations, and a system was developed in which clusters of wooden piles were driven into the ground through an upper layer of mud and peat until they rested on one of the harder layers of sand below the surface. Foundation piles could go as deep as 60 feet, a fact that elicited a riddle from Rotterdam's Erasmus about "a city whose inhabitants live on the tops of trees like birds."

Because taller, thinner houses meant a more intensive use of land, Amsterdam remained the same size physically from 1425 until 1580. Nevertheless, despite the fact that the 16th century was one of the most turbulent in the entire history of the Low Countries, due to the Reformation and resulting religious and political struggles that resulted in the outbreak of the 80 Year's War with Catholic Spain in 1568, commerce in the Northern Netherlands continued to expand, and Amsterdam saw a steady stream of immigrants coming for work.

However, it was with the fall of Antwerp to the Spanish in 1585 that prosperity positively exploded in Amsterdam. Within a short period, Amsterdam took over the position of this South Netherlands major trading city (Antwerp had taken over from Bruges, when that city's river Zwin silted up). Experienced Antwerp merchants and craftspeople, as well as poor Protestants and rich Portuguese Jews, sought refuge and work in Amsterdam, which gave impetus to trade. Amsterdam had acquired a large merchant fleet, and expanded its cargo-carrying trade commissioned by merchants abroad, especially in the Baltic, with grain from Poland and Prussia. The Dutch, through their Amsterdam port, became the carriers of Europe, and their fleet was larger than those of England, Scotland, and France combined.

From 1595 onward, Amsterdam regularly sent explorers to find new sea routes, particularly to the East Indies, where precious spices and other exotic goods could be obtained. This led, in 1602, to the establishment of the United East India Company, a limited liability company that obtained a monopoly for the trade in territories east of the Cape of Good Hope in south Africa. Soon, its Dutch ships swarmed over the seven seas, and the company became the most commercially successful organization in the world, with trading posts all over the globe.

As a result of these activities, Amsterdam, in the early 17th century, developed into the main staple market in the world, with buffer stocks of a wide range of commodities kept in long rows of tall, handsome warehouses, sometimes tilting slightly forward, so that bales of goods being raised on the hoisting beams wouldn't brush the building. Goods from weapons to corn and spices to art treasures could be acquired in Amsterdam. As early as 1578, Prince Willem of Orange foresaw the city's success, predicting: "Amsterdam shall prosper, and shall rise above all other cities."

With Amsterdam the biggest trading town and depot of the 17th century, the recruiting of inexpensive labor became ever more important to merchants. Between 1570 and 1640, Amsterdam's population increased from 30,000 to 139,000. In 1609, a decision was reached to undertake a considerable expansion of the city, which included the construction of the concentric pattern of canals (Herengracht, Keisersgracht, and Prinsengracht) that continues to give the city such a distinctive shape. Also in 1609, the Amsterdam Discount Bank was established, where not only merchants, but princes, towns, and foreign governments opened accounts. Especially after the end of the 80 Years' War (with the Peace of Munster, 1648), Amsterdam became *the* international center for finance, a position it maintained well into the 18th century.

With all this wealth, art, especially painting, became an accepted, expected form of acquisition. With an active artistic environment free from the restriction of guilds, Amsterdam was a wide-open market for painters. Among the masters most closely associated with the city were Ferdinand Bol, Govert Flinck, and Jacob van Ruisdael. But the grand master painter in Amsterdam, and widely acknowledged as such in his lifetime, was Rembrandt. One of Rembrandt's first major commissions came from an Amsterdam merchant family—in 1631, the portrait of Nicholas Ruts (now in the Frick Collection, NY). By 1632, Rembrandt had moved permanently from Leiden to Amsterdam, which offered not only a wider artistic scope, but also the probability of more profitable portrait commissions. His first commission after the move was a group portrait (*The Anatomy Lesson of Professor Tulp*) for the surgeons' guild that avoided the problem of just a series of posed portraits by including the dramatic event of a dissection in progress. Rembrandt's own Amsterdam house (see *What To See and Do*) was an easy walk from the new Guildhall of the militia companies' building, the Kloveniersdoelen (the site of the present Doelen Karena Hotel on Nieuw Doelenstraat) for which he was commissioned to paint the company of Captain Frans Banning Cocq at the precise moment that he is giving his lieutenant the command for the company to march. The work, Rembrandt's most famous and today the centerpiece of Amsterdam's Rijksmuseum, came to be called *The Night Watch,* although a major restoration in 1975 revealed the scene to be daytime one. Rembrandt never left Holland, claiming there was enough inspiration in his native land. From Amsterdam, he took long walks across the city and out along the river Amstel finding scenery that suggested paintings and, especially, landscape drawings (he made about 250 landscape drawings and etchings in his lifetime, nearly all of them of Amsterdam and its surroundings). When

Rembrandt died in Amsterdam in 1669, not much attention was paid. He is buried in the Westerkerk (as is his son Titus), though the specific site is unknown.

Amsterdam's prosperity lasted through the 18th century, even though its port was surpassed in importance during that period by London, Hamburg, and Bremen. Napoleon Bonaparte's army occupied Holland from 1795 through 1813. In 1806, he sent his brother Louis Napoleon, despite his disinclination—he even pleaded that the Dutch climate would be hazardous to his health—to rule the conquered country. Living first in The Hague, then Utrecht, Louis Napoleon finally settled most happily in Amsterdam in 1806, and turned what had been the Stadhuis (town hall) on the Dam since it opened with great pomp and pageantry in 1655) into the Royal Palace it remains today. He filled it with a priceless collection of Empire-period furniture, most of which remained when Bonaparte, fed up with his brother's too sympathetic approach to his subjects, recalled Louis to France in 1810, and solved the Dutch "situation" by absorbing the Netherlands into France.

In 1813, the French troops of Napoleon left Holland in a state of collapse, and Amsterdam's maritime glory all but gone. This stagnation ended in 1876, when the Noordzee Kanaal (North Sea Canal) (see *Haarlem, In The Area*) was cut straight through the dunes roughly along the river IJ (pronounced "eye") that flows through Amsterdam to give the city a short shipping connection directly to the sea. Other transportation connections also led to Amsterdam's revival. The first railway line, to Haarlem, was opened in 1839, and soon afterward, to Utrecht. In 1889, the grand Centraal Station was built on an artificial island not far from the site of Amsterdam's earliest settlement.

The upturn in the economy helped to remove one of the causes of poverty in Amsterdam, but a new Poor Law in 1854 was necessary, and the second half of the 19th century saw an increasingly organized welfare policy implemented. Schools were seen as the gateway through which a pauper child might pass and be transformed into a decent, upright member of society, and in a short time, education became the city's largest item of net expense. Housing, sanitation, and social questions remained concerns that were actively confronted in the city.

The Second World War hit Amsterdam hard. Of the city's 86,000 Jewish residents (out of 140,000 in the country) at the beginning of the Nazi occupation, almost all of whom were transported outside the country to camps, fewer than 10,000 returned. The first roundup, and subsequent deportation to Germany, of Jews (400 men and boys) in Amsterdam by the Nazis took place in mid-February 1941. On February 24th, workers of all religions met in Amsterdam to discuss a protest, with the dock workers in the forefront of the action. A general work stoppage (nothing short of treason to the Nazis) was begun the next morning. Every single factory, workshop, and office emptied; no trains, garbage or mail trucks ran, and Amsterdam fell as silent as a city can. By the afternoon, the strike had spread to a 15-mile radius around Amsterdam. In response, Nazi troops were sent out in Amsterdam to arrest or shoot strikers, and within a few days they succeeded in suppressing the strike. This Amsterdam action was the single instance of broad-based support for the Jews against their oppressors in occupied Europe during the war. When the war was over, Queen Wilhelmina paid a lasting tribute to the Amsterdammers' stand by adding the words "Heroic, Resolute, Merciful" to the Amsterdam city coat of arms. Another lasting tribute to the resistance of the Amsterdammers is on the **Jonas Daniel Meijerplein,** near the site of the Jewish deportations during the war, and across from the **Jewish Historical Museum** (see *What to See and Do*), the moving sculptured figure of *The Dock Worker* by Mari Andriessen.

Although the southern part of the Netherlands had been liberated by then, during the winter of 1944–45, Amsterdam and the rest of northern Holland had to endure further hardship. The period is remembered as the Hunger Winter, for there was no fuel, gas, electricity, or transport. Reportedly highly untasty tulips were dug up, mashed, and made into soup. Some 20,000 died of the cold and hunger in Amsterdam alone, and their bodies piled up at the Zuiderkerk because it was impossible to bury the dead, with no wood for coffins and no gravediggers with the strength to work.

The years following the war were spent in the long process of recovery and rebuilding. Numerous urban and industrial projects were undertaken in Amsterdam, with much of the development taking place in the southeast section of the city. The plan for reclamation of land from the IJsselmeer progressed with the Flevoland polder province, with the Almere complex of cities becoming brand new "bedroom communities" to Amsterdam. Fortunately, unlike cities such as The Hague and Utrecht, Amsterdam planners avoided the process referred to by the Dutch as *cityworming* (the building of a new exclusively commercial complex or "mall" in the centrum), keeping instead to the traditional mixed-function urban concept. After 1960, Amsterdam's harbor (which currently handles about 27 million tons annually, making it Europe's fourth busiest harbor, after Rotterdam, largest in the world, Hamburg, and Bremen) activities increasingly moved west, as a result of which the town and harbor became separated. Present town-planning by the Amsterdam City Council is creating offices, museums, hotels, and housing along the river **IJ** (behind the Centraal Station) and the eastern docklands in order to stop further migration from the city center.

Since the 16th century, Amsterdam, as well as being a strikingly beautiful and successful commercial center for Holland, has played another important role in Dutch society, one well put into words by William Z. Shetter in his book *The Netherlands in Perspective* (see *Benelux*

Bibliography at back of book). He writes, "Amsterdam is called a *lastige stad*, a term that is difficult to translate, because although *lastig* means something like "bothersome," the phrase is used in a way that emphasizes the city's vital role in being a progressive, and even radical, cutting edge, however uncomfortable that may be."

GUIDEPOSTS
Telephone Code 020

Tourist Info — VVV, Stationplein 10, 6266444 Mon.–Sat. 9 a.m.–5 p.m.); Easter–Sept. Mon.–Sat. 9 a.m.–11 p.m., Sun. 9 a.m.–9 p.m. (except 11 p.m. Jul.–Aug.); Oct.–Easter Mon.–Sat. 9 a.m.–6 p.m. (Sat. 5 p.m.), Sun. 10 a.m.–1 a.m. & 2–5 p.m. A small VVV office is at Leidsestraat 106: slightly shorter hours.

City Transport — GVB (tram, bus, Metro info.): Stationplein: Daily 7 a.m.–10:30 p.m. (except Sat. & Sun. 8 a.m.).

Trains — Central Station Information Office: Mon.–Fri. 8 a.m.–10 p.m., Sat., Sun., Hols. 9 a.m.–6 p.m.; 6202266 (international), 06–8991121 (national).

Emergency — Medical, central doctors service: 6642111. Police: 6222222; main police station: Elandsgracht 117, 5569111.

Post Office — Postkantoor (main post office): Singel 250–256; 5563311; Mon.–Fri. 8:30 a.m.–6 p.m. (Thurs. til 8:30 p.m.), Sat. 9 a.m.–noon.

Telephone/Fax — Telehouse (international calls, telegrams): Raadhuisstraat 46–50; 6743654; 24-hrs. daily; Tele Talk Center (international calls, telefax): Leidsestraat 101; 6208599; 24-hrs. daily.

Taxis — Taxicentrale: 6777777. It's best not to count on being able to hail a cab. There are taxi ranks at the CS, Rembrandtsplein, Leidseplein, across from the Concertgebouw at Museumplein, and major hotels.

Tours — Holland International, Rokin 54; 5512812. American Express, Damrak 66; 5207777 Keytours Holland, Dam 19; 6235051.

Books — The American Discount Book Center (specializing in books from the U.S. and U.K.) is at Kalverstraat 185; 6255537. The Atheneum Bookstore on the Spui has books in English; the Atheneum Newsstand next to it has a large selection of magazines from around the world.

WHAT TO SEE AND DO......................

It would be impossible to provide information on all there is to see and enjoy in Amsterdam. Certainly, many of your lasting impressions won't come from specific attractions, but from activities as offhand as an evening drink at a canalside cafe with a wondrous view of light-outlined bridges. From about mid-March through October, bridges, facades, towers, and trees along sections of the city's renowned ring of canals and other historic buildings are illuminated, from sunset to 11:30 p.m. (somewhat later at mid-summer, when, because of the northern latitude, it remains light until nearly 11 p.m.). Many, but not all, museums are closed Monday year-round. Some also close January 1, Christmas, and April 30 (Holland's National Day).

The Amsterdam VVV publishes a number of informative, interesting walking tour brochures in English, including a *Walk Through* series for *Maritime Amsterdam, Jewish Amsterdam,* and the *Jordaan.* The booklet *Amsterdam in the Footsteps of Vincent Van Gogh* (who lived in Amsterdam for just over a year in 1877–78, returning many times thereafter, and made his love for Amsterdam plain in letters to his brother Theo) covers places associated with the artist. There are also brochures on *Sculptures of Amsterdam I* and *II,* and *"Amsterdam School" Architecture in Amsterdam-South.* Prices are about Dfl. 2.50 apiece.

Knowing the key transportation and entertainment "hubs" will facilitate familiarity with Amsterdam. **Centraal Station** (CS) is an arrival point for many: all who travel by train, and those who fly in to Schiphol Airport and take the excellent rail connection into the city. A substantial number of city tram lines originate at the CS. Straight down the **Damrak** from the CS, past what was the port in the earliest era of the city, is **Dam Square,** with its Monument, Royal Palace, and Nieuwe Kerk. The Damrak continues as the **Rokin** to **Muntplein,** with the Munt Tower and its carillon (concerts Fri. noon–1 P.M.). Midpoint on the Rokin where the road narrows and the Amstel river from here out from the center has been left unfilled, a right turn brings one to the **Spui** and the **Beguinhof.**

With the Rokin at one's back, a left turn from the Munt into Reguliersbreestraat leads shortly to **Rembrandtsplein,** with its congregation of cafes. Carrying on, one comes to the **Blauwbrug** across the Amstel. To the left is the **Stopera** (the combined new Stadhuis, or town hall, and **Muziektheater,** behind which is **Rembrandt's House;** straight ahead across the bridge is **Waterlooplein,** and the **Jewish Historical Museum.** Turning right past the Munt, one enjoys the block-long **floating flower market** before arriving at Leidsestraat, a left turn onto which leads, after crossing the city's three concentric canals (**Herengracht, Keizersgracht,** and **Prisengracht**) to **Leidseplein,** a center of Amsterdam social life, with its restaurants, terrace cafes, and the best place from which to watch the people parade. Just beyond, past the landmark American Hotel, is the Singelgracht, over which a left brings one to the **Rijksmuseum** and **Museumplein.**

Rijksmuseum • *Stadhouderskade 42, Tues.–Sat. 10 a.m.–5 p.m., Sun. & hols. 1–5 p.m.; closed Mon.; 6732121; trams 6, 7, 10* • Built in 1885 by P. J. H. Cuypers, the Rijksmuseum is the cornerstone of Holland's permanent art exhibits, with the largest and finest collection of Dutch paintings in the world. The museum dates from an 1808 decree by then-ruler Frenchman Louis Bonaparte, brother of Napoleon, and was first housed at the Dam, in the former Stadhuis, turned into the Royal Palace by Louis. Rembrandt's *Night Watch,* the artist's best-known work, around which the museum was designed, has its own room (Room 224, top floor) with interpretive exhibits located nearby, and other rooms of his works, including *The Jewish Bride* and *Self-Portrait as the Apostle Paul.* The top floor is where the masterpieces of Dutch 15th–17th painting are, with rooms allocated to multiple works by **Frans Hals** (including *Merry Dinker*), **Jan Steen** (including *Feast of St. Nicholas*), **Vermeer** (*The Milk Maid, Woman Reading a Letter, The Love Letter, The Little Street*), and **Jacob van Ruisdael** (*Windmill at Wijk bij Duurstede* and *View of Haarlem*), **Pieter de Hooch** (*Woman with a child in a Pantry and Courtyard behind a House*), and **Nicolaes Maes** (*Old Woman at Prayer*).

Also on the top floor are Flemish works (**Rubens, Van Dyck**), Spanish (including Dutch-born **Anthony Moro, Goya,** and **Murillo**) and Italian (**Fra Angelico, Tiepolo**). In the Applied Arts section, there are three rooms of Delftware. Dutch painting of the 18th and 19th centuries, including Impressionism, The Hague School, and the Amsterdam School are on the ground floor. If you have time to see more, the Rijkmuseum has sections on Dutch history, Asiatic art, sculpture, and applied arts (including Flemish and Dutch tapestries). There is a detailed floor plan, brochures and catalogs available in English, a museum shop, and a restaurant.

Rijksmuseum Vincent van Gogh • *Paulus Potterstraat 7; Tues.–Sat. 10 a.m.–5 p.m., Sun. & hols. 1–5 p.m.; closed Mon.; 5705200; trams 2 & 5 from CS* • Opened in 1973 as a permanent home for a collection by Vincent van Gogh (1853–1890) of more than 200 paintings, 500 drawings, graphic art, and letters, and some works by his friends and contemporaries, including Gauguin and Toulouse-Lautrec. Van Gogh, who had a troubled, truncated life, and created most of his marvelous works in a mere five years just prior to his death more than a century ago at age 37, today is as popular a painter as any who ever lived. Although he executed many of his most memorable pieces outside Holland, primarily in France, his work is deeply rooted in the Dutch artistic tradition. He dropped the name *Van Gogh,* signing only Vincent to the paintings he considered worthy, because he found that outside of Holland no one could pronounce it correctly. Among the best-known paintings at the museum are *The Potato Eaters, Vase with Sunflowers, The Bedroom/Arles,* and *Crows in the Wheatfields* (for other Van Gogh works in Holland, see the Kroller Muller Museum, Otterlo).

Stedelijk Museum • *Paulus Potterstraat 13, corner Van Baerle Straat; Mon.–Sun. 11 a.m.–5 p.m.; 5732911; trams 2 & 5 from CS* • Opened at the end of the 19th century, in the 1950s the Stedelijk became one of the first museums in Europe to collect and exhibit contemporary art. Today, it is one of the most influential modern art museums in the world. Chronologically, the collection begins with works of "classic" modern artists, **Manet, Monet, Cezanne, Van Gogh, Matisse, Chagall, Picasso,** and advances through the early decades of the 20th century, when new visual "vocabulary" replaced the traditional use of perspective and began letting go of the ties to visible reality in favor of the abstract, non-representational, art of Dutch-born **Mondriaan,** and **Malevich.** Shown through the sweep of the Stedelijk collection, such changes can be seen as logical, even inevitable. Since the early 70s, when the Van Gogh Museum was opened next door and most of that artist's work moved to it, the Stedelijk has been devoted exclusively to modern art, and new acquisitions always strive to present the latest developments in visual art. The Stedelijk began collecting photography in 1958, following the museum's highly successful exhibit of *The Family of Man* by Luxembourg-born **Edward Steichen** (see Clervaux Castle, Lux., the Family of Man exhibit). Saturdays at the Stedelijk at 3 p.m. Sept.–June, there are free concerts in the series *Music of Today;* films, videos, lectures, and performance art are frequently on offer. Basic floor plan in English; museum shop.

Oude Kerk • *Oudekerksplein; April–Oct. Mon.–Sat. 11 a.m.–5 p.m., Sun. 1:30–5 p.m., Nov.–March Mon.–Sat. 1–3 p.m., Sun. 1:30–3 p.m.; tower accessible Jun 1–Sept. 15 Mon., Thurs. 2–5 p.m., Tues., Wed. 11a.m.–2 p.m.; 6249183; year-round concerts Sat. 4–5 p.m. on 47-bell Hemony carillon (restored 1990), one of the finest in Holland; frequent summer evening organ concerts* • The earliest parish church in Amsterdam (c. 1300), the Oude Kerk was built on an artificial mound close to the Amstel. Various rebuildings brought the church to its large present size by the first half of the 16th century and, with the 1578 *Alteration*, the Oude Kerk was transferred from the Catholic to Protestant rite. Closed temporarily in 1951 because of the imminent danger of its collapse, the Oude Kerk was completely restored between 1955–1979. The medieval church has the largest wooden roof (15th century, painted) in the Netherlands. **Dirck Crabeth** is credited with some of the fine 16th and 17th-century stained-glass windows; the **Vater/Muller organ** (the sound is exceptional) dates from 1724–36. Rembrandt's wife **Saskia** was buried beneath the stone that reads: Saskia 19 Juni 1642. Among the interior details, note the antique-decorated **Kerkmeesters Kamer** (vestry room). The Oude Kerk rests in a Linden-tree shaded cobbled square in the oldest part of Amsterdam, complete with cafes, bicycle and pedestrian traffic, and a few red-light district "shop windows."

Koninklijk Paleis (Royal Palace) • *Dam; daily June 15–Sept. 1, 12:30–4 p.m., call for possible additional times; 6248698* • When the Peace of Munster was signed in 1648, finally officially ending the 80 Years' War with Spain, Amsterdam was the wealthiest city in the world; laying the foundation stone late the same year for a monumental Stadhuis (today the Royal Palace on Dam Square) was an appropriate proclamation. Built on 13,000 piles, the massive, free-standing sandstone (all imported and virtually "emptying" two quarries) neo-classical Jacob van Campen building was called by contemporary poet Constantijn Huygens the "eighth wonder of the world" (a tired phrase today, but one that carried more weight in the 17th century). The Stadhuis was filled with the works of the Golden Age's finest sculptors and artists. Atop the facade, Atlas shoulders the world, as the Dutch then undoubtedly felt they did economically; inside, one flight up, the huge marble Citizens Hall has maps of the two hemispheres inlaid in the floor, so that visitors to the Stadhuis could appreciate how much of the world was Dutch. Many large allegorical sculptures decorate the hall, and frescoes and paintings are inclined to subjects favoring Greek and Roman gods. Nowhere are the moral lessons in the decorative work of the building more evident than in the Bankruptcy Office, where, in addition to reliefs showing rats gnawing at unpaid bills, the decor features the fatal Fall of Icarus. Perhaps **Meindart Hobbema** (1638–1709), one of the last born of the great 17th-century Dutch artists, should have taken note. Hobbema painted many excellent rural landscapes as a young man, but marriage seems to have changed his style. As a result of his wife, who was hired as cook to the Burgomaster of Amsterdam, who resided in the Stadhuis and entertained in great style there, Hobbema was able to get the job of wine-measurer for the city. Perhaps life became too easy, for Hobbema didn't paint much after that and, it is said, he and his wife died with little to show for it. The "classical" treatment in the Royal Palace is even carried to the softly piped-in music. The handsomely furnished former Magistrate Court Room and Burgomaster's Chamber can be visited, as well as rooms where pieces of the valuable Empire furniture collection that Louis Napoleon, installed as King of Holland in 1808 by his brother Bonaparte, used to decorate the building when he confiscated it as a royal palace. Louis' rule was too sympathetic to Dutch ideas, for which Napoleon removed him from the post, but the famous furniture and the status of the building as a royal palace remain. A good brochure in English is given out, and there is an explanatory video.

Dam • In the center of Dam Square, which has been the heart of Amsterdam since its founding c. 1270, is the **Nationaal Monument,** which commemorates all who died from 1940–45. The Queen lays a memorial wreath there on May 4th, on the eve of Liberation Day, May 5th.

Nieuwe Kerk • *Dam; open conditionally Mon.–Sun. 11 a.m.–5 p.m.; 6268168; concerts on the 1655 organ in summer* • Since it was begun about the year 1400, the "new" in its name comes only in reference to the century-older Oude Kerk. The deed of foundation was signed in 1408 by Frederik van Blankenheim, Bishop of Utrecht, who thus seems to have approved the division of the growing town of Amsterdam into two parishes: the Old Side, with the Oude Kerk, and the New Side, with the Nieuwe Kerk. The progressive enlargement of the church seems to have been stimulated by the unedifying rivalry between the Old and New parishes. In 1565, when the Oude Kerk acquired its magnificent tower and carillon, the Nieuwe Kerk reacted by laying up a massive foundation for a tower of its own. The project was delayed by the 80 Years' War. Finally, after being badly damaged by fire in 1645 (as a result of which few interior furnishings date from before then), rebuilding plans called for the construction of a tower for the Nieuwe Kerk. But the ending of the 80 Years' War caused a burst of building fever for a Stadhuis (Town Hall, now the Royal Palace) from 1648–55, and, when not enough funds could be found for *that* grandiose structure next door to it, the Nieuwe Kerk seems to have lost its last chance for a tower. In addition to the wonderfully painted classical cases of the two 17th-century organs designed by Jacob van Campen, and the huge carved pulpit, placed mid-church, Calvinist-style, is the monumental black marble tomb of Admiral de Ruyter (1607–1676), who died in a naval battle in Sicily while defeating the French fleet, was embalmed, and then sent home to Amsterdam, where thousands attended his funeral at the Nieuwe Kerk in 1677. Though now a "decommissioned" church, all reigning Dutch monarchs since King Willem I in 1815 (through Queen Beatrix, 1980) have been inaugurated in the Nieuwe Kerk, a city honor upon which Amsterdam rests its claim of being the country's capital. In the narrow **Gravenstraat** behind the Nieuwe Kerk are a number of tiny old shops. Do peek into #18, *De Drie Fleschjes* (the three little bottles), a small 17th-century pub.

Amsterdam Historisch Museum • *entered via decorative archway at Kalverstraat 92, from St. Luciensteeg 27, or through the Beguinhof (see next); daily 11 a.m.–5 p.m.; 5231822* • Whichever route one takes to it, the Amsterdam Historical Museum, with its extensive complex of buildings and courtyards, is a delightful discovery. Perhaps the pleasant surprise unfolds best from Kalverstraat, coming through the site occupied in 1414 by the sisters of the order of St. Lucy; the cowbarn of their convent is now the museum cafe **In de Oude Goliath** (to the right), inside of which is a giant wooden sculpture of Goliath, which from about 1650 to 1862 was a major attraction in an amusement park in Amsterdam's **Jordaan** district. To the left, one sees a courtyard wall with lockers for the belongings of boys of the Burgher Orphanage, which was established here in 1580 after the convent was taken over by the city under the 1578 Dutch law that confiscated all Catholic Church property. The Amsterdam Burgher Orphanage occupied the site until 1960, when it moved to new quarters on the edge of town. The building was then extensively restored, and opened as the historical museum in 1975.

To the left of the entrance, which is in a courtyard at the end of the passageway through the orphanage, is one of the most exciting public pedestrian passageways one could ever hope to encounter: the **Civic Guard Gallery.** The large-scale mini-museum walkway contains a priceless collection of huge civic guard and guild portraits, mounted on the outside brick walls of the handsome old institution, all safely encased under glass. The "museum street" is a stunningly effective and innovative use of space. Inside is a basically chronological treatment of Amsterdam's 700-years-plus history; borrow a written guide in English at the ticket counter for the general idea behind the exhibits, although many are multi-media or wonderful works of art (old views of Amsterdam, maps, prints) that have been donated to the museum or which came from former city institutions. Some of the Amsterdam themes that are imaginatively covered are city expansions, trade and industry in the 14th and 15th centuries, navigation in the Golden Age, and the history of the Dam as the center of public life since the city was first settled. Retrace your steps to the Civic Guard Gallery and head through it for the Begijnhof.

Begijnhof • *accessible from the Spui or from the Amsterdam Historical Museum's Civic Guard Gallery; daily, use Spui entrance after* *museum hours* • The full diversity of Amsterdam's sights becomes evident when one enters this peaceful, picturesque place, inhabited since 1346, when it was established as a pious community by the Sisters of St. Begga. Unlike those at the neighboring St. Lucy Convent, the Beguines were left in peace after the Alteration of 1578. Most of the houses in the courtyard were privately owned, either by Beguines or outsiders, and the city did not confiscate this private property, especially since many of the Beguines belonged to prominent Amsterdam families. The Beguine Church, which had been consecrated in 1419, was another matter, however, and it was taken over by the town. After years of being rented out as a warehouse, the city leased the church to the Presbyterians, Scottish, and English Calvinist Separatists living in Amsterdam who did not want to join the Church of England (it remains the Scottish/English church today).

Some of the English pilgrims worshipped here in 1608, moving to Leiden in 1609; some of them sailed from Delfshaven in 1620 (depicted in a stained glass window), boarding the *Mayflower* in England, and reaching Plymouth in the New World. The Beguines continued to live, and worship, in their garden square, but the Mass had to be celebrated in secret, and different houses were used. In 1655, the parish priest bought two houses and converted them into a permanent chapel for the Beguines. (City permission was granted on condition that outwardly nothing would betray the presence of a church.) Today, the Catholic Chapel can claim its identity in the Begijnhof. The land in the center of the garden-like Begijnhof was used as a bleaching-field until at least the mid-18th century. It is surrounded today by 17th- and 18th century (restored) housefronts, with old gables (neck, clock, and step-style) and old gablestones, some of which have been set in a wall near #34. This is the **Houden Huis** (wooden house), with its original wooden exterior, c. 1475, Amsterdam's oldest surviving house.

Anne Frank House • *Prinsengracht 263; Mon.–Sat. 9 a.m.–5 p.m., Sun. & hols. 10 a.m.–5 p.m., in June, July, Aug. open all days until 7 p.m.; 6264533; trams 13 & 17* • Anne Frank would have celebrated her 64th birthday in 1993. Instead, she died of typhus at the age of 16 in the Bergen-Belsen Nazi concentration camp. Because of a diary she kept during the two years that she, her family, and four others lived in the secret annex upstairs in this 200-year-old canal house, Anne Frank has a face among the millions of Jews who died during the Second World War. Visitors can see the small secret annex in the upper back of the house, where eight people had to endure two years in close confines before their whereabouts were disclosed to the Nazis. Among the touching details are black-and-white magazine pictures of movie stars and young English princess Elizabeth that Anne had pasted on her bedroom wall. There are two flights of very steep stairs to enter the museum. A video and brochure, in English, set the scene historically, and visitors then go "behind the bookcase" and up to the hidden rooms. Exhibits on the lower floors show photographs of Anne and her family before they fled into hiding, and convey details of the Nazi occupation in Amsterdam and life at the concentration camps. The Anne Frank Foundation seeks to prevent discrimination and violations of human rights in the world.

Not long before the group in hiding was betrayed to the Nazis, Anne wrote in her diary: "It's really a wonder that I haven't dropped all my ideals because they seem so absurd and impossible to carry out. Yet I keep them, because in spite of everything I still believe that people are really good at heart."

NOTE · · · This is one of the most popular sites in Amsterdam, and waiting lines can be long; plan an early start to avoid them.

Westerkerk • *Prinsengracht, corner Raadhuisstraat and Westermarkt; May 15–Sept. 15, Mon.–Sat. 10 a.m.–4 p.m.; tower accessible June–Sept. Tues, Wed., Fri., Sat. 2–5 p.m.; carillon concerts Tues. from noon–1 p.m.; 6247766; tram 13, 17* • Built between 1620 and 1630 in the Dutch Renaissance style, it is considered to be the masterpiece of architect Hendrick de Keyser. The distinctive 265-foot (85 meter) tower is topped with the Imperial Crown of Maximilian of Austria, a right that Amsterdam received from the Hapsburg Court in 1489. Rembrandt's unmarked grave, and that of his son Titus, are in the Westerkerk. (From 1660 until his death in 1669, the artist lived in a modest quarters at Rozengracht 184, nearby.) Standing at the corner of the church is a small modern sculpture of Anne Frank, which often has fresh flowers laid at its feet. Rising high above the statue is the colorfully crowned steeple of the Westerkerk, which, though only doors away from the windows of Anne's Secret Annex, could not be seen since the windows were painted to prevent the captive residents from being seen by neighbors. But its 47-bell carillon was a comfort to Anne, who wrote in her diary of "the (chiming) clock at the Westertoren which I always find so reassuring."

On the Keizersgracht side of the Westerkerk is Amsterdam's simple triangle-shaped pink granite Homomonument (Gay Monument). Nazis required that homosexuals in occupied Holland wear a pink triangle badge.

Jordaan • Across from the Westerkerk on the Prinsengracht is a Canal Bike dock, and on the far side of the Prinsengracht the distinctive Jordaan neighborhood begins. Noted now for the bohemian, bizarre, and beautiful, and its relaxed and creative character, the Jordaan was developed in the early 17th century, at the same time as the **Grachtengordel** (canal belt), but was purposefully left unplanned in comparison with the great concentric pattern, and allowed to grow up as a working-class, artisan, tradesman, and, very early on, immigrant district, with smaller and squatter houses, and narrower streets and canals. *Jordaan* probably comes from the French "jardin" (garden), since many of its streets have horticultural names. Before long, it deteriorated into an overcrowded slum, a scene of repeated bubonic plague epidemics, and extreme poverty; in the 1890s, with 90,000 inhabitants, it was Europe's most densely populated city quarter. A century later, with 19,000 residents, the Jordaan's been gently gentrified, fortunately not to the point of losing its unique character. Bounded by the Prinsengracht, Rozengracht, Lijnbaansgracht, and the delightful Brouwersgracht, the Jordaan contains some of the city's most characterful cafes, small boutiques and bistros, and hidden *hofjes* (almshouses). The *Brouwersgracht* (brewers' canal) is the point from which construction on the three concentric canals began about 1600.

Nederlands Theater Museum • *Herengracht 168; Tues.–Sun. & hols. 11 a.m.–5 p.m., closed Mon.; 6235104* • Exhibits primarily concern Dutch theater tradition, and downstairs is a miniature theater from 1781. The real reason for you to visit, however, is the 1638 canal house's exquisite decor detail, particularly wall and ceiling paintings and plaster work in the marble hall and monumental staircase from when it was rebuilt in the Louis XIV-style in the 18th century.

Willet-Holthuysen Museum • *Herengracht 605; Mon.–Sun. 11 a.m.–5 p.m.; 5231870* • Built for the daughter of one of Amsterdam's Burgomasters in 1689, and left by the Holthuysen family to the State in 1889, this double-width canal house has furnished rooms reflecting the 18th and 19th centuries and a fine tiled and brass and copper-utensil-adorned 18th-century basement kitchen. One room features a c. 1740 painted ceiling by Jacob de Wit, another an Aubusson wall covering. Two lounges are virtual art galleries. Be sure to reach the top floor, which has a cozy and intimate feel. The back bedroom, overlooking the garden, is set for sewing, a task lighted from the largest window I've ever seen in a house. The floor-to-ceiling windows of the enchanting garden room are on the first floor at the rear. The formal French-style garden behind the house also can be viewed (through iron railings) from Amstelstraat (between Rembrandtsplein and the Blauwbrug).

Museum van Loon • *Keizersgracht 672; year-round Mon. 10 a.m.–5 p.m., Sun. 1–5 p.m., closed rest of week; 6245255* • At least the severely limited opening hours for this fine furnished late 17th-century canal house come on a day when many of Amsterdam's other museums are closed. One is free to wander around the house at will, with the help of a detailed explanatory booklet (in English). Built in 1671–72, the first tenant of the house was the successful painter **Ferdinand Bol** (once a pupil of Rembrandt). The French influence in the decor of the personable house reflects that style's popularity in the early 1800s because of Napoleon's rule (1795–1813) of the country, and the house, as much as possible, has been restored to its late 18th-, early 19th-century state. The garden behind the house also has French flavor in its formal style.

Amsterdam Stadhuis • *Amstel 1; Mon.–Fri. 8 a.m.–6 p.m., Sat. 10 a.m.–6 p.m., Sun. and hols. noon–6 p.m.; 5523458* • The **Normaal Amsterdams Peil** (N.A.P.), a.k.a. **Amsterdam Ordnance Datum** (A.O.D.), was established three centuries ago and based on the average high watermark of the Zuiderzee, which was then Amsterdam's connection to the North Sea; it is still the "water table" referral point for all construction in the Netherlands. The A.O.D. bronze knob, mounted in a passage of the Stadhuis, marks ground zero level; the three watercolumns on view show the high or low tide of the North Sea at the particular moment at IJmuiden; the high or low tide at Vlissingen (in Zeeland, to the south); and the highest level reached during the Zeeland floods in 1953. The Stadhuis shares its setting on the Amstel with the **Muziektheater,** from which there's a splendid view of the evening illuminations along the river during intermission and after performances.

Rembrandt House • *Jodenbreestraat 4; Mon.–Sat. 10 a.m.–5 p.m., Sun. & hols. 1–5 p.m.; 6249486* • Holland's most famous artist lived here from 1639–1660, and the house, which dates from 1606, contains a nearly complete record of Rembrandt's etchings. Rembrandt's development in etching, a form for which he is less familiar, can be seen in the works displayed. The museum also shows some paintings by his own teacher Pieter Lastman and his pupils.

Jewish Historical Museum • *Jonas Daniel Meijerplein; daily 11 a.m.–5 p.m.; 6269945; tram 9 from CS, Metro to Waterlooplein* • Across from the Portuguese Synagogue on the J. D. Meijerplein is the Ashkenazic Synagogue Complex, whose four components date from 1670 to 1752 and now form the Jewish Historical Museum. The museum, which opened in 1987 and won the 1989 Council of Europe Museum Prize for its imaginative architectural restoration, stands in the former Amsterdam neighborhood Vlooyenburg (built about 1600), into which moved large numbers of Sephardic Jews from Portugal and Ashkenazic Jews from Germany. A glass-roofed passage connects the four synagogues, added as the Amsterdam Jewish community expanded; one, the Grand (1670), is the oldest public synagogue in western Europe. Exhibits cover the Jewish life cycle, and highlight the social history of the Jews in the Netherlands. English brochure, museum shop, Kosher coffee shop. Outside, on the Meijerplein, seek out *De Dokwerker (The Dock Worker*—see *History)*, a Mari Andriessen statue, at once powerful and powerless.

Nederlands Scheepvaart Museum (Netherlands Maritime Museum) • *Kattenburgenplein 1; Tues.–Sat. 10 a.m.–5 p.m., Sun. & hols. 1–5 p.m., closed Mon.; 5232222; bus 22 or 28 from CS* • Located in the 1656 former arsenal of the Admiralty of Amsterdam, the national maritime museum was opened in 1973. The museum aims to present an overall picture of Dutch shipping, past and present, with a focus on overseas trade, naval warfare (and fine stirring paintings), navigation, and cartography (great globes and maps). There are plentiful models of ships from the Dutch East and West Indies companies, clipper ships, up to the proud passenger liners of the Holland-America Line. Set off in a separate section is the early 18th-century, oar-powered *Royal Barge*, used as recently as 1962 for the occasion of the silver jubilee of Queen (now Princess) Juliana. Museum floor plan in English, exhibit descriptions in Dutch only. Cafe with harbor view; excellent book and gift shop.

Moored next to the museum, among several ships of interest, is the recently-completed (it was five years in the construction) full-size replica of the 18th-century merchant ship of the Dutch East India Company *De Amsterdam,* which sank in the English Channel on its maiden voyage in 1749. The interior has been recreated as authentically as possible to give visitors an insight into what life would have been like aboard the vessel.

Museum Amstelkring "Our Lord in the Attic" • *Oudezijds Voorburgwal 40; Mon.–Sat. 10 a.m.–5 p.m., Sun. & hols. 1–5 p.m.; 6246604* • Located in the attics of three contiguous mid-17th-century canal houses in the oldest section of Amsterdam is a full-scale richly decorated Catholic Church—in hiding. With the coming of the **Alteration** in 1578, which made Protestantism preeminent, and Catholicism technically illegal, the city of Amsterdam, governed by business interests, in general ducked the issue of religion by allowing the practice of the Catholic religion—as long as it wasn't obvious. This led to the rise of many so-called "hidden churches," of which this is the last in Amsterdam (where there were once about 60). A museum since 1888, and appearing much as it did in 1735, **Our Lord in the Attic** has a poker-face exterior and downstairs parlor. There is little to prepare one for the visual shock of the large three-adjoining-attics area at the top of an unprepossessing staircase: a Baroque altarpiece (with Jacob de Wit paintings), pews and a balcony, confessional, stowaway pulpit, and separate sacristy, all on a scale substantial enough to have supported a full-time resident priest. One of the many intriguing items in the church is a small silver box in the shape of a coffin. Since Catholics at the time could not be buried in consecrated ground, hallowed earth was kept in the box and scattered, three spoonfuls per person, over the bodies of deceased Catholics before their coffins were closed.

Red Light District • Examples of Amsterdam's traditional tolerance abound around the **Our Lord in the Attic** church, which is located in the center of the city's red light district, which has been sanctioned in the same area (adjacent to the town's original site on the Dam) since the 14th century. How a city manages its sin may be a good measure of its maturity; in Amsterdam, one senses an unruffled, reasoned approach to prostitution, rather than the over-reactive, adolescent attitudes that do nothing to improve the situation which prevail in many other places. Along and in streets off the quaint, canaled **Oudezijds Voorburgwal,** women sit in small shop-like windows, offering themselves as merchandise. The process may be shockingly direct to some, but it keeps the business of sin behind plate glass, limiting its spillage into streets and normal city life. Medical checkups and other professional aid and advice for prostitutes are encouraged by officials (and made wide use of), and the *Red Thread* organization works to protect the women's dignity. Thus, in Amsterdam, for all concerned, including tourists, there's a certain safety associated with the practice of "the world's oldest profession."

SHOPPING

As you'd expect with such long-established pragmatic practitioners of trade, prices are set in Holland. No need to think about bargaining (except at flea and antique markets). The VVV sells several excellent shopping/walking tour brochures for those who want to do it 'til they drop: *On The Lookout Between the Canals, On the Lookout in The Jordaan, On The Lookout for the Chic and Beautiful, On the Lookout for Art and Antiques,* and *On the Lookout for the Amsterdam Open-Air Markets* (pamphlet). Prices shown always include the 18.5% VAT or btw tax. (See *Practical Travel Info.* at beginning of book for advice regarding tax refunds.) Basic hours are 9 a.m.–6 p.m., except Sat. when most close at 5 p.m. Virtually all are closed all day Sun., and many don't open until 1 p.m. Mon. Late-night shopping is Thurs., till 9 p.m.

Amsterdam has been in the diamond trade since 1586 (for the history of Amsterdam's and Belgian Antwerp's involvement with diamonds, see *Decorative Arts/Traditional Crafts* in front of book), and the *Amsterdam cut* is known for its quality. The **Amsterdam Diamond Center** (Rokin 1; open daily; 6245787), and several other diamond-cutting houses can be visited for free tours and demonstrations of the "four Cs" qualities of the shining gemstones. Many sell jewelry, as well as unmounted stones, in their showrooms.

In the European city that has done more to protect its historic architectural heritage than any other, you'd expect to find an active antique trade. More than 100 antique shops can be found on and just off Amsterdam's short **Nieuwe Spiegelstraat**. As an appropriate backdrop to the objets d'art in the shop windows is the Rijksmuseum, which dominates the view at the end of the street. Art and antiques have kept close company in Amsterdam since the opening of the Rijksmuseum in 1885, within a couple years of which the first antique shop had opened on Nieuwe Spiegelstraat. Amsterdam has over 140 art galleries, most of which specialize in contemporary art, for which the city is considered one of the leading ones in Europe. The galleries are scattered throughout the Centrum.

One of Amsterdam's main shopping areas is the pedestrian **Kalverstraat** (it means "bullock street," and cattle were once driven to market along it), one of the city's earliest streets. Running parallel to the Rokin, between the Dam (location of the prestigious **De Bijenkorf** store) and the Munt Tower, it has major department stores (**Vroom & Dreesman**) and many boutiques. Just beyond the Munt Tower, which is home to a **De Porceleyne Fles** Delftware shop, on Reguliersbreestraat, is **Hema,** for colorful, imaginative housewares and, from its small food section the makings of a picnic: fresh bread, cheese, sandwiches, *vin ordinaire.* The Kalverstraat has Centrum convenience, but not quite the cachet, of **P.C. Hooftstraat** and **Van Baerlestraat** in the museum quarter, which have boutiques carrying fashionable internationally renown names. **Focke & Meltzer** on P.C. Hooftstraat carries the delftware of **De Porceleyne Fles** and other fine china and crystal. The enjoyable Jordaan district has small shops with diverse wares tucked here and there.

You'll probably run across enough "typical Dutch souvenirs" during your strolls around the city, but a cut-above-the-average and a useful congregation of Dutch artisans and their output can be found in a complex, near the Sonesta Hotel. Nearby is **De Klompenboer** (wooden shoe farm) at Nieuwezijds Voorburgwal 20, in case you want to purchase a pair.

Amsterdam's markets include the **Flower Market** at Singel Canal, between Koningsplein and Muntplein, Mon.–Sat. 9 a.m.–5 p.m. The city's largest general goods and produce street market is on **Albert Cuypstraat,** Mon.–Sat. 9 a.m.–5 p.m. The long-standing flea market, not quite what it once was, is at **Waterlooplein,** Mon.–Sat. 10 a.m.–7 p.m. Sundays, go to Nieuwemarkt for open-air antiques May–Oct., 10 a.m.–4 p.m. The enclosed many-stall **Antique Market de Looier** is at Elandsgracht 109, Sat.–Thurs. 11 a.m.–5 p.m., closed Fri. Nearby, at Looiersgracht 38, is **Rommelmarkt** (flea market), same hours. A **stamp** market (*Postzegelmarkt*) on Wed. and Sat. from 1–4 p.m. lends character to the scene by Nieuwezijds Voorburgwal 280. Artists offer diverse works Apr.–Oct., Sun. 11 a.m.–6 p.m. at the Spui and on Thorbeckeplein.

ACCOMMODATIONS........................

Some of the most charming hotels, often on canals, in Amsterdam (and other Dutch cities) have been made out of one or a series of one-time private houses; these have lots of character, and lots of steep stairs, since it's often difficult (and always expensive) to install elevators. Staff help with luggage, so that needn't be a concern when you consider whether to avail yourself of this distinctive Dutch-style accommodation. In the selection of hotels for the book, both convenience and setting have been strongly weighed. In cities, where business travelers are inclined to be absent on weekends, inquire about weekend discount rates, which may be as much as 50%. Especially at more moderate hotels, always inquire when booking if credit cards are accepted.

Deluxe

★★★★★ **De L'Europe** • *Nieuwe Doelenstraat 2–8, 1012 CP; 6234836, fax 6242962* • Approaching a centennial on its superb site, arguably the best combination of scenery and convenience of any hotel in the city, the Hotel de l'Europe faces the Amstel and Munt tower in the confident knowledge that she is an Amsterdam grande dame. Old-world, but not old-fashioned, despite its fine six-story Victorian facade. The excellent reputation of its Excelsior restaurant kitchen is well-deserved. There's been recent renovation and redecoration, with dining, afternoon tea, and drinks on a wraparound canal-level terrace, and health club with pool (in surprising classic Roman bath-style) and sauna. You need to ask for a waterview; facing the Muziektheater instead of the Munt is quieter. The hotel has 101 rooms; seats in the elegant elevators; bidets in the bath; minibars; in-room safes.

★★★★★ **Ramada Renaissance Amsterdam** • *Kattengat 1, 1012 SZ; 6212223, fax 6275245, U.S. & Can. 800–228–9898* • Located in one of the city's oldest neighborhoods, with crooked, cobbled little streets, dominated by the great green dome of the desanctified 17th-century Round Lutheran Church, the Ramada Renaissance, until recently the Amsterdam Sonesta, is located in a 1975 building that incorporates historic monuments into the property. The 425 guest rooms feature rich contemporary materials and furnishings, and five-star amenities. The service provided by the professional, friendly young Dutch staff is refreshing.

Amsterdammers, as well as guests, enjoy the public places, the authentic "brown" **Koepel Cafe** (with outside terrace in nice weather), and the Sunday morning **Koepel concerts** in the Round Lutheran Church (see *Events and Festivals*), which also serves as the hotel's unique conference center, the **Boston** nightclub, and **Splash,** its health club.

★★★★★ **Pulitzer** • *Prinsengracht 315–331, 1016 GZ; 5235235, fax 6276753* • Recently acquired by the Italian Ciga Group, whose renovation plans for the property were uncertain at press time, the Pulitzer is expected to continue to delight guests with its assemblage of historic buildings (19 of them, mostly 17th-century) and its imaginative integration of them into an inviting whole, complete with glass-enclosed connecting corridors and central tree-shaded garden courtyard. Much of the art and furniture is modern, as is the plumbing, but despite those changes, there's a timeless charm to this Pulitzer prize. (In fact, it takes its name from *the* Joseph Pulitzer's grandson, who had a vision for the then-decaying canalside houses and opened the hotel in 1971.) The 195 guest rooms are all unique, with old beams, brick, and, at least until recently, a rather rustic charm. A full range of anemities and services are provided; the canalside coffeeshop is highly pleasant, as is the cozy bar. The location puts one in the center of the picturesque, and close to much else of interest in Amsterdam.

★★★★★ **Golden Tulip Barbizon Palace** • *Prins Hendrikkade 59–72, 1012 AD; 5564564, fax 6243353, res. U.S. & Can. 800–333–1212* • Located in the oldest part of Amsterdam, the Barbizon Palace is one of the newest and most successful of the city's modern hotel/historic house marriages. Incorporating 19 monument facades, including one of Amsterdam's only two remaining timber houses at Zeedijk 1 (c. 1550), the Palace presents a highly individual face to the Centraal Station across from it; architects created an elegant interior with a blend of Dutch, French, and even Roman elements. Marble floors, columns, and balustrades give the lobby a stately look, completed by an arched transparent roof. More than half of the 263 guest rooms are contained in the old houses and are split-level with old oak beams. Minibar, in-room safe, hairdryer, telephone with modem hook-up, health club, VIP club room, and 24-hour room service are among the amenities. The gourmet restaurant **Vermeer** has a 17th-century ambiance, and there's a typically Dutch pub.

★★★★★ **Amstel (Inter-Continental)** • *Professor Tulpplein 1; 6226060, res. U.S. & Can. 800–327–0200* • This highly regarded Amsterdam hotel landmark, fronting on the Amstel, has reopened following a top-to-toe renovation into an 80-unit all-suite property (very expensive). The historic features of the handsome foyer have been retained, while a swimming pool with view on the Amstel River and full health club have been added. There's a new business center, and **Le Rive** restaurant has been expanded.

★★★★★ **Apollo** • *(Trust House Forte International)* • *Apollolaan 2, 1077 BA; 6735922, fax 6739771, U.S. & Can. 800-225-5843* • This gracious, contemporary hotel sits at the confluence of three tree-lined canals, faced by many of the highly pleasant public spaces, including the picture-windowed country-house-like lounge. The 217 rooms are smart in appearance, generous in size, and have the range of amenities you'd expect, along with 24-hour room service; ask for an even number if you want to face the canals. The Apollo, situated in a quiet, out-of-the-center corner of town, offers free parking, friendly and helpful front-desk service, and has informal, formal, and terrace cafe restaurants facing the canals. It's a three-block walk to the nearest tram into the Centrum.

★★★★★ **Golden Tulip Barbizon Centre** • *Stadhouderskade 7, 1054 ES; 6851351, fax 6851611, res. U.S. & Can. 800-333-1212* • The 1920's facade of this unpretentiously elegant hotel is an example of the Amsterdam School architecture, and the soft colors and lighting in guest and public rooms a reflection of the French Barbizon School. The youthful Dutch staff focuses on friendly service. The Barbizon overlooks the lively Leidseplein, and is well located for walking to museums, shopping, dining, and trams. Its 242 comfortable, contemporary-style rooms have double-glazed windows, air conditioning, minibars, safes, hairdryers; there's 24-hour room service, ice-making machines on every floor, concierge, valet parking, a well-equipped health club, and business services center. **Cafe Barbizon** is open for conveniently long hours, as is the skylighted lobby bar.

★★★★ **American Hotel** • *Leidsekade 97, 1017 PN; 6245322, fax 6253236* • The thoroughly European American Hotel has occupied its prominent canaled corner of Amsterdam, just off the Leidseplein, since the 1880s. The 188 comfortable guest rooms are replete with Art Deco details, as is the two-story lobby. Amenities include fitness center (sauna, weight machines), newsstand, room service, and characterful cafes: terrace, canalside, the Nightwatch bar. Its most famous feature is the flagrantly Art Deco **Cafe Americain** (open 11 a.m.–2 a.m.), a roomy rendezvous favored by the Dutch, and enjoyed by all, for coffee with newspapers, pastry, light and full meals, and after dinner drinks.

First Class

★★★★ **Grand Hotel Krasnapolsky** • *Dam 9, 1012 JS; 5549111, fax 6228607* • The location couldn't be more in the heart of Amsterdam for this traditionally Dutch hotel, all recently renovated, and enlarged by 37 deluxe rooms to 316. Brought back to its 1880 airy elegance is the **Winter Garden** restaurant where breakfast (included) is served. At the marble-topped tables of the **Krasserie** lobby cafe/bar (where a photo of Queen Wilhelmina hangs), which overlooks Dam Square and across to the Royal Palace, one sits close to the heart of the city, but a bit removed from its bustle. Fitness center; concierge; 24-hour room service; hotel parking garage.

★★★★★ **Amsterdam Marriott** • *Stadhouderskade 21, 1054 ES; 6075555, fax 6075511, U.S. & Can. 800-228-9290* • Sometimes the lobby seems as animated as the Leidseplein, which the hotel overlooks, and you can watch the street scene from **The Terrace** glass-enclosed sidewalk cafe. A cozy, quieter nook is **De Library** lobby cocktail bar, and there are both informal and more formal restaurants. Museums, shops, trams, and other restaurants are within an easy jaunt. The 400 spacious rooms and baths come with all the service (24-hours) and amenities (minibars, air conditioning, etc.) that you associate with the name Marriott. The best views are in the front rooms on upper floors.

★★★★ **Doelen Karena Hotel** • *Nieuwe Doelenstraat 24, 1012 CP; 6235632, fax 6221084, U.S. & Can. 800-365-6935* • The outer walls of the 17th-century Doelen Hall, once the civic guard hall for which Rembrandt's huge *Night Watch* was commissioned (in 1638) and where it hung (until moved to the Town Hall on the Dam in 1715), were incorporated into the present hotel, which opened in 1883. The original richly ornamented marble lobby, the superb views of the Amstel and Kloveniersburgwal canal (which half of its 86 guest rooms overlook), and setting in one of the most scenic sections of Amsterdam, give the hotel plenty of character. Many of the guest rooms have been renovated, and have a light, modern appearance; many have sitting areas, all have pants press, hairdryer, minibar, in-room coffee/tea maker. Small restaurant overlooks canal; cozy bar, also with views, has old Dutch ambiance.

★★★★ **Schiller Karena** • *Rembrandtplein 26-36, 1017 CV; 6231660, fax 6240098, U.S. & Can. 800-365-6935* • Built in 1892, with art-nouveau detail in the stained glass, chandeliers, and mirrors of the large, gracious, plant-filled lobby lounge and restaurant, the Schiller is a historic landmark on the Rembrandtplein. The rooms are all different; some have balconies overlooking the large green, cafe-rimmed square. Pants press and coffee tray among amenities in rather standard but comfortable rooms. A glass-enclosed terrace cafe fronts the hotel along the Rembrandtplein.

★★★★ **Jan Luyken** • *Jan Luykenstraat 54, 1071 CS; 5730730, fax 6763841* • Located in three former houses on a tree-shaded street, the hotel has a quiet location near the art museums, shopping, Concertgebouw, and beyond the sounds of but close to the lively Leidseplein. The property's 65-room (all with bath, though I saw some very small tubs, minibars, and in-room safes) size means personal attention from the very pleasant, helpful staff at the front desk. Elevators, though some rooms are a fair distance from them. There's an attractive breakfast (only, included) room, and a typically Dutch-style cozy lobby bar with small garden terrace where snacks, soup, and toasted sandwiches are served.

★★★★ **Scandic Crown Hotel Victoria** • *Damrak 1–6, 1012 LG; 6234255, fax 6252997* • Almost every visitor to Amsterdam since 1890 has seen the stately Victorian facade of the Victoria Hotel, now enlarged and updated with a new lease on life as the Scandia Crown Victoria. Steps from Centraal Station, yet in the city stream, the hotel has 321 traditional, comfortable rooms; those in the original building are larger, more gracious; non-smoking rooms and executive floor available. Business center; health club; parking garage. The cozy **Tasman Bar**, and glassed-in **Terrace** on the Damrak where one can watch the world go by, are Amsterdam standards.

Moderate

★★★ **Ambassade** • *Herengracht 335–353, 1016 AZ; 6262333, fax 6245321* • Centrally located in seven 17th-century patrician canalside houses, the Ambassade is a delight from one's first step into the elegant, welcoming lobby. Though somewhat less stylish than the public rooms (there's an elegant French-style salon), each of the 47 bedrooms (some 65% of which face the canal, made cheerful with p.m. sun) is distinct and immaculate, decorated with pretty prints and antiques. Breakfast (included) in an elegant canal-front room; light meals available from the 24-hour room service. Elevators in each building promised by 1992. Very popular with those who have discovered it, so reserve as far ahead as possible.

★★★ **Het Canal House** • *Keizergracht 148, 1015 CX; 6225182, fax 6241317* • These two charming mid-17th-century mansions (26 rooms, all with modern tile baths) are filled with an eclectic collection of the long-standing friendly American owner's auction-acquired antiques and Dutch prints. Convenient, prestigious location. Breakfast (only) served in a quite stately garden-view salon. Rooms overlook canal or garden (illuminated at night). Elevator to most rooms, small lobby bar.

★★★ **Hotel Borgmann** • *Koningslaan 48, 1075 AE; 6735252, fax 6762580* • From the terrace tables behind this roomy 1902 home, one is surrounded by the greenery and bird songs from Vondelpark. The big windows almost bring the outside in to the luxurious, but fresh and cheerful country-house-like lounge, where breakfast (only) is served, and bar service is available. The 15 twin rooms (rooms in back or front of house are largest) and 3 singles each have a minifridge, trouser press, hairdryer, TV, telephone, and bath or shower. Very friendly service. No elevator. On-street parking. Nearby tram, museum district.

★★★ **Owl Hotel** • *Roemer Visscherstraat 1, 1054 EV; 6189484, fax 6189441* • A block from the Leidseplein, and just behind the Marriott Hotel, this light, bright contemporarily decorated 34-room hotel has a quiet location, with a small plant-filled relaxing lounge and bar that open onto a garden. The five-floor, 100-year-old building has an elevator; the generous-sized double rooms all have shower (some bath), TV, telephone; breakfast (only) is included. Very central, near arts museums, trams.

★★★ **Avenue** • *Nieuwezijds Voorburgwal 27, 1012 RD; 6238307, fax 6383946* • Opened in 1990 in a restored warehouse of the United East India Company, the six-story hotel has 38 rooms (12 superior—recommended because of larger size), and a pleasing contemporary wicker and wood look, some beamed ceilings. Breakfast included; restaurant; elevator; credit cards; hairdryers in all rooms. On tram lines; easy walk to Centraal Station, Damrak.

★★ **Vondel** • *Vondelstraat 28–30, 1054 GE; 6120120, fax 6854321* • This mid-19th century, family-run house-hotel has 30 rooms, all with private bath or shower, telephone, and color TV. Located less than a block from the lively Leidseplein, the hotel itself has a quiet location, and has only light bar service in the lounge. Within walking distance of museums; trams at Leidseplein to Centrum and CS. Breakfast (included) room; two saunas in garden; personal attention. No elevator, but several rooms on ground level.

★★ **Amsterdam Wiechmann** • *Prinsengracht 328, 1016 HX; 6263321* • Located in two restored canal houses, the cheerful, family-style hotel has 36 simply-decorated rooms, all with telephone, toilet, bath/shower, many have canal views; TV in cozy lobby lounge. There's a wonderful corner breakfast (included) cafe with wide windows overlooking two canals. Three storys, steep narrow stairs, long corridors, no elevators, but help with baggage. No credit cards.

★★★★ **Atlas** • *Van Eeghenstraat 64, 1071 GK; 6766336, fax 6717633* • Situated in a quiet, leafy neighborhood at the edge of Vondelpark, the Atlas' 23 all-different rooms are housed in a large traditional Dutch art nouveau residence. A block from tram to Centrum, within walking distance of art museums, shopping, restaurants, Leidseplein cafes. Huge windows in reasonable rooms, each with modern bath. Elevator, friendly 24-hour room service, laundry service, safes at front desk, small lobby restaurant-bar, credit cards accepted.

★ **Washington** • *Frans van Mierisstraat 10, 1071 RS; 6796754, fax 6734435* • The generous-sized rooms (both with and without private modern marble bath facilities) in this recently renovated house-hotel, decorated with antiques and orientals, ornamented with wood wainscotting and other details, are often filled with the sound of musicians, guest performers at the nearby Concertgebouw. On a residential street, close to museums and trams, the hotel features friendly service, breakfast (only); no elevator; guests have own front door key.

★★ **Agora Hotel** • *Singel 462, 1017 AW; 6272200, fax 6272202* • Great location on a canal, steps from the Flower Market, the Spui, and the Beguinhof. You do need to be able to handle steep stairs (help with luggage) to be able to take advantage of the Agora. The small Dutch-style canal-view lobby evolves to a cheerful breakfast (only) room farther back, where coffee and soft drinks are served during the day. The traditionally decorated bedrooms, all different and with private facilities, are inclined to get more interesting architecturally the higher up you go, but it's a hike; ask to be nearer ground level if you prefer. Close to sights, shops, trams.

Inexpensive

★★★ **Rho** • *Nes 11–23, 1012 KC; 6207371, fax 6207826* • It's not lovely to look at from the outside, though the location, just steps from the Dam, couldn't be much more convenient. Once you step into the lobby of this 1908 former theater (renovated as a hotel in 1989), however, with its soaring, curved skylit ceiling, you're bound to be intrigued. The 61 rooms are very functional, often generous in size, as are the tile bathrooms (open showers with curtains), and feature telephone and TV. Elevator (four floors), parking available. The intriguing former theater lobby is the breakfast (only) room, light and airy, with potted palms, stained glass, globe lights. Take a drink up to the balcony from the lobby bar to see further signs of the building's past life as a theater.

★★★ **Toro Hotel** • *Koningslaan 64, 1075 AG; 6737223, fax 6750031* • The 23 recently renovated rooms in this turn-of-the-century mansion on a quiet avenue overlooking Vondelpark are comfortable in size, decor, and in-room amenities: minibar, TV, telephone, hairdryer. Public rooms have charming details, antiques, chandeliers, stained-glass windows, a terrace, and garden. Breakfast room (or served in your room) and lobby lounge with drinks service; credit cards; elevator; on-street parking; two blocks to tram to Centrum.

★ **Seven Bridges** • *Reguliersgracht 31, 1017 LK; 6231329* • Located on a lovely canal, close to but beyond the sound of the lively Thorbeck and Rembrandtsplein, this 200-year-old house is clean, bright, and cheerful. Most of the rooms have private shower, all have radio, some TV, no telephones. Room 3 on the garden is especially nice. Breakfast served in rooms.

★★★ **Hotel The Bridge** • *Amstel 107, 1018 EM; 6237068* • The scenic location on the Amstel, near the "Skinny Bridge," is only viewed from two rooms (large and old-fashioned), but at the far end of the long corridor on the ground-floor, on which all 26 rooms are located, are eight cozy, modern, quiet rooms facing the "unknown canal" that represent good value. All rooms have private bath facilities, toilet, and telephone (no TV); continental breakfast included in the Italian restaurant next door. Drinks available off small unusual lobby created in days when the hotel was a marble factory.

★★ **Rokin Hotel** • *Rokin 73, 1012 KL; 6267456* • Very centrally located, close to the Dam. For both quiet and comfort above the very-basic decor of its other rooms, ask for one of the ten better-standard doubles located in a canal house at the back of the hotel (where there are also hotel "apartments" for longer stays). No elevator; breakfast (only) included. Major credit cards (except Diners).

RESTAURANTS

The Dutch invariably breakfast at home, so visitors will find few places that serve more than coffee early in the morning except hotels, which begin serving by 7 a.m. A Dutch buffet breakfast *(ontbijt)* will include various breads, sliced cheeses and meats, juices, cereals, milk, perhaps boiled eggs, yogurt, fresh fruit, and coffee or tea. A picturesque little cafe on a tree-shaded square on the Singel canal that does serve breakfast (with eggs), outside in good weather, is the **Cafe-Eethuisje De Roef** *(Stromarkt 4, 8:30 a.m.–9 p.m.; 6274515; inexpensive)*, at end of Kattengat, just past the Sonesta Hotel. Breakfast is also served at **Greenwoods** *(Singel 103; Mon.–Fri. 9 a.m.–7 p.m., Sat., Sun. 11 a.m.–7 p.m.; 6237071; inexpensive)*, as well as light lunch and tea in the big-windowed, canalside, cozy, crowded cafe. Remember that dinner is taken relatively early in Holland, and even in the best restaurants, many kitchens close by 9:30 p.m. The better the restaurant, the better idea it is to make reservations.

Even if Amsterdam does boast that you "can eat out in any language" there, its Dutch restaurants deserve to come first. **Haesje Claes** *(Spuistraat 275/other entrance N.Z. Voorburgwal 318; open Mon.–Sat. noon–midnight (kitchen closes at 10 p.m.), Sun from 5–9:30 p.m.; 6249998; inexpensive)* offers the Dfl. 19.75 Tourist Menu in an appealing dark wood, gezellig atmosphere dating from 1520 that makes it a favorite in the neighborhood. Hearty (including Dutch pea soup, hutspot) to simple (omelets) choices. Also offering the Tourist Menu and Dutch flavor and fare is **Oud Holland** *(Nieuwe Zijds Voorburgwal 105; Mon.–Sat. from noon, lunch & dinner; 6246848; inexpensive)*. **De Roode Leeuw** hotel-restaurant *(Damrak 93; open from noon for lunch and dinner daily; 6249683; inexpensive)* offers a Dutch kitchen and a front-row view of the city from its glass-enclosed terrace. **Die Port Van Cleve** *Nieuwe Zijds Voorburgwal 178; 6240047)*, which had been serving meals for nearly a century before it added 100 hotel rooms, offers a choice of two fine Dutch restaurants. **De Poort Restaurant** *(from 11 a.m. daily, lunch and dinner; inexpensive)* is the more relaxed, with plants, stained glass, and an old tiled fireplace; a specialty is Dutch *biefstuk* (beef steak) and every one served since 1870 has been numbered: if yours ends in 00, it's free, and so's the wine. Across the hall is the **De Blauwe Parade** *(daily, lunch from noon, dinner from 6 p.m.; expensive)*, traditional with its solid old oak and leather furniture; it was a tasting room in the mid-1500s for the beer brewery that became *Heineken*, but has become even more notable, since 1886, for its wonderful Delft blue and white *De Porceleyne Fles* wall tile tableaux of children in 17th-century court dress celebrating the gathering of grapes for wine (the restaurant *does,* appropriately, have a fine wine cellar to accompany the excellent Dutch cuisine). **Hollands Glorie** *(Kerkstraat 220; daily from 5–10 p.m., closed Mon. Nov.–Mar.; 66244764; inexpensive)* is small and pleasantly cluttered with old copper and brass utensils, tiles and antiques, with candles lighted at each table. A la carte choices include mussel cocktail, smoked eel, pork cutlet, and beef steak, and there's a *prix fixe* menu. **Restaurant Bodega Keyser** *(Van Baerlestraat 96; Mon.–Sat., noon–11:30 p.m., closed Sun; 6711441; moderate)* opened in 1905 next door to the still-new **Concertgebouw** and has been inseparably associated with concertgoers ever since (so much so that its clocks are set slightly ahead so patrons won't miss the first movement of the program, and its kitchen remains open for post-concert diners). Keyser's is also convenient for patrons of the neighborhood's fashionable shops and art museums. The typical Dutch decor of the front-of-the-house cafe, with its wood furniture, carpets on the table, brass lamps, newspapers, and outside tables when the weather's warmish, is also open for morning coffee; fresh Dutch seafood, especially *Sole a la Meuniere* are specialties, also served at the clothed and candlelit tables in the rear. Last, but certainly not least in Dutch atmosphere, is **D'Vijff Vlieghan** *(Spuistraat 294; daily from 5 p.m.; 6248369; very expensive),* situated in five 17th-century canalhouses. The series of seven dining rooms, each furnished in a different Renaissance-style, creates an intimate whole, upstairs and off passageways, most cozy in candlelight. The traditional Dutch cuisine has recently improved, the result of "nouvelle" nuances.

Even more than traditional Dutch dishes, Indonesian fare seems to be the national food of Holland; most Dutch have a favorite restaurant for it, and the selections are located in various sections of the city. Waiters are usually very helpful in explaining the dishes, and many restaurants have menus translated into English. Just across the street from D'vijff Vlieghan is **Kantjil** *(Spuistraat 291; daily 11 a.m.–11 p.m.; 6200994; inexpensive),* one of Amsterdam's most recent Indonesian restaurants, with a pleasant plant-filled, airy, light wood slightly Deco decor, and tables with wicker chairs on the sidewalk terrace. A perennially popular choice is **Sama Sebo** *(P.C. Hooftstraat 27; daily lunch, dinner; 6628146; inexpensive)* very friendly, helpful service, small, authentic, and on everyone's list of one of the best Indonesian restaurants in Amsterdam. **Indonesia** *(Singel 550, at Muntplein; open daily from noon; 6232035; inexpensive)* is long-established in its upstairs high-ceilinged, gracious, almost colonial setting, staffed by helpful Indonesians. **Djawa** *(Korte Leidsedwarsstraat 18; open daily from 5 p.m.; 6246016; inexpensive)* is another tasty, traditional choice for Indonesian fare, located just off the Leidseplein. In the Jordaan neighborhood is **Speciaal** *(Nieuwe*

Leliestraat 142; 6249706), which looks far more special and intimate inside than out. This is where many Amsterdammers "in the know" go for Indonesian.

You certainly don't have to go to a seafood restaurant for fish in this sea-minded country, but it's nice to know where the Dutch choose to go—**De Oesterbar** *(Leidseplein 10; open daily from noon; 6232988; moderate).* Fish, some of the edible variety, some not, swim in tanks on the ground floor, which is more cozy and less expensive than the restaurant upstairs. **Le Pecheur** *(Reguliersdwarsstraat 32; Mon.–Fri. lunch and dinner, Sat. & Sun. dinner only, from 5 p.m.; 6243121; moderate)* has a trendy, tasteful interior, and a wonderful garden terrace with a view of townhouses for outdoor dining.

French/continental cuisine is served at some of the most highly regarded restaurants in Amsterdam. **'T Swarte Schaep** (The Black Sheep) *(Korte Leidsedwarsstraat 24; open daily from noon; 6223021; expensive).* A calm traditional Dutch backdrop for continental cuisine and singular service, its leather-chair comfort quite removed from the casual liveliness of the Leidseplein cafes it overlooks. Lunch (set menu) and dinner (kitchen open until 11 p.m., late by Dutch standards). **Le Ciel Bleu** *(Hotel Okura, Ferdinand Bolstraat 333; open from 6:30 p.m.; 6787111; expensive)* offers fine French cuisine with the most far-reaching view over Amstedam. **Ciel Bleu Bar** *(6 p.m.–1 a.m.)* is a bar atop the Okura, highest view of the night lights. Hotel de l'Europe's exclusive **Excelsior** *(Nieuwe Doelenstraat 208; daily, lunch from 12:30 p.m., dinner from 6 p.m.; 6234836; expensive)* serves a Menu de la Saison, a gourmet Alliance Menu and, since the opening of the nearby Muziektheater, a Theater Menu. For post-theater and later, less-expensive dining, the Europe's **Le Relais** is a fine choice. **De Silveren Spiegel** *(Kattengat 4; Mon.–Sat. lunch and dinner, closed Sun.; 6246589; expensive)* is situated in an enchanting 17th-century house opposite the Ramada Hotel's Koepel Cafe, whose patrons benefit from having a view of the restaurant. The decor of either dining floor does justice to the fine French food. The appealing old **Restaurant De Bols Taverne** *(Rozengracht 106; Mon.–Sat. noon to midnight; 6245752; moderate)* serves a good choice of international dishes, as well as a very broad selection of the liqueurs made by the company from which it takes its name, and other Dutch drinks.

All the world seems interested now, but Amsterdam for many years has had a great following for Japanese food. The city's best Japanese restaurant is **Yamazato** *(Hotel Okura, Ferdinand Bolstraat 333; open daily for lunch, from noon, and dinner, from 6 p.m.; 6787111; expensive),* which overlooks a miniature Japanese garden and serves a wide range of traditional Japanese dishes. The Japanese-owned Okura emits an Oriental calm that's complemented by its somewhat out-of-center canalside locale. The hotel also has the **Teppan-Yaki** steak house (lunch/dinner; expensive) and a sushi bar.

Cafes seem to sprout on Amsterdam sidewalks whenever the weather comes even close to cooperating. The word "cafe" also indicates a restaurant of a certain style, so some of the establishments listed below may focus more on food, others on setting (menus are always posted, so you'll know which is which). Its location surprises people, but the **Ie Klas Grand Cafe Restaurant** at Centraal Station *(Spoor/platform 2b; daily 9:30 a.m.–11 p.m., Sun. 10:30 a.m.; 6250131; inexpensive)*, once the First Class waiting room and now restored to past lofty-ceiling splendor, and a dark-wood cafe next door, also serves a more-than-acceptable menu, within sound of the pleasant rumble of the trains. A thoroughly European setting. Sat. 7–10 p.m. live jazz, Sun. brunch with live classical music. **De Knijp** *(Van Baerlestraat 134; daily noon–3 p.m., 5:30 p.m.–midnight; 6714248; inexpensive)*, close to the Concertgebouw and museums, is a light-hearted art deco/brown cafe combination that is a neighborhood charmer. The eclectic, cozy decor matches the menu: Zeeland oysters to sate, pate to pastries.

Het Land van Walem *(Keizersgracht 449; daily from mid-morning; 6253544; inexpensive)* is an artsy, reading-newspapers sort of coffee-house, and it sprawls along the canal at small tables when the weather warrants. There's a charming courtyard garden sometimes used for dining. The delightful dowager-Dutch **Royal Cafe De Kroon** *(Rembrandtsplein 15; daily 10 a.m.–1 a.m.; 6252011; inexpensive)* is up two flights of graceful curving 1898 steps to the huge airy rooms and glassed-in balcony overlooking the tree tops of Rembrandtsplein. For tea, sweets, or more substantial treats. The **Cafe de Jaren** *(Nieuwe Doelenstraat 20; daily 10 a.m.–1 a.m., 2 a.m. Fri., Sat.; inexpensive)*, resting between the De l'Europe and Doelen Karena hotels, has a wonderful view over the Amstel to the Musiektheater, from terrace level and upstairs. Serving soups, salads, sandwiches, and more substantial fare. Located at the edge of the colorful Jordaan neighborhood on one of the loveliest stretches of canal in the city, **De Belhamel** *(Brouwersgracht 60; daily noon–midnight, kitchen open noon–2:30 p.m., dinner 6–10 p.m.; 6221095; inexpensive)* serves as a special stop for a drink, with an intriguing intimate two-tier interior with faux marble columns and art nouveau details. Informal menus, daily specials, desserts. Two other cafes worth noting, as much for location as the edible offerings, although those are certainly worthy, are **Cafe Luxembourg,** facing squarely on the Spui, and **Brasserie De Bock,** with split views of the Spui and the Singel. For food before or after a visit to the Rijksmuseum, or an antique expedition in the shops of the Nieuwe Spiegelstraat, stop at the Cafe **Hans en Grietje** *(Spiegelgracht 27; lunch 11:30 a.m.–5:30 p.m., open til 1 a.m. for light fare; 6246782; inexpensive)*. The cheerful canalside cafe, which serves sate, omelets, uitsmijters, and hamburgers, has a wonderful view of the Rijksmuseum.

For platter-size Dutch pancakes, savory or sweet, head for either **The Pancake Bakery** *(Prinsengracht 191; daily noon–9:30 p.m.; 6251333)* in the roomy beamed and bricked basement of an old canalside warehouse, or tiny, four-tabled **Upstairs** *(Grimburgwal 2; Tues.–Sun. 9 a.m.–7 p.m., closed Mon.; 6265603)* up two ship-steep flights. For tasty, quick *broodjes* (sandwiches), follow in the tracks of Amsterdammers to **Eetsalon van Dobben** *(Korte Reguliersdwarsstraat 5; daily, from 9:30 a.m., 11:30 Sun.; 6244200)*, near the Rembrandtplein, or one of **Broodje van Kootje's** two locations: Leidseplein 20 and Spui 28, open daily 9:30 a.m. until late.

Although you'll seek them out more for their atmospheric flavor and drinks than for food, most of Amsterdam's famous "brown cafes" (or *bruine kroeg*) do serve snacks. The name brown cafe comes from the tobacco-stained walls and ceilings, cozy carpeted tables, and perhaps sawdust on the floor, and the "gezellig" ambiance of it all. You'll probably find them to be a cross between an English pub, a French cafe, and an American bar, and although the atmosphere of many may feel like the home of loosely knit family, the ranks are usually open to strangers, and of course everyone will be able to hold an avid conversation in English. Although visitors will find their own favorites, the following are certainly among the most interesting. It is said that a coffin-maker around 1600, selling drinks to earn a little extra money, marked the beginings of **Papeneiland** *(Prinsengracht 2; 11 a.m.–1 a.m.; 6241989)*. The Prinsengracht is home to several other brown cafes: **De Eland** *(#296; noon–1 a.m.)* and **Van Puffelen** *(#377; 11 a.m.–1 a.m.)*, but **Pieper** *(#424; 10:30 a.m.–1 a.m.; 6264775)* is one of the most famous. **Frascati** *(Nes 59; 10 a.m.–1 a.m.; 6241324)*, near Dam Square, is fashionable, and particularly comfortable for women to visit. And **Hoppe** *(Spui 18; 8 a.m.–1 a.m.; 6240756)* has a split personality; **Hoppe zit,** the saloon-like seated section of the 1670 establishment, located on the left-hand side, and, on the right, **Hoppe staan,** a standing bar, with sawdust on the floor inside, and a rack for drinks outside in season. Also in the Jordaan is **Cafe Nol** *(Westerstraat 109; open 8 p.m.–2 a.m.; 6245380)*, a splendidly decorated cafe, where, especially on Friday and Saturday nights, amazing scenes occur. Those who like *kitsch* should not miss Cafe Nol.

ENTERTAINMENT AND EVENTS..

English-speaking tourists can avail themselves (at the VVV, Dfl. 2.50) of the bi-monthly magazine *What's On in Amsterdam* or *Amsterdam This Week,* for daily calendars of entertainment events, as well as listings of museums, galleries, rental car agencies, etc. The **Amsterdams Uit Buro (AUB)** on the Leidseplein and the **VVV's Theaterbespreekbureau,** Stationsplein, open Mon.–Sat. 10 a.m.–4 p.m., will book seats in advance for most concert, opera, ballet, and theater performances (in person sales only).

Concertgebouw *(Van Baerlestraat 98; Box Office 6718345; trams 2, 5 from CS).* Recently renovated in honor of its centennial, the Concertgebouw, celebrated worldwide for its acoustics, is home to Amsterdam's renowned **Concertgebouworkest** (Conductor Riccardo Chailly). Concerts by it and visiting companies and performers regularly sell out; contact or visit the Box Office to see what's available. Chamber music is presented in the Kleine Zaal. From Sept. to June, there are free Wed. lunchtime concerts (12:30–1:15 p.m.); varied programs from full symphony to duets.

Beurs de Berlage *(Damrak 62A; 6265257)* is the architecturally intriguing home (English tours on request at 6258908) of the 140-musician **Netherlands Philharmonic Orchestra.** The Netherlands Chamber Orchestra and other guest artists perform in the new "glass box" Aga Zaal there. **Muziektheater** *(Waterlooplein 22; 6255455)* This white-marble-and-glass rounded building at a curve on the Amstel in the heart of the city is Amsterdam's latest cultural landmark. The amazingly intimate, 1600 red-plush seat Musiektheater is the home for the **Netherlands Opera Company** (Director Pierre Audi) and the **Dutch National Ballet** (both of which create whole new productions each year for the June-long Holland Festival. Some tickets for every performance are reserved for same-day sale at the Musiektheater Box Office. Schedules for the **Holland Festival,** whose varied cultural programs are focused in Amsterdam, are available in advance from Netherlands Board of Tourism offices.

Year-round at the Amsterdam Sonesta Hotel's **Round Lutheran Kerk Koepelzaal** are 11 a.m. Sunday morning concerts. Very popular with the Dutch, they are always well-attended, and a *kopje koffie* (cup of coffee) beforehand is included in the Dfl. 6 price. The great domed 1668 church, long a landmark in the neighborhood, was restored in the 1970s by the National Monuments Committee and the Ramada Hotel. The Ramada and the church, which also serves as the hotel's handsome conference center, are connected by underground passage.

During July and August, **organ concerts** (Amsterdam has 42 historic church organs) are given in the following churches: Oude Kerk; Nieuwe Kerk (Dam); Engelse Kerk (Beguinhof); Oude Lutherse Kerk (Spui, part of University of Amsterdam); Westerkerk; and Sint Nicolaaskerk. Consult the VVV or events calendar listings for details.

IN THE AREA.....................................

Several tour operators (their offices are congregated along the Damrak, opposite the Beurs van Berlage) offer half and whole-day motorcoach excursions to various places in the area. Look carefully at the respective brochures or itineraries and ask questions as to how much time you will actually have at the sights you most want to see. It is possible to get to the major places on your own on public transportation, so consider this alternative. Alkmaar (see below), although an architecturally appealing old town, most warrants a visit on Friday mornings (May–Sept.) for its colorful (usually crowded) cheese market activities, and is accessible by train. On many commercial tours from Amsterdam are the former fishing towns of Volendam and Marken. I cannot recommend them (*especially* Volendam) since they exist almost exclusively to fulfill tourists' desires (lots of locals in traditional costumes worn just for you, and you can even wear one and have *your* picture taken in it, wooden shoe factories, and other gimmicky offerings). It's all a pretty successful show (one I'll cover briefly in the chapter on Old Zuiderzee Villages), but there's far more authenticity of atmosphere elsewhere.

Bloemenveiling Aalsmeer (Aalsmeer Flower Auction) • *Aalsmeer, Legmeerdijk 313; (02977) 34567; open Mon.–Fri. 7:30–11 a.m., closed Sat., Sun., hols.; fee)* • Catch Aalsmeer bus from near front of Amsterdam CS, beginning at 6 a.m.; there is a short bus transfer in Aalsmeer to the flower auction (ask driver for details). Buy a return (round trip) bus ticket for best buy. Allow 1 to 1 1/2 hours to get there. Never have tourism and commerce combined for more beauty. The Aalsmeer complex, located a few miles south of Amsterdam, covers 47 acres (so big that some workers "commute" within it on bikes). A special visitors' gallery has been erected, from which visitors can watch the colorful auction spectacle (from 8–9 a.m. is the best); there are multi-lingual information signs, push-button commentary around the route, and an explanatory brochure to help you understand the unique auction process is given out on arrival. Trains of carts with bundles of cut flowers wind through the building on computerized rails, each variety in its own area. The whole process proves it's possible to put a pretty face on business (see *The Bulb Field Business* chapter).

Zaanse Schans • *(Zaanse; site open at all times, special attractions open daily April 1–Nov. 1; rest of year weekends only; (075) 162221; no fee)* • Located nine miles (15 km.) northwest of Amsterdam near Zaandam, Zaanse Schans (established as a museum village in 1960) is a picturesque and pleasant 17th-century Dutch six-windmill country village on the river Zaan, a truly "living" museum since its houses have inhabitants. Characteristic of the community, which faithfully mirrors the one in Zaan c. 1700, are the tidy green-with-white-trim wooden houses. Among the points of interest to be visited are a cheese farm, a wooden-shoe workshop, an old grocery store, a clock museum, a tin artisan, two windmills, and an antique shop. There are boat excursions on the river. There is a Dutch pancake house, **De Kraai** *(daily 9 a.m.–6 p.m. Feb.–Sept., 10 a.m.–5 p.m. Oct.–Nov., closed Mon. in Nov.)*, on the premises, as well as the restaurant **De Hoop op d'Swarte Walvis** *(Mon.–Sat. lunch noon–2:30 p.m., dinner 6–10 p.m., closed Sun.; (075) 165629; expensive)* with a well-respected kitchen and atmospheric antique interior, with terrace dining in good weather. From Amsterdam CS, it's a 15-minute train ride to Station Koog-Zaandijk (in the direction of Alkmaar), from which it's about a ten-minute walk to Zaanse Schans. Half-day coach excursions to Zaanse Schans are available from Amsterdam.

If you are traveling by car in the area, some of the lovely waterland villages to include are Westzaan, De Rijp, Wormer, and Jisp. In Zaandam, now quite urbanized, is the Czar Peter cottage, lived in by Peter the Great in 1697, when he came to Holland to learn ship building. He created such a stir in the then small town that he had to remove himself to Amsterdam, where he could remain relatively anonymous as he learned the trade.

Alkmaar Cheese Market • *Waagplein (Weigh House Square); Fri. mid-April–mid-Sept. 10 a.m.–noon; approximately 1/2 hour by train from Amsterdam CS, more than 1/2 mile from Alkmaar station to town center* • The attractive old town of Alkmaar, which received its charter in 1254, was frequently caught in the crossfire of struggles involving the Dutch provinces of Holland, Friesland, and Gelder. But Alkmaar is still proud of its citizens' successful stand against the Spanish seige in 1573. The moated and canaled sections of "inner" Alkmaar, within the old grassy green ramparts, retain much of the look they would have had then. While it's probably not the place for an overnight stay, Alkmaar is much more than its Cheese Market; however, since many of the town's other attractions open to coincide with the market, Friday mornings are the recommended time for a visit.

The Cheese Market usually attracts large crowds around the Waagplein to watch the colorful carryings-on. Plan to arrive enough in advance to get the good tourist information in English (walking town tour brochures, background on cheese market tradition and procedure, map) available from the VVV, located in the **Waaggebouw** (weigh house), which also houses a **cheese museum** *(April 1–Oct. 31, Mon.–Sat. 10 a.m.–4 p.m.)*. Cheese begins arriving at the market after 7 a.m., and the market-manager allocates certain sections of the square to various sellers. The four companies of porters, in white costumes and lacquered straw hats in red, green, blue, or yellow according to their company, are members of the Cheese-Carriers' Guild, which dates back to the early 17th century, although cheese was being weighed in Alkmaar as early as 1365. The market undoubtedly is continued in its present form largely for tourists, but the business conducted is serious nonetheless. After inspection and weighing, the lots of cheese (primarily the cannon-ball-shaped Edamms, here in their natural wax covering, not wrapped in red cellophane for export) are carried off on wide wooden barrows to the buyers' warehouses. Payment is likely to take place over coffee, or something stronger, in the cafes around the square.

The Waaggebouw dates back to 1341, and served both as a chapel and hostel for needy wayfarers. In 1581, Prince Willem the Silent of Orange restored to the town so-called weighing-rights (in part to reward the town for its brave stand against the Spanish in the 1573 seige); the need for more marketspace caused the chapel (which probably had been turned over to the town when the Protestant Dutch Reform Church became the declared religion in 1578) to be rebuilt as the still active weigh house. The 1599 tower has a **carillon** *(concerts on Fri. 11 a.m.–noon during cheese market season, year-round Sat., market day, noon–1 p.m.)*. The tower clock has a pair of jousting knights who charge each other on the hour chime. Plan to stay and wander awhile in town after the cheese market: Enjoy the early 16th-century double-stairway Stadhuis, the Vismarkt (fish market), the picturesque old facades along the Oude Gracht, the small narrow streets, canal bridges, and hofjes. The gothic Grote Kerk (St. Laurens) 1470–1520, which contains the tomb of Count Floris V (died 1296), is noted for its small organ (1511), one of the oldest in regular use, and the 1643 organ designed by Jacob van Campen.

Accommodations/Restaurants in the Area

★★★★ **Chateau Marquette** • *Marquettelaan 34, 1968 JT, Heemskerk; 02510–41414, fax 02510–45508; first class* • Located between Alkmaar and Zaanse Schans is a gracious country castle restaurant-hotel. Chateau Marquette's 68 tasteful contemporary guest rooms, all with spacious modern bath and full amenities, were added in a separate building from the castle. Bicycles available for guests; sand dune trails only 1.5 miles away. The a la carte restaurant, open daily from 6 p.m., Sunday brunch from 11:30 a.m., is located in the moated castle, whose dining rooms and salons have superb architectural details and antique furniture. The kitchen prepares continental cuisine, and offers several menus.

HAARLEM

Guidelines for Haarlem

SIGHTS The **Frans Hals Museum** and, on Haarlem's gargantuan Grote Markt, **St. Bavokerk** (1400–1550) with its famed organ, are the city's stellar stops. Throughout the appealing city, fine architecture from the 17th and earlier centuries, both on grand and smaller scales, is in evidence.

GETTING AROUND Once you get to the **Grote Markt** (a 15-minute walk from the train station), the heart of Haarlem, prime sights are located pretty compactly, the Frans Hals Museum being the farthest point, about a 10-minute walk. Several bus routes from the station stop near the Grote Markt, and there are taxis at the station.

SHOPPING Old print, antique, and other shops are located around St. Bavo's church along the Oude Groenmarkt, and in the streets that radiate out from the Grote Markt. There are shops at the Frans Hals Museum and at St. Bavo's church. During the growing season, there's a Saturday flower market on the Oude Groenmarkt.

ACCOMMODATIONS Hotels in the town are limited, but there's a choice of two comfortable properties with fairly convenient city locations.

RESTAURANTS The variety of settings and types of food available will match travelers' taste, time, and pocketbook preferences.

ENTERTAINMENT AND EVENTS With Keukenhof gardens and the bulb fields nearby, the spring season (Apr. 1–end May) is easily the area's busiest. There are weekly evening concerts on the **St. Bavokerk Christian Muller organ** mid May–mid-Oct., with an additional afternoon concert a week in July and Aug. (see *St. Bavo's, What to See and Do*). Concerts by participants in Haarlem's biennial (1994, 1996, etc.)

International Organ Improvisation Competition are played nearly daily in July on the St. Bavo's organ. Concerts on the third Suns. of the months Sept.–May and on occasional candlelight evenings are given at the Frans Hals Museum (call for specifics and reservations). In early June (check with VVV for date), Haarlem holds its annual **Luilak,** an all-night giant flower and plant sale on the Grote Markt (4 p.m.–8 a.m.).

ARRIVING Haarlem is on the main Amsterdam-Rotterdam rail line, some 15 minutes from Amsterdam by frequent service; its 1908 station is a monument building. There are good road and motorway connections.

IN THE AREA Several intriguing attractions are located close to Haarlem: to the south are the **bulb fields** and **Keukenhof** garden, **Zandvoort,** a favorite North Sea resort, and **Cruquius,** an old steam water pumping station, with a museum that shows how the Haarlemmermeer was drained. To the north, pretty **Spaarndam** village has a statue that illustrates the story of the boy with his finger plugging a dike. The busy trio of locks at **IJmuiden** sends ships up the *Noordzee Kanaal* to Amsterdam. West of Haarlem are bicycle paths through the dunes at the **National Park de Kennemerduinen,** and footpaths (only) in the dunes of **Amsterdamse Waterleiding** reservoir south of Zandvoort.

TRAVEL TIPS It's not necessary to overnight in Haarlem to attend an evening organ concert at St. Bavo's; regularly scheduled evening trains until nearly midnight provide plenty of time to return to Amsterdam, Rotterdam, or points in between. The Frans Hals Museum, unlike many in Holland, is open Mondays.

Haarlem in Context

By the 10th century, Haarlem had become a township on the Spaarne River, on which the Counts of Holland levied tolls. The Counts' early fortification here is recalled in the name **Gravenstenenbrug** (Counts' fortress bridge) that spans the Spaarne today. By the 13th century, the town had acquired considerable status, as reflected in its coat of arms: a silver sword among four stars, crowned by a cross. The crown and sword had been presented to Haarlem by German Emperor Frederick II as reward for the city's help in occupying Damiata in 1219 during the Second Crusade. The "Damiaatjes," a set of chimes in St. Bavo's belfry, are a further recognition.

In 1245, Count Willem II presented Haarlem with a city charter, from the precincts of his hunting lodge on the 't Zand (now the Grote Markt), where jousting tournaments were held. The site of the lodge, destroyed by city fires in 1347 and 1351, was given to the town, which built a Stadhuis (town hall) there by the end of the 14th century. From the 15th through the early 17th century, there were many alterations and additions to the Stadhuis; City Architect Lieven de Key designed the wing along Zijlstraat in 1620–22, and drew up plans for the last major rebuilding (1633), which gave the facade the Italian Renaissance elements it still retains. Haarlem's couples today have their civil marriages in the medieval Knights' Hall (Gravenzaal), which, when ceremonies aren't on the calendar, visitors can view (facing the Stadhuis, its entrance is around the corner to the left). Behind the Stadhuis is a monastery, destroyed by the 14th-century city fires, now somewhat restored. The name Prinsenhof refers to a residence built on the site in 1590 by the Prince of Orange after the church had been plundered and damaged beyond repair in 1578 in Reformation tumult.

A significant piece of Haarlem's 15th-century history is kept alive by a statue on the Grote Markt near St. Bavo's of **Lourens Coster** (1370–1440), a native with a well-substantiated claim (1423) to being at least a co-inventor (with Germany's Gutenberg) of the art of printing with moveable type. Coster is buried in St. Bavo's, the exact location unknown. Holland's first newspapers were published in Haarlem and, more than 550 years after Coster's typesetting here, Haarlem remains a printing center, full of book publishers, editors, and newspapers. Also calling Haarlem home is the firm Enschede, which prints postage stamps and paper currency, not just for Holland, but for other governments, too. (In case you hadn't noticed, Frans Hals' portrait appears on the Dutch blue 10-guilder note).

As with the rest of Holland, 16th-century Haarlem was keenly affected by the northern Netherlands revolt against Spain, known as the Eighty Years' War. In 1572, with a population of 20,000, Haarlem was larger and more important than Amsterdam (not until the 17th century did Amsterdam eclipse Haarlem), and thus served as a symbol of resistance for the Dutch. In December 1572, Haarlem was beseiged by Spanish troops, under Frederick of Toledo, son of the dread Duke of Alva. For awhile, the Haarlemmers held out, managing to ice skate in and out of town on canals and rivers to acquire supplies. The Spanish were ordered to wear iron cleats to be able to pursue, but that proved unsuccessful. However, spring came and, with the canals and river melted, the Spanish gradually gained the upper hand. The Spanish Navy stationed in the Haarlemmermeer to the north of the town effectively blocked the town's only outside line of supply. Subsequent attempts by Willem the Silent to provide relief, and heroic efforts by the Haarlem women under the leadership of Kenau Simons Hasselaer, proved unsuccessful, and citizens were forced to capitulate in July 1573. They agreed to surrender on condition that a general amnesty be granted if 57 of the town's leaders were handed over. The terms were accepted, but several days later the Spanish wrought wholesale massacre in Haarlem, killing some 1800 of the Holland garrison stationed there, all the Calvinist leaders, and many more. Several months later, Haarlem citizens at least had the satisfaction of knowing they had made victory costly for the Spanish. Unable to equip their forces adequately after the expenditures at Haarlem, the Spanish, in their subsequent attempt to subdue the nearby town of Alkmaar by seige, failed, marking the beginning of a downward turn in the Spanish domination of Holland.

Haarlem had more to suffer that drastic decade. In 1576, still under Spanish rule (Haarlem was occupied for five years following the seige), fire destroyed large parts of the town. Shortly after the Spanish vacated Haarlem in 1578, Dutch Protestant purges in the town succeeded in destroying the treasures in churches and religious houses that had survived the flames. St. Bavo's church, which had escaped the fire, passed into Protestant hands.

But the Reformation also produced positive results for Haarlem. After the Spanish conquest of Antwerp in the South Netherlands in 1585, many Flemish and Wallonian Protestant refugees fled north. The specialized skills and capital of the many Flemings who settled in Haarlem significantly affected Holland's social, cultural, and economic development, helping pave the way for the soon-to-appear "Golden Age."

In the 17th century, Haarlem occupied a fairly small, narrow strip of land, bordered on the west by a row of dunes that separated the town from the North Sea, and on the east by the large Haarlemmermeer lake, drained in the 19th century (see *Cruquius, In The Area*). The river Spaarne, which flows through the town south to north, passes through the east side of Haarlem. Boatyards, breweries, and numerous windmills that served as sawmills and in the baking, brewing, tannery, and cloth trades, lined its banks. Due to the generally poor road conditions, transport then was mainly by water, and the Spaarne formed a vital link between towns in the northern and southern regions of the Holland province. A canal to Amsterdam was dug in 1632, and one to Leiden in 1656. The canals linked up with others, forming an extensive waterway network. The waterways were bordered by bridlepaths along which horses roped to barges towed them. Hourly boats between Haarlem to Amsterdam ran on Europe's earliest published transportation schedules.

The clean dune water between Haarlem and the North Sea was partly responsible for the success of two of the city's major early industries. Water sources were important in the production of beer, and in 1628 the number of breweries in Haarlem had reached 50 (and would reach 150, though none remain today). The quantity of beer consumption was high (and alcoholic content low) in this period, not only in Haarlem, but elsewhere in Holland, because the quality of most drinking water was poor.

A second significant industry was linen. Haarlem damask graced tables in several European courts, where its sheen, patterns, and whiteness were much admired. The latter quality was the result of lengthy bleaching in the grasslands outside Haarlem, where the linen, after many rinsings in the river Spaarne, was spread out to bleach in the clear coastal light. Town linen-makers eventually polluted the river, which ruined the quality of Haarlem beer, causing brewers to begin using the clean, naturally sand-filtered dune water on the other side of town.

The same coastal light that so successfully bleached Haarlem's linen attracted artists, and in the 17th century, a specialty of the Haarlem School was landscapes. But the town's major art figure concentrated on portraits. Frans Hals, who had been born in Antwerp about 1580, and come north as had many other Flemish to find freedom from the Spanish, spent the rest of his long life working in Haarlem.

Possibly because so little is known about Frans Hals (*much less* than has actually been written about him), even late 17th-century biographers were highly imaginative in reconstructing his life. The myths that have been perpetuated are exceedingly hard to correct with fact. One glaring inaccuracy is that Hals as an old man lived in the *Oudemannenhuis* (old men's almshouse), whose Governors' group portraits he painted. It may make a good story but it's untrue. Hals never lived at the almshouse; the rented house in which he lived at the time of his death (1666) was in Ridderstraat (off Kruis Straat). In an historical irony, the Oudemannenhuis today is the Frans Hals Museum.

Also coming to Haarlem from Flanders was Ghent-born architect **Lieven de Key** (c. 1560–1627), who by 1593 had been appointed city stonemason and bricklayer. Probably well before he oversaw the construction of the Oudemannenhuis in 1608, he had been elevated to Haarlem's City Architect. His **Vleeshal** (Meat Hall), built on the Grote Markt in 1602/03, is one of the outstanding works of the Dutch Renaissance style. Built in brick with gray stone decorative detail, the Vleeshal has a strong horizontal element in its facade design, which keeps it down to earth, in contrast to its Grote Markt neighbor, the Gothic Grote Kerk, that reaches for heaven. With the arrival of Lieven de Key, South Netherlands Renaissance architecture was introduced to Haarlem. His buildings, and those built under his supervision, show many elements typical of the Flemish style: porches, prominent towers, balconies, balustrades, projecting sandstone cornerstones on facades, gable recesses, and scroll and iron mounting work. These ingredients are found in many buildings on, and in the vicinity of, the Grote Markt, as well as in the Bakensserkerk, the Nieuwekerk, and De Waag (weigh house). The Grote Markt itself is the only such "southern Netherlands-style" square north of Holland's major rivers, thus confirming Haarlem as the most Flemish-appearing city in the "northern Netherlands."

On the St. Bavo side of the Vleeshal, note the ornamental steer and rams heads, sculpted in expensive imported Belgium stone (Holland has no stone quarries), to show what business was conducted within.

Today, the restored Vleeshal is a part of the Frans Hals Museum and used for special exhibits and lectures. This is also true for the Vishal (1768), which abuts St. Bavo's.

Nieuwe Gracht was dug in the 17th century to give Haarlem the substantial enlargement of city limits it needed. With its expanding population in the 17th century, Haarlem's churches were no longer capable of caring for the increasing number of needy: the Golden Age meant prosperity for Holland overall, but its benefits didn't necessarily trickle down to all people. Haarlem's prosperous private citizens without children, sensitive to the plight of the poor, often provided material assistance in the form of hofjes, modest individual almshouses around a central courtyard. Twenty hofjes existed in the city by the end of the 17th-century, and 18 remain to be seen by visitors today.

One of Haarlem's most unusual is the 18th-century (1768) **Hofje van Oorschot,** with the usual family coat of arms over the door of the main building that housed the Governors' Room. Unlike most hofjes that are sheltered from the street behind an enclosing courtyard wall, however, Oorschot is on view from the street (Kruis Straat) through a tall open iron railing. This was the result of objections from rich merchants living across the street, who didn't want to look out on a bare brick wall along the sidewalk; architectural arrangements were duly made for the hofje and its garden to be open on three sides to the street.

Haarlem, in the 19th and 20th centuries, has quietly prospered, growing in population to 150,000, content in its role as provincial capital of Noord Holland.

GUIDEPOSTS
Telephone Code 023

Tourist Info.	VVV, Stationsplein 1; 319059
Parking	Limited meter parking at the station by the VVV; inquire there about car parks near the sights you plan to visit.
Trains	Schedules and information in the station.
Buses	Local buses 1, 2, and 3 stop at Grote Markt.
NZH Buses	Bus stop for most routes (including bulb fields, Keukenhof garden, Zandvoort beaches) is in front of train station.
Bike rental	At train station.
Taxis	Available in front of station.

WHAT TO SEE AND DO.....................

If ever a small city brought body and soul together in a single place, Haarlem does at the Grote Markt. Expansive is hardly a sufficient word for the enormous brick paved main square, around the reaches of which are some of the town's most memorable buildings, including the soaring gothic Grote Kerk (St. Bavo's), which manages to be big enough not to be swallowed up by the size of its setting. The Haarlem we enjoy today is a proud product of Holland's 17th-century Golden Age, when only Amsterdam competed with it as an art center, and when it was able to enjoy the talents not only of its native citizens, but also those of the Flemish who emigrated here.

Frans Hals Museum • *Groot Heiligland 62; open Mon.–Sat. 11 a.m.–5 p.m., Sun., hols. 1–5 p.m.; closed Christmas; 319180, fee* • The *Oudemennenhuis* (old men's house), built in 1608 under the supervision of municipal architect Lieven de Key from the proceeds of a public lottery held in Haarlem in 1606, served as an almshouse for 200 years, and then as an orphanage for another 100, until opening as a museum in 1913, restored to its 17th-century architectural authenticity. Of particular note is the magnificent Renaissance-style corridor, whose squared black and white marble floors, edged with blue and white tiles, seem to recreate one of the delicate Dutch interiors painted by Vermeer of Delft. The reconstruction of the 17th-century garden accentuates the harmony of the whole museum, a fortunate combination of the skill of an architect and the genius of a painter from the same period.

The greater part of the life work of Frans Hals has, alas, been scattered around the world. Nevertheless, particularly in group portraiture, considered one of the crowning accomplishments of the Dutch school of painting, Hals is well-represented here. There is a series of five Civic Guard group portraits, most notably the *Banquet of the Officers of the Civic Guard of St. Adrian* (1633), a striking contrast to the group portraits of the *Governors of St. Elizabeth Gasthuis* (1641), and the well-known governors and governesses of the Oudemannenhuis (the museum when it was an almshouse), both painted in 1664, when Hals was older than 80. These important works show the bold, fluent brushstrokes which gave Hals' portraits (Hals captured all segments of Haarlem society from prosperous merchants and military officers to fisherboys and pub crawlers), in particular, such a feeling of the moment. French Impressionists Manet and Monet made special journeys to Haarlem to see these paintings. And Vincent van Gogh, obviously influenced by Hals' remarkable rapid and free brushstroke style, wrote: "What a joy it is to see a Frans Hals, how very different from paintings in which everything is carefully and uniformly smooth."

Hals is the centerpiece of the museum, but many other outstanding Dutch painters and styles (landscape, seascape, still life, everyday life scenes, church interiors) are on view. Since Haarlem is so close to the bulb-growing district, in one area of the museum, paintings, drawings, and tiles have been assembled and designated the **tulip route** (with English brochure) to show the enthusiasm (and madness) that the flower has caused (see *Tulipmania* in chapter *The Bulb Field Business*). And there's a *Doll House* (never meant to be used by children) dating from 1750, filled with over 3000 tiny decorative and artistic treasures.

St. Bavo's or **Grote Kerk** • *Entrance on Oude Groenmarkt 23; Mon.–Sat. 10 a.m.–4 p.m.; 324399* • Built between 1390 and 1520 (the date on the face of its tower clock), Haarlem's Gothic Grote Kerk is one of the largest in Holland. Construction of the church was not constant; work often had to be suspended due to lack of funds. Considering the number of individuals who orchestrated the work, St. Bavo's shows a remarkable harmony. A stone lantern tower designed by Keldermans was built in 1506, but had to be pulled down in 1514 because it was judged to be too heavy. In 1518 a new tiered tower was erected, constructed of wood and covered in lead. The most recent major restoration of the church was completed in 1985.

Approaching the entrance (#23) on Oude Groenmarkt (old vegetable market), one sees centuries-old small shuttered shops snuggled into the sides of St. Bavo; with pure Dutch practicality, the shutters open from top to bottom to form a shelf upon which to display wares. The church is entered through a narrow passage beautifully adorned with old blue and white tiles. For centuries after it was built, the church was always open, used by Haarlemmers as a passage from one part of the city to another. Such unhindered entrance was the reason for Dog Whippers (who have a chapel in the church), whose job it was to remove troublesome dogs from the premises. The town brewers also had a chapel.

Among other church aspects of interest are the *Graf van Frans Hals* (the artist's grave), on view through the choir screen, a masterpiece of medieval craftsmanship made in 1517 by Jan Fyerens, a brass founder from Mechelen (Belgium). When candles are mounted in the screen and lit, it resembles the *Burning Bush*. The tomb of the well-known painter of Holland's hulking Protestant church interiors, **Pieter Saenredam,** is elsewhere in the church. Sticking half-way into one church wall is a cannon ball, left as a reminder of the Spanish seige in 1572–73. The carved oak pulpit, always center stage in Dutch Protestant churches, dates from 1679; its brass hand rails are in the shape of snakes slithering down, meant to represent Satan fleeing from the Gospel.

It's hard to turn away from the 5068-pipe Christian Muller 1748 organ, considered one of the most important instruments in the world, and certainly one of the most beautiful, in its towering (almost 100 ft. high), sculpted case. Handel played the organ on two visits, prior to Mozart's in 1766 at the age of 10; Dr. Albert Schweitzer, a fine organist, sat at the console, too. When the organ was installed, the huge stained-glass window that had decorated the wall had to be bricked over (observable from the exterior, by the Vleeshal). There are guided tours of the church May–Sept. Sat. 11 a.m. and 2 p.m. Free one-hour organ concerts are offered Tues. nights 8:15 p.m. mid-May–mid-Sept., and Thurs. 3 p.m. in July and Aug. (please confirm).

Teylers Museum • *Spaarne 16, open Tues.–Sat. 10 a.m.–5 p.m., Sun. 1–5 p.m., closed Mon.; 319010, fee* • This is Holland's oldest museum, with a musty, archives-like 18th-century atmosphere to support the fact. It was founded in 1778 by a wealthy silk merchant who had no family to inherit his eclectic arts and sciences collection. The original five directors left the accumulated results of their hobbies and individual interests to the museum, and Teylers left enough money in his will so that future directors could keep on acquiring assorted stuff. Teylers is quite famous for its fossils, and plays tribute to the Age of Enlightenment (in which Teylers lived) with its physics exhibits (limited English explanation on scientific exhibits). But perhaps of most interest is its exceptional selection of master drawings by Michelangelo, Raphael, Rembrandt, Jacob van Ruysdael, Correggio, Claude Lorrain, and paintings of The Hague School. The Oval Room, where minerals are displayed, is of visual interest, and the entire museum is, according with Teylers' wishes, lit only with natural light.

Corrie ten Boom Huis • *Barteljorisstraat 19 (Ten Boom Clock and Watch Shop); Mon.–Sat. 10 a.m.–4:30 p.m. Nov. 1–Apr. 1 11 a.m.–3:30 p.m., closed Sun. and hols.; 310823.* • This is a different edition of Anne Frank's secret annex living space in Amsterdam during the World War II Nazis occupation of Holland. In the ten Boom home, above the ground floor family watch repair shop, Corrie ten Boom, then in her 50s, served as the leader of a Dutch resistance group of 80 people, and offered a "safe" house to fugitives, Jews, and other people hunted by the Nazis, smuggling them on to other havens, through an underground network that saved many lives. Eventually the ten Boom family of Haarlem was betrayed, with the Gestapo raiding the house and arresting six family members, three of whom died as prisoners. Corrie survived Ravensbruck concentration camp and, for the rest of her life, traveled the world with her "calling," testifying of God's love. She died in 1983 at the age of 91.

The house, a typical Dutch town dwelling, has been left as it was for much of Corrie's life. The carefully created hiding places are preserved, and the whole story is told in Corrie's book *The Hiding Place* (see *Bibliography*). There's no fee for the 45-minute guided tours (a clock sign on the watch shop door tells the time of the next one), though at the end you get a bit of proselytizing, and a donation toward the spiritual ten Boom Foundation is welcomed.

ACCOMMODATIONS..........................

First Class
★★★★ **Carlton Square** • *Baan 7, 2012 DB; 319091, fax 329853, U.S. Sales Office 800–223–9815* • Haarlem's newest, largest (97 rooms), and most luxurious hotel is located out of the center, facing a park but within fairly reasonable walking distance of the Grote Markt. The restaurant **Cafe de la Paix** is a la carte, and the **Whiskey Bar** has a British ambiance.

Moderate
★★★★ **Golden Tulip Lion D'Or** • *Kruisweg 34, 2011 LC; 321750, fax 329543, U.S. sales office 800–333–1212* • This long-established hotel is located close to the railway station and across from the bus terminal (front rooms will get noise). Rooms are more or less similar in layout, but make sure you ask for a modernized one with lighter, brighter colors and decor. Lobby lounge has Scandinavian-style modern furniture, perfectly cheerful though not luxurious.

Inexpensive
★★ **Carillon** • *Grote Markt 10, 2011 RC; 310591, fax 314909* • This small (37 beds) very modest hotel, with its location right on the Grote Markt, gives a warning with its name. If you're noise sensitive, remember that the memorable location comes with striking bells from the carillon of St. Bavo's, every quarter hour, all night long.

RESTAURANTS................................

Sooner or later you'll be on Haarlem's Grote Markt wanting "a little something," and the **Cafe Restaurant Brinkmann** *(Grote Markt; open daily 9 a.m.–midnight, kitchen closes at 11 p.m.; inexpensive)* could hit the spot. A Delft tile tableau, mounted to mark the cafe's 50th anniversary in 1929, decorates the entryway to the art nouveau/continental-style place, with lighted candles at the table even at lunch, stained glass, plants. If you take a window seat, while you partake of something off the varied menu of sandwiches, uitsmijters, pizza or pasta, burgers or steak with salad, quiche, or just coffee and pastry, you can enjoy a great view of the Grote Markt out the grote windows. Just a few doors away is **Cafe Mephisto** *(Grote Markt 29; daily noon–9 p.m., Mon. only noon–3 p.m.; inexpensive)*, a trendy, pleasant place with art-nouveau details such as a stained-glass ceiling, mirrors, lamps, dark wood, and fresh flowers. Omelettes, uitsmijters, and other tasty light meal fare.

If you're coming from the train, you won't even have to wait for the Grote Markt, since you'll pass several good choices along the route. Closest to the station is what a Dutch friend described as one of the best Indonesian restaurants in Holland, **Mooi Java** *(Kruisweg 32; open daily 5:30–10 p.m.; 323121; inexpensive)*. It has a low-key authentic Indonesian atmosphere, with batik tablecloths and cane chairs. Continuing straight, Kruisweg becomes Kruis Straat before becoming pedestrianized as Barteljorisstraat, which runs into the Grote Markt. **Cafe 1900** *(Barteljorisstraat 10, open Mon.–Sat. 10 a.m.–mid., Sun. 5 p.m.–midnight; 318183; inexpensive)* is a trendy, but basic, art deco delight, a copy of a Parisian cafe, with dark wood detail, little marble tables and straight wooden cafe chairs, and interesting lighting fixtures. Good choice for informal fare from coffee to uitsmijters. Walk a few doors down to satisfy your sweet tooth at **Tearoom H. Ferd. Knipers** *(Barteljorisstraat 22; open Mon.–Sat. 9 a.m.–5:30 p.m., closed Sun.)*. As Haarlem's best pastry shop, it's where Dutch women "of a certain age" share a pick-me-up pause while shopping.

For a proper sitdown meal—for which you'll want to allow time—on the Frans Hals Museum side of the Grote Markt is **Restaurant Peter Cuyper** *(Kleine Houtstraat 70; open Mon.–Sat. noon–3 p.m. and 6–10 p.m., closed Sun., last week Dec., and first 3 weeks Aug; 320885; moderate)*, situated in restored 16th century townhouse with courtyard (dining outside in decent weather). Lots of Dutch atmosphere with candles, fresh flowers, copper lamps, amid the architectural details and oak furniture. The cuisine is French (preparation a cross between classic and nouvelle), the food Dutch: local salmon, lamb, and chocolate from Haarlem's own factory. Just around the corner from the Frans Hals Museum in a lovely old street is **De Vrome Poort** *(Nieuw Heiligland 10; open Wed.–Sun. 5–10 p.m., closed Mon., Tues; 317285; moderate)* gives a spring-like impression in its small cozy space, complete with Dutch door and lace at the windows. Fresh Dutch food prepared with a French touch.

IN THE AREA..

Spaarndam • In this picturesque old Dutch fishing village with 17th-century houses and gables, built along a typical Dutch dike, a 600-year-old lock on the river Spaarne (which flows through Haarlem) is decorated with a small bronze statue that represents the tale of the boy who plugged a hole in a dike with his finger. Most Americans grew up with the story (most Dutch didn't) of the brave boy who, seeing a small leak in a dike, saved Haarlem from inundation by thrusting his finger into the hole, staying there all night until he was discovered in the morning and the hole could be properly plugged. The tale is told in the 1865 novel *Hans Brinker or The Silver Skates* by American Mary Mapes Dodge, though it wasn't Hans Brinker himself who performed the supposed heroic deed (so implausible that perhaps that is why the Dutch have never paid it much heed). Nevertheless, after nearly a century of American visitors inquiring about the location of the brave act, Dutch tourism officials took over. In June 1950, while several hundred Haarlem school children sang, Princess Margriet (sister of Queen Beatrix), then 7, performed her first public function by unveiling the sculpture designed to satisfy the inquirers.

Cruquius Museum • *Cruquiusdijk 27/32, south of Haarlem, just to east of Heemstede; open April–Sept. Mon.–Sat. 10 a.m.–5 p.m., Sun. and hols. noon–5 p.m., closes at 4 p.m. in Oct. and Nov., closed Dec.–Mar.; 023-285704)* • As early as 1641, plans had been drawn up to drain the huge *Haarlemmermeer* (lake), although they called for no fewer than 166 windmills to do the job, which wasn't considered feasible. Not until 1839 did the Dutch Parliament put into action a drainage plan that could be followed through. Cruquius was one of three steam-driven pumping stations used to reclaim the polder land between 1849 and 1852. Made redundant in 1933, Cruquius, a monument in Holland's history of hydraulic engineering and a relic of the Steam Age, was given new life as a main exhibit in a museum providing insight into Holland's perpetual push to gain land from the sea.

An interesting model shows what the Netherlands without its dikes and drained polder land would look like: for starters, there'd be lots less of it. Also shown are the stages by which Holland has reclaimed land from the sea, the earliest in 1456 near Alkmaar. The Haarlemmermeer project of the 19th century drained the land (13 feet below sea level) on which Schiphol Airport now rests. There are also maps and models showing the history of pumping land dry with windmills (some in the region are still used for that). There's an English translation of exhibit notes that visitors can carry around with them. Tickets and refreshments from the tea house in the former chief engineer's cottage next door. Cruquius is accessible by bus from Haarlem.

IJmuiden • The *Noordzee Kanaal,* dug (by hand) from 1865–1876 along the early course of the IJ river to preserve Amsterdam's future as a deep-water port, links that city with the sea at IJmuiden, a distance of 13 miles (22 km). The three locks (dating from 1876, 1896, and 1930, respectively) make for interesting viewing; the 1930 Noordersluis is one of the largest in the world: 1300 ft. long, 50 ft. deep, 160 ft. wide, and the Noordzee Kanaal as a whole is larger than the Panama Canal. The steady stream of huge containers led by tiny tugs, barges, and other craft, seen closer at hand here than at Rotterdam (see *Harbor Cruises*), impresses one with the supreme economic importance of sea trade to Holland. A free, continually running (allowing for ship traffic, which has the right of way) 24-hour 5-minute car ferry crosses the Noordzee Kanaal near Velsen-Zuid (the entire old village center of which is registered as a national monument). If you aren't heading farther north, turn left when driving off the car ferry for a fascinating drive back across the Noordzee Kanaal atop the locks: Pay attention to the traffic lights! On the south side of the canal, at the IJmuiden fishing harbor (largest in the country), visitors are welcome Mon.–Fri. 7–10 a.m. at the fish auctions, and any time at one of several **fresh fish restaurants.**

Frans Roozen Bulb Growers • *Vogelenzangseweg 49, Vogelenzang; Apr. and May, daily 8 a.m.–6 p.m., July–Oct. Mon.–Fri. 9 a.m.– 5 p.m.; 02502–7245* • South of Haarlem is the "old" bulb district. (It's old only in relation to the "new" bulb district, less well-known to visitors, that has been developed in the far north of Noord Holland province.) Among the many professional bulb nurseries that were established around Haarlem in the 1780s was that of the Frans Roozen family, still a pioneer in cultivating and marketing bulbs. During April and May, in the Frans Roozen greenhouses, show gardens, and bulb fields, some 1000 varieties of bulbs (700 of which are tulips) are grown as a "living catalog:" bulbs can be ordered for home delivery. The place isn't overly commercial (albeit a bit gimmicky with its small windmill in the middle of the garden), is free and, with its close-up view of bulb fields in bloom, makes a good supplement to Keukenhof in the spring. From July–Oct., many summer flowering bulbs are on display in the garden and greenhouses.

Zandvoort • Second only to Scheveningen (The Hague) as a Dutch beach resort, and the favorite with Amsterdammers, Zandvoort is well-served by both train and bus from Haarlem and Amsterdam. There are 38 pavilions along the lively broad sandy beachfront, as well as a section reserved for nude bathers. Recreational facilities range from bike paths in the dunes to the north (bike rental at Zandvoort train station, reservations recommended in summer season) to a casino.

LEIDEN

Guidelines for Leiden

SIGHTS   Leiden has the timeless Dutch beauty that comes with canals, picturesque gables, and a working windmill in the center. **Leiden University** (Holland's oldest, 1575), numerous bookshops, cafes, sites associated with America's **Pilgrim Fathers** who lived here 11 years before sailing for the New World, landmarks from Rembrandt's early life, and interesting museums, give the town broad appeal.

GETTING AROUND   Walking is the best way to see the town, even though its historic center is not as compact as some. Public buses or taxis from the station can supplement your feet. One-hour canal cruises (June, July, Aug. only) pass some of the main sights. The VVV offers guided walking tours of the city Sun. afternoons June to Sept.

SHOPPING   Leiden serves as the main shopping town for the surrounding region, and has a full range of department and smaller stores. Late-night shopping (til 9 p.m.) Thurs.; general market along Nieuwe Rijn in city center Wed. and Sat. 9 a.m.–5 p.m.

ACCOMMODATIONS   In-town hotels are limited in number, and run from modern first-class accommodations to moderate old canal-fronted townhouses.

RESTAURANTS   A full range of fare from formal French and cozy candlelit bistros to casual cafes catering to students.

ENTERTAINMENT AND EVENTS   Leiden is a lively student town with brown cafes and some music clubs. The VVV prints a monthly events calendar. Oct. 3 is celebrated annually in observance of the end of the **seige of the city** by the Spanish in 1574. A church service on the U.S.'s Thanksgiving Day in St. Pieterskerk commemorates the Pilgrim Fathers' stay in Leiden.

ARRIVING   Leiden lies more or less midway on the main Amsterdam-Rotterdam train line, with Haarlem 15 minutes to the north, The Hague 15 minutes to the south. There are trains every quarter hour in each direction, and several hourly to/from Schiphol Airport, located just off the A 4 motorway. Leiden's canals account for the many one-way and pedestrianized streets, making driving complicated. Your best bet is to arrive by train; if you come by car, park it (legally) and forget it.

IN THE AREA Leiden lies at the southern boundary of Holland's main **bulb field district,** which normally is in bloom from late March to mid/late-May (see *The Bulb Field Business*). The main train line from Leiden north to Haarlem towards Amsterdam (*not* the Schiphol/Amsterdam line) passes through the fields. A bus from Leiden station stops at Keukenhof gardens. Windmill cruises (three hours, mid-June to early Sept.) depart from Leiden and take in the surrounding countryside.

TRAVEL TIPS Leiden's students are assertive cyclists who assume the right-of-way, even over pedestrians.

Leiden in Context

Much of what distinquishes Leiden—the same *Leyden* as it was written in periods past—today stems from events that took place in 1574, though the town has a considerably longer history. Traces of Roman settlements have been found near Leiden, but essentially the area remained one of almost inaccessible below-sea-level marsh through much of the first millennium after Christ. One wonders why the Vikings bothered to plunder so persistently. About the year 1000, a stronghold and refuge from high water, as well as from confrontations with the powerful bishops of Utrecht who by then ruled the region, was built on a small island between two branches of the Rhine River. Around this *Burcht*, which still stands in the center of town, a village grew, and, by the 11th century, when the Counts of Holland settled there, Leiden's continuance was assured.

About 1100, the danger of flooding from the Rhine at Leiden (the name means *place on the waterways*) was diminished by the construction of the first dikes, which also served as city walls. Gradually, craftsmen and brewers augmented the population of farmers and fishermen, and Leiden became the most important market town in the area. In 1266, Count of Holland Floris V awarded Leiden a city charter with extra all-important privileges, including toll-freedom and exemption from certain taxes, which fostered further growth in trade and population.

By the early 14th century, new canals had been dug to encompass the larger town. Leiden's textile industry, having received a boost from immigrating Flemish weavers, became famous far afield for the excellent quality of the woolen cloth it produced. In common with much of Europe, Leiden was plagued in the second half of the 14th century by outbreaks of the Black Death, which severely reduced its population.

Nevertheless, the city enjoyed relative prosperity until succumbing to a long-lasting economic recession about 1500, led by a decline in the cloth trade.

In 1572, Leiden, together with 11 other important cities in the northern Netherlands, joined Willem I (the Silent), Prince of Orange, in opposing Spanish rule. Such support ran the risk of confrontation: In 1573, Spaniards laid seige to Haarlem (successfully), then Alkmaar (unsuccessfully), and the Leijenaars prepared themselves. The town's earliest cornmills lay outside the city, but early in 1573 these were all demolished to keep them from falling to the Spanish, and eight new ones were built on the city walls. Large supplies of food were stored within the town in anticipation of a seige, and, late in 1573, Spanish troops did indeed surround Leiden. But the town's preparation paid off, and citizens suffered little deprivation before the Spanish, quite suddenly, withdrew in March 1574. Just as unexpectedly, however, her troops having only temporarily been needed to fight elsewhere, the Spanish reappeared around the city walls in late May. Stores, so carefully set aside the previous year, had not been replenished, and this time food shortages in Leiden occurred alarmingly soon.

In what may be the most famous Dutch stance during the 80 Years' War with Spain, Leijenaars held ground courageously. As August advanced to September, food shortages reduced many in the city under seige to eating rats. Willem of Orange had pledged help to Leiden and, though severely ill with a fever at his residence in Delft, he directed defense plans, partly with the communications aid of carrier pigeons from the Leiden home of three brothers at 94 Rapenburg (still known as *Het Duyvenhuis,* the pigeon house). Knowing he had 200 Dutch vessels on the North Sea ready to rout the Spanish, still camped in relative comfort around the walls of Leiden, Willem made what was a drastic decision for a Dutchman: to breach dikes that had been built up over centuries in order to defend Leiden from the sea. The desperate deed was done. The dikes were cut in 16 places, and the sunken land surrounding Leiden flooded. But the water didn't come in deeply enough to sail the ships, which required a minimum 28-inch draught, over the countryside fields and roads to Leiden. In fact, the wind changed direction, blowing the sea away from Leiden.

Within the city, the situation worsened by the day, as hundreds of starved citizens became thousands. Edible leaves had been stripped from the trees. Horses, then dogs and cats, and finally cows—kept until they were too emancipated to produce milk—were slaughtered and distributed in as small portions as possible among the population. When such conditions brought the plague upon the people, some finally seemed ready to capitulate, since it had been weeks since the dikes had been severed, with no relief in sight. It was reported that Leiden's Burgemeester (mayor) Adriaan van der Werf, who believed death by starvation preferable to dishonorable surrender, offered the restive citizens his body for food "as far as it will go," thus stunning and/or shaming the citizens into continuing their resistance.

A full two months after the dikes had been damaged, 131 days after the Leiden seige had begun, with at least 6,000 citizens dead, a fierce southwest storm swept Holland. The North Sea surged, finally carrying Willem's Dutch naval force through the broken dikes to within winning distance of the Spanish on the night of October 2, 1574, and the relief of Leiden finally was realized.

In the morning, October 3, during a search of the abandoned Spanish positions, one city marksman, Ghijsbert Corneliszoon Schaek, found a huge kettle of *hutspot* (hotchpotch), a stew of beef, carrots, potatoes, and onions, which gave survivors of the seige their first fresh food in months. (The reputed iron kettle, often attributed to having been found by an orphan—it makes a good story—is on display at Leiden's Lakenhal Museum.) Shortly thereafter, "seabeggars" arrived from south of the city on the Vliet with ships loaded with white bread and herring for the starving citizens. To this day, those are the favored foods during the local October 3 celebrations and street fairs.

For their brave endurance of the seige, Willem offered the people of Leiden exemption from taxes for a certain period, or the establishment of a university. Despite what citizens in heavily taxed Holland might do today, Leiden residents then took a long-range view and chose to have the first Dutch university. The inauguration took place in February 1575, with an elaborate parade and floating procession on the river. Leiden quickly became the most important Protestant university in Europe, attracting the finest minds in Europe, and making Holland a leading center of scientific learning and art. Since 1581, when the Catholic Church in Holland was outlawed, the university has been headquartered in the former convent of the White Nuns on the Rapenburg canal.

Most deservingly, Leiden experienced better times following its relief from the seige. The manufacture of cloth once more became the driving force of the city's economy. Ironically, this was somewhat due to the Spanish, who still occupied the southern Netherlands (today's Belgium). After they overtook Antwerp in 1585, among the many Flemish refugees who came north to Holland were numerous skilled textile workers who settled in Leiden and provided fresh impulse for its industry. Leiden entered the 17th-century Golden Age as one of the biggest industrialized places in Holland, and possibly Europe's largest textile manufacturing town of the time. The impressive 1597 Stadhuis on Breestraat (whose facade fortunately survived a 1929 fire) was designed by Lieven de Key to reflect the prosperity of Leiden at this period.

Because Leiden had successfully struggled with Spain for her own spiritual freedom, and because the town had a special reputation for welcoming exiles fleeing persecution in other lands, it seems quite natural that English "separatists," seeking to escape the rigid edicts of James I, wanted to settle there. After months of trying to arrange passage to religiously tolerant Holland, one group of English managed, after several false, near fatal starts, to escape from Boston, England, across the North Sea to Amsterdam. Among the group of pilgrims were 18-year-old William Bradford, who would later serve as governor of Plymouth Colony (Massachusetts) for many years, and William Brewster, who had served in Holland in 1587 with Queen Elizabeth's secretary of state, and later would become the pilgrims' spiritual leader in the New World.

They and others, upon discovering disagreements among the English separatists in Amsterdam, petitioned the liberal Leiden leaders for residence permits for 100. These were granted, "provided such persons behaved themselves," and by May 1, 1609, the pilgrims had moved to Leiden. A measure of Leiden's true support is the lack of attention the city burgemeester paid to English authorities who, learning that Leiden had admitted the "separatists," protested for their return.

Trained for the most part only in farming, the pilgrims in many cases had to accept jobs of physical labor, particularly in the textile industry, which employed most workers in town. Having lost much of their personal property through theft or seizure while trying to get from England to Holland, many of the English had to work long hours at subsistence level just to survive. So hard did they have to work that, despite their strong religious conviction, they were unable to establish their own meeting house until May 1611.

At that time they bought **De Groenpoort** (the green gate), which stood on a site that has been occupied since 1683 by the **Jean Pesijnhofje** almshouse, across from the great Pieterskerk (church). The Groenpoort served as the pilgrims' church and as a parsonage for their English religious leader, John Robinson and his family. Small "cottages" were built around its courtyard as houses for the least well-off members of the English congregation. A plaque near the gate of the Pesijnhofje indicates that here "John Robinson lived, taught, and died—1611–1625." The lovely enclosed garden with its small surrounding houses, today rented to student and elderly couples, is open to the public.

Unlike many of his pilgrim parish peers, William Brewster was well educated. He was able to tutor in English at Leiden's University, and eventually established a small printing press—an evangelical enterprise. The *Pilgrim Press* was located near Pieterskerk on Stincksteeg (Stink Alley, now renamed William Brewster alley), and is indicated today by an explanatory tablet.

Continued poverty and concern about the corruption of their youth, who were growing up without English identity and under the less religiously strict influence of Dutch neighbors, caused growing discontent among the pilgrims. When William Brewster had to flee Holland to escape arrest for one of his Pilgrim Press religious essays (James I's officials had tracked down the typeface), he returned to England under the surname of Williamson. There, he began making arrangements for the pilgrims' passage to the New World. The Separatists in Leiden would probably have read Captain John Smith's enthusiastic *A Description of New England* published in 1616, and hoped to have better success with "converting" the natives there to their religious outlook than they had had in Holland. Recalled William Bradford later in his *History of Plymouth Plantation,* the young and strong pilgrims who left "Leyden, a fair and bewtifull citie," did so "not out of any newfangledness or such like giddy humor—but for sundry weighty and solid reasons."

On the last day of July 1620, 54 of the English group from Leiden—35 of them "saints," those going for religious reasons, and the remaining "strangers," those who sought commercial opportunity in the New World—boarded barges by the Vlietbrug (near the Pilgrim Documentation Center, see *What To See and Do*), and sailed south down the Vliet to Delftshaven (now a picturesque old harbor in a quiet corner of Rotterdam). There, they departed, after prayer, aboard the *Speedwell* for England, where they met up with the good ship *Mayflower.*

John Robinson, the pilgrims' spiritual leader in Leiden, remained behind, since the majority of his parish had not opted to head for the New World, with its rigors, at that time. He had hoped to follow eventually, but died in 1625, and was buried in the Pieterskerk. A memorial on the outside wall of the massive old church reads: ". . . whence at his prompting went forth the Pilgrim Fathers to settle New England." As the pilgrims had foreseen, many of the English who remained in Leiden (and the majority had) became assimilated into Dutch society. Robinson's son Isaac was one of the last of the Leiden pilgrims to emigrate to Plymouth (Massachusetts), in 1632.

Dutch influence on the pilgrims who established America's first permanent English colony at Plymouth is hard to pinpoint, but there can be little doubt that some of the Dutch civil laws and precedents the pilgrims had experienced in Leiden were incorporated into the idea of the separation of church and state that, even under the religious-minded pilgrims, was established in America from the start at Plymouth. Those who want to might see a Leiden connection between the pilgrims' celebration of a Thanksgiving feast with the Indians, and the annual three days of feasting and prayer they would have observed over October 3 in thanksgiving for the relief of Leiden from the Spanish seige. Today, Thanksgiving services still are held for both occasions in Leiden's Pieterskerk: on October 3, and on the U.S. Thanksgiving Day in November. The ecumenical service is a meaningful remembrance of the pilgrims' past.

Leiden was one of Holland's thriving centers for painting, and the birthplace of **Lucas van Leyden** (1489?–1533). During the Golden Age, many important painters began their lives, and came into and continued their art, in Leiden: **Jan van Goyen** (1596–1656); **Rembrandt** (1606–1669); **Willem van der Velde the Elder and the Younger** (1611–1693) and (1633–1707); **Gerrit Dou** (1613–1675); **Jan Steen** (1625/26–1679); **Gabriel Metsu** (1629–1667); and **Frans van Meiris** (1635–1681). Jan Steen, son of a Leiden brewer, and trained as one himself, is known to have owned a tavern in 1672 on the Lange Brug. It is reputed—though so much inaccurate biographical data has been perpetuated about Holland's great masters that this needs to be taken as perhaps just a good tale—that, because he was his tavern's own best customer, the tavern that was meant to support Steen at his painting in fact produced bills that had to be paid for in paintings. One biographer wrote, "For a long time his works were to be found only in the hands of dealers in wine." Steen is buried in the Pieterskerk.

Rembrandt was Leiden's greatest son. His father was a fairly prosperous miller, whose surname Van Rijn indicates that the family had lived for some generations beside or near the Rhine River, as it did in Rembrandt's day. (His birthplace, and residence for most of his 26 years in Leiden, on Weddesteeg, near the Rembrandt Bridge, is marked by a tablet.) The eighth of nine children, Rembrandt seems to have been the most promising, and was sent to Leiden's Latin School. (In the egalitarian Dutch provinces, it was not unthinkable that a miller's son could aspire to a profession.) The Latin School (built by Lieven de Key in 1599 and used as a school until 1864) was located near the Pieterskerk and, since Rembrandt would have been receiving his schooling in the same period as the pilgrim sojourn in Leiden, he could easily have passed one or another of the pilgrims on the street. The purpose of the Latin School was to prepare young men for Leiden University, then the equal of any in Europe, and while Rembrandt matriculated there, he seems to have left shortly thereafter, having determined to pursue painting.

Rembrandt's first Leiden art instructor is unknown. The second, under whom he served a three-year apprenticeship, was the Leiden painter Jacob van Swanenburgh, who taught Rembrandt the fundamentals, but seems not to have made an important impression upon his pupil; his specialties of architectural scenes and views of hell were two subjects to which Rembrandt never subsequently turned his hand. With Rembrandt showing great talent, his father sent him to Amsterdam for further study under **Pieter Lastman,** then one of the Netherlands' foremost painters of historical scenes. At the age of 18 or 19, Rembrandt returned to Leiden and set himself up as an independent master, developing rapidly as a painter, perfecting his etching technique, and soon surpassing most other Dutch artists.

Leiden was a bustling town during the six or seven years that Rembrandt had his studio there, working closely with artist Jan Lievens (who had also studied under Lastman in Amsterdam), and having several students, Gerrit Dou being the most important. With 50,000 people in 1620 (70,000 by 1670), Leiden was second in size in Holland only to Amsterdam (110,000). Architecturally, Leiden was typically Dutch: narrow houses, with gabled roofs and bright-colored shutters, lined the canals and streets, but if Rembrandt recorded it, no such scenes have survived. Visitors found Leiden conspicuous for its cleanliness, even in well-scrubbed Holland, but, paradoxically, the town also had an abominable stench rising from almost currentless canals that often were clogged with sewage, which perhaps contributed to Leiden's periodic outbreaks of the plague (several deadly epidemic diseases). Some years the death toll was so high that the town's earthen ramparts had to be used as supplemental cemeteries.

In the Leiden of the 1620s, almost all workers, largely illiterate and underpaid, were associated with the town's textile trade; their living conditions would have fostered Rembrandt's great sense of humanity. He also felt the full influence of the population contrasts at Leiden University, where he saw a parade of students and philosophical professors from countries throughout Europe, many from noble families, whose foreign clothes fed his eye for the picturesque, exotic, and sumptuous details in dress that he put in his paintings the rest of his life. In 1632, Rembrandt left Leiden for Amsterdam, where he won almost immediate fame and wealth.

Scientifically, especially due to its University, Leiden attained and maintained a position of prominence in Europe during the Age of Reason, and on into the Enlightenment. The **Museum Boerhaave** pays tribute to **Christian Huygens,** a 17th-century scholar whose most notable achievement was the invention of the pendulum clock, which improved significantly the accuracy of navigation for the all-important Dutch East India Company ships. Also honored is **Antony van Leeuwenhoek,** who invented the first microscope, also on display.

A century-and-a-half after the pilgrims departed Leiden, another piece of early American history was connected with the town. Under initial encouragement from the province of Friesland, the Dutch were the first to recognize the thirteen colonies' proclamation of freedom from Britain, and to send them much-needed financial aid. (Pragmatic Dutch commercial shipping companies operating out of the Caribbean during the American Revolution actually sold supplies to both sides.) When the war was over, George Washington appointed John Adams of Massachusetts (a descendant of *Mayflower* pilgrim John Alden and later 2nd president of the U.S.) the first U.S. Ambassador to Holland. Adams, his wife Abigail, and son John Quincy (6th U.S. president) came to Holland in 1781, at which time John Quincy, then 14, was enrolled at

Leiden University. Abigail Adams wrote in a 1786 letter of a visit to the Pieterskerk: "I visited the church at Leyden, in which our forefathers worshipped . . . I felt a respect upon entering the doors."

By the time of the Adams' appointment to Holland, Leiden's economic cycle had turned down again, the population reduced to 30,000, the town in physical disrepair. Not as devastating as the 1574 Seige, but nonetheless drastic, was the 1807 explosion: a ship loaded with a cargo of 37,000 pounds of gunpowder, illegally moored in the city center, exploded violently, making ruins and rubbish of hundred of homes and buildings and killing 151, with hundreds more wounded. (Canadians will be reminded of the Halifax explosion.) The Van der Werf Park memorializes the site.

Economic conditions have ebbed and flowed during the 19th and 20th centuries, but today, Leiden (population 109,000), used to taking a long hard look at itself, appears at least as lovely as it ever has. Many of the town's fine old buildings, saved from urban-renewal razing because of its improverished periods, have seen recent renovations, and several reconstructions are completed. Leiden is enjoying a promising present, while preserving a lovely look of the past.

GUIDEPOSTS
Telephone code 071.

Tourist Info	VVV, Stationplein 210, 2312 AR, 146846; 1 Apr.–31 Aug. Mon.–Sat. 9 a.m.–8 p.m., Sun. 10 a.m.–4 p.m.; 1 Sept.–31 Mar. Mon.–Fri. 9 a.m.–5:30 p.m., Sat. 10 a.m.–3 p.m., Sun. closed.
Bike rental	Bicycle depot next to railway station, 131304; Van der Laan, Merelstraat 13, 155915.
Rowboat rental	Jac. Veringa, near Rembrandtbrug, 149790.
Canal cruises	Jac. M. Slingerland, Quay Beestenmarkt, 134938.
Parking	Carparks indicated on VVV city map; at Stationplein (across from VVV), including Beestenmarkt, Lammermarkt (near De Valk, convenient to De Lakenhal Museum).
Auto. Assn.	ANWB, Stationweg 2, 146241.
Train	Information in station hall.
Bus	NZH (local and regional bus services), Stationplein 5, 134441.
Emergencies	Police 144444; medical 122222.

Shopping   Pedestrianized Haarlemmer Straat, Breedstraat, and side streets

Taxis   Listed in VVV city brochure. Available at train station.

WHAT TO SEE AND DO......................

Leiden is worthy of a more lingering look than many travelers allow time for. The activities of university students, who live throughout the city, give Leiden a lively evening atmosphere, which isn't the case in some older Dutch downtowns, making it a good choice for an overnight alternative, and a useful, less expensive base from which to make day trips. If your time in Leiden must be limited, you can use the order in which the sights are listed below as a *suggestion* of relative importance (always subject to your own interests). No matter how short your stay is, start at the VVV across from the train station. In addition to a map, which you'll find necessary in this town, there are other excellent English-language booklets on the pilgrims, town history, museums, and several self-guiding walking tour brochures: *A Pilgrimage through Leiden; Leiden, a town of Monuments; Leiden, a true Dutch Heritage; Following in Rembrandt's Footsteps;* each includes many of the basic town landmarks.

Municipal Museum "de Lakenhal" • *Oude Singel 32; open Tues.– Sat. 10 a.m.–5 p.m., Sun. and hols 1–5 p.m., Oct. 3 10 a.m.–noon; closed Jan 1, Dec. 25; 254620* • The handsome *Lakenhal* (Cloth Hall) was built in 1640 to serve as the center of Leiden's wool textile industry and headquarters of the preeminent Cloth Guild; aspects of the cloth trade are shown in five sculptured plaques on the facade, and the courtyard was used for the rigorous inspection of the cloth that preserved its high reputation. Turned into Leiden's municipal museum in 1874, it now houses displays in elegant rooms with beamed ceilings, tiled fireplaces, and oak floors. The historic sections cover the Seige of Leiden, with a huge wall tapestry map of the city in the 16th-century, and the famous *hutspot*; wonderful period rooms include a delightful tiled kitchen (where there are many more 17th-century Dutch tiles) and the distinguished Governors' Room with fine old furniture. The excellent painting collection has works of the town's famous artists: Lucas van Leyden's triptych *The Last Judgement* (1527), works by Rembrandt, Jan Steen, Gerrit Dou, and Jan van Goyen's *View of Leyden,* which shows what the town looked like at the time the pilgrims lived here.

St. Pieterskerk • *Pieterskerkhof; ask at the VVV about opening times* • This elephantine 15th-century edifice, the sometime house of worship for the English pilgrims, has been restored and now functions as a conference center and setting for Leiden student exams, as well as for special services (particularly on October 3 in memory of the end of the seige of 1574, and Thanksgiving Day to commemorate the pilgrim connection). The "minimalist" Protestant interior decoration includes many interesting grave slabs flush with the floor; on the exterior is a memorial to John Robinson, religious leader of the pilgrims. Opposite that memorial is the **Jean Pesijnhofje,** an almshouse built in 1683 on the site of the pilgrims' **De Groene Poort,** restored in 1979 and still in use today as housing for old and student couples. Near the Pieterskerk, on **Pieterskerkchoorsteeg** (Peter's Church Choir Alley) is a plaque over the door to William Brewster Alley, where his Pilgrim Press operated.

Pilgrim Fathers Document Center • *(Vliet 45; open Mon.–Fri. 9 a.m.–noon, 2–4:30 p.m., closed Sat., Sun., holidays, and Oct. 3; 120191* • The center houses a permanent exhibition of photocopies of personal records documenting details of the pilgrims' lives in Leiden. Marriage and tax records, an edition from Brewster's Pilgrim Press, and other items pertaining to Leiden's entire 17th-century English community—with tags designating those who sailed on the *Mayflower*—can be examined. An informative 20-minute film on the pilgrims and the religious times in which they lived is available in English.

Leiden University • *Rapenburg 73; 148333* • Since shortly after its founding (1575), in 1581 when all Catholic property was confiscated in Holland, the University's adminstrative headquarters have been housed in the former convent of the White Nuns on Rapenburg canal (at the *Nonnenbrug,* Nuns' Bridge). It may be possible to enter the university building at the entrance, in which case seek out the examination waiting room with its walls covered with the names and dates of those who agonized over the results. Of possible interest is the **University History Museum** *(open Tues.–Thurs. 1–5 p.m., closed Oct. 3, hols.),* which contains exhibits regarding University history and, mostly, student life.

Founded in 1587, the University's **Hortus Botanicus** (Botanic Gardens, entrance Rapenburg 73), among the oldest in Europe, was under the initial directorship of Carolus Clusius, the same man who had been presented in Vienna with the first tulip bulbs to reach Dutch soil (see *Bulb Field Business* chapter). *(Open daily Mon.–Sat. 9 a.m.–5 p.m., Sun. 10 a.m.–5 p.m., closed Sat. Oct. 1–Apr. 1, Oct. 3, Dec. 25–1st Mon. after New Year's.)* In addition to the ancient trees, gardens, and canal, there are extensive greenhouses with wide-ranging plants from around the world in the climate-controlled environments.

Windmill Museum De Valk • *Binnenvestgracht; open Tues.–Sat. 10 a.m.–5 p.m., Sun. and hols. 1–5 p.m.; closed Mon., Jan 1, Oct. 3, Dec. 25; 254639; fee* • Although *De Valk* comes last, that's only out of respect for Leiden's other substantial sights. I've always found *De Valk* (the falcon) one of Leiden's most interesting sights (and the best windmill museum in Holland), and it's so centrally situated in town that it would be hard to miss. An authentic tower-style flour mill dating from 1734, De Valk is seven stories, beginning with a former miller's living quarters on the ground floor, which all will enjoy, though the exhibits on higher stories, which can only be reached via narrow flights of ship-steep stairs may not be a wise choice for those with a concern about heights. Heading up, one passes the all-wood working mill parts, a self-service slide show (English) about Leiden and windmills (some 70 of the approximately 900 remaining windmills of the 9000 that once existed in Holland are located in the greater Leiden region), exhibits on the historic function and importance of windmills (with much information in English), and reaches the reefing stage (5th flight). Here, 45 feet up, on the wide wooden outside platform (from which there's a 360-degree view), is the wheel by which the miller turns the sails (with a span of 88 feet) into the wind. Wonderfully, the sails at Leiden are set free in the wind most afternoons from Apr. 1 to October 1.

For those settling into Leiden with lots of time, there are several other respected museums that can be visited, including the **National Museum of Natural History,** the **National Museum of Ethnology,** and the **National Museum of Antiquities,** which has the Egyptian A.D. 1st century Temple of Taffeh, presented to the Dutch in 1969 in thanks for their contribution to rescuing Nubian treasures that would have been lost due to the construction of the Aswan Dam.

ACCOMMODATIONS......................

The hotels listed are all centrally located. With the exception of the new Golden Tulip property, all are in old townhouses. Guest houses, which may not be in the center of town, can be contacted and booked at the VVV.

First Class
★★★★ **Golden Tulip Leiden** • *Schipholweg 3, 2316 XB; 221121, fax 226675, (1–800-333-1212)* • This is Leiden's newest, largest (102 beds), most modernly luxurious center city hotel, situated across from the railway station, on the right (center city) side of the tracks.

Moderate

★★★ **De Doelen** • *Rapenburg 2, 2311 EV. 120527* • A handsome building on a handsome canal near the university, this nine-room hotel still has the feel of the 15th-century patrician house it was converted from, with features such as old beams, antique tiled fireplaces, dark oak wainscotting, and other old Dutch details in its nooks and crannies. There is no elevator, and needless to say, no two rooms are alike (prices vary somewhat too). A couple of rooms overlook the canal. Some rooms are fairly old-fashioned in dark wood old Dutch, and others are lighter, more modern, with less character. The hotel's restaurant is well-respected locally, with a walled garden cafe.

★★★ **Hotel Mayflower** • *Beestenmarkt 2, 2312 CC; 142641* • This 14-room family-run hotel has modern decor with touches of Dutch: stained glass, tiles, paintings in the bright, comfortable little lobby, off of which are a breakfast room and bar. Large modern baths and light wood furniture produce an airy feel to bedrooms. Two rooms have view of the canal and the square the hotel faces, but rooms in the back will prove quieter in this very centrally located hotel, four blocks from station. Elevator.

Inexpensive

★★ **Nieuw Minerva** • *Boommarkt 23, 2311 EA, 126358, fax 142674* • Eight row houses, c. 1600, with 40 rooms that vary considerably: some in older part are cozy and nice, some modernized and very ordinary; all have private toilet and shower. No elevator *yet* on my most recent visit. Cozy, friendly, slightly tired, eclectic Dutch-style lobby. Two locally popular restaurants (moderate and inexpensive), one with less formal menu, quicker service; both serve lunch and dinner.

RESTAURANTS..................................

Though limited in number, the restaurants in Leiden will certainly serve your needs. Hotel restaurants and cafes should be kept in mind, since they need to be of a high enough standard to attract a local clientele as well as overnight guests. The "three-course fixed-price menus" and "dish-of-the-day" will represent the best values. If you're looking for a proper restaurant meal, it's always a good idea to call for reservations, since seating capacities can be small and service deliberately unrushed.

A Leiden standard because of its longevity, location, looks, and food is **Oudt Leyden** *(Steenstraat 51–53; restaurant only closed Sun.; 133144; rest. expensive, pancake house inexpensive/moderate)*, where you get two choices at one address. Long established in a trio of town houses on the main street from the station into the Centrum, the restaurant offers nouvelle-style continental cuisine, with attentive service and handsome atmosphere. The **'t Pannekoekenhuysje** at the left entrance offers the typical Dutch platter-size pancakes and other traditional Dutch specialties.

Sharing space on the same alley just a few doors from the Pieterskerk, where the pilgrims sometimes prayed, are two of Leiden's best bistros, which may put tables out in front when the weather's nice. **De Bisschop** *(Kloksteeg 7; 125024; expensive)* offers a pleasant dining space replete with flowers and a prix-fixe menu, among the a la carte dishes. At **La Cloche** *(Kloksteeg 3; 123053; expensive)* fare is apt to be fresh and French in an old house that has been most successfully "smartened" with white rattan and other tasteful details. **La Grand** *(Herengracht 100; 140876; closed Mon.; moderate),* as one of the Neerlands Dis restaurants, is a solid choice for Dutch dishes.

Two *eet-cafes* recommended for informal fare and touching shoulders with students are **De Grote Beer** *(Rembrandtstraat 27)* and **Pardoeza** *(Doezastraat 43).* According to residents, the town's best Indonesian food can be had at **Surakarta** *(Noordeinde 51; 123524; inexpensive).*

THE HAGUE

Guidelines for The Hague

SIGHTS The Hague, seat of government for the country (though not the capital) and residence of *H.M. Queen Beatrix,* has much of appeal for all ages and interests. There are a number of art museums, including the exquisite **Mauritshuis** mansion with its masterpieces of Golden Age painting, and the **Gemeentemuseum,** with the largest collection of Dutch artist Mondriaan's works in the world. Other choices range from a museum of instruments of torture, a composite Dutch town constructed at 1:25 scale **(Madurodam),** the **Peace Palace,** and the Parliament's **Ridderzaal,** one of Europe's best preserved pieces of Gothic architecture. In appearance, The Hague differs considerably from a typical Dutch town of canals and narrow, gabled houses: having been a diplomatic center throughout its history—today more than 60 nations have embassies or consulates here—led to a more expansive, park-like layout. The decorum of The Hague "downtown" is contrasted at the coast, with

Scheveningen's North Sea resort trappings of **Pier, Promenade,** casino, and even a nudist beach.

GETTING AROUND As you'd expect in a city its size (population 450,000), sights in The Hague are spread out, but many are bunched in the **Centrum** (city center), and can be reached on foot from the **Centraal Station** (CS). The Hague has a fine **tram** and **bus** network, and the CS is close to stops on several routes, including the tram to Delft, less than five miles away. Trams also run to the center of town and on to Scheveningen from The Hague's **Hollands Spoor** (HS) station. The 1-, 2-, and 3-day local transportation passes, tickets, and maps of the city system are available at the information *(i)* booth at the CS, and the main **VVV** tourist office is next door to it in the Babylon Shopping Complex. Though you may see less orthodox bureaucrats in business suits riding bicycles to work, The Hague's two-wheeler traffic isn't as distracting as in some other Dutch cities; (bike rentals at the HS station and in Scheveningen.)

SHOPPING A cosmopolitan diplomatic capital, The Hague is a sophisticated shopping center, with a focus on antiques and boutiques, but running the gamut from market stalls to quality department stores featuring avant-garde goods.

ACCOMMODATIONS From the seaside at Scheveningen to the heart of The Hague, choices range from rooms in grand century-old "establishments" with superb service to small home-like hotels.

RESTAURANTS Indonesian food is in plentiful supply, since The Hague is the heartland of the Indonesian community in Holland. But from *hutspot* (hotch-potch) to haute cuisine, and from *nieuwe haring* (fresh herring) stands in the courtyard of the Binnenhof Parliament compound to seafood in view of the fishing fleet at Scheveningen, you'll find most anything you want in the way of eating in The Hague.

ARRIVING The Hague is somewhat closer to Rotterdam than Amsterdam on the main rail line between those two cities (a trip which takes slightly over an hour). Trains run in both directions several times hourly, as do trains to/from Schiphol Airport (a half-hour ride). For purposes of visiting The Hague by foot, **Centraal Station (CS)** should be your stop if you have a choice, although there's more frequent service to the **Hollands Spoor** (from which there are trams and buses to the *Centrum,* about one mile). The Hague can be reached via motorway and other major roads.

HOLLAND · · 197

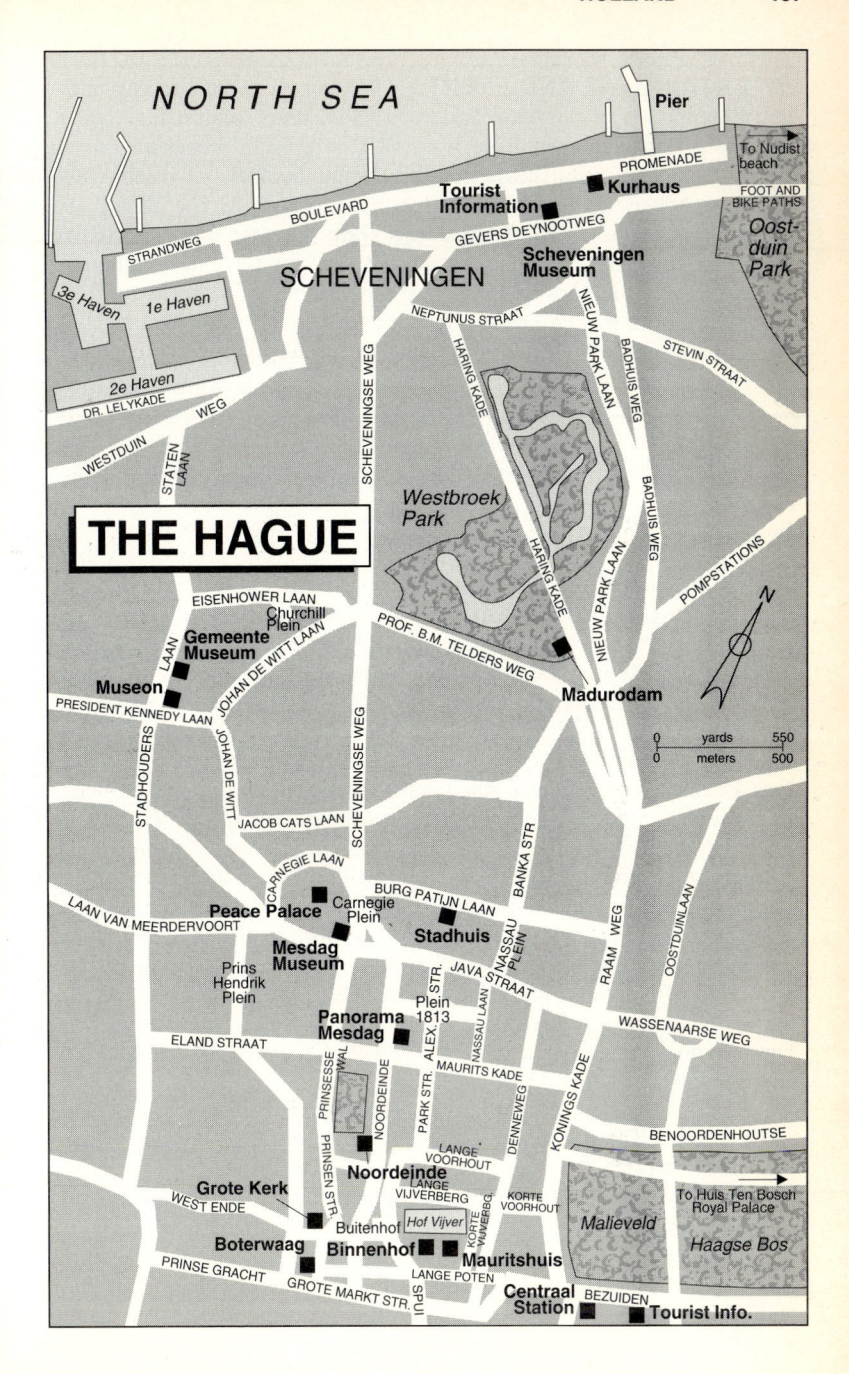

THE HAGUE

Map locations:

- North Sea
- Pier
- To Nudist beach
- Foot and Bike Paths
- Promenade
- Boulevard
- Strandweg
- 3e Haven
- 1e Haven
- 2e Haven
- Dr. Lelykade
- Westduin Weg
- Staten Laan
- Tourist Information
- Kurhaus
- Gevers Deynootweg
- Scheveningen Museum
- Scheveningen
- Neptunus Straat
- Haring Kade
- Nieuw Park Laan
- Badhuis Weg
- Stevin Straat
- Oostduin Park
- Scheveningse Weg
- Westbroek Park
- Pompstations
- Eisenhower Laan
- Churchill Plein
- Gemeente Museum
- Museon
- Johan de Witt Laan
- President Kennedy Laan
- Prof. B.M. Telders Weg
- Madurodam
- Stadhouders Laan
- Johan de Witt
- Jacob Cats Laan
- Carnegie Laan
- Burg Patijn Laan
- Banka Str
- Raam Weg
- Peace Palace
- Carnegie Plein
- Stadhuis
- Nassau Plein
- Oostduinlaan
- Laan van Meerdervoort
- Mesdag Museum
- Prins Hendrik Plein
- Java Straat
- Wassenaarse Weg
- Panorama Mesdag
- Plein 1813
- Alex. Str.
- Nassau Laan
- Eland Straat
- Maurits Kade
- Denneweg
- Prinsesse Wal
- Noordeinde
- Park Str.
- Konings Kade
- Prinsen Str.
- Lange Voorhout
- Benoordenhoutse
- Grote Kerk
- West Ende
- Lange Vijverberg
- Korte Voorhout
- To Huis Ten Bosch Royal Palace
- Buitenhof
- Hof Vijver
- Malieveld
- Haagse Bos
- Boterwaag
- Binnenhof
- Mauritshuis
- Prinse Gracht
- Lange Poten
- Grote Markt Str.
- Centraal Station
- Bezuiden
- Tourist Info.

Scale: 0–550 yards / 0–500 meters

ENTERTAINMENT AND EVENTS In addition to the ongoing after-dark illumination of the main buildings (Binnenhof, Mauritshuis, etc.), The Hague/Scheveningen have a number of colorful occasions worth noting. The VVV publishes a monthly events booklet *(VVV Info),* and will book tickets (in person only) for performances in The Hague and elsewhere in Holland. The **Nederlands Dans Theater,** an authoritative dance company that has acquired an excellent international reputation, and the **Residentie Orkest** *(Den Haag Philharmonic),* are housed, respectively, in the Dutch Dance Theater and the Dr. Anton Philips Hall, a successful and striking cultural complex on the Spui in the center of the city.

TRAVEL TIPS The center of The Hague tends to be quiet and relatively unpeopled at night, though it's perfectly safe to wander around.

The Hague in Context

It is on the site of the *Binnenhof,* (Inner Court) more than 750 years ago, that the Counts of Holland built a structure that would become the seat of government for the vigorous democracy of the Netherlands. That building, probably a hunting lodge, situated beside a pond in woods between coastal dunes and low-lying waterlogged land, was begun by Floris IV, Count of Holland from 1222 to 1234. The place is first mentioned in 1242 as *Die Haghe* (the hedge), from which comes the city's formal name, *'s-Gravenhage* (the counts' hedge), found mostly on maps; in conversation, the Dutch shorten it back to *Den Haag.* Though he never lived there, Floris's son Count Willem II, elected King of the Romans and German Emperor at Aachen in 1247, impressed with the German nobility's regal standard of living, began to build a castle more in keeping with his status. His son Floris V, who by then also numbered Zeeland among his territorial possessions, was able to add the *Ridderzaal* (Hall of Knights), an impressive Scheldt-style Gothic building, by selling off his inherited rights to the Scottish throne for a handsome fee. The building complex became the *Binnenhof* and was the Count's preferred residence by his death in 1296.

The first Counts of Holland to occupy the Binnenhof with their entire court and families were Albrecht of Bavaria and his son Willem VI, in about 1400. The settlement immediately surrounding the palace was greatly expanded during this period since it had to be largely self-sufficient. Stables, livestock, vegetable gardens (planted on what today is the *Plein*), a saddlery, smithy, bottling room, bakery, and chapel all existed within the Binnenhof. Outside the core settlement was the *Buitenhof* (Outer Court), where craft and trades-people kept close, in the hope of commissions. Today's *Plaats* was a meeting place just outside the court gate (now the Prison Gate or *Gevangenpoort,* a museum of torture instruments), the *Vijverberg* was a playground among the trees, and the *Kneuterdijk* served as tournament grounds. The *Lange Voorhout,* an entry into the Hague Woods, often was brightened with the canopies of tents in which court guests who could not be accommodated at the Binnenhof palace camped. When farms grew up slightly farther afield, The Hague could actually be called a village.

Holland and Zeeland, together with the rest of the Low Countries, came under the rule of the Dukes of Burgundy during the mid-15th century, but day-to-day administration remained with the *Stadholder* (regional ruler), who resided in The Hague. The Burgundian Dukes kept court in Brussels, but the peripatetic nature of their business brought them regularly to the Binnenhof. On two occasions Philip the Good held magnificent banquets in the Ridderzaal for the knights of the Order of the Golden Fleece (who also attended services in 1456 at the *Grote Kerk* near the Buitenhof.

By the early 16th century, sovereignty over the Low Countries had passed to Emperor Charles V. By now, The Hague was a prosperous "open" place, with many mansions among its parks. To this day, The Hague looks unlike most other old Dutch towns. This is the result of never having been a fortified town (where because space was scarce, taxes on homeowners to pay for the upkeep of the town walls often were based on the width of a dwelling, which led to narrow, deep, tall houses). Without the space constrictions imposed by city walls, The Hague was set out with wide tree-lined avenues, and mansions amid park settings. Emperor Charles V, ruler of Spain, Burgundy, and the Low Countries, found The Hague pleasing, and sought to protect its natural beauty, but his son Philip II had little love for any part of Holland, and had other things on his mind when he sent his Spanish forces through The Hague.

Its lack of defensive walls came home to haunt The Hague during Holland's 80 Years' War with the Spanish. When the Spanish marched north, the government in the Binnenhof under Stadholder **Willem the Silent,** Prince of Orange, fled to nearby, somewhat-safer Delft, which was walled. The Hague lay in the pathway to the Dutch cities destined for seige (Leiden, Haarlem, and Alkmaar), and passing troops, friend and foe, burned and abused it. At one point, Delft burgers proposed burning down what remained of The Hague in order to force the Spanish out of their camping site in the *Haagse Bos* (Hague Woods) but Willem defused the idea, suspecting it to be inspired by selfish motives to move the government to Delft.

After Willem's Spanish-inspired assassination in Delft in 1574, the executive of the States of Holland resolved to meet only in The Hague. (This decision was politically possible since The Hague had never had a seat in the assembly of the States because it had never received a town charter, and thus aroused less jealousy than the selection of any *offical* town as the seat of government would have). In 1588, the States General, which represented all the seven united Dutch provinces, selected The Hague as its headquarters for the same diplomatic reason and, thenceforth, nearly all bodies associated with the government of the Netherlands have located themselves in or around the Binnenhof.

As The Hague entered the 17th century, it quickly grew in importance, attracting to its democratic court nobility, merchants, musicians, craftsmen, and architects. The Hague became one of the most important diplomatic posts for foreigners, a prime gathering point for international statesmen, so much so that one contemporary Englishman wrote of it as "the whispering gallery" of Europe by the time the Republic of the United Netherlands had won full recognition when the 80 Years' War was officially ended by the Peace of Munster in 1648.

When **Willem II** died in 1650, several provinces, including powerful Holland, decided not to appoint a new Stadholder. Instead, a role of Grand Pensionary was instituted, the holder of that title being the effective leader of the Dutch Republic. **Johan De Witt** served with distinction in the office of Grand Pensionary, and the Dutch overseas empire increased substantially during his leadership. Simultaneously, Johan's brother **Cornelius** distinguished himself as a naval commander who had fought the English and French fleets.

Despite this, the brothers' policies became unpopular in 1672, and Cornelius, unjustly accused of plotting against young Willem, Prince of Orange, was imprisoned in the Gevangenpoort. In one of the country's least laudable incidents, political enemies sent a message to Johan under Cornelius' name, asking him to come to the prison. Though friends and his daughter feared a trap and urged him not to go, the loyal Johan felt he had a duty to his brother if he were in need. The message had indeed been false, and now both brothers were under arrest. De Witt disparagers plied the impassioned masses assembled outside the prison with brandy and wine, maneuvering them into a riotous mood. Although legitimate cavalry troops were sent to control the crowd, they were cleverly tricked into leaving, and the storming of the prison by an enraged, drunken mob commenced. They found Cornelius lying down, racked with pain from days of torture, unable to stand, and his brother Johan reading to him from the Bible. Both brothers were hauled from the cell, shoved down the stairs, and became separated from each other. In the street below, Cornelius was struck on the head and trampled to death. Johan lasted a few minutes longer, before a pike was driven into his face, and he was shot in the neck. It is said that as he fell he managed to clasp his hands in the direction of heaven. Steps from the Gevangenpoort prison museum (where the De Witt cell is on view), on the Plaats, is a statue of Johan De Witt.

Later in 1672, when France invaded Holland, and threats along its coast came from the combined fleets of the French and English navies, the States General once again turned to the House of Orange for leadership. This was **Prince Willem III** (1650–1702), who, in addition to being the Dutch Stadholder, was also to become King of England and Ireland, through marriage to Mary, daughter of James II, with whom he became joint ruler. Naturally, Willem's joint position made The Hague even more of an international meeting center for diplomats and merchants. Even after Willem's death in 1702, splendor continued at the court in The Hague. The pomp and pageantry included mock sea battles on the Hofvijver lake by the Binnenhof, royal processions through the streets with flaming torches, fireworks displays, and outings to Scheveningen.

During the French rule of the Netherlands from 1795 through 1813, the matter of The Hague not being an official town was rectified by an unexpected supporter. In 1806, Napoleon had his brother Louis Bonaparte, who had tried to resist the invitation, come to Holland to act in his place as ruler. Louis arrived at The Hague, which doesn't seem to have suited him. But before he left, first for Utrecht and then Amsterdam, Louis awarded The Hague its first full civic charter.

In 1818, one Jacob Pronk opened a wooden bathing "machine" establishment on the dunes at Scheveningen. This consisted of guests "curing" themselves by sitting in sheltered tubs of "seawater with healing power" atop the dunes. Later, Pronk placed two bathing machines right in the surf, with attendants close at hand to help the daring participants. The business was so profitable that it was taken over by Scheveningen village leaders in 1828, and seaside resort activities have been a main business ever since. Scheveningen's outer and first inner harbor were dug in 1904, and fishing remains a mainstay of the economy. The harbor is home to one of the largest herring fleets in Holland, and for the opening of the season in May on *Vlaggetjesdag* (flag day), the fleet is decked out in colorful pennants and more fishermen's wives than usual wear the local costume (long black dress, striped apron, black shawl, and ornamented starched-white headcover). It's still tradition that the first barrel of *nieuwe haring* (fresh herring) is delivered with great ceremony to the Queen.

The **Peace Palace,** completed in 1913, was an outgrowth of a call for international peace by **Czar Nicholas II of Russia** on August 28, 1898, during a conference for peace that he had called in The Hague. In the U.S., **Andrew Carnegie** heeded the call and donated $1.5 million for a building to house various international institutions.

As the seat of government, The Hague had responsibility for, and a resulting influence over, the administration of colonies, particularly for the supremely important Indonesia. The island archipelago of Indonesia (today, the fifth largest country in the world, based on population) was given its independence in 1949, at which time Indonesian nationals were given the opportunity to move to Holland. The majority who did so settled in the Hague, as did a number of retired Dutch military officers who served in Indonesia, and returning executives who had worked in corporations there.

Though its population today has reached 450,000, in certain respects The Hague remains a small town, although its stores and restaurants, and their clientele, reflect the cosmopolitan character of the town that the International Court of Justice calls home. Travelers to The Hague today can't help but notice the city's curious condition of split personality. The Hague favors diplomacy, dignity, and decorum, royal residences, elegant townhouses, well-endowed museums, and well-tended lawns. In The Hague, the Dutch prefer to stand on ceremony and take pride and pleasure in their history and heraldry. Yet, mere minutes from the staid, stately center of the city proper is its seaside escape valve: Scheveningen.

At **Scheveningen** (pronounced approximately SCKAY-ven-ing), propriety can be dropped—though some *Hagenaars* don't, as attested to by those who stride the North Sea beach in business suits and shoes. Scheveningen boasts a resort full of activities, from wind-screened cafes on the sand to sunbathing pits in the sand to a gambling casino. From the seafront Promenade and Entertainment Pier that reaches out over the waves, it's a few minutes' walk north to a naturist (nudist) beach, while just to the south is the centuries-old fishing village where fishermen's wives still wear their traditional Dutch costume.

In The Hague, there's larger-than-life pageantry when Queen Beatrix arrives in a golden coach drawn by eight matched horses and uniformed honor guard to open Parliament in September. In another corner of the city, ordinary mortals can play Gulliver among the Lilliputians in the 1:25 scale miniature Holland at Madurodam. The Hague's duality provides residents, as well as travelers, with a two-for-one experience, and it's certain that The Hague celebrates rather than suffers its split personality.

GUIDEPOSTS
Telephone Code 070

Tourist Inf. VVV *In The Hague:* Koningin Julianaplein 30 (in Babylon shopping center, next to CS): open Mon.–Sat. 9 a.m.–9 p.m., Sun. 10 a.m.– 5 p.m. (from mid-Sept.–March, closed Sun, other days 9 a.m.–6 p.m.); *In Scheveningen:* Gevers Deynootweg 126; same hrs. as above except open Sun. year-round, mid-Sept.–March other days til 8 p.m.; Tel: 3546200.

Emergencies	Police: 3222222
	Physician (general info) 3455300
	Dentist (day, night, weekend) 3974491
	Pharmacies (evenings & weekends) 3451000
Lost & Found	Police (Mon.–Fri. 9 a.m.–3:30 p.m.: 3108015
Transport Inf.	HMT (public transport) 3429201
Money	Exchange office at Centraal Station open daily 9 a.m.–9 p.m. (Sun. 10 a.m.)
Books	American Discount Book Centers (for U.S. and U.K. titles): Spuistraat 72; 3642742

WHAT TO SEE AND DO......................

Because attractions in The Hague are spread out, they are grouped below by location. Those listed under *The Hague Centrum* are all within roughly a mile of one another. A booklet from the VVV, a self-guided walking tour *Along Seven Centuries of Hague Architecture* (Dfl. 2.50), begins at *Het Plein,* behind the *Binnenhof,* and discusses some 45 sites enroute.

The Hague Centrum to Peace Palace

Mauritshuis • *Korte Vijverberg 8; Tues.–Sat. 10 a.m.–5 p.m., Sun. 11 a.m.–5 p.m., closed Mon.; 3469244; fee* • Adjoining the Binnenhof and facing the Hofvijer, a small lake with swans, a fountain jet, flowing flower boxes, and tree-shaded banks, is the recently restored Mauritshuis, acknowledged as one of the finest small museums in the world. Ensconced in a small 17th-century classical mansion, the Mauritshuis imparts a sense of intimacy and welcome, making you feel as if you're visiting an extraordinary private collection. The Mauritshuis owns about 900 works, of which some 350 are exhibited at any one time (head for the upper floor for the Golden Age favorites). The core of the collection, which numbers 10 Jan Steens, three Vermeers (including *View of Delft*) and 14 Rembrandts (including *The Anatomy Lesson*), consists of paintings acquired since the 18th century by the princes of the House of Orange. Some of the paintings were seized by Napoleon in 1795, but returned in 1816, after his defeat at Waterloo in Belgium. In 1822, the paintings were first put on display in the Mauritshuis, where they could be seen on Wednesdays and Saturday mornings by anyone "who was well-dressed and not accompanied by children." There is a fine museum shop and cafe in the basement. An oddity the museum enjoys is the payment of your entry fee when you exit.

Binnenhof • *Information Center, Binnenhof 8a; Mon.–Sat. 10 a.m.– 4 p.m., in July and Aug. also open Sun; closed hols.; for booking conducted tours 3646144; fee* • The heart of The Hague is the historic Binnenhof, a complex of portals, courtyards, and palaces built beginning in the 13th century, which is the home of the Dutch Parliament. Tours include 1st and 2nd Chambers when Parliament is not in session, and the *Ridderzaal* (Hall of the Knights), a huge, high-ceiling banqueting room, which is one of Europe's medieval architectural treasures. Its decorations include 17th-century Flemish tapestries, a large rose window with the coats of arms of Netherlands counts and dukes, leaded-glass windows with the coats of arms of the principal Dutch cities, and the flags of the 12 Dutch provinces. Today used as the throne room for the Queen's annual opening of Parliament and state receptions, the Ridderzaal was used by Napoleon as a stable. The Information Center has a slide show in English and permanent exhibitions on Holland's government and the Royal Family.

The Royal Tour • *Mon.–Sat. April 1–Sept. 30, except third Tues. Sept., res. from VVV 3546200; 1:45 p.m.; fee Dfl. 19* • is a three-hour afternoon coach excursion that passes the palaces and other points of interest connected with the House of Orange in The Hague, and includes a half-hour visit to the *Ridderzaal* (Knight's Hall) at the Binnenhof.

Lange Voorhout • This grassy L-shaped mall in the center of The Hague is lined with theaters, banking houses, embassies, and the landmark Hotel des Indes. Purple crocuses carpet it in the spring and, in summer, it's the setting for al fresco antique markets. The beauty of this mid-city green space has long been cherished; it's said that early in the 16th century, while he was still ruler of the Low Countries, Emperor Charles V sought to ensure the continuation of the Lange Voorhout's loveliness by ordering that any man who cut down a tree along the avenue would have his right hand cut off as punishment. **Lange Voorhout Palace** is being renovated to host special exhibits in connection with The Hague's Gemeentemuseum. All but one of the buildings along the Lange Voorhout give it an architectural elegance: the modern United States Embassy sticks out like a *non*-classic sore thumb.

The Hague Historical Museum • *Korte Vijverberg 7; Tues.–Sun., hols., noon–4 p.m., closed Mon.; 3646940; fee* • Opened as a museum only a few years ago, this restored mansion is worth stepping inside just for the lovely views out its huge windows overlooking the Hofvijver lake and Lange Voorhout. There's an explanatory floor plan to the exhibits of paintings, portraits, townscapes of The Hague (still recognizable centuries later), and other memorabilia detailing the history of The

Hague (plan in English but not exhibit notes). Nevertheless, the museum is interesting overall, and its setting superb. There's a museum shop.

Museum Bredius • *Lange Vijverberg 14; Tues.–Sat. noon–5 p.m.; 3620729* • Comprised of the fine private painting collection of Abraham Bredius, a former director of the Mauritshuis Museum, the newly reopened Bredius Museum is in new quarters, a beautifully restored manor house facing the Mauritshuis across the Binnenhof's picturesque lake which is lined with large pink-blossomed horse chestnut trees. Bredius collected works by Dutch painters, particularly those of the 17th century; pieces on display include those by Rembrandt, Steen, Van Ostade, and several wonderful ones by Dutch "little masters" Simon Verelst and Hendrik Aerts.

Gevangenpoort (Prison Gate) • *Buitenhof 33; year-round Mon.–Fri. 10 a.m.–4 p.m., from April–Sept. also Sun., hols. 1–4 p.m.; 3460861; fee* • Guided tours every hour on hour; last tour at 4 p.m., extra tours Jul. and Aug.; 10-minute narrated (English) color slide show. Located across from the Binnenhof is the 14th-century former main gate to the complex, which doubled as a prison until 1828. Since then it has served as a museum, containing what is possibly Europe's most comprehensive collection of torture instruments (not that Holland's early treatment of prisoners was more heartless than elsewhere in Europe). A fascinating and frightening insight into the dispensing of justice in earlier days is quietly made very real by the excellent English-speaking guide. He explained that innocents unfortunate enough to find themselves imprisoned often had to suffer through torture before they were believed, and even if an innocent were to survive three days of torture on the rack, the stretcher, thumb screws, etc., he would probably have been an invalid for the rest of his life. If one were guilty, there was no reason not to confess *before* torture: beheading provided a more humane ending. Simple confinement was relatively rare, and the rich could often buy their way out, say by purchasing bricks to repair a city wall.

Schilderijenzall (Prince Willem V Picture Gallery) • *Buitenhof 35; Tues.–Sun. 11 a.m.–4 p.m.; 3182487; fee* • By 1771 Stadholder Prince Willem V of Orange, an enthusiastic art collector, had outgrown his Binnenhof living quarters because of his paintings and bibelots. He bought this house across the street and in 1773 had the first floor converted to a picture gallery, and opened it to the public on certain days (making it Holland's first public museum). Only a few of the paintings here now were in Willem's original collection; he donated much of it to the State in 1815, and the paintings wound up in the Mauritshuis, which had been bought especially for the purpose of displaying the collection. Most paintings on view are 17th-century Dutch, but reflect 18th century tastes (idealized landscapes, opulent still-lifes, and sophisticated genre paintings) and layout, arranged frame-to-frame from floor to ceiling.

Grote Kerk • *Grote Kerk Plein 10; mid-May–mid-Sept. Mon.–Sat. 11 a.m.–4 p.m.; 3658665* • West along the Groenmarkt (vegetable market) from the Buitenhof is the Grote Kerk (St. Jacobskerk), which suffered from fires in 1402 and 1539, but still can be said to date largely from the mid-15th century. In the choir are two stained-glass windows thought to be the work of Gouda artist **Dick Crabeth** (16th century). The **Huygens** (Constantijn and his astronomer son Christiaan) family vault is in the church. Next to the Grote Kerk, dating from 1565, though enlarged twice since then, is the picturesque **Oude Stadhuis** (old town hall). It is used for civil wedding ceremonies and is not usually open to visitors.

Noordeinde Palace Garden • *Public entrance at rear of palace on Prinsessewal; open at all hours* • The garden, good-sized and gracefully landscaped with a lake, and royal stables, are behind the Palace Noordeinde, a neo-classical in-town palace built in 1563 where the widow of Willem the Silent and her children lived after his assassination in 1584 (see Delft, Prinsenhof). Since 1984, Queen Beatrix and her staff have had their offices in the elegant Palace Noordeinde, from which the Queen leaves in her golden horse-drawn coach on *Prinsjesdag* (third Tues. in Sept.) to open Parliament. The palace also has guest rooms for state visitors. Facing the palace is an equestrian statue of Willem the Silent and, across from it, a statue of former Queen Wilhelmina dominates the small square where, under the spreading chestnut tree, there is a stamp market on Wed. p.m. and Sat. a.m. Its proximity to the palace makes Noordeinde one of The Hague's most elegant shopping streets. Following Noordeinde northwest, the road becomes Zeestraat (for Panorama Mesday, following). Just to the east is **Plein 1813**, a monumental roundabout that celebrates Dutch independence from the French. Radiating from it are symmetrical tree-lined avenues that form the heart of The Hague's embassy area.

Panorama Mesday • *Zeestraat 65b; Mon.–Fri. 10 a.m.–5 p.m., Sun., hols. from noon; 3642563; fee* • One of the founding figures of The Hague School was H. W. Mesdag (see Mesdag Museum, following). In 1880, he and a group of artist friends painted a protest against authorities who had decided to cart away the sand dunes at Scheveningen to construct a housing project. The result: the protest made its point, and what is probably the largest canvas in the world—45 feet high, 400 feet in circumference—remains housed in the Panorama Mesdag Museum, specifically designed to display the recently restored painting. At the museum, after progressing through several rooms of smaller works by Mesdag (his subject was almost always Scheveningen: its seascape, fishing fleet, and classic views of women in the local costume waiting on the shore) and his wife (Sina van Houten), visitors pass through a tunnel, and emerge at the top of a flight of stairs in the center of a painted in-the-round scene as seen from atop the dunes at Scheveningen. The details of Dutch fisherfolk life as it was a century ago are marvelous. A taped commentary (multi-lingual, with English) gives some history on panoramas (cycloramas), a popular painting form from the period (though few have survived), appreciated both as a work of art and as a historical document. Panorama Mesday, in which the sense of optical illusion is extraordinary, is made even more realistic since it employs no artificial light; when it's gloomy outside, the beach scene inside is appropriately gray, since the only light that enters the museum comes through a glass dome. Near the exit is the permanent exhibit *The Panorama Phenomenon.*

Mesdag Museum • *Laan van Meerdervoort 7F; Tues.–Sat. 10 a.m.–5 p.m., Sun. and hols. 1–5 p.m.; 3635450; fee* • The nearby H. W. Mesdag Museum is the late Dutch painter's private collection displayed in the townhouse that was his studio. A former banker, **Mesdag** (1831–1915) became a painter (winning a gold medal for a seascape at the 1870 Paris Salon) in a group that collectively became known as *The Hague School* (including Jozef Israels, Anton Mauve, J. W. Bilders, Paul Gabriel, Willem Maris, Willem Roelofs). Not only an avid painter, Mesdag also supported other artists financially, and was a fervent collector. The museum has the most important collection of paintings of the Barbizon School (Corot, Millet, Daubigny, Rousseau) outside of France, as well as many works from the Hague School, which was much influenced by the Barbizons. No English documentation at museum.

Peace Palace • *Carnegieplein 2; Mon.–Fri. 10 a.m.–noon, and 2–4 p.m., guided tours at 10, 11, 2, 3; 3469680; fee; take Tram #7* • Despite its relatively recent appearance on the scene (completed in 1913), the Peace Palace has become a symbol of The Hague. Home of the Permanent Court of International Law (since 1922) and the Academy of International Law (since 1923), the Peace Palace was built with a $1.5 million donation by Scottish-American steel-magnate Andrew Carnegie after the first international conference for the suppression of war was held in The Hague (at Huis ten Bosch) at the insistence of Czar Nicholas II of Russia. As a result of the conference, the Permanent Court of Arbitration was established, and its need for a suitable home reached the ears of Carnegie. The foundation stone was laid in 1907, during a second peace conference in The Hague (held in the Ridderzaal). The Peace Palace is built in the Flemish Renaissance style (by architect Louis Cordonnier of Lille, France, whose design won out over 200 competitors), and the ornate interior is rich in contributions of materials and national craftmanship from dozens of countries. The bronze entrance door is from Belgium, the marble statue *Justice by Peace* from the U.S., the stained-glass windows in the Great Hall from the U.K.

En Route to Scheveningen

Gemeentemuseum • *Stadhouderslaan 41; Tues.–Sun. 11 a.m.–5 p.m., closed Mon.; 3381111; fee; take Tram #10* • The paintings of a relatively recent Dutch master are highlighted at the Gemeentemuseum (municipal museum), which has the world's largest collection (154) of works by **Piet Mondriaan** (1872–1944). The unique group is particularly strong in Mondriaan's early works, which show his movement from early dark landscapes, through his "blue" period, to the totally abstract primary color blocks and black line-pieces for which he is most known, and was most influential. Dutch painter **Karel Appel,** a member of the COBRA group who has lived in New York for many years, has donated more than 50 drawings to the museum. The building (1935) itself was the swan-song of the grand old man of modern Dutch architecture, **H. P. Berlage**. The **Hall,** with its concrete skeleton visible, is the hub of the museum, whose tiles, lighting (all natural, even in the showcases), colors, and other details all bear the Berlage stamp. The 19th- and 20th-century collections contain paintings and sculpture from many European masters, as well as from The Hague School.

Museon • *Stadhouderslaan 41, Tues.–Fri. 10 a.m.–5 p.m., Sat., Sun., hols. noon–5 p.m., closed Mon.; 3514181; fee; take Tram #10* • This remarkable museum, whose exhibition materials cover "every aspect of life" is "typically Dutch" in terms of its well-done displays, and overall philosophy, which stress equality with the idea that "the more you know about people, the more tolerant you'll be." *The Earth, Our Home* is a hit exhibit, and those on human activities on the planet might be something like *So Many People, So Many Hats,* a collection of hats from around the world, or *Everyone has a Right to a Home,* with examples from Bedouin tents to temples to townhouses. Most exhibits have English explanations and, even without them, the message would be meaningful.

Madurodam • *Haringkade 175; daily 9 a.m.–10:30 p.m. except closes 11 p.m. June–Aug., 9:30 p.m. Sept, 6 p.m. Oct–early Jan., closed early Jan. to March; 3553900; fee; Trams #1, 9* • The Hague's most whimsical attraction, Madurodam, is located midway between the town's seat of power and the sea. A miniature man-made Holland, at 1/25 scale, Madurodam fills four acres with replicas of 150 of Holland's most famous buildings (including The Hague's Binnenhof), arranged into a tiny working town complete with trains, mini-marching bands, a bicycle jam, a small Schiphol airport with KLM craft, and a pint-size port of Rotterdam. The attention to detail at Madurodam delights the child in every adult, and children are enchanted to feel as big as Gulliver among the Lilliputians at Madurodam. **Note:** Madurodam's endearing detail is not as visible under the mini-town's night lights, and the script of its evening sound and light show, which I had looked forward to, seemed contrived. I recommend a daylight visit to Madurodam, and a visit to the real Binnenhof for its romantic after-dark illumination.

Scheveningen

If you find the name of this seaside resort hard to pronounce, apparently you're in the company of almost everyone in the world who isn't Dutch. And the Dutch have even put their lives on the line over that fact. During Holland's World War II occupation by the Nazis, in order to determine if the person to whom they were speaking was Dutch or German, members of the Dutch resistance asked the other person to pronounce *Scheveningen*—it's the "sch" sound that makes or breaks it. If the person did so satisfactorily, it was assumed he was Dutch. (A backup tongue-twisting test sometimes used by the Dutch on the Nazis was the word *Massachusetts*—how's *that* for an international outlook!).

Kurhaus • *Steigenberger Kurhaus Hotel (see hotels), Gevers Deynootplein 30; 3520052* • The 1885 Kurhaus is as much a Scheveningen monument as it is a five-star hotel. The magnificent and enormous Kurzaal, with its restored frescoed, gilted, and skylighted domed ceiling, and Corinthian columns supporting the balcony, has been the scene of many memorable events in the past century. Many important people, either performing in the concerts that have long been a tradition in the Kurzaal—the Berlin Philharmonic (under the baton of von Karajan), Bruno Walter, Stokowsky, violinist Yehudi Menuhin, Leonard Bernstein (who wielded his baton here in his European debut), singer Marlene Dietrich, Edith Piaf, Jacques Brel, Maurice Chevalier, Vladimir Horowitz, Charles Aznavour, to name a few—or passing through the great hall to meetings or other business—Churchill, Truman, Crawford, Kissinger, Brandt, Hepburn, NATO meeting attendees—have filled more than one leather-bound hotel guestbook. So, whether you're a guest or not, this is the one interior that's a "must see" in Scheveningen.

Promenade/Boulevard • The broad Promenade/Boulevard, which runs for a mile or more parallel to the beach and open North Sea, just above the sandy Strand, is lined with glass-encased, wind-sheltered cafes and coffee houses, souvenir and snack kiosks, and a huge, heated, artificial wave swimming pool/exercise complex.

The Pier • *at the Promenade; 3543677* • The present Pier opened in 1961, rebuilt after the preceding pleasure jetty had been deep-sixed by the Nazis. The Pier reaches out more than 400 yards over the North Sea, offering dining, sun terraces, an amusement arcade, a 45-meter-high belvedere (viewing tower), a fishing platform, and shops on its four "islands." There are fireworks from the Pier on Friday nights at 11 p.m. in summer. A quiet corner in one of the eateries at its end is a good place from which to watch the sun sink into the North Sea at day's end.

Museum Scheveningen • *Neptunusstraat 92; Tues.–Sat. 10 a.m.– 4:30 p.m., open Mon. in summer; 3500830; fee* • Located in an old school, the museum, since its formation in 1952, has been about the fishing life and history of Scheveningen for Scheveningers. There's a focus on the fishing way of life, photos of old Scheveningen, and local traditional costumes. Coffee is available at an authentic old fishermen's pub on the premises.

SHOPPING

Most department and clothing stores are located in the Centrum (around and off Spui Straat, Hoog Straat, Grote Markt Straat), which has a number of pedestrian streets. The **Passage** is an elegant enclosed shopping arcade. Antiques shops line the **Denneweg,** behind the Hotel Des Indes on Lange Voorhout, and **Noordeinde,** the street named for the palace on it that serves as the Queen's official office. There are some 100 to haunt in The Hague. (Ask at the VVV for the brochure *Antique Walk.)* Antiques, curios, art, books and bric-a-brac also are sold at the open-air market on Lange Voorhout Thurs. and Sun., mid-May–end Sept., 9 a.m.–9 p.m. From Oct. 1–mid-May, the market is Thurs. only, and moves to the nearby Plein. Late-night shopping (9 p.m.) in The Hague is Thurs., with most stores closed Sun. In Scheveningen, especially on and near the beach, opening hours for the plentiful casual shops are longer: seven days a week and, from mid-March–mid-Oct., up until 10 p.m.

ACCOMMODATIONS..........................

The two deluxe properties described here won't save you much money over similar properties in Amsterdam, but both have stellar settings, the character and charm that can come with 100+ years of history, and standards of service on which they pride themselves. If you'll have to be content just to walk through their lobbies, make sure you do. There's no lack of other comfortable corners to book yourself into, keeping in mind that pleasant, less expensive small hotels in Scheveningen (most are family establishments) in summer are in high demand from Dutch, German, and many other tourists, since this is Holland's premier coastal resort. Make reservations as far ahead as possible, and check about minimum length-of-stay requirements in summer. Especially busy is the second weekend in July, when the **North Sea Jazz Festival** (four days) fills the town with music and fans. The VVV will help with accommodations if you decide on the spot you want to stay overnight. Hotels have been separated under The Hague and Scheveningen.

The Hague

Deluxe

★★★★★ **Hotel des Indes (Inter-Continental)** • *Lange Voorhout 54, 2514 EG; 3632932, fax 3451721, res. U.S. & Can. 800–327–0200* • Kings, presidents, and statesmen from many countries can attest to the fact that the Hotel des Indes has always held a grand position in The Hague. Built as a lavish town house by a baron, upon his death the family sold it to a local hotelier, and the palatial building was born as the *Hotel des Indes* (a name chosen to combine both French chic and the exoticism of the Dutch East Indies). Many of the baron's original furnishings remain intact in public rooms: massive crystal chandeliers, glittering mirrors, and rich brocade wall coverings. The magnificent central lounge, still *the* place to take tea, has seen many special guests pass through: Lindbergh, Czar Nicholas II, Eisenhower, Stravinsky, the Dutch spy Mata Hari, and Bing Crosby. The great Russian ballerina Anna Pavlova died here of pneumonia. With only 77 rooms, service can be as attentive as you expect, and the location in this "city of Royal Residence" on the lovely Lange Voorhout is superb. **Le Restaurant,** with its white-glove service, is well-regarded for its classical French flair and fare. The lobby bar is a cosmopolitan meeting place, and the lobby an after theater or symphony rendezvous. Parking available.

First Class

★★★★ **Hotel Corona** • *Buitenhof 39–42, 2513 AH; 3637930, fax 3615785, res. U.S. 800–221–1074, res. Can. 800–344–4034* • Parliament is just around the corner and, with a handsome terrace cafe in front for those who want to be seen and heard, and widely-spaced tables at the hotel's outstanding restaurant inside for those who don't, the Corona is understandably popular with Dutch politicians. The hotel, with its 26 rooms, all of which were recently renovated in contemporary style with pastel colors, dates from the early 1900s (although the building in the 18th century was a lively coffee house), and its handsome marble and mahogany lobby gracefully reflects its age. Parking available close to hotel.

Moderate

★★★★ **ParkHotel Den Haag** • *Molenstraat 53, 2513 BJ; 3624371, fax 3614525* • Built in 1910 as a hotel, the breakfast (included) room overlooks the Noordeinde Palace gardens; some of the 114 guest rooms have balconies with views on to the garden. The Park is conveniently tucked into an antique-and-print-shop-lined street near the center of The Hague. Dignity, not flash, dictates the decor, which has a mix of modern and traditional furniture, and some nice architectural details, including a *Jugenstil* (art nouveau) five-story stairwell in yellow brick. Rooms are spacious, and have large marble baths. There's a lobby bar, but no in-hotel restaurant since there are so many others in the vicinity. The hotel has its own parking garage.

Scheveningen

First Class

★★★★★ **Kurhaus Hotel (Steigenberger)** • *Gevers Deynootplein 30, Scheveningen 2586 CK; 3520052, fax 3500911, res. U.S. 800–777–5848* • Scheveningen's Grande Dame by the Sea, the Kurhaus went from the very real threat of the wrecker's ball (in the early 1970s) to a glittering celebratory ball in honor of its salvation, complete renovation, and centennial in 1985. The huge **Kurzaal,** with its magnificent painted, skylit ceiling, the dome of which seems to reach halfway to heaven, is headquarters and highlight of the hotel, and the wonderful North Sea views out the enormous windows simply reinforce the sense of being someplace special. And I love the unlikely and light-hearted contrast of the blue sculpture of a mermaid sitting in an easy chair reading a book amid the grandeur. The ambiance of the evening buffet in the Kurzaal is ineffably European: live piano music floats into the lofty space, and you can enjoy an eating experience that can be drawn out to save the setting. (A breakfast buffet in the same superb setting is included for overnight guests). Of the Kurhaus' 241 guest rooms, the best ones face the sea, with French windows opening out onto small wrought-iron balconies. A number of rooms are modest in size, but there's plenty of room to spread out on the property. There's a terrace cafe from which to survey the sea and the Pier, and large wave pool, sauna, and exercise complex. Off the Kurzaal, under a red awning, is **Casino Scheveningen,** which, while perfectly enjoyable if you like casinos, isn't as elegant as the Kurzaal; there are 24 tables for French and American Roulette, Blackjack, and Baccarat for the big spenders *(open daily 2 p.m.–2 a.m., dress code).* The **Kandinsky Restaurant,** in a striking Art Deco room with six original lithographs by the artist, is the hotel's a la carte restaurant, with many of its 60 seats overlooking the sea.

★★★★ **Carlton Beach Hotel** • *Gevers Deynootweg 201, 2586 HZ; 3541414, fax 3520029, res. U.S. 800–223–9815* • This 108-room, 76-apartment modern eight-floor hotel fronts directly on the North Sea (moderate supplement for full sea view), and all rooms have balconies. It is located at the end of Scheveningen's built-up beach, and has a pleasantly remote feeling by being the last property before the long line of sand dunes north on up the coast for as far as you can see. Two restaurants, bar, and an indoor fitness center (exercise machines, sauna, steam bath, swimming pool) are among its facilities, and there's free parking for guests. Near all tram lines to The Hague. All rooms have hairdryers, mini-bar or kitchenette. Buffet breakfast included.

Inexpensive

★★★ **Bel Park** • *Belgischeplein 38, 2587 AT; 3505000* • Two rambling turn-of-the-century homes on a green roundabout in a residential neighborhood make this a homey, pleasant choice. It's a 15-minute walk to the Pier, with a tram nearby. Airy, light, and freshly painted, all 14 rooms (and a two-room suite) have shower and toilet, with price varying somewhat with size. No elevator, but wide straight stairs. Free on-street parking.

★★★ **Hotel Petit** • *Grote Hertoginnein 42, 2517 EH; 3465500, fax 3463257* • This is a family-style hotel not far from the Peace Palace, on the Scheveningen side. The late 19th-century house (18 rooms) was renovated in 1988; rooms are generous in size and have desks and sitting areas; all have shower or bath and mini-bar. The house is three floors (elevator to top floor), with stained glass in the stairwell. In a nice residential area (on tram and bus route) near embassies, and guests are of many nationalities. Terrace cafe in front in season; restaurant.

★★★ **Aquarius** • *Zeekant 107, 2586 JJ; 3543543, fax 3543684* • Only a road separates these three connected houses that have been made into a 21-room hotel from the boulevard and beach. Some rooms front sea, several have balconies from which one gets a view of the Pier. Room decor is fairly basic; all rooms have private toilet and curtained shower. There's a breakfast room, pleasant restaurant with three-course menus, and a few tables on the seafront terrace outside. No elevator. Near trams. Parking available.

★★★ **City Hotel** • *Renbaanstraat 1–3, 2586 EW; 3557966, fax 3540503* • Above the restaurant, with terrace cafe, several blocks from the beach and VVV, are six rooms, small, clean, decorated in white wicker with pastel floral prints. Around the corner in this residential quarter of Scheveningen are two houses with some 20 rooms, owned by the hotel, with pay phone and antiques in the small lobby (you are given your own front door key, no elevators). Breakfast is served at restaurant.

★★★ **Esquire** • *Van Aerssenstraat 43–65, 2582 JG; 3522341, fax 3520195* • Several blocks from the Scheveningen inner harbor (with its fish restaurants), this family-run hotel has 30 rooms in seven small houses on a quiet residential street. No elevators, but eight of the rooms are on the ground floor. Rooms have modern utilitarian furniture, and modern tile baths. Breakfast is served under a skylight behind the bar and restaurant (where you can "just say what you'd like" according to the owner).

★★ **Hotel Seinduin** • *Seinpostduin 15, 2586 EA; 3551971, fax 3557891* • Located a block from the boulevard along the beach (near the point from which Mesdag painted the Panorama), a pleasant walk to the Pier. All 18 rooms have shower, toilet, telephone, TV, and minibar. Convenient to VVV and trams. Basic but pleasant. On-street parking.

RESTAURANTS.................................

Several of the hotels mentioned in the previous section have highly-regarded restaurants, and these should be considered among your dining choices in The Hague. Booking is recommended for the better restaurants. An appetizing aspect of the Dutch colonial inheritance is the large number of Indonesian restaurants; this is especially true in The Hague, which has as many as a hundred. **Garoeda** *(Kneuterdijk 18a; open daily; res. at 3465319; inexpensive)* is the one Indonesians themselves, and Hagenaars who have lived there, consider the best, and its location couldn't be much more in the center of things. The dignified atmosphere lends itself to the ceremony of the *rijsttaffel*, but you can dine with fewer dishes if you desire. **De Salon** *(Molenstraat 52; 3654030; closed Mon.; inexpensive)*, which stands out with its distinctive Jugenstil brick exterior, also stands out with Hagenaars for reasonably priced bistro/grill-style meals in the center of town. Located by the picturesque Oude Stadhuis (and in appropriate weather there is a terrace cafe out front from which to view it) is **'t Goude Hooft** *(Groenmarkt 13; open daily; 3469713; inexpensive)* which, in addition to the outdoor tables, has its cozy cafe where the three-course Tourist Menu (Dfl. 19.75) is served, and a restaurant upstairs where Dutch specialties are on the menu. Though it serves continental cuisine, **'t Gemeste Schaap** *(Raamstraat 9; closed Thurs.; 3639572; moderate)* has a delightful old Dutch interior not far from the Grote Kerk. Whether or not you attend a performance in The Hague's Music and Dance Hall, **Cafe Piccolo Mondo** (small world) at the Dr. Anton Philipszaal proves intriguing, since it's shaped like an ice cream cone.

Behind the Lange Voorhout is the cozy **Oude Haagsch Pannekoekhuis** *(Maliestraat 10, off Denneweg; 3462474; inexpensive)*, where you can treat yourself to a plate-size pancake, sweet or savory (my favorite is cheese and chunk ginger) amid a typical old Dutch decor of red-and-white-checked tablecloths and old brass and copper utensils. You can almost count on seeing a Dutch grandmother treating the family. Finish the meal with coffee or a Heineken on the terrace of the pub a few doors down, overlooking a picturesque, unusual canaled corner of The Hague. Even if you're on the hunt for Dutch or English antiques along the Denneweg, you might get the taste for Italian. If so, you won't have far to go to find **Panino Teca** *(Denneweg 41; open daily, 3652026; inexpensive)*. For the same urges in the vicinity of the Peace Palace or Mesdag Museum, try **Il Vesuvio** *(Laan van Meedervoort 14; open daily; 3603735; inexpensive)* for great pizza.

In Scheveningen, local patrons love the **Vispaleis** (fish palace): it's their favorite herring stand at the second inner harbor (Dr. Lelykade). Close at hand are **'t Kokkeltje** *(Dr. Lelykade 11; open daily; 3523300; inexpensive)* and **Ducdalf** *(Dr. Lelykade 5; open daily; 3557692; inexpensive)*. Both offer a wide variety of seafood (herring, sole, North Sea gray shrimp, Zeeland oysters) and it would be hard for it to be fresher, since the fishing fleet and fish auction house are at the next harbor over.

In Voorburg

★★★★ **Vreudg & Rust Restaurant-Hotel** • *Oosteinde 14, 2271 EH, Voorburg; open daily for lunch noon–2:30 p.m., dinner 6:30–10:00 p.m.; for res. 3872081, fax 3877715* • This highly-touted restaurant, within walking distance of the charming old center of Voorburg, a suburb of The Hague, is a 1751 mansion that sits on parkland that runs down to the river Vliet. Refurbished in 1989, the 14 rooms feature such individual details as beamed ceilings, red marble baths with heated marble floors, fine plaster work, and crystal sconces. *First Class/deluxe.*

In Wassenaar
★★★★ **Auberge de Kievet** • *(Stoeplaan 27, Wassenaar-Zuid; open daily lunch noon–3 p.m., dinner 6–10 p.m.; for res. (01751) 19232, fax. 10969* • A countrified mansion-inn in a fashionable, wooded suburb of The Hague, Auberge de Kievet is known first for its restaurant, though the 26 guest rooms are no less comfortable for that. *First Class/Deluxe.*

ENTERTAINMENT AND EVENTS......................................

Queen's Birthday • *30th April* • This national holiday is celebrated in the Queen's hometown with a fun fair and street festivities on the Lange Voorhout.

Vlaggetjesdag (Flag Day) • *mid-May at Scheveningen harbor* • The opening of the herring season, with ''dressed'' fishing fleet ships, food, music, traditional crafts, and boat trips.

Fireworks • *11 p.m. from Scheveningen Pier Fri. evenings July–mid-Aug.; late Aug.* • International Firework Festival with several shows per night (check for dates and time).

North Sea Jazz Festival • *July* • This four-day event at various venues in The Hague is the most prominent jazz festival outside the U.S.

State Opening of Parliament • *third Tues. in Sept.* • Queen Beatrix, herself a resident of The Hague, arrives at the Binnenhof in a golden coach drawn by eight matched horses, attended by an honor guard, to give the details of the government's plans for the coming year in a speech to the first session of Parliament in the Ridderzaal.

The Hague Christmas Market • Ten days in the middle of December on Het Plein.

Inquire at the VVV about Friday evening **organ concerts** at various churches in The Hague, and about concerts in the Kurzaal at the Kurhaus in Scheveningen.

DELFT

Guidelines for Delft

SIGHTS Delft's intimate old center is dense with delicate impressions. Along stretches of its tranquil tree-shaded canals, the luminescence seems to have been supplied by the town's 17th-century master painters, and charming street scenes of daily life that served as subjects for those artists can still be seen. Delft's ancient **Grote Markt** (main market square) is one of the most magnificent in the Benelux, anchored by the **Nieuwe Kerk** (new church, from 1381), and the **Stadhuis.** The **Prinsenhof,** where Willem the Silent *(Father of the Fatherland)* lived, and was slain in 1584, is an atmospheric in-town "palace" museum, just steps from a canalside mansion museum filled with fascinating old Dutch tiles. Most visitors head for **De Porceleyne Fles,** the only one of Delft's famous blue and white ware factories to have survived from the 17th century.

GETTING AROUND Delft is definitely a place to slow your touring pace to a saunter. To be seen and savored as it should, you must walk the compact, picturesque canal-laced city. Buses and trams serve the surrounding suburbs, but not the *Centrum* (old center). Canal boat excursions and tours by horse-drawn tram can supplement, but shouldn't substitute for, your feet in old Delft, especially in and around the **Grote Markt,** and along the **Oude Delft, Hippolytusbuurt, Voldersgracht,** and **Koornmarkt** canals. For a unique view (and great photographs) of Delft, create your own canal cruise on rented pedal boats and kayaks. If you want to join the bicycle brigades—Delft is a university town with 16,000 students and corresponding number of two-wheelers—rent one at the rail station. That's where you'll find taxis, too.

SHOPPING Delftware, the blue and white porcelain that's virtually synonymous with the town, should rightly top your shopping list, which is just as well since it's hard to avoid it in the shops on and just off the Grote Markt. As mentioned before (see *Delftware* in *The Benelux Cultural Legacy: Decorative Arts/Traditional Crafts*), the product's so pretty that the commercialism isn't offensive, though the profusion of choice (and range of quality and price) can cause confusion for the buyer.

ACCOMMODATIONS There's an adequate choice of moderately priced, friendly canal-front hotels in the center of old Delft.

EATING OUT In Delft, you can dine as well as anywhere in Holland. Or catch quicker nourishment around the Markt or along one of the canals, at one of the many cafes, some of which offer outside tables when the weather is cooperative.

ENTERTAINMENT AND EVENTS The VVV tourist office, located on the Markt, will have the latest listings, but you can count on live carillon concerts on the famed Hemony bells of the nearby Nieuwe Kerk on Tues., Thurs., and Sat., 11 a.m.–noon; in summer, there's also a weekly evening carillon concert (check with VVV). Buy a coffee or beer at one of the cafes to secure the equivalent of a front-row seat. Inquire, too, at the VVV about the organ concert schedule at the Oude Kerk. Delft's annual *Art and Antique Fair* (ten days in mid-Oct.), held at the Prinsenhof, is considered one of Europe's most prestigious.

ARRIVING Located between Rotterdam and The Hague, Delft is an inter-city stop on the frequently-serviced main Rotterdam-The Hague-Amsterdam rail line. The Delft station, at Van Leeuwenhoeksingel 41, decorated in old blue-and-white tiles, is slightly outside the center, a 10- or 15-minute walk to the Markt. Regional buses and taxis congregate conveniently at the station. Tram #1, which connects Delft with the center of The Hague and Scheveningen (5 miles), has a Delft stop on Phoenixstraat, a 5–10-minute walk to the Markt. If arriving by car, take exit Delft-Noord or Delft Pijnacker off the A13(E19) motorway. Non-metered parking is available on the Phoenixstraat (just outside the old center).

TRAVEL TIPS *Not* recommended as the way to see Delft, but if **De Porceleyne Fles** is on your "must see" list and your time very limited, it's wise to get a taxi from the rail station to the factory (a fair walk, none of it within the pretty old center). The factory (at which there is on-street parking if you arrive by car) will call a taxi when you're ready to leave, and you could ask the driver for a quick ride through old Delft before being dropped back at the station.

Delft in Context

Although a small settlement had existed previously, the real history of Delft begins with the 1075 arrival of Duke Godfried van Lotharingen, called Govert the Hunchback, who built a fortress, probably on the site where the Stadhuis is today, and had the first canals of Delft dug (the patterns of which are essentially the same today). Under the administration of successive Counts of Holland, Delft had become a center for the exchange of agricultural goods between the village and the surrounding countryside by the early 13th century. In 1226, under Count Willem II, Delft received its first charter, which included the right to hold a weekly market, which it still does (Thurs., on the Markt). Present-day names, such as the Beesten (animal) Markt, recall when pigs were sold there; today, that square's atmosphere, especially in the evening, is more like Paris' Place du Tertre. Delft was granted permission in 1389 to excavate the Delfshavense Schie, which provided a direct connection with the Maas River at Rotterdam, an undertaking that contributed substantially to the inland town's prosperity.

As early as the 13th century, the brewing of beer had developed as an important industry in Delft. By the second half of the 14th century, Delft beer boasted markets not only in Holland, but also in Flanders and Germany. The water in Delft's canals, it seems, was especially well-suited to the preparation of beer and, by the 15th century, Delft had nearly 200 beer breweries.

Another Delft industry of the day, second in success only to brewing, was cloth weaving. It expanded to the manufacture of tapestries (see the Tapestry Hall of the Prinsenhof) and carpets in the 16th century, when emigrating Flemish weavers, fleeing difficulties caused by Catholic Spanish rulers there, settled in Delft. Street names are reminders of those days: *Voldersgracht* (Fullers Canal); *Raam* (Frame); and *Versersdijk* (Dyers' Dike).

As well as being distinguished as a center of resistance and headquarters for Willem (the Silent) of Orange during the war with the Spanish, Delft was the birthplace of some of the developing Dutch nation's proudest figures. The admirals **Piet Hein** (1577–1629) and **Marten Tromp** (1598–1653) achieved national victories that still warm the hearts of Dutch sailors, and both are buried with appropriate monuments in Delft's Oude Kerk. The town's **Hugo de Groot** *(Grotius)* (1583–1645), jurist and statesman who established the principles of international law (see *Benelux Cultural Legacy, The Muse*) is singled out by a statue in the center of Delft's Markt. When Holland wrested itself free from the Spanish, at least on its soil, in the late 16th-century and began to flourish, Delft was well-positioned to share in the prosperity.

In 1572, during the Eighty Years' War engagements in Holland, military leader Willem took up residence at the **Prinsenhof** in Delft (relocating from the Binnenhof in The Hague, which was less protected). Having the Prince of Orange present within its walls conferred great prestige upon Delft. He'd been an inspiring leader when Holland's major towns rose with him to resist the Spanish in the early, most trying years of the Eighty Years' War for the Dutch. He especially shone in the liberation of Leiden from its bravely resisted beseigement, and while living in Delft, became generally known affectionately as Father Willem and, more grandly, *Het Vader de het Vaderland* (Father of the Fatherland), the true and trusted leader of the now Protestant northern Netherlands.

Thus the events of July 10, 1584—a familiar date to all Dutch—at Delft's Prinsenhof were especially tragic. That night, heading to the dining room with his wife Louise de Coligny and guests, Willem passed a man who he recognized as a Protestant emissary from the French court who he had previously received. In fact, unbeknownst to Willem, the man, Balthasar Gerard (Geraerts) had been to the Prinsenhof the previous Sunday, lingering in the courtyard. When a guard asked what his business was, Gerard, remaining anonymous, gave the seemingly guileless reply that he had no business there, what he really wanted was to be in the church opposite (the Waalse Church, still used today), but lacked appropriate stockings and shoes. The guard kindly conveyed his need to Willem, who had given the guard money for the would-be worshipper. As it came out later, however, Gerard did not buy footwear with the prince's money. Instead, he made a long-planned purchase of pistols and bullets, for he was no Protestant emissary from France, but a Catholic fanatic from Burgundy who was out to collect the reward that the Spanish King Philip II had put on Willem's head. That July evening, Gerard, having obtained entry to the Prinsenhof under false pretenses, waited in hiding. Their dinner done, Willem, leading his party up to his chambers, had only mounted two steps when Gerard stepped out from behind a curtain and fired three bullets, two of which hit Willem, passing through his body, leaving holes in the wall behind him. The beloved 51-year-old leader of the Dutch people, fell, his supposed final words learned by all school children: "My God, have pity on me and my poor people." The *teychenen derkoogelen* (marks of the bullets), still visible at the bottom of the stairs in the Prinsenhof, have been so enlarged by Dutch visitors touching them that they are now protected behind glass.

Gerard, who escaped briefly in the ensuing confusion, was soon captured by guards and taken to the prison cell in Delft's Stadhuis on the nearby Markt. In the Belfry (that survived a fire in 1618 and was incorporated into the replacement, built in 1620), Gerard was imprisoned to await trial and sentencing in a cell that required him to remain constantly in a prone position. On the Markt, four days later, Gerard was drawn, quartered, and beheaded, his head placed on a pike in public.

The 17th-century Golden Age glowed in Delft. In 1602, the Dutch East India Company established its headquarters here, and the owners began to make trading arrangements with China to import that country's popular blue and white ware to Europe. Millions of pieces reached Holland through the Delft-based company between 1602 and 1657. Delft artisans, in trying to imitate the pretty pieces to get in on the profits, developed their own fine product, and the town's fledgling pottery industry took off. By the middle of the 17th-century, nearly 30 factories were producing blue and white (and other patterns), which became known simply as Delftware. The manufacture of tiles took an enormous upturn, and they can still be seen in old homes, restaurants, and taverns throughout Holland on fireplaces, in kitchens, and to edge walls where they meet the floor. Tiles became so typical in homes that they can be seen in some of Vermeer's paintings.

Moving at a parallel with the 17th-century momentum of the pottery industry in Delft was painting. The Delft School's greatest masters were **Jan Vermeer** (1632–1675) and **Pieter de Hoogh** (1629–1684). De Hoogh, a genius at genre, was born in Rotterdam and had moved to Amsterdam by the time of his death, but he called Delft home during the most productive period of his life when he created his memorable and intimate interpretations of domestic life. Genre painter **Jan Steen** also lived for a while in Delft, though he did not belong to the Delft School; for some years from 1654 onward, he managed the beer brewery *De Slange* in the Oude Delft. Delft's Golden Age legacy was led up to by several significant local painters: **Anthonie Palamedeszoon** (genre scenes), **Paulus Potter** (famous for his landscapes with animals), **Gerrit van Houckgeest, Cornelis van Vliet,** and **Emanuel White,** known for their church interior paintings.

Most important of all was **Carel Fabritius** (1622–1654), Rembrandt's most accomplished student, and a painter who had a strong influence on Vermeer, although no proof of any formal painter/pupil relationship exists. Already recognized, and considered a painter with enormous potential promise, Carel Fabritius was killed at the age of 32 in the 1654 Delft calamity, the *Delft Thunderclap*. At half past ten the morning of October 12, a gunpowder magazine (located in the northern part of the old town) containing some 80,000 pounds of powder left over from the Spanish war blew up. It killed hundreds of people and completely destroyed or did great damage to at least half the buildings of the town. The blast buckled the stout walls of the Nieuwe Kerk, which stood diagonally across the street from **Mechelen,** the house on the Markt (roughly where #62 is today) where Vermeer lived most of his life, and the setting for, and where he created, most of his paintings. In the explosion, Carel Fabritius was buried beneath the rubble of his house, along with his family and the man who was sitting for his portrait.

It is Johannes (Jan) Vermeer who, today, we associate most closely with Delft. It has been suggested that the high finish of Vermeer's enamel-smooth paintings reflects the glaze of Delft porcelain, an omnipresent influence in the town during his lifetime. In the autumn of 1632, Vermeer, second child of Reynier Janszoon Vos and his wife Dymphna, was listed in the baptism register of Delft's Nieuwe Kerk, which stood only steps across from Markt from the family residence Mechelen. Mechelen was an active establishment: his father kept a tavern there, designed and sold cloth from there, and, the year before Jan's birth, had been registered by the Guild of St. Luke as a Master Art-Dealer. Vermeer was undoubtedly influenced by the paintings his father handled as an art dealer (many of the works bought and sold would have come from nearby Utrecht, a Catholic city whose school of artists were more closely connected to Italy and Caravaggio, with his dramatic use of light), as well as the works he could see at studios of artists in Delft. It is likely that Vermeer began as an apprentice at about the age of 15, although nothing is known of his art education. The register at Delft's Stadhuis notes his marriage on April 5, 1653, to Catharina Bolnes, who came from a prosperous family in Gouda. Jan and his wife lived with his parents at Mechelen, remaining there for most of their marriage (which produced 11 children in 20 years). In December 1653, Vermeer was listed as a Master Painter in the local Guild of St. Luke.

We know of Vermeer's interest in music from the subjects of his paintings. Living as he did across from the Nieuwe Kerk, the installation in the tower there of a carillon of 36 Hemony Brothers bells ("the latest thing") in 1663 must have been of interest, perhaps inspiration, since he would have heard them all day long.

Vermeer was well-respected by his contemporaries: twice he served two-year terms on the board of the Guild of St. Luke. Because the Dutch have always kept meticulous records of financial transactions, it can be deduced that Vermeer lived a frugal life, but his financial condition deteriorated near the end of his life. In 1672, he and his family were forced to rent out Mechelen and moved to a smaller house (on nearby *Oude Langedijk*). When he died three years later in 1675 (and was buried in the Oude Kerk), Vermeer left his wife and eight minor children with almost no money.

Of the several dozen paintings (there was little else) his wife Catharina possessed at the time of his death, some 29 were Vermeer's own (only 32 of his entire life's work are known to exist today). Catharina seems to have made great efforts to keep her husband's paintings, but there was no way to make ends meet, and she declared herself bankrupt in April 1676. Designated as receiver for the estate was Delft native **Antonie van Leeuwenhoek,** born the same year as Vermeer, a town clerk to the Delft bailiff, who, on the side, liked to muse over matter under the microscope and, who, through his improvements on that instrument, is credited with giving the world the first accurate description of red blood corpuscles and is responsible for the first drawing of bacteria in 1683. (Although his works aren't in as many museums as Vermeer's, some are on view at the Museum Boerhaave in Leiden). Leeuwenhoek seems to have been unsympathetic in his dealings with

Vermeer's widow. At the sale of the bankrupt estate, a woman merchant named Jannetje Stevens managed to have 26 paintings by Vermeer seized and held as security against a family debt of 500 guilders "for groceries supplied." Catharina protested, and it was agreed that if she immediately paid 342 guilders, the art works would be returned to her. But there are no records that tell whether Catharina ever saw her husband's paintings again.

In 1696, an Amsterdam auction catalogue listed 21 paintings by Vermeer, with an average asking price of 70 guilders. That catalogue comprises one of the few historical foundations that critics have for determining genuine Vermeers to this day. The 1696 auction in Amsterdam marked the last time for nearly 200 years that Vermeer's work received any but the most incidental public attention; Vermeer was all but ignored during the 18th and most of the 19th centuries, and even detailed scholarly volumes about the painters of Holland's proud Golden Age of art gave his work no mention. Attention to Vermeer didn't begin again until 1842, when the French aristocrat Thore-Burger, during a visit to Holland chanced to see *View of Delft,* which hung in a gallery in The Hague, and was so impressed by the painting that he devoted much of the rest of his life to making Vermeer well known.

By the time Vermeer died in Delft in the second half of the 17th century, Amsterdam and Rotterdam, because of the superior size and location of their ports, had taken over progressively more of the Dutch nation's trade. Although its famous pottery industry continued strong, the rest of Delft slowed down. The number of breweries in the city shrank from 200 to 15. Just before Vermeer's death, Holland as a whole also saw a complete change in its fortunes. In 1672, Louis XIV of France, who resented the Dutch for their prosperity and coveted their Rhine River ports on the North Sea, sent his armies into the Dutch Republic. In a matter of months, they had swept through most of the country. The French invasion closed the books on the Golden Age, and the country went into a decline that affected every phase of life, including the art market, which completely collapsed. Delft's economy came to a standstill. In the 18th century, even Delftware was in decline, and most of the pottery factories closed. The town became one of retired residents, and a bastion of conservative Calvinism.

A dormant Delft saw the dawn of a new age in the mid-19th century, fostered by the founding of the *Koninklijke Akademie* (Royal Academy),—now the Technical Academy—in 1842, and the linking of the town to the national railway network in 1847. For the sake of expansion, ancient town ramparts were sacrificed, but powerful protests against the further mutilation of the old town—the Oude Delft canal had been threatened with being filled in to make way for a tram track in the center—in large measure prevailed. Today, as you cruise along Delft's flower box-decorated canals, or absorb the sights on foot, you see well-preserved monuments, such as the former **East India Company** headquarters (originally three 16th-century houses), the former **St. Barbara Cloister,** founded in 1405, and the 1650 **Vleeshal** (now both renovated as student clubs), the 1770 **Waag** (Weigh House, used today as a theater), the **Visbanken** (still in use as a fish market, since 1342), and the picturesque **Oostpoort** (the last remaining of Delft's eight 14th-century city gates), located throughout the prosperous town. Delft's population, which had been 23,000 during the days of Vermeer, and fell to 13,000 by the beginning of the 19th century, now numbers 90,000 (greater Delft), and its 16,000 students from the Technical University make a lively contribution to contemporary life in Delft.

GUIDEPOSTS
Telephone Code 015

Tourist info	VVV Markt 85, 2611 GS; 126100; open Mon.–Fri. 9 a.m.–6 p.m., Sat. 9 a.m.–5 p.m., Sun. 11 a.m.–3 p.m. (from Oct. 1–March 31 closed Sun.)
Markets	Thurs. general market on the Markt 9 a.m.–5 p.m. (poultry to produce, nuts to knick-knacks); flower market at same time along Hippolytusbuurt canal; flea market along canals in town center Sat. end Apr.–end Sept., often to the accompaniment of barrel organs and street musicians.
Parking	Metered parking on the Markt (except during Thurs. market), near to the VVV, which has map showing other in-town locations. Free parking on Phoenixstraat by windmill, just outside of old town to west.
Canal Cruises	*Rederij Brands,* Wijnhaven. From week before Easter to mid-Oct.; daily 10:30 a.m.–5:30 p.m.; 45 mins.; 126385.
Pedal Boats & Kayak Rental	Rotterdamseweg 148 (near De Porceleyne Fles); rentals by the hour; 571504.
Horse-drawn Tram	On the Markt; Easter–Sept.; daily except Thurs. (market day); 561828.
Bike Rental	At the station. Maps of ANWB signposted cycling routes (Delfland and Westland) available at VVV.

Taxis At the station.

WHAT TO SEE AND DO......................

Delft is a destination deserving of an overnight stay, even though it's practically in The Hague's backyard. During the day, explore quiet courtyards, quaint interiors, gardens, and gables. Sunlight sifting through ancient trees highlights fascinating Dutch facades and produces fantastic reflections in the waters (green in summer, dark in winter) of the canals, crossed by humpbacked bridges—all redefined by Delft's special quality of light. After the motorcoach crowds have called it a day, a medieval atmosphere moves back to the Markt, and seeing the monuments around its expanse illuminated after dark is a special experience. The Markt, the showplace of Delft, marked in the center by a statue of native son Hugo de Groot (Grotius), who is most definitely meant to be honored but is unintentionally dwarfed by the scale of the long marketplace (still used as such on Thurs.), has one grouping of Delft's premier attractions, while a cluster of others can be found on the lovely Oude Delft canal, only several interesting walking blocks away. On national Dutch holidays, opening hours are different, so check with the Delft VVV.

Prinsenhof • *St. Agathaplein 1 (entrance off Oude Delft); open Tues.–Sat. 10 a.m.–5 p.m., Sun. & hols. 1–5 p.m. (Mon. open 1–5 p.m. June–Aug. only); 602358* • The Prinsenhof is one of the Dutch nation's most historic buildings, and one of Delft's loveliest, just off the Oude Delft canal in the St. Agathaplein, an old cobbled courtyard with chestnut trees, a 15th-century chapel, and an ambiance of Burgundian days, when the earliest sections of the building were erected as a cloister. The Prinsenhof has the sad celebrity of being the place where Prince Willem the Silent, having lived there from 1572 when he became the leader of the Dutch Protestant revolt against the ravages of Spanish Catholic rule in the early days of the Eighty Years' War, died from an assassin's bullet in 1584; the event gives the buildings its credentials as the cradle of Dutch liberty (see *History*). The fascinating building is a labyrinth of rooms and corridors of unusual beauty, filled with fresh flowers and antique portraits, paintings, and furniture, primarily reflecting Delft's history, particularly in the period of the Eighty Years' War. At the reception desk is a detailed English text with the history, layout of building, and description of exhibits, which you can take around with you.

Museum Lambert van Meerten • *Oude Delft 199; hours same as Prinsenhof; 602358* • Nearby on the Oude Delft canal is a charming old patrician canal-side mansion, whose owner Lambert van Meerten set out to make a museum of the decorative arts at the end of the last century. The core of the collection is old Dutch tiles. The tiles, whole walls' worth of individual squares, or grouped together in tableaux (there's a 200-tile representation of a naval victory set in the wall above the stairs that lead from the spacious entry hall), show the full range of artisans' skill and imagination in this traditional Dutch medium from the 16th–18th century. The house has lovely details, heavy oak shutters, leaded window glass, lovely carved wood molding and wainscoting, oak-beamed alcoves, 17th-century Hindeloppen paneling from Friesland, and the so-called Leyden room, whose atmosphere is reminiscent of Vermeer. This is a truly delightful corner of old Delft.

Oude Kerk (Old Church) • *Heilige Geestkerkhof; April 1–Nov. 1, Mon.–Sat. 10 a.m.–5 p.m.; 123015* • The foundations were first laid in 1240, though the stone church and tower one sees today dates from about 1500. The squat, squared tower leans noticeably, more than six feet (two meters) off the perpendicular. During a dozen-year restoration, which was completed in 1961, glazier Joep Nicolas, who had worked in the U.S., was commissioned to make entirely new windows for the church. The church's largest bell, *Bourdon* by name, cast in 1570 and weighing ten tons, is rung only on the most important occasions, the last being the funeral in Delft of Wilhelmina, the former queen, in 1962. Among the prominent persons buried in the Oude Kerk is Vermeer (a simple stone); there's a memorial to Leeuwenhoek, and impressive tombs of the great Dutch naval heroes Piet Hein and Maarten Tromp. Hein's tomb, a marble effigy of the captor of the Spanish silver fleet (1628) in a chapel with doric columns of black and white marble, is the work of Pieter de Keyser, eldest son of the famous architect Hendrick de Keyser, who had designed Willem the Silent's mausoleum in the Nieuwe Kerk. Tromp's memorial, a baroque monument executed by Pieter de Keyser's brother Willem from a design by Jacob van Campen, features an effigy in full armor, with a relief of the naval battle at Terheyde, in which Tromp met his death. (In Dutch sea lore, Admiral Tromp is remembered for supposedly once hoisting a broom to his masthead to proclaim that he had swept the seas clear of the English.)

Het Wapen van Savoye • **(Gemeentelijke Archiefdienst** or **Municipal Archives)** • *Oude Delft 169; Tues.–Fri. 9 a.m.–4 p.m. (Thurs. til 9 p.m.); 602341* • This former 16th-century house now exhibits changing displays related to Delft's history. A shop sells reproductions of old paintings, drawings, and maps in notepaper and postcard form.

Also note next door the **Gemeenlandshuis van Delfland** (Delfland Water Authority) at Oude Delft 176. This former home (no visits) is Holland's finest surviving example of 16th century gothic architecture.

Nieuwe Kerk • *Markt; Apr. 1–Nov. 1, Mon.–Sat. 9 a.m.–5 p.m., closed Sun., Nov. 1–Apr. 1, Mon.–Sat. 10 a.m.–noon, 1:30–4 p.m.; 123025* • The Niewe Kerk, begun in 1381 and completed in 1496, is designated the "new church" only in comparison with Delft's tilting-towered Oude Kerk, whose origins go back to the year 1240. In the Niewe Kerk crypt are buried all members of the Dutch royal family, the House of Orange. Willem the Silent's mausoleum, designed by Hendrick de Keyser, and years in the making at a staggering cost, shows a white marble recumbent figure, at the foot of which is the effigy of his devoted dog. So the story goes, Willem's dog refused food and water after his master's death, and died within days. Willem's monument is directly above the House of Orange royal burial vaults (not open to the public). The most recent ruler to be put to rest was former Queen Wilhelmina, who died in 1962 and, at her own decree, had an all-white funeral.

For visitors interested in an energetic climb, the 357-foot tower is open in summer. The panorama of the Dutch countryside from the top reveals flat green grazing fields speckled with cows, rooftops in The Hague nearby and, beyond, sand dunes and the thin blue line of the North Sea. In the Niewe Kerk tower is a Hemony 48-bell carillon, one of the finest of many in Holland.

Stadhuis • At one end of the Markt stands the magnificent 17th-century Stadhuis, or town hall. The tower dates from the 15th-century, saved from a fire (1618) that destroyed the rest of the building. Inside, a massive marble staircase leads to the council chamber, which also serves as the site for the civil wedding ceremonies that are required by Dutch law. Among the items on display is a 17th-century map of Delft, showing a remarkably similar layout to what it is today. If timing is fortunate, you might see a wedding party arriving at the Stadhuis in horse-drawn carriages (though you can visit the building only if no such ceremonies are scheduled).

Not of such importance as the sights described above if your time is limited, but of possible interest if you are lingering longer are:

Paul Tetar van Elven Museum • *Koornmarkt 67; May–Oct. 1, Tues.–Sat., 1–5 p.m.; 124206* • This 18th-century canalside patrician house was the home of Delft painter **Paul Tetar van Elven** (1823–1896), who was born in Antwerp, and taught drawing at Delft. It retains a 19th-century atmosphere in its interior. Contents in the period rooms include a fine collection of porcelain, an artist's studio furnished in the old Dutch manner, ceiling frescoes, and paintings and drawings by the former owner.

Royal Dutch Army and Arms Museum • *Korte Geer 1, Tues.–Sat. 10 a.m.–5 p.m., Sun. 1–5 p.m.; 150500* • While museum contents, exhibits revealing Dutch military history through realistic figures (and armies of "toy" soldiers), stylish suits of armor and more modern military dress and paraphernalia, and dioramas (no English descriptions) won't be of interest to everyone, the building (a handsome renovated 17th-century arsenal) and location may well be. The arsenal is located on an extension of the west side of Delft's Koornmarkt, just across the curve of a canal water from the *Zuidwal* (south wall), the place from which Vermeer took his *View of Delft*, which shows the museum, town towers, the soft, reflective light, and huge sky, hovering somewhere between full sun and showers. (The *View of Delft* is at the **Mauritshuis** next door in The Hague.)

Nusantara Museum of Ethnology • *Sint Agathaplein 4, Tues.–Sat. 10 a.m.–5 p.m., Sun. and Mon. June–Aug. only, 1–5 p.m.; 602358* • Located across from the Prinsenhof, this museum has a collection of objects from the Dutch East Indies (Indonesia). It particularly focuses on the range of arts and crafts representing the diverse cultures within Indonesia, the former Dutch colony which gained its independence in 1949.

SHOPPING................................

There's a full complement of department and other stores at in-town *In de Veste* pedestrianized shopping center, and in and off the Markt are smaller, more personalized shops, such as the butcher and the baker. But, since this *is* Delft, presumably it's the candlestick maker (of blue and white ware) that you've come to see. Begin with at least a look at the best: De Porceleyne Fles handpainted works. You'll notice the difference in quality of decoration between these pieces and the factory-made ware at the many shops that line the Markt, and also the difference in price.

Royal Delftware Factory De Porceleyne Fles • *Rotterdamseweg 196. Apr. 1–Nov. 30 Mon.–Sat. 9 a.m.–5 p.m., Sun. & hols. 10 a.m.–4 p.m.; Dec. 1–Mar. 31, Mon.–Fri. 9 a.m.–5 p.m., Sat. 10 a.m.–4 p.m., closed Sun.; 560234* • De Porceleyne Fles (the porcelain bottle), founded in 1653, schedules potter's wheel and handpainting demonstrations (by one of the firm's 150 artists) frequently during the day, to give you an idea of the personal attention that goes into producing each piece of the factory's ware, distinguished on the bottom by the mark of a jar and initials "JT" to attest to its authenticity. The show rooms are so prettily arrayed that it feels like a museum (and indeed, some of the unique pieces are as expensive as museum objects). Around tiled fireplaces and in a superb display cabinet presented by the Dutch King William III sit blue and white (and other polychrome patterns) jugs and ginger jars, bowls and bud vases, and tiles and teapots.

There are some seconds (25–40% off) on sale at the factory, although the Royal Delft store with the largest selection of seconds in town (also good selection of first quality pieces) is **De Backer vd Hoeck** (*Markt 62, Apr. 1–Oct. 30, open daily 9 a.m.–6 p.m., 142227*), which will mail purchases anywhere. There is also a branch of the shop at Markt 30 (open year-round) in the back room of which is a fine collection of colorful tiles; many are seconds, but with careful inspection, you'll find ones that are fine for yourself or as gifts.

Atelier de Candelaer • *Kerkstraat 13. Apr. 1–Sept. 30: Mon.–Fri. 9 a.m.–6 p.m., Sat. 9 a.m.–5 p.m., Sun. 10 a.m.–6 p.m.; Oct. 1–Mar. 31 Mon.–Sat. 10 a.m.–5 p.m. 131848* • In a picturesque corner of Delft just off the Markt behind the Nieuwe Kerk, this two-person studio sells the fine pieces of handmade Delft produced on-site.

ACCOMMODATIONS

The hotels listed are all very centrally located, only a short walk from the Markt, but on residential streets with canals. Staffs are friendly and very able in English.

Moderate

★★★★ **Delft Museumhotel** • *Oude Delft 189, 2611 HD; 140930, fax 140935* • This is Delft's most recent hotel, though it's in two contiguous 17th-century houses. The traditional brick, big-windowed, dignified facade shelters a friendly staff and lobby and public rooms that are updated in ambiance. Each of the 28 guest rooms in the hotel proper is different, many with original details. There are 25 additional rooms in a new addition at the back, which are larger and slightly more expensive, that offer views of the gardens. There is a lobby cafe for breakfast (no restaurant) and snacks during the day, and a bar-lounge (that looks out on Delft's Oude Kerk). Prices vary slightly with room view (eight face canal, or garden) or suite, all with modern tiled bath and shower. Nice sense of character, winding corridors.

★★★★ **De Ark** • *Koornmarkt 59–65, 2611 EC; 157999, fax 144997* • Housed in three restored canal houses in a lovely residential section of central old Delft are 16 rooms (seven with canal view, others face garden), all different, large, often sunny, neat, though with rather nondescript modern furniture. Never mind. There's plenty of dutch *gezellig* (coziness) about the place, and the friendly front desk is staffed 24 hours. The bricked, beamed dining room with corner fireplace provides a Dutch buffet breakfast, and well-prepared, tasty dinners if you desire. There's parking for a fee, and several one-bedroom suites in the annex across the street (canal).

★★★ **Leeuwenbrug** • *Koornmarkt 16, 2611 EE; 147741, fax 159759* • Also on the same charming canal (quite quiet, one-way traffic), all 33 rooms in this three-floor elevatored hotel, which has a mix of traditional and modern decor and details, are different, some with beams, mantels, or other details; five face canal; each with modern bath and/or shower; five rooms are in the new additional canal townhouse next door, with huge windows. There's a cozy lobby lounge with newspapers, books, and TV (also in all rooms), that faces canal. Breakfast only, but there's a lobby bar that's open til 1 a.m. Pay parking next to hotel.

RESTAURANTS

You can dine handsomely (and historically) in Delft. But if you prefer a simply savory or sweet snack, you won't have to forgo a scenic setting to do so.

Restaurant De Prinsenkelder, or the Princes' Cellar *(Prinsenhof, entrance Schoolstraat 11; Mon.–Fri. noon–2:30 p.m., and 6–9:30 p.m., dinner only on Sat., closed Sun.; 121860; expensive)* is in the attractive brick vaulted basement of the Prinsenhof. Meathooks can still be seen in the ceiling, which shows that while the building served as a cloister and as the home of Willem the Silent, this was the food and wine cellar. The atmosphere for the first class, local Dutch food carefully prepared and presented in the French style (fresh sauteed eel, fillet of tuna with Dutch shrimp, ginger with cream) is historic, romantic, very Dutch, and definitely Delft.

Another touch of old Delft is the **Restaurant "Het Straatje van Vermeer"** *(Molslaan 18; Tues.–Sat. noon–3 p.m., and 6–10 p.m.; reservations at 126466; expensive),* which has a cozy ambiance of Dutch decor with antiques, old tiles, and copies of Vermeer paintings on the walls. Reserve for dinner, since the restaurant does serve groups, and you want to be seated in a room with other individual parties. Menus and a la carte choices include a full range of continental and Dutch dishes.

For more informal fare, begin at the Markt. **Monopole** *(Markt 48)* is just one of many cafes there, helping to fill the vast space with outdoor tables and chairs when the weather warrants, and providing an excellent vantage point from which to survey the superb setting. You can sit as long as you want over a coffee, juice, or beer, and maybe you'll be thinking you're in heaven if the carillon in the Nieuwe Kerk begins a carillon concert (Tues., Thurs.—market day and quite a different scene—and Sat. at 11 a.m.). Light meals and snacks available from early morning until well into the evening. Across the Markt, about midway along its length, is a **Banketbakkerij** or pastry shop *(corner of J. Gerritstraat, open Mon.–Sat. til 5:30 p.m.)*, which also sells bread, chocolates, and Holland's *hopjes* (coffee-flavored caramels). Head for the back of the shop, up a few stairs, to the tiny tea room (where you only need buy a cup of coffee). It has four check-clothed tables, a huge old tiled fireplace, walls hung with old wooden cookie molds, all overlooking a little canal.

Nearly next-door neighbors on the lovely Oude Delft canal are two local favorites. **Kleyweg's Stads-Koffyhuis** *(Oude Delft 133; 124625; closed Sun.)* for breakfast, lunch, dinner, or coffee, served outside on a barge moored along Delft's oldest, possibly most picturesque, canal if you like. A tasty variety of sandwiches, pancakes, and other light meals is served. The **Stadspannekoeckhuys** *(Oude Delft 113, 130193, open daily noon–10 p.m., closed Mon. in winter)* is another good choice for platter-size Dutch pancakes and quick meals. Back at the Prinsenhof Museum is the **Koffiekelder de Nonnerie** *(St. Agathaplein, off Oude Delft, 121860, closed Mon.)*, a cafe in the cellar that serves coffee and lunch, in the garden when the weather's right.

ROTTERDAM

Guidelines for Rotterdam

SIGHTS Despite a history as lengthy as its neighboring Dutch towns, Rotterdam has an entirely different appearance and personality, largely a result of the leveling of its center by the German *Luftwaffe* on May 14, 1940. Rotterdam's city skyline, especially at the waterfront, is contemporary and striking; sections along its **port,** the largest and busiest in the world, look like a grown-up "Erector" set, with cranes locked in their skyward saluting position. Commentary on cruises points out just how state-of-the-art the port is. On land and water, imaginative planning is much in evidence, as you'll discover when visiting the several excellent **museums** and exceptional examples of **modern architecture.** Rotterdam's one preserved historic section has U.S. pilgrim ties: picturesque **Delfshaven** is the port from which the English Separatists who had been living in Leiden departed on the sea journey that led them to Plymouth, Massachusetts.

GETTING AROUND   The broad boulevard **Coolsingel,** running north/south through modern Rotterdam's center, and continuing to the port as **Schiedamsedijk** from the point where **West Blaak** and **Blaak** make an east/west crossing, provides a basic orientation to the city. Many of the major sights are on or near these streets, though several may be too far to reach on foot, in which case there's a good **tram/bus/Metro** network (and helpful system map). A Dfl. 8.25 day-pass is available from the city transportation booth on Stationplein. The VVV, which has a city information booth at Centraal Station, runs an hour-long **city tour** from there (daily 1:15 p.m. Apr. 1–Sept. 30), on an historic tram; it provides a good look at the city's many faces. **Spido Havenrondvaarten** *(Willemsplein at waterfront; 4135400; tram 5 from CS, Metro: Leuvehaven)* has a selection of frequently scheduled port cruises (1¼ and 2¼ hrs. and longer, multi-lingual commentary). A combination tram/cruise package takes approximately 2½ hours.

SHOPPING   **Lijnbaan** (opened in 1953), the first center-city pedestrianized shopping precinct in Europe, was a truly revolutionary concept in its era, with more than a mile-long mix of shops, boutiques, and cafes, some under cover. It remains a pleasant shopping area and city passageway, with gardens and sculpture. On and around the **Beursplein,** by the bold blue-green *World Trade Center* on Coolsingel, is where the major department and clothing stores are found. On **Nieuwe Binnenweg,** one of the city's oldest shopping streets, are a number of antique and curio shops; in Delfshaven on Voorhaven is **Adriaan Groenewond Antiques,** considered the best of its kind in the city. Stores are generally closed Mon. until 1 p.m.; late night shopping is Fri., til 9 p.m. Rotterdam's **general market,** also with antiques and curiosities, is Holland's largest: Tues. & Sat. 9 a.m.–5 p.m. on the Mariniersweg and surrounding streets; there's also a book, stamp, and coin market on Grotekerkplein. Tues. & Sat. 9:30 a.m.–4 p.m.

ACCOMMODATIONS   There's variety enough to meet your personal comfort/cost ratio, from five-star international to cozy neighborhood two-star.

EATING OUT   All aspects of Rotterdam are present in its restaurants: architecturally intriguing contemporary or cozy historic settings for continental or typical Dutch cuisine, and the flavors of foreign kitchens you'd expect to find in an international port.

ENTERTAINMENT AND EVENTS Rotterdam's monthly events and exhibitions calendar *Agenda* (in Dutch only) is available from the VVV or hotels, where someone can translate the listings for you. The **Rotterdams Philharmonisch Orkest** (James Conlon, Conductor) resides in **De Doelen,** which opened in 1966 in the center of the city (box office 4132490). In the 1980s, acclaimed English conductor Simon Rattle (City of Birmingham Symphony Orchestra) was principal guest conductor for Rotterdam, a musical company he describes as "exciting." On Wed., Oct.–May, free half-hour **lunch concerts** are presented at De Doelen, beginning at 12:45 p.m. Lunchtime **organ concerts** (12:45–1:15 p.m.) are held in St. Laurenskerk Fridays, with other musical performances in the church on Thurs. (except Jan., Feb.). The annual international **Rotterdam Film Festival** is held in Jan./Feb.

ARRIVING Rotterdam is served at least four times hourly by train on the Amsterdam—The Hague—Rotterdam line, a branch of which runs to Schiphol Airport, and is also connected by rail with Gouda and Utrecht; all use Centraal Station. The City's **Zestienhoven Airport** offers various intra-European air connections. Those arriving at **Hoek van Holland** via ferry from England can take the boat train directly to Rotterdam (about a half hour). By motorway, Rotterdam is 76 km. (47 miles) south of Amsterdam, 103 km (62 miles) north of Antwerp in Belgium. Because of the massive size of its port, two tunnels (the *Benelux* and the *Maas*) are part of the complex highway system that serves and encircles Rotterdam.

IN THE AREA **Kinderdijk,** in the countryside near Rotterdam, provides windmill fans with 19 in a single scenic setting. The picturesque old port of **Dordrecht,** 20 km. (12 mi.) south of Rotterdam (sometimes considered the southernmost city of the Randstad), lies somewhat off today's main tourism track, at the cross-river-roads of Holland's inland waterways. **Spido Cruises** to the waterworks and waterways of the region are available from Rotterdam, as are maps for self-driving routes of the extensive Rotterdam port from the city to the North Sea.

TRAVEL TIPS Rotterdam is surrounded by an efficient but complex motorway network that is dense with drivers determined to get where they are going as rapidly as possible—all of which can be confusing for the uninitiated motorist. Arrival in the city by train is recommended. If you do come by car, get specific *place names* to look for on exit ramp signs.

Rotterdam in Context

Rotterdam, like Rome, wasn't built in a day, but it was laid waste in one. In the very year Rotterdam should have been celebrating its 600th anniversary (festivities commemorating its receiving civic rights in 1340 had been planned), the sudden events of a single catastrophic day, May 14, 1940, overshadowed the city's entire history. Six hours of Nazi air bombardment leveled six centuries of progress in Rotterdam, destroying more than 25,000 homes and many historically significant buildings, killing hundreds, and leaving another 100,000 homeless. And it was wanton waste on the part of the Nazis (who had invaded Holland from the German border to the east four days before on May 10), since earlier that same May 14 the Dutch had signaled for a truce in order to discuss surrender terms.

A city's history is reflected in its facades, and you can count on one hand the buildings in the center of Rotterdam that pre-date 1940: the Stadhuis (built in 1920 in the Dutch-Renaissance style); the Main Post Office; the Schielandhuis (see *What To See and Do*), and St. Laurenskerk (Grote Kerk). Of all the other historic monuments destroyed, only the cinder-sided St. Laurens church, with its scarred but still-standing tower, a symbol to the city, was cast to play the part of the phoenix in Rotterdam, and allowed to be resurrected from the rubble to rise again on the city skyline. For the rest of its rebuilding, in striking contrast to the post-war plans in Europe's other badly bombed cities, Rotterdam opted for the radical and imaginative concept of creating a whole new contemporary city from the ashes of the old one. Lewis Mumsford, the American architect and city-planning critic, wrote in his classic book *The City in History,* "Not every (bombed) city rose to the challenge of its destruction as determinedly and as skillfully as Rotterdam," adding, "The word 'renewal' is a tame one to describe the resurgence of Rotterdam."

Such a fresh start was made possible by the foresight of the Rotterdam city government which, almost immediately after the Nazi bombing, expropriated the ruins of the bombed buildings and the sites on which they had stood, becoming sole proprietor of 415 acres in the heart of Rotterdam (former owners received fair compensation for the value of their property as of May 9, 1940, the day before the invasion). A year after the official end of the war, the provisional city council of Rotterdam approved the so-called "Basic Scheme" for the city, which banned industry from the center, cut by two-thirds the number of residences in what had been a severely overcrowded city center, and built in spaciousness by widening downtown streets and planting plenty of flowers. Of the centralized pedestrian Lijnbaan, shopping plaza, first of its kind in the world, Mumford reviewed it as "exemplary in almost every way." (The Lijnbaan may appear pleasant but ordinary to today's visitors, but it should be appreciated for its conceptual contribution to the present multi-malled landscape worldwide.

Its citizens' reputation for hard work is evident in the half-kidding comment that in Rotterdam "shirts are sold with the sleeves already rolled up." Never was their shirt-sleeve stamina needed more than after the Second World War. Within five weeks of the liberation of Rotterdam, work on reconstruction of the port had begun (the Nazis had blown up half the port's machinery and equipment in 1944), with no argument from citizens that the port took precedence over other rebuilding, since the prosperity of the city, and indeed much of Holland, depended upon shipping.

A brief look back to its beginnings reveals that Rotterdam was first settled in about the year 1000, at a dam on the small river Rotte, where peasants and fishermen gradually became involved with local trade and fishing. A flood in 1164 swept away the wooden huts of the early hamlet, but residents were determined to fight for its survival come hell *or* high water. In 1299, Rotterdam was officially recognized by its feudal overlord, Wolfert van Borsselen, as an urban entity, the 19-feet-below-sea-level town having become protected by dikes, and adept at driving stilts (wooden piles) into silt for building foundations. The Counts of Holland gave Rotterdam city rights in 1340. The city was almost completely consumed by fire in 1563, which barely left time to rebuild before it joined other Dutch cities in support of Willem I (the Silent) against the Spanish in 1568.

In his own times, as he remains in the 20th century, **Erasmus** (1466–1536) was Rotterdam's favorite native son, though an illegitimate one since his father was a priest. (See Erasmus under *"Benelux Cultural Legacy: The Muse".*) Fortunately, he didn't let that happenstance hamper his life, obviously believing the words he later wrote: "No one is injured save by himself." Erasmus was one of the first persons since the end of the Roman Empire to earn his living by the pen, and Rotterdammers past and present seem to see their own straightforward selves in many of his words. His *Adages* adapted from antiquity sayings are familiar to us all: "As plain as the nose on your face," "Call a spade a spade," "Caught in his own snare," and "In the country of the blind, the one-eyed man is king."

Located on the delta of two significant river systems, the Rhine and the Maas (Meuse), Rotterdam's physical position played the leading part in its prominence, but history had a supporting role. At the end of the Eighty Years' War and the Peace of Westphalia (1648), the River Scheldt and Antwerp's port were closed. Sea traffic turned north to Rotterdam (and Amsterdam), from which time Rotterdam, until then just one of the "small towns" of Holland, and its port gradually began to grow. Another substantial boost for its shipping trade came Rotterdam's way when Holland blockaded the River Scheldt from 1830–39, after

Belgium had seceded from the Kingdom of the Netherlands set up in 1815 by the Congress of Vienna. Much of what had been Antwerp's shipping trade, mostly from the Dutch colonies, again was diverted to Rotterdam. With this incentive, the harbor at Rotterdam developed further, but was hindered by silt at the mouth of the Maas, which prevented the entrance of large vessels. This was more than inconvenient as Europe progressed through the Industrial Revolution and into an age empowered by steam. The present-day preeminence of Rotterdam's port is due to the construction of the **Nieuwe Waterweg** (1863–1872), and subsequent plan of continual dredging. After 1872, Rotterdam offered ships a 30 km. lock-free entry from the sea to the city.

Beginning in the 20th century, Rotterdam has carried out successive programs of port development, water management, and industrialization that have made the city the powerhouse of the Dutch economy. Overcoming the damage done during the Second World War, the port of Rotterdam quickly regained its pre-war tonnage. Ironically, Rotterdam's recovery largely grew out of its role as the main furnisher of raw materials by river barge to West Germany during that country's postwar "economic miracle." The process of digging new deep water harbors, the reverse of Holland's more usual land-creating efforts, produced the port/industrial complexes of Botlek and Europort, and put the port at Pernis on its way to becoming the largest oil refinery complex on the continent. By 1962, Rotterdam had edged up on, and surpassed New York (until then the busiest harbor) in total tonnage to become the largest port in the world. Radar facilities were installed to enable ships to enter the port from the North Sea even in zero-visibility fog. Actually 20 miles (37 km.) inland from the North Sea, Rotterdam is, more accurately, a series of ports along that length, which is lockless and bridge-free (two major motorway tunnels, the Benelux and the Maas, pass under the port in the city).

Today Rotterdam services 32,000 sea-going vessels and 180,000 inland waterways barges annually, handling 292 million metric tons of bulk cargo, putting it well ahead of its two nearest international rivals, Kobe, Japan, and New York. In Europe, the port of Rotterdam handles more trade than the ports of Le Havre, Bremen, Hamburg, Antwerp, and Amsterdam combined. Even more importantly for its future, Rotterdam is the best-equipped transport, distribution, and trade center in Europe, and is linked to the continental hinterland by a sophisticated network of waterways, roads, railway, and pipelines, since the onward travel of goods from the port is as important as their arrival by ship. As the needs of the transport world evolve, Rotterdam is prepared to meet the challenge of offering the best and most efficient harbor service to exporters and importers of raw materials and goods.

Apart from its "no contest" claim in comparative port size, Rotterdam's competition with the city of Amsterdam is keen. There's no casualness about the two cities' confrontation in *voetbal* (pronounced "football," what we in America call soccer), when Rotterdam's *Feijenoord* team faces off with Amsterdam's *Ajax*. Since its original postwar rebuilding, Rotterdam has had a chance to come full circle in city-planning concepts, and again is taking the lead by re-evaluating some of its ground-breaking urban planning ideals and ideas. **Waterstad** (water city) is the name of the combined new recreational attractions along the riverfront: **Tropicana** with its indoor swimming pool and sub-tropical environment; open-air museum of inland shipping; Sunday art market; **IMAX** theater; **National Econocenter;** and assorted pubs and restaurants. That certainly makes Rotterdam the right place for Holland's future National Museum of Architecture. The words "stronger through strife" were added to the city's shield after the war, and Rotterdam's "sleeves-ups" citizens—who now number 575,000, and come from 124 countries—seem to have proved themselves to be just that.

GUIDEPOSTS
Telephone Code 010

Tourist Info	VVV, Main Office, Coolsingel 67. Open year-round Mon.–Fri. 9 a.m.–6 p.m. (except Fri. to 9 p.m., Sat. 9 a.m.–5 p.m., Sun. 10 a.m.–4 p.m. (except closed Sun. Oct.–Mar.). Closed Dec. 25, 26, Jan. 1. VVV at Centraal Station (Rotterdam info. only) open daily 9 a.m.–10 p.m. (except Sun. open 10 a.m.), closed Dec. 25, Jan. 1. 4136000.
Port Tours	Spido Havenrondvaarten, Willemsplein; 4135400. The 1¼ hr. harbor tour is year-round, varying schedule; additional cruises daily Apr.–Sept.
Emergencies	Police, ambulance: 06–11.
Post Office	Coolsingel 42, 4542221. Open Mon.–Fri. 8:30 a.m.–7 p.m. (except Fri. 8:30 p.m.).
ANWB	AAA associate organization: Westblaak 210, 4140000.
Parking	Public garages (look for "P" signs) in center around Centraal Station, Lijnbaan.
Transport	Information on public transportation in Rotterdam and greater region: Stationplein, 4546890.
Taxi	Rotterdam Taxi Base: 4626060; taxi ranks at Centraal Station, Hilton, on Coolsingel.

WHAT TO SEE AND DO......................

During its mid-20th-century rebuilding, Rotterdam humanized its contemporary core with plenty of public sculpture, though the most moving piece is a wrenching reminder of WW II: *Devasted City* (**Ossip Zadkine,** 1952, Plein 1940, behind the Maritime Museum). The human figure, with a gaping hole in its torso that simultaneously symbolizes a "person without a heart" and a "city without a center," its hands raised to the sky, expresses both horror and hope. Far less thought-provoking, but a perennial personal favorite, is the shy yet sturdy *Monsieur Jacques* by **L. O. Wenckebach,** 1959, on Coolsingel (whose "twin" greets visitors at the entrance to the Kroller-Muller Museum in Otterlo). **Rodin's** *L'homme qui marche* meets shoppers at the pedestrianized Korte Lijnbaan. On Grotekerkplein is one of Rotterdam's most beloved sculptures, of native son *Erasmus,* who was born near this square in Oct. 1469. The statue (by **Hendrik de Keyser,** 17th century), which thankfully survived the bombing and thereafter was safely sequestered for the duration of the war, portrays Erasmus reading a book. **Umberto Mastrianni**'s *Kiss* near Centraal Station has been renamed *Goodbye* locally. Many of Rotterdam's museums are free on Wed. (and for children under 16 at all times).

Boymans-van Beuningen Museum • *Mathenesserlaan 18; Tues.–Sat. 10 a.m.–5 p.m., Sun. & hols. 11 a.m.–5 p.m., closed Mon., Jan. 1, Apr. 30.; 4419400; Tram 5, Metro: Eendrachtsplein* • This is the only museum in Holland with collections of both fine and applied art from the 14th century to the present, and there are probably few museums in the world where one can find works by artists Van Eyck, Da Vinci, Van Gogh, and Andy Warhol under one roof. The Boymans-van Beuningen Museum, its 250,000-piece collection well-respected worldwide, is the beautifully blended result of private donations (many from local Rotterdam families) and selective acquisitions. One of the showpieces is Pieter Bruegel the Elder's **The Tower of Babel** (c. 1563), and another Rembrandt's portrait of his son Titus. (Because the Boymans has so many of his drawings, the institution and scholars associated with it have become leading authorities in studies on attributions to Rembrandt.) Among artists represented in the Old Masters department are Hieronymous Bosch, Rubens, Lucas van Leyden, Jan Steen, Jan van Goyen, Karel Fabritius, and Frans Hals. The print and graphics galleries contain important works by artists from Durer to Dali, and among the many renowned representatives in between are Picasso, Magritte, Max Ernst, Man Ray, Kokoschka, and Kandinsky. There is a large bookstore, and reproductions are available in many forms; the coffee shop has a garden terrace.

The Boymans museum was an interested party in an intriguing chapter of art history that involved a modern Dutch "master painter." **Hans van Meegeren** wielded his brush so well that he created six "Vermeers" that even experts became convinced were long-missing works by that 17th-century Dutch genre master. In 1937, the Boymans Museum paid $286,000 for one of them. And during World War II, German Field Marshall Hermann Goring, an art collector, acquired another. However, when the war was over, Van Meegeren was criminally charged with having cooperated with the Nazis by sending a Vermeer out of the country to Goring, and this forced him to decide which was worse: to be charged as a forger or denounced as a collaborator. In the post-war climate, it seemed far safer to be a forger, so Van Meegeren admitted that Goring's "Vermeer" was a fake. Yet, still, experts on Dutch master artists, studying the works that Van Meegeren said were his, refused to believe that the paintings weren't genuine. Only by actually painting a *new* Old Master before the eyes of judges was Van Meegeren able to convince the art world that he was a master forger. Finally, he was believed, then convicted, given a year in prison, and died of a heart attack before he was able to serve his sentence.

Delfshaven • *Trams 4, 6, Metro: Delfshaven* • Although this picturesque old district (a protected historic area since the late 1960s and largely restored) was incorporated into Rotterdam in 1866, it was created as a port for Delft in the 14th century. Delft, which needed a port to maintain its economic viability, received permission to create a shipping channel along the river Schie to the Maas in 1389. The project served its purpose until it was sacked in 1488, barely surviving. Delfshaven was important in the 17th century for Delft's East India Company ships, but leaders in Delft began to be protective of their town, and refused to let Delfshaven develop. Dutch naval hero Piet Hein was born here (Piet Heynstraat #10) in 1577 (not surprisingly, a statue of him stands nearby). Perhaps Delfshaven's most memorable moment in history came on August 1, 1620 (Gregorian calendar), when the so-called *Pilgrim Fathers,* who had been living in Leiden, set sail from here aboard the *Speedwell,* via England (where they met up with the *Mayflower,* which proved more seaworthy), eventually reaching America and establishing Plymouth Colony. The 16th-century **Oude Kerk** (Aelbrechtskolk 20; 4774156), where the pilgrims most probably prayed before their departure, is rarely open to individuals (there is a service on Thanksgiving Day), but there's a commemorative plaque by the door. Inside is a stained-glass window of the *Speedwell* and a memorial dedicated to the pilgrims. A Hemony carillon was placed in the tower of the restored Regency-style church in 1963; inquire at the Rotterdam VVV about summer carillon and organ concerts. Next door to the Oude Kerk is the **Raadhuis** (town hall, from the days when Delfshaven was independent), dating from 1580. In the attractive old **Zakkendragershuisje** (Sack Carriers house), Voorstraat 13, is a working pewter artisan's shop. At the end of Voorhaven is a working, grain-grinding windmill that can be visited, including its outside "balcony," from which there's a nice view. Across the Voorhaven footbridge is the new **Museum voor Naieve Kunst** (Museum of Naive Art) *(Voorhaven 25; Mon.–Sat. 9: 3 a.m.–4:30 p.m., Sun. 1–4:30 p.m.; 4766611), also an art gallery.*

Delfshaven's **De Dubbelde Palmboom** *(Voorhaven 12; Tues.–Sat. 10 a.m.–5 p.m., Sun. & hols. 1–5 p.m., closed Mon., Jan. 1, Apr. 30; 4761533; tram 6 from Coolsingel, Metro: Delfshaven)* is a part of the Rotterdam Historical Museum. Located in a restored (1975) 19th-century warehouse with brick floors and beamed ceilings, the museum has interesting exhibits on living and working in the Rotterdam region in the pre-and post-industrial eras, attractively arranged in rooms on nine levels connected by wooden ramps (and elevators) working their way up into the eaves, where the cafe **De Bonte Hond** is housed. There are cards in English explaining exhibits in each room.

Prins Hendrik Maritime Museum • *Leuvehaven 1; Tues.–Sat. 10 a.m.–5 p.m., Sun. & hols. 11 a.m.–5 p.m., closed Mon., Jan. 1, Apr. 30; 4132680; Trams 1, 3, 6, Metro Beurs/Churchillplein* • Meant to provide insight into maritime history as a whole, and the story of shipping in Europe, the Netherlands, and Rotterdam in particular, the Maritime Museum (opened in 1986) fulfills its mandate by multi-media means: a series of diverting five-minute videos on shipping that bypass the need for language; ship models of all sorts (kits for even smaller models of ships such as the Holland America Line's *Rotterdam* are on sale in the excellent museum shop, which also sells old shipping posters, books in English, etc.); old paintings and prints; charts showing the comparative sizes of sea-going craft; and equipment (there's a highly popular periscope, and a complete ship's bridge). Ramps (good for accessibility) from one floor to another are suggestive of ship gangways, and pass windows with fine views out to the harbor, and the museum's berthed exhibits: steam tugs, sailing vessels, and the delightful restored Royal Dutch Navy warship *De Buffel*. As shipshape as you'd expect a Dutch crew to keep her, *De Buffel* sailed under steam from 1868 to 1896 (the engine and copper tubing gleam as if new). You'd expect the deluxe quarters of the Commandant and officers, but what was truly progressive was the impressive living standards for the sailors. As for the brig in *De Buffel*'s bowels: I've *paid* to sail transatlantic in cabins less large. Rotterdam's Maritime Museum shows that, as with music, ships and the sea stir emotions that transcend language.

St. Laurens or Grotekerk • *Grotekerkplein; June–Sept. Tues.–Sat. 10 a.m.–4 p.m., Oct.–May Thurs. only noon–2 p.m.; 4131494* •

Built in the 14th and 15th centuries in the Dutch late-Gothic style with wide lofty aisles and timber barrel vaults, St. Laurenskerk was badly damaged in the May 1940 bombing. Throughout the war, with the rubble from the bombings eventually removed, St. Laurens' burnt shell and tower (with the 1660 49-bell carillon unharmed) stood as a sentinel on the bare Grotekerkplein. A particularly important link between Rotterdam's past and present, St. Laurenskerk was rebuilt following the war, but it was the only reconstruction that the citizens opted for, making instead the quite radical choice to create a new city center from scratch. The church rebuilding was completed in 1968, with a new organ (one of the church's three) dedicated in 1973. St. Laurenskerk, the Dutch Reformed Church of Rotterdam, is known for its church choir.

Kijk-Kubus (Public Cube House) • *Overblaak 70; Jan.–Mar. Sat. & Sun. 11 a.m.–5 p.m., Apr.–Dec. Tues.–Fri. 10 a.m.–5 p.m., Sat. & Sun. 11 a.m.–5 p.m., Jun.–Sept. also open Mon. 10 a.m.–5 p.m.; 4142285; Tram 3, Metro Blaak* • The group of 38 "cube" houses, of which the Public Cube is one, situated in the central Rotterdam city district of *Blaak,* are collectively called "Het Blaakse Bos" (the Blaak Woods), due to the houses' other nickname, "tree dwellings." Seeing them, I didn't find it surprising that the cube houses had garnered so many descriptive names, since they are so unexpected, so imaginative, in their shape and setting. Designed by architect Piet Blom and built in 1984, the cube houses serve as an upper-level "bridge," linking the waterfront, particularly the picturesque and popular pub-lined *Oude Haven,* to the town: Rotterdam's Centraal Library, the general street market's Mariniersweg, and older post-W.W. II residential areas. As you wander astonished beneath the cube-shaped houses, tipped 'til they're resting on one corner point, you can't help wondering what they're like as for-real living spaces: can the floors *possibly* be level? All is answered in a visit to the intriguing "model" home. I will say that the windowed top point of the cube made me want to spend a night lying on the floor looking up at the stars.

Another building that deserves your notice is **the Pencil,** so-called because the building, with its steeply graded, lead-colored roof, does resemble a point-up stubby pencil. The aforementioned **Centraal Library** *(Hoogstraat 110; Tues–Sat. 10 a.m.–9 p.m., Mon. 12:30–9 p.m., Sat. 10 a.m.–5 p.m., closed Sun; 4338911)* has a bit of Paris' Pompideau Center about it, with large bright yellow exterior ventilation tubes branching off to various floors. Architects Bakema and Van den Broek built the seven building layers with a sloping glass front and each floor getting smaller, appearing like a pyramid when viewed from the interior ground floor. Central escalators are designed to cascade down like a tiered waterfall.

Euromast & Spacetower • *Parkhaven 20; March–Sept. daily 10 a.m.–9 p.m., Oct.–Feb. daily 10 a.m.–6 p.m., except Spacetower 11 a.m.–4 p.m., weekends only in Jan. and may be closed at other times due to weather conditions; 4364811; Tram 6 or 9, Metro Dijkzigt, bus 39* • Now a recognized silhouette on the city skyline, the Euromast was built in 1960, but in 1970 the Spacetower was added, since the 27-story Erasmus University Medical Faculty (observe the large gleaming white, rather shiplike structure on West Zeedijk), built in the interim, had robbed the Euromast of the 360-degree view that it advertised. Now at 600 feet (185 meters), the Spacetower's unmarred views over city and port seem secure. A bit pricey (Dfl. 12.50), but the panorama from the Space-cabin's comfortable couch-seating, aimed outward, as it ascends and descends (in a total of five minutes) while slowly revolving is wonderful in good weather. And, I was told, you can stay seated and go up and down again for the same price. Note that there's an outside flight of stairs (and observation deck) at the Euromast level (340 feet) to reach the Spacecabin. In the Euromast are both formal and informal restaurants, and at the base it has a gift shop.

The Euromast sits in portside **Het Park,** site of the 1960 *Floriade* exhibition. Just to the east, also abutting the harbor, is **Het Nieuwe Werk,** a gracious, gardened section of the city. This is the neighborhood where shipping companies have their corporate headquarters and countries their consulates, especially in the mansions along **Park Laan.** The lovely mansion at #14 is a **Museum of Taxation,** and the avenue's other inhabitants make jokes about that being where the *real* resources of Rotterdam are. Next door is the **Veerhaven,** the harbor from which Rotterdam's much-admired Admiral Piet Hein (1577–1629) sailed and later made his legendary seizure of the Spanish silver fleet. Across the Nieuwe Maas from here, the massive green copper-topped building that looks as if it's on an island, is **Kop van Zuid,** the former embarkation halls for Holland-America Line's transatlantic and other ocean-going liners.

Schielandshuis Museum of History • *Korte Hoogstraat 31, Tues.– Sat. 10 a.m.–5 p.m., Sun. & hols. 1–5 p.m., closed Mon., Jan. 1, Apr. 30; 4334188; Tram 1, 3, 6, Metro Beurs/Churchillplein* • Housed in the recently restored classical-facaded **Schielandshuis** (1665), the only historic building to survive the destruction of the city center in 1940, this section of Rotterdam's Historical Museum sticks out in the cityscape in a most welcome way. It was in this building, probably built from a design by architect Pieter Post, that the original Boymans Collection of art had been installed in 1849, completely destroyed in an 1864 fire, which also badly damaged the building. The Schielandshuis has only recently recovered from the overly-hasty restoration following that fire, as it was needed to house the City Archives as well as the Boymans collection renaissance, until it burgeoned to such a size as to require quarters of its own (1938). Today, the Schielandhuis' exhibits focus on the development and cultural and art history of Rotterdam, including a section on the May 1940 bombing, and the far-reaching effects that had on the city. Among the museum's art work is the **Atlas van Stolk collection** of prints and drawings on the history of the Netherlands, two panels of a 1540 altarpiece from the St. Laurenskerk when it was still a Catholic Church, and a two-meter model by Hendrik de Keyser of the wooden steeple that topped the church between 1619 and 1645. Famed jurist **Hugo de Groot** (Grotius), who once served in the position of Pensionary for Rotterdam, is represneted by the leather bricklayer's doublet he wore on his flight to Antwerp after his escape from Loevestein Castle (see *Benelux Cultural Legacy, The Muse/Literature*). The top floor is devoted to antique items of everyday living. There is a museum shop (English museum guide), a garden courtyard cafe, and a restaurant, **De Pappegay** (see *Restaurants*).

ACCOMMODATIONS

Deluxe

★★★★★ **Hilton International Rotterdam** • *Weena 10, 3012 CM; 4144044, fax 4118884, U.S. 800–445–8667, Can. 800–268–9275* • This is where you come in Rotterdam for turn-down service, uniformed reception staff, and 24-hour room service. The lobby is one of the gathering places in the city, especially for late-night entertainment: disco and casino (open 2 p.m.–2 a.m.). The 248 well-serviced rooms, including non-smoking rooms, three executive floors, and some with views of the Stadhuis handsomely illuminated at night, are decorated in the muted tones of high quality, first class international decor, with hair dryers and mini-bars. **Le Restaurant** serves Dutch and international cuisine. Business services, parking available.

First Class

★★★★ **Parkhotel** • *Westersingel 70, 3015 LB; 4363611, U.S. 800–223–6510, Can. 800–424–5500* • Predominantly a business hotel during the week, the Park is located by Museumpark, not far from the Boymans Museum, and within walking distance of transportation, shopping, and most central sights. Of the 154 rooms, 60 are in the new wing, upgraded with air conditioning, mini-safes, double-glazed windows, and lightwood decor. Non-smoking rooms available. An art work passage connects the new and old sections of the hotel, which has a library corner in its fire-placed modern lounge. The well-kept, less expensive (moving them down into the moderate-price category) rooms in the older part of the building have larger bedrooms and baths, luxurious spreads, mini-bars, hairdryers. Fitness facilities available, free-parking behind hotel; room service 6 a.m.–1 a.m. There's an a la carte restaurant and a casual grill-cafe.

★★★★ **Atlanta** • *Aert van Nesstraat 4, 3012 CA; 4110420, fax 4135320* • Very centrally located, on the corner of the Coolsingel, though the convenience could bring some traffic noise (quieter rooms at back). The Atlanta is, of course, a post-war construction, with a traditional lobby that's elegant in an old Dutch way, with a cozy "brownish" bar with leather chairs and couches; the restaurant serves 6–10 p.m. The 170 rooms are comfortable and reasonably roomy, the largest on the sixth floor.

★★★★ **Hotel Inntel** • *Leuvehaven 80, 3011 EA; 4134139, fax 4133222* • The newest addition on the hotel front in Rotterdam comes with harbor and port views, a location from which all city attractions are walkable, or within a quick hop on the tram, located across the street. The 150 light, tidy rooms, all with small, modern bathrooms with tubs and wall-mounted showers, remote TV and telephone, feature big windows. Red leather couches, marble, mirrors, stainless steel, recessed lighting, and windows are the ingredients of the cheerful lobby. There's a lobby restaurant, where breakfast (included) also is served; the **Waterway Bar** has snacks 5 p.m.–1 a.m., with a harborview, and skyline lights after dark. The top floor fitness center has a pool with large windows facing harbor; sauna, solarium. No room service. In all, a very pleasant place.

Moderate

★★★★ **Scandia** • *Willemsplein 1, 3016 DN; 4134790, fax 4127890* • This one-time Scandinavian seamen's hotel, still under Scandinavian ownership, has been turned into a hospitable, clean, comfortable, no-frills general hotel. Close to and half-facing the port, near the Spido port-excursion piers, the four-story hotel has 52 rooms with light decor; rooms vary in size (and price accordingly); some doubles have only a tile stall shower, and some suites are quite special at the price. All have mini-bar, TV, tel. There's room service during restaurant hours: 7 a.m.–10 p.m.

★★★ **Van Walsum** • *Mathenesserlaan 199, 3014 HC; 4363275, fax 4364410* • Built 100 years ago as a house, this family-owned-and-operated hotel, with flower boxes on the front, is situated on a pleasant tree-lined neighborhood avenue, near public transportation, and, for walkers, within range of Delfshaven and the Euromast. The 26 rooms, many with old plaster details on ceiling, all have modern tile shower (some with bath), TV, tel.; some have a mini-fridge in room. The warm, welcoming Dutch atmosphere carries from the lobby bar, and small restaurant, secluded garden terrace, where drinks and breakfast (included) can be served in summer. Parking available.

Inexpensive

★★ **Bienvenue** • *Spoorsingel 24, 3033 GL; 4669394, fax 4677475* • Located two blocks out the rear door of the Centraal Station, on a residential street fronting a quiet canal, this 1920s house has ten rooms, half with private shower and toilet. The cheerful, family-run hotel is basic, but very clean and neat; beds have firm mattresses. Front rooms overlook canal and lawns, there's a garden in the back. No elevator; pay telephone at reception. The lobby lounge/reception/breakfast (only) room is one flight up, with window boxes, canal view.

RESTAURANTS............................

Restaurant Old Dutch (*Rochussenstraat 20; Mon.–Fri. 11:30 a.m.–midnight, closed Sat., Sun.; 4360344; very expensive*) has an authentic old Dutch atmosphere, right down to the stale smell of cigars. If you don't mind that, or the rather steep prices, the Old Dutch will provide traditional (Dutch/French cuisine) and tasty dining. **La Villette** (*Westblaak, 160; Mon.–Fri. noon–10 p.m., Sat. dinner only, closed Sun.; 4148692; moderate*) features refined award-winning nouvelle cuisine and cordial service in a gracious fairly formal setting. Located in Het Park, not far from the Euromast, with views of the Nieuwe Maas, **Restaurant Parkheuvel** (*Heuvellaan 21; lunch noon–3 p.m., dinner 6–10 p.m., closed Sun.; 4360530; moderate*) also serves nouvelle cuisine that ranks among the best in Holland, complemented by an excellent wine list. **Zochers'** (*Baden Powell Laan 12; open daily for lunch, dinner till 9:30 p.m.; 4364249; inexpensive*) also is located in Het Park, in the former mansion of the restaurant's landscape architect namesake. Varied fare, snacks, exotic drinks, and a Sunday morning brunch buffet with classical music. Outside dining terrace overlooks the formal box gardens.

For dining with a impressive view day or night, there's the **Panorama,** 320 feet high in the Euromast (*Parkhaven 20; daily noon–10 p.m., 5 p.m. in winter; 4364811; inexpensive*) for buffet lunches and dinner, or lighter fare. **Silhouet** (*4364811; moderate/expensive*) is the a la carte restaurant (also aperitif bar) in the Space Cabin, serving French-accented continental cuisine. With another wonderful view of Rotterdam's new skyline, at ground-level near Willemsbrug (lighted at night) and other port and harbor lights, **La Meuse** *(at Tropicana. Maasboulevard 100; Mon.–Fri. noon–11 p.m., Sat., Sun noon–7 p.m.; 4020700; moderate)* has a three-course menu with wine for about Dfl. 50. There's also a meal with a view right in the center of the city, on the 23rd story of the **World Trade Center Restaurant** *(Beursplein 37; Mon.–Fri. noon–9:30 p.m., closed holidays, Sat., Sun.; 4054465; moderate)*. And in the basement of the Schielandshuis Historical Museum, is **De Pappegay** *(Korte Hoogstraat 31; lunch noon–4 p.m., closed Mon.; 4117232; moderate)*.

At Delfshaven, there are several dining choices. For fish or mussels, head for **Le Harve** *(Havenstraat 9a; daily, lunch, dinner til 10 p.m.; 4257172; moderate)*, and speak up for a window table. **Eethuis de Parel** (The Pearl) *Voorhaven 54; Wed.–Sun. 5–11 p.m., kitchen til 9 p.m., closed Mon., Tues.; moderate)* will offer fish, but also meat and vegetarian dishes overlooking the canal from which the Pilgrim Fathers sailed. **Cafe "Oude Sluis"** *(Havenstraat 7; daily; 4773068; inexpensive)* has real working class "brown cafe" character and, from the small back terrace or tables on the bridge, a great view of the old harbor.

If you want informal fare in the area of the city that Rotterdammers are most fond of, head for the **Oude Haven.** There, against an eclectic backdrop of the Cube Houses, the Pencil, and the boats in the picturesque harbor, is a neighborhood conglomerate of pubs and restaurants, most of which spill out onto the terraces in good weather. The establishments located around the Oude Haven each have their own character, but **Pardoen** *(Spaansekade 62; daily, kitchen closes at 8 p.m., but open for drinks much later; 4130910; inexpensive)* is typical in its personableness in service and setting. Uitsmijters, omelets, salads, toasted sandwiches, etc. **Cafe de Unie** *(Mauritsweg 34; daily; inexpensive)* is characterized by post-modern minimalist decor and has a *De Stijl* facade in primary colors. Situated on a canal, with a very large front window, it's a good place for snacks or meals while watching the world go by. Another colorful cafe is **'t Oude Tramhuys** *(Westersingel, at intersection with Nieuwe Binnenweg; inexpensive).* **Stationplien 45** presents patrons with several international choices, entirely appropriate for a port city that welcomes sailors, businesspeople, and travelers from around the world. The names foretell the cuisine: **The Royal Beefclub, Don Quijote, Viking, Chez Francois, New Yorker,** and **Tokaj** (Hungarian). The kitchens are open until 10 p.m., inexpensive. For the foreign cuisine that really isn't foreign in Holland (Indonesian), a good choice in Rotterdam is **Dewi Sri** *(Westerkade 20; daily, until 10:30 p.m.; 4360263; moderate)*.

IN THE AREA..................................

Kinderdijk • At no other single site in the world will you find as many windmills as near the Dutch town of Kinderdijk (near Alblasserdam), nine miles SE of Rotterdam. In about 1740, 19 mills were built here to drain excess water from the Alblasserwaard polders. Although nowadays power-driven pumping engines do the job, the mills remain well-preserved. The rural Kinderdijk site is always open (no fee) and, though often crowded during the day in season, presents an essentially unspoiled setting. From Apr. through Sept., one of the mills is open to visitors daily, except Sun., showing its antique interior with furnishings, and mechanical workings. Every Sat. afternoon in July and Aug., the mills are put into operation. During the second complete week in Sept., the mills are illuminated at night. From May through Oct., there's the possibility of a cruise in the mill region (01859–12482).

Dordrecht • From the **Groothoofd** gate of this handsome old port city (town rights were granted in 1220), one overlooks the Merwede and the Oude Maas, the busiest river junction in the world. A walk along **Wijnstraat** (named for the staple rights awarded in 1299, which meant that all the wine brought to Holland by ship had to be first unloaded in Dordrecht) passes many delightful 16th- and 17th-century Dutch facades, decorated with lace curtains on the windows. Along **Nieuwe Haven,** one gets a good picture of life aboard a barge, a large number of which are moored here, and the **Museum Mr. Simon van Gijn** *(Tues.–Sat. 10 a.m.–5 p.m., Sun. & hols. 1–5 p.m.; 078-133793)* here is a patrician house with period rooms including an 1800 kitchen, tapestries, silver, tiles, and pewter. The **Statenzaal** (States Hall) in the **Hof** (Court) was the site of the signing of the first documented resistance to the Spanish in 1572. The **Dordrechts Museum** *(Museumstraat 40; Mon.–Sat. 10 a.m.–5 p.m., Sun. & hols. 1–5 p.m.; 078-134100)* has a 17th-century collection that includes works by Nicolaes Maes, Jan van Goyen, and Aelbert Cuyp, and paintings of The Hague School, and those of Dordt artist Ary Scheffer. The **Grote Kerk** *(May–Sept. Tues.–Sat. 10 a.m.–noon, 2–4 p.m.)* mostly dates from the late 15th century, although the massive tower was begun in 1339 in the Brabant Gothic style. The 1626 49-bell carillon usually is played Fri. 11 a.m.–noon, Sat. 2–3 p.m.; the organ dates from 1671. There is a fine marble pulpit (1756) with a magnificent wooden canopy.

Rotterdamse Havenroute • The ANWB (Dutch auto club), in conjunction with the Port of Rotterdam publishes a Rotterdam Port Route booklet in English, with detailed information and directions intended to give the automobile-driving traveler the clearest possible picture of the vast installation. Inquire at ANWB or the VVV.

Spido's Delta Works and Seven Waterways Cruise • On Wed. and Thurs. in July and Aug., Spido runs nine-hour (beginning 10 a.m.) excursions from Rotterdam that take in, by way of water, locations including the Nieuwe Maas, Oude Maas, Haringvliet, Hollands Diep, the Pernis Oil refineries, the sluices near Hellevoetsluis, Willemstad, Dordrecht, and the windmills of Kinderdijk.

GOUDA

Guidelines for Gouda

SIGHTS Gouda's lovely **Grote Markt** (market square) is one of the largest in Holland and, at its center, stands the **Stadhuis,** which may be the oldest Gothic town hall (1450) in the country. **St. Janskerk/ Grote Kerk**), with the longest nave in the Netherlands and some of the country's most remarkable stained-glass windows, is just off the Markt, across the street from **St. Catherina Gasthuis** museum. Much of the center of the canal-laced town has been designated a preserved historic area.

GETTING AROUND Walking is the best way to get a feel for this pleasant town, and the only way to see the very center. The train station, just outside the old canal-encircled town, is within reasonable walking distance of the Grote Markt. Taxis and local regional buses are based at the station.

SHOPPING This town of 61,000 is the shopping center for a much greater regional population. Local specialties include clay pipes (both decorative and practical), candles, pottery, and what travelers most associate with the name of the town—cheese.

ACCOMMODATIONS Hotels in Gouda are very limited, your best bet being **Keizerskroon** *(Keizerstraat 11–13, 01820-28096; inexpensive),* with a dozen or so bedrooms, some with private toilet and shower. Located in the old center, just a few minute's walk from the Grote

Markt, it is clean, VVV-approved, has a restaurant, car park, TV in rooms, and accepts major credit cards. The VVV office may be able to suggest alternatives if there is no room at this inn.

RESTAURANTS For informal munching as you walk around, buy some *Goudse Siroopwafels* (treacle-filled waffles), which, though sold all over Holland, originated here. For sit-down casual fare, try **Old Dutch** *(Markt 25; inexpensive).* **De Zes Starren** *Achter 14; Mon.–Sat. noon–3 p.m., 5–9 p.m., closed Sun.; 16095; moderate)* is the small, stylishly old Dutch-decorated restaurant in the former kitchen of *Het Catherina Gasthuis Museum*, which was a hospital in centuries past. **Mallemolen** *(Oosthaven 72; Tues.–Sun. 5–9:30 p.m., closed Mon.; 15430; expensive),* used by local Dutch when they want to celebrate in style, has a intimate old Dutch atmosphere and serves traditional French dishes.

ENTERTAINMENT AND EVENTS A **cheese and old handicrafts market** joins the regular general one on the Markt from 9:30 a.m.–noon on Thurs. from late June to late Aug. The rest of the year, area cheesemakers mostly sell their great homemade wheels of Gouda informally off the backs of their farm trucks parked near the **Waag** (weigh house) during the Thurs. and Sat. markets. Concerts on St. Jan's 49-bell (many of which are original) 1676 Hemony **carillon** are played by the town carillonneur Thurs. 10–11 a.m., Sat. 11:30 a.m.–12:30 p.m. from Apr.–Sept. **Organ concerts** are presented by visiting players on St. Jan's great organ (a 3850-pipe instrument built between 1732 and 1736 by Jacob Francois Moreau of Rotterdam that is used on alternate weeks). **Gouda bij Kaarstlicht** (Gouda By Candlelight) takes place annually on a Tues. evening between Dec. 13 and 20 from 7–9 p.m. During it, the darkened windows of the Stadhuis and buildings surrounding the Markt are gradually lighted in sequence with candles, while Christmas carols are sung by Gouda choirs and a large public crowd standing in the square. The memorable event was initiated a number of years ago when, on the occasion of its 100th anniversary, the **Gouda candle factory** made a presentation to the town of a substantial number of candles and this ceremony was conceived for their use.

ARRIVING Gouda is located about 15 miles (25 km) northeast of Rotterdam, 21 miles (35 km) southwest of Utrecht. There are trains to Gouda from both cities; trains from Amsterdam connect through Utrecht. If you are traveling in the area by car, there are many pleasant country roads to and from Gouda, especially the route from Gouda to Schoonhoven (see below) via **Haastrecht** (with its lovely 17th-century stepped-gable Stadhuis) and along the **Vlist**.

IN THE AREA **Oudewater,** with an intriguing witch story to tell and small streets of appealing 16th-century Dutch Renaissance facades, and **Schoohoven,** also a pleasing old place with a long tradition of silver craftmanship, are located in the pretty countryside surrounding Gouda, much of which is traversed on roads built along the tops of dikes. Both towns are accessible by bus from Gouda.

TRAVEL TIPS If you plan a trip to Gouda on a summer Thursday, you'll also catch a morning carillon concert, as well as the only opportunity in the year to see the *inside* of the Waag (weigh house), as part of the cheese market. Although the market ends for the day by 12:30 p.m., plan to stay longer to savor the city's other sights.

Gouda in Context

Gouda (pronounced HOW da), long a merchant town, was granted a charter in 1272 by Count Floris V. During the 14th and 15th centuries, it was a center for the cloth trade, and in subsequent centuries production of a variety of other items became prominent, including clay smoking pipes, pottery (today, much blue and white delftware is produced in Gouda), candles, and cheese. The humanist and theologian Erasmus was educated in Gouda—and probably conceived here, according to a plaque at **Het Catherina Gasthuis** that reads in scholarly Latin: *Desiderius Erasmus Goudae Conceptus Rotterodami Natus Anno 1457*. What the plaque doesn't add is that his father was a Catholic Priest.

GUIDE POSTS
Telephone code (01820)

Tourist Info	VVV Gouda, Markt 27; Mon.–Fri. 9 a.m.–5 p.m., Sat. 10 a.m.–4 p.m.; 13666.
Bike Rental	Railway station, Stationplein; 19751.
Markets	On the Markt, Thurs. 9 a.m.–1 p.m., Sat. 9 a.m.–5 p.m.
Buses	Bus station near rail station, just outside old center to the north. Bus 85 goes to Oudewater (seven miles, about 25 mins.) through pretty typically Dutch countryside approximately half-hourly during the day; Bus 197 to Schoonhoven is through equally interesting Dutch scenery.
Parking	Parking on Markt on non-market days. Metered

parking behind Waag (weight house) and by Kleiwegplein, near station.

WHAT TO SEE AND DO......................

The heart of the city is the slice-of-pie-shaped Markt, on or near which are most of the major places of interest. Gouda is very pleasant to explore on foot, especially the area behind the St. Janskerk and Het Catherina Gasthuis, where one finds small canals, bridges, gardens, and hofjes tucked away. The public library and municipal archives, housed in a former orphanage (1643) at Spieringstraat 1, are particularly appealing, as is the Willem Vroesenhuis (1614), a former old men's hofje. The old **Vismarkt** (fish market) and corn exchange sit on the Lange Gouwe canal, just a short way from the Markt.

St. Janskerk • *Achter de Kerk—behind the church; March 1–Oct. 31 Mon.–Sat. 9 a.m.–5 p.m., Nov. 1–Feb. 28 10 a.m.–4 p.m.; 12684* • Although the original stone church on the site was 14th-century, the cross-shaped church with the wooden arched roof that we see today is mostly 16th century, rebuilt after substantial destruction was caused to the earlier structure by lightning in 1552. That reconstructed church has the longest nave in the Netherlands, and its dramatic length (123 meters/403 feet) so dominates the town that Gouda has been described as "a church with a town." The main reason most people visit St. Jans (dedicated to John the Baptist) is to see its stunning stained-glass windows. Numbering some 70 in all, the earliest windows date from 1555, and were in many cases given as bequests by the citizens of Gouda, who had raised money to rebuild the structure following the 1552 fire. As well as showing scenes from the Bible (especially the life of John the Baptist and Christ: Nos. 9–19), the windows also are a record of Dutch history. The brothers **Wouter** and **Dirck Crabeth** designed and executed the best of the windows, which are world-famous for their size (up to 20 meters/66 feet high), brightness (the huge windows catch lots of light), color composition, and perspective.

Since Holland was still a Roman Catholic country at the time the church was rebuilt, it was appropriate that the first person to respond positively to the request to donate a window was the Bishop of Utrecht, whose *Baptism of Christ* by John (Dirck Crabeth) was placed in the center of the choir in 1555. Philip II of Spain, who ruled the Netherlands, also gave a window in which he and his consort, England's Mary Tudor, are portrayed. St. Jans remained Catholic until 1571, and in that period 22 windows were installed, 14 by the Crabeth brothers. In 1572, the town of Gouda joined the side of the Reformation. Although no new windows were installed for 20 years because of the troubled religious times, fortunately, the church escaped Iconoclastic backlashes and destruction. Not only did the windows survive, but between 1593 and 1603, Protestants finished the project begun by the Catholics, though from this point the windows reflect the history of Holland more than that of the Bible. *The Relief of Leiden* is depicted in window 25, and shows Willem the Silent. The windows were seen as being threatened again in the 20th century by forward-thinking city fathers, who removed all the windows in 1939 in anticipation of war with Nazi Germany. They were stored at first in the cellars of local farms, and later removed to bunkers beneath sand dunes for safety. After the liberation, it seemed right to add another window as a witness to both the occupation and the liberation. A detailed booklet about the windows is available in the church. Services in the Dutch Reformed Church are held Sun. at 10 a.m. and 5 p.m.

Het Catherina Gasthuis • *Achter de Kerk 32 or Oosthaven 9; Mon.–Sat. 10 a.m.–5 p.m., Sun., hols. noon–5 p.m.; 88440* • A former hospital for transients and the local needy, and continuing to function from the 14th century until 1910, the building, while in places dating back to the 14th and 16th centuries, is largely from the mid-17th century. As a town museum, it contains the usual regional historical material, as well as religious art (including 16th-century altarpieces, a *Doubting Thomas* by Wouter Crabeth, and other works from Gouda churches) and paintings (including an important collection of Barbizon and Hague School works from the 19th and 20th centuries), though plenty of pleasure comes from the building itself. A chalice and eucharist dish of silver-gilt with enamel decoration, presented by Jacqueline of Bavaria to the Gouda Civic Guard in 1425, is one of the museum's treasures. Rooms of interest include an old dispensary, a kitchen equipped in the late 18th-century manner, an original furnished 17th-century women's Regents' Room, a torture room in the cellar, and a "mad room" for the troublesomely insane. (Once numerous, this is the last of such rooms intact in Holland (with a self-starting Dutch slide show about the history of the care of insane people in Holland.) At the Oosthaven entrance, an English booklet on the museum is available.

Stadhuis • *Markt; Mon.–Fri. 9 a.m.–noon, 2–4 p.m., closed Sat. & Sun; 13800* • An extensive restoration completed in 1952 resulted in the reappearance of the facade of Gouda's free-standing 1450 Gothic Town Hall, the side walls distinctive with shutters in Gouda's colors of red and white. The Stadhuis was built by Jan Kelderman, probably a member of the famous family of sculptor and architects by that name in the southern Netherlands (today Belgium) city of Mechelen. The front is ornamented with a double set of steps (1603) and representation of counts and countesses of the House of Burgundy, while the rear, which faces the Waag (weigh house) has a handsome stepped gable and had a scaffold, used as late as 1860, now the balcony for the civic wedding chamber behind it. Though always meant to house the town authorities, the building also originally served as the meat hall at ground level, since keeping a close eye on the slaughter of animals so as to prevent contamination was an important task of city leaders. At the corner of the front facade toward St. Janskerk is a sundial, and near it, a 1961 addition of a carillon that plays a tune every half hour, upon which the figure of Court Floris appears to reenact his presentation to Gouda of its city charter in 1272.

Waag • *Markt; last week of June to last week of Aug. Thurs. 9:30 a.m.–noon only, not open at other times* • Built by architect Pieter Post in 1668, Gouda's weigh house, which is used for its original function during Gouda's summer Thurs. morning cheese markets, is distinguished by a fine sculptured relief on the front by Batholomeus Eggers that shows the weighing of cheese.

De Moriaan • *Westhaven 29; Mon.–Fri. 10 a.m.–5 p.m., Sat. 10 a.m.–12:30 p.m. & 1:30 p.m.–5 p.m., Sun. & hol. noon–5 p.m.; 13800* • This 17th-century merchant's house is set up as an old tobacco shop with inventory on the marble shelves, on which sit black and white containers, a black and white tile floor, tile-lined shelves, and brass scales. De Moriaan has an impressive collection of old Dutch tiles, Gouda pottery (even now there are nearly 100 potters in town), and plentiful old smoking pipes, from the funny and frivolous to the fine and beautiful. Clay pipes actually were introduced to Gouda by English soldiers stationed here around 1600. An English soldier founded the first pipe factory, after which the Dutch adopted the trade that has become a tradition in the town.

SHOPPING..

The famous Gouda cheese *(Goudse kaas)* carries the name of the town, and has more ages than man, as you'll see at **Hoogendoorn,** a cheese-and-wine delicatessen on the Markt, across from the Stadhuis. Beginning with the youngest *(extra jonge),* the taste gets somewhat sharper with each stage: *jonge, jonge belegen, belegen, extra belegen, oude* to *overjarig* (which crumbles in your hand). The shop works closely with the town cheese board, and sells all sorts of factory and local farmers' cheeses *(boerenkaas).* The place to find the town's well-known candles is **Gouda Kaarsen** *(Achter de Kerk 9).* The city's celebrated clay pipe-making and decorating is demonstrated at **Adrie Moerings** *(Peperstraat 76; Mon.–Sat. 9 a.m.–5 p.m.; 12842),* the personable potter whose hand-made pipes and hand-thrown pots are for sale.

IN THE AREA..

Heading toward Schoonhoven from Gouda, via Haastrecht, you are on the northeast edge of a region called the **Krimpenerwaard,** real Dutch polder countryside. Along the **Vlist,** on this stretch of which there are two well-restored windmills, are beautiful willow trees and reeds. Behind the high dikes, along the tops of which one drives, it's a "downward" look onto old thatched farm houses and lush meadows that feed the cattle from whose milk is made the *Boerenkaas,* which one sees *Te Koop* (for sale) along the roadsides. It's good bicycling country.

Oudewater • This quaint, quiet (pop. 7000) town of mostly late 16th-century Dutch Renaissance buildings with fascinating facades, tiled roofs, step gables, and brick bridges crossing the canal that runs between cobbled streets down the middle of the Markt, is nothing if not peaceful. And that's quite a contrast to the days when Oudewater was the scene of salvation for tens of thousands of women during a lengthy witch hunt (primarily in the 15th and 16th centuries) that left in its wake nearly a million dead before the fear and fury were spent. To understand that furor, and the significance of Oudewater to those accused of being witches, you'll need to dip into diabolology with me for a moment.

Belief in the "existence" of witches was first officially acknowledged at the time of the Inquisition, a tribunal established by the Roman Catholic Church in the 13th century for the discovery, suppression, and punishment of heretics. From that, there arose an elaborate diabolology, or devil lore. Thirteenth-century Italian scholar St. Thomas Aquinas was the first to dogmatize the belief in witches, who were thought to be handmaidens of the Devil. Much fear was attached to possible association with witches, who were believed capable of causing thunder, crop failure, even the Black Death, all certain signs of Satan's strength.

Following the Spanish version of the Inquisition—the reorganization of the Catholic Church under the Spanish sovereigns in 1478—belief in and fear of, witches reached epidemic dimensions. In 1490, a book appeared that codified the campaign for exterminating witches. Published under the auspices of Pope Innocent VIII and Emperor Maximilian, *Malleus Malleficarum (Hammer of the Witches)* was written by righteous men who sincerely believed it was better for the innocent to suffer than for the guilty to escape. It defied all present-day criteria for acceptable evidence, presumed guilt, advocated torture to obtain confessions, and suggested ways to confuse prisoners. If accusers wished to remain anonymous, they were allowed to do so, since witch-sleuthing was considered a service to God that justified every expedient. Those accused were hunted down and exterminated like vermin. With mere rumor basis enough for accusation, whole regions could be quickly infested by witch fever. Whether his determination to get a divorce (the idea had been inconceivable before then) by fair means or foul gave other men ideas during the height of the witch craze is unknown, but no less a heavyweight than Henry VIII (1491–1547) probably was instrumental in putting the thought into some men's minds of ridding themselves of no-longer-loved wives by planting an anonymous accusation of witchcraft against their spouse.

The era is notorious for cruel and prolonged torture to wring confessions from those suspected of witchcraft, usually women. So agonizing could the torture be that one inquisitor is said to have boasted that he would be able to extort a confession from the Pope. Often under torture, body and soul simply came apart. In addition to torture, three tests were used to determine if the accused was a witch. The test of tears was based on the well-known "fact" that witches couldn't cry. A priest or judge placed his hand on the suspect's head and told her to shed tears; if she couldn't, she was bound to be burned at the stake. In the water test, the suspect was bound by rope and lowered into a river. If the woman sank, although she most probably also drowned, she was proclaimed innocent. If she floated, that was considered proof that she was light enough to fly at night on the Devil's business.

It was believed that the Devil gave witches the supernatural power to fly, and assumed that those who had been given this Satanic gift must be light enough to get airborne. Thus the test of weight was the third, and perhaps most widespread, test for witchcraft. Public scales were set up all over Europe, each with its own official weighmaster. Women who weighed less than an arbitrarily agreed upon amount were positively pronounced witches and sentenced to the stake. With the court-ordered weighing being a matter of life or death to the accused, many weighmasters also became masters of the bribe. Some became so greedy that if not offered money, they would automatically "rig" the scales so that the accused would not weigh enough to be set free. There are even recorded cases in which revengeful unbribed officials signed certificates stating a woman to be completely weightless.

In Oudewater, trial by weighing was the only one used. When a suspect came in to be weighed, she went into a dressing room with the town midwife, and was stripped and searched, to see if she had any hidden weights on her person. When this check was completed, the suspect had to put on a long white robe and was then measured for height. She had to weigh in kilograms the number of centimeters she measured above one meter. Furthermore, the build of the body was also considered at Oudewater, and if her weight "was in accordance with the natural proportions of the body," a woman was given a certificate that acquitted her of witchcraft. The weighmasters at Oudewater had a reputation for being honest, and unsusceptible to bribery.

In 1545, near the height of the witch craze in Europe, Spanish King and Holy Roman Emperor Charles V himself grew concerned over the excesses of the devilish storm that had been unleashed by the extremism of the Spanish Inquisition. In Holland, he had occasion to attend a witch trial in Polsbroek. A suspect was being weighed there and the weighmaster, who had been bribed, declared that the woman weighed only 2.5 kilos (5.5 lbs.). The emperor did not believe this, and took the woman with him to Oudewater. There, he even surreptitiously enticed the weighmaster with gold ducats, but they were refused, and when the women was weighed she was found to be 50 kilos, and acquitted. Impressed with the honesty, Charles V gave Oudewater the privilege of issuing certificates, valid throughout his vast European empire, which stated that the bearer could never again be accused of witchcraft.

No one had been before, or ever was thereafter, judged to be a witch for weighing too little at Oudewater. After Charles V's pronouncement, thousands upon thousands of women came from as far away as Sweden and Sicily, Poland and Gibraltar to pay the set fee to step onto the scales in Oudewater, and to step off free.

In 1613, the government of the Seven Provinces, having declared themselves free of the Spanish who still ruled the Southern Netherlands (Belgium), abolished all witch trials. But, in actual fact, the last certificate issued for the Oudewater *heksenwaag* (witches' scale) was dated June 12, 1729.

Though witches weren't burned at Oudewater, the town (which received its rights in 1295) itself went up in flames in 1575. Hence, the handsome **Heksenwaag and Museum** *(Leeuweringerstraat 2; Apr. 1– Oct. 31 Tues.–Sat. 10 a.m.–5 p.m., Sun. noon–5 p.m.; 02460–3400)* dates from the late 16th c., as does much of the town. Entering the building, one immediately notices the huge wooden scale, which was not destroyed in the fire, and, at more than 500 years old, is the Oudewater original. Should you choose to step on the scales (almost everyone does, even former Queen Juliana couldn't resist, and the weighmaster is discrete with the results, which will surprise non-metric Americans by taking off 10% of their poundage), your copy of the *Testimony of the Act of Weighing in the Weigh-House at Oudewater* will be in English. Most exhibits in the museum of witch documentation upstairs aren't, but with the background provided above you should be able to find items of interest.

Next to the Waag, at Markt Oostzijde 14, is the step-gabled **De Boerenbakker,** a bakery and tea room with a terrace cafe in front and a few tables in back overlooking a garden. Ask for the local butter cookie specialty, *Heksenwaagjes*. On the other side of the Heksenwaag is an *ijs salon* (ice cream shop), in front of which are two canalside benches, one always occupied by a family that sits in sculptured silence. Save time to browse about town: the lovely Stadhuis dates from 1588 (although its tower is 14th century, a survivor of the fire), and there are several antique shops.

Schoonhoven • This small attractive old fortress (pop. 11,000) on the banks of the River Lek has been known as "silver town" for the several centuries that silver craftspeople have made it a major business. The silver industry flourished here, particularly in the 18th and 19th centuries, manufacturing silver articles, especially the ornaments worn with traditional costumes. The **Nederlands Goud, Zilver, en Klokkenmuseum** *(Kazerneplain 4; Tues.–Sun. noon–5 p.m.; 01823–5612)* has a fine collection of Dutch silver, including some rare pieces made in Schoonhoven as early as the 17th century. As well as silver tea sets, decorative boxes, "sewing things," and some gold objects on display, there's an outfitted silversmith's workshop and a history of hallmarks in the Assay Office. The clock room collection, with timepieces from all over Holland, ranges from small pocket watches as old as 17th century, to the substantial 16th-century works of a tower clock from Breda. The **Waag** (1616) on the Dam in front of the museum, with a wide overhanging roof where open carriages of goods waiting to be weighed could remain dry, is now used as a *pannekoekhuis* (pancake house) in summer.

The VVV, which has a map and walking guide to the town in English, resides in the basement of the Stadhuis, begun in 1452, with a 50-bell carillon (1775) in the steeple. In front of the Stadhuis, which is on the in-town Haven (harbor), Schoonhoven has preserved the site of a 1597 witch-burning, in which the victim was Marrigje Ariens, a woman who sought to cure people with the herbs she gathered and prepared; a circle of stones marks the sad spot. The "honor" of Holland's last case of witch burning, in 1608, probably goes to nearby Gorinchem. That date was "relatively civilized" by contemporary standards, considering that the Salem witch trials in Massachusetts took place in the 1690s, the last English witch was burned in 1716, and the last witch known to have died at the stake in Europe did so in Switzerland nearly 200 years later, in 1782. Following the harbor down from the Stadhuis to the river leads to the **Veerpoort** (1601), the only remaining town gate of the original five.

UTRECHT

Guidelines for Utrecht

SIGHTS The Randstad's easternmost city is the country's fourth largest (pop. 230,000), capital of the province of Utrecht, carrying Roman-origin credentials. Utrecht (pronounced *EW trecht*) was in medieval times the only center of importance in the northern Netherlands, a history that shows in its attractive, atmospheric, and well-preserved old center. An ancient bishopric and present archbishopric, with a bevy of beautiful old churches including the city-symbol **Dom Tower** and its slightly-separated cathedral, Utrecht also offers a unique system of lower-than-street-level canals whose quays are set with inviting cafes, musical and other unusual museums, and an historic university (the largest in Holland), whose students lend a lively perspective to the city.

GETTING AROUND Utrecht is served by buses and trams, although you won't need to make use of them in the old center where most of the attractions are located. Every Sunday **Bus Line M** takes the attractive *Museum and Green Line* run through Utrecht. Sundays from mid-May to mid-Sept. there's a **VVV guided walking tour** on a different theme (*courtyards and almshouses, canals and wharves, churches around the Dom,* etc.) in the center of Utrecht, beginning at 10:30 a.m. (and also at 1:30 p.m. from late June–late July), departing from **Stadkasteel Oudaen** (Oudegracht 99). In July and Aug. the VVV organizes various **bus tours** that provide an overview of the various districts of the city. At the VVV you can rent a **self-guided cassette tour,** and buy a tour brochure to the churches of this one-time ecclesiastical capital. **Canal tours** and **Canal Bikes** offer different views of Utrecht.

SHOPPING For shopping in high style, Utrecht's **La Vie** enclosed complex with fountain and waterfall offers a wide range of luxury wares at elegant department stores such as **De Bijenkorf** (sometimes called the "Harrod's of Holland"); exclusive boutiques abound on Vie Straat and Oudkerkhof. Other major Dutch and European stores (**Vroom & Dreesmann, C & A,** etc.) are on adjoining Vredenburg and in the **Hoog Catharijne** center by Centraal Station. **Hema** can be found on the **Oudegracht,** as can **De Sleate,** a Dutch chain that sells remaindered and other books (plenty in English) and posters. **Lichte Gaard** and **Vis-**

markt are streets with ample antique shops. A large general market is held on the Vredenburg Wed. and Sat.

ACCOMMODATIONS Utrecht, a venue for major international trade congresses and industry fairs—many held at the *Royal Exhibition Center (Jaarbeurs),* the largest trade marketplace in Europe—has several modern international chain hotels to serve attendees of the same, who number nearly a million annually. Thus, there's no lack of hotel rooms (though the city *can* be completely booked during major fairs), but properties that are cozy, comfortable, and central are limited.

RESTAURANTS Being a genial gathering spot for both students and business and pleasure travelers, Utrecht has a broad assortment of restaurants and cafes.

ENTERTAINMENT AND EVENTS Concerts of all kinds are presented in the **Muziekcentrum,** where the VVV has its offices. Its and other programs and events are listed in the biweekly guide (in Dutch) *Uit in Utrecht.* Concerts by the carillonneur can be heard year round Sat. 11 a.m.–noon at the Dom Tower, which has the largest and one of the finest instruments (dating from 1669) in The Netherlands. Frequent organ concerts are held in summer in the city's many churches. In June, there's the **Festival Theater a/d Werf** with street and indoor theater and musical performances. Sept. brings a festival of ancient music.

ARRIVING With its location in the center of the Netherlands, Utrecht is the country's main rail junction. (As such, it's the logical location as headquarters for the country's railroads and the **Dutch Railway Museum,** see below under *What To See and Do*). Amsterdam, to the northwest, is about 30 minutes away on any of the frequent trains; Rotterdam, to the southwest, is a bit farther. Utrecht has a rail connection to Schiphol Airport. Buses serve Utrecht province, but a car is recommended (and may be necessary) for reaching many of the region's castles, riverside villages, and quiet spots of scenic beauty.

TRAVEL TIPS If you didn't come to Utrecht to see its city shopping malls (however fine they may be), don't be discouraged as you come out of the super-modern Centraal Station and have to negotiate through the **Hoog Catharijne** (the largest covered shopping center in Holland, one of the largest commercial centers in Europe—so big it's been divided into *kwartiers*/quarters as if it were a city unto itself) to reach the VVV. Once there, it's only a brief two blocks to the **Oudergracht,** and all the old canalized center-city picturesqueness you could want. Utrecht's evening appeal, with light and laughter emanating from the waterside cafes, should also be experienced.

IN THE AREA If you're traveling by car, to the northwest of Utrecht (in the direction of Amsterdam) are a couple of Holland's many midcountry castles, and the many-mansioned banks of the **Vecht River** through the delightful villages of **Breukelen, Loenen,** and **Ouderkerk.**

Utrecht in Context

Utrecht received its present name indirectly from that of its Roman predecessor *Trajectum ad Rhenum* (ford on the Rhine), which was founded in AD 48 on the site now occupied by Dom Plein. The settlement came into disuse after a flood in 839 re-routed the waters of the Rhine into the Lek River, and the place name became *Oude Trecht* (old ford). Well before the flood, Frankish King Clovis had constructed a church here, c. 500. But the beginnings of real importance for the province arrived with **St. Willibrord,** a monastic native of Northumbria, who became the first Bishop of Utrecht in 696. He became so influential that the town was known for some period within the Frankish and Frisian parts of the considerable Utrecht bishopric territory as Wiltaburg (see also Echternach, Luxembourg, a town that arose around an abbey founded in 698 by the same St. Willibrord). About the year 700, St. Willibrord had two churches built in Utrecht, the one dedicated to St. Martin proving to be a predecessor to the present Domkerk. From his base in Utrecht, Willibrord converted most of the north of the Netherlands to Christianity. After the destruction from raids by Norsemen (who sacked the city in the early 10th century) and Frisians was stemmed by erecting defenses that provided a sense of security that attracted a growing population, Willibrord's successors became increasingly powerful as overlords to large land holdings.

Utrecht was under the protection of the Germanic Holy Roman Empire (and often served as an imperial residence), which meant its powerful Prince Bishops were a constant challenge to the authority of the Counts of Holland. Increasingly, the politically-minded prelates also alienated the growing wealthy Dutch merchant class, and, in 1527, Bishop Henry of Bavaria sold his secular rights to the substantial Utrecht territory to Emperor Charles V. Charles proceeded to build a castle for himself in Utrecht on what is today the **Vredenburg** (the castle was demolished in 1577 in a citizens' revolt against the unpopular Spanish rule of the Netherlands by Philip II, son of Charles V).

As a youth, Charles, who had been born in the southern Netherlands in Ghent, had had as tutor Adrian Florisz, a native of Utrecht who was one of the most educated men of his era. While later serving as bishop in Tortosa, Spain, he was elected **Pope Adrian VI** (1522). In

Utrecht, there was great rejoicing over the honor of having a man from the city chosen pope (Adrian remains the only Dutch pope and, until 1978, had been the last non-Italian pontiff). In 1517, Adrian had had a house built for himself in Utrecht (the **Paushuise** or Pope's House, corner of *Kromme Nieuwe Gracht* and *Nieuwe Gracht*) and had wanted nothing more than to return to it and his city, but died in Rome (Sept. 14, 1523) not long after his election without ever having seen the house, which today is used for official city functions.

Practically from its founding, Utrecht has been a city of churches and bishops. About the year 1025, Bishop Adelbold built yet another new church on the site originally chosen by St. Willbrord for his **St. Martin's** (and site of today's Domkerk). His successor, Bishop Bernold, used the site as the centerpiece for his enterprising undertaking of a *kerkenkruis* (cross of churches), in which four churches, with Adelbold's ecclesistical edifice at the crossing point, formed the shape of a cross in the city. The four new churches, named for the four major churches in Rome at the time, are **St. Pieters** at the east arm of the cross, **St. Jan's** (N) and **St. Paul's** (S), with **Mariakerk** (St. Mary's) on the west, completing the cross in 1080. Fire, the Reformation, and other city troubles have taken a toll over the centuries, but the basic plan is still in evidence. However no sole church structure has in its foundations more of Utrecht's history than the **Domkerk** (See *Domkerk, What to See and Do*).

The **University of Utrecht,** second in age only to Leiden and today the largest in the country, was founded in 1636 at a location close to the Domkerk. In the 17th and 18th centuries, the university was popular with Scottish students, including James Boswell, who studied civil law here in 1763. Having the Dutch House of Orange on the English throne in the person of William III (joint ruler with Mary, daughter of James II) led to many ties between the two countries: Utrecht native son **Godert de Ginkel** (1630–1703), later Earl of Athlone, was a general in William III's forces in Ireland.

Utrecht university's present auditorium is the Dom Cathedral's former Chapterhouse, which was the site for the signing of the **Union of Utrecht (1579),** which made the northern Netherlands officially Protestant. The bells of the Domtoren rang out when it was announced that the Union was signed here by **Count Jan van Nassau** (brother of Willem the Silent, who did not attend and originally disapproved of the Union, feeling, in his broadminded way, that it overlooked too many of the interests of the Roman Catholic people) for the province of Holland, and by other representatives for the provinces of Zeeland and Utrecht. With Utrecht's strong Catholic presence, understandably there had been opposition to overcome by those ecclesiastics who feared a close alliance with Holland, where the Protestant Calvinists were in control. Utrecht supporters of the union went so far as to literally lock up one of the

Catholic priests of a Counter-Union movement until the Union of Utrecht had been duly signed on January 23. (On May 3rd, Willem finally expressed cautious approval of the Union, having been persuaded that no better union was possible under the given circumstances). Although not originally intended as such, the 1579 Union of Utrecht virtually became the constitution for the Republic of the Seven United Netherlands (1588–1795.)

In 1559, the Church in Rome had raised the bishops of Utrecht to archepiscopal rank, but the honor turned out to be short term, since within a year of the singing of the Union of Utrecht, the Catholic See in Holland was dissolved. Under French Napoleonic rule of Holland (1795–1813) the Catholic Church's legal status was restored, though the archbishopric was not revived until 1851. (When Louis Bonaparte ruled as King of Holland (1806–1810) for his brother Napoleon, he reigned from Utrecht for a brief period, using what is now the library of the university as his palace.) Today, the Dutch Roman Catholic archbishopric of Utrecht is alive and well, and inclined to cause the Vatican consternation with the independence of its ideas.

GUIDELINES
Telephone code 030

Tourist Info	VVV Utrecht, Vredenburg 90 (in the Muziekcentrum); Mon.–Fri. 9 a.m.–6 p.m., Sat. 9 a.m.–4 p.m.; 314132.
Canal cruises	**Utrechts Rondvaartbedrijf,** Oudegracht 85, 319377.
Canal Bike	Oudegracht, opposite Stadhuis; 333626; Apr.–Oct., 9 a.m.–7 p.m.
City Transport	Information can be obtained at the GVU kiosk on Stationplein; Mon.–Fri. 6:30 a.m.–8:30 p.m., Sat. & Sun. 8:30 a.m. – 6:30 p.m.; 317962. Also at the VVV.
Post/Telephone	Neude, Mon.–Fri. 8:30 a.m.–7 p.m. (Thurs. to 8:30 p.m.), Sat. 9 a.m.–noon.
Police	Paardenveld, 325911.

WHAT TO SEE AND DO......................

Utrecht's below-the-street wharfs, built beginning in the 12th century, when the water level of the river and canals through the city was still changeable, provide a unique and distinctive look to the center.

Domkerk (Dom Church) • *Domplein; daily May–Sept. 10 a.m.–5 p.m., Oct.–Apr. Mon.–Sat. 11 a.m.–4 p.m., Sun. 2–4 p.m.; 310403* • Entrance to the lacy-facaded, flying-buttressed Gothic St. Martin's Church (Dom Cathedral), whose foundation stone was laid in 1254 (atop the site where St. Willibrord had built a church, which, in turn, had topped the city's original Roman settlement site), is in the remaining section of the structure's once-lengthy nave. The nave was said to be completed in 1505, though this did not include a roof; a temporary one was placed on the nave between 1505 and 1512, after which work on the cathedral was suspended, not for the first time, but, due to war and economic difficulties, forever. The Reformation and rise of the Dutch Republic culminated in 1579 with the Dom's conversion from Cathedral of a Catholic Archbishop to "ordinary" Dutch Reform Protestant church. On August 1, 1674, Utrecht was hit by a tornado, and the double-aisled nave of the Dom collapsed. The Dom tower, which by plan had always been basically detached structurally from the church, was undamaged by the storm, but thereafter stood much distinctly separated. For undocumented reasons, the rubble that resulted from the "whirlwind" destruction of the nave was not cleared away until 1826 (when you think of the *generations* that lived their whole lives with that massive mess, it certainly puts a new perspective on a month's dust under the bed at home). Once the rubble *was* removed, the Domplein was laid out with tinted stones showing the outline of the collapsed nave). For centuries, the play of light in the soaring, spacious Choir and High Choir has been the glory of the Dom. The most recent restoration, begun in 1979, was completed in 1988. The picturesque *cloisters* (14th and 15th century) connect the cathedral with the former Chapterhouse (1495), in which the *Union of Utrecht* was signed in 1579. Over the windows in the cloister, a popular place to rest or listen to a carillon concert from the Domtoren, are carved scenes from the life of St. Martin.

Domtoren (Dom Tower) • *Domplein; Apr. 1–Oct. 31 Mon.–Fri. 10 a.m.–5 p.m. (last tour 4 p.m.), Sat. 11 a.m.–5 p.m., Sun. noon–5 p.m., Nov. 1–March 31 Sat., Sun. only; 919540/919528* • When the 112-meter/367-foot Domtoren was finished in 1382 (from the beginning the plan had been to attach it only superficially to the church, on which construction was expected to last much longer), only four churches in Europe had taller towers: England's Salisbury, Bruges' Our Dear Lady, and the churches of Freiburg and Lubeck in Germany. Its straight lines to the sky are possible because the buttresses are within the body of the structure. Many climb the 465-step tower, beginning at the deceptively broad, straight **stately stair,** which was built for the bishop to reach the St. Michael's Chapel near the base. Rising up the Domtoren, one gets a closeup look at the 50-bell carillon. The Domtoren has served as model for a number of other church towers in Holland, including the Martini Tower in Groningen, St. Jans in Maastricht, Tower of Our Lady in Amersfoort, Tower of the Great Church in Zwolle, and the Grote Kerk in little Loenen (see *In The Area*).

Van Speelklok tot Pierement (National Museum for Musical Clocks to Street Organs) • *Buurkerkhof 10; multi-lingual guided tours on the hour Tues.–Sat. 10 a.m.–5 p.m., Sun. & hols. 1–5 p.m., closed Mon., most major hol.; 312789)* • In the 1980s, Utrecht's 15th-century "citizens' church" or **Buurkerk,** the largest Gothic parish church in Holland, took a new lease on life (a 500-year lease, in fact) as a museum in which "everything makes music." Here, Holland celebrates its singing-tower (carillon) clocks and street organs in a collection that includes automatic musical instruments from the 18th–20th centuries. (These are true musical instruments, with some form of "program" replacing the musically-skilled human hand; in principle, any musical instrument can be automated, and throughout history many attempts—both successful and unsuccessful—have been made, beginning in the 14th century in the Netherlands with the development of mechanical clockwork and striking works). This is definitely a museum where you'll want to join a tour (one strikes every hour, on the hour, for about an hour) since during one you get to hear up to 20 of the enchanting exhibits play. There are multi-melody mantel clocks and marvelous music boxes that play disks (forerunners of CDs), automated chamber and church organs, and pneumatically-operated pianolas, whose player-rolls reproduce actual performances of famous master pianists such as Saint-Saens, Chopin, and Fauré. Instruments range in size from the miniature mechanisms of musical watches to the large barrel-operated *orchestrions,* meant to replicate an orchestra's sounds. The rise of radio and gramophones in the post-1929 depression period brought an end to the 400-year era of string-playing automatic instruments.

The Buurkerk is a building worth enjoying in its own right, since its careful restoration and conversion to a museum conserved its architectural integrity and valuable frescoes. The innovative interior design created acoustically independent galleries in a free-standing form so that the church could be returned to its original condition at any time. That shouldn't be soon, since the museum really did sign a 500-year lease. Also at the museum is a collection of **barrel organs,** from early 17th-century examples of portable ones to the still-popular street-style Dutch specialty (early each June, Utrecht stages a street organ day), to the huge, handsomely carved and painted fairground organs (a German and French musical tradition) and dance hall organs. The museum has a video that shows more instruments in action if you haven't heard enough, and there's a cafe and shop.

Centraal Museum • *Agnietenstraat 1; Tues.–Sat. 10 a.m.–5 p.m., Sun. & hols. 1–5 p.m.; 315541* • Holland's oldest municipal museum (1838), the Centraal has a rich resource in its half-dozen 17th and 18-century period rooms, and **Jan Scorel** (1495–1562) is one of the leading lights among the Utrecht painters represented. Among others are **Abraham Bloemaert** (1564–1651) and sons, and Gerrit van Honthorst **(1590–1656).**

Het Catharijneconvent • *Nieuwegracht 63; Tues.–Fri. 10 a.m.–5 p.m., Sat., Sun., & hol. 11 a.m.–5 p.m., closed Mon.; 313835* • Two years after it opened in 1979, the International Council of Museums presented Het Catharijneconvent with its Museum-of-the-Year prize. With Utrecht a past and present Dutch ecclesiastical center, the contents appropriately cover the country's history of Christianity (both Catholic and Protestant), and represent the largest collection of medieval art (sculpture, paintings, illuminated mss., breviaries, religious relics, and vestments) in Holland.

Nederlands Spoorwegmuseum (Dutch Railway Museum) • *Maliebaan station; Tues.–Fri. 10 a.m.–5 p.m., Sun. and some hols. 1–5 p.m. closed Sat.; 306206* • You can catch a special 10-minute train from the CS (or walk) to the 1874 *Maliebaan,* a "retired" station where exhibits keep track of Holland's more than 150 years of rail history (the first line opened in 1839 between Amsterdam and Haarlem). On three covered platforms and five tracks, beautifully restored rolling stock, steam, electric, and some horse-drawn tramway cars; on *Spoor 1* (platform one) stand a row of seven locomotives; both the beginning (1864) and end of the line (1945) are British achievements. Nostalgic paintings and prints decorate part of the old railway hall. This is a well-done museum at the country's rail crossroads that even non-train buffs will find interesting, considering that trains are such a tradition in Europe. There's a comprehensive booklet on all aspects of Dutch trains, from the historic to the futuristic, available in English, and refreshments await in the old **Wagons-Lits** restaurant car.

Rietveld-Schroderhuis • *Hendriklaan 50A; Tues.–Sun. 12:15–5 p.m.; visits only with prior reservation by telephone 517926; bus #4* • Despite Holland's many buildings of interest across several centuries, this is the one example of Dutch architecture to be incorporated in the World List of Protected Buildings. An important monument in the Dutch art movement **De Stijl,** the house was built in 1924 by architect and furniture designer Gerrit Rietveld, and contains both his simple bold lines, brightly colored geometrical chairs, and other furniture he designated for it. Rietveld's work has a strong tie with nature. Visits must be arranged ahead of time because of the limited space inside the house.

Museum voor het Kruideniersbedrijf (Grocery Museum) • *Hoogt 6, Tues.–Sat. 12:30–4:30 p.m.; 316628* • This is the Dutch equivalent of an old penny-candy store, with women in aprons serving your choices of sweets from great glass jars (there are some 25 different kinds of licorice, a favorite in Holland). A free museum of sorts, with old kitchen and cooking utensils is upstairs, but the real delight is downstairs, especially if a crowd of Dutch children come in after school. For sale are tins of tea and biscuits, prettily decorated with Holland scenes.

ACCOMMODATIONS..........................

First Class
★★★★ **Scandic Crown Hotel** • *Westplein 50, 3531 BL; 925200, fax 925199* • Located on the non-historic side of the tracks, though only steps from Centraal Station, the gleaming glass 120-room Scandic Crown is convenient to the Jaarbeurs Complex for trade fairs, a short walk to the VVV, and not much farther from Utrecht's old center. Its Scandinavian style is carried through from room decor and restaurant specialties to the fact of a sauna in the fitness room. Non-smoking rooms, parking available.

Moderate
★★★ **Malie** • *Maliestraat 2, 3581 SL; 316424, fax 340661* • This friendly, stylish 30-rooms-in-adjoining-restored-houses hotel is owned and operated by a young couple who are trained in hotel management and show it. The residential neighborhood property is a short bus ride, or longish walk, to the city center. Each airy, neat, individual room has shower, TV, telephone, reading lamps; several overlook the garden, and two have private terraces. Prices vary slightly with size—go on, splurge! The breakfast (only, included) room looks on to the garden, and there's a lobby bar with comfortable leather couches, magazines. Elevator, bus #4 to Centrum.

★★★ **Smits** • *Vredenburg 14, 3511 BA; 331232, fax 328451* • Sitting close to the site of Charles V's short-lived 16th-century castle on the Vredenburg, the recently renovated five-story, 87-room property is close to the station, sights, and shopping. All rooms have shower; ask for a tub/shower if you want one. Since the hotel faces the Vredenburg, where the Wed. and Sat. markets get an early start, rooms on the back are a quieter choice. There's an attractive lounge bar (with live piano music many nights) and a restaurant that serves all three meals (buffet breakfast included for guests). Elevator, major credit cards.

RESTAURANTS..................................

The starting and stopping point for eating and drinking in Utrecht is the **Oudegracht,** with its cafes on the canal terraces and eateries within the wharfs (in which case their address reads *onder,* or under, the building on main street level above). With menus posted and prices kept pretty reasonable by the city's student population, making a choice here isn't very chancy. Nevertheless, you might want to know that **Il Pozzo** is the Oudegracht's largest and most famous terrace cafe and, locally, *the* place to be seen, although crowds also tend to follow the sun in their search for cafe seats. Il Pozzo's name reflects the strong Italian influence in Utrecht, as does **Venezia,** the Oudegracht location for Italian *ijs* (ice cream). **La Pizzeria** *(Voorstraat 23; noon–2 p.m., 5–11 p.m., closed Sun. & Mon. til 5 p.m., closed hol.; 316021; inexpensive)* claims the honor of being Utrecht's oldest Italian restaurant, and dishes up pasta, veal in a variety of styles, and Italian wines, as well as pizza.

Cafe de Paris *(Drierharingstraat 16; noon–2 p.m., 5:30–10 p.m., closed Sun. & hols.; 317503; moderate)* is an enterprise of one of the enterprising Fagel brothers, who operate a handful of highly respected independent restaurants around Holland. The menu is limited but choice, French-influenced, and served in a Belle Epoch setting. Also offering a good range of French fare is **Polman's Huis** *(Keistraat 2; daily noon–11 p.m.; 313368; inexpensive),* which occupies a desanctified 17th-century church with Art Deco accents and huge floor-to-ceiling mirrors, and serves up music most evenings. Another historic setting for supping is the restored medieval mansion (which also had a life as an old men's home) **Stadskasteel Oudaen** *(Oudegracht 99; daily 5:30–11 p.m.; 311864; moderate),* whose upstairs restaurant serves continental cuisine and a four-course menu. At ground floor is a fashionable bar, and there's a cafe, both of which are open for morning coffee.

Back on the Oudegracht, or, rather one level down from it, look for **Tantes Bistro** *(Oudegracht a/d Werf 61; daily 5–11 p.m.; 312191; inexpensive)* that serves French-style food, but also Dutch dishes, in an old vaulted canalside cellar. Nearby is **De Werfkring** *(Oudegracht a/d Werf 123; Mon.–Sat. noon to 8 p.m., closed Sun. & hols.; 311752; inexpensive),* where the vegetarian dishes are healthy, tasty, and priced for a student's pocket. That's also true of the plate-size delicious Dutch *pannekoeken* (pancakes) and other light items at the 14th-century **De Oude Muntkelder** *(Oudegracht a/d Werf, beneath the main Post Office; Tues.–Sat. noon–8:30 p.m., closed Sun. & Mon.; 316773; inexpensive),* at which there's outside canalside terrace or inside seating. At **Victor Consael** *(Neude; open daily 10 a.m.–10 p.m. in summer, 8 p.m. winter; 316377; inexpensive),* a Utrecht family institution since 1850, you can get *poffertjes* (rather like doughnut holes sprinkled with sugar) and waffles, as well as pancakes.

For a snack "to go," stop at the Jewish bakery **De Tarwebol** on Zadelstraat, near the Buurkerk. To end the day on a completely different note, you might drop in to **Fellini** *(Stadhuisbrug; Wed.–Sun. 10 p.m.–4 a.m.)*, a disco located in the extensive ancient cellars underneath the Stadhuis (town hall). The restoration has made the cellars truly beautiful, and, even if you don't plan to dance, it's a special place to see during a stop for a drink.

IN THE AREA..................................

Slot Zuylen • *signposted to the right on east bank of Amsterdam-Rijn Kanaal, five km./three miles northwest of Utrecht, near Maarssen, Tournooiveld 1, Oud Zuilen; mid-Mar.–mid-Nov. daily, tours at 10 & 11 a.m., 2, 3 & 4 p.m., Sun. 2, 3, & 4 p.m., closed Mon.; 030–440255* • A castle with a substantial moat surrounded by woods, originally built in the late 12th century but given a facelift in the 18th (though still one of Holland's most characteristically medieval castles), its contents include fine furniture, tapestry, porcelain, and pictures. James Boswell visited and established a long-lasting friendship with Isabella van Zuylen here in 1763–64, while he was a student at Utrecht university; she later married a Swiss and became known as a novelist under her married name Isabelle de Charriere. A main feature of the fine garden, to which the public has free access, is a serpentine wall.

Kasteel De Haar • *5 km./3 miles further north at Vleuten-Haarzuilens; Kasteellaan 1; March–mid-Aug & Oct.–mid-Nov., tours more or less hourly 10:30 a.m.–4:30 p.m., Sun. 1:30 p.m., closed Mon.; 03407–1275* • The flamboyant-by-design neo-Gothic **De Haar,** which definitely lives up to a brochure claim of being "an unexpected occurrence in this down-to-earth Dutch landscape," dates from the turn of this century having been first built in 1165, enlarged in 1287, destroyed in 1482, rebuilt in 1505, and badly damaged by the French in 1672, after which it was left relatively alone and in ruins. Marriage of the heir (Baron Etienne van Zuylen van Nyevelt van de Haar) in 1887 to a Baroness de Rothschild provided funds to restore the ancestral home. In 1892, the commission was given to **P.J.H. Cuypers,** the famous, prolific, and authoritative architect of Amsterdam's Rijksmuseum and Centraal Station. There were altercations and alterations, as much over matters of taste as finance; funds seem, in fact, to have been close to unlimited, since hundreds of laborers and artists worked, sometimes day and night, from 1892 through 1912 to complete the task, and to ensure the necessary supply of bricks the Baron built a brick factory. He also dismantled the entire village that had grown up near the castle over the centuries but was now, he felt, too near the castle to allow for the forested hunting grounds and gardens he had planned, and moved it two kilometers away. (He "built" the forest by transporting and transplanting mature-only trees.) While the castle was being rebuilt, the owners took a sort of second honeymoon around the world, buying whatever they liked as furnishings to stock it. Architect Cuypers felt it was all too eclectic, and expressed his thoughts by weaving into the library decoration such sayings as "Nothing in excess" and "I hope you won't regret it." In fact, the castle contains valuable works of art, none more worthy than the dining room's 17th-century Flemish tapestries after a design by David Teniers the Younger. The hall is a lofty landmark of the castle: a celebration of Van Zuylen prominence in the Middle Ages, it features ten family statues set into the carved sandstone towering tiered galleries that rise to a gilted oakwood ceiling based on a former one at the Palace of Justice in Rouen, France. Stained-glass windows in the hall have scenes from the De Haar history. It isn't an Everyman's idea of home, but one has to say it's impressive. The family-anecdotal tours, which include details about the style of living when the family and its high-society guests take up residence each Sept. (the castle is centrally heated and the plumbing is thoroughly modernized) includes the grand rooms on the ground floor and a bedroom or two. Allow time to enjoy the lovely Versailles-style formal gardens. There's revival in Haarzuilens village (which can reached by a walk through the woods from the castle if you like) at cafe-restaurant **De Vier Balken** *(Brinkstraat 3; 03407–1268; lunch and dinner, closed Mon.)*, a pleasingly rustic atmosphere with tasty Dutch dishes from salads to steaks.

The **River Vecht** flows from Utrecht almost to Amsterdam and, during medieval days, nobility from **Het Sticht** (the old name for the province of Utrecht) and the bishops of Utrecht built fortress-castles along the Vecht in order to defend the region from attacks from provocators from the province of Holland. During the devastating time (1672–73) of the French occupation of the region, virtually the entire region of the Vecht was destroyed. Many Amsterdam merchants, however, retained enough riches from the East Indies trade of the Golden Age to line the river once again with marvelous buildings, this time ornate summer mansions with landscaped lawns and teahouses. (The daily ceremony for tea, first introduced in Holland c. 1610, and becoming wildly popular in the course of the 17th century, as engaged in at these riverfront gazebos [and thus visible to "sightseers on the water"] was meant to be showy.) Although few of these are open to the public, these remain well-preserved in private use and the exterior can be enjoyed by those traveling in the area by car, cruise boat, or bicycle.

One of the most beautiful villages on the Vecht is **Breukelen,** from which the New York City borough "Brooklyn" gets its name; yes, there's a bridge, a pretty little drawbridge that no one mentions selling. Breukelen, too, was largely demolished by Louis XIV's forces in 1672, with the stones being used to build defensive works. However, the shortly thereafter rebuilding doesn't seem to have cost the village much of its narrow-streeted charm.

South of Breukelen, on the west side of the Vecht, is the **Restaurant-Hotel Hofstede Slangevegt** *(Straatweg 40, Breukelen; lunch noon– 2 p.m., dinner 5:30–9:30 p.m., except Sat. & Sun. dinner only, closed Tues; 03462–61525; moderate),* an elegantly cozy traditional restaurant with river terrace and conservatory. The locally popular restaurant has three-course prix fixe lunches and dinners. If you don't mind mixing with the family owners, there are several rather ordinary rooms (inexpensive), but two on the river, with balconies, private shower/toilet.

Another village long on loveliness is **Loenen** (pop. 7000), with its many 18th-century houses. The design for the 15th–16th-century Dutch Reform Church tower was taken from Utrecht's Domtoren, though in 1741 the foundation had to be propped up with peat to correct a lean, which from some angles is still noticeable. Two intimate and tempting local dinner dining choices are **Tante Koosje** *(Kerkstraat 1; 02943– 3201; closed Wed.)* in a house beside the church, and **Restaurant 't Amsterdammertje** *(Rijksstraatweg 119; 02943–4813),* cozy with wooden tables, candles, and ivy draped around the mirrors. Continue on toward Amsterdam through **Ouderkerk aan de Amstel** (Old Church on the Amstel), another authentic old Dutch village that's a pleasant place to pause for some refreshment at one of the many cafe terraces along the river.

NORTHERN HOLLAND: AN INTRODUCTION

The north of the Netherlands includes the provinces of Friesland, Groningen, and Drenthe. The northern provinces are anchored by the cities of Leeuwarden, capital of Friesland, and Groningen, capital of its same-name province.

Friesland has an atmosphere of landed nobility and wealth. Cows (the famous *Frisian black and whites,* bred and exported around the world) have for centuries been so important to the province's economy that a statue of one (named *Us Mem*—"our mother") stands near the station in the center of Leeuwarden. The countryside is studded with prosperous farmhouses, distinctive in that both the family living quarters and barns are sheltered under a single huge roof. Black glazed tiles (as distinguished from the more common ones in orange terracotta) were symbols of wealth and used over the home section of the structure. The Frisians were early settlers of the sea-embattled land in the north, living first on man-made mounds *(terps)* meant to keep them above the high water level; by the year 1000, they had developed an extensive network of dikes. In addition to Dutch, Friesland has had its own language (today, a compulsory course in the province's primary schools) and body of literature for centuries; *Frisian* is described as being "a brother to the English language and a cousin to Dutch." The Frisian people have long been friends of the United States. In 1782, while still an independent province, Friesland was the first government to recognize the newly-formed United States of America as a country (there's a plaque stating that fact in the historic Provincial House in Leeuwarden). The Frisians also strongly urged the Dutch government to loan the young America some much-needed capital. Friesland has always seemed separate from the rest of the Netherlands, its location on the far side of the former **Zuiderzee** (now the enclosed *IJsselmeer*) adding to its sense of remoteness. The road atop the enclosing **Afsluitdijk** (opened in 1932) provided a more accessible driving route to the province and opened Friesland to more outside influence, but, even today, few residents of Holland, and fewer visitors, know much about this interesting and attractive area.

Groningen, at the "top" of Holland, has far-stretching fields, rows of poplars permanently bent by the winds off the shallow *Waddenzee*, and horizons marked by "mountains" of clouds. The only town of any size in the province, Groningen, was a center of activity by the 11th century, and today retains the inner-city waterways that were its moats in earlier eras. The landmark of the attractive historic city center is **Martinikerk,** a lovely church largely 15th-century in appearance, though begun in the 13th. The distinguished **University of Groningen** was founded in 1614.

Mooi Drenthe ("lovely Drenthe") is the way this northeastern province, the least well-known of the country's twelve, often is described. With Drenthe's heathland, inland sandbanks, peat fens, and woods, the phrase is apt, and certainly more descriptive than Drenthe's other epithet: "the forgotten province." The most intriguing attractions in Drenthe are reminders of its prehistoric (c. 3000 B.C.) inhabitants, great megalithic burial chambers known as *Hunebeds,* many of which survive (especially along the Hondsrug ridge that runs northwest from Emmen).

As interesting as the "far" north of Holland may be, it is the "near" north, with its picturesque old fishing villages around what formerly was the **Zuiderzee** (South Sea, now the IJsselmeer lake) that usually is most rewarding for visitors. Of particular interest are **West Friesland** (the northeast section of today's North Holland province) and, across the Afsluitdijk that closed off the Zuiderzee, the **southwest corner of Friesland.** Most visitors also want to know how the new polder province of **Flevoland,** which exists in a region that until 1932 was under the tidal waters of the Zuiderzee, came to be reclaimed from the bottom of that sea.

OLD ZUIDERZEE VILLAGES AND THE NEW POLDER PROVINCE

Following two centuries of sinking land, rising seas, and mounting floods, the great storm of **1287** breached the sand dune barrier between the North Sea and what had been an inland lake north of Amsterdam. The flood produced by the storm (which killed 50,000 in Friesland alone) created the **Zuiderzee,** whose tidal shores became the site for the many flourishing fishing villages and seafaring towns that gave the region its identity. Their Zuiderzee connection became the chacteristic quality of these quaint and handsome seashore communities. So strong was the shaping force of the Zuiderzee on life around its rim that 60 years after the great **Afsluitdijk** (barrier dam) sealed it off from the North Sea in 1932, you can still sense the salt in the air of the picturesque old ports, now filled with recreational sail boats instead of commercial sailing ships.

For many visitors, sentimental regret for the passing of the "sailing on the tide" seafaring tradition of the Zuiderzee villages is offset by a fascination with the story of the creation of a whole new province of polderland from what used to be the bottom of the sea. The tale is exceptionally well told—in multiple languages—at the **Informatiecentrum Nieuw Land** located in **Lelystad,** the capital of the new Flevoland polder province.

Guidelines for Old Zuiderzee Villages/New Polder Province

SIGHTS There's a great deal of scenic variety in the region covered in this chapter, from compact waterland villages to prosperous towns that sent forth sea captains around the world in the 17th century. The open-air **Zuiderzee Museum** at Enkhuizen gives an impression of daily life and work in the Zuiderzee region during the period of 1880–1930. The 300-year old craft of making Dutch tiles and porcelain can be seen in **Makkum,** and Hoorn's **West Fries Museum** is one of the region's most attractive sources of local history. You can also encounter traditional costumes, thatched farmhouses, a village where farmers ferry cattle from one grazing field to another on flat-bottomed boats, castles, and cloudscapes above Friesland's vast and verdant reaches that make you catch your breath.

GETTING AROUND To reach the sights in this section requires a car, although certain places are served by train: Hoorn, Enkhuizen, and Lelystad more or less conveniently from Amsterdam; Groningen, Leeuwarden, Harlingen, and Kampen via trains through Utrecht. This being Holland, local and regional buses go to literally every village, but a traveler with limited time will not want to waste it waiting at remote countryside crossroads to make the next bus connection. A word of caution about driving on the provincial roads. Many are single lane in each direction; the flatness of the polder terrain, combined with the speed at which local drivers go, can fool you about on-coming car distances, so be wary when planning to pass. Also, the smaller the rental car you can manage with, the more you'll save on the vehicle, and the easier it will be to navigate it on tight turns in tiny villages.

SHOPPING The larger towns on this route (Hoorn, Harlingen, Kampen) have the most varied selection of shops for basic and specialty goods. There's a museum shop with gift items at Enkhuizen's **Zuiderzee Museum. Hindeloopen,** once famed for its painted furniture, has a number of shops with smaller items in its distinctive style. **Makkum** has traditional Dutch tiles and porcelain.

ENTERTAINMENT AND EVENTS Wednesdays from early July to mid-August, there are **folklore markets** in Hoorn. Thursdays (mid-June to mid-August), the West Frisian Folklore markets are held in Schagen. Also on Thursday afternoons in July and August, in both Enkhuizen and at the **Zuiderzee Museum,** large groups from various Zuiderzee villages dress in traditional costume and perform live music. An historic steam train runs between Medemblik-Hoorn-Enkhuizen from May–Sept.

(02290–16653). From mid-April–late May, **bulb fields** bloom around West Friesland. Every 3rd Sunday of the month from Easter to September Naarden celebrates **Civil Guard days** in medieval costume at its Vesting Museum. In Purmerend on Thurs. in July and Aug. from 11 a.m.–1 p.m. a small **cheese market** with handicrafts is held. The Dutch are fond of taking guided hikes through the **Waddenzee mud flats** in summer.

ACCOMMODATIONS Given the limited quantity and size of hotels in the area, reservations are suggested, and are a must in the summer months when the Dutch and other Europeans come here on holiday. (Even those arriving by private sail boat—which many do—often opt for a hotel with hot shower.)

RESTAURANTS Seafood is bound to come to mind as you circle the former Zuiderzee and see the wealth that fishing brought to its villages and towns. Most hotels have a more-than-reputable restaurant.

TRAVEL TIPS Keep a stash of *guilders* and *kwartjes* (25-cent pieces) on hand for parking meters, so you can make the most of short stops in towns.

THE ROUTE..................................

This exploration of old Zuiderzee villages (including places of interest inland) and the new polder province of Flevoland, heads north from Amsterdam, following the map in a roughly clockwise route through the fishing villages of **Monnickendam, Marken,** and **Edam.** It then proceeds up the west side of what today is the IJsselmeer to the important towns of **Hoorn** (explorer Willem Schouten put his hometown's name on the map by naming the southern tip of South America Cape Horn) and **Enkhuizen.** After crossing the **Afsluitdijk** into Friesland, with stops at **Harlingen** and **Franeker** (from which a motorway continues northeast to Leeuwarden and Groningen) the route drops south to the small and picturesque ports of **Makkum** and **Hindeloopen** that lie along the northern coast to the IJsselmeer, and then inland to the southeast to lovely little lakeside **Sloten,** the smallest of Friesland's 11 towns. Without neglecting **Blozijl** (now bound into the mainland by polder), and the pleasing oddities of **Giethoorn** and **Staphorst,** the road continues to **Urk,** once an island, but now also absorbed into the mainland. Both **Kampen** and the well-preserved formerly fortified city of **Elburg** have roads leading onto **Flevolande,** the new polder province (the *In-*

formatiecentrum Nieuw Land, in the capital **Lelystad,** details how Holland has reclaimed over 400,000 acres from the former Zuiderzee in the last 50 years). As you leave the new land, there are last looks at the old: fortifications and castles at **Naarden** and **Muiden,** almost at Amsterdam's door. The mileage for the entire route is remarkably manageable, and even the rural roads are well paved and signposted. You can easily meander for much of a week, or take the shortcut dike-top road from Enkhuizen across the IJsselmeer to Lelystad (Rt. N302, 28 kms./17 mi.) for an edited edition of the tour. Therefore, decisions about an itinerary can be based upon your interests, and the amount of time you have.

ON THE ROAD

Leaving Amsterdam *Centrum* via the *IJ Tunnel* north, look for signs for **N247** (or **Volendam**) in the next few miles, and exit there. That's the end of motorways for the remainder of the route, unless you choose otherwise on select stretches.

Broek-in-Waterland

About six miles from Amsterdam—less than a half hour by car, even if you're negotiating heavy central Amsterdam traffic out of the city—you'll arrive in *Waterland,* a lovely water-logged region of canals and small villages with typical wooden houses often painted green with white trim. With its large wooden houses, ornamental summer and domed tea houses, and gracious gardens, the village of Broek-in-Waterland (pop. 3,000) is a charming witness to 18th-century prosperity. Just past the church, built in 1628 and recently restored *(open from May–mid-Sept. 10 a.m.–4 p.m.),* at the far end of the village, there are several wooden shoe *(klompen)* and cheese-maker cottages *(De Domme Dirk)* that are friendly and non-commercial in comparison with the ones you'll see on the road to Volendam. Broek was the setting for the 1865 story *Hans Brinker, or The Silver Skates.* Hans and friends regularly *skated* into Amsterdam, but today there's an attractive sea dike cyclists' route from Amsterdam along the IJsselmeer to Broek and Monnickendam; inquire at the Amsterdam VVV for the *Waterland Cycle Route* (English) booklet. Broek-in-Waterland is so convenient to, yet such a complete change from, Amsterdam that one of its restaurants (**Neeltje Pater**) is a luncheon favorite out of the city for chauffer-driven business clients. Across the road is the more reasonably priced **De Witte Swaen** *(noon–9 p.m., closed Mon.)* for Dutch pancakes.

Monnickendam

VVV in the 15th-century **Grote Kerk,** *the first building you come to; April–Oct. Mon.–Sat. 10 a.m.–noon, 2–5 p.m., rest of year 4 p.m.; pop. 10,000* • Just 12 km./7 mi. north of Amsterdam, Monnickendam's center is the Middendam, with the 17th-century **De Waegh** (Weighhouse), now a pleasant **pannekoekhuis,** *(11 a.m.–10 p.m. daily April 1–Oct. 31; open Fri.–Sun. only Nov. 1–Mar. 31; 02995–1241; inexpensive).* Nearby is the 16th-century **Speeltoren,** with the second oldest carillon in Holland. **Restaurant "De Posthoorn"** *(Noordeinde 39; 02995-1471; inexpensive/moderate)* has a quietly stylish, attractive antique-decorated traditional old Dutch interior, with candlelit tables even at lunch, and serves three-course luncheon menus that feature such favorite starters as Zeeland oysters, smoked eel, eel soup, and fish or chicken salad, but will also prepared a light choice of omelet or salad. With a terrace on the harbor, near the herring smokehouses, is the **Cafe-Restaurant Stuttenburgh** *(Haringburgwal 2; 02995–1869; inexpensive)* which features service from 10 a.m. of pancakes to fresh fish, and a *gezellig* (cozy) interior filled with antique music boxes.

Marken

From Monnickendam, you can drive atop a dike to the former island of Marken, whose land was resurrected from the Zuiderzee by nuns and monks in the 13th century. Since the mid-1900s, it has been a peninsula connected to the mainland by causeway. The village's typical green wood and white-trim cottages sit in a crescent facing what used to be open sea; they retain a far-reaching waterview across the IJsselmeer. If you arrive in the late afternoon or evening, and linger over a drink at **De Taanderij** *(Havenbuurt 1; 02996–1364),* a terrace cafe at one end of the crescent, you may get a personal impression of the tiny village, where traditional costumes are worn "for the tourists." Perhaps one shouldn't fault the villagers for their successful "switch-to-tourism-to-survive" business sense, after their former sea fishing industry foundered with the sealing off of the Zuiderzee in 1932. There's a **Marken Museum** *(Kerkbuurt 44; Easter–Nov. 1, daily 10 a.m.—5 p.m.; Sun. noon–4 p.m.),* fitted out as a typical fishing family would have lived up to about 1932. You may manage a pleasant visit to Marken (the coaches have to park outside the village, which is mostly pedestrian). The commercialism at the nearby, much larger town of **Volendam** is harder to ignore, however, and best avoided.

Edam

VVV in 1737 Stadhuis on the 1569 Damplein; Mon.–Sat., Apr.–Oct., 10 a.m.–5 p.m.; Nov.–Mar., 1 a.m.–12:30 p.m., Mon.,–Sat.; closed

Sun; 02993–71727; pop. 25,000 • Its name is familiar for having originated, centuries ago, the recipe for the region's most widely produced type of cheese. Edam's cheese market *(Wed. mid-July–mid.-Aug., 10 a.m.–noon)* at the 18th-century **Kaaswaag** *(itself open daily 10 a.m.–5 p.m.)* is a small, tourist-oriented affair (Alkmaar is the main cheese market for the cannon-ball shaped edams see *Amsterdam, In the Area*). However, the wonderfully picturesque town merits much meandering to see its canals, drawbridges, grassy ramparts, and many fine facades; it's conveniently small, but always seems to offer another enticing corner to turn. Edam received its town rights in 1357, at which time it was walled and a toll-free canal to the Zuiderzee constructed. From 1573–1922, an important weekly cheese market was held there (records from 1649 show that Edam exported a half million cheeses that year), and its cheese-aging warehouses are still active. **Dam Square** is the center, but the recently restored 15th-century **Grote Kerk** *(Grote kerkstraat; April–Oct., daily 2–4:30 p.m.)*, tucked in a corner of the town is perhaps Edam's proudest possession. It is the largest triple-ridged church in Europe, with a fine carved-oak choir screen, and has 30 early-17th-century windows that give the interior lovely lighting. Edam's oldest brick house (c. 1530) is now the **Town Museum** *(Damplein 8; April–Oct., Mon.–Sat., 10 a.m.–4 p.m., Sun. 2–4 p.m.);* inside you can see the typical construction, which must be sturdy to support its "floating cellar," a brick box-shaped room that floats freely on ground water that is rumored to have been devised by a retired sea captain owner who wanted to sleep rocking on water. The VVV sells *A Stroll through Edam* in English. If no other restaurants have already caught your eye on your tour about town, **"Rimi"** *(Prinsenstraat 5; 02993–71630)* is recommended locally for casual fare, while the **Cafe-Restaurant "Hof Van Holland"** *(Lingerzijde 69; 02993–72546)* has a more elegant decor and extensive menu.

ACCOMMODATIONS ★★★ Hotel "De Fortuna" • *Spuistraat 1; 02993–71671; inexpensive* • This cozy complex of five restored 17th-century houses (about 30 rooms) around a garden and flowered terrace overlooks a canal at the edge of the historic town. Most rooms have a private shower and toilet, many have a TV and telephone with cheerful modern room decor; there are steep stairs (no elevators) to negotiate in some cases. Breakfast (included) is served, but no other meals; drinks are available to guests only. On-street parking.

Hoorn

VVV in the 1613 stepped-gable "Statenpoort," Nieuwstraat 23, year-round, Tues.–Fri., 10 a.m.–12.30 p.m. & 1:30 p.m.–5 p.m., Sat. 10 a.m.–2 p.m., Mon. 1:30–5 p.m., closed Sun., except Jul. & Aug.,

Mon.–Sat. until 6 p.m.; 02290-18342; pop. 56,000, 5,000 in old center; 20 km./12 mi. north of Edam • In the 12th century Hoorn was a shipping stopover between Denmark and Bruges in Flanders. In the 14th century, it received town rights, after which markets and a legal system were established. With the local economy strong in sea trade in the 15th, 16th, and 17th centuries, especially from the Dutch East and West Indies companies, Hoorn embellished its mansions, warehouses, hofjes, and admiralty buildings to reflect the prosperity of those times. A building in the old center that can't help but hold your attention with its fanciful Dutch Renaissance facade is the 1632 provincial government building that now houses the **West Fries Museum** *(Rode Steen 1; Mon.–Fri. 11 a.m.–5 p.m., Sat. & Sun. 2–7 p.m.; 02290–15783)*. Also intriguing on the inside, the handsome museum houses period rooms (including a tiled kitchen and loft), with furniture, fine and decorative arts, old maps and ship models, old panelling, tapestries, and civic guard portraits, and has a charming garden. Many Dutch "naive-style" painters have come from the West Fries section of Holland and a permanent display of their delightful art recently was added to the museum. Walk from the museum down to the **Old Haven,** where the striking semicircular 1532 (restored 1905) **Hoofdtoren** (old defense tower) dominates what is now a yacht harbor. Across from it is the terrace cafe **Het Schippershuis** *(02290–15202)* for a drink or lunch with a view. The VVV has a brochure in English **(Walking in Hoorn)** that features the harbor and *hofjes* (almshouses, of which there are many in Hoorn, founded by the wealthy merchants), and gives a map, descriptions of sights, and a good bit of history. During the first half of the 17th century, Hoorn, and Holland, may have become too prosperous for their own good: In the second half of the 17th century, Hoorn's prosperity began to decline, partially as a result of the **Anglo-Dutch Wars,** which reflected an English attitude expressed by Samuel Pepys in his diary of 1665 that "all were mad for a 'Dutch war' which would, it was hoped, ruin Dutch trade."

Enkhuizen

VVV Stationplein 1; 02280–13164; pop. 20,000; 16 km./9 mi. northeast of Hoorn • How appropriate that a museum dedicated to life as it was around the former Zuiderzee should be reached by boat—and boat alone. From Enkhuizen's train station (parking included in museum admission) boats embark every few minutes for the few-minute cruise past the steepled skyline of the town to the **Zuiderzee Museum** *(mid-April–late Oct., daily 10 a.m.–5 p.m., last admission 4 p.m.; 02280-18260)*. The site of the Zuiderzee Museum, which opened in 1983 and promptly won the *European Museum of the Year Award,* is the former working harbor site from which the 35 km./21 mi. dam/road from Enkhuizen to Lelystad (on the then-new East Flevoland polder on the other side of the IJsselmeer) was built in 1965. The Zuiderzee Museum is dedicated to the socio-historic purpose of recreating work and domestic life as it was in the region during the half century prior to the 1932 construction of the **Afsluitdijk** (see below). Through its 135 houses and workplaces, collected from Zuiderzee villages and towns, the museum has been assembled to create a complete and charming urban setting, with canals, churches, alleyways, and gardens. There's a detailed, color-illustrated guidebook in English that describes the specific buildings, and also provides interesting background tidbits, such as: rain water, used for drinking and cooking (well-water being good enough only for cleaning and outdoor needs), was most pure when it ran into collection barrels off roofs made of tiles that were glazed, and hence didn't grow moss. As you wander through this Zuiderzee "village" you'll find many folk more than willing to chat about their activities: the man in the smokehouse bending over his hot oakwood fire; a fisherman sitting on a lawn "doing penance" (mending nets); or the attendant at **Apotheek De Grote Gaper** ("The Big Yawner"). Having explained that the large carved wooden head with mouth open and tongue stuck out was typical of Dutch signage used since the Middle Ages to indicate a drugstore or chemist's shop, he made sure I didn't miss the wonderful collection of 40 such heads in the room behind "his" old shop, originally from Hoorn. There are several eateries at the museum, including the **Pannekoekenhis Taveerne de Meermin** *(02280–10291)* which features light meals, a menu, and soup of the day, in addition to pancakes, and a pub with an outdoor terrace overlooking the IJsselmeer.

The actual town of Enkhuizen, to which you can return by foot from the exit *(uitgang)* of the museum if you wish, is an historic treasure itself, dating back almost a millennium. Coming on foot from the museum, you'll see the restored **Peperhuis** (1625), which was owned by the Dutch East India Company from 1682. Walk along the tree-shaded, sun-speckled **Zuider Havendijk,** and the **Zuiderspui,** which ends at a white pedestrian drawbridge that crosses to the 1540 **Drommedaris Tower** with its 1677 Hemony carillon *(concerts Sat. 4–5 p.m.),* both easily enjoyed from the terraced cafes opposite. Enkhuizen has a second Hemony carillon in the green copper-crowned **Zuiderkerk** (1450), with additional concerts. In summer, Enkhuizen is the Dutch port with the largest number of traditional sailing ships: large-masted old wooden craft that make a fine sight when under sail in the IJsselmeer, which you can view from atop the town's grassy ramparts.

ACCOMMODATIONS ★★★ Die Port van Cleve • *Dijk 74; 02280–12510; inexpensive* • This friendly, slightly old-fashioned, 20-room family hotel is cozy and pleasantly located, in the old town facing the old port, an easy walk to the most interesting part of town and still not far from the station if you've come by train. Bedrooms are functional, with tile toilets/showers. Its old Dutch decor restaurant and terrace cafe are congregating places for visitors and town dwellers alike.

RESTAURANTS For fine dining **Restaurant Die Drie Haringhe** *(Dijk 28; noon–2 p.m., 5 p.m.–10 p.m., closed Tues.; for res. 02280–18610; moderate)* offers fare from *lapin* (rabbit) to *lotte a la gember* (lotte fish with ginger) in an upstairs setting of old brick, wood beams, and candlelight on the white-light-strung old harbor, across from the illuminated Drommedaris, whose carillon chimes the quarter hours. There's a cafe in the **Drommedaris** evenings.

From Enkhuizen, enroute to the Afsluitdijk, to the south and north are some of the **bulb fields** that increasingly have been planted in the northern part of North Holland province. If you're here in season (more or less mid-April–mid-May), keep your eyes open. You also might make a turn into tiny **Twisk,** a pretty village entirely under preservation. Among the noteworthy buildings are distinctive dome-shaped farmhouses, a 14th-century church, mansions with particularly elegant front doors and chimneys, and the requisite canal bridges. If you are tracking down all tempting touring options, consider that from **Den Helder** (home of the *Netherlands Royal Navy* and **Het Torentje,** the museum that documents its history from 1813), **Texel** (pronounced *TES sel*), the first and largest of the **Waddenzee islands** off the northwest coast of Holland, is only a quick car ferry away. Texel is well-known for its birds (especially spoonbills) and sheep (its lamb is advertised in many a Dutch restaurant), and there are some bulb growing fields in-season. Surrounded by sand dunes, Texel's several towns (the capital is Den Burg) are a popular place for summer and camping holidays. In the Texelstroom, at the leeward side of the island (opposite what used to be the mouth of the Zuiderzee), the heavy-laden ships of the *Dutch East India Company* rode out rough seas three centuries ago.

The Afsluitdijk

The 30-kilometer/19 mile Afsluitdijk *(barrier dam),* which runs from Wieringen to the coast of Friesland and sealed the mouth of the **Zuiderzee** (South Sea), was built between 1927 and 1933 using traditional methods with contemporary technology. No hydraulic engineering project—not even the mammoth and amazing *Delta Plan* in Zeeland, whose planning began 20 years later and was 30 years in the actual execution—has ever appealed so much to the imagination of the Dutch people as the Afsluitdijk. It also impressed the *American Society of Civil Engineers,* though members took their time (50 years) to put the fact on a plaque there. Plans for damming the Zuiderzee and reclaiming large sections of the land within the enclosed area date back to 1667 and one Hendric Stevin. Many highly ambitious schemes surfaced during the 19th century, but it was the plan of Dr. Cornelis Lely that eventually met with approval from Parliament (finally pushed into action by burst dikes and floods that did great damage around the Zuiderzee in 1916). Dredged clay loam, sand, stone, straw and reeds were the ingredients that sealed off the sea five years after the dam was begun, the last gap closed in the presence of Queen Wilhelmina. The long blast of ships' horns sounded the sea's death toll midday on the 28th of May, 1932. Soon the dam was topped off with a two-lane road and cycle path. Locks allow ships to pass in and out to the Waddenzee and sluices discharge excess water. Today, it's a four-lane motorway that runs between North Holland and Friesland. At the point at which the last gap was filled, there is a lookout tower with visitor parking, cafe, a pedestrian crossover (and vehicle turnaround), and monuments. Be prepared for stiff breezes at this highly-exposed piece of man-made real estate.

Harlingen

VVV Voorstraat 34; Mon.–Fri. 9 a.m.–6 p.m., Sat. 9 a.m.–1 p.m. & 2–5 p.m.; 05178–17222; pop. 16,000; 100 km./60 mi. from Amsterdam • Arriving on the mainland after crossing the Afsluitdijk, head north on Rt. N 31/A 31 for Harlingen, which, since the construction of that barrier, has the distinction of being Friesland's only seaport (the town is situated outside the dam). Since it is still a bustling seaport, it has a commercial look at first, with its piers and port, but head into the old center to **Noorderhaven,** and dispose of your car at one of the parking meters there. The entire Noorderhaven, several blocks of buildings with fine 16th–18th-century facades on both sides of this in-the-town harbor, is a preserved historic monument, with the 1736 Stadhuis at #86. One block away is Voorstraat, the town's attractive tree-lined main street, on which is located the **Hannemahuis***#56, open April–Sept., inquire at VVV #34 for hours*• an imposing patrician house museum with the local treasure trove, among which will be found mementos from the whaling expeditions from the 16th century onwards (which originated from Harlingen), a silver collection (much of it the work of members of a guild founded here in 1648), and locally-produced tiles from the 16th–20th centuries. **Makkum** (see below) was only one of many Friesland tile factories in the 16th and 17th centuries, and Harlingen tiles were well known after 1600. Having disappeared long ago, the craft was revived in 1973 by the **Aardewerk en Tegelfabriek** *(Voorstraat 84).* The Hannemahuis also has a lovely garden. A walk atop Harlingen's several piers affords a fine view of the Frisian landscape, as well as across the Waddenzee with its shipping traffic.

Franeker

VVV in the 17th and 18th century 't Coopmanhus Municipal Museum, Voorstraat 51; pop. 13,000 • Heading inland from the sea only a short distance is **Franeker,** another historic town which from 1585 was the proud possessor of a university until Napoleon suppressed it in 1811. **Pieter Stuyvesant** (1592–1672), a Frisian, studied there before his travels to Nieuw Amsterdam (New York). The VVV in the **'t Coopmanhus Museum** (which has exhibits of local history and objects, but only a brief explanation sheet in English) can supply a town map and English-language leaflet on the highlights in the town. Certainly Franeker's (and one of Holland's) most unusual attractions is located in the old and intimate house of self-educated Eise Eisinga. Sitting across from the 1591 **Stadhuis** on Raadhuisplein, a sign on the facade reads: **Planetarium** *(April–Sept., Tues.–Sat. 10 a.m.–12:30 p.m., 1:30–5 p.m., May–Aug., also Mon. 1–5 p.m.; 05170–3070),* and that is what Eisinga built in the ceiling of his living room here between 1774 and 1781. Once you know (from the excellent booklet in English on sale at the Planetarium and tour given by the custodian) that Eisinga wrote a 600-page volume on mathematics at age 16 and was calculating eclipses at age 18, his accomplishment can be understood as the work of a genius. After an extraordinary planetary alignment in 1774 had led a Friesland minister to predict that two planets would collide and destroy the universe, Eisinga decided to build a planetarium that would give his contemporaries a better insight into the science, rather than superstition, of the sky. Keeping his everyday job as a woolcomber, he spent seven years at night by candlelight with amazing accuracy and complexity, creating dials for day and year, movement of the planets, moon and sun, the date, all with cogwheel clockwork. Since its completion it has been open to the public because Eisinga wanted to convince the public that the solar system would not collapse. Astonomers and engineers from around the world, even NASA officials, still come to see it. Eisinga's own star rose and set: from rising through Franeker ranks as officer of the civic guard and member of the town council, he became embroiled, against his will, in civil discord and could preserve his personal liberty only by going abroad, away from his Planetarium and family. For eight years he remained in exile, but finally returned to teach at Franeker's university. Eventually, Eisinga wound up with a State stipend for himself, and his son upon his death, as caretaker of the Planetarium, which the government had bought.

From Franeker, **Leeuwarden** *(VVV, Stationplein 1; 058–132224)* is only 20 km./12 mi. As well as being an interesting historic and canaled destination and the provincial capital, it has the only five-star hotel in Friesland.

ACCOMMODATIONS ★★★★★ **Oranje Hotel** • *Stationsweg 4; Leeuwarden; 058–126241, fax 058–121441; moderate* • The hotel was practically rebuilt for its reopening in 1986, with 78 thoroughly modern guest and bright, pleasant public rooms. The lobby lounge/bar is the community congregation point, and its **L'Orangerie** restaurant *(dinner only; moderate/expensive)* has both prix-fixe menus and *à la carte* choices. The **Taverne** offers more casual meals. The hotel is within sight, but out of sound of the station, and a short walk from the historic center.

Makkum

VVV in 1698 **Waaggebouw** *at Pruikmakershoek 2; 05158–1422; pop. of greater area 3,500* • With a sharp turn south at the end of the Afsluitdijk, you're almost immediately in Makkum. A delightful former Zuiderzee fishing village, Makkum now has mostly pleasure craft in its harbor. Makkum made its name in ceramics because of the particular quality of the sea clay found here (see at front of book under *Dutch Tiles* under *The Benelux Cultural Legacy: Traditional Crafts and Decorative Arts*). Tichelaar's Koninklijke Makkumer Aardewerk en Tegelfabriek or, more simply, **Royal Makkum** *(Turfmarkt 59; Mon.–Fri., 9 a.m.–5:30 p.m., Sat. until 4 p.m.; 05158–1341)* is a ten-generational ceramic factory that was awarded use of the title "Royal" in 1960. Guided tours (approx. a half-hour long) of the factory's biscuit-fired and hand-painted process are given Mon.–Thurs., 10 a.m.–4 p.m., and on Fri. until 3 p.m. Makkum ware comes in several multi-colored patterns, without emphasis on the blue and white of Delftware. In addition to many practical and ornamental items, a wide variety of historic-patterned and modern tiles are produced. The shops at the factory and in the center *(Het Makkumer Tegelhuis, Markt 19)* charge the same substantial prices for their first quality ware that you'll find in Amsterdam or The Hague, but do ask about the "seconds" for sale. The VVV, which distributes a small map of the town, is located in what is the local museum, worth a visit if you have time after first taking an explorative turn around the pretty canaled-corners of this atmospheric town.

Workum

VVV in the 1650 **Waag** *at Merk 4; 05151–1300; pop. of greater area 4,500* • A seaport in the 15th century, Workum is centered around an attractive cobbled main square (the **Merk**) on which stands the Stadhuis (15–18th century), and the **Waag**, which is decorated with grotesque statuary. Leaving the Merk via the Begine drawbridge, you'll come to the *Doltewal,* a canal lined with pleasure craft at the back of the village. **De Gulden Leeuw** is a pleasant terrace cafe at Merk 2.

Hindeloopen

VVV in the 1619 Oostertoren at the Haven; 05142–2550; pop. 900 • This exceptionally charming village is worth allowing plenty of time in which to wander and wonder. Once occupied by captains who sailed the seven seas from its small harbor, and formerly famed for the decorative painted wooden furniture that carried the town's name, Hindeloopen claims neither distinction today. Nevertheless, the legacies of both activities—sea commanders' homes and *likhuzen* (small houses behind the captains' main homes used by wives and children during the summer in the absence of the masters, a feature unique to the village), and ateliers where smaller items painted in the historic Hindeloopen style are crafted and sold—will hold your attention. There's one essential stop, the **Hidde Nijland** museum *(March 1–Nov. 1, Mon.–Sat., 1 a.m.– 5 p.m., Sun. & hol., 1:30–5 p.m.)* in the former **Stadhuis** (begun in 1683). Here you'll see what you can't buy anymore: the Scandinavian/Oriental-influenced genuine Hindeloopen painted furniture. The rooms reveal a variety of furniture, wall panelling, and utensils painted in both traditional and mourning colors. Visit the VVV for a leaflet in English with map and town sights; it will indicate the 18th-century mansion that now has a cafe in a canalside garden. Parking is outside the village, either at the Hidde Nijland museum, from which you can walk into town "by the back door," or at the other end of town just before the Haven; blue "P" signs are posted.

Stavoren

VVV Voorstraat 80; 05149–1616; pop. 1,000 • Lying on the projecting southwest point of Friesland, Stavoren isn't on the way to anywhere, except the passenger (only) ferry to Enkhuizen, with its harbor a stopover point for summer sailors. Stavoren itself is pleasant but unexceptional; however, since hotels are limited in southwest Friesland, it's worth mentioning the one here.

ACCOMMODATIONS ★★ **De Vrouw van Stavoren** • *Havenweg 1, 8715 EM; 05149–1202, fax 05149–1205; moderate* • has a dozen basic tidy rooms, some with private toilets and showers. There's a pleasant restaurant inside, and dining *al fresco* on the rear patio. The name of the hotel refers to a statue across from it of the "Vrouwe (woman) of Stavoren," who looks out to the offshore reed-grown sandbank known as the **Vrouwezand**. As the popular local story goes, a rich merchant's wife asked a ship captain to bring back from his distant destination the most precious cargo he could find. The captain returned with a hull full of wheat from Danzig (a commodity which made the Netherlands very wealthy in the 16th and 17th century). However, such mundane merchandise was obviously not what the woman had hoped for, and, in a fury, she ordered the ship's contents tipped into the Zuiderzee at the Stavoren harbor mouth. It is said that the wheat, when it germinated, caused the formation of the sandbank that eventually ruined Stavoren's harbor.

Sloten

VVV Dubbelstgraat 125; 05143–583; pop. 600 • This is the smallest of the Friesland's 11 towns, a fact which only gives its attributes—a moat, dike (on which is a high-water warning cannon), canal through the cobbled center of town (open to residents'-only cars), old sluice gates, and 17th and 18th-century facades and step-gabled houses—all the more appeal. The Stadhuis dates from 1757 and, under its Fries name **Stedhus Sleat,** contains a museum *(Heerenwal 48; Easter–Sept.; Tues.–Fri. 10 a.m.–noon, 2–5 p.m., Sat. & Sun. 2–5 p.m.)*, which only shows that no place is too small to have one.

Giethoorn

VVV Beulakerweg a/b ark; 05216–1248; pop. 2,500 • Known for its tree-lined canals—there are no roads, only foot/bicycle paths along the canals, and arched bridge over them—on which most everything in the many-islanded village must be transported in flat-bottom boats, tiny rural Giethoorn is without doubt picturesque. The first inhabitants in the mid-13th century named the place **Geytenhorn** for the masses of wild goat horns which they found, probably the result of the animals' drowning deaths in earlier floods. The village acquired its characteristic appearance from haphazard peat digging. Earlier residents cut peat turfs in the most accessible places, making hollows that filled with rain, forming ponds and lakes—and required further ditches and canals to be dug to transport the peat. The area became a series of islands, with short steeply-arched footbridges built to connect them, yet allow for boats to pass beneath them. In the fields on the fringes of Giethoorn, reeds are grown for thatch (cut in spring), which is seen on many a local roof, and sold for that purpose all over Holland. Open, covered, motorized, manual, group tour or self-hire "punters" are prominent in Giethoorn, which can get very crowded (especially on summer weekends), reducing its otherwise quite considerable charm. One way to avoid the crowds is to stay overnight on the fringe of the village and walk to it in the evening or early morning. There are car parks outside the village, which is accessible only by foot or boat. Various residents tout home-exhibits as museums, though none is necessary to see, the grassy green and gardened village houses being artful and interesting enough. A stop at one of the terrace cafes along the paved footpathed main canal is as good a way as any to set the scene in your mind.

ACCOMMODATIONS: ★ **Hotel-Pension De Jonge** • *Beulakerweg 30, 8355 AH; 05216–1360; inexpensive* • This basic, but clean and modern 20-bed property has central heating, some rooms with private facilities, and a restaurant (breakfast, included) that at lunch and dinner specializes in *pannekoeken* (Dutch pancakes). No elevator, two floors.

Blokzijl

VVV Kerkstraat 12; June 1–Sept. 1, Mon.–Sat., 9 a.m.–6 p.m.; 05272–414 or 286 • Once directly on the coast but now land-bound as part of the *Noordoostpolder* (northeast polder), Blokzijl, like so many former Zuiderzee towns, today has mostly pleasure craft in its harbor, which by a system of canals remains connected to the recreational waters of the IJsselmeer. Blokzijl's cobbled alleyways, stolid-steeped church, and harbor crescent rimmed by 17th-century merchant houses topped with typical step, neck, or bell gables, tell a tale of one-time prosperous trading days. Nearby **Vollenhove** is another former Zuiderzee town which offers 17th-century appeal around its port.

ACCOMMODATIONS ★★★ **Hotel Kaatje bij de Sluis** • *Zuiderstraat 1; 05272–1833, fax 05272–1835; hotel is closed Mon. & Tues. nights, month of Feb.; first class* • Located beside the town's busy lock (Room 2 looks straight out at it), this light-hearted, light-colored, 8-room, three-story townhouse-hotel understandably requires reservations (at least a month in advance in summer). Rooms, decorated in pastels and white, with minibar, terry robes, hairdryers, in-room coffee makers, old map prints, and appealing gray and pink tile in the bath and toilet, can be better than a home-away-from-home. Breakfast (included) is served in the garden terrace, shaded by old trees, or glass-enclosed room overlooking the garden and sluice (where coffee and drinks are available during the day). Upon checking in, hotel guests invariably make reservations for a meal at the hotel's restaurant—below.

RESTAURANTS Kaatje bij de Sluis • *(Brouwerstraat 20; noon–2:30 p.m., 6–10 p.m., closed for lunch Sat., closed Mon. & Tues. and month of Feb.; for res. 05272–1833, fax 05272–1836; expensive)* • Just across the drawbridge (which goes up and stops traffic on a regular basis) from the hotel is its restaurant, possibly the better known of the two establishments. The award-winning cuisine is served in a romantic, but spirited setting appropriate for the imaginative dishes from soup to sweets: *Soupe de courgettes aux Escalopes de Poissons* (zuchini soup with assorted fish), *Tarte a l'Ananas et Sorbet au Citron* (pineapple tart and lemon sherbert).

Staphorst

This inland town, a bit off the beaten track, has a reputation for traditional costumes and old-time religion in strict Protestant Dutch Reform style. The pattern of Dutch life represented in this strictest of Calvinist farming communities is a significant part of the country's heritage, but the elements can be experienced elsewhere under easier circumstances. The people in Staphorst don't want you taking pictures of them in costume (women and children, and some males regularly wear traditional attire) on any day of the week, and don't even want you in town on the Sabbath Sunday, when they march to church and back home on several occasions—and when they might do physical damage to your camera. Staphorst's lengthy main street is lined with large old thatched farmhouses (which once served for both owners and their animals) set amid modern store fronts and milk factories. If you're looking for coziness to accompany the quaintness of the lifestyle, this isn't the place to look, and your curiosity isn't appreciated. But it will undoubtedly be fed from hearing stories of Staphorst behavior, such as the public shaming of adulterous members of the community by parading the hand-bound couple through town in a manure cart while people lining the street pelt them with dung. And, there's the "open bedroom window" policy for suitors of eligible daughters, who can't get married in the Reformed Association church in Staphorst *until* they are pregnant. In this closed community, where marriage with outsiders is forbidden, women accept the circumstances as expressed in local farming paraphrase: "No farmer can buy a cow until he is sure of the calf." There's a farming museum **Museumboerderij** *(Gemeenteweg 67; April 1–Nov. 1, 10 a.m.–7 p.m., Mon.—Sat.; 05225–2526)* that shows the typical Staphorst style of decor, costumes and the local weaving of material for them, a *klompen* or clog maker, and has a garden.

Urk

VVV in Museum "Het Oude Raadhuis," Wijk 2, April 1–Sept. 30, Mon.–Fri., 10 a.m.–5 p.m., Sat. 10 a.m.–1 p.m.; Feb., Mar. Oct., Mon.–Fri. 10 a.m.–1 p.m.; closed Nov.–Jan.; 05277–4040; pop. 12,000 •
Since the reclamation of the northeast polder in the IJsselmeer, the greater part of Urk, once an island in the Zuiderzee, has been enclosed by the new land and become land-bound. The sealing off of the Zuiderzee did not bring about the decline of Urk that had been predicted. Determined to continue with sea fishing, Urk fishermen expanded their field of activity (their catch now comes from as far afield as the Danish and Span-

ish coasts) by building one of the largest and most modern fleets in the world, and using the sluices in the Afsluitdijk for access to the North Sea. Two generations ago fishing was a job learned at sea, but nowadays no Urk fisherman goes to sea without thorough training at the local nautical college. Urk also developed an important fish auction, and is flourishing with fish processing factories. A busy harbor with more than 150 "beam-trawler" fishing vessels gives Urk an air of modernity about its quays, though visitors can enjoy the contrast of seeing an old man in his baggy black traditional costume sharing the setting. In the small residential streets of this architecturally varied town, the more brightly-colored dress of the old women (the only ones who regularly wear the costume these days) may be seen, as they chat in the front gardens of their homes; church on Sunday brings out the greatest number of costumes.

For some time in the 17th and 18th century, the island of Urk belonged to the city of Amsterdam, which had bought it in order to maintain its important Zuiderzee coastal navigational marks (such as the first light beacon in 1617), in order to avoid the treacherous "Shallow of Enkhuizen" sandbank. Near the newer present lighthouse landmark (beyond which is a long line of modern "turbine" windmills) is the **Kerkje aan de Zee** (little church on the sea), inside which a plaque lists all the ministers who have served there since 1629. Nearby, also sharing the point of land that overlooks today's IJsselmeer, is Urk's **Vissersmonument,** a statue of a wind-blown woman in Urk costume looking out to what still appears to be open sea. Just down the road in **Het Oude Raadhuis** is the town museum showing Urk's long history with the Zuiderzee. Quite naturally, fish is the speciality at most Urk restaurants. A cozy local favorite, with lace at the curtains indoors and an outside terrace with IJsselmeer views, is **De Kaap** *(Wijk 1, daily lunch to 10 p.m., 05277–1509, inexpensive),* with its well-known "all you can eat" fish plates. A passenger ferry (no cars, but bicycles allowed) sails between Urk and Enkhuizen several times daily in season *(early May–early Sept. daily except Sun.; 1.5 hours one-way; 05277–3407).*

Kampen and Zwolle

Though larger, two towns to the southeast of Urk offer charm and more than their fair share of history if you have time to explore them. **Kampen** *(VVV Oudestraat 85; 05202–13500)* is a former Hanseatic town with a well-preserved town center that was begun in the 13th century. Among the sights to seek out is the Stadhuis with its remarkable **Magistrates Hall** dating from the 16th century (English booklet), and displaying a complete set of full-length portraits of members of the royal Dutch *House of Orange* from Willem the Silent. St. Nicolaaskerk dates from c. 1500 in its present shape and size, and has a famous organ from 1742, on which summer concerts are held *(Sat. in July & Aug. at 3 p.m.)*

Zwolle *(VVV Grote Kerkplein 14; 038–213900)* also is an old Hanse town, whose golden age was the 15th century. It has appealing remnants of two sets of fortification walls, bastions, towers, and old town gates. In 1980, Zwolle was instrumental in renewing the *Hanseatic League* association (some 70 northern European towns were trading partner members in the period from the 1200s to 1669) and members now meet regularly in those cities on a rotating basis.

ACCOMMODATIONS: ★★★★ **Grand Hotel Wientjes** • *Stationsweg 7; 038–254254, fax 038–254260; first class* • This 50-room, third-generation family-owned and managed hotel has been a landmark on the regional scene since its opening in 1929 in a former burgomaster's residence. Guestrooms are comfortable and the young staff friendly and service-minded. The Grand Wientjes' kitchen is also well-regarded.

Elburg

VVV Jufferenstraat 9; 05250–1520; pop. 750 inside the moat • Elburg is a monument in itself, one of the best-preserved towns in Holland. Its appearance is in large part from the 16th century, but there are many touches from the 14th, when Elburg was one of the earliest members of the **Hanseatic League.** At the end of the 14th century, Elberg moved inland, behind walls, and its unique rectangular town design was laid out by Arent thoe Boecop, steward of the Duke of Gelders. You can enjoy the original moat around the old center by walking atop the grassy and wooded ramparts that rim most of the town; a section of old city wall still has houses built into it. If you can manage the climb up the **St. Nicolas** church tower (156 steps) you'll be rewarded with a remarkable view down on this picture-tempting compact, intact town, in good weather, a 20-mile vista across the flat, flat land of neighboring Flevoland. The church has carillon concerts on Saturdays from 3–4 p.m., and the Elburg Town Choir Boys sing there Wednesdays in July and Aug. from 11 a.m.–1:45 p.m. The VVV has a *Do-It Yourself Guided Tour of Elburg* booklet in English and a map. Across the street from the VVV is the 15th-century **St. Agnes Convent,** housing Elburg's interesting local museum. The heart of the town is the **Vismarkt** (concert bands Wed. evenings in summer), with terrace cafes and restaurants spread out at every corner.

ACCOMMODATIONS: ★★ **Het Smeede Hotel** • *Smedestraat 5; 05250–3877; inexpensive* • Located in a well-restored old house in the heart of historic Elburg, the spotlessly clean, 14 crisp-yet-cozy bedrooms are walk-up (help with the luggage if needed), with private facilities, telephone, writing table, and TV. There is no lobby to speak of in this friendly, family-owned-and-operated hotel; breakfast (only, included) is served on the ground floor.

Harderwijk

VVV Havendam 58; 03410–26666 • The **Veluws Museum** in this former Hanseatic town on the Zuiderzee *(Donkerstraat 4; May–Sept., Mon.–Fri., 10 a.m.–5 p.m., Sat. 1–4 p.m., closed Sun., and Sat. during rest of year; 03410–14468),* located in an 18th-century merchant's house, offers a 12-minute slide show in English that presents a history of Harderwijk. The **Markt,** the former fish market, is an attractive cobbled rectangle, tree-shaded and surrounded by fine facades, in the soul of the old center of the town; you'll find a quiet terrace cafe or two. Whether or not you stop in Harderwijk, take the **N302** from it across the *Veluwe meer* (the very edge of the old Zuiderzee) to the new Dutch polder province of Flevoland.

Flevoland

VVV Lelystad, Agorahof 4; 03200–43444; 50 km./30 mi. from Amsterdam • Flevoland province was established on January 1, 1986, its polders (reclaimed land) adding more than 238,000 acres to the small country's total. The "new" area consists of the eastern section ("dried" between 1950–1957) and the southern (1959–1968). The entire **Zuiderzee Project** has produced five polders, and 616,730 acres, since 1930. Today, Flevoland sometimes is spoken of as the granary of western Europe for its corn fields that grow golden in summer. Other Flevoland crops of particular importance are oilseed rape (which blankets the fields in brilliant yellow in May), pearl onions (which you can smell in the air), sugar beets, potatoes, and flower bulbs (there's a Flevoland bulbfield route). Flevoland's capital **Lelystad** is named for Cornelius Lely (1854–1929), who developed the plan for the Zuiderzee Project. His original objectives (developed in the 19th century) were finally adopted and set out in the *Zuiderzee Act of 1918:* To reduce the length of coastline, thereby reducing the risk of flooding; to improve water management, including the creation of a fresh-water basin; to improve the lines of communication (roads); and to increase the area of agricultural land. The first three of these goals were met in large measure upon the completion of the **Afsluitdijk** in 1932. The agricultural needs could be met only upon the production of polderland. *The* place to head for an appreciation of the technology that went into making this polder province lies just outside Lelystad, **Informatiecentrum Nieuw Land** *(signposted; April 1–Oct. 31, daily 10 a.m.–5 p.m.; Nov. 1–Mar. 31. Mon.–Fri., 10* *a.m.–5 p.m., Sun. 1–5 p.m., closed Sat.; closed Dec. 25, Jan 1.; 03200-60799; full exhibit information in English).*

Begin your visit by watching the excellent slide show (English and other language versions) with background on the formation and control of the Zuiderzee and the polderland. The center also has lots of English language literature; for those who want the whole story, ask for the publication *Planning and Creation of an Environment*. Exhibits tell a highly interesting story about the creation of polderland in Holland from the 13th to the 20th century, and detail the actual "drying" process of a Dutch polder. As an underwater dike is built, electric and diesel pumping stations work round the clock to drain the area. The main waterways planned for the finished polder are dredged while the polder is still submerged; smaller canals and dividing-ditches are dug after the polder has been drained. Immediately following drainage, the swampy soil is sown by airplane with reed seed; reed serves to break up and ripen the soil for cultivation while also preventing the growth of weeds. Following the reclamation phase, agricultural engineers usually grow field crops on the new soil for about five years, a transition period needed for the soil to mature and become suitable for later use. Rapeseed usually is the first crop sown because its deep roots promote soil aeration. Later crops may be flax, grass, peas, and dwarf beans. After the maturation period, when the land is destined for farming and fruit-growing, it is let to private individuals for those purposes on a short or perpetual lease (actual ownership of the land is retained by the Dutch government). Large expanses of woods also have been planted in Flevoland.

The uses to which the new polderland have been put were carefully considered. Agriculture was the primary purpose to which the earlier North-East polder, created between 1937–1942, was put. This also was the case with East Flevoland, which was dry by 1957, although towns, too, were planned. The first inhabitants of Lelystad, pioneers who had to build a whole community from scratch, picked up the keys to their brand new homes in September 1967. The very high birth rate and resulting population crunch in Holland in the 1960s led to the South Flevoland polder (dry by 1968) being planned for more heavy urbanization. By 1975, the dike road between Enkhuizen and Lelystad was completed. It was meant to serve not only as a means of transportation across the IJsselmeer, but as part of the drainage process for the last scheduled element of Lely's original plan, the **Markerwaard** polder. The Dutch, however, began raising their voices over the need for preserving open areas for water recreation (especially their beloved sailing). The demands, accompanied by a decline in the 1980s of Holland's birth rate and an increase in intensive agriculture production elsewhere in Holland (not to mention agricultural surpluses mounting throughout the European Community), have put plans for draining Markerwaard on hold for the time being.

Naarden

VVV Adr. Dortsmanplein 1b; 02159-42836; pop. 16,000 • When you've had your fill of polders, head southwest for Amsterdam. Past the polder city complex of Almere, back on the "mainland," are two more chances for a look at old Zuiderzee villages. First, head for **Naarden,** a fortress town dating from 1350. Its distinctive six-pointed-star bastion, ramparts, and double-moated fortifications took shape when the Dutch rebuilt the town after the troops of Louis XIV, who had captured it in 1672, were forced out in 1673 by Willem III. A visit to the **Vestingmuseum** *(Turfpoortbastion; Easter-Oct., Mon.-Fri.; 10 a.m.-4:30 p.m., Sat. & Sun., noon-5 p.m.)* takes you into the casements, which display dioramas, old prints, and cannon, and offer an opportunity to mount the grassy ramparts for a view. An even finer view of the fortification pattern comes from atop the tower of the **Grote Kerk** *(April 30-Sept. 30, Sat.-Thurs., on the hour from 1-4 p.m.)*

The late Gothic Grote Kerk (essentially 15th century) is worth seeing inside for its 20 Old and New Testament ceiling panels, painted between 1510 and 1518. In 1572 the Spaniards massacred the entire population of Naarden, ransacked the city, and partly burned it down, but spared the church. Noted for its acoustics, it is the site of a renowned annual performance of **J.S. Bach's** *St. Matthew's Passion* on Good Friday. Ask the VVV about weekly evening organ concerts in summer. The VVV has several brochures with information in English, including the self-guiding *Naarden Gabletour*. A bus from the nearest railway station serves Naarden.

Muiden

VVV Kazernestraat 10; 02942-4754; pop. 7,000 • Also a former fortress town on the Zuiderzee, with locks and a harbor now filled with private pleasure craft, Muiden is best known for its romantic-looking castle **Muiderslot** *(Herengracht 1; April 1-Sept. 30, Mon.-Fri., 10 a.m.-5 p.m., Sun. 1-5 p.m., Oct. 1-Mar. 31 until 4 p.m., 1-hour guided tours only, depart several times an hour, last tour an hour before closing)*. Built by Count Floris V in the 13th century, it is decorated with a valuable collection of furniture and paintings from the 17th century, the period when the great Dutch poet and historian **Pieter Corneliszoon Hooft** lived here as sheriff of Muiden and castellan of Muiderslot. P.C. Hooft gathered about him here a group of leading artistic figures and scholars (including **Grotius,** the poet **Vondel,** and **Constantijn Huygens**) which became known as the **Muiden Circle.** Guided tours (which require climbing a fairly steep flight of hollowed brick stairs at the beginning but otherwise is easy) are pleasantly anecdotal and unrushed. There's an herbal garden in front of the castle. Muiden is close enough to Amsterdam (public transportation available), and popular enough with Dutch from even farther afield, for its cafes and pubs to be busy; on warm nights, terrace tables are spread out along the little harbor, in sight of Muiderslot. **Eethuys-Cafe Graaf Floris V van Muiden** *(Herengracht 72; 11 a.m.–10 p.m.; till midnight for drinks; 02942–1296; inexpensive),* an atmospheric old brown cafe a short walk from Muiderslot, makes a good stop for salads, soups, fish, and tasty snacks.

CENTRAL HOLLAND: AN INTRODUCTION

One of the most noticeable characteristics of the countryside in the central part of Holland is that, east of Utrecht, most of the land lies *above* sea level. The landscape has large stands of forest primeval that haven't undergone the scourge of centuries of saltwater floods. Thousands of acres of trees adorn Apeldoorn's **Royal Park** and the **National Park De Hoge Veluwe,** both of which fill much of the triangle formed by three of the principal cities in the center of Holland: **Arnhem, Apeldoorn,** and **Amersfoort.** In addition to old trees, the landscape in this region is lightly rolling, rather than water-surface flat as in the west of the country.

Within the Netherlands, province names tend to be used to define districts, which is not particularly helpful for the unfamiliar traveler. In any case, in the center of the country the most outstanding attractions cut across provincial boundaries, although many lie within the largest, and largely rural, Dutch province of **Gelderland.** The city of **Utrecht** certainly has a central location in the country, but since it is also a component of *Randstad Holland,* it has been included in that section. Also, for the purpose of travel logistics, some smaller places often considered "central" Holland are covered in this book in the *Old Zuiderzee Village-New Polderland Province* chapter. Center of Holland sights lying *bezuiden de Moerdijk* ("below the rivers") have been included in the **Southern Holland** section under *North Brabant* province. (The *Index* at the back of the book is a quick reference.)

ARNHEM, APELDOORN, AND AMERSFOORT

Guidelines for Arnhem, Apeldoorn, and Amersfoort

SIGHTS Several of the most interesting and important museums in the country are situated in central Holland, in or near the towns of Arnhem, Apeldoorn, and Amersfoort, which is how they are arranged here. The rich fruit orchards of the **Betuwe** ("good land") and the country's largest national park, **De Hoge Veluwe** ("bad land"), with its drifting sand dunes, heathland (in bloom late August through September), and woods, add another scenic dimension.

GETTING AROUND The three main cities are served by train. From the rail station in each there are local buses that serve most of the other attractions, towns, and villages covered. However, it must be mentioned that depending upon public transportation, reliable though it is in Holland, will slow you down. A car is certainly recommended if you want to cover more than one of the major sites included here in one day. Taxis, while practical within Arnhem from the station, or for Het Loo from the Apeldoorn station, will be expensive to the **Kroller-Muller Museum** because of its rural location. Bicycle hire is possible at the city train stations, though again here an assessment of time and distance will need to be made. If you take a public bus (from Arnhem station), check with VVV for season and specific times: usually there is a direct bus to the museum July–Sept., year-round public bus to Otterlo or Hoenderloo (3.4 and 4.0 km./approx 2 mi., respectively, to Visitor Center), from which bicycle rental and taxis are available. At the **Visitor Center** *(Bezoekerscentrum)* in the center of the national park **De Hoge Veluwe,** one of the famous little fleet of 400 "white bikes" (one speed, no basket or provision for parcels, no time limit) is available to you for free (a service to cut down on car traffic in the national park) on a first-come basis; weekends can be busy, but there's also back-up paid bicycle hire on the premises. The **Kroller-Muller Museum** is an easy and enjoyable bike ride from the park Visitor Center, and there are plenty of paved cycle routes of different duration in De Hoge Veluwe.

SHOPPING The three cities in this chapter are the main shopping centers in the region. **Het Loo** palace has an excellent gift shop, the museum shop at the **Kroller Muller** has a wide selection of art books, prints, and cards, and there's a gift shop at the Arnhem **Openluchtmuseum.**

ENTERTAINMENT AND EVENTS Check with VVV about the Amersfoort carillon concerts in the **Onze Lieve Vrouwetoren** and **Belgian Monument** and organ concerts in the **1534 St. Joriskerk.** The cities of Arnhem and Nijmegen commemorate Operation Market-Garden each September. In Spakenburg traditional costume and crafts fairs take place on the last two Wednesdays in July and the first two in August.

ACCOMMODATIONS With the assumption that many of you will be traveling by car in this region, several country castles and inns have been included. With the exception of the **Keizerskroon** across from Het Loo in Apeldoorn, country accommodations in the area will prove more interesting than their in-town counterparts.

RESTAURANTS Many museums discussed in this chapter have a cafe and/or restaurant (as is often the case, especially in museums outside of cities, throughout Holland). There are some fine country restaurants in the region, located in settings from sophisticated rustic to castles.

ARRIVING Holland's public transportation and information coordination will impress you anew. At **Arnhem** (pop. 130,000), local and regional buses and the VVV *(Stationplein 45, 085–420330)* are located at the train station, as is true in **Amersfoort** *(VVV Stationplein 27, 033–635151, pop. 100,000),* and **Apeldoorn** *(VVV Stationplein 6, 055-788421, pop. 144,000).*

IN THE AREA Many visitors come via Arnhem to visit the exceptional **Kroller-Muller Museum** (with its 278 Van Gogh's and other great 19th-and 20th-century paintings and sculpture) set in the Dutch national Park **De Hoge Veluwe. Oosterbeck** has an **Airborne Museum** about the Market-Garden operation of Sept. 1944. The more geographically spread-out smaller attractions in the center of the country have been included under the most appropriate of the three cities.

TRAVEL TIPS Remember that throughout Holland VVVs in major towns and cities (identified with an "i" sign) can supply you with quite detailed and up-to-date information about museum hours and public transportation in other regions. That way you can plan a day trip ahead of time with the help of your "home base" VVV, thus having the details about public transportation/opening hours, etc. for your destination which will mean easy coordination (allowing more time to enjoy what you came to see and do.

ARNHEM ....

Even though the soaring-towered 15th-century **Grote Kerk,** whose 230-foot tower (with 54-bell carillon, concerts 10 a.m. Friday), restored after its destruction in 1944, includes flying buttresses embellished with modern gargoyles resembling Mickey Mouse, Donald Duck, and the local pastor (whose dispute with the stonecutter inspired this "tribute") makes Arnhem infamous; despite its lovely parks, fountains, and squares, such as the attractive **Korenmarkt,** a lively scene of cafes and students whenever the sun shines; and even though vistas over the Rhine River beckon, Arnhem is most closely associated with the eight-day September 1944 battle that bears its name.

"In Britain the epic fight of the 1st Airborne Division at Arnhem tends to be thought of as a separate action. In fact it was only a part of a much larger operation spread over more than fifty miles and involving far larger forces than a single division. It was, moreover, Hitler's last victory and one he should never have been given the chance to win. It was the end-product of inter-allied rivalries and, above all, of the arrogance and vanity of the newly promoted Field Marshal Montgomery." This is how Michael Glover opens his chapter on Arnhem and Operation Market-Garden in his book *A New Guide to the Battlefields of Northern France and the Low Countries* (see Bibliography: Random Readings at the back of book). Although it saw small successes, Operation Market-Garden was largely doomed to failure from the start; that failure came with the battle of Arnhem. From the Belgium border, the advance had to take place along a single main road that ran for most of the distance on a causeway with no possibility of vehicles moving off it, hereby essentially creating a front of one tank. Market-Garden was envisioned by Allied planners as a final push over German troops that were seen as irredeemably broken for a swift capture of the German Ruhr, due east, and final victory in the war. The Market aspect of the two-part operation (drawn up separately in Belgium and England) was the dropping of the Airborne Corps to advance over the Arnhem bridge, while the advance was the Garden. It was understood from the start that only total success would serve the purpose, a point that emphasized the risky nature of the project, risky even before allowing for such events as the breakdown of radio communication (which among other things led to the landing of a large supply drop straight into the hands of the Nazis) and bad weather that delayed the dropping of the Polish Parachute Brigade. Two days before it was set to be implemented, General Eisenhower, originally a supporter of Market-Garden, was so convinced that it had become inoperative that he sent his chief of staff Lieutenant-General Bedell Smith to dissuade Montgomery from undertaking it. Having been accused of being over-cautious in the Normandy campaign, Montgomery was out to demonstrate that he could take risks and was "the greatest general in the world." Comments Michael Glover, "Fifteen thousand allied casualties was a high price to pay to prove that he was wrong." Glover continues, "The courage and endurance of everyone engaged—British, American, Polish, German and, in particular, the members of the Dutch Resistance—should not blind anyone to the fact that Market-Garden was a disastrous failure. What is worse is that it was a predictable failure."

In the center of Arnhem, only a short distance from Arnhem's 15th-century Stadhuis and Grote Kerk, is **Airborne Plein,** a sunken garden traffic rotary with some ruins from the city bearing the date 17 September 1944, that leads into Nijmeegseweg (the road south to Nijmegen), which shortly crosses the Rhine River over "the bridge too far." The in-town end of the now rebuilt and renamed **John Frost Bridge** (also still known as the **Rijnbrug**) was taken and defended gallantly for three days and four nights by the 2nd Battalion of the 1st Parachute Brigade, but in the end for nought.

Nederlands Openluchtmuseum • *Netherlands Open-Air Museum; Schelmseweg 89, at northern edge of Arnhem, off the A12/E35 road, or north from the Willemsplein by Arnhem train station on Zijpendaalseweg on bus #3; daily 9 a.m.–5 p.m., 10 a.m. Sat. & Sun. from late March to Oct. 31; 085–576111* • Admired as one of the world's best open-air museums, this Dutch edition was founded in 1912 with a half-dozen houses. Since then, it has grown to 75 buildings, dismantled brick by brick, stone by stone, or peat turf by turf in their original locations throughout the country and reassembled with the same care at the museum, representing all walks of ordinary life as practiced in the not-so-distant past. There are no guided tours, which is just as well since you want to be at leisure to explore at will, sampling the authentic settings, sometimes through "hands-on" means, as the mood strikes. There is an excellent English guide, with a map, both short and detailed descriptions of each site, and recommended routes for from one to four-hour length visits. But essentially it's an informal place that invites you to stroll at will, by the windmills, in the herb garden, through the traditional costume exhibit. The distinctly different farmsteads from various regions around Holland, separated by beech woods, garden plots, a drawbridge perhaps, are well worth visiting, from a day laborers' one-room cottage, a c. 1700 *los hoes* without a dividing wall between the barn and human living space, and a prosperous 18th-century Frisian "head, neck, and body" building. There's a one-room school buildings, dovecote, eelmonger's hut, and a c. 1820 tradesman's house from Zaandam does double duty as a gift shop. A restaurant, pleasant pancake cafe, and snack stall on the beech-wooded landscaped acres will keep you refreshed.

IN THE AREA..

Since it was central to the Arnhem action of the Market-Garden Operation, Oosterbeek is the place with the most to see. Leaving Arnhem from the Willemplein in front of the station via the **Utrechtstraat,** along which (at No. 85) a plaque notes that this was the German security headquarters for the area from 1940–1944, and opposite No. 68 is the Dutch war memorial. Crossing into **Oosterbeek** *(VVV Utrechtseweg 216),* passing many of the parachute and glider landing fields (the **Airborne Monument** stands at the edge of them), the cumulative memorials, historical markers, museum, and, finally, the war cemetery, provide a haunting commentary on the events of September 1944.

Oosterbeek Airborne Museum • *Utrechtseweg 232 in Oosterbeck suburb west of the city; Mon.–Sat., 11 a.m.–5 p.m., Sun. & holidays, noon–5 p.m., closed Christmas and Jan 1; 085-337710* • Located in the former Hotel Hartenstein, which served as the headquarters for both armies at one time or another, the Airborne Museum recreates the circumstances and situations of the battle by means of excellent audio-visual (in English) presentations, dioramas, photographs, and other materials that recount the downhill course of the misguided mission. Next to the Museum is the **Klein Hartenstein** *(Utrechtseweg 226, 085-342121),* an excellent cafe-restaurant with bar, fireplace, and terrace. In Oosterbeek, Stationweg leads north to the **Oosterbeek Military Cemetery,** where the majority of British casualties from Market-Garden rest. The **Tafelberg Hotel,** which can also be visited, was used as the emergency hospital in the film *A Bridge Too Far* about the battle.

National Park De Hoge Veluwe • *Bezoekerscentrum or Visitor Center; Marchantplein; daily April 1–Oct. 31; 10 a.m.–5 p.m., Nov. 1–Mar. 31 Sun. & hol. only 11–6 p.m.; 08382-1627* • Much of the land contained by the rough triangle formed by Arnhem, Apeldoorn and Amersfoort is made up of Holland's largest national park, **De Hoge Veluwe.** In the center, near the village of Otterlo, is one of the country's most outstanding art museums. The 13,300 acres of natural parkland of heath, woodland, sand dunes, and fen, as well as the magnificent collection of man-made treasures, were a gift to the Dutch nation from Anton Kroller, a business success story in Rotterdam, and his wife Helene Muller, who turned her attention to collecting art (see Kroller-Muller Museum, below). They lived in the **St. Hubertus Hunting Lodge** *(in park 6.5 km./4 mi. from Visitor Center; May 1–Oct. 31 10–11:30 a.m. & 2–4:30 p.m. daily)*, after it was designed in 1913 by Dutch architect H. P. Berlage to be a stone visualization of the 8th-century life of Belgian St. Hubert, patron of the hunters (Kroller originally purchased De Hoge Veluwe as his own private hunting domain, and the fauna, including red deer, roe, and wild boar, are still protected in the park). One of the design considerations of the equally individualistic interior was the control of light and brightness to correspond to the level of "enlightenment" in St. Hubert's life at the stage a given room is meant to portray. Berlage also designed much of the furniture (Henri Van de Velde, architect of the Kroller-Muller Museum, collaborated on some pieces) and the pond in front of the lodge. Among the many park services offered are free *white bikes* (near Visitor Center; daily 8 a.m.–sunset, Apr. 1–Oct. 31) for use on a first-come basis within the park to visitors who arrive by car or public transportation in order to cut down on motorized traffic in the park; the **Koperen Kop Restaurant** *(near Visitor Center; daily 9:30 a.m.–6:30 p.m., except 4:30 p.m. Nov. 1–Mar. 31)* with a spacious dining room and sunny terrace; the **Groene Winkel** (green shop), by the visitor center, sells books, posters, "green" souvenirs; miles of walking and cycle paths; and an observation high stand "hide" from which to watch male deer at close range.

Kroller-Muller Museum • *Tues.–Sat., 10 a.m.–5 p.m., Sun. 11 a.m.–5 p.m., closed Mon. & Jan 1, year-round; sculpture park: April 1–Nov. 1 10 a.m.–4:30 p.m., Sun. 11 a.m.–4 p.m.; 08382–1241* • Much more than the tip but scarcely the entire iceberg of art in this museum is the collection of 278 works by Vincent Van Gogh. There are too many treasures in the superb, predominantly 19th- and 20th-century collection for them to all be on display at one time, but many of the major paintings by Van Gogh, including "The Potato Eaters" (and other peasant protraits from his Dutch period in Nuenen—see North Brabant), "Sunflowers," and "Self Portrait," 1887, as well as several Arles-era scenes, are kept on view. The museum opened in this Belgian Henry van de Velde-designed building in 1938, built by the Dutch nation in exchange for the gift of the contents by Helene Muller. The museum was extended by W. G. Quist in 1977. In addition to **Van Gogh,** there are pre-Impressionists, including **Corot** and **Courbet;** Impressionists such as **Seurat, Renoir,** and the Dutch **Jongkind;** post-Impressionists; and many later modernists including **Picasso, Mon-**

driaan, **Braque, Gris,** and **Leger.** There are a small number of Old Masters as well.

The Kroller-Muller **sculpture garden** is Europe's largest (47 acres) and its pieces begin pleasing from the front lawn of the museum. At the start of the path is Wenchebach's endearing hat-in-hand "Monsieur Jacques" (whom you might have been introduced to in Rotterdam). Among the many nature-ensconced works are ones by **Rodin, Henry Moore, Epstein, Giacometti, Lipchitz, Maillol, Nevelson, Serra,** and **Oldenburg;** an open pavilion by **Rietveld** houses several works by **Barbara Hepworth.**

APELDOORN

Although the name Apeldoorn is first documented in 793, it wasn't until the building of the **Royal Palace Het Loo** (1685–1692) that the city attracted any attention. From that time, the construction of comfortable houses began, because many wanted to live in the shadow of Dutch royalty. The burgeoning park-like city remains surrounded by the King's former hunting ground, the *Royal Forest* (nearly 25,000 acres). Het Loo had unusual appeal because Dutch society did not traditionally support an ostentatious royal court lifestyle, which is understandable given their essential Protestant Calvinist character. In fact, as the building of Het Loo began, Dutch painters were creating the *"Vanitas,"* still lifes that warned against a concentration on possessions above considerations of the soul. And, in case you're recalling the splendid marble Royal Palace on the Dam in Amsterdam (1648–1655), remember that it wasn't built as a royal palace at all, but as the Stadhuis for a flourishing city in which "commerce was king" and thereby worthy of such a *tasteful* display of wealth. In fact, it was the influence of history and English royalty that helped hasten Het Loo (meaning "open place in the woods") palace into being. Mary (daughter of James II of England) and her Dutch husband Willem accepted an invitation to undertake an armed expedition to England against her Catholic father in 1688. James had forfeited support in England by his Catholic and unconstitutional rule, and on his flight, Willem and Mary were invited to be joint rulers as King and Queen of England, Scotland, and Ireland. (Again, in 1690, Dutch Protestant Willem of Orange, as England's King William III, was called upon to battle Catholic James II, then on Irish soil, in the *Battle of the Boyne*. The orange band on the Irish flag comes from this encounter with Holland's House of Orange). In 1684 Willem had purchased the 15th-century manor house now called **Het Oude Loo** *(restored, open to public, as are its gardens in April and May)* as a hunting lodge. In 1685, Willem and Mary lay the foundation stone of **Het Nieuwe Loo.**

Perhaps even the new palace would have seemed small by Mary's English standards, a "come down" unless she appreciated its intimate scale. Het Loo did, however, have some amenities that most English castles of the time wouldn't have had: indoor plumbing and sliding windows. The decoration of the interior and the layout of the gardens were designed by **Daniel Marot** (1661–1752, and, incidentally, an ancestor of actress Audrey Hepburn), a French Huguenot who fled to the Netherlands in 1685. Once he became King of England, Willem competed with contemporary Louis XIV of France (who was at war with Holland at the time). In the royal rivalry, at least for the loveliness of its gardens, Het Loo was said to surpass *Versailles*. Two globes, one of heaven and one of earth, served as water fountains, and were fed by the waters of the Rhine. Symmetry was the word for both the building and garden design.

Het Loo was drastically altered in 1807–09 when it was designated a summer residence by **Louis Napoleon,** whose brother Bonaparte had him installed as King of Holland from 1806–1810 during the French occupation from 1795–1814. The garden was changed to the then-fashionable English landscape style, and the facade was altered with Empire-style shuttered windows. The Dfl. 80 million restoration from 1975–1984 was undertaken with the idea of restoring both the palace and gardens to their original design.

Het Loo is a palace of subdued splendor compared to some of the continent's castles, but that actually makes it easier to relate to, to imagine people actually living here. In fact, Het Loo was renovated with the idea of accurately depicting its three centuries of royal residency by the House of Orange, from Willem III and Mary II through frequent use as a royal family summer residence over the centuries, to **Queen Wilhelmina** (1880–1962), who came to live year-round at Het Loo after a 50-year reign, following her 1948 abdication in favor of her daughter Juliana (whose own country house-like palace **Soestdijk**—no visitors, but clearly visible from the road—is located in nearby Baarn). Wilhelmina lived at Het Loo until her death, after which she lay in state in the palace chapel. After the 1953 hurricane, Wilhelmina offered shelter at Het Loo to flood victims (see *Southern Holland, Zeeland*), and also provided aid there to Dutch nationals forced to flee from Indonesia under President Sukarno (1945–1967). The last royal resident of the palace was **Princess Margriet** (sister of Queen Beatrix) and her husband, Mr. Pieter Vollenhoven, and their four sons, who departed in 1975 so that the extensive restoration process prior to Het Loo's reopening as a national museum could be accomplished.

During restoration, Het Loo was painstakingly brought back to the original design of the celebrated Daniel Marot, who had overseen every detail, from the sculpted marble garden urns down to the many different damask wall coverings. Wall and ceiling panels and marble and faux marble (fashionable then) floors and columns were uncovered, tapestries were restored. Visitors are struck by the lack of corridors at Het Loo; one apartment leads directly to another as was the 17th-century style. Although the 17th century predominates, some of the rooms used by the royal family in the late 19th and 20th centuries have been left as they were enjoyed by more contemporary members of the House of Orange (some of Wilhelmina's childhood toys have been left in one room), and a tour of Het Loo can be made in a roughly chronological order.

Appropriately, among the first apartments one is led to are those of Willem and Mary. Much of the furniture in their two separate apartments (between which is located the Audience Hall) is not the original (though the pieces are period) because a great deal of destruction occurred during the two French occupations. The King's and Queen's gardens, carefully planned for the view out their respective windows, couldn't have brought much more pleasure to Willem and Mary than they bring visitors today. Rooms of particular interest because of their intimacy include Mary's Cabinet, a bright tiny corner room overlooking gardens on two sides, with pieces of the blue and white Delftware that she collected on the mantel, and Willem's corner-room library, which contains darkwood cases between the windows and a mirrored and plastered oval ceiling. The long Picture Gallery also offers a view out onto the garden, where the formal box-hedged parterres ringed with flowers appear as large flowered Dutch tiles at that distance. A typical Dutch detail at Het Loo is the bountiful use of fresh flowers in wonderful arrangements displayed throughout the palace.

Your visit to Het Loo is self-guided (plentiful English-language documentation on interior and garden available, descriptions on actual exhibits in Dutch only). From April 1–Oct. 31, a recommended 25-minute video film in English is shown in the Delft-blue-decorated Grotto as an introduction on aspects of Het Loo's history, restoration, interior design, and furnishings. Concerts are held in Het Loo the last Friday of every month at 8:15 p.m. and the last Sunday of every month from 2–4 p.m. (res. and tickets required, contact the palace or VVV). A map of marked, varied-length walking routes in the palace park is available at the museum entrance.

Two dining possibilities are offered at Het Loo. The **Balzaal Paleis Het Loo** *(10 a.m.–5 p.m., closed Mon. and Nov.–April; 055–212244; inexpensive)* is located in part of the West Wing; the restaurant takes its name from the fact the space was a ballroom in the early 20th century. Its ceiling and panelling remain as decor for your dining. On the walls of the restaurant are five gold-leather hunting scenes of c. 1650 Flemish origin, representing the hunting of lion, boar, deer, heron, and women. **Theehuis Paleis Het Loo** *(10 a.m.–5 p.m., closed Mon.; inexpensive)* A self-service restaurant in one of the "garages" of the royal stables that house the vintage carriages, coaches, and cars once used at Het Loo.

ACCOMMODATIONS ★★★★ **Hotel De Keizerskroon** • *Koningstraat 7, 7315 HR; 055–217744, fax 055-214737, for res. in U.S. 800–223–6510, in Canada 800–424–5500; First Class* • De Keizerskroon ("the emperor's crown") came by its name legitimately, when Czar Peter the Great, visiting royalty at Het Loo, ignored the protocol of staying at the palace and stayed instead with his servants at the inn next door which advertised *"A l'auberge, on traite proprement"* (at the inn everyone is treated well). That's still the case today, though the hotel has burnt and been rebuilt since Peter's days and now is a modernized hotel with 100 well-lit, colorful rooms, with windows that open, some with balconies, all with hair dryers and a basketful of amenities in the bath. The cozy leather-bound-furniture lobby has a modern fireplace, at the corner of which is a charming sculpture of a girl reading. The hotel has a parking garage and an indoor swimming pool. The hotel **De Keizersgrill** *(noon–10:30 p.m.; moderate)* is bright and beckoning, with painted wall panels of Het Loo's gardens.

IN THE AREA..................................

Deventer • *VVV Brink 5, pop. 65,000* • A short distance to the northeast from Apeldoorn is an old Hanseatic League town with a well-preserved historic center, often called the **Bergkwartier,** with many houses in the Gelderland-Overijssel style of the 12th–16th centuries. The **Waag** (weigh house, 1528) has a museum of local history. Across from the essentially 15th-century Grote Kerk is the late 17th-century **Stadhuis,** in which hangs a picture of a Deventer town council meeting painted by Gerard Terborch (1617–1681) who, as burgomaster then, appears presiding over the meeting.

Zutphen • *VVV in the 14th-century Wijnhuis—with Hemony carillon—on Groenmarkt, pop. 32,000* • To the southeast of Apeldoorn is Zutphen, also a former Hanse town with an attractive historic center. **St. Walburgskerk** *(Grote Kerk),* noted for the 15th- and 16th-century wall and ceiling paintings, is also renowned for its gothic *chained library* (where original manuscripts remain fastened to old reading desks), the oldest in western Europe, in the former chapter house (1564).

RESTAURANTS De Echoput • *Amersfoortseweg 86, Hoog Soeren; 10 a.m.–midnight, kitchen closes 10 p.m.; 9:30 p.m. Sun., closed Mon. and Sat. for lunch; for res. 05769–248; expensive* • A

Member of Alliance Gastronomique and Relais Gourmand, this place may be somewhat unprepossessing in appearance, but wait for the palette to pass judgment. The "nouvelle with solid French classic base" (as the owner describes it) highlights the several *prix-fixe* menus and *a la carte* dishes, of which game is a specialty in-season. If the weather cooperates, you can dine on the terace surrounded by the royal forests of neighboring Apeldoorn.

AMERSFOORT

The lovely medieval heart of Amersfoort *(VVV Stationplein 27; 033– 63515; greater pop. 100,000)* was first fortified after receiving enfranchisement in 1259 from Henry of Vianden (Luxembourg), then bishop of Utrecht. Amersfoort has the picturesque distinction of being the only city in Europe to have a double ring of canals around its old center. Described in one source as making "no significant appearance in Netherlands history," Amersfoort is and appears ancient enough to have provided the settings and props for any number of dramatic historical roles (such as the one neighboring Arnhem was cast for in World War II), but certainly is better preserved today for the fact that it didn't. For example, the so-called *muurhuizen* (wall houses) were built where the first town walls (1381) were dismantled in 1451 when a larger second wall had been completed, and are a unique feature from early Amersfoort. Much within those second walls preserves a medieval picture. **Het Havik,** the former harbor of Amersfoort and center of the old town, is now a canal lined with beautiful house facades (and a flower market on Friday mornings). There's also a **Friday morning fish market** on Groenmarkt by St. Joriskerk, at which women in traditional costume from nearby Spakenburg (see below, *In the Area*) may be preparing and selling their fresh wares.

Onze Lieve Vrouwetoren • *Onze Lieve Vrouwekerkhof; check with VVV for summer hours of admission* • The 100-meter/328-foot church tower dates from the 15th century, though it has been restored several times since; it has a 47 mostly-Hemony-bell carillon that used to belong to an attached chapel until that unfavored building blew up in 1787 while being used as an arsenal. The unlucky chapel's outline was put into the pavement in the square when it was redone. There's a Friday morning carillon concert from 10–11 a.m. for market day.

Museum Flehite • *Westsingel 50; Tues.–Fri. 10 a.m.–5 p.m., Sat. & Sun. 2–5 p.m., closed Mon.* • The museum, which is housed in three old wall houses, the right-hand one of which is in large part original, has exhibits on the history of Amersfoort and its surroundings, and has a large model of the historic town center. The restored **Pieters en Bloklands Gasthuis** (hospital), located diagonally across the road from the Flehite, is also a part of the museum (ask about access). The men's ward, dating from the early 16th century, has retained its original character, including its wooden bedsteads or sleeping cupboards, old tiles, and locked oaken chests where individuals kept their earthly belongings. It is unique in Holland and well-worth the effort to visit.

De Keppelpoort • *Grote Spui; June 24–Sept. 1 Mon–Fri. 10 a.m.– 5 p.m., Sat. & Sun. noon–5 p.m.* • Built at the beginning of the 15th century as part of the second town rampart, **De Koppelpoort** is a paired, combination land and water gate by the River Eem. The restored treadmill inside was powered by men to lift and lower the heavy partition gate.

De Nederlandse Beiaardschool • *The Dutch National Carillon School; Grote Spui 11, 3811 Ga; 033–752638 with a reservation open to the public during Flehite Museum hours in summer, other seasons by special arrangement, contact VVV* • The Amersfoort school, and the one in Mechelen, Belgium, are the only carillon schools in the world (see chapter on Carillons in front section of the book). Since its founding in 1953, Amersfoort has had more than 250 students from 11 countries, who have in the course of their studies played on most of Holland's 182 carillons. The main school building, in a particularly attractive part of the old center, houses offices, campanological display, library, and practice keyboards. The school has keyboard computers on which students are encouraged to compose contemporary carillon music. Although the Onze Lieve Vrouwetoren carillon is close by, most playing lessons, and practice time, are scheduled at the **Belgian Monument** at the Amersfoortse Berg (woods) at the southeast edge of town. The Monument, which commemorates Belgium's gratitude to Holland for helping with its refugees during World War I, has a light four-octave Eijsbouts carillon. Director of the school Jacques Maassen is the *stadsbeiaard* for the town of Breda, and American Todd Fair, carilloneur for Amsterdam's Oude Kerk, is on the faculty. Diplomas and performing artists' diplomas are granted; a week-long summer academy is held.

IN THE AREA..

South of Amersfoort are a castle and a village worthy of attention if you are ambling by auto (also accessible by bus from rail stations in

Amersfoort and Utrecht CS). To the north is the "costume town" of Spakenburg. A couple of castle hotels and a renowned restaurant are also there.

Kasteel Huis Doorn • *Langbroekerweg 10, Doorn 3941 MT, 13 km. south of Amersfoort; Mar. 15–Sept. 1, Mon.–Sat., 9:30 a.m.–5 p.m., Sun. 1–5 p.m.; 03430–12244* • When Germany's ex-Kaiser Wilhelm II was forced into exile in 1918, being a cousin of Dutch Queen Wilhelmina, he turned to Holland for help and Parliament gave him permission to settle in. He bought this 14th-century, largely reconstructed in the 18th century house from actress Audrey Hepburn's great aunt, a Dutch baroness. Although it's a pleasant mansion, it certainly would have seemed a great come-down to Wilhelm when he arrived with his 58 wagon-loads of belongings from the palaces of Germany, including two loads of *silver* (some of the elaborate pieces are on display). Other treasures with which the Kaiser arrived are the **Gobelin tapestries** in the dining room, and display cases with an exceptional collection of *snuff boxes* that once belonged to Frederik the Great of Prussia. Huis Doorn is decorated in 1920s style and has been left largely as it was when the former Emperor, who lived here from 1920 to 1941, died. (When he died, Nazi forces then occupied Holland and Hitler ordered a full military funeral for him). Wilhelm was a proud man and placed plenty of pictures of himself all over the house; the magnificant crystal-edged mirror in his bedroom must have framed his image nicely. Perhaps pleasure in his face was compensation for having been born with a much shorter left arm, which shows quite clearly from his military uniforms on display. Be sure to see Wilhelm's study/library, a lovely, liveable book-lined round room with views of the grounds in three directions. Most remarkable is the riding saddle on stilts in which he sat while working at the stand-up desk; Wilhelm believed that no man could be mentally alert unless he was sitting absolutely erect. The park surrounding the castle provides for pleasant strolling among old oaks and beechtrees and groves of rhododendrons. From the terrace of the former **Orangerie,** now a tea room, there's a pleasant view back to the castle. Restoration of Huis Doorn underway at press time is expected to be finished by the end of 1992.

Wijk bij Duurstede • *VVV Markt 24, in the 1662 former Stadhuis; 03435–75995, open Mon. 1–4 p.m., Tues.–Sat. 10 a.m.–noon, 1–4:30 p.m.; pop. 15,000* • The Dutch visit this lovely old town largely to enjoy its *gastronomy* and *galleries,* and just in case you think it might ring a bit hollow with that description, local residents say that "people never leave because it is so pleasant here." There are no set sights save for the ancient tree-shaded Markt, and small cozy streets (printed walking-tour in English available from the VVV), though many visitors make their way to the romantic ruin of 12th-century moated **Duurstede Castle,** with its historic restored square **Donjon** (defensive dwelling tower), a typical early construction in the region. David of Burgundy, bastard son of Philip the Good, became Bishop of Utrecht in 1456 and took possession of Duurstede Castle, intending to make the fine John the Baptist church (recently restored) on the Markt equal to the Utrecht Dom in splendor, but failed to finish his plan. Down by the dijks on the rivers (Wijk is where the Neder Rhine becomes the River Lek) is Holland's only still existing windmill built on a gate in the city wall, and carries the name **Rijn en Lek** (Rhine and Lek; 1659). Many people mistakenly think it is the windmill in the marvelous moody-skied masterpiece painting by Jacob van Ruisdael entitled "Molen at Wijk bij Duurstede" (c. 1665) in Amsterdam's Rijksmuseum. That specific windmill, which stood close by, was demolished in the first half of the 19th century, but you can ask to have the **windmill base** pointed out to you as you walk along the bank to enjoy the river views.

RESTAURANTS Restaurant Duurstede • *Maleborduurstraat 7; noon–2 p.m. & 6–10 p.m., closed Wed.; 03435–72946, fax 03435–74614; moderate* • Chef and owner Paul Fagel (one of eight brothers who cook in the famed Dutch family of restauranteurs) has housed his well-regarded kitchen in an ancient stone building, in a pleasant home-like split-level setting, with bar in the basement and dining room upstairs. The old beamed ceilings, bright contemporary art and decorative details are as imaginative a combination as Fagel's *prix-fixe* and *a la carte* offerings, which show Italian and seafood influences. **Restaurant 'T Schippershuys** • *Dijkstraat 5; Tues.–Sun., 10 a.m.–9 p.m., closed Mon.; 03435–71538; inexpensive* • This stylish 1840s space with wood floors, high ceilings, big windows and a terrace on the Rhine/Lek riverfront across the street is close to the site of the Ruysdael windmill base and the picturesque existing city wall windmill. Tasty menu choices include omelettes, uitsmijters, salad nicoise, and pancakes. **Cafe-Bar 't Hoff** • *Markt 15a; daily, lunch to late night; 03435-74848; inexpensive* • It's not surprising that there's the aroma of beer in this air of this small pub, since it's been serving the same since the end of the 15th century. Light dishes and snacks are served inside under the ancient wooden ceiling or at the terrace at the back, where there's a view to the town's castle and a *jeu de boules* may be brewing.

Spakenburg • *11 km./7 mi. north of Amersfoort, served by public VAD bus from station every half hour* • A former Zuiderzee fishing village, whose fishermen have mostly taken to eel fishing, building and chartering traditional Dutch sailing boats (which keeps the little harbor full of ship masts), and also preparing and selling fish in costume at weekly markets all over Holland. About 800 women in the village (out of a population of about 20,000 for the combined township of Spakenburg and Bunschoten, which is inland and therefore has a farming character) wear traditional costume everyday, the youngest doing so about the age of 40. Most have inherited some of the costume parts from family members, and so the clothing is antique and valuable, as well as sentimental. One woman explained to me that those who wear traditional costume in Spakenburg daily "really wouldn't feel dressed in anything else." These women even wear the costume on holiday in other countries on the continent. Others in the village will wear the dresses on special occasions, such as family weddings, birthdays, anniversaries, and also tourist ones, such as the last two Wednesdays in July and first two in August when Spakenburg hosts its annual market and traditional crafts days. While not extreme, the community is very religious and there are those who don't even watch television on Sundays. However, such is the passion for *voetbal* (soccer) across all segments of Dutch society that when there's an important match being shown, if a Spakenburger for religious reasons can't bring himself to watch the match on Sunday, he'll record it on his VCR for Monday viewing.

Museum 't Vurhuus • *Oude Schans 47; end April–mid Oct. Mon.–Sat. 10 a.m.–5 p.m.; 03499–83319* • This appealing little museum is arranged to show the various intricacies associated with traditional costumes and their evolution (for adults and children) in Spakenburg and next-door neighbor village Bunschoten in a c. 1915 setting of shop and typical fisherman family living room, which also includes interesting household decorative details, such as the tiled fireplace.

ACCOMMODATIONS/RESTAURANTS IN THE AREA:

★★★ **Kasteel 't Kerchebosch Hotel-Restaurant** • *Arnhemse Bovenweg 31, Zeist; 03404–14734, fax 03404–13114; hotel; moderate* • A turn-of-the-century, neo-Grothic, former country house of a nobleman, who created the eclectic decor from antique details and materials gathered from old monasteries, castles, and churches (such as doors from Utrecht's Dom cathedral). Set in quiet park surroundings, the 30 rooms include 14 in the house and the rest in a new wing added at the rear in 1976; all have moderate amenities, although there is no elevator, which accounts for the only-three-star rating. Among the facilities (open to the public) are a bar lounge *(daily 8 a.m.–12:30 a.m.)*, bistro *(Wed.–Sun., 6–10 p.m.)*, and specialty restaurant, where breakfast (included) is served, open for lunch and dinner daily.

★★★★ **Kasteel De Hooge Vuursche Hotel-Restaurant** • *Hilversumsestraatweg 14, Baarn; 02154–12541, 02154–23288; hotel: first class* • This Cuypers-designed late 19th-century house as a hotel has retained a residential graciousness. The public rooms have hardwood floors, high ceiling elegance, and delicate architectural details. There are garden and fountain views out the large lounge windows, and each of the 20 guestrooms has its own restful, uncluttered character amid a soft-colored decor. There's 24-hour room service and luxury amenities in the rooms. The formal traditional French cuisine *a la carte* restaurant is open for lunch and dinner daily, and there are tables on the terrace overlooking the lake.

★★★★ **Auberge de Hoefslag** • *Vossenlaan 28, Bosch en Duin; for res. 030–251051, fax 030–285821; hotel: first class; restaurant: expensive to very expensive* • A countryside restaurant of charm and style that works wonders with local market produce, all created by **Martin Fagel** of the renowned Dutch restaurant family. If you're expecting to be too pleasantly satiated after dining to want to drive, De Hoefslag also is an inn, with 34 rooms; breakfast's included.

SOUTHERN HOLLAND: AN INTRODUCTION

In its use here, Southern Holland includes the provinces of **Zeeland, North Brabant,** and **Limburg,** all lying "below" the great *Rhine, Maas,* and *Waal* rivers, which flow from the interior of the continent to empty into the North Sea near Rotterdam.

Even Dutch tourism officials use the term "Southern Holland" in their foreign-language literature, since it's a convenient phrase for referring to this less-well-traveled section of the country. However, it's precisely in this region that the resident Dutch want to make the point that their country is **The Netherlands,** *not* Holland, which, technically, is only two provinces, North and South. Travelers in these southern provinces who use the word "Holland" when speaking of the country may encounter occasional explanations (always given with a smile). When I find myself in Zeeland, North Brabant, and Limburg I attempt to be sensitive to the issue by trying to remember—not always successfully—to use the name "Netherlands."

The Dutch provinces in the south of the Netherlands are linked by ties to Belgium, on which they all border. Here, history left the boundaries a bit blurred; not—since the mid-19th-century—politically, but psychologically. Rule by the Burgundians and the Spanish lasted longer in the once so-called southern Netherlands (today's Belgium), and the cross-cultivation across the southern Dutch border (which, in any case, shifted for centuries), left a greater impact upon the personality of the people there than elsewhere in today's Netherlands. The differences between the Dutch in the north of the country and those in the south may not *leap* out at you, but only the most casual passer-through will not notice the change in mentality and mood between the Holland "north of the rivers" and the Netherlands south of them.

ZEELAND

Well-named, **Zeeland** (sea land) is as much water as land, and much of what land there is lies below sea level. The southern section of Zeeland, **Zeeuwsch Vlaanderen,** is connected to the European continent at Belgium's border, but to the rest of its own province only by car ferries, across the watery finger of the **Westerschelde,** which points inland to the Belgian port of Antwerp. **Walcheren,** with the provincial capital **Middelburg,** and **Noorde** and **Zuid Beveland,** form Zeeland's largest "island grouping," some linked by modern dikes and dams, and others, once attached to the mainland, now sliced from it by canals, but reconnected by bridges. **Zeelandbrug,** Europe's longest bridge at 5,022 meters/3.1 miles, reaches gracefully across the **Oosterschelde,** the mouth of which has been given "the teeth" of the massive 65 concrete pier-*Stormvloedkering* (storm surge barrier), the final complex part of the most impressive hydraulic engineering plan ever undertaken in the world (see **Delta Expo,** below). Interest in that project has brought a new public to beach-blessed Zeeland, though the remote-seeming province's contact with the greater world still comes mostly in the form of summer holidaymakers.

From an early date, Zeeland shared in the trade prominence and prosperity that its access to the sea provided. Historically, the province of Holland (today's North and South Holland combined) also included Zeeland, which had been annexed by Holland in 1323, following long disputes over its territory by the counts of Holland and Flanders. Basically, Zeeland, Holland, and Flanders shared a similar history for some 500 years up until 1436, at which time Holland itself was annexed into the wide holdings of Duke Philip of Burgundy. Early trade in *wool* and *cloth* with England and Scotland created wealth for the region, a fact attested to by richly-adorned public buildings such as the **Middelburg** and **Veere stadhuizen.** It certainly was a boon for Zeeland business when, in 1444, Lord of Veere Wolfert van Borssele married Mary, one of the six daughters of James I of Scotland, a match which led the way to Veere's monopoly in the Scottish wool trade, which lasted until the French occupation of Holland of 1795.

Meanwhile, many Zeeland towns were involved in the seiges of the Dutch seven-province struggle against the Spanish. **Vlissingen,** an ancient town of little previous importance, was chosen in 1556 as embarkation port by Spanish King Philip II, who left the Netherlands embittered against his Dutch subjects, accusing Willem the Silent of treachery. When the Spanish attacked in the 1570s, Vlissingen was one of the first towns to revolt against them.

Low-lying Zeeland has a long history of floods. One of the worst was the St. Elizabeth Flood of 1421, which destroyed 72 Zeeland villages and drowned some 10,000 inhabitants. Though fewer human lives (1,835) were lost during the **hurricane of February 1, 1953,** which breached many of Zeeland's dikes, 200,000 livestock died, some 485,000 acres of the country's most fertile farmland were submerged in salt water, and 48,000 homes were damaged, many beyond repair. That catastrophic storm, combined with the degree to which the Dutch had raised the science of hydraulic engineering, resulted in a "never-again" stance that subsequently produced the **Delta Project.** (In February 1990 a hurricane again struck the coast of Holland—the same storm caused death and devastation also in the UK, Belgium, and inland in Luxembourg,— but, with the Delta Project in place, it was only beaches, not breaches, that required repair from sea damage.)

What must have made the disastrous hurricane of 1953 even more devasting for Zeeland was that it came so soon after the enormous flood damage sustained by the province during World War II's deliberate **bombing** by the RAF in September/October 1944 to unearth the Nazis from their bunkered positions in Walcheren, from which they controlled the Westerschelde entrance to the port of Antwerp. (Following the successful Normandy invasion in June 1944, the Allies had a particular need for Antwerp as a port for landing supplies for the rest of their continental campaign.) Beginning in September, bombs rained down on Walcheren's dikes, the aim being to breach them and literally flood the Nazis out. By the end of October 1944, the RAF had succeeded in causing several serious breaches in the dikes at Westkapelle, Veere, Vlissingen, and Rammekens. Most of Walcheren lay under sea water (where it remained for more than 13 months, during which time most trees, as well as all other vegetation, died). Walcheren was freed by

Allied troops (including the *2nd Canadian Division*), landing at **Vlissingen** and **Westkapelle** (*Landing Monument* and other memorials) on November 1, 1944. By the end of 1944, work was begun on repairing the breaches, although it wasn't until February 1946 that the last gap in the dikes of Zeeland closed. And the entire job of reconstruction had not been fully completed when the 1953 hurricane struck.

Today it's possible for travelers as well as residents to put to rest that troubled past, and enjoy Zeeland's peaceful rural setting of dignified farms, remote sand dunes, quaint quiet old towns, a quality of light that's a delight, and long-repaired dikes lined with full-grown rows of fast-growing "replacement" poplars.

Guidelines for Zeeland

SIGHTS Situated in the southwest of the Netherlands, cut by the Eastern and Western Scheldt rivers, Zeeland is made up of areas that originally were islands. That geographical fact created a certain isolation, which, while mitigated today by connecting roads resulting from the Delta Project, produces within the province more vestiges of older customs (such as *traditional costumes*) than are visible in Randstad Holland. Zeeland's location between Flanders and Holland involved it in important mercantile enterprises in the 15th–17th centuries, a fact reflected in rich and refined buildings such as the stadhuizen in **Middelburg** and the villages of **Veere**. Other historic towns such as **Zierikzee, Goes, Tholen,** and **Sluis** will make your camera-shutter-finger itchy. **Vlissingen** is a busy long-established port and resort. Today, Zeeland's beaches are busy in summer, and her former sea fishermen have turned their focus to cultivating the famous *Zeeuws oysters* and *mussels*. The ingenious **Delta Works,** the definitive protection for the province against a too-assertive sea, attracts visitors from around the world.

GETTING AROUND Without question, a car is the best way to capture the essence of the area. There's a quite extensive Zeeland provincial bus service: tiny Veere can be reached from Middelburg, for instance. Inclusive day train trips from major stations to the **Delta Expo** are run by the Netherlands Spoorwegen several times weekly. Bicycle rentals are available at Middelburg station (reservations in summer suggested) and many private locations throughout Zeeland. Two-wheelers are common commuting means for Zeelanders, and you're liable to come across Walcheren women in traditioinal dress (cap with lace "blinkers" and golden coils, black shawl, voluminous skirts, and black and white overskirt) pedalling with a full load of parcels.

SHOPPING The main shopping centers in the region are Middelburg, Vlissingen, Zierikzee, Goes, and Hulst. Some shops close for lunch (generally 12:30–1:30 p.m.); most are closed on Sunday, although there's an exception for shops in some towns in Zeeuwsch-Vlaanderen, which keep open to compete with the nearby Belgium shops that open Sundays.

ENTERTAINMENT AND EVENTS Although traditional costumes are seen less and less frequently in Zeeland, they are still worn with some regularity in Walcheren and South-Beveland, the best bet to see them being at the weekly general markets (in Goes on Tuesday, Middelburg and Zierikzee on Thursday, Vlissingen on Friday), or Sunday mornings en route to a rural church. *Tilting at the Ring,* a traditional "tournament" game with horses (that also amounts to something of a flower festival), is held once in July and once in August (check with the VVV for specific dates).

ACCOMMODATIONS One should book well-ahead during the peak summer season. Vlissingen has the most hotels, and the most liveliness, no doubt because of its port. Most Zeeland hotels are the small, family-run sort. The **Zeeland Provinciale VVV,** upstairs from the Middelburg VVV on the Markt, *(Mon.–Fri. 8:30 a.m.–noon and 1:15–5 p.m.; 01180-33051)* can help with bed and breakfast-type accommodations (most plentiful, and most heavily booked, in summer).

RESTAURANTS There's nothing more appropriate to grace the tables in Zeeland than the "fruits of the sea," and nothing fresher, more varied, or more delicious. Specialties are shellfish (oysters, mussels, North Sea "gray" shrimp, lobsters, winkles). A number of fish are also landed here (sole, turbot, eel). Traditional locally-produced sweets include *bolus* (sweet rolls) and *babelaars* (buttery candies). Do not neglect the restaurants in hotels in Zeeland, since it is through customers' stomachs that those establishments often attract overnight guests.

ARRIVING Zeeland borders on Belgian Flanders, and is an easy driving distance from the Flemish cities of Bruges, Ghent, and Antwerp. Daily car-ferries run between Sheerness, in Kent, England, and Vlissingen (Flushing) in Zeeland. Locations in Zeeland that can be reached by train are limited to Middelburg, Goes, and Vlissingen, via Roosendaal on a main line south from Rotterdam.

TRAVEL TIPS If you visit Zeeland by car, or car ferry at Vlissingen, a glance at a Benelux map will show it's only a short drive across the border to the Belgium's Flemish "art" cities: Bruges, Ghent, and Antwerp. If you come to Middelburg by train, a plan to combine that Zeeland city with a Flemish itinerary is equally sound: retrace your rail route to Rosendaal, and hop a quick direct train south to Antwerp-Mechelen-Brussels, etc.

ON THE ROAD ....

Middelburg

VVV, Markt 65, population 39,000; telephone code 01180 • Bombed by Nazis on May 17, 1940 (three days after the leveling of Rotterdam), Middelburg's center lay largely destroyed at the end of the war. The town, sitting on the slightly elevated land that makes its Lange Jan tower visible from afar, did, however, escape the flooding that followed the 1944 Allied bombing. With careful post-war rebuilding, the devastation disappeared, and today Middelburg goes about its business with an appealing, quietly proud air. **Lange Jan** (Abbey Tower) *(Easter–Oct. 1, Mon.–Sat., 10 a.m.–5 p.m.; 82255)* The tall (85-meter/280-foot, 207-stair), crown-topped, "singing" tower of the abbey is the landmark not only of the town, but the whole of Walcheren, from most parts of which it is visible. Its carillon (concerts Thursdays noon–1 p.m., extras in summer) sounds rebound about the pedestrian streets, and it's impossible to tell where the wonderful music is coming from—if you didn't know; the enclosed Abbey courtyard (with cafe) is a fine place for listening. Originally constructed in the first half of the 14th century, the tower burnt down many times, most recently in the Nazi bombing of May 1940, when in its flaming crash it also wrecked the **Abdijkerken** (Abbey churches) near its base. The three churches were rebuilt as one, complete with **Lange Jan,** reconstructed and re-crowned.

Stadhuis • *Stadhuisstraat 2; Mon.–Fri. 10 a.m.–noon, 1:30–4:30 p.m., except Thurs. 1–5 p.m., times of conducted tours posted on information board outside main entrance; 26251)* • Middelburg's other outstanding monument, her Stadhuis, stands at a corner of the cafe-rimmed Markt. The original of this opulently-sculpted Gothic edifice was begun in 1452. With carved oak moldings and high vaulted ceilings it was an impressive headquarters for the town's important cloth guild. When the Nazis bombed the center of Middelburg on May 17, 1944, it's said that the Stadhuis continued to burn for two weeks, keeping the ground around it too hot to walk on. The re-creation of the marvelous, many-figured (25 counts and countesses of Holland and Zeeland) facade, which originally had taken several generations of the Flemish architect family Keldermans of Mechelen to finish, was completed in 1967. The hall has a number of antiques to admire, including Delft vases and 17th-century Makkum tiles. The civic wedding room has two Brussels tapestries (c. 1600), and there are two more from Bruges in the large Banqueting Hall, which was originally used as the first cloth-market in the Netherlands. The "star" of the Aldermen's room, generally considered the most beautiful in the Stadhuis, is a large 17th-century Dutch "cushion" cupboard of rosewood and ebony.

The Abbey Complex • *conducts multi-lingual tours May 1–Nov. 1, Mon.–Sat. 1:30 & 3 p.m.; also at 11 a.m., Tues.–Fri., July & Aug.* • The Abbey was founded by canons from Belgium in 1127, occupying buildings on this site from 1150 until 1574, when Willem the Silent's troops "secularized" it by turning the complex over to the States of Zeeland. The abbey churches were required to change from Catholic to Protestant practices. The 1940 bombings almost entirely destroyed the Abbey buildings, but they have been faithfully restored. Zeeland's provincial goverment meets in the Council Chamber of the abbey each month, and other organizations share quarters. One is the **Roosevelt Study Center** *(Abbey 9; Wed. & Thurs. 9:30 a.m.–12:30 p.m., 1:30–4:30 p.m.; 01180-31011)*, a research resource that also has a permanent exhibit of photographs, clippings and other memorabilia on Theodore (especially his 1910 trip to Europe as reported in the Dutch newspapers—translated bits), Franklin (his roles in the WPA and World War II), and Eleanor ("First Lady of the World"). Claes Maertenszoon van Rosevelt and his wife Jannetje sailed from Zeeland in the 1640s, settling in the colony of Nieuw Nederland in the city of Nieuw Amsterdam (New York), and became the founders of an American dynasty.

Zeeland Museum • *Abbey 3; year-round, Tues.–Fri., 10 a.m.–5 p.m., Sat.–Mon., 1:30–5 p.m.* • Located in the 16th-century "canons' quarters" wing since 1972, the museum's core collection of curiosities was assembled by the Zeeland Society beginning in 1769. The tapestry room may be considered the highlight. The seven tapestries, each 4 meters/13 feet high, with a combined total length of 30 meters/99 feet, were made around 1600 by Flemish weavers working in Middelburg. They were commissioned by the States of Zeeland, who decided that the battle between the Zeelanders and the Spanish should be recorded for posterity in a memorable manner. The two largest (whose restoration is currently underway) depict dramatic sea battles off Bergen op Zoom and Rammekens. The remaining beautifully colored and bordered tapestries, whose size permits a remarkable wealth of detail, have all been restored in recent decades (a process that took much more time than the ten years it originally took for their creation). The folklore room, in the beamed, steep-roof attic, shows the regional traditional dress, how it has modified over time, and the differences between the Catholic and Protestant costumes. There is also a display of objects related to the cultivation of the *madder plant,* whose roots yield a red dye that was an important ingredient in the region's cloth trade. In the 17th and 18th century rooms are elegant examples of furniture, Delft blue, and a striking portrait of Admiral de Ruyter by Ferdinand Bol (1667). Although the museum exhibits themselves are described only in Dutch, an English-language explanation sheet is available.

ACCOMMODATIONS ★★★ Le Beau Rivage • *Loskade 19, 4331 HW; 01180-38060; inexpensive/moderate* • is a friendly house-size hotel, well-located along the town side of the Walcheren Kanaal, within walking distance of the station or town center. It has a small restaurant and lounge-bar; nine rooms, all individual, with bath; parking; no elevator.

★★★★ Hotel Du Commerce • *Loskade 1; 4331 HV; 01180-36051, fax 01180-12386; inexpensive* • is on the Walcheren Kanaal (canal), across from the station. The 40 bedrooms have a basic but comfortable decor, all with private shower/bath. The hotel has a restaurant and bar.

RESTAURANTS Het Groot Paradijs *(Damplein 13; noon–2 p.m., 6–9 p.m., closed Sun., Mon.; 26764; moderate)* occupies a fine house on a handsome square, and serves select seafood and other carefully-prepared cuisine in a setting of beamed ceilings and brass chandeliers. **De Huifkar** *(Markt 19; noon–11 p.m., closed Sun. in winter; 12998; inexpensive to moderate)* provides a rustic touch in the center of town, with brick, beams, candlelight, and ladderback chairs. Zeeland's seafood is also a speciality here, sole and mussels merit attention. Closeby is **De Ploeg** *(Markt 55; noon–9 p.m., closed Wed. in winter; 34690; inexpensive)* with outside tables (in season) from which to view Middelburg's marvelous Stadhuis and sample the varied menu.
De Kabouterhut Pannekoekhuis *(Oostkerkplein 7; noon–9 p.m., closed Mon. except school vacations; 12276; inexpensive)* is an informal friendly place where lines are liable to form for its platter-size fare. **De Abidij** *(Abdijplein 5; 10 a.m.–3 p.m., closed Sun.; 35022; inexpensive)* is a pleasant resting point for coffee, snacks, or light lunch, amid the museums of the Abbey complex.

Veere

VVV Markt 21, pop. 1,000 • When Veere, four miles northeast of Middelburg, was at the height of its importance, thanks to a marriage bond between Mary, a daughter of James I of Scotland, and Wolfert van Borssele, lord of Veere, in 1444, the population of this wonderfully quiet (if there's no tour bus making a quick stop) backwater reached 9,000. It later (1541) become a "staple port" whereby all Scottish trade to Europe had to pass through its harbor. From the grassy ramparts and brick paths that encircle much of this petite patrician village, one can observe the lingering legacy of those prosperous days, though the red roof tiles may be muted in the mist. The Delta Project ended Veere's days as a sea fishing port, but sailing and watersports have taken over on the Veerse Meer (Veere Lake), and the village sports a yacht harbor instead of a fishing one. Standing by the Veerse Meer by the 14th-century De Campveerse Toren, the 14th-century **Grote Kerk** is an elephantine hulk on the horizon on the other side of the village. The Cisterne, or village well, was constructed in 1551 on the orders of Maximilian of Burgundy, who had promised the Scottish wool merchants a supply of good drinking water; the well stored the rain water collected off the roof of the Grote Kerk. The Gothic **Stadhuis** *(Markt; 01181-253)*, dating from 1474, and slender Renaissance steeple topped with a gilded ship weather-vane (added in 1599), are still recognizable as they appear in old prints. The facade, renovated in the 1930s and suffering no bomb damage during the subsequent war, is decorated with statues of lords and ladies of Veere. Inside is a museum containing objects related to town history and a celebrated cup left by Maximilian when he came to inspect the Cisterne; the council chamber is adorned with **Gobelin** tapestries and paintings.

Schotse Huizen • *Scottish Houses; Kaai 25 & 27; April 1–Sept. 30, Mon. 1–5 p.m., Tues.–Sat. 10 a.m.–5 p.m.; 01181-744* • In exchange for Veere having a monopoly on all importing, storing, and trading of Scottish wool, Scottish traders living there received certain privileges: their own legal system, their own chapel in the Grote Kerk, and housing. The Schotse Huizen are the only two buildings occupied by Scottish traders to have been preserved from this period (which ended with the Napoleonic occupation in 1795). In addition to being private houses, they also served as business premises. **Het Lemmeken** ("the little lamb," which refers to the gablestone decoration indicating the wool trade), the finer of the two houses, was built in 1539, and is an important example of 16th-century Dutch architecture with its wall clamps, fanlight, and adorned arches above the windows. The Museum is entered next door via the front room of **De Struys** (once a twin to "Het Lemmeken" but losing out in later remodeling) where one is greeted by one of the finest pieces in the collection: the late 17th-century Zeeland "star cabinet," which is inlaid with ivory and many varieties of wood. There is an interesting set of scultpures by a Mechelen artist c. 1516 of lords and ladies of Veere that were originally on the Stadhuis facade and originally painted in bright colors. Among the pieces of fine furniture, porcelain, jewelry, and old watercolors of Veere when it was a trading and fishing port, one also appreciates details of the setting: the huge blue and white tiled hearth hung with brass and copper utensils, high beamed ceilings, shiny tile floors, brick walls and, from the top floor, which is a fishing museum, the wind whistling in the gables as one looks out over the tiled roofs and gardens of the town and the wide waters of the Veerse Meer.

ACCOMMODATIONS ★★ **De Campveerse Toren** • *Kade 2, 4351 AA; for res. 01181-1291, fax 01181-1695; inexpensive* • Dating from the mid-14th century, when it was built as part of Veere's fortifications, **De Campveerse Toren** began being used as an inn not long afterwards. A favorite place with the Dutch for their civil marriage ceremonies, the Restaurant-Auberge, open year-round, has six basic rooms in the ancient inn building (No. 1 has a curved end wall with windows onto water and ramparts on three sides) and 11 in historic next-door annexes; most rooms have view of harbor, many have private bath. Centuries ago, the inn advertised: "simple night's accommodations but an absolute night's rest."

RESTAURANTS De Campveerse Toren Restaurant • *(See above; moderate to expensive)* • is renowned as a romantic (window booths with views on the water, beams, brick, candlelight, and a walk-in fireplace) setting for remarkable food, far more than for its hotel (although I recommend both). England's Edward IV enjoyed his food and stay here in 1471. Breakfast must not have been included in the price of his bed (as it would be today), however, because records note that Edward, presented with the bill for his boiled eggs for breakfast, felt that he had been overcharged. "Are eggs so rare in Holland?" he is said to have asked the innkeeper. "No," was the reply, "but kings are."

Also well-documented (the menu and bill rest in the town archives) is a banquet enjoyed here on June 21, 1575, by Willem the Silent, Prince of Orange, and 30 guests on the occasion of his marriage (his third) to Charlotte de Bourbon. The royal repast included two peacocks and two heron, three pheasant, an undisclosed number of suckling pigs, a whole calf, hams, joints of beef, lobster, and turbot, washed down with a river of Rhine wine (156 liters/165 quarts), and an additional 268 liters/284quarts of assorted French wine and beer. Included in the bill were charges for candles, peat for the fires, the hire of cutlery and several serving wenches, a lost napkin, the innkeeper's time and trouble, and broken glasses (reported to be a fair number). De Campveerse Toren obviously oversaw a successful affair, since eight years later Willem returned for a repeat with his fourth wife, Louisa de Coligny. De Campveerse Toren's romantic and royal restaurant reputation has continued. Prince Ranier of Monaco brought Princess Grace here for a leisurely evening meal shortly after they were married. Wonderful food and well-garnished dishes, from smoked eel, "sea vegetables," and seafood to anything else off the continental menu.

D'Ouwe Werf • *Bastion 2; lunch & dinner; 01181-493; moderate* • is attractively noticeable across the narrow harbor via a little bridge—a white house with a usually well-peopled terrace in front for a lovely view back over Veere, prix-fixe menu, and fresh a la carte seafood and shellfish.

Goes

VVV at station, pop. 31,000 • is the main town of Zuid Beveland, with a large rectangular Grote Markt with some fine facades. The West and Oost singels (canals) mark the old moats and ramparts around the old center. To the east of Goes is Yerseke, renowned in Holland for its *Yerseksche Oesterbank* (oyster beds), and mussel beds too, which rest up against the Zuid Beveland banks of the Oosterschelde.

Delta Expo

On Neeltje Jans island, follow signs for Burgh-Haamstede/Oosterscheldewerken from Brouwersdam or Zierikzee; daily April–Oct. 10 a.m.–5 p.m., Nov.–Mar. same hours but closed Mon. and Tues. and Christmas; 50-minute boat trips in the Oosterschelde near the Storm Barrier from April–Oct. only, every hour from 11:30 a.m.–4 p.m., res. necessary 01115-2702 • The immediate impetus for the most extensive hydraulic engineering project ever undertaken in history was the hurricane of February 1, 1953, in which 1,835 people drowned in Zeeland; the sea came within inches of overreaching sandbagged dikes near Vlaardingen, the result of which would have been to send the bottled-up water that surged through the English Channel and across the North Sea barreling over the Randstad, flooding Rotterdam, The Hague, Leiden, and dampening the threshold of Amsterdam. Exhibits at the Delta Expo, located on the former construction island for the final stage of the 30-year Delta Project, make real the need for such a system, and show the state-of-the-art engineering expertise used in its realization.

Hydro-engineering, a science of which the Dutch have become the undisputed international masters (Dutch consultants were prominent in developing England's Thames Barrier, and are now widely sought as consultants worldwide in areas vulnerable to the impacts of an accelerating sea-level rise, as under the "greenhouse effect") is presented in a brief historical perspective at the Delta Expo that gives visitors a 2000-year overview of Dutch-style sea water-management from pre-Roman times to the present. Landscape maquettes and "wet" tidal models, slide presentations, instruments, and other multi-media assemblages also bring the mammoth Delta Project into focus. A good starting point for visitors is the introductory film (in Dutch, with English subtitles—and there's an excellent multi-lingual leaflet for the whole Expo). The film explains that the Delta Project called for a series of dams that would reduce the length of the Zeeland coastline by some 700 kms./420 mi., thus eliminating the need for and risk from damage to the many smaller dikes and dams previously required to keep the sea at bay. (A similar concept had been envisaged 400 years earlier, but had to bide its time.) The film shows that it took a complex combination of equipment, computers, cables, underwater TV cameras, purpose-built boats, and many quality control experts to complete the huge storm barrier. Construction of the 65 18,000-ton (dry weight) underwater piers required the round-the-clock pouring of concrete from March 1979 until the beginning of 1983 to ensure that the quality of the materials was uniform and the tight construction schedule met. Special "mattresses" were laid once the shifting sands were scrapped down to the rock bed, and upon these rested the enormous concrete piers, 40 meters/130 feet high, fitted to centimeter-precision. Movable steel barriers (each 42 meters/138 feet wide) are suspended between the piers, and in normal circumstances remain open, allowing the tide to flow through. If the water level increases to a dangerous level, all 62 barriers can be closed in about an hour. The Storm Surge Barrier, which can, when necessary, halt the flow of the 1.1 billion cubic meters of water that pass through the Oosterschelde with each turn of the tide, was opened in October 1986 by Queen Beatrix in ceremonies that inspired awe and relief.

The other dam constructions of the Delta Project had to be completed before that final and most complicated segment, the Oosterschelde storm barrier between Schouwen and Noord Beveland, could be completed. When the project was begun in the late 1950s, preserving the environment hadn't yet become a concern. But by the second half of the 1960s, environmental groups and representatives of the fishing industry pointed out that permanently damming the Oosterschelde would mean the end of a unique natural environment, as well as the loss of the financially-significant trade in oysters, mussels, and fish. The Dutch Parliament decided to take another look at the expensive segment already underway. A special committee was commissioned to perform a new study, and came back with a new concept: the Oosterschelde should not be permanently closed off, and in fact should be kept open most of the time, but be able to be closed when there was a risk of flooding.

That decision saved a highly developed ecosystem, many species of fauna and flora, allowed for the existing salt and fresh water areas to remain stable, and, of course, kept the economically important shellfish and fishings industries alive.

The roof of the exhibition center (which has a cafe and restaurant) affords a magnificent view over the mouth of the Oosterschelde. Your visit to Delta Expo should include a walk into the interior of one of the great concrete piers of the storm barrier, an experience that reinforces the enormity of the work and the force of the water it seeks to control. Now it's tourists who flood this section of Zeeland.

Zierikzee

VVV at Havenpark 29; 01110-12450 • at the north end of the Zeelandbrug, in Duiveland, is a long, narrow town, with carillons that strike the hours at either end. Head for the Oude Haven, with its park, and road leading to a picturesque drawbridge and old towers. Zierikzee has three towers (Nobelpoort, Noord and Zuidhavenpoort) which date from the early 14th-century extension of the town along the harbor.

Stadhuismuseum • *Meelstraat 6; May 1–Sept. 30 Mon.–Fri. 10 a.m.–noon & 1–5 p.m.; 01110-13151* • Located in the spired 1554 building, among its historical exhibits and traditional costumes, the town hall is particularly noted for its *Schutterszaal* (Militia Room), which features an impressive "overturned" original oak roof that resembles the massive hull of a ship. It is also noted for its municipal silver collection, recalling the days from the 14th–18th centuries when the town was an official assayer of silver.

The Maritiem Museum • *Mol 25; May 1–Sept. 30, and school holidays, Mon.–Sat. 10 a.m.–5 p.m.; 01110-13151* • is housed in the restored brick, step-gabled 1526 Gravensteen, whose facade is decorated with wrought-iron latticework. This old prison's original cells are preserved, and other exhibits tell of the rise and fall of Zierikzee's fishing and merchant shipping industries.

ACCOMMODATIONS/RESTAURANTS ★★★ Hotel Mondragon • *Havenpark 21, 4301 JG; 01110-13051; inexpensive* • With just under a dozen rooms, most with private bath, the Mondragon is wonderfully situated in the loveliest part of pretty old Zierikzee, by the park, old harbor, and historic towers. The hotel has a restaurant and bar just down the street.

Restaurant Mondragon • *Oude Haven 13; daily lunch and dinner; 01110-2670; moderate* • is scenically situated on the old harbor, and has a lovely traditional decor. Seafood's the suggestion, starting with the freshest oysters you've ever likely to slide down.

To the north of Zierikzee, **Dreischor** is worth a visit. It is the most attractive of several unusual *ring-villages:* its church (1340–1475) sits in the center of the village on a moat-surrounded grassy circle. The village's small stadhuis dates from 1637. **Brouwershaven** is a small interesting town, the center of which (the broad **Markt**) includes the small port where Count Floris V built a dam in 1285. Willem the Silent had it walled in 1582 (now dismantled). The facade of the **stadhuis** is 1559, a young face on an older building, and the **Grote Kerk** is basically the result of rebuilding in the 14 and 15th centuries. Silting, the result of flooding in 1682, relegated the town to its present sleepy but pleasing status.

NORTH BRABANT

Brabant was born as a part of the duchy of Lower Lorraine, which was created in the 10th century amid the territorial reshufflings that followed Charlemagne's death. In 1190, Lower Lorraine ruler Duke Henry I took upon himself the new title Duke of Brabant. The **Duchy of Brabant** (which included much of what today is the Dutch province of North Brabant and the Belgian provinces of Brabant and Antwerp) lasted from then until 1430, when Duke Anthony died childless, leaving the title to Duke Philip the Good of Burgundy. From that time, Brabant's history merged with the Netherlands.

During the *Eighty Years' War* (1568–1648), Brabant was split in two, the southern section being retained by Spain (and eventually becoming the Belgian provinces of Brabant and Antwerp), while the northern portion was merged with Willem the Silent's Dutch Protestant rebellion. North Brabant became part of the United Provinces under the *Treaty of Munster* (1648), but only as a "land," not a self-governing province. During the occupation of the Netherlands by Napoleon (1795–1814), the two Brabants were reunited. But, with the establishment of the Kingdom of the Netherlands in 1815, Brabant was again separated into its Dutch and Belgian parts, this time North Brabant having full status as a Dutch province.

Historically, the people in North Brabant have been predominantly Roman Catholic (today 85% are so "on paper, not in practice" was the way it was put to me). After the rebellion of the Dutch against Spanish rule in the northern Netherlands, the success of Protestants there led to difficulties for North Brabant's Catholics. They felt that the Protestant leaders of Holland's *States General* in The Hague regarded them as a "colonial" territory, and that the economic well-being of the region was largely neglected.

Traditionally a "poor" province, in that the sand and clay soil from the region's rivers is not fertile enough to support the population economically, North Brabant has come into economic strength in this century largely due to development at **Eindhoven.** There, in 1891, Dr. Anton Philips founded a firm that produced electric light bulbs. As **Philips,** now a world-recognized name in electronic products, grew, Eindhoven became a "company town," such was the firm's influence in attracting talented people and bringing related industry to the region.

Guidelines for North Brabant

SIGHTS Special places of interest are spread out in North Brabant, a roomy province, much of it woodlands, heath, and peat fen, extending west to east along the Belgian border from the Scheldt River to Limburg, and north to the Merwede and Maas river boundary. In **Eindhoven** *(VVV Stationplein 17, 040-449231; pop. 192,000)*, there's 20th-century art at the respected **Van Abbemuseum,** and a wonderful exhibit of the wonders of technology at Philips' **Evoluon.** Places where the past is palpable are the small fortified river towns of **Willemstad** in the west of the province, **Woudrichem** in the center, and **Grave, Ravenstein,** and **Megen** to the east. From Woudrichem it's possible to take a boat to **Loevestein** *(in summer, Mon.–Fri. once an hour from 10:30 a.m.–4:30 p.m.; from 12:30 p.m. Sat.; no boats Sun.)*, the c. 1360 castle/prison *(open April–Oct. Mon.–Fri. 10 a.m.–5 p.m., Sat.–Sun., 1–5 p.m., guided tours every half hour, last 4 p.m.)* from which Grotius made his famous escape (see *Benelux Cultural Legacy, The Muse*). **Oirschot** (northwest of Eindhoven) has the most attractive and best preserved market square in Brabant (with cobblestones, shady old trees, gas lamps, and the dignified calm of centuries), and the entire town center is a national monument, including the Stadhuis (1463) and Gothic St. Pieterskerk (1465–1500). **Bergen op Zoom,** a historic town in the west of North Brabant, where the dunes meet the heath, has a Grote Markt that's carefree with cafes in summer, and buildings that reflect its past, including the last 15th-century **Markiezenhof** palace, now a museum.

GETTING AROUND Since sights of interest to the traveler are scattered, a car is nearly necessary for seeing your selected sites in a reasonable time frame. As everywhere in Holland, there is excellent provincial bus service, but it is time-consuming. Trains serve the major towns: 's Hertogenbosch (Den Bosch); Breda; Eindhoven; Bergen op Zoom. Boat cruises (tel: 566773) from Den Bosch to **Heusden** *(Tues., Thurs., Sat. 11 a.m. mid-June through Aug.)* and **Woudrichem** *(daily at 10 a.m. mid-June to late Aug.)* leave from the Dommel, near the town's train station.

SHOPPING Obviously, branches of main Dutch stores will be found in the centers of cities and major towns, virtually all located on pedestrian streets.

ENTERTAINMENT AND EVENTS Breda celebrates the pre-Lenten **Carnival** with the most vigor in North Brabant, though Bergen op Zoom and Den Bosch hold their own. In addition to its annual **Art and Antiques Fair,** Breda hosts the colorful **National Tattoo** at the end of each August, and a jazz festival then as well, with performances set mostly in the Grote Kerk. In mid-August, the Grote Kerk is decked out in flowers for *Breda Flora.* Den Bosch has an important annual vocalist competition, and in September Tilburg and Eindhoven have jazz festivals.

ACCOMMODATIONS While there are pleasant town and country choices in the two, three and, occasionally, four-star categories, five-star luxury is not available (except for a business hotel in Eindhoven). As elsewhere in Holland, the local VVVs are the most up-to-date accommodations authorities.

RESTAURANTS Anchovies from Bergen op Zoom can raise a thirst for Brabant-brewed beer. In May and June, asparagus is the traditional treat, and locally-favored sweet specialties include the Den Bosch "Bossche koek" (cake). Both rural bistros and highly-regarded restaurants reflect a Burgundian fondness for fine food.

TRAVEL TIPS When exploring by car in regions near rivers, check your map carefully, and ask questions locally, to make sure of the location of bridge and/or car ferry crossings.

ON THE ROAD ....

's Hertogenbosch

VVV Markt 77; Mon–Fri. 9 a.m.–5:00 p.m., Sat. 4 p.m., 123071; pop. 90,000; telephone code 073) • North Brabant's provincial town is the pleasant smaller city of **'s Hertogenbosch (Den Bosch,** pronounced Den BOSS). Its center is the enclosed triangle of the **Markt,** which has a bronze statue of painter **Hieronymus Bosch** (1450–1516) who was born there. The Markt plays host to Wednesday and Saturday morning markets (on Wed. accompanied on the **Stadhuis** Hemony carillon from 10–11 a.m.). The Stadhuis has a remodeled classic Dutch facade (1670) and interior wall paintings, tapestries, and other objects in the Council Chamber worth seeing (normally open during business hours).

The village of 's Hertogenbosch ("the dukes' woods") grew up around the early 13th-century **De Moriaan,** built by Henry I, Duke of Brabant (who conferred a charter on the town in 1185) as a hunting lodge. It now houses the VVV on the Markt. There, you can pick up a leaflet *Wandering around Old Den Bosch,* which will send you to, among other places, the restored **Uilenburg Quarter,** a canal, arched bridge, gallery, boutique, and bistro pedestrian neighborhood not far from the Markt. Much of the core of the city is closed to vehicular traffic, and public sculptures to notice along the way make the walk to the town's most outstanding attraction a pleasure.

Sint Janskathedraal (St. Janskerkhof; check at VVV for hours) The finest example of late Gothic architecture in Holland, this could be your sole reason for a visit to Den Bosch, especially since it was fully restored to splendor not long ago. Sint Jan's, built between 1380 and 1552 under the auspices of the Bishop of Liege, took its share of shuttling back and forth between Catholic and Protestant rites, but finally settled with Catholicism (thanks to Napoleon) in 1810; in 1929 the Pope conferred the status of basilica upon the structure. The building's blend of Romanesque brickwork and Perpendicular-style carved stonework has been compared to that of England's Lincoln Cathedral. Sint Jan's tower's progression through various architectural ages can be seen as it ascends, from Romanesque base to slender 17th-century Baroque spire, with Gothic bringing up the midsection. The small figures, a hundred individual *gargoyles* groping about the buttresses, are one of the most distinguishing details of the exterior (copies of some of the small figures are sold as souvenirs in town). Inside, the double-aisled nave, which appears especially lofty owing to the lack of capitals in the main arcade, carries one's view to the choir. Among the specifics that warrant attention are the solid copper 1492 font, the many restored flat floor tombs, the north transept's two grisaille works by **Hieronymus Bosch,** and, near the south transept, the "Altar of Passion," an Antwerp retable from 1500. The monumental 17th-century *organ* casing by Symons and Schysler with an 18th-century instrument by Heyneman is one of the largest and most beautiful in Europe. Concerts on the 48-bell carillon are given Wed. noon–1 p.m., and the tower can be climbed on certain days in summer (inquire within).

Noord Brabant Museum • *Verwersstraat 41; Tues.–Fri., 10 a.m.– 5 p.m., Sat. & Sun., noon–5 p.m.* • Established in 1837, and moved into the restored and enlarged 1769 Government House palace (until recently the residence for provincial governors) a hundred and fifty years later, the Museum has displays on all facets of North Brabant life as befits a building with the Brabant coat of arms on its facade. Among the many exhibits are two early "dark" period Van Gogh's painted in Brabant, and views of Den Bosch over its long history.

ACCOMMODATIONS ★★★★ **Golden Tulip Central** • *Markt 51, entrance Mr. Loeffplein 98, 5211 RX; 125151, fax 145699, res. in USA 800-333-1212; First Class* • A modern hotel with a fine location on the Markt (entrance at the back), the Central has 122 rooms; many on the higher floors have fine views of the square. Breakfast (not included) is served in the hotel's 14th-century vaulted cellar. The comfortable indoor-outdoor lobby cafe fronts the Markt. There's also a restaurant. Parking garage next door.

RESTAURANTS Raadskelder • *Stadhuis cellar; 136919; moderate* • restaurant in the venerable brick vaults of the Stadhuis basement serves a full menu of well-prepared, traditional fare in the soft light of wrought-iron chandeliers. There's a bar-lounge if you want the atmosphere but just a drink. **Pumpke** • *Parade 37; daily; inexpensive* • has outside tables on a square from which you can face the splendid structure of St. Jans. Enjoy the view over coffee or a light meal.

Heusden

VVV Engstraat 4, daily in summer 10 a.m.–5 p.m., 04162-2100; pop. 2,000 within fortified town • Here there are no "must-see" museums, just the pleasure of enjoying an enchanting old fortified town on the river Maas with more than 400 historic buildings that have been recently and lovingly restored. The centuries-old streets, cobbled market, tucked-away squares, stepgables, gablestones, the windmill by the little former fishing harbor (now for yachts), and, of course, the view across the river and over the canals of this former Roman settlement won't fall short of your scenic needs. There are unearthed ramparts and town walls from the 17th century on which to walk *around* the town. Heusden has bus service to/from Den Bosch.

ACCOMMODATIONS ★★★ **"In Den Verdwaalde Koogel" Hotel-Restaurant** • *Vismarkt 1, 5256 BC; 04162-1933, fax 04162-1295; inexpensive* • is a step-gabled delight dating from the 17th century, all of its 13 rooms restored outside and inside, each individually decorated, with private toilet and shower, TV, telephone, and mini-bar. The spirit of service of the management ("In North Brabant, you're only a stranger once"), setting (an interior of tasteful contemporary furnishings amid brick and old beams), and a terrace cafe on the lovely main square in sight of the historic harbor windmill, all assure a pleasant stay. And so does the reputable kitchen of the restaurant *(lunch and dinner daily, noon–2:30 p.m., 6–9:30 p.m.)*, which offers various multi-course daily menus, and full *a la carte* selection, especially the house paté, lamb, and the lovely, lean, local pork (the province has 3.2 pigs for every person).

RESTAURANTS • In addition to **In Den Verdwaalde Koogel** above, try **De Pannenkoekbakker** *(Vismarkt 4; 04162-2100)* for savory or sweet meal-on-a-plate Dutch pancakes, or **Cafe Havenzicht** (harbor view) *(Vismarkt 2; 04162-2723)* for a variety of appealing informal fare on the square or inside.

Breda

VVV near station, Willemstraat 17, Mon.–Sat. 9 a.m.–6 p.m., 5 p.m. Sat.; 222444; pop. 120,000; telephone code 076 • One of the chief, and most attractive, towns in the province, with most of its monuments in the old center, Breda has a long, turbulent history as a fortified town near the border of Belgium. There has always been a quiet corner in Breda, however, at the **Beguinhof,** whose history goes back to 1267, and situation on the present site dates from 1531. Small brick houses, restored in 1980, encircle the ancient garden courtyard, decorated with a delightful contemporary statue of two beguines by Amsterdam sculptor Hans Bayens. Behind the Begijnhof is Breda's large in-town *Valkenberg Park.*

The **Castle of Breda** grew from the first stronghold built by the *Heren* (Lords) *of Breda* on the site in 1198, and was later enlarged into a grand palace by the famous Italian architect Tomaso Vincidor of Bologna. From the castle, **Charles II,** who had lived in Breda in exile for some time, set forth in the *Declaration of Breda* (1660) the terms upon which he would sit on the throne of England. The *Treaty of Breda* (1667), also signed at the Castle, awarded the colony of *Nieuw Amster-*

dam (New York) to the English. Since 1828, the castle has housed Breda's important **Royal Military Academy** (no visitors except during the late August evening performances of the colorful **National Tattoo** in the forecourt). The Lords of Breda who lived in the Castle were the scions of the Netherlands' House of Oranje-Nassau. Count Hendrik III of Nassau, a tutor and counselor to Emperor Charles V, was an influencial ruler in the early 16th-century, and did much to aid the reconstruction of Breda following the town's great fire in 1534.

Not far from the Castle is the **Spanjaardsgat** (Spaniards Gate), two heptagonal towers with watergate that were added to the 16th-century fortifications of the city in 1610. Its name stems from an inaccurate association with a historic event that took place in Breda on Shrove Tuesday in 1590. In 1581 Breda had been occupied by the Spanish, who had a stronghold in the nearby southern Netherlands (now Belgium). The surprise attack was probably in retaliation for the town's role in the *Compromise of Breda* (1566), the first document signed by Dutch noblemen denouncing Spanish dominion. However, in 1590, in a Trojan-horse kind of caper, Maurice of Nassau was able to retake the town when 80 of his men, hidden under peat turves in the barge of Adriaen van Bergen, who supplied the Spanish garrison with fuel, were towed into the center of town under the unknowing noses of the occupying forces, who were quickly overpowered (the Spanish retook Breda in 1625.)

The heart of Breda is the **Grote Markt,** where the citizens go to market Tues. and Fri. mornings, drink beer at the many cafes, and, for one long weekend of the year, revel at *Carnival*. In the **Stadhuis** (1767) is a large reproduction of the famous Velasquez painting "Las Lanzas," which shows the surrender of Breda to the Spanish commander Spinola in 1625. At Grote Markt 19 is **Het Lam,** an exceptional 17th-century building that houses the municipal museum *(Wed.–Sat., 10:30 a.m.–1 p.m., Tues., Sun., Hol. 1–5 p.m.)*. The neighboring former meat hall carries sculpted heads of cattle on its facade.

At the northern end of the Markt is the **Grote Kerk,** begun in the 13th century and noted for its many monuments, triptych by **Jan van Scorel** (1495–1562), and copper lattice-work. The church has played an important role in the history of the Oranje-Nassau dynasty; all the related lords of Breda prior to Willem the Silent are buried here, their tombs memorials to history as well as works of art. Beneath the magnificent alabaster mausoleum of Count Engelbert II (who died in 1504), is buried his grandson, **Rene de Chalons,** the first Prince of Oranje-Nassau (died 1544). In 1552 his successor Willem the Silent, Prince of Orange, who became known as the "Father of the Fatherland," had the vault enlarged, probably for himself. However, when Willem was assassinated at the Prinsenhof in Delft in 1584, Breda was still held by the Spanish, and thus Delft's Nieuwe Kerk became the burial site for Willem and all succeeding members of the House of Orange. The church's lacy-looking tower (97 meters/318 feet) has a carillon (concerts twice a week), and can be climbed (276 steps). A 25-year renovation was completed in 1969; originally built in 1509, the tower burned when struck by lighting in 1694, and was replaced as a gift by King Willem III.

ACCOMMODATIONS ★★★ **De Klok** • *Grote Markt 26, 4811 XR; 214082, fax 143463; moderate* • If you want to be in the midst of the grandeur of the Grote Markt, stay in a front-facing room at this small (23 room) unpretentious hotel, which has its own cafe and bar, and private facilities in most rooms, TV in all. There's an elevator, but no parking.

RESTAURANTS Offering a view of the Grote Kerk, a superb Renaissance setting of its own, and exceptional food (a combination that's hard to beat), is **Auberge de Arent** *(Schoolstraat 2; lunch and dinner; for res. 144601; expensive)*. The restaurant space has a high, painted ceiling, a Baroque fireplace, and fresh-flower-decorated tables set out on a black and white checkerboard marble floor. French and Dutch-inspired dishes, well-served from a choice of *prix-fixe* or the *a la carte* menus. The **Cafe Franciskaner** *(Grote Markt 23; daily; inexpensive)*, only one of a number of establishments on the congenial, cafe-cluttered square, is a local favorite for *koffie en gebak* (coffee and pastry) or other snacks.

Baarle-Nassau-Baarle-Hertog

VVV St. Annaplein 10, 04257-9921; pop. 7,500; bus service from Breda, 19 km/12 mi.) • This *one town-two country* place arouses the curiosity of almost everyone who hears about it, and the civic complications that arise from its geo-political status raises smiles in those of us for whom the world is overly bureaucratic. Parts of the town are legally Dutch and others legally Belgian. Different laws apply in the two sectors. Thus, there are two burgomasters, two stadhuizen, two police forces, two school systems, and two taxes systems; townsfolk buying chocolate and cigars go to Belgian shops, where a lower rate makes them cheaper. The nationality of a house that straddles both Belgian and Dutch territory—a common occurrence, since the town's numerous small enclaves of land criss-cross all over the map—is determined by the location of the front door; a house number plate indicates by its design which country one's in. Naturally, there's at least one edifice in which the front door itself opens on both Belgian and Dutch soil. One such building, **Het Huis op Loveren 2 en 19,** is the former Swan Inn, whose records show that

Grotius (see *The Muse* under *The Benelux Cultural Legacy*) spent the night of March 22–23, 1631, en route on his escape from Loevestein prison to Antwerp. Even jurists as learned as Grotius (considered the father of international law) haven't solved all the problems associated with Baarle-style situations: When the going gets complicated, transactions take place at the **Cafe Het Hoekske**—through which the national frontier runs, as indicated by a painting on the outside wall—in the presence of both a Dutch and a Belgian notary.

Historians aren't entirely sure why Belgian enclaves exist in Dutch territory, though the confusing condition is said to have its roots in inheritance disputes in 1198, between Duke Henry I of Brabant, who had the Baarle-Hertog lands, and Godfrey, Lord of Breda, who, with the additional identity of Count of Nassau, held the Baarle-Nassau estates. At the *Peace of Westphalia* (1648), the Baarle that had belonged to Nassau was given to the northern Dutch United Provinces, and the part that had belonged to the Duke (Hertog) was awarded to the southern Netherlands (now Belgium). This singular situation remained unchanged even after 1843, when the frontier of the at-long-last legally separated countries of Holland and Belgium was formally established. Over the centuries many attempts have been made to find a remedy for what outsiders consider an abnormal and untenable condition, but which some of the local populace refer to as a "precious inheritance." Its circumstances did save Baarle-Hertog from the German occupation suffered by the rest of Belgium in World War I. Then, in spite of Dutch Baarle surrounding itself with barbed-wire fencing to signal *its* neutrality, Belgian Baarle in October 1915 established a radio station which made the village an important outpost for Allied espionage.

Neunen

Ardent fans of **Vincent van Gogh** will find interest in this otherwise ordinary town of 20,000, a suburb to the southwest of Eindhoven. The **Van Gogh Documentation Center** *(Papenvoort 15; Mon.–Fri., 9 a.m.–noon & 2–4 p.m., except closed the first and third Fri. of the month)* gives a picture of the period when Vincent lived and worked here, with exhibits of photographs, reproductions, and numerous original works of art produced during his Nuenen period. The Center, opened by Vincent's nephew Vincent (son of the artist's supportive brother Theo) in 1976, has a self-guiding brochure to the places in Neunen that are associated with Van Gogh. Many have hardly changed, and are recognizable in his paintings and drawings. Vincent came to Neunen, where his father was minister of the Protestant Dutch Reformed Church on Papenvoort, in 1883, at the age of 30. He lived at #26 on the Main Road (still standing, dated 1764 in iron numbers, today the church rectory) with his parents for much of that period, until 1885 when he left the town. His parents furnished a shed in their back garden (visible from the road behind the house) as a studio for Vincent, who worked intensely on his art while he lived in Nuenen. At the time, this Kempen region of Brabant relied mainly on agriculture and weaving, and Vincent often helped with tilling the soil. His admiration for the peasants and the way in which they literally ploughed their way through the heavy work and their hard life increased, and he created many well-known paintings and drawings of them. It was in Nuenen that Van Gogh produced the works of his early "dark" Dutch period, under the influence of Rembrandt and his effects of light and shadow *(chiaroscuro)*, and painted his first masterpiece (both in Vincent's and art historians' opinion): *The Potato Eaters* (April 1885). He left Nuenen (then a community of about 2,000 people who, other than the peasant workers he befriended, generally regarded Vincent as an odd character) after a painful love affair that was ended by the family of his beloved, Margot Begemann, who then tried to take her own life.

Note: Van Gogh was born in the North Brabant town of **Zundert** (several miles south of Breda, close to the Belgian border), but his childhood home has been demolished (although near the site is the small Vincent van Gogh Plein, with a statue *Vincent and Theo* by **Ossip Zadkine**). There's little else to see except, in the graveyard of the church where his father was minister, a marker for a year-older brother *Vincent* who died in infancy (the re-use of a Christian name under such circumstances was quite common in those days).

LIMBURG PROVINCE

Limburg Province essentially is a north-south strip of land that stretches roughly 50 kms./30 miles along the border in the southeast of the country that Holland shares with Germany. The Dutch Limburg forms a wedge into Belgium's Limburg province. The two Limburgs once were one, under the early bishoprics of Tongeren, then Maastricht, and finally Liège. Under the *Treaty of Munster* in 1648, the Spanish kept the southern portion of Limburg, but the Dutch United Provinces in the northern Netherlands received Maastricht and all Limburg east of the Maas (Meuse) River. In 1814, the two Limburgs were rejoined under the short-lived Dutch-Belgian United Kingdom of the Netherlands. In

1830, all of Limburg except Maastricht joined in the Belgian uprising against Dutch rule. Thereafter, Limburgers in the north regarded themselves as Belgian until divided again by the 1839 *Treaty of London,* under which the borders of the present Dutch Limburg province were set.

The northern part of Limburg province is made up largely of small industrial towns with rather uninspiring landscape, and travelers will find few sights of sufficient interest to warrant a stop. Exceptions include **Thorn,** cobbled, medieval, and known as the "white village," an epithet derived from its all-painted-white buildings. There's an interesting 13th-century Gothic abbey church with Baroque interior *(open daily, 9 a.m.–6 p.m., Easter–Oct.).* Also worthy of a while is the old center of **Sittard,** around whose spacious Markt (parking, terrace cafes, shops) stand a number of 16th-century half-timbered structures. In the town center of **Heerlen** is the **Thermen Museum** *(Tues.–Fri., 10 a.m.– 5 p.m., Sat., Sun., hols. 2–5 p.m.; 045-764581)* with Roman baths, excavated in the 1970s, imaginatively on view from a bridge above, and museum of related exhibits (descriptions in English) and maps of the important Roman roads that led through Heerlen.

It is the south of Limburg that is the far more physically attractive portion of the province, with wooded rolling hills unlike the landscape anywhere else in Holland. The summer holiday heart of the region is **Valkenburg,** a bustling, family-style place, with countless hotels, casino, and new *Thermae 2000* spa complex. But for most travelers, the most attractive, interesting, and historic place in Limburg by far is **Maastricht.** Only 125 miles from Amsterdam, diagonally across the country, Maastricht seems far more distant in the difference of its ambience.

MAASTRICHT

Guidelines for Maastricht

SIGHTS Maastricht, with a population of 115,000, has an appealing and compact old center, with narrow cobbled streets, quaint squares, and some 1,450 protected historic monuments, the oldest from Roman days. The mellow yellow stone buildings of local marl in the restored pedestrian **Stokstraat Quarter** are from the 17th and 18th centuries, and many have sculpted gable stones. Maastricht, with its assemblage of churches (Romanesque and Gothic) and cafes, is ringed by rampart walls (built in 1229, 1350, and 1516 respectively), atop which one can circle much of the town. The riverfront adds interest to the city, which is divided by the Maas, and connected by the St. Servaas Bridge, the first version of which was a 13th-century wooden span with nine arches.

GETTING AROUND Maastricht's mood is best met on foot; walking allows for poking into picturesque corners, glancing up at gables and gablestones, and making spontaneous stops where and when your senses are engaged. The VVV offers guided 1½ hr. **walking tours** of the city *(daily at 2 p.m. on holiday weekends, and July and Aug.; Sat. only April–June and Sept.–mid Nov.).* The VVV also rents a "walkman" cassette taped tour of the city, sells the architecturally detailed book *A Walk Through Maastricht,* and supplies other self-guided walking tour literature. City buses provide coverage of the outskirts, and you can go by river cruise boat to see the St. Pietersburg caves. Taxis and rental bicycles can be had at the station.

SHOPPING For such a relatively small city, Maastricht has surprisingly sophisticated shops, ranging from boutiques to bakeries. Many of the main department and other stores are located on and just off the pedestrianized **Grote Straat,** which leads to the **Vrijthof** (main square). General markets are held on Marktplein in front of the Stadhuis Wednesdays and Fridays. Summer Saturdays from 10 a.m.–4 p.m. there are flea, antique, and art markets on the Markt. Late night shopping (9 p.m.) is on Thursday.

ENTERTAINMENT AND EVENTS Available free from the VVV is the monthly events calendar *Maastricht Maandagenda;* there's a summary listing in English. Cafes, concerts, and **pub crawls** cover the favored evening activities. Maastrichtenaars enjoy the fact that their city has a church for every *week,* and a pub for every *day,* in the *year.* A number of the pub/cafes have live music, and many remain open until 2 a.m. In summer, weekly evening organ concerts (usually Tuesday) are held at one of several churches. The well-known male choir **Mastreechter Staar** has free open rehersals (except July and Aug.; details from the VVV). Maastricht is in **Carnival** country, the southern section of the Netherlands that is largely Roman Catholic and makes much of pre-lenten festivities; some museums are closed from the Saturday before through *Mardi Gras* (the Tuesday before the Ash Wednesday start of Lent, dates vary). The Burgundian food festival of **Preuvenement** fits in with the city's intense interest in cuisine.

ACCOMMODATIONS Maastricht offers a small but solid choice of hotels in the city. Many are family-owned and operated; all deliver friendly, personal service. In the surrounding Limburg countryside are several castle/manor house-style hotels with renowned restaurants.

RESTAURANTS Without contest, this region is the cuisine capital of The Netherlands. Fresh produce and attention to preparation make it hard to find less than fine food at any eatery, but some restaurants really star on taste tests.

ARRIVING Tucked into the far southeast corner of the Netherlands—which gives it almost a central continental location—Maastricht is a Dutch destination that can easily be included in an itinerary featuring France, Germany, Switzerland, and, of course, Belgium and Luxembourg. Maastricht is readily reached by rail, road, and air. There are hourly train arrivals from Amsterdam, an *Intercity* that takes about 2.5 hours. Rail connections from The Hague and Rotterdam have a convenient cross-platform change at Eindhoven. Maastricht also is served hourly by trains from Belgium's Bruges, Ghent, Brussels, and Liège, and other international points. Via motorway, Maastricht is 215 kms./125 mi. by road from Amsterdam, and lies roughly halfway between Brussels and Cologne. Maastricht's modern airfield offers, among other service, several flights daily to/from Amsterdam on *NLM Cityhopper* (contact **KLM** for flight information) and to/from London.

IN THE AREA The only U.S. military cemetery in the Netherlands is at nearby *Margraten*. Old fortified farms, villages with half-timbered buildings, and country castles scattered in the pleasantly rolling hills of southern Limburg. Liège, the capital of Belgium's French-speaking Wallonia, is only 20 kms./12 mi. (see under Belgium).

TRAVEL TIPS If you don't plan to have a rental car in this rural region of the Netherlands, you needn't worry about missing the province's most important historic and sightseeing highlights, since these are in Maastricht itself. The cruise along the River Maas to Liège, Belgium, is *not* recommended, since the riverside scenery does not justify the length of time the trip takes (several hours one way); if travelling to Liège, take a quick train instead.

Maastricht in Context

Maastricht isn't a name that readily rolls off the tongues of tourists, even those fairly familiar with Holland, but it's nonetheless—and, perhaps, decidedly more—worthy of discovery for that. Maastricht is the Netherlands' oldest, southernmost (it lies well below Belgium's northern border), and most unexpected city. For starters, the people of Maastricht practice an almost unDutch-like indulgence in the good life, exhibiting a Burgundian *joie de vivre,* and focusing on fine food, drink, and fun. As one resident put it, "We don't have a lazy mentality, but we do enjoy life." That attitude contrasts sharply with the "Black Stocking Church" (the conservative, very religious element of the Protestant Dutch Reformed Church found in the north of the country), which undoubtedly would be shocked by the attitude held *here:* "Catholicism allows you to enjoy yourself."

In Maastricht and surrounding Limburg, features commonly associated with Holland—water-logged land, windmills, wooden shoes—make way for other characteristics in the intriguing territory of this tricultured corner of the country. With **Aachen,** Germany (the ancient city inseparably associated with Charlemagne and the Holy Roman Empire), and **Liège, Belgium** (the capital of French-speaking Wallonia), each only a dozen miles (20 km.) away, Maastricht merchants have long accepted *marks* and *francs* as freely as *guilders,* providing a foretaste of the European monetary dexterity anticipated under the EC's "single market" economic initiatives.

The Maastricht "mentality" encompasses the foreign influences of its nearby neighbors. As one guide put it, "In Maastricht we live and let live. Sometimes those who are surrounded only by their own kind become judgmental, but this doesn't happen in Maastricht where so many things mix." Many Maastrichtenaars might be called chauvinists, in that they love their city above all others, but, as one city official put it, "People like us who live in places where their history has gone back and forth feel European or international, not overly nationalistic." Another expressed it this way: "We don't feel we're crossing a border when we go to Belgium or Germany, but we do feel we've come home when we get back to Maastricht."

Maastricht was founded by the **Romans** about 50 B.C. Its name derived from the Latin *Mosae Trajectum,* meaning "site where the Maas could be crossed." The settlement, which grew to become a walled *castellum* (fortified district), was located on important roads, the foremost of which ran from the English Channel and North Sea ports to Cologne, and was known as the "Appian Way of the North." Towards the end of the 4th century, after 400 years of occupation during which Maastricht became a center of Christianity, the Romans and their army withdrew to return to Rome, leaving the city vulnerable to attack by

Frankish tribes and, later, the Norsemen. Their raids were among the first of more than twenty beseigements suffered by Maastricht over succeeding centuries, the most recent being the four-year Nazi occupation during World War II. That ended in September 1944, when the 30th Infantry "Old Hickory" Division of the *U.S. 1st. Army* made Maastricht the first town in the war-ravaged Netherlands to be freed.

From A.D. 380 to 721, Maastricht was a bishop's seat, becoming so when **St. Servaas,** fearing the Frankish tribes, transferred the see from Tongeren (the oldest town in Belgium) to Maastricht before he died. A small chapel was built on the site where he was buried, and several centuries later a cathedral named for him began taking shape there. **St. Hubert,** Maastricht's last bishop, transferred the see to Liège in 721 (which eventually led to an era of great power for the prince-bishops there).

Maastricht came under the influence and favor of Charlemagne's Frankish Empire when the Holy Roman Emperor made his base at nearby Aachen (Germany). Having survived the turbulent centuries following the death of Charlemagne (in 814), Maastricht became, in 1204, a joint possession of the dukes of Brabant and the prince-bishops of Liège. With feudal fending required to keep itself intact, Maastricht erected its first protective ramparts in 1229; it wasn't long before the town outgrew them, and a second set was added about 1350 (sections of each still stand). These were the earliest of many bastions that eventually made Maastricht one of Europe's most strongly fortified cities—with its strategic position, the armies of the Spanish, French, English, and Germans too often over the centuries beat a path to the city's sturdy town gates.

In 1576, Maastricht joined with Willem the Silent's other Dutch supporters in the rebellion against the Spanish. But, in 1579, Spanish leader the Duke of Parma paid the city back with a four-month seige and ruthless sacking. Secular war Maastricht saw plenty of, but, because it had the traditions of both Protestantism (through the House of Orange) and Roman Catholicism (being within the realm of the nearby Bishop of Liège), the city escaped the sacred outbursts of the *Iconoclast* and other religious outbreaks of the Reformation. Eventually, most of the citizens settled on the Catholic faith (about 90% of the population today).

In 1673, the city fell to the French, in one of Maastricht's most famous beseigements due to its cast of characters. That year, French king and army commander Louis XIV stood on a hilltop watching his forces, among which was **D'Artagnan,** a captain in the **Musketeers** (and inspiration for Alexandre Dumas' novel *The Three Musketeers*), and the 6,000 troops of England's Duke of Monmouth, who had pledged aid to Louis against the Dutch United Provinces. During the seige Captain John Churchill (later Duke of Marlborough, ancestor of Winston Churchill) was rescued by D'Artagnan, who lost his life in doing so.

D'Artagnan is remembered by a statue, supposedly marking the spot at which he fell, in Maastricht's **Waldeckpark**.

In 1795, the once-again occupying French made Maastricht the capital of the newly-created **Department of the Lower Meuse**. After Napoleon's defeat at Waterloo (1815), Belgium and the Netherlands were ordered to unite under the Dutch King William I. But, after battling over the union for nine years (1830–1839), the two countries adopted a partition. Some citizens in Maastricht, perhaps because of the logic of their geographic location, at the time wanted to join with Belgium, but the Dutch garrison that occupied Maastricht decreed otherwise. Thus, the ancient province of Limburg was split in two, with Maastricht remaining a part of the Netherlands.

Today it's possible to say that Maastricht has the best of both countries: Dutch-style tidiness and tolerance, combined with a Belgian-style appreciation for the fine art of the kitchen and "cafe-society."

GUIDEPOSTS
Telephone code 043

Tourist Info	VVV, Het Dinghuis, Kleine Staat 1; Mon.–Sat. 9 a.m.–6 p.m. (from end June–August til 7 p.m., also Sun. 11 a.m.–3 p.m.); Carnival and some holidays 11 a.m.–3 p.m.).; 252121). Bookings for guided walking tours of city, tours of limited access sites, St. Pietersburg caves, casements, Derlon Museum Cellar, river cruises, day coach trips VVV shop with maps, pamphlets, books, prints, posters, gifts.
Parking	Parking garage beneath Vrijthof in center.
Post Office	Corner of Vrijthof and Statenstraat, Mon.–Fri. 8 a.m.–7 p.m., Thurs. til 8 p.m., Sat. 9 a.m.–noon.
Emergency	Police 292222, health 293333.
Bike rental	At the Railway Station bicycle stall, 6 am–midnight, 1 am Sat. & Sun. 211100. Dfl. 7 per day, Dfl. 28 per week.
Cruises	Stiphout Cruises, Maaspromenade 27; daily Maas River cruises from mid-April–Sept., on the hour 10 a.m.–5 p.m., Sun. 1–5 p.m., 55 mins.; 254151.
Taxis	In front of the rail station.

Recreation The VVV has information on the full range of recreational opportunities in Maastricht, including fishing (license required)), archery, tennis, Jeu de Boules (public courts, sets can be rented), and Kayak Tours Limburg for kayak day trips on safe "white-water" on un-canalized stretches of the Maas.

WHAT TO SEE AND DO......................

The whole of Maastricht city center is a protected area due to its wealth of historic buildings (at least 1,450). New and renovated buildings by law must be adapted to their surroundings. The old city is a strolling, cafe-sitting, settling-in at a cozy restaurant paced place. Students at the city's faculties for translation studies, music, and hotel management contribute to the city's atmosphere. **Vrijthof Square,** Maastricht's largest square by far, is generally considered to be the center of the city. The expansive space is surrounded by interesting structures, not the least of which are an uninterrupted row of terrace cafes (sidewalk cafes) settled along its east side. Use the VVV brochure *Maastricht Fortifications Walk* as your guide for a walk on the city walls, the **Pesthuis** being a good place to mount the ramparts. For a good view back to the ramparts, visit **Waldeckpark,** near Tongerseplein. Note that the 17th-century Waldeck Bastion is where Chevalier D'Artagnan, the famous French musketeer, was felled June 25, 1673. **Grote Looiersstraat** (with its French-flavored, tree-shaded center mall where you may see men playing *jeu de boules*) and **Ezel Markt** (with its donkey sculpture and fine view of the pretty 17th-century **Huys op den Jeker,** which straddles that stream) are two delightful corners of the city to see. Year-round many historic buildings are floodlit after dark, and from mid-June to mid-September and on bank holidays, additional monuments are illuminated, from dark until the wee hours.

Het Dinghuis • *Kleine Staat 1; same hours as VVV, given above* • Today the headquarters of Maastricht's VVV tourist office (ground floor), Het Dinghuis, dating from about 1470, with its beautiful stone gable and a timbered wall on the Jodenstraat side, is the most striking example of Maastricht's many saddleback buildings, with steeply slanting roofs that provided much needed storage space for staples to ensure survival through the sieges that have been so much a part of the city's history.

Bonnefanten Museum • *Dominicanerplein; Tues.–Fri., 10 a.m.–5 p.m.; Sat., Sun. & hol. 11 a.m.–5 p.m.; 251655* • The collection of Maastricht's main museum, housed in a modern building, includes rich archaeological holdings: The Maas valley has been a timeline of cultures for more than a quarter of a million years, and Maastricht is one of the very few European cities that has been inhabited continuously since the Roman period. Also shown are fossils found in the area's marl caves (the table-land was formed 80 million years ago). Maastricht's **Natural History Museum** displays a particularly wide variety of fossils that were found in the local St. Pietersberg caves. Napoleon once found there the fossilized head of a massive lizard (known as the "Meuse Lizard"), which experts estimate must have been 20 meters/66 feet long. It was so admirable that he was willing to exchange 500 bottles of fine French wine for it. The Bonnefanten Museum's fine arts collection includes sculpture from the Romanesque and Gothic periods, Italian paintings of the 14–16th centuries, 16th–18th century paintings from the southern Netherlands, including several Brueghels, and an expanding contemporary section. Also of interest is the maquette (model) of Maastricht, a modern copy of a 1748 "relief model" of the city (the original is in Paris' Hotel des Invalides) that French officers built as a military seige study, with descriptive slide show.

Spanish Government House • *Vrijthof 18; Wed. 2–5 p.m., Thurs. 10 a.m.–1 p.m. & 2–5 p.m., from April 1–Oct. 31 also Sat. 10 a.m.–1 p.m.; 292201* • This 16th-century furnished mansion, once headquarters for Spanish officials, has a rich collection of Dutch, Flemish, French and Italian antique furnishings and decorative art.

Derlon Museum Cellar • *Hotel Derlon, Onze Lieve Vrouweplein 6; Sundays 1–5 p.m., or through VVV tours* • Since there had been Roman and medieval finds in this oldest part of Maastricht before (in nearby **Op de Thermae** square the outlines of a Roman bath are indicated on the pavement), prior to excavation (1983) for the most recent hotel on the site, a major archaeological investigation was carried out by the municipality. The astonishing result, the discovery of a 6-meter/20 feet deep virtually undisturbed stratum of the city's history from the first century to the 14th, was in large part preserved through altered building plans, and is on public display as a unique cellar museum beneath the modern Hotel Derlon. On view are a 1st-century cobbled Roman road, a 2nd-century Roman temple square, and a wall that is part of a 4th-century Roman fort (castellum) that once covered the entire Stokstraat quarter.

Stadhuis • *Markt 78; Mon–Fri. 8:30 a.m.–12:30 p.m. and 2–5:30 p.m.; 292222* • Built in the years between 1659–1664, the building is one of the most important works by Dutch architect **Pieter Post.** The interior (the imposing domed entrance hall is open to the public, possibly other rooms), with its original antique furniture and parquet floors polished to a glowing patina, could easily be a museum in its own right. The rooms feature tapestries (Gobelins and Brussels), stucco work, painted ceilings, leather wall hangings, and mantelpieces. The Stadhuis tower dates from 1684, and contains a carillon (bought before the tower was even built) of 43 bells, 17 of which were cast by the Hemony brothers. It's regularly played on Fridays from 11:30 a.m.–12:30 p.m. by the town carillonuer, with additional concerts scheduled in summer. The **Markt,** the square in front of the Stadhuis, is the scene of Wednesday and Friday markets, and a 1902 sculpture with an eternal gas flame that honors the Maastricht chemist S.P. Minckelers (1784–1824), the inventor of gas lighting.

St. Servaasbasiliek • *Vrijthof; daily 10 a.m.–5 p.m. (4 p.m. winter, 6 p.m. summer* • St. Servaas, a massive Romanesque church, reopened in May 1990 following several years of large-scale interior and exterior restoration that produced a magnificent result. The body of this medieval cruciform basilica dates from c. 1000, but its soul and name come from St. Servaas (St. Servatius), the first bishop of Maastricht, who moved the bishop's See from Tongres (in Belgium) to Maastricht in the late 4th century. The Treasure Chamber has been part of the basilica since A.D. 827, and its collection of reliquaries is renowned, the showpiece being an arm in silver that contains an arm bone belonging to the apostle Thomas, a gift from the Crusader Godfrey of Bouillon (see Belgium, Bouillon) in 1099. St. Servaas has a carillon upon which some summer concerts are played.

St. Janskerk • *Vrijthof Square; June 15–Sept. 15, Tues.–Fri. 11 a.m.–4 p.m., also on Sat. in July & Aug.* • Although St. Jan's, dating from the 14th century, is Maastricht's finest Gothic church, its 256-foot spire (which, above the plain stone building, is a surprising red color, the result of a mineral covering used to make the surface harder) is not entirely successful in its attempt to match the soaring grace of Utrecht's Domtoren, after which it was modelled. Originally built to be the parish church to St. Servaas, St. Jan's was designated the Netherlands Protestant Church in 1632. Thereafter, the alley (now much-widened) between St. Jan's and the Catholic St. Servaas has been called "Purgatory." In clear contrast to St. Servaas' elaborate decor, the interior of St. Jan's is plainly Protestant, with bare stone walls and columns, fine old tombs set flat into the floor, and mid-church Louis XVI pulpit. The tower can be climbed.

Onze Lieve Vrouwekerk • *(Church of Our Dear Lady) Onze Lieve Vrouweplein; open daily (not during services). Treasure-house (entrance through church) open daily 11 a.m.–5 p.m., Sun. 1–5 p.m. Easter to mid-Sept.; 251851* • Entry to the church from the square is to the left of the formidable **westwerk** (c. 1000), an almost windowless, fortress-like wall, via the **Stella Maris** side chapel (c. 1500). The essence of centuries' worth of incense clings to the candlelit interior, the most notable feature of which is the choir with its richly-carved capitals. The church's Treasure includes magnificent reliquaries, procession banners, church silver, and other ecclesiastical art and crafts.

St. Pietersberg Caves • *Mount St. Pietersberg; two miles south of Maastricht; guided tours (only), one hour, several times daily June–mid-Sept., reduced schedule rest of year, must be booked through VVV; 252121* • Since the St. Pietersberg caves were interesting enough to merit inclusion in Roman historian Pliny's writings in A.D. 50, and have generated interest among most of the city's guests in the two succeeding millennia (the cave walls are a virtual "visitors' book," so we know), you can feel confident about putting them on your list of Maastricht "musts." The limey labyrinth of 45-foot deep galleries cut in marl-limestone (a soft chalky building stone that hardens in the air) has numerous names carved in its soft walls, the earliest from 1037, among which are Sir Walter Scott, Voltaire, princes of the House of Orange, and Napoleon. For a thousand years (until 1875), stonecutters carved huge blocks of limestone from here, expanding its already considerable, natural size to over 200 miles (20,000 passages) of dark, silent, and cool caves (a constant year-round temperature of 50 degrees F.). Guides tell the story of four 17th-century monks who went in unescorted, having affixed a thread at the cave entrance to find their way out; but that "lifeline" broke and their days ended wandering within the caves.

For those who could find their way within them, the caves have served as a place of refuge; in the 18th century they harbored Austrian and Italian mercenaries hired to help the Dutch combat the French invaders, and in World War II they were readied to shelter up to 50,000 people from Nazi bombing, but never needed to be put into use. Deep in these caves, Rembrandt's "The Night Watch" was hidden from the Nazis during the war, rolled up in a specially prepared copper drum. When the war was over and the huge 13 x 16-foot painting was being restored before being rehung in Amsterdam's **Rijksmuseum** it was discovered that the picture, darkened from the smoke of peat fires in rooms where it had previously hung, actually showed a daytime scene.

ACCOMMODATIONS..........................

The city hotels listed are all within a mile or so of one another, but the actual location of the property you choose will affect your experience of the city. Since Maastricht has a new convention center just outside the center and good European transportation connections, it is increasingly attractive for congresses, and hotel reservations are suggested.

Deluxe
★★★★★ **Hotel Maastricht** • *De Ruiterij 1, 6221 EW; 254171, fax 616044* • Located on the banks of the Maas, facing across the river to the silhouette of the historic city center (which is just a few minutes' walk across the St. Servaas Bridge), this attractive, modern, full-service 112-room property with several restaurants, including the **Kobe** Japanese steakhouse, is Maastricht's most deluxe. Some of the many riverview rooms, which feature a decor of lively colors and marble baths, have balconies, and there also are split levels and apartment accommodations. The terrace cafe on the river overlooks the city and the steady stream of barges heading upstream into the heart of Europe.

First Class
★★★★ **Hotel Derlon** • *(Onze Lieve Vrouweplein 66, 6211 HD; 216770, fax 251933, res. in U.S. 800-344-1212.)* • Located on the historic, intimate-yet-lively square that's home to Our Beloved Lady church, a street away from the restored pedestrian Stokstraat, and near the ancient city ramparts, the Derlon couldn't be better or more charmingly situated. Several bedrooms in the modern but tastefully styled, service-oriented 42-room hotel overlook the cafe-cluttered, colorful scene on the square, where patrons gather until the wee hours of warm evenings. It is a special place that rests above Roman ruins that are one of the city's most significant early sites (see Hotel Derlon Museum under What To See and Do).

Moderate
★★★ **Hotel Du Casque** • *Helmstraat 14, 6211 TA; 214343, fax 255155* • There has been an inn on this site on the Vrijthof since the 15th century, though the present facade and interior of this family-run 43-room (6 rooms face on square) hotel are modern renovations. The lobby is small and unprepossessing, rooms clean and spacious. Breakfast (only, included). Parking.

★★★★ **Hotel Beaumont** • *Wycker Brugstraat 2, 6221 EC; 254433, fax 253655* • This family-run (3 generations) traditional 85-room hotel lies mid-way between the railway station and the old heart of Maastricht

(10-minute walk). Many of the rooms have been recently refurbished. Its restaurant, **Alsacien,** off the lobby bar, is a favorite locally. Indoor parking.

Inexpensive

★★ **Maison Du Chene** • *Boschstraat 104, 6211 AZ; 213523, fax 258082* • A hotel/restaurant since 1985, with a cozy, especially recommended French brasserie (*daily, noon–2 p.m., 6:30–10 p.m.; moderate*) on the ground floor, this hotel has 21 tidy, modernly-outfitted bedrooms in three old townhouses, most with shower/bath. There's a European flavor with friendly service, and it's in an excellent location (just off the Markt with Maastricht's City Hall).

★★★ **Hotel Bergere** • *Stationsstraat 40, 6221 BR; 251651, fax 255498* • Behind the historic facade and lobby with a stylish cafe are 40 guestrooms with recently modernized amenities. It's a short walk to the railway station and a pleasant, somewhat longer one across the Maas to the old center. Elevator; free parking; non-smoking rooms.

RESTAURANTS..

Residents around Maastricht revel in fine dining, and this strong gastronomic tradition has resulted in the restaurants of southern Limburg province, *en masse,* garnering more recognition than those of any other region of Holland. Local Limburg food favorites include *white asparagus* (fresh in May/early June), fruit flans *(Limgurgse vlaai),* fresh water *trout,* game, and Belgian-style chocolate *pralines.* As in Belgium and Luxembourg, in Maastricht less-than-good meals practically are nonexistent.

For fine dining, **'t Hegske** *(Heggenstraat 3a; 5–11 p.m., closed Tues; for res. 251762; moderate)* is a tiny antique-congested restaurant just off centrally-located St. Amorsplein. The romantic six-tabled candlelit interior—with another eight under the skylighted enclosed terrace with softly splashing fountain—specializes in fish and meat prepared in the French style. **Restaurant Jean Le Bruche** *(Tongersstraat 9; noon–2 p.m., 6–10 p.m., Sat. dinner only, closed Sun., Mon.; for res. 214609; expensive)* serves up selections such as lamb, fish, and duck salad in an intimate French country home decor. Nearby is **Pater Noster** *(Tongersstraat 42; noon–2 p.m., 5–11 p.m., closed Mon., no lunch weekends; inexpensive)* for good Dutch food. At **Au Coin des Bons Enfants** *(Ezelmarkt 4; noon–2 p.m., 6:30–10 p.m., closed Sun., and Sat. for lunch; for res. 212359; expensive),* whether you opt for open log fire elegance indoors or the rustic courtyard when the weather's fine, the

French/Belgian fare will agree with the setting. Split-level **Sagittarius** *(Bredestraat 7; 6–10 p.m., closed Sun., Mon.; for res. 211492; moderate)* specializes in seafood *(bouillabaisse, scampi, sole, smoked salmon)*, though the meat dishes also merit attention; both are served with a smile.

Lovers of shell fish and seafood also can seek out the chic but relaxed **Restaurant L'Escale** *(Havenstraat 19; 5 p.m.–midnight, closed Sun., Mon., hol.; for res. 213364; moderate)*, one of several excellent eateries clustered in the area between the lovely *Onze Lieve Vrouweplein* (on which the restaurant also offers outside terrace dining) and the *Op de Thermen* (site of old Roman baths), both just off handsome Stokstraat. Sharing the same building (and phone and hours) with L'Escale is **Le Vigneron** (inexpensive), a cozy darkwood bistro which offers a large selection of wines by the glass, and menus of traditional French dishes that include wine. **'t Plenkske** *(Plankstraat 6; noon–10:30 p.m., closed Sun.; for res. 218456; expensive)* offers light and bright glassed-in, or outdoor patio, dining overlooking the Op de Thermen; regional dishes from Maastricht, Liège, and France fill the bill of fare. **'t Klaoske** *(Plankstraat 20; noon–2:30 p.m., 6–10:30 p.m., closed Sun.; for res. 218118; moderate)* has more of an old Dutch look and feel, and the traditional country cuisine makes it a long-standing local favorite; it offers weekday business luncheon specials.

There are plenty of places in Maastricht for lighter, less formal fare. The oldest pub (1673) on the vast Vrijthof is the **In Den Ouden Vogelstruys** *(The Old Ostrich; Vrijthof 15; 9:30 a.m.–2 a.m.; 214888; inexpensive)*. This traditional cafe bar, with its rustic wooden interior and terrace cafe, has a faithful local following and is a good, yet limited choice for a hearty or light lunch or dinner of Dutch specialties (pate, choucroute garnie, soups, sandwiches of cheese and Ardennes ham). Next door is **Panache** *(Vrijthof 14; daily 10 a.m.–11 p.m.; 210516; inexpensive)*, one of the **Neeerlands Dis** restaurants that promises tasty, traditional dishes (*tournedos-poivre* to pastries). Moving along the row of cafes that anchor the Vrijthof one comes to **Monopole** *(Vrijthof 3; daily 10 a.m.–10 p.m.; 214090; inexpensive)* which features light fare and drinks on its terrace.

With more than 365 of them, Maastricht's pubs come in every variety. Many serve food (an excellent value, all *inexpensive*) amid their special and individual ambiance, making them cafes as much as a bars. Without doubt the smallest is **De Moriaan** *(Stokstraat 12; 4 p.m.–2 a.m., closed Sun., Mon.; 211177)* with 3½ tables inside, a terrace on the Op de Thermen outside, and good spaghetti. Close by is **In de Karkol** *(Stokstraat 5; noon–2 a.m., closed Sun., Mon.; 217035)*. On the extension of the Stokstraat is **In 't Knijpke** *(St. Bernardusstraat 13; daily 6 p.m.–midnight; 216525)* which calls itself a cafe cheese-cellar; with the brick vaulted-ceiling room candlelit and mellow music an accompaniment to the likes of onion soup, mussels, pate, and escargot, need I add it's atmospheric and friendly. With a stirring view from its terrace tables of the fortress-like West front of the O.L. Vrouwekerk (memorably illuminated at night) across the square, **Charlemagne** *(O.L. Vrouweplein 24; daily 9 a.m.–11 p.m.; 219373)* is a popular place. At the corner of the square is **De Bobbel** *(Wolfstraat 32; 11 a.m.–9 p.m., midnight on weekends, closed Sun; 217413)*. **Cafe Sjiek** *(St. Pieterstraat 13; daily 5 p.m.–2 a.m.; 210158)* has a cozy interior of stained glass, wood, candles, and flowers, and in good weather customers spill out across the street to a terrace cafe on lawns in view of fragments of ancient city walls *(terrace kitchen hours, noon–9 p.m.)*. Choices run the gamut from soups and salad nicoise to crab and steak.

IN THE AREA..................................

Southern Limburg Province • The Netherlands' Limburg Province is popular with the Dutch and other Europeans for country (especially summer) holidays. Here are the country's highest hills, commonly called the "Dutch Alps" (though, to put the topography in perspective, their top elevation of 1000 feet still comes short of New York City's *Empire State Building*). If you have a car to explore this gently rolling land, you'll find it dotted with fine old (some 17th century) fortified farmsteads *(boerderij),* built around courtyards and closed to the street side by gates. Villages such as Epen, Epenheide, and Gulpen have handsome half-timbered buildings tucked into them. The castles found across the countryside originally formed a defensive line during the area's turbulent earlier times, but once their protective elements were no longer politically important, many were architectually embellished. Sometimes castles and fortified farms stood side by side, as one sees at **Kasteel Erenstein** in Kerkade (see below). Having a car will enable you to indulge in some of the countryside restaurants for which South Limburg is renowned. Some are set in castles that also offer guestrooms, but, frequently the establishments are sought out first and foremost for their food. Definitely reserve—for meals as much as for rooms.

Netherlands American Military Cemetery • *Margraten; 04458-1208* • The only American military cemetery in the Netherlands, the site was liberated on Sept. 13, 1944, by the *U.S. 30th Infantry Division* during the *First U.S. Army*'s drive towards Germany. The cemetery was established on Nov. 10, 1944, by the Ninth U.S. Army as one of the first used for the interment of Americans who had fallen on German soil. A peaceful resting place for 8,300 (including 40 pairs of brothers buried side by side), there is row upon row of graves marked by white Italian marble Latin crosses or Stars of David, and an observation tower (149 steps) that offers a panorama of the cemetery and countryside.

ACCOMMODATIONS/RESTAURANTS IN THE AREA

★★★ **Kasteel Wittem Hotel/Restaurant** • *Wittemerallee 3, Wittem 6268 AB; for res. 04450–1208, fax 04450-1260; hotel: Moderate; restaurant: expensive* • Set in a hilly landscape of ancient trees 20 kms./ 12 mi. from Maastricht, Castle Wittem has a history that dates back to about 1100, and Willem the Silent, Prince of Orange, who rescued it from the Spanish (who, under Charles II, had shown good taste in their conquering) in 1568 and then used it as a base for counter-attack. The castle was restored in 1611 with money given in compensation for damage suffered during that struggle, and again in 1972, in cooperation with the *Commission for Ancient Monuments*. Its 12 guestrooms located atop stately staircases and winding castle corridors (no elevators) are roomy, individualistic, and mostly recently renovated with marble baths and English country-style decor. Inquire about the two tower rooms. There's a terrace for drinks by the double moat, in which a black swan swims. **Kasteel Wittem Restaurant** offers creative classic French cuisine in a setting of silver candlesticks, leather chairs, and beamed ceiling. Excellent service and wine list. Inclusive gastronomic weekends.

★★★ **Kasteel Erenstein Hotel/Restaurant** • *Oud Erensteinerweg, Kerkrade 6468 PC; for res. 045-461333, fax 045 460748; hotel: First Class; Restaurant: expensive, closed Sat. for lunch* • The 45 modern, well-furnished guestrooms are located in an imaginatively restored 270-year-old *boerderij* (a fortified farmstead built around a central courtyard), which is a protected national monument. Breakfast (not included) can be served in your room or in the glass-enclosed winter garden (former courtyard), open during the summer. There's a health club: whirlpool, sauna, steam, and hot tub (fee). Across the road, the renowned **Kasteel Erenstein Restaurant** is in the early 14th-century Renaissance chateau's grand hall (traditional, intimate, elegant); the cuisine is French, the menu *a la carte* or *prix-fixe*.

Chateau Neercanne Restaurant • *Cannerweg 800, 2 miles outside Maastricht; daily noon–2:30 p.m., 6:30–9:30 p.m., closed Mon.; for res. 043-251359; expensive* • Located on a hillside, overlooking the River Jeker and the Belgium border, Chateau Neercanne was built in 1698, and one of its first houseguests was Czar Peter the Great. Since restoration in 1955, Chateau Neercanne has elegantly housed one of the region's preeminent restaurants. The internationally-renowned French cuisine uses only fresh ingredients (in season, herbs and vegetables come from its own garden) and focuses on seasonal and regional specialty dishes for the *a la carte* and *prix-fixe* menu offerings. In addition to the romantic setting of the dining room (Venetian glass chandeliers, Baroque wallpaper, leisurely gracious service) and broad stone terrace for use in fine weather, there's an Auberge in the vaulted cellar of an adjoining building where one can have lunch. The natural marlstone cellars extending into the hillside behind the castle hold one of the most choice selections of wine in the country (and, in neighboring caves, NATO installations).

Bruges by day. *Opposite*, Bruges by night. *(Photos courtesy of Tourist Office for Flanders)*

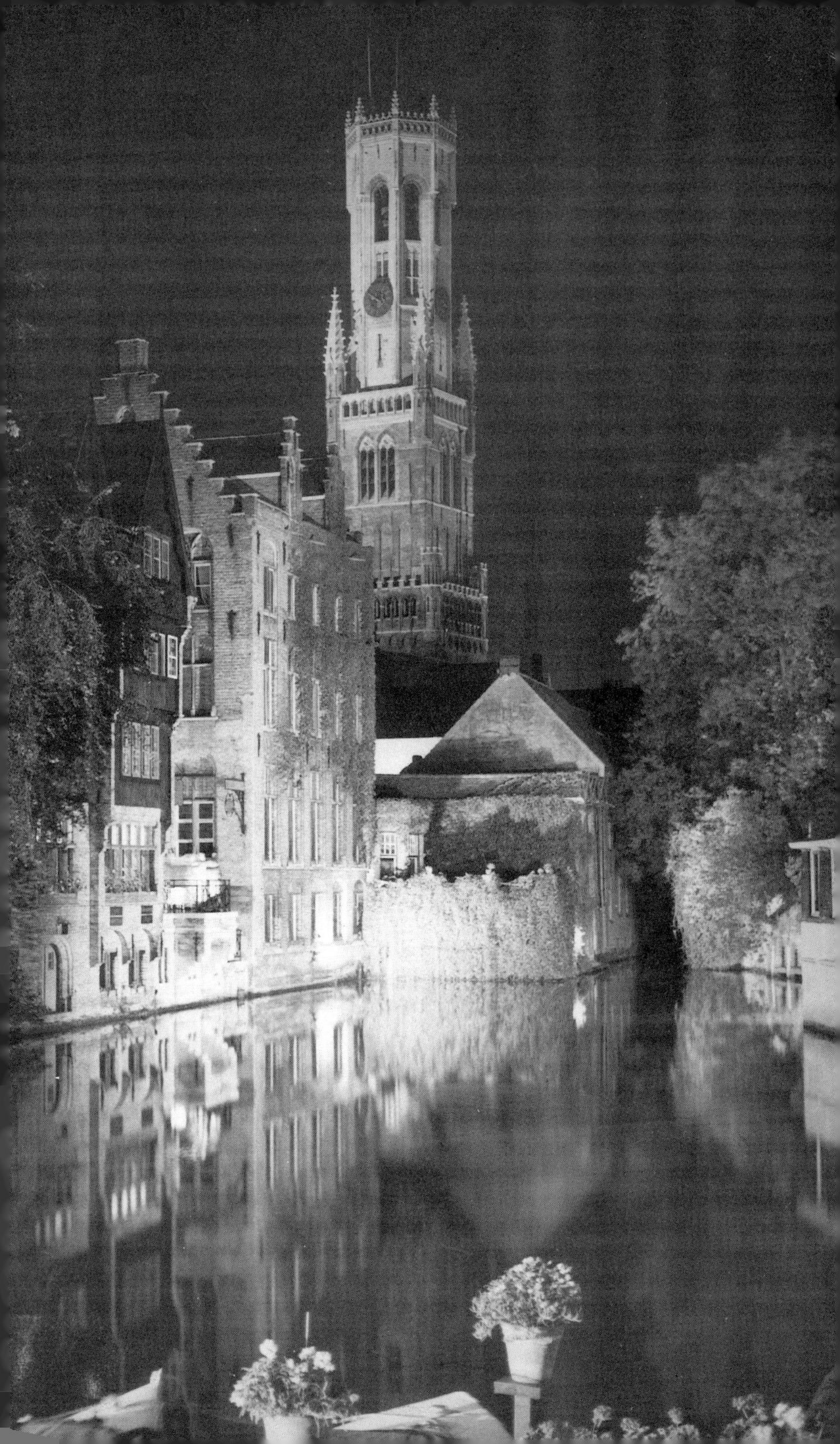

Opposite, The Hague: Frivolous. The Pier and Promenade at the North Sea-side resort of Scheveningen. *Below,* The Hague: Formal. The *Binnenhof* complex of government buildings and the *Mauritshuis* museum facing the *Hofvijver* in the center of the city. *(Photos courtesy of Netherlands Board of Tourism)*

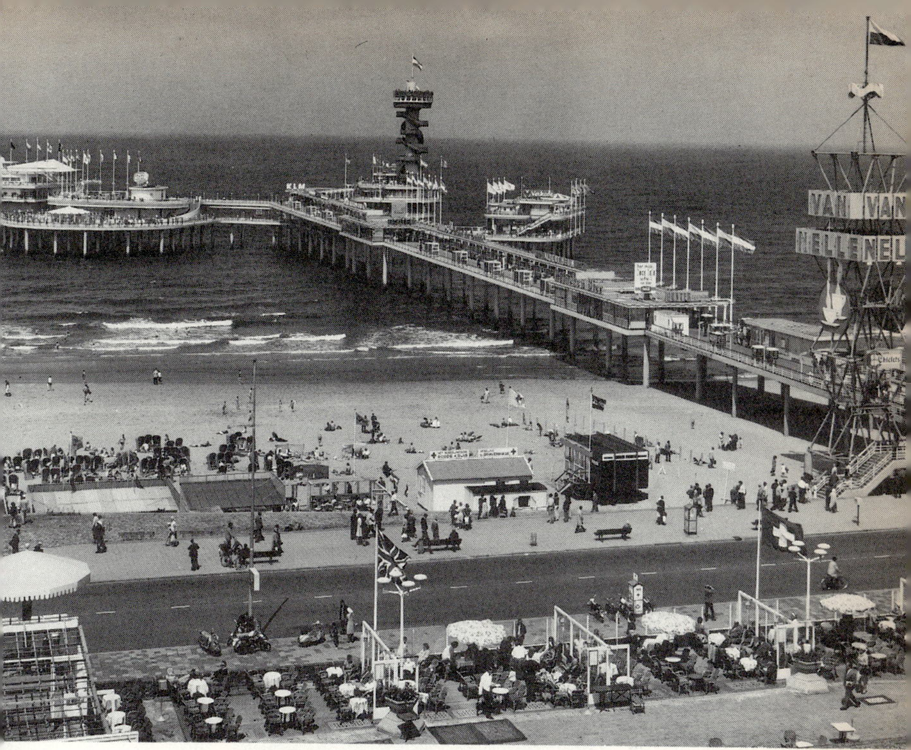
VAN VAN
NELLE NEL

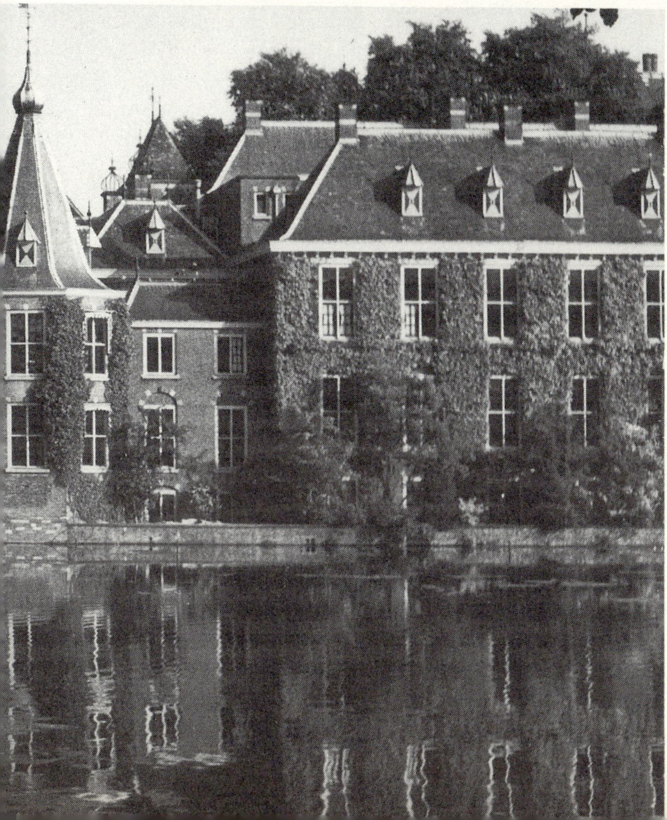

Gathering places: Galerie de la Reine, Brussels. *(Photo courtesy of OPT, Office of Tourism in the French-speaking Community of Belgium)*

Festival market in front of the Stadhuis at Antwerp's Grote Market. *(Photo courtesy of Antwerp Office of Tourism)*

Cafes on Onze Lieve Vrouweplein (with the *westwerk* of O.L.V. church in background), Maastricht. *(Photo courtesy of Maastricht VVV)*

Exterior of Bock casements, Luxembourg City. *(Photo courtesy of Luxembourg National Tourist Office)*

Interior of Bock casements, Luxembourg City. *(Photo courtesy of Luxembourg National Tourist Office)*

Antwerp Cathedral at night. *(Photo courtesy of Antwerp Office of Tourism)*

BELGIUM

INTRODUCTION

The Belgian Landscape

Though small (30,500 sq. kilometers/11,775 sq. miles), Belgium has a remarkable variety of scenery, with countryside that changes character every two or three dozen miles. Clockwise from the northwest, where the North Sea fronts Belgium's sand dune and broad beach coastline, the country is bordered by Holland to the north, Germany to the east, Luxembourg to the southeast, and France to the southwest. The north (**Flanders**) and south (**Wallonia**) of Belgium are not only different from each other linguistically and culturally (see *The Belgian People* below), but geographically. In general the north is much flatter, with some areas, especially in the province of West Flanders, lying below sea level. There, the land had to be reclaimed from the sea; between the 8th and the 13th centuries, a 12 by 30 mile wide strip of low-lying coastal land was, through the use of sluices, transformed from salty swamp into fine polder farmland that remains among Belgium's richest. Rows of sentinel-like trees that form wind breakers along the cross-country canals are one of the distinctive sights in this part of Flanders.

The **Kempen,** in northern Belgium, is a large section of land between the Schelde and the Maas rivers that reaches through the provinces of Antwerp and Limburg. The terrain changes from moorland, heath, and lakes to extensive pine forests and orchards as one moves west to east. West Flanders' **Heuvelland,** a presently peaceful district of lakes and walking trails south of Ieper, was the heart of Belgium's battlefield in World War I.

Wallonia, roughly the southern half of Belgium, also is varied, but overall more wooded and hilly than Flanders. This section of the country has an industrial sash stretched across it from Liège to Tournai, and in the past was prominent for its coal production.

A large area of Wallonia is covered by the forests of the **Ardennes.** The most elevated area (600 meters/1600 feet, with winter skiing)

BELGIUM · · · 357

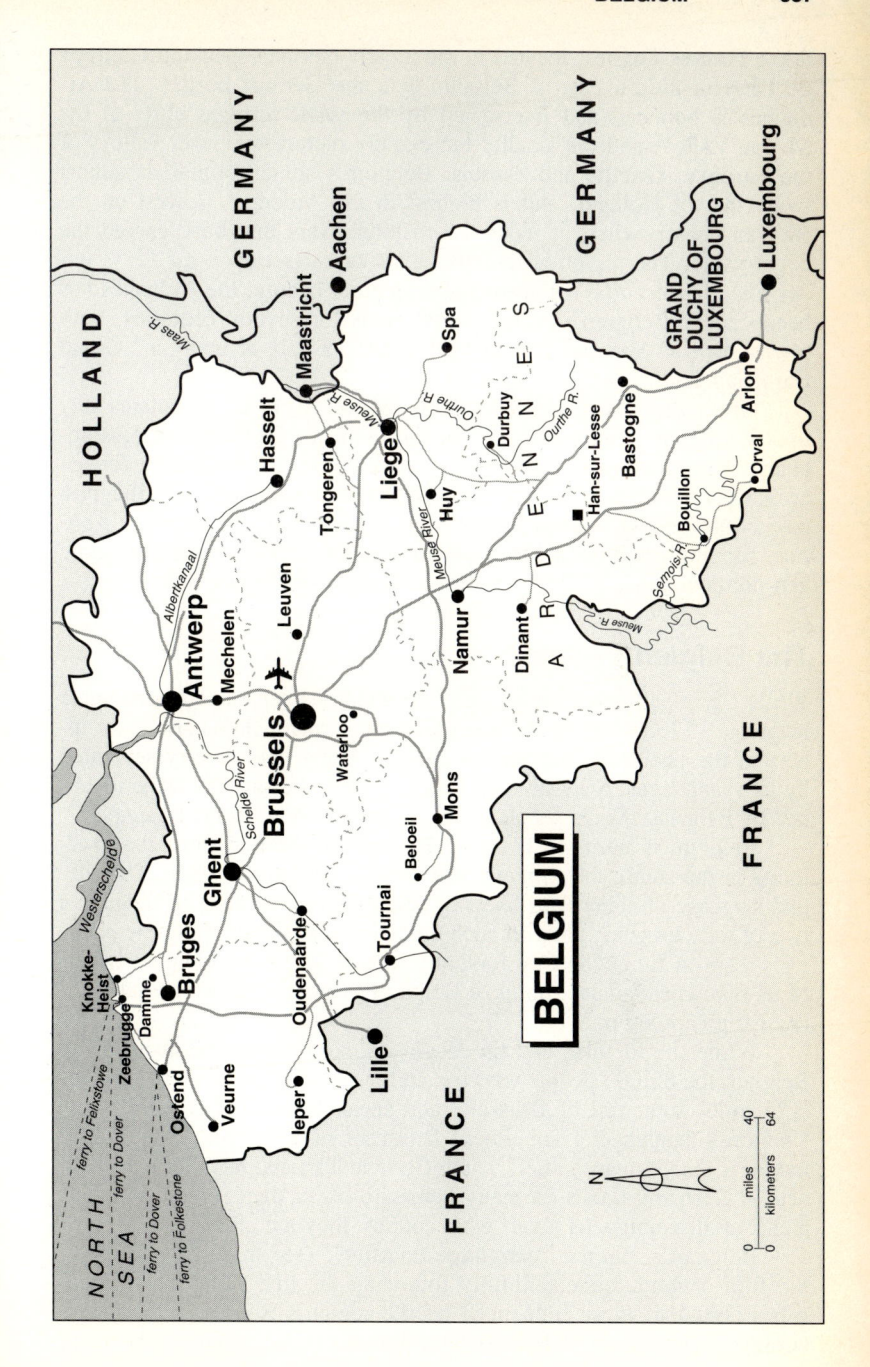

is the **Hautes Fagnes,** located in the mostly German-speaking **Cantons de l'Est** in the far east of Belgium near the German border. The Ardennes is bounded and intersected by the castle-fortified cliffs of the **Meuse Valley,** and the smaller but equally picturesque river valleys of the **Sambre, Ourthe** and **Semois.** Belgium's annual rainfall is almost twice that of Holland, and is highest in the Ardennes (lowest on the Belgian coast), where it feeds the rushing rivers that have carved the countryside. The region is famous for its caves (see *Han-sur-Lesse* under *The Meuse Valley*). Because of its natural beauty, the Ardennes has been one of Belgium's major tourist areas for several centuries, with towns such as Spa and Dinant having been a part of many a "Grand European Tour."

Physically, there are few places where rivers or mountains distinctly separate Belgium from Holland, France, Germany, or Luxembourg. This circumstance has left the country open to invasion by foreign armies for virtually all of its recorded history. Yet, internally Belgium has a very clearly defined border: one of language. Its *language frontier,* running roughly east to west through its center, makes the single geo-political entity of Belgium one nation *divisible* culturally.

The Belgian People

While "England and America are two countries separated by the same language" (according to Irishman George Bernard Shaw), Belgium inherited the decidedly stickier situation of being one country separated by two languages. Stickier still, Belgium could be said not to be inhabited by Belgians: As the people there say, the situation "is not so simple."

Belgium is home to both the **Flemish** in the north and the **Walloons** in the south; the former speak *Dutch,* the latter *French.* The second language of either is as likely to be English as the other of Belgium's two official tongues. Only in such crucial areas as supporting the country's team in European Cup football (soccer), or speaking up on behalf of its renowned cuisine, do most Belgians overcome their regional identity for a national one.

While the Flemish and the Walloons can be tentative about being Belgian, the 85,000 people who live in the mostly rural Eastern Cantons (125 miles southeast of Brussels) and speak German (Belgium's truly "minority language") are ardent believers in Belgium. Though they live near the German border, watch German TV, and buy German products in Germany (taxes on many items are lower there), these Belgians aren't at all ambiguous about what country they are citizens of.

Belgium's internal **"language frontier"** (see map) dates back to the fifth century, quite faithfully following the line along which local tribes split into those influenced by the region's Roman or Germanic heritage. The Celtic **Belgae,** whom Julius Casear noted as the most

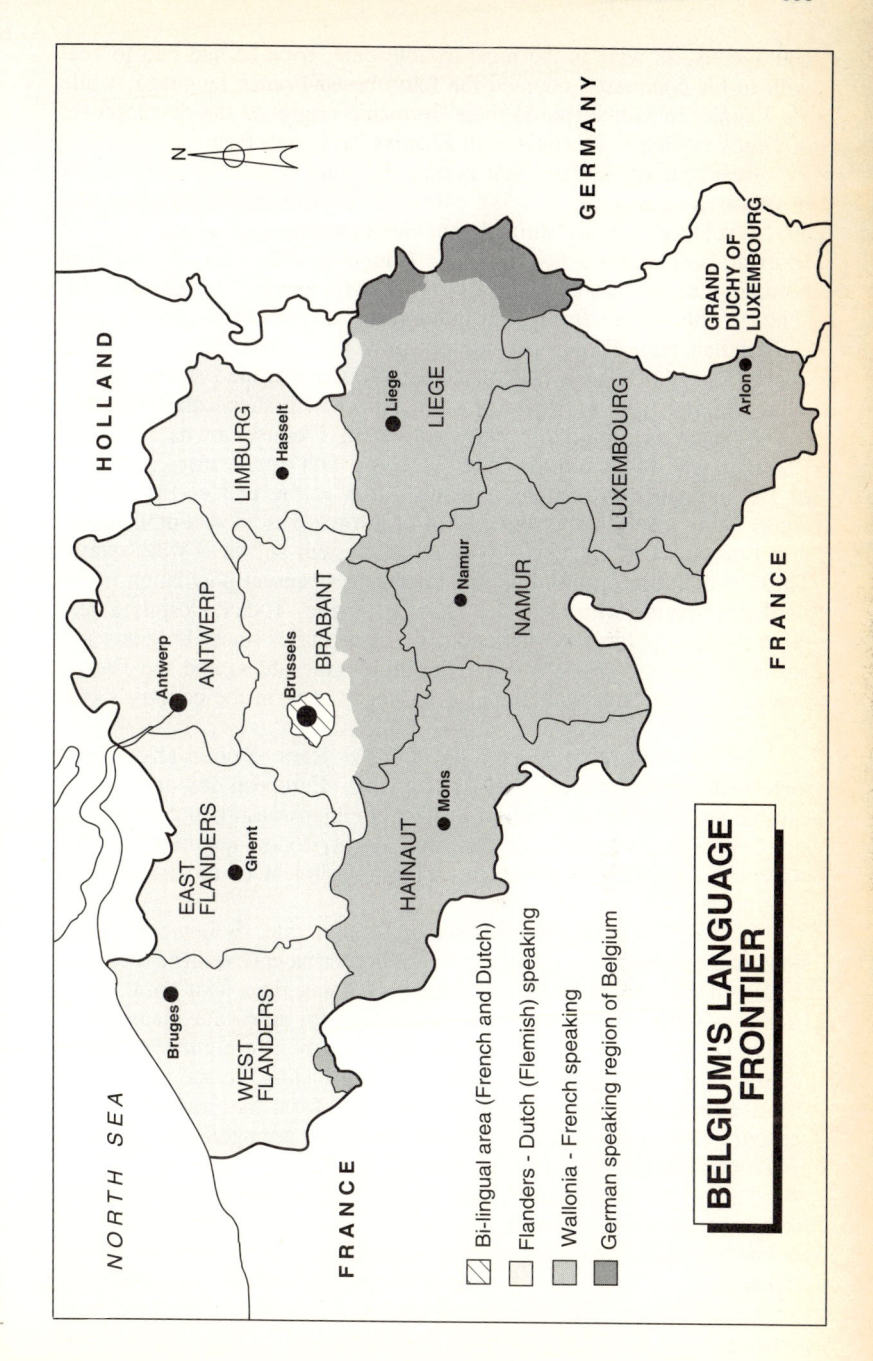

BELGIUM'S LANGUAGE FRONTIER

- Bi-lingual area (French and Dutch)
- Flanders - Dutch (Flemish) speaking
- Wallonia - French speaking
- German speaking region of Belgium

courageous, as well as the most troublesome, tribe he had had to deal with in his conquests, adopted the Latin-based *French* language, while the **Franks** remained true to their Germanic origins in the development of *Dutch* (which is identical with *Flemish* in written form).

Residents of the land that is now Belgium were forced by history to follow a constantly changing course of leadership; the region gradually developed identity through *duchies* (such as that of the Duke of Brabant) and *counties* (as under the Counts of Flanders). By the time northern Europe was evolving out of the Middle Ages in the mid-15th century, the people from both cultural areas had come under French Burgundian rule. French became not only the favored language of the upper class, but also a fashion copied by the educated *bourgeoise* (a name derived from *burghers* or town citizens), a social class that virtually began in Belgium's early-to-flourish Flemish towns. (Though "bourgeoise" today means "middle class," and often carries overtones of the ordinary, we should remember that at the end of the Middle Ages, being a self-supporting citizen of a town was an accomplishment in a Europe where the serf-driven feudal system still held wide sway). Thus, at that time, it was only the uneducated peasant population in the rural countryside who used the Flemish tongue. Today, despite a plethora of socio-political permutations in the centuries since, Belgians still are basically bourgeoise in their life style and values, and the French language still retains something of an upper hand in the country's culture.

Belgian culture developed during 2000 years of often all-too-intimate exposure to that of other—occupying—European countries. As a captive audience for its foreign leaders, Belgians absorbed certain outside fashions, but maintained their own deeply-rooted qualities over the centuries, up to the relatively recent establishment of an independent Belgium in 1830.

In the course of centuries under foreign rule, Belgians on both sides of the country's internal bicultural border have developed a certain indifference to government and a habit of doing their own thing. As a friend in Bruges describes it: "Belgians look for an escape clause from government because for generations of occupation foreigners made all the rules for them. Even today, Belgians are inclined to see all government, even their own, as 'foreign.' Coming from that attitude, many see our 'black money' system—under-the-table arrangements to avoid government taxes—as a kind of national sport."

Though conservative in many ways, Belgians openly admit to not liking regimentation. They may appear undisciplined because of their aversion to rules. Again, my Bruges friend traces this to Belgium's past: "Historically, since Belgians were not ruled by Belgians, they got used to ignoring leaders, and that carried over to an avoidance of rules. Belgians don't like building codes, or following traffic signs." He's the first to admit that this "leads to disorganization," but returns to the point that it's a trait that "comes out of history."

Belgium has a population of approximately 10 million: 5.7 million are Dutch-speaking Flemish; 3.1 million are French-speaking Walloons; and about one million are residents of Brussels (where a large majority is French-speaking). An additional half million are foreigners: Eurocrats and diplomats (many countries post diplomatic missions in triplicate to Brussels, one each to the European Community, NATO, and the Belgian royal court), as well as immigrant workers (many from Africa, especially Zaire, formerly the Belgian Congo).

As the above figures show, today Belgium's Dutch-speaking Flemish population is decidedly in the majority. Until the last decade or so, however, French speakers more than overcame their numerical inferiority through their dominance of the country's culture. While recent legislation of various language issues, and the implementation of a form of federalism, have worked towards equalizing Belgium's two communities, French cultural dominance is still strong, and remains part of the Belgian "problem."

During the Reformation in the 16th century, most of Belgium's Protestants eventually headed north to Holland to escape the harsh intolerance of the region's Roman Catholic ruler Philip II of Spain. With nearly all the remaining population Catholic, religion served as a bridge linking Belgium's two cultures. A large number of Belgians still are self-professed Catholics (particularly in Flanders), but, during the 20th century, anticlericalism increased so substantially (especially in Wallonia) that eventually the various religious/anti-religious movements wanted their own political parties.

Whether or not they choose to participate in either actively, *religion* and *politics* affect every Belgian's life. Belgium's political parties represent the same ideological tendencies as those elsewhere in Europe: *Christian Democratic* (called Social Christian); *Conservative* (called Liberal); *Socialist;* and *Green.* When their community's economic situation strengthened in the 1960s, the Flemish began insisting on a stronger voice in the Belgian national government (for more on the Flemish Movement, see *Flanders: An Introduction*). This resulted in each of the main political parties breaking into two sections, duplicating themselves along linguistic cultural community lines. Since then, *compromis à la Belge* has been an even greater fact of Belgian political life. Despite coalition governments (all but unavoidable due to the splintering of political parties), the language issue often comes ahead of other considerations, and often has led to a falling out, and subsequent "fall" of the current coalition.

The introduction to Belgium of **federalism,** in 1988, gave important decision-making powers to the regions of Flanders, Wallonia, and Brussels. Federalism has helped both to stabilize Belgium's political situation and to overcome the lingering linguistic divisions. In the past, when Belgium's internal petty rivalries and hostilities have periodically ignited, it sometimes has seemed that the country would split. Though often predicted, however, it hasn't happened and under federalism, is now much less likely to.

Whatever cause for cursing the Flemish and Walloons have between themselves, they stand in similarly estranged circumstances with respect to their contiguous, supposedly culturally-related neighbor countries. In France, there's little acceptance of the French-speaking Walloons as French (in large measure due to their perceived inelegant pronunciation of the language), and in Holland the Dutch are inclined to think of the Flemish as rather embarrassing country cousins who speak a dialect. Uncomplimentary Belgian jokes, again often taking as their subject a perceived inability to properly use the French or Dutch languages, are told over the borders in both France and Holland. So, in the end, Belgium's internal "situation" is so peculiarly its own that it *almost* creates a national consciousness. The Belgians, well aware of the jokes told at their expense, take them pretty well. Only the few extremists in either community ever have thoughts of actually merging with France or Holland (though the issue was the subject of *The Times* of London's annual front-page *April Fools Day* article in 1992). Some Belgians even manage a smile at the irony that for all the energy expended on gaining the right to speak their respective languages *inside* their country, *beyond* their borders, Belgians' ability to speak those languages may be regarded as laughable.

Other ironic aspects of their internal language situation take place at the same time. Belgians find themselves becoming increasingly internationalized through their role in the EC. In 1986, for example, a small farming village in Flanders, *Fourons,* that lay near the Walloon language boundary (and thus, though Dutch-speaking, had a large number of French-speaking residents and was a "protected French-language minority"), made headlines. Its French-speaking mayor, Jose Happart, regularly refused to take a required examination that would have revealed his poor knowledge of Flemish (fluency in both Belgian languages is legally required in order to hold any government job in Belgium). Happart expressed his feelings with the logic: "Why should I conduct all official acts in Flemish if most people here speak French?" Flemish officials responded "because Fourons is in Flanders," a not unreasonable insistence given their hard-won right to administer affairs on *their* soil in *their* language. Through media coverage, Happart became a hero in Wallonia, a fiend in Flanders. Today Happart, an elected member of the *European Parliament,* still speaks up on Belgian issues of respective languages and regions; however, after a recent lively television debate with a leading Flemish politician, Happart posed a new perspective on the subject by saying, on record, that "after all, everybody will speak English in 20 years."

With their complicated internal socio-politics, it's no wonder that Belgians remain fond of their folklore. Folkloric celebrations in Belgium are loosely referred to as "carnivals." *The* carnival, **Mardi Gras,** is, of course, one of the year's highlights, especially in **Binche,** 30 miles south of Brussels. Then, the Walloon town teems with the prancing figures of the "Gilles," members of a male society who break out annually in dazzling costumes, complete with elaborate eight-pound ostrich-plumed headgear. Although some of Belgium's carnivals are seriously religious (among them Bruges' **Procession of the Holy Bood** and Veurne's brown-cowled, cross-carrying participatory **Process of the Penitents**), many more are only slightly so (as in a David and Goliath encounter that is an annual affair played out by **"giants"** at Ath). They may also be permeated with pagan traditions, reflect bygone 15th-century Burgundian days, or suggest the 16th-century influence of the Spanish empire.

Historians believe that Belgium's folkloric festivals originated in pre-Christian spring fertility rites, and sun worship (still practiced by many northern Europeans, though in costumes more appropriate for the beach). The introduction of the pageantry element into Belgian folk history can be pinpointed precisely. In response to the **Reformation,** Ghent-born Emperor Charles V, who ruled over much of continental Europe, is credited with creating festivals beginning in 1549 to show the "romance" of Roman Catholicism, in contrast to the puritanism of the Protestant approach to life. Brussels' annual July **Ommegang,** a florid Flemish historical "walkabout" in the Grand Place, is Belgium's grandest show of this kind of carnival. Ostend's **Blessing of the Sea** is a straight-forward celebration of the town's fishing industry and longtime maritime flavor. Most Belgian carnival celebrations are fanciful and cheerful, but the meanings of some can meander into the macabre, their enactment giving a glimpse of the *grotesque,* a quality that has been reflected in the area's art over the centuries, from Bosch and Brueghel to the 20th-century surrealists Ensor, Magritte, and Delvaux.

Belgian's relationship with their country may be complex, but individual passions are clear cut. To a person, they appreciate the good things in life, including food and drink. It's a trait said to have held since the country's Burgundian days five centuries ago. Along with the *de rigueur* fervor for football (soccer), cycle-racing stirs the souls of Belgian participants and spectators alike; the annual Flemish **Ronde van Vlaanderan** cycle race is one of the runners-up in excitement to the **Tour de France.** Many Belgians find pleasure in specialty interests. Radical adult puppet theater (the **Toone Puppet Theater** tucked into Brussels' ancient l'Ilot Sacre district is the best known of the "establishment" puppet theaters, see under *Brussels, Entertainment and Events*) doles out strong satire (usually not in English). Comic strip art is so popular that there's a museum, the **Belgian Comic Strip Center,** in Brussels (see under *What To See and Do*) devoted to it. (Pierre Culliford, a Belgian artist better known under the professional name of **"Peyo,"** is creator of the *Smurfs*, the internationally popular little blue characters that reflect the local fondness for cartoon and comics art). Most unusual of all may be the near-mania in certain circles for pigeon racing. Before becoming aware of that sport I had, most mistakenly, assumed that the caged pigeons I saw at the Sunday morning *Bird Market* on Brussels' Grand Place were destined for dinner tables. The much more interesting story behind the contents of those cages is that Belgium is home to the world's largest number (some 120,000) of *colombophiles* (pigeon fanciers), who get passionate about the 25,000 pigeon races held each year. Betting on the birds can involve substantial sums.

Unlike their Dutch neighbors to the north, Belgians were not shaped by the sea. While Dutch merchants spent the 17th century garnering wealth by sailing the world, Belgians made their money as at-home industrialists. The Belgian character is clothed in a bourgeois life-style and fed by conservative capitalist ideology. Belgium's prudent and productive market economy runs by methodical, non-spontaneous means. An historically strong belief in free trade results in the basically hard-working labor unions occasionally calling strikes to keep the populace aware of their contribution.

Beyond doubt, Belgians and Belgium defy easy definition. But while the country's internal situation can be frustrating and fraught with overtones for residents, visitors with a little insight into the complex nature of the country's bicultural society can enjoy observing the whole intriguing situation.

Belgium: An Historical Perspective

Between 57 and 50 B.C. Julius Caesar conquered the northern sector of tri-parted Gaul, the land lying in the basins of the Scheldt and the Meuse rivers. At the time, it was inhabited by Gallo-Celtic tribes, including the Belgae. *Romans* named the region **Gallia Belgica** and occupied it until the 5th century. From the 3rd century, however, Rome's hold began to weaken, and the *Franks* (a loose federation of German tribes) began to penetrate the area. Eventually, the Franks colonized the lower Scheldt, leaving only a forested stretch from the Scheldt to the Ardennes separating them from the *Wala* (Walloons, or romanized Celts). Virtually the same ethnic and linguistic frontier runs through the center of Belgium today.

Once the Romans departed, **Clovis,** who was born in 465 in Tournai (then the capital of the Frankish Merovingian kings), conquered all of Gaul (except Burgundy and Provence), having declared himself Christian and gained the support of the Church. After his death in 511, the Gallic territory became splintered, with what today is Belgium being a remote corner. In 751 **Pepin the Short** ousted the last weak Merovingian and, in seeking to reassemble the realm, founded the Carolingian dynasty. Pepin's son **Charlemagne,** who reigned from 768 to 814, wound up being declared Emperor of the West by the Pope in 800, with lands reaching from Denmark to southern Italy and from northern Spain to the Oder. Under Charlemagne, Belgium had an important position in the empire.

Fierce fighting broke out between Charlemagne's grandsons, however, and what had been achieved during his reign was lost in the partitioning of the region. As a result of the warring, the 843 **Treaty of Verdun** divided the "Belgian" area between Charles the Bald and Lothair. Charles, King of West Francia (more or less France as we know it) received the territory west of the Scheldt (which would become Flanders, and included a part of what is Walloon territory today). Lothair, whose lands bordered the Rhine and the Rhone, received the remainder, which was to become the Duchy of Lower Lotharingia (Lorraine).

The dissolution of the Carolingian Empire led to the founding of numerous principalities (many of them keeping their names as modern provinces) whose powers were determined by frequently changing alliances. In 864 the Flanders countship came into being and, through marriage between dynasties, it became strong and unified. Lotharingia broke up into a number of minor courts and principalities.

While much of Europe still slept in the Dark Ages (also known as the Middle Ages, lasting until about 1450), Belgium began awaking. The **rise of towns** in Flanders led to new structures for society by redistributing the population from the countryside where the feudal system still flourished. By 1100 Flanders was firmly established, with Bruges, Ghent, and Ypres rapidly becoming city-states through the power of the privileges bestowed upon them by Flemish counts. A mastery of mercantilism resulted in wealth that encouraged and supported an active artistic environment. In the 1200s, Ghent and Bruges had become so independent-minded that they hardly recognized the Counts of Flanders' authority, much less that of the French King, to whom Flanders was allegiance-bound.

In 1302 French King-to-be Philip the Fair decided to do away with Flanders (by invading it and overpowering the Count) in order to annex the region's riches to France. Flemish citizens quickly showed how fiercely they were willing to fight for their freedom. Led by weaver Jan Breydel and butcher Pieter de Coninck, a rough-and-ready crowd of trades and craftsmen met at **Kortrijk** to confront an army of France's finest mail-clad knights. The Flemings were armed primarily with devices called *goedendags* ("how do you do's"), small spiked balls of iron that were swung on four-foot chains in circles over their heads and let loose to slash the enemy. Though the French were contemptuous of their lowborn opponents, they couldn't defeat the brave Flemish citizens. At battle's end, the French dead numbered 63 nobles, including commander Robert d'Artois, and 700 knights, from each of whom was removed a pair of golden spurs, ornaments which gave the battle its name. Still regularly reenacted as one of Belgium's colorful folkloric events on the site in Kortrijk that is marked by a monument, the **Battle of the Golden Spurs** is significant for being the first occasion on which common citizens defeated well-armed and protected knights; it thereby made medieval military and social history, and indicated the beginning of the end of the era of chivalry.

During the 14th century, various developments combined to bring about instability in Flanders. There were local guild rivalries and tyranny by the urban oligarchy over the rural peasantry. Changing trade patterns affected Flanders' all-important cloth industry and led to the emigration of many weavers of England. The marriage of Margaret (heir of Count of Flanders Louis de Male) to Philip the Bold of Burgundy resulted in the end of Flanders as a separate state, and the beginning of **the Burgundian period** in 1384. The Dukes of Burgundy, who ruled the region until 1473, united almost the whole of the Netherlands.

Under the tenure of **Philip the Good** (1419–1467) there was an increase in trade and luxury, and the first flowering of Flemish painting occurred (**Jan van Eyck** was court painter to Philip). Philip was set on having monarchical status: In 1421 he bought Namur; in 1430 he inherited Brabant, Limburg, and Antwerp; in 1433, after deposing the previous ruler, he took over Hainaut, Holland, and Zeeland; and, in 1443, he bought Luxembourg. For an extra measure of authority, in 1456 Philip had his nephew Louis de Bourbon elected Bishop of Liège, and made his bastard son Bishop of Utrecht. In the meantime, he forced Bruges and Ghent (which mounted an unsuccessful revolt in response) to surrender many of their privileges. This after having honored their superior wool-weaving by establishing the *Order of the Golden Fleece* in Bruges in 1430.

Philip was succeeded by his son **Charles the Bold,** the richest and most ambitious prince of his day. He, too, held the nobles and cities in check, and, in his desire to be a king, married Margaret of York, sister of Edward IV of England. Over-extending himself in a military campaign in Lorraine, Charles was killed at Nancy in 1477. He left extensive lands in turmoil to his daughter Mary, whom the Flemish held virtual hostage until she signed the *Great Privilege* charter that granted far-reaching rights to the provinces. In the same tempestuous year that her father died, Mary (in response to demands from the French king to marry *his* son) arranged to marry Maximilian of Austria, whereby the Netherlands passed from the Burgundians to the **Hapsburgs** of Vienna.

Mary and Maximilian had a son, Philip the Fair, to whom Maximilian, upon his election as Holy Roman Emperor in 1494, handed over the Netherlands and other lands, including Spain. Philip died young, and in 1506 the Burgundian land inheritance from his mother passed to his six-year-old son Charles, who had been born in Ghent.

Charles, who would be one of the dominant figures of European history, spent his childhood under the governorship of his aunt Margaret of Austria, who established herself and Charles in Mechelen. In 1515, the Netherlands' States General declared Charles (then 15) of age to lead their lands; in 1516 he also became King of Spain and, in 1519 Emperor, having inherited the Hapsburg empire holdings from his grandfather.

As Charles V (Charles Quint), and later Holy Roman Emperor, he ruled over greater European domains (from Spain to Hungary, and from Sicily to the Netherlands) than any single person before or since. In 1530, Charles V appointed his sister, Mary of Hungary, as regent of the Netherlands. She exacted heavy taxes in order to support the wars that Charles waged elsewhere (particularly in France) to keep his empire intact. In 1540, Ghent rebelled against paying for such wars, but Charles personally suppressed the uprising and, in keeping with his aim to diminish the ancient privileges of towns that impaired the power of his crown, he rescinded many of Ghent's rights.

But the business of managing his empire militarily became increasingly overshadowed for the Roman Catholic Charles by concern about the Protestant **Reformation.** First Martin Luther in Germany (from 1520 on), and then John Calvin in Switzerland, attacked the Catholic Church's corruption, in selling of indulgences and the self-indulgent lives of priests and the Pope. From Switzerland, the austere fundamentalist beliefs of *Calvinism* spread to Belgium (and on to Holland, where, after 1550, Calvinism was the prevailing religion). In Belgium, Calvinist orators attracted and converted thousands in the forests outside towns from Bruges to Liège and Antwerp to Tournai. The number of Protestant converts increased continually. Charles tried to hold back the tide by first prosecuting individual "heretics," and then moving to more wholesale action under the **Edict of Blood,** which decreed death for those convicted.

In 1555, an exhausted (perhaps ill; he died in 1558) Charles abdicated in favor of his son Philip II of Spain. A contemporary painting of the actual ceremonial event shows the cast of main characters (Charles entering on the arm of Willem the Silent of Orange; Philip II; Duke of Alva; the Counts of Egmont and Hoorn) for the upcoming tragedy: the *Revolt of the Netherlands,* or the **Eighty Years' War.** It is said that at the end of his father's abdication address in the throne room of Brussels' Coudenberg Palace, Philip, who could speak neither Dutch nor French, had his acceptance speech read by another. Philip never learned either language, and wound up loathing the "Lowlanders," never setting foot in the Netherlands again after 1559 (though he lived until 1598). He did, however, favor Flemish art, and had many works by **Hieronymus Bosch** (1474–1516) sent to Madrid; Utrecht-born and Belgium-educated painter **Antonio Moro** (c. 1519–1576) was frequently called upon to paint Spanish Court portraits.

The year prior to assuming power in the Netherlands, Philip II had married Queen Mary Tudor of England (1516–1558), herself a Catholic with a passion against Protestants (the treatment of whom earned her the epithet "Bloody Mary"). Philip's narrow-minded religious views fanned smouldering religious controversies into flames, spreading Protestantism further. He countered the Reformation in every way he could, ordering the ruthless persecution of all Protestants (and many others he accused of heresy).

For their part, Protestants participated in events such as the **Iconoclastic Fury** of 1566, a month-long spree during which hundreds of Catholic churches throughout the Netherlands were broken into, statues smashed, religious images burned, and tombs opened. Antwerp was particularly hard hit by damage from extreme Calvinists; to this day one sees churches there with empty niches and disfigured statues. Which leads one to wonder how much of the Netherlands' early artistic legacy was lost. One extremist action provoked another. Within a year (in 1567), Philip sent the fanatical **Duke of Alva** (a.k.a. Alba) to the Netherlands with an army of 10,000 Spanish troops. He outlawed Willem of Orange, garrisoned the towns with his troops, and quickly set up the so-called **Council of Blood,** which he used to execute many of the nobles, including Counts Egmont and Hoorn, who had become Protestants.

Dutch Prince Willem (the Silent) of Orange, who had lived in Brussels (having been brought up there at the court of Charles V), unable to convince Philip II of Spain to follow a moderate course in the Reformation rather than persecuting the Protestants, left Brussels in 1568, collected troops, and headed north to Holland to lead an armed resistance from there. Protestant rebels under **Willem of Orange** began to see some success beginning in 1572 with the capture of Vlissingen (Flushing) in Zeeland. By the end of the year, they controlled most of the province of Holland and Willem had been declared Stadholder. The Duke of Alva concentrated on stamping out the simultaneous uprisings in the southern Netherlands (today's Belgium). In 1573, just before his return to Spain, Alva's soldiers, unpaid and mutinous, unleased their anger in the brutal sacking of Antwerp known as the "Spanish Fury." Alva's Spanish replacement, Luis de Requesens (who died in 1576 and was in turn replaced by the Duke of Parma) continued the fighting in the Netherlands, mostly against Willem's forces in the Protestant-controlled north (Holland), since the south seemed ready for compromise.

In 1579, the signing of the *Union of Arras*—which declared faith in Catholicism and loyalty to Philip II—by the deputies of certain southern regions ended the last hope for unity between the northern and southern Netherlands. It was followed shortly by the *Utrecht Union of the Seven United Provinces,* which established the Protestant northern Netherlands (roughly, today's Holland) as separate from the southern Netherlands. Most Protestants had fled either to Holland or England by the time the Duke of Alva had finished his reign of religious persecution, (Amsterdam had to tear down its walls and expand the city to accommodate all the immigrants).

Before his death in 1598, Philip II ceded the Belgian province to his daughter Isabella who, married to Archduke Albert of Austria, was made an archduke in her own right. The "Reign of the Archdukes" (until 1621) was a period of economic recovery and great intellectual and artistic brilliance, led by Baroque Age genius Pieter Paul Rubens.

The southern Netherlands was returned to Spanish rule in 1621 and became contested territory between the Hapsburgs and the Bourbons during the *Thirty Years' War* (1618–1648). The war ended with the *Treaty of Munster,* which gave official acknowledgment of the United Provinces' (Holland) full independence, and secured Spanish agreement to the condition that the Scheldt be closed. Antwerp quickly went into ruin, and the trade and prosperity shifted northward to Holland.

During the 17th century, it became increasingly important to France's Louis XIV (who had married the Spanish Infanta) to have the Spanish Netherlands be subject to him. He went so far as to invade Holland but was unsuccessful. England could be counted on to oppose the French Louis's plan, and all parties wound up one way or another in the *War of the Spanish Succession* (1702–1713). In the *Treaty of Utrecht* signed in 1713, France finally abandoned all claim to the Spanish southern Netherlands, which passed to the Austrian Hapsburgs.

The region remained essentially independent as the Austrian Netherlands, undergoing little more change than the name of the sovereign, which for much of the period was Maria Theresa. Her popular and enlightened Brussels representative, **Charles of Lorraine,** ushered in a period of prosperity and renewed interest in culture. Transportation networks were constructed, agriculture was modernized, and industry (especially coal) was encouraged. Maria Theresa's successor, Joseph II, was (for reasons of personality more than policy) unsuccessful in his dealings with Belgium. In 1792, war broke out between Austria and revolutionary France; by 1794, Austria had been defeated and Belgium was once again under French occupation.

It was with a measure of acceptance that Belgium became a dependency of France in 1795. However, by the time conscription had been introduced, the Church persecuted (by anti-religious revolutionaries), and the government centralized, Belgians no longer found favor with the French. Under **Napoleon**'s rule from 1799 to 1814, a few positive elements were added under his *code of civilization* (among them the metric system and the first plan for numbering buildings for street addresses). After the Corsican Emperor suffered a final defeat in 1815 on their own soil at Waterloo, however, the idea of true independence loomed large for Belgians. But Britain had other ideas, fearing that Belgium was too weak to resist if the French made new attempts to control the region's ever-important North Sea ports.

The *Congress of Vienna* ordered Belgium incorporated into the **Kingdom of the Netherlands.** The plan was described—even by the diplomats of the day—as being solely for "the convenience of Europe," rather than the welfare of the Belgians, and proved, unsurprisingly, unpopular. Two points in particular doomed it from day one. The Belgian Catholic Church, especially strong in Flanders, could not tolerate the Dutch Protestant approach to religion. Secondly, all Belgians refused to accept mere equal representation in the *Netherlands States General* when, at the time, they had twice the population of Holland. In addition, though Dutch, King Willem, following the social form of the day, spoke French, which offended the Flemish; also, he paid particular attention to the industrial development of the rich coal fields in Wallonia while virtually ignoring Flanders's economic well-being (in Flanders, only the port of Antwerp, recovering rapidly after being reopened by Napoleon, benefitted from trade as a part of the Kingdom of the Netherlands).

By 1828, the two Belgian communities and opposing political parties had put aside their differences in common hostility to Dutch rule. Within weeks of the French Revolution of 1830, the Belgians held a brief one of their own, demanding of the European powers—this time successfully—that their independence and "perpetual neutrality" be recognized. The crown of the new constitutional monarchy was offered to and accepted by German Prince **Leopold of Saxe-Coburg,** an uncle and strong influence over England's Queen Victoria. Holland's Willem did not give in to the arrangements willingly and, ironically, the new King Leopold I was forced to call upon France for military reinforcement to flush him out of Belgium.

No sooner had the Belgians achieved the right to be their own political leaders than they became leaders in the **Industrial Revolution** on the continent. Europe's first steam-operated locomotive and rail line, running between Brussels and Mechelen, began in 1835. Belgians also invented the tram, and in the 19th century built tram networks all over the world.

Leopold II, who did much to foster Belgium's growth and transport systems, came to the throne in 1865. A colonialist to the core, he tried to get the Belgian government interested in acquiring a piece of Africa and, when he couldn't, decided to do so himself. In 1879 Leopold had H. M. Stanley (of "Dr. Livingstone, I presume" association) make agreements with some African chiefs to open up trading stations in an area he called the **Congo Free State.** Using his own resources,

Leopold established what amounted to a personal fief: eight times the size of Belgium, with three times the population. The resources he realized in return (copper, cobalt, timber, diamonds, and uranium, among others) made Leopold one of the richest men in the world. Eventually, even his own countrymen charged him with exploitation, however, and, in 1908, the African territory became the **Belgian Congo** colony under a largely reluctant Belgian government rule.

In 1960, the Belgian government granted independence to the Congo. The manner in which it did so reinforced its relative uninvolvement from the start: Belgium simply walked away, leaving only a few indigenous university graduates, doctors, and trained administrators to cope with the change. Renamed **Zaire,** with the capital *Kinshasa* (it had been *Leopoldville* under the Belgians), the newly independent country began life largely in a state of political and social disarray; the internal violence that has dogged it since has been attributed by some to the unprecedented speed with which Belgium cut its colonial connection. In any case, most Belgians agreed with the independence decision at the time, despite the resulting loss of 4% of national income. Today, Zaire continues to be burdened with backwardness and political corruption, but businessmen who seek its still considerable natural resources keep themselves largely unconcerned about the social conditions of the country.

In Belgium, the 19th century proved relatively calm and stable. A rising demand for social rights and equal education was evident in the demands of the **Flemish Movement** (see *Flanders: An Introduction*). After the *Workers' Congress* at Brussels in 1886, socialism gained a new following. Even art got into the act, as the *art nouveau* style was specifically adopted by those sympathetic to socialists. Art Nouveau architect Victor Horta created a marvelous headquarters for the Workers' Congress in the **Maison du Peuple** (built 1895, demolished 1966).

Most other issues fell away when Belgium, whose neutrality had been guaranteed by the Great Powers in 1839, was, nevertheless, invaded and occupied by the Germans at the beginning of the **Great War** (1914–1918). The "language situation" surfaced on the Ypres Salient in the form of the *Flemish Front Movement*. At issue was the fact that although an estimated 80% of Belgium's trench-confined conscripts were Dutch-speaking, few of the disproportionately large number of French-speaking officers knew the language of their soldiers, some of whom were punished for failing to obey commands they could not understand.

The German occupiers found that the conflict between Belgium's two language communities played into their hands. But working to keep Belgians together in battle was the brave leadership of the beloved **King Albert and Queen Elizabeth,** who based themselves at De Panne on the small southwest strip of Belgian soil which—with the help of hundreds of thousands of Allied troops in the trenches around Ypres—remained free for the duration (see *De Panne* and *Ypres* under *The Belgian Coast*). World War I devastation in Belgium included the loss of much magnificent medieval architecture, though the people rebuilt many of the monuments in their original exterior splendor.

Reconstruction from the First World War had not been fully completed when the Second began, with the Nazi invasion of Belgium (and Holland) on May 10, 1940. But for his death in a tragic climbing accident in 1934, King Albert I might have had to see his country through another war. Instead, his son Leopold III was seated on the throne. Leopold had married the extremely popular Princess Astrid of Sweden in 1926, but, a year after the royal couple was crowned, Astrid died in a motor accident in a car driven by her husband. Tragedy was to rule Leopold's reign.

During **World War II,** many Belgians were deeply troubled by the feeling that their king was not behaving in the best interests of the nation. **Leopold III,** stiff and inclined to ignore his ministers' advice, probably never would have won the affection felt by the Belgians for his father, King Albert, who symbolized Belgium's strength under prolonged fire in World War I. Leopold, in contrast, surrendered his armies and permitted himself to be taken prisoner 18 days after the Nazis invaded Belgium. His initial "wait and see" stand probably had been based on a belief that he could do more for his people from *within* Belgium than in exile, but it proved wrong on all counts. Staunch Leopold supporters point out that, once a prisoner, he successfully pleaded with Hitler for a less restrictive occupation (no *Gestapo* were stationed in Belgium, and conditions there were much easier than the ones the Dutch had to endure). But the bottom line was that, once a prisoner in his palace at Laeken and seen receiving mild treatment himself from the Nazis, Leopold was forever compromised in the eyes of his Belgian people. This was particularly so when his actions (probably more passive than pro-Nazi) were contrasted with those of Holland's Queen Wilhelmina (who had gone to England with her government and, once the Dutch got over the shock of her fleeing, from outside her country, was able to serve as a stirring symbol of resistance for the Dutch). Leopold spent the war being shifted from one place of imprisonment to another, to Germany in 1944 for safe-keeping after the Allied Normandy invasion, and finally to Salzburg, Austria, where he was found in 1945 with his 15 year-old son Prince Baudouin.

In exile in Switzerland, Leopold—whose brother Prince Charles had been asked to take over as regent for Belgium—knew he could not wear the Belgian crown again without the issue being resolved. Just short of ten years after the Nazis had invaded Belgium in May 1940, the **Royal Question** was posed to the people: *Should Leopold return to the Belgian throne?* He won the plebiscite, but by a 57 percent of the population that so closely followed the bicultural lines of the country—

in general, he was favored by Flemish Catholics, rejected by Walloon anticlerics—that, had Leopold insisted upon reclaiming the crown, Belgium might have seen civil war. Leopold's son **Baudouin** was quietly given constitutional powers and acceded as king in 1951 when he turned 21. More than one Belgian murmured under his breath: "The crisis is dead. Long live the King."

Well before the end of the war, in 1944, from their headquarters in exile in London, the governments of Belgium, Holland, and Luxembourg began talks about a post-war border-free economic union between the three. The name coined was *BENELUX* (BElgium, NEtherlands, LUXembourg), and it marked the beginning of a new era for Europe (see also *Introduction* to this book). The promise of the Benelux association led to one double its size: the six-membered **European Coal and Steel Community,** which was established to pool coal and steel production within the Benelux countries plus France, Germany, and Italy. The 1951 plan, fashioned by farsighted French planner Jean Monnet and proposed by Luxembourg-born and raised Robert Schuman, by then the French foreign minister, was called by Walter Lippmann "the most audacious and constructive initiative since the end of the war."

By 1957, yet another new stage in European integration had been reached, with the signing of the *Treaty of Rome* that established the **European Economic Community** (Common Market). The new international body eventually designated **Brussels** as its capital. (Belgium was small enough so that the privilege conferred upon its capital did not unleash jealousies among the other larger members). Today, the European Community (EC) has doubled its membership since the old Coal and Steel Community days to a full dozen, and new heights of European economic cooperation have been scaled with the single-market initiative.

The anniversary of the founding in 1950 of the European Economic Community is observed in Brussels each May 9th (Eurocrats have dubbed it *St. Schuman's Day,* after Common Market co-architect Robert Schuman). As far as Belgium is concerned, it's certainly a day worth celebrating, since the EC has changed the course of the country, and particularly its capital. After centuries of being a pawn of Europe's empire builders, Belgium has the satisfaction of knowing that its voice is heard as an equal in the European Community. And Belgium's crossroads capital has become virtually the capital of Europe.

Belgium is unique among the bilingual countries of the world in that its two main language groups are so nearly equal in numbers and area. Even more unusual is the extent to which bilingualism has, in the second half of the 20th century, been regulated by legislation. This process has continued under *federalism,* which was written into the constitution in 1980. Due to the complexity of Belgium's circumstances, a correctly calibrated federal formula is still evolving but separate and equal regional governments have been established for Flanders, Wallonia, and Brussels. Despite an often wasteful, excessively expensive overlapping of resources, the change to federalism overall has been deemed largely successful. Nevertheless, a lot of energy that could go into more far-reaching endeavors is expended to maintain Belgium's bicultural balancing act. For example, bilingual switchboard operators for the Belgian Senate must say "Le Senat/De Senaat" when answering the phone on Mondays, Wednesdays, and Fridays, and "De Senaat/Le Senat" on Tuesdays, Thursdays, and Saturdays. (Sundays, they rest).

Long-term Prime Minister **Wilfried Martens,** who has been able to calm the frictions between Belgium's Dutch, French, and German-speaking communities, has refined and developed the concept of federalism, and made it the bedrock of a political philosophy that has kept him in almost unbroken power since 1979. The national parliament and central government have responsibility for *international affairs, security, defense, consumer protection, labor, social security,* and *overall economic* and *monetary policy* (which must deal with Belgium's large chronic national budget deficit).

The recovery of the Belgian economy in the 1980s was one of the world's success stories. Despite an unemployment rate above the EC average, small 10-million-people-strong Belgium is surprisingly well-poised economically for the 1990s. Eleven of the country's corporations, a mix of metals, merchandising, banking, and utilities, make it on to *Forbes* magazine's list of the 500 largest companies outside the U.S. Belgium is the highest *per capita* exporter in the world: fully 70% of the GNP leaves the country as exports. The only worry with that is, as *Forbes* points out, "If its trading partners catch colds, Belgium gets pneumonia." Belgium recently found out that, even as the seventh most active financial center in the world and the fourth largest in Europe, it isn't invulnerable to international corporate raiding. Several once-proud family-run operations are now in the hands of foreigners.

Many of the internally-traumatic turns of 20th-century Belgian history have barely been noticed beyond its borders. In any case, on the world stage, they pale beside the significance that Belgium has assumed in the latter part of this century as one small but equal state in the European Community. With Brussels moving from the *de facto* to the *de jure* capital of Europe as capital of the European Community, the country has a high visibility. Today, Belgium—which, perhaps more than any other EC country, is loosening the ties of its own nationalism—eagerly awaits Europe's economic integration, which will, among other things, ease the exit of its own exports even more. Belgians are the first to characterize the European adventure in deregulation as an evolutionary, not revolutionary, process—and that suits their essentially conservative character just fine.

Keys to the Kingdom

TOURIST OFFICES Belgium now has parallel and autonomous governmental departments for all functions, including tourism, for both language communities: in Flanders, it's the **Vlaams Commissariaat-Generaal for Toerisme,** or VCGT, and in Wallonia the **Office for the Promotion du Tourisme de la Communauté Française,** or OPT. Each publishes its own tourism literature (although, when interests overlap and for national "theme" brochures, say castles, information is published jointly); all is available off the Grand Place at Rue Marché aux Herbes 61 *(513.30.30)*. Brussels, being distinct from either of the above departments, has its own tourist office, with offices in the magnificent **Hôtel de Ville** on the Grand Place, the **Tourist Information Brussels** *(T.I.B.; 513.89.40)* handles all materials and matters related to Brussels. At both, you'll be well served with English-language literature, at least for major cities and attractions. Elsewhere in Belgium, local tourist offices, indicated with an "i" for information and usually centrally located in towns or cities at or near the rail station or *Grote Markt/Grand Place* (main square), will provide materials on their area and possibly the greater region, so long as it is part of the same cultural community.

LANGUAGE: As you can tell from the background given above, the bilingual/bicultural issue has shaped Belgium. As a visitor, however, you needn't make more of it than your natural curiosity leads you to. English is widely spoken in all Belgian tourism areas. Brussels is officially bilingual (all street signs and public facilities must be designated in both French and Dutch), though French predominates. The city's large multi-national community (members of the European Community and NATO missions, diplomats, the staff of international corporations) often meets, linguistically speaking, in English.

Travelers may observe that language can be a sensitive subject *between Belgians*. For visitors to *this* foreign destination, it almost can be an advantage *not* to know the local languages. The use of English will not offend members of either community, whereas an attempt at French in Flanders or to a Flemish-speaking person in Brussels, on in Dutch to a Walloon, could. You can't rely on a surname to tell whether a Belgian is Flemish or French. The use of English establishes straight away that you are *not* Belgian, a vastly preferable situation to being mistaken for a member of one community who refuses to use the language of the other.

USEFUL VOCABULARY: See English/Dutch/French lexicon at the back of this book.

ALTERNATIVE PLACE NAMES: An aspect of travel in Belgium is that the names of places located in one language community often are translated into the other community's version. This means that you may see roadsigns directing you to such perhaps heretofore unknown corners of the country as **Doornik** (which is the Flemish version of the Walloon city of **Tournai**) or **Malines** (French for the Flemish city of **Mechelen**). The country **Belgium** is written either **Belgie** or **La Belgique,** and the officially bilingual city of **Brussels** (the only place with a real right to two names) is **Bruxelles/Brussel.** Selected place names are listed below alphabetically under the region Flanders (North) or Wallonia (South) in which they actually are located, with the other language-group name (and a third, English version, if such exists) in the second column.

Flemish Belgium

Local Flemish	French/English
Aalst	Alost
Antwerpen	Anvers/Antwerp
Brugge	Bruges
De Haan	Le Coq
De Panne	La Panne
Gent	Gand/Ghent
Halle	Hal
Ieper	Ypres/Wipers
Ijzer	Yser
Kempen	Campine
Kortrijk	Courtrai
Leie	Lys
Leuven	Louvain
Lier	Lierre
Maas	Meuse
Mechelen	Malines
Oostende	Ostende/Ostend
Oudenaarde	Audenarde
Schelde River	Escaut/Scheldt
Tongeren	Tongres
Veurne	Furnes
Vlaanderen	La Flandre/Flanders
Zeebrugge	Zeebruges

Walloon Belgium

Local French	Flemish
Ath	Aat
Bruxelles	Brussel/Brussels
Hainaut	Henegouwen
Huy	Hoei
Liège	Luik
Meuse River	Maas
Mons	Bergen
Namur	Namen
Nivelles	Nijvel
Soignies	Zinnik
Tournai	Doornik
Wallonie	Walloon/Wallonia

Just to prepare you, Belgians also feel free to change the names of places near to but beyond their borders, at least on their internal signage. See below.

German/English	French	Dutch/Flemish
Aachen	Aix-le-Chapelle	Aken
Trier	Trèves	
Koln	Cologne	Keulen
	Paris	Parijs
The Hague	La Haye	Den Haag
	Bois le Duc	's Hertogenbosch
	Nimegue	Nijmegen
	Lille	Rijsel
Dunkirk	Dunkerque	Duinkerken
Flushing		Vlissingen

THE FLAG(S): The national flag of Belgium consists of broad vertical bands in black, gold, and red, the historic colors of the Brabant province. Equally (perhaps more) inspiring to Belgians are the honored emblems of the Flemish and Walloon communities. In the north, banners showing the rampant lion symbol from the medieval coat of arms of the Counts of Flanders fly proudly over the land. To the south, the strutting cock, a symbol of courage used steadily in the centuries since Caesarean Gaul, oversees Wallonia.

WEATHER: Average High and Low Temperatures by month in Brussels (in Fahrenheit)

WEATHER IN BRUSSELS—Lat. N50°50'—Alt. 190'

	JAN.	FEB.	MAR.	APR.	MAY	JUNE	JULY	AUG.	SEPT.	OCT.	NOV.	DEC.
Low	30°	33°	35°	40°	46°	52°	55°	55°	52°	44°	38°	33°
High	39°	43°	49°	57°	64°	70°	73°	72°	67°	56°	48°	42°
Days with No Rain	16	13	16	14	15	13	15	15	14	14	12	15

NATIONAL HOLIDAYS: New Year's Day; Easter Monday; Labor Day (May 1); Ascension Day (in May); Whit Monday; National Day (July 21); Assumption Day (in August); All Saints' Day (Nov. 1); Armistice Day (Nov. 11); Christmas Day. **Note:** In Belgium, which doesn't have the "blue laws" that effectively close Holland every Sunday, many stores have opening hours on Sundays.

HOTEL AND CULTURAL PERFORMANCE RESERVATIONS
Belgium Tourist Reservations (BTR) provides a free booking service for hotels of all categories throughout the country. You can telephone

(from the U.S. 011-32-2-230-50-29, from the U.K. 010-32-2-230-50-29) or write (Post Office Box 41, 1000 Brussels 23) giving your accommodations requirements: dates; town or location; whether you'll be traveling by public transportation or car; amenity and price category preferred; number of people in your party; and number of rooms (twin beds or double/*grand lit*), with or without bath. BTR responds to your requests promptly, usually telephoning you back to give you the details, and following up with a mailed written confirmation. The system runs on good faith; no deposit is required, although your major credit card number will be taken if the hotel accepts such. To contact BTR from within Belgium, the telephone number in Brussels is 230.50.29. The reservation system is widely used by Europeans and the British, though it is less well known in North America: in 1990, BTR processed 90,000 reservations in Brussels alone.

BALCONOP (an acronym for BAllet, CONcert, and OPera) will make reservations for performances at Brussels's **Monnaie Theater,** the **Société Philharmonique de Bruxelles** and the **Opera Royal de Wallonie,** among other companies. The address of BALCONOP (a division of the Service Artistique of OPT) is Rue Marché-aux-Herbes, 61, 1000 Brussels, upstairs from the all Belgium tourist information office on the ground floor (telephone 518.14.94, fax 513.69.50).

RAIL TRAVEL: Belgium built the first European rail line—between Brussels and Mechelen in 1835—and today has the most dense national rail network in the world. Train travel to cities is highly recommended, especially since, once there, attractions usually are best appreciated on foot. The frequency of trains between Brussels and other towns of reasonable size and importance is two or three times an hour; smaller places usually are served by at least one train an hour from the nearest major town. Here are some sample rail travel times from Brussels to other major towns in Belgium; Mechelen 20 mins.; Antwerp 30 mins.; Ghent 45 mins.; Bruges 55 mins; Tournai 60 mins.; Liege 65 mins.; and Ostend 75 mins. For information on all train travel within and beyond Belgium, contact S.N.C.B. (Société Nationale des Chemins de Fer Belges) in Brussels (219.26.40).

DRIVING: It must be said that Belgian drivers as a group are considered by other citizens on the continent to be less than adept at driving (and the butt of jokes on that score). More seriously, the driving accident and fatality rate in Belgium is seven times that of the U.S. (while the statistics for Holland are very similar to those in the U.S.) The situation is undoubtedly contributed to by the fact that until 1967 no demonstration of driving skill was required, since no driving licenses were issued in Belgium. Plans to harmonize driver standards and traffic laws throughout the EC have been greeted with relief by all, but meanwhile the word in Belgium is be wary and understand the rules of the road there as well as you can.

Road conditions vary considerably throughout the country; the country's motorways are always well maintained, but rural roads, especially in the Ardennes, may not be as well looked after. The **Royal Automobile Club de Belgique** is located in Brussels at Rue d'Arlon 53 (230 08 10).

TRAVEL DISTANCES: Brussels, with a central situation in Belgium, as well as within the Benelux and Europe, posts the following traveling distances to other cities.

City	Miles	Km
Amsterdam	122	198
Frankfurt	254	409
Koln (Cologne)	125	203
London	201	325
Luxembourg City	127	205
Paris	181	292

CITY SIGHTSEEING TOURS: Introduced within the last few years as an alternative to large mortorcoach tours of Belgian cities are the mini-vans of the **Sightseeing Line** company. Beginning several times daily at central sites in Brussels, Bruges, Antwerp, and Ghent, the mini-vans, which hold about a dozen passengers, are much better suited to the not-made-for-motor-vehicles streets in these old cities. The vans enable the tour to encompass some medieval sections of the cities that would be impossible for larger coaches to traverse. The commentary for the driving route is taped in each of nine languages (tourists select the correct channel on their headsets), which means that everyone gets the full story told at each attraction passed. Also, if you run into an inner-city traffic jam, the tape can be stopped and relaxing classical music substituted until the tour (which, without such delays, may run from 60 to 90 minutes) recommences. For details, ask for Sightseeing Line brochures at local tourist offices.

LIQUOR LICENSING LAWS: Although loosening, Belgium's liquor license laws still limit the sale of alcoholic beverages to wine and beer in a number of establishments. Places that do restrict the sale of high alcohol-content spirits usually also offer diverse aperitifs such as vermouth, sherry, and *kir* (white wine with *cassis*).

THE ROYAL FAMILY: The present (and fifth) constitutional king of the Belgians, **Baudouin,** was born in 1930, exactly 100 years after Belgium gained its national independence. He ascended the Belgian throne at the age of 21 in 1951 when his father, Leopold III, abdicated (see above under *An Historical Perspective*). In 1960, King Baudouin married Spanish noblewoman **Fabiola** Mora y Aragon, who is infinitely more popular with her subjects than were the Spanish rulers of the region several centuries ago. King Baudouin and Queen Fabiola are scrupulous in their efforts at an even-handed attitude toward the two Belgian cultural communities. Nevertheless, the royal family, since it represents the Belgian nation as an entity, is not of surpassing importance to many of the country's Flemings or Walloons.

There are no children from the royal marriage. The eldest child of Baudouin's brother Albert (Prince of Liège), Prince **Philippe,** born in 1960, has been educated as heir to the Belgian throne. King Baudouin and Prince Albert's older sister, Josephine-Charlotte, is married to Grand Duke Jean of Luxembourg.

BRUSSELS

Guidelines for Brussels

SIGHTS Brussels's **Grand-Place,** with its inspiring 15th-century **Hotel De Ville** (Town Hall, with **Tourist Information Brussels—T.I.B.**) and gilt-highlighted guild houses (late 17th century), is Europe's most magnificent square—and car-free at last. It's the starting point for all city sightseeing, to be followed by the small surrounding medieval market streets of the **Îlot Sacre,** including the restaurant-clogged **Petit Rue des Bouchers.** Belgium's finest collection of Flemish "primitives" paintings, as well as wonderful works from the Netherlands' 16th and 17th centuries, and the Belgian Surrealists, are at the **Musées de l'Art Ancien et Moderne** on **Place Royale,** which is near the **Royal Palace.** The sights around the **Grand Sablon** include its antique shops and weekend outdoor market, art galleries, church, and the **Petit Sablon** with its restful statue-ornamented garden. Among Brussels' varied architecture are fascinating samples of the turn-of-the-century **art nouveau** style, especially the former house of Belgium's most famous exponent, Victor Horta. City attractions are varied, and sometimes surprising. The **after-dark illumination** of monuments creates lasting impressions; the Grand-Place aglow will leave you spellbound.

GETTING AROUND Belgium's capital city is well equipped for conveying people from one to another of its 19 *communes*. **Metro** is the fastest, most decorative means (see *Bourse Station/Metro art* under *What To See and Do* below); buses are next best, then trams (colorful but slow, they're gradually being done away with since street cars interfere excessively with Brussels's notorious traffic). Metro and transportation system maps are available from the T.I.B., as are 24-hour tickets (BF 180) for unlimited use of city Metro, buses, and trams. Fares shown on taxi meters include tip. Parking in Brussels is as eventful as in any too-traffic-congested old European city. Metered spaces have varying rules (have BF 5 and 20 pieces handy); paid car parks (indicated by blue **P** signs) can be found at **Blvd. de Waterloo, Place de la Monnaie,** and **Place Rogier.**

SHOPPING Brussels isn't London, Paris, or Rome, but the best designer names from each can be found in the luxury specialty shops and designer boutiques in the **Haut de la Ville** (Upper Town) along the chic **Blvd. de Waterloo** and **Avenue de la Toison D'Or.** The big-name chain and department stores are clustered primarily in **Blvd. Aldolphe Max** and the pedestrianized **Rue Neuve.** Late night shopping is Friday, til 8 p.m., though smaller shops and grocery stores that close at lunchtime may remain open until 7 or 8 p.m. other nights, too. Travelers should inquire of shopkeepers about the conditions for duty-free purchases.

ENTERTAINMENT AND EVENTS The Tourist Information Brussels's publication *BBB Agenda* (for sale) has a timetable of events in the city, including opera, ballet, and concerts; the T.I.B. also can arrange bookings. See, too, events listings in *The Bulletin,* Brussels's English-language weekly newspaper. Cafes, nightclubs, and cinemas (some 35, showing a varied range of films in their original language) are clustered in the upper town between Porte Namur and Place Louise, and the lower town between the Place de la Bourse and Place Rogier.

ACCOMMODATIONS Brussels offers plentiful hotel choices in all prices—which have risen across the board in the last several years in this European capital. Because of the startup in September of European Community (EC) meetings, as well as fall trade congresses and corporate conventions, hotel rooms then and in October can be scarce.

RESTAURANTS If gourmets worldwide consider Brussels one of the top cities for food (restaurants number nearly 1,400), you'll hardly want

382 · · · BELGIUM

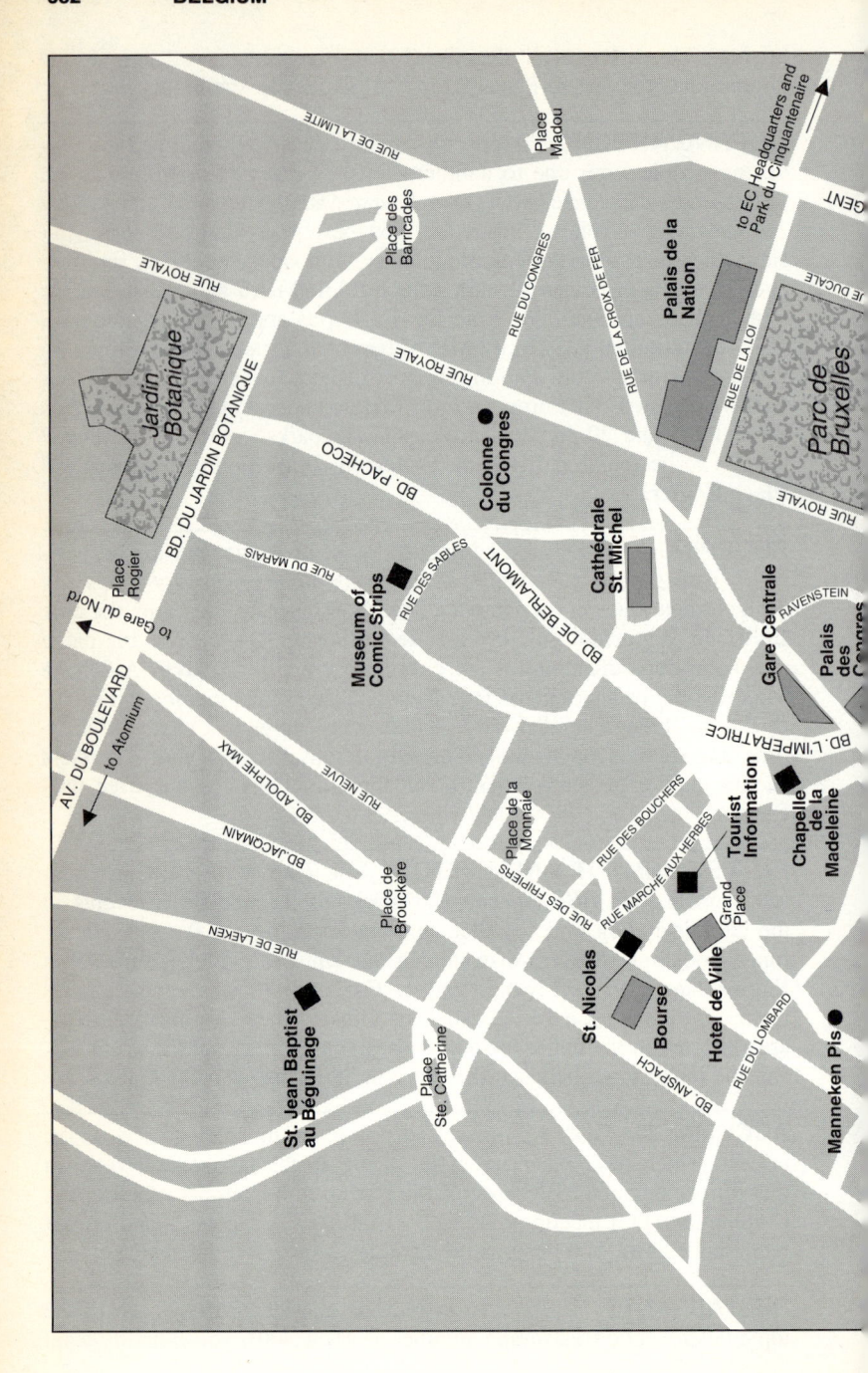

BELGIUM · · · 383

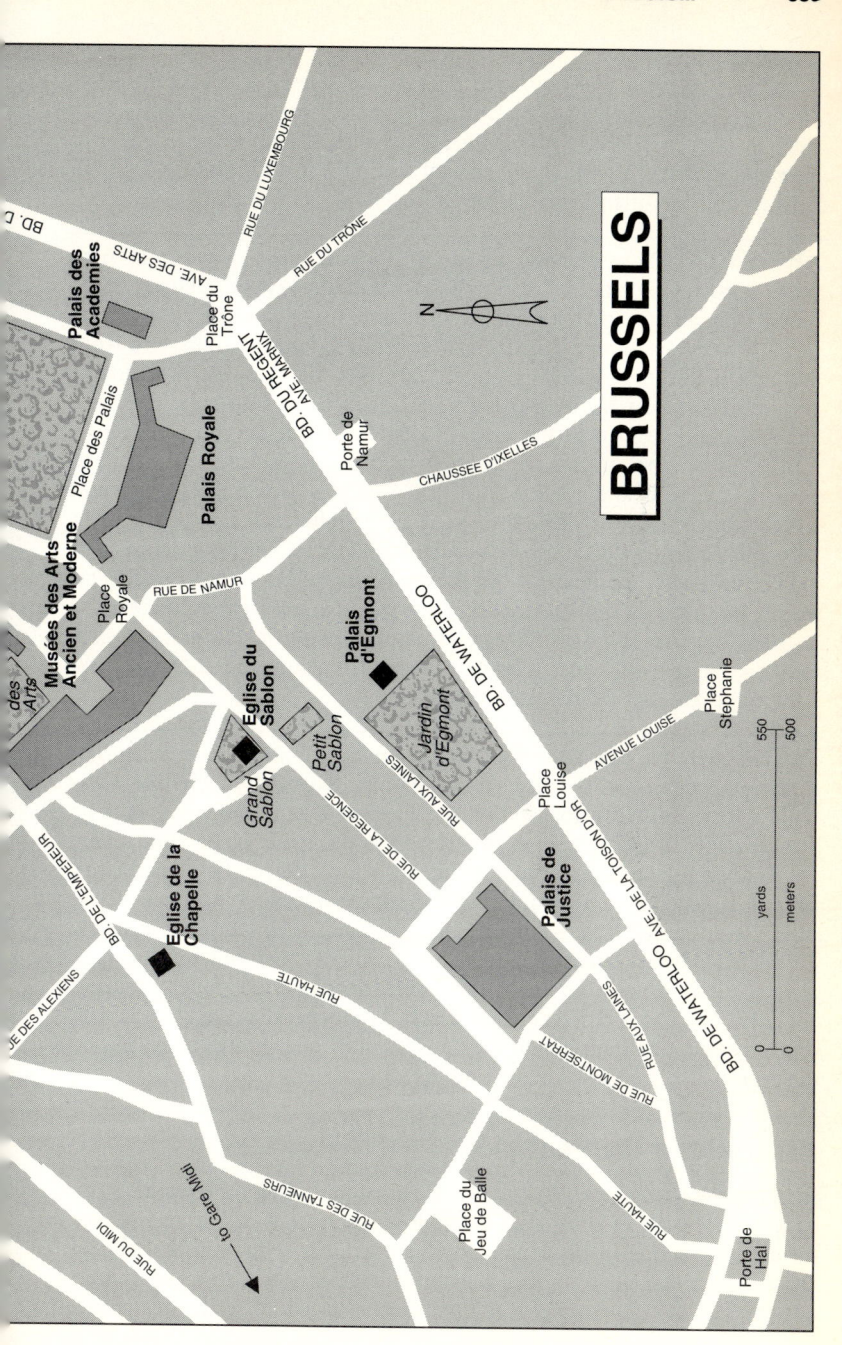

to leave without assessing the city's celebrated cuisine for yourself. Whether you want *frites* (French fries) from stands, *alfresco* meals of *moules* (mussels) at tables set out along ancient alleys, Belgium's beef stew in beer specialty (*vlaams carbonada*) in an atmospheric cafe, or an extraordinary repast at an elegant dining "institution," it will be hard to find less-than-fine food in Brussels.

ARRIVING Those arriving by air fly into Brussels' **Zaventem Airport,** 9 mi./14 km. northeast of the city. **Sabena World Airlines** is the major Belgian carrier, with both transatlantic routes and air connections onward to many European cities. There's thrice-hourly rail service from the airport into the city (20 minutes, fare BF 70), with the first stop at Brussels' **Gare du Nord** (North Station), then **Gare Centrale;** one train an hour continues on to the **Gare du Midi** (South Station), the city's third main station. If you are arriving in Brussels by train, and already have reservations at a hotel, you'll find it helpful to know before arrival which train station is closest to your hotel, although the Metro links with all stations, and all have taxi stands. Gare Centrale is closest to the Grand-Place, the heart of old Brussels, and to both the Brussels and the all-Belgium tourist information (Rue Marché aux Herbes 61) offices. As the *de facto* capital of Europe, Brussels is well-linked with the continent's major motorways. Ferries arriving from England at Ostend and Zeebrugge are met by Brussels-bound trains.

IN THE AREA Located in a magnificent building on the eastern outskirts of Brussels at Tervuren is the **Musée Royal de l'Afrique Centrale** which, formerly focused on the *Belgian Congo,* now has exhibits on the whole of Africa. South of Brussels is the rural battleground where the Emperor Napoleon, much to the relief of the early 19th-century European heads of state, came but did not conquer at **Waterloo.**

TRAVEL TIPS Brussels's museums, offices, and other attractions usually close at noon for up to two hours, so plan your midday touring accordingly. The **Art l'Ancien** and **Art Moderne** museums have coordinated their one-hour lunch closures so that one or the other of the underground-connected sections remains open.

Brussels in Context

Imagine the scene, seen by an American acquaintance in Brussels, visiting his Belgian in-laws: two Bruxellois conversing, a French-speaker forming questions in his language to a Fleming, who was replying in Dutch—both continuing in that manner without missing a meaning. That's not the way the city's *official bilingualism* is meant to work, of course. What the scene, granted extreme, shows is that Brussels (Bruxelles,

Brussel) remains a capital concern to members of both Belgium's major cultural communities.

Geographically, Brussels lies well within Dutch-speaking Flanders, but, socially, it is overwhelmingly French in its orientation. According to William Z. Shetter, author of *The Netherlands in Perspective,* "The power of Brussels to radiate and extend French influence is a source of constant anxiety to the Flemish." By law, no count is made, but it's known that Brussels' French-speaking Belgian-nationality residents outnumber the city's Dutch-speakers by an estimated 4 to 1. The 1962 guarantee of equal language rights for the Flemish did not erase French-outlook favoritism in Brussels, and only very recently has the Dutch language become an accepted route to advancement in business and government there. If one could put language aside, the Bruxellois are more of an amalgam: while a majority may *speak* French, most *think* like the Dutch, the result being a cultured business acumen.

In addition to having to absorb the complexities of its indigenous inhabitants' bicultural existence, Brussels, with a population of just under one million, is nearly 25 percent foreign, many MEPs (Members of the European Parliament), diplomats, multi-national corporate executives, and their families. It sounds like the making of a melting pot but, according to Brussels-based *Financial Times* reporter Lucy Kellaway, it's not so simple. In an article in that British newspaper, Kellaway explains: "Each nationality keeps to itself, remaining true to all its prejudices, persuasions, and preferences. . . . Outside work they stick to themselves. They live in little pockets, send their children to national schools, and, distance permitting, go home to their own countries at weekends. . . . While (citizens of EC) member states mix little with each other, they do not mix with the Belgians at all. . . . Language is only partly to blame for this isolationist behaviour. After all, anyone who works in the Commission must be able to speak French, and most people can muster decent English and probably another language too."

While this picture of human nature, almost reminiscent of a colonial lifestyle, may be discouraging to those in the EC who seek to drop their narrow nationalist identities in order to see the "big-picture" Europe, it perhaps proves reassuring to citizens of individual countries in Europe—and travelers from abroad—who have worried that union in the European Community might mean the end of the cultural idiosyncrasies.

Brussels, today one of Belgium's three federalist regions (with Flanders and Wallonia), celebrated its millenium in 1979, which puts its founding back in 979, when Charles of France, Duke of Lower Lotharingia, built a fortified structure on the island of Saint Gery on marshy land called **Bruoscella.** In 1041, ducal successors built a new castle on the highest land, becoming early residents of the **Haut de la Ville** (Upper Town) at **Coudenberg,** site of the present Royal Palace. Brussels first had fortified walls in 1100, and the first version of its Cathédrale Saint Michel appeared in 1225. To embrace the continuing growth, a second series of city walls (where the *inner boulevard* ring road now runs) was finished in time for Brussels' quadricentennial in 1379.

Entering the 15th century, Brussels gained in stature as a residence of the ambitious **House of Burgundy,** which became the most powerful state between France and Germany, acquiring nearly all the secular lordships of the Netherlands. The first stone of the Hôtel de Ville was laid on the Grand-Place in 1402, in response to the need for Brussels to have grander buildings for use by the Burgundian dukes. Their court attracted large numbers of French knights to Brussels, and the French language became fashionable among the Netherlands nobles.

In 1430, Burgundian **Philip the Good,** called "the equal of kings and emperors," took possession of Brabant, thereafter moving his capital from Dijon to Brussels. The city achieved remarkable economic growth by turning to the production of luxury goods: lace, paintings, tapestries, jewelry, and church furnishings. Artists and craftsmen of great renown flocked to the increasingly ostentatious court. Under Philip, **Jan Van Eyck** became court painter, and **Rogier van der Weyden** (Rogier de la Pasture) was appointed Brussels' town painter.

Charles V (Quint) confirmed the political and administrative preeminence of Brussels by himself settling in the city at the palace of Coudenberg in 1515, and, in 1530, officially moving the Netherlands' court there from Mechelen. As capital of the Netherlands' 17 provinces (land that today includes parts of both Belgium and Holland), and with a central location within the immense Hapsburg empire which ruled the Netherlands, Brussels received great benefits. The original **Ommegang** (still annually reenacted on the Grand-Place) was a brilliant pageant marking the grand entry procession of Charles V and his son Philip II, King of Spain, into Brussels in 1549. But Brussels also had the unenviable inevitability of being at the center of the **Reformation.**

The stage was set for the **Eighty Years' War** by the 1555 abdication of Holy Roman Emperor Charles V at Brussels' Coudenberg Palace. Power over the 17 Netherlands' provinces passed to his son Philip, a fanatic Catholic. In Brussels to receive rule from his father, Philip thereafter oversaw the Netherlands long distance from Spain, dispatching orders and officials to collect unpopular financial taxes and tributes, suppressing Protestants, and installing his half-sister Margaret, Duchess of Parma, as regent in Brussels. Philip's harsh policies inflamed newly-converted Protestants, who were filled with anti-Papist preaching from Calvinists and Lutherans. A wave of religious rebellion swept the Netherlands. The first action of the Eighty Years' War came on April 5, 1566, when hundreds of Netherlands nobles marched through the streets of Brussels to the home of Margaret of Parma to protest religious persecution. Many carried beggars' bowls that once had signified that their support for the king would last until they were reduced to beggars. Taunted as *geuzen* (beggars) as they walked past regime loyalists, the nobles and their followers adopted the term as a rallying nickname. The year 1566 also produced extremist Protestant crowds that attacked Catholic churches and their contents. Brussels' **Cathedrale St. Michel** suffered severe damage, and relics in the **Eglise Notre-Dame du Sablon** were destroyed.

Spanish response to the wide-spread destruction was brutal. In 1567, Philip II sent the **Duke of Alva** (Alba) and 10,000 troops to the Netherlands to replace the Duchess of Parma. In Brussels, Alva established the *Council of Troubles* for trials of sedition against Netherlanders (who called the court the **Council of Blood**). By 1568, groups of 30 to 50 people at a time were being condemned to die, their property confiscated by the Spanish Crown. In only a short time, the tally of the dead reached 8,000.

Perhaps because the earliest resistance to Spanish religious oppression had come from the Netherlands nobility, when the Dutch **Counts Egmont** and **Hoorn**—both of whom had previously served with honor in the armies of Charles V and Philip II—went to Brussels to seek relief for Holland from the persecution of the Protestants there by the Spanish King's representative, Alva wouldn't listen. At 10 a.m. on June 5, 1568, on Brussels' Grand-Place in front of the *Maison du Roi* (which never housed a king, only the Spanish law court), a silent, shocked crowd saw Egmont and Hoorn beheaded. Afterwards, it is said, many people pushed past the Spanish guards to dip their Belgian lace-trimmed handkerchiefs in the blood of the first martyrs of the war. (Some time later, a memorial commemorating the infamous execution was erected on the spot in front of the steps where it took place; the statues of Egmont and Hoorn and fountain from it were moved to the peaceful *Place du Petit Sablon* when the garden there was laid out in 1890). The tide turned in 1576 when **Dutch Prince Willem of Orange** was able to drive the Spanish out of Brussels, and the city enacted anti-Catholic laws that virtually abolished all outward signs of the religion.

From 1585, however, by which time the religious struggles between the Spanish and the Dutch had caused a split between the northern and southern Netherlands provinces, Brussels was reoccupied by Spanish forces and served as the capital of the southern Spanish Netherlands. Thereafter, the city, and most of the rest of what is Belgium today, remained basically loyal to Spain and Catholicism. The pro-Catholic **Counter-Reformation** brought a wave of Jesuits, priests, and nuns to Brussels, and the arrival of Philip II's daughter Archduchess Isabella, who, jointly with her husband Archduke Albert of Austria, was appointed ruler of the Spanish Netherlands in 1598. Life in Brussels again flowed around a fashionable court, and the city became a haven for political exiles, such as the sons of beheaded Catholic English King Charles I.

As Spanish influence flagged at the end of the 17th century, **Louis XIV of France** embarked on an imperialist adventure through the Netherlands. In 1695, he ordered his 70,000-man army to fire cannon and mortars from the heights of Anderlecht on central Brussels. Forty-six hours later, Brussels had lost nearly 4,000 houses, 16 churches, and many major buildings, including all those surrounding the Grand-Place, with the exception of the **Hôtel de Ville** which, miraculously, withstood the onslaught. The Bruxellois response was to build a more magnificent main square than before, a goal they accomplished in four short years. French efforts in the **War of the Spanish Succession** (1701–1714) finally went down in defeat due to England's Duke of Marlborough, John Churchill (Winston's ancestor), and Austria's Prince Eugene; this brought the southern Netherlands under Austrian Hapsburg rule.

The Austrian era began oppressively, and social confrontations culminated in the beheading of Brussels' guild leader **Francois Anneessens** in 1719. But **Charles of Lorraine,** a genial Austrian ruler (dispatched from Vienna's Hapsburg household of Maria Theresa), oversaw the era after the 1745–1748 **War of the Austrian Succession** (during which France conquered nearly the whole of the country before losing it again to Austria). Under Charles, the physical face of Brussels around the Place Royale changed to *neo-classical,* as the Royal Palace, Palais de la Nation, and Parc de Bruxelles took shape. Maria Theresa's son, Joseph II, who ruled from 1765–1790, had a well-intentioned plan for reform, but his over-hasty and insensitive implementation aroused a spirit of revolt.

Under the influence of the French Revolution and the leadership of **Henri van der Noot,** the people of Brussels took arms, and in a national uprising, declared the **United Belgian States** (the first use of the "Belgian" name in modern times) in January 1790. The life of the independent republic was short-lived; by agreeing to restore some civil rights that had been rescinded by Joseph II, Austrian Emperor Leopold II was able to reoccupy the country. Between 1792–94, in yet another turnaround of rulership, the French Revolutionary Army under Napoleon Bonaparte beat the Austrians for Belgium *and* defeated Holland. Both Netherlands countries became dependences of France (and were united as the **Batavian Republic** from 1795 to 1808). With the exile of Napoleon to Elba in 1814, the *Congress of Vienna* was set to bind Belgium to Holland again when its plan had to be postponed because of the reappearance of the French Emperor.

Cannon fire from the fields of **Waterloo** (only a dozen miles away) could be heard in Brussels during the day of the battle on June 18, 1815. Many who had gathered light-heartedly at the Duchess of Richmond's "Waterloo" Brussels ball for guest-of-honor the Duke of Wellington (who danced until dawn on June 16), were, on the 18th, sure that Napoleon would bring bloodshed all the way to Brussels. Those fortunate enough to find passage fled to Antwerp on barges.

After the Battle of Waterloo in 1815 (see *Waterloo* under *In the Area* below), despite Belgian protestations, Holland's Prince Willem became ruler of Belgium as king of the **Kingdom of the Netherlands,** since the European powers, still meeting at the **Congress of Vienna,** were anxious to keep a strong, established, buffer state between themselves and France. Brussels became co-capital (with The Hague) of the new kingdom. But, beneath the surface, Belgians breathed **revolution,** which came in 1830 in Brussels. An opera performance of Auber's *The Mute of Portici,* which carries a strongly suggestive patriotic message (see *Theater de la Monnaie* under *What To See and Do* below), inspired Belgians to take to the streets of Brussels after an August 25, 1830, performance. Some raised the Brabant flag—the same tricolor of black, gold, and red that the new country adopted soon after—over the Hôtel de Ville. Young intellectuals and others rioted, sacking the homes of government ministers, raiding bakeries for bread and bars for alcohol, and destroying machinery in factories. Brussels' Burgomaster Vanderlinden d'Hooghvorst formed an 8,000-man militia that quelled the riot but didn't stop the movement. Joined by volunteers from the provinces, the Bruxellois fought a rebellion against 14,000 Dutch soldiers who arrived in September. The **Parc de Bruxelles,** in front of the *Palais de la Nation* where the Dutch government had its Brussels headquarters, was the scene of some of the fiercest fighting. On September 27, 1830, a free **Kingdom of Belgium** was finally declared, with Brussels named the capital. In July of 1831, the keys to the city were handed over to the new King Leopold of Saxe-Coburg, who swore allegiance to the Belgian people on the steps of *St. Jacques sur Coudenberg* church on **Place Royale.**

The energy released with the achievement of Belgian independence produced plentiful signs of progress and prosperity in the capital of the new kingdom. The **Free University of Brussels** was founded in 1834; in 1835, continental Europe's first passenger steam locomotive chugged out of Brussels (to Mechelen); and the Royal Library opened in 1837. Later in the 19th century, the covering of the Senne River took place, largely for sanitary reasons, but it made possible the construction of Brussels' central boulevards (today's **Anspach, Adolphe Max,** etc.). The **Palais du Justice** (built between 1866–1883 by Joseph Poelaert), a Greco-Roman domed domain larger than St. Peter's in Rome, if nothing else showed civic confidence and added to the 1880 exhibition at the **Parc du Cinquantenaire** in celebration of the free country's 50th birthday.

During World War I the Nazis violated Belgium's declared neutrality, and used the senate chamber of Brussels' Palais de la Nation (Parliament Building) for its wartime tribunal. In that chamber in 1915 the Nazi Tribunal condemned courageous English nurse Edith Cavell to death by firing squad. She had been running a training school for nurses in Brussels and, uncowed by threats, had willingly harbored and further helped Belgians and Allies seeking to escape across the border to neutral Holland (she is crediting with helping 130 prisoners escape). Brussels was again occupied in World War II (from May 1940–September 1944).

During 1944, government ministers who had fled from Belgium, Holland, and Luxembourg, and were all operating in exile from London, settled on the idea of the **Benelux,** a mutually beneficial, barrier-free customs and trade, which, when officially instituted in 1948, helped put the devasted economies of the three countries on the fastest possible post-war recovery track. The **Benelux** proved a harbinger of European evolution, and, in 1959, Brussels was selected as the capital of the **European Economic Community.** Brussels also blossomed from hosting the extremely successful **World's Fair in 1958,** with **Atomium** being the symbol of its nuclear energy theme. In 1967, Brussels was chosen capital of NATO (North Atlantic Treaty Organization). Those developments forever changed the face and mentality of the city. On the domestic front, in 1980, under a new Belgian form of government, Brussels found itself one of the country's three federal regions (together with Flanders and Wallonia).

While the internationalism of Brussels is intriguing to travelers—it's the "company town" for European government, and TV news anchors in countries throughout Europe begin their coverage with "Today in Brussels . . ."—it also can create a certain dissatisfaction for the resulting lack of a single, well-defined foreign identity. Even its own Belgian population doesn't allow Brussels to present a single culture to visitors—though two foreign flavors for one destination could be considered a bonus. The simple fact is that Brussels is complex.

More than most places, Brussels is the result of its history, which includes happenings in this last decade of the 20th century. They are all revealed on the physical face of the city, nowhere as clearly as in the mixed architectural course the city has followed during the second half of this century. What some call a carelessly-conserved architectural heritage, others explain by saying that Brussels wants to be more in the present than just a pretty face from the past. That shouldn't be a worry, since Brussels, as capital of the EC, heads the world's largest economic block, the 340 million citizens of an evolving single market Europe.

Brussels's longstanding city symbols, the surprisingly smaller-than-life boy statue mascot **Mannekin Pis** and the **Atomium** molecule multiplied many billion times its size, both seem to have had to step slightly aside for the **EC flag** (a circle of 12 gold stars representing the 12

European community member nations on a field of blue) as the city emblem one sees everywhere. But, ever interested in being innovative as well as true to its history, Brussels has adapted: Mannekin Pis has had his wardrobe updated with an official EC outfit.

GUIDEPOSTS
Telephone code 02

Tourist Office — **Tourist information Brussels (T.I.B.):** Hôtel de Ville, Grand-Place, B-1000 Brussels; 513.89.40; daily 9 a.m.–6 p.m. (from Oct. 1–March 30 closed Sun.), closed Christmas, New Year's.

Emergencies — Accident: 100; police 101: doctors on duty: 479.18.18, 648.80.00; dentists on duty: 426.10.26, 428.58.88

Airport — General info. 02/722.30.00; SABENA World Airlines: reservations 511.90.30, information 720.71.67

Trains — Information for all trains in Belgium and in Europe: 219.26.40

Metro, Tram, bus — Information day and night: 515.21.11.

Lost Property — Lost property office for metro, buses, trams: 515.23.94, Ave. de la Toison d'Or 15, 9:30 a.m.–12:30 p.m.; for property lost in a taxi, apply to police station nearest point of departure or call 721.31.11

Tours — **ARAU City Tours:** in English on such themes as **Brussels 1900, Brussels in the 1930s, Surprising parks and squares,** 513.47.61 or 512.56.90. **Sightseeing Line:** 14-seat minibus tours in English (headset) through Brussels' smaller streets, schedule, info. 513.89.40 (T.I.B.)

Taxis — Available at taxi ranks, or by telephone order: **Taxis Oranges** 513.62.00; **Taxis Verts** 511.22.44; tip is included in meter price.

Post Office — Main office: **Centre Monnaie** Mon.–Fri. 9 a.m.–5 p.m. money orders, 8 a.m.–8 p.m. stamps; Sat. 9 a.m.–noon. (Sat. in July & Aug. 9 a.m.–8 p.m. for stamps only.)

Telephone/Telex	Main city office: Blvd. de l'Imperatrice 17, daily 7 a.m.–10 p.m., 513.44.90
Local Newspaper	*The Bulletin,* a Brussels weekly in English; events information.
English books	W. H. Smith, Blvd. Adolphe Max 71, 771.92.00

WHAT TO SEE AND DO......................

By law, the names of Brussels' streets, buildings, etc. must appear in both official languages (as you'll see on the T.I.B. map), but here, solely for simplicity's sake (and with, I hope, the forgiveness of the Flemish), I often have used only the French. Except for scattered attractions (included at the end), major sights are grouped under three main centers: the **Grand-Place;** the **Place Royale;** and the **Grand Sablon.**

Grand-Place and Surrounding Area

Grand-Place • *Grote Markt, main square* • It's difficult to overstate the impact the Grand-Place makes as you enter it on foot from any of the confined cobbled streets that lead there. Suddenly, you are assaulted with splendor on a staggering scale, an impression strengthened not only by the great size of the square, but the architecturally-harmonious appearance of the whole. In the disaster-turned-triumph of the 1695 French bombardment, except enemy cannons leveled everything around the Grand-Place except what they sought most: the soaring spire of the Hôtel de Ville. Immediately, plans were made to build even grander guildhouses and, between 1696 and 1699, many were completed. Baroque and beautifully embellished, with statue-studded gables, pilasters, and balustrades, the gold-leaf detail of the decor glowing in the sun or gleaming under night spotlights, the guildhouses surround Brussels' immense (120 by 75 yards, 110 by 70 meters) main square. Most of the buildings served as headquarters for the business and social meetings of Brussels' guilds, identified by the appropriate patron saint or insignia on the facade; all have stories (inquire at the T.I.B. about its audio-tours of the Grand-Place) though none has a more varied history than the **Maison du Cygne** (swan) at No. 9. Rebuilt in 1698 as a house for Peter Fariseau (a founder of the Brussels opera), it became in 1720 the butchers' guildhouse. In exile from Germany, **Karl Marx** (1818–1883) moved with his family into the building in about 1846 and, having met Friedrich Engels in Brussels, undoubtedly wrote some of their jointly-published (1848 in Belgium) *Communist Manifesto* under its roof. So perhaps it's appropriate that the *Belgian Labor Party* was founded in the Maison du Cygne in 1885. Today, it houses an elegant restaurant of the same name whose prices are most certainly capitalist, not communist.

Centerpiece of the Grand-Place is the **Hôtel de Ville/Stadhuis/Town Hall** *(multi-lingual guided tours only, April–Sept., Tues.–Fri., 9:30 a.m.–12:15 p.m., 1:45–5 p.m., from Oct.–Mar. closes at 4 p.m., Sun. 10 a.m.–noon, 2–4 p.m., tours cancelled in case of City Council sessions or receptions, last tour a half hour before closing time, closed Mon., Sat., some hols; 512.75.54)*, one of the largest (197-foot/60-meter facade) and finest Gothic buildings in the Benelux. With a 295-foot/90-meter openwork spire by Jan van Ruisbroek, topped with a figure of Archangel Michael, patron saint of the city, it was completed in 1454. Included in the guided tour of the interior are reception halls laden with decorative treasures: 15th-, 17th-, and 18th-century Brussels' tapestries, Gothic wood carvings, and fascinating full-length portraits of the likes of Charles V and Philip II.

Museum of the City of Brussels • *Maison du Roi, Grand-Place, directly opposite the Hôtel de Ville; Mon.–Fri. 10 a.m.–12:30 p.m., 1:30–5 p.m. except 4 p.m. Oct. 1–Mar. 31; Sat., Sun., hols. 10 a.m.–1 p.m.; 511.27.42* • Despite a lack of English explanation, much here will capture your attention, including the building itself (though, singly among those on the Grand-Place, it is not as old as it looks). Destroyed in the 1695 bombing, it remained a shattered shell (and eyesore) until rebuilt in 1763; but it was reconstructed in such an ordinary and unharmonizing style that it became neglected and had to be virtually demolished and rebuilt again in 1873, then under the patient efforts (22 years worth) of City Architect Victor Jamaer, who used old engravings as his guide but added the galleries and the tower. The ground floor displays 16th- and 17th-century Brussels' tapestries, including one made from a cartoon by Rubens, 15th-century carved-wood retables, 14th- and 15th-century stonework saved from Brussels's buildings, and 18th- and 19th-century Brussels faience, all highlighted by **Pieter Breugel the Elder**'s *Marriage Procession*. The first floor also presents a history of Brussels's city design and development, shown through items such as a model of the 17th-century town and paintings and prints showing the Senne river harbor before it was filled/covered in the 19th century. The main attraction of the second floor is the display of several dozen of the 400-odd outfits in the wardrobe of Brussels's mascot **Manneken-Pis** (see below). The costumes periodically donned by the two-foot-tall statue range from Roman centurian to American cowboy. Maurice Chevalier penned and published a song to Manneken-Pis in 1949 and gave him an outfit complete with a straw hat of the type the French songster was famous for. On some dates Manneken-Pis is dressed ceremonially: each

Sept. 3, in thanks for their liberation of Brussels on that date in 1944, he wears the uniform of the Welsh Guards.

L'Ilot Sacré • *The Sacred Isle* • This old section of the lower town, a network of narrow cobbled streets built on the once-marshy land where Brussels was born more than one thousand years ago, covers the area immediately north of the Grand-Place. Its pedestrian back streets carry the names of the businesses conducted here since medieval days: *Marché aux Herbes* (herb market), *Rue des Bouchers* (butchers' street), *Rue de Beurre* (butter street), *Rue de Poivre* (pepper street). Today, L'Ilot Sacre is indeed considered to be sacred, to be protected from the demolition and development that have wreaked more havoc on Brussels's buildings than the cannonballs and bombs of any war since the 17th century. One of Brussels's most appetizing tourist sights is the restaurant region of Rue des Bouchers and Petit Rue des Bouchers: it's often said that if visitors haven't eaten out at least once here they can barely say they've been to Brussels.

Eglise St. Nicolas • *Rue de Beurre 1; daily 8 a.m.–6 p.m., except Sat. 9 a.m.–6:30p.m., opens hol. at noon; 511.17.75* • whose origins (the choir is 14th century) go back as far as the activities of the area's merchants, to whose patron saint the church is dedicated, lies at the edge of L'Ilot Sacre. Small shops still abut its sides in the medieval manner. Extensively restored in 1955, St. Nicolas is rich in art works: the *Vladimir Icon* of 1131, paintings by Bernard Van Orley, and one attributed to Rubens.

Art in the Metro/Bourse Station • *Blvd. Anspach;* Art in the Metro *brochure in Dutch and French only* • From 1976, when the first stations of the Brussels Metro opened, until 1984, when the city's Museum of Modern Art opened on Place Royale, the only real museum of contemporary art in the Belgian capital was underground in the system's shiny new stations. When Metro construction began in 1969, an art-loving politician helped direct its decoration, moving city planners to a totally innovative approach because, as one spokesman said, "we did not want to have a stereotype Metro, with kitchen or bathroom-type tiles and every station the same." The Ministry of Transport not only solved much of Brussels's enormous urban traffic problem, which had come to impact the quality of life in the city, but also improved the quality-of-life dimension of the Metro stations (elsewhere so often anonymous, monotonous, user-unfriendly underground spaces). About 1% of the Metro budget was set aside for commissioned works from jury-invited contemporary Belgian artists who, once asked, were given freedom to express themselves in the station space and often were involved right along with the construction. Artists were asked to use materials that would stand up to the underground environment.

Bourse is only one of some three dozen Metro stations that displays some of the 50 works of original art, but since it's central, we'll begin a Metro art inventory there. A large oil painting of old Brussels trams, painted by Belgium's grandfather of Surrealism **Paul Delvaux,** is quite in character for the artist who has used train stations as symbols for years. As with several stations, Bourse has more than one art work; **Pol Bury** created a *Moving Ceiling* out of 75 welded stainless steel cylinders. At the *Comte de Flandre* station, **Paul van Hoeydonck**'s *16 x Icarus* group of figures "fly" from the ceiling. (Van Hoeydonck, who lived in the U.S., has the distinction of being the world's only artist to have a work on the moon: his small statue *Fallen Astronaut* was placed on the moon's surface by *Apollo 15*'s Armstrong in 1971.) Since the opening of the new *Stockel* station in 1988, riders have been delighted by artist **Van Herge**'s colorful comic strip figures lining both long walls. The entire *Alma* station reflects nature: pillars are painted as tree stumps and the ceiling is a puffy cloud-filled sky. *Vandervelde* is a fantasy landscape, with the second-largest ceiling fresco in the world (following, of course, the Sistine Chapel). *Aumale* features the world's largest photographic work of art. It depicts scenes showing the Anderlecht neighborhood outside as it was before and after demolition to make way for the station. *Hankar* station has Roger Somville's 500-square-yard/meter acrylic wall and ceiling painting called *Notre Temps,* showing the contradictions of "our times" in vividly colored scenes: an all-night cafe where people discuss the future of the world, motorcyclists refusing to take part in the everyday battle of life. At *Merode,* Roger Raveel's large oil panel painting *Ensor: Vive La Sociale,* with its faceless people (in the style of painter Ensor), bright colors, and mirrors, is meant to raise questions. Many of the stations feature sculptures; at *Stuyvenbergh,* **Yves Bosquet** has mounted statues of the Royal Family against one wall. With the variety of materials used (Station *Louise* has a tapestry), there are stations that do have tiles, but there's nothing of the bathroom about them: *Tomberg*'s are yellow ceramics with a blue line design; *Merode* has a wonderful wall of blue, red, yellow, and brown tiles; and *Roodebeek*'s tiles mix with marble in striking black and shades of gray vertical stripes.

It's nice to know that in this city, which has commissioned works from celebrated artists for more than 500 years, the Ministry of Transport is continuing the tradition today and has enabled many of Belgium's best artists to carry out work which many of the artists themselves consider to be of decisive importance in their careers. In addition to its aesthetic appeal, the Brussels Metro has statistics that show it has greater passenger security, less graffiti and vandalism, and fewer suicides than the underground transportation systems of comparable-size cities.

Theatre de la Monnaie • *Place de la Monnaie* • So-named because, until bombed by Louis XIV's army in 1695, the **Munt** (Mint) had stood here, and the Theatre de la Monnaie that replaced it played a role in Belgian independence. In February 1829, the opera *La Muette de Portici* by French composer **Daniel Francois Auber** premiered at the theater at a gala attended by the Dutch royalty of the Kingdom of the Netherlands. The opera's libretto told of Neapolitans' struggles against oppressors, and the climatic aria *Amour Sacre de la Patrie* (Sacred Love of the Fatherland) was vigorously applauded by the Belgians, whose emotions obviously had been stirred because of their own unhappy enforced union with Holland since 1815. The audience's reaction caused the opera to be withdrawn from the repertoire for 18 months. When it was staged again on August 25, 1830—only a month after Parisiens had overthrown the French monarch—following the provocative line *Rendsnous l'audace et la fierte* ("give us back boldness and pride"), intellectuals were inspired to join workers outside on the Place de la Monnaie in demonstrating against underpayment and unemployment. Those who fell in the ensuing month-long revolution (see *History*, above) are buried beneath a monument at the **Place des Martyrs,** a quiet square two blocks north of the theater off Rue d'Argent. The Theatre de la Monnaie standing today was designed by Joseph Poelaert following a fire in 1855; it has recently been lavishly restored.

Sainte Catherine/Saint Géry district • Just across Boulevard Anspach from the Bourse is a less explored area of old Brussels, an extension of the narrow market streets found in the Ilot Sacre. A landmark is the large **Eglise Sainte Catherine** (*Place Saint-Catherine; 7:30 a.m.– 7 p.m., 5 p.m. in winter; 513.34.81*), built in 1854 by Joseph Poelaert in a mixture of styles. A 17th-century belfry from a former church stands nearby, as does the **Tour Noire,** a survivor from the city's 12th-century walls. Running parallel to each other north from the church are **Quai au Bois à Brûler** and **Quai aux Briques,** once quays on either side of the subsequently-covered Senne River, an area known as the **Marché aux Poissons** (Fish Market) and noted for its seafood restaurants (see *Restaurants,* below). The area's open space and fountains provide a pleasant surprise. Nearby is the **Eglise Saint Jean Baptiste au Béguinage** (*Place de Béguinage; Tues., Thurs., Fri., Sat. 9 a.m.–5 p.m., Sun. 10 a.m.–5 p.m.*), built from 1657–1676 by Luc Fayd'herbe; its three-gabled Flemish-Italian Baroque facade is one of the finest in Belgium (it, and that of Sainte Catherine, are both beautifully floodlit at night).

Adjoining the Sainte-Catherine district to the south is **Saint-Géry,** within which is **Les Halles,** an 1881 neo-Flemish renaissance marketplace used as a wholesale meat market as recently as 1977 and subsequently saved from demolition by ARAU (see *Tours* under *Guideposts,* above). Today Les Halles (which renovating-architect Jacques Zajtman admits was influenced by London's Covent Garden) is an upmarket assemblage of clothing, craft, and chocolate shops, and gathering place for the gregarious and street performers. The 32 boutiques and interior stalls are bathed in a special glow by the natural light that pours in through the glass/wrought-iron roof. A mezzanine-level bar runs the length of the building, providing a viewing and drinking stand overlooking shoppers on the floor below; in the low-arched cellars is a restaurant.

Manneken-Pis • *Rue de l'Etuve at the corner of Rue du Chene, some 100 yards/90 meters southwest of the Grand-Place* • Manneken-Pis, an unexpectedly small, scarcely two-foot-tall/just over a half-meter-high statue of a naked young boy urinating into a fountain struck such a strong chord with Bruxellois that city fathers in 1619 commissioned a bronze replacement from Jerome Duquesnoy the Elder to replace a similar 15th century stone statue. Many legends exist concerning the origins of Manneken-Pis, but, even leaving such speculations aside, the story of the statue-turned-city-symbol is absorbing.

His singular popularity and position as city mascot have made Manneken-Pis the subject of a series of kidnappings over the centuries. The first attempt, intercepted, was made by British soldiers in 1745. That effort seems to have inspired French soldiers in 1747, but their plot, too, was uncovered before it played out. However, to recompense Brussels for his soldiers' seizing of the statue, King Louis XV bestowed upon Manneken-Pis a title and gold-embroidered brocade court costume, complete with sword and feathered hat, to wear on festival days. Before long, other groups, both Belgian and foreign, were following suit, gifting Manneken-Pis with sufficient garb to make him the city's best-dressed citizen, one necessitating a wardrobe keeper (see *Grand-Place, Maison du Roi,* above). The most damaging kidnapping incident occurred in 1817 when a supposed ex-convict pulled the statue from his street-corner niche and broke it into pieces. Fortunately, the fragments were found and reassembled to form a mould from which the present statue was cast. In 1956, after yet another attempt, Manneken-Pis was bolted in place and equipped with a burglar alarm. During a snowstorm a few years later, however, the alarm bells froze, and prank-minded students from Antwerp were able to make off with him, though he was returned unharmed the next day.

Galleries Saint Hubert • *entrances off Rue du Marché aux Herbes, Rue des Bouchers, and Rue d'Arenberg; always open* • At the end of Rue des Bouchers, one enters a different era. The Industrial Age made possible the art of glass and metal that found one of its earliest and finest expressions in the skylighted Galleries Saint Hubert, Europe's first covered shopping walkway, built in 1847 by J. P. Cluysenaer. Not only was the arcade an early all-weather environment but it provided pedestrians with through passage in an alley-area that over the centuries had become choked with impasses. The airy and attractive glass-vaulted arcade splits into the flag-festooned yet elegant **Galerie de la Reine** and **Galerie du Roi,** housing boutiques, cafes, and a theater.

Brussels has other 19th-century arcades: **Bortier Arcade,** browsed for its bookshops, connects Rue de l Madeleine to Rue Saint-Jean; **North Arcade,** with a broad selection of shops, connects the pedestrian Rue Neuve and the busy Boulevard Adolphe Max at the northern end of the Place de Brouckère; and **Hirsch Arcade,** though not flourishing, still supports a secondhand bookshop and print and etching shop that have been there since the second World War, runs at right-angles to Place des Martyrs and Rue d'Argent.

Belgian Center of the Comic Strip • *Rue des Sables 20; daily 10 a.m.–6 p.m., closed Mon. and 1/1, 11/1, 12/25; 219.19.80* • Opened in 1989, this museum links two distinctively Belgian forms of creative expression. The setting is a 1903 former textile warehouse that was designed by Brussels's leading art nouveau exponent, architect Victor Horta; the contents are what Belgians call the *Ninth Art,* the social phenomenon and genuine art form of the comic strip. The museum was once the Waucquez Warehouse, the only one remaining of six art nouveau department stores that Horta built in Brussels; it, too, was very nearly lost to the wrecker's ball when the store went out of business in 1965 and buyers couldn't be found for the building, leaving it abandoned to weather and vandals until the middle of the 1980s. Fortunately, visionaries in the '80s seeking a place to gather the fantastic examples of their unusual art form saw the possibility of doing so under the historic Waucquez roof, which was subsequently restored. The displayed comic strips and audio-visual exhibits (more than 60 years of creativity are documented) usually are in French and/or Flemish only, but their visual appeal and that of the wonderful building, with its magnificent lobby, ornamental grand staircase, art nouveau details, and space and light on all three floors, make the museum thoroughly worthwhile. There's also a shop with curios and posters, and an attractively ornamented brasserie (omelets, pasta, salads, chicken and seafood dishes, beverages including wine and beer, kitchen open until 3:30 p.m.). The museum's location, Rue des Sables, in an area of central Brussels now in transition back to respectability, once teamed with pedestrian traffic because of the public stairs at the end of the street which still lead to the upper town.

Place Royale and Surrounding Area

Cathédrale Saint-Michel • *Place Sainte-Gudule; Easter to Oct. 31, 7 a.m.–7 p.m., Nov. to Easter, 7 a.m.–6 p.m.; 217.83.45* • The cathedral, whose triforium is especially lovely when illuminated, has stood on its sloping site between Brussels's lower and upper town since the mid-13th century; the twin truncated towers, a rarity in Belgium, give it a strong French appearance. Overall, the massive building has a simple Brabant-Gothic style, with the nave and transept dating from the 14th and 15th centuries. Though elevated in rank to cathedral only in 1961 (when it became the seat of the Archbishop of Brussels-Mechelen), St.-Michel, long known as Belgium's national church, has been the setting for all the country's great religious occasions since the time of Duke Philip the Good of Burgundy. An extensive, and extended, restoration-in-progress makes it uncertain as to what will be on view to visitors, but the 16th-century stained-glass windows in the south and north transepts, created from cartoons by **Bernard van Orley,** are a treasure to search out, as are those of the same period in the **Chapel of the Blessed Sacrament,** donated by Charles V and his family, whose granddaughter Archduchess Isabella and her husband are among those buried in the crypt. Also buried in the cathedral is one-time Brussels's city painter **Rogier van der Weyden** (1400–61) and Margaret of York (d. 1322), daughter of England's Edward I. A superb carved-wood Baroque pulpit by Hendrik Verbruggen (1669) shows Adam and Eve being expelled from Eden, and six splendid 17th-century tapestries by Van der Borght sometimes are hung in the choir, often in summer, when chamber concerts may be given in the Chapel.

Rue Ravenstein • Exiting the Victor Horta-designed Gare Centrale (Central Station) through **Galerie Ravenstein,** with its arcade and rotunda, leads to Rue Ravenstein. Across it, just to the left of Horta's **Palais des Beaux-Arts,** is **Rue Baron Horta,** formerly the **Escallier Belliard,** on which was located **Pensionnat Heger** to which **Charlotte Brontë** (1816–1855) came in 1842–43, first as a student, then remaining as a teacher, having fallen unrequitedly in love with Monsieur Heger. Brontë's Brussels experiences appear as background in her novels *Villete* and *The Professor,* in which Rue Ravenstein is called Rue Fossette. At the top of Rue Ravenstein is the 15th-century **Hotel Ravenstein** (now a restaurant, see *Restaurants,* below), Brussels's last surviving mansion from the Burgundian period, with a picturesque interior that's been carefully restored. In it was born **Anne of Cleves,** the "'Flemish Mare,'' fourth wife of Henry VIII. Further up is the top of the Mont des Arts.

Mont des Arts • Erected between 1954 and 1965, Mont des Arts is another route from the lower town to the upper, with stairs and garden through its center, convention center to the left and Royal Library to the right, to the **Place du Musée** with the impressive Louis XVI-style palace of Charles of Lorraine at the summit. Its lavish exterior decoration features statues and bas-reliefs celebrating the arts and sciences.

Museum of Ancient Art/Art Ancien; Museum of Modern Art/Art Moderne • *Rue de la Régence 3 for access to both museums; daily 10 a.m.–5 p.m.; lunch closings are coordinated so that when one closes for an hour the other remains open; closed Mon., 1/1, 5/1, 11/1, 11/11, 12/25, and election days; 513.96.30; catalogues in English* • Simply stated, these museums are the most important collections in Belgium, a country noted for its art. The Museum of Ancient Art, whose focus is on the **Flemish "Primitives"** rather than classical ancients, concentrates on the art of the 15th–17th centuries in the Netherlands, with some contemporary paintings from Italy and elsewhere included for comparison. Highlights from the rich collection in which virtually all major Netherlands artists are represented include *The Annunciation* by the **Master of Flemalle,** *Portrait of Anthony of Burgundy* and *The Lamentation* by Brussels' mid-15th-century City Painter **Rogier van der Weyden** and a room devoted solely to five major works and a fragment by **Pieter Breughel the Elder** (the most important grouping of his works outside of Vienna). In an adjoining room are copies and adaptations of his work done by his son, **Pieter Breugel the Younger,** who was born just a short distance from the museum in 1564. Often called "Hell Breugel" for his own painted visions of life after death, he is responsible through his carefully copied versions of having preserved now-lost original works by his father (who died when his son was only five). Among the copies here are the *Massacre of the Innocents* and *Festival of Flanders,* which, though not of the genius of the father's originals, are masterpieces in their own right. The great works in the 17th-century Dutch gallery are displayed in a lovely carpeted and skylighted setting.

The Museum of Modern Art, opened in 1984, and connected—compliments of **Alphonse Balat** (1875–1885)—to the older, neo-classical museum building by passageways and escalator, is a stunningly successful creation of multi-level exhibit space in the form of a glass half-bowl curved to catch the natural light, and set some eight levels in and beneath the courtyard of Charles of Lorraine's palace. Belgium's entire cast of 19th and 20th-century painters and sculptors is covered, among which is a collection of 26 major works by **René Magritte,** including *Empire of Lights* and *The Domain of Arnheim* (kept by his widow until her death in 1986). A well-marked, color-coded museum plan (comprehensible even in its French/Flemish form) helps make the most of your time. There's a good shop and cafeteria.

Place Royale • This area of the upper town took its shape and neo-classical appearance in the 18th century as Hapsburg rulers instituted a grand Paris-influenced plan meant to make Brussels look a little less like Vienna's country cousin. At the center of the square is an equestrian statue of **Godfrey de Bouillon,** leader of the First Crusade in 1096 (see *Bouillon* under *Wallonia, The Meuse Valley*). Close by is the **Royal Palace** (open to visitors for a period each Aug./Sept., check with T.I.B. for dates, times), currently used for state receptions, royal audiences, and as the King's office (the royal residence is in suburban **Laeken,** see below). The palace was built in the 1730s, more or less on the site of the former **Palace of Coudenberg** (which burned in 1731) that had been used by the Dukes of Brabant from the end of the 11th century, and their descendants including Emperor Charles V. The present Royal Palace was expanded and renovated by Leopold II at the beginning of this century.

The marriage of King Baudouin and Queen Fabiola took place in 1960 in the regal 500-foot Throne Room, certainly a setting worthy of the royal affair with its exquisite mosaic parquet floors, gleam of a dozen Val-Saint-Lambert Belgian crystal chandeliers (which in turn glow in the gold-edged mirrors), plasterwork friezes, and wall-and-ceiling ornamentation. The Goya Room is decorated with antique Brussels tapestries based on cartoons by the 18th-century Spanish painter.

Facing the Royal Palace is the **Parc de Bruxelles** *(open daily 6 a.m.–9 p.m.).* Laid out in its present French park form in 1835, it was previously the park for the Dukes of Brabant and was famed throughout Europe as a hunting wood and warren with ponds, fountains, and grottos. During the Belgium "revolution" of 1830, the park was the scene of armed exchanges between Belgians and Dutch King Willem's forces. Today, the espaliered Linden trees, their leafy limbs linked Brabant-style to form a green trellis, shady strolling promenades, and fountains, provide a peaceful, pleasant separation of Monarch and State (the **Palais de la Nation/Parliament** being at the opposite side of the park from the palace). **The Belgian Parliament** *(public entrance at rear, Rue de Louvain 7; guided visits can be arranged on weekdays between 10 a.m. and 4 p.m. when there are no sessions, call the Senate 515.82.11 or the House 519.81.11.; English language literature available).* As a guide pointed out, "The country of Belgium doesn't exist by the grace of God as does the United Kingdom; we Belgians exist by the grace of the Great Powers." Included on a tour of the impressively-furnished building, built between 1779 and 1783, is the rich red Senate Chamber and the green-toned House of Representatives, both of which conduct all business with simultaneous translations of Dutch into French and vice versa.

The nearby **Congress Column** *(Place du Congres, Rue Royale)* commemorates the National Congress of 1831, which proclaimed the Belgian Constitution. The large bronze figures represent freedom of the press, education, religion, and association. An eternal flame at the base pays homage to unknown soldiers from the first and the second World Wars, both represented by both a Fleming and a Walloon.

The Sablon and Marolles Districts

Place du Grand-Sablon/Grote Zavel • *Rue de la Regence, a short distance southwest of Place Royale* • Far more refined than its name in French ("sandy wasteland") suggests, the Sablon is an elegant, elongated square, encircled by smart antiques and art shops, trendy bars and restaurants. It first became fashionable in the 16th century. It's at its most colorful on weekends, when the red and green-awning stalls of the antiques market are set at the top of the square.

Eglise Notre-Dame du Grand Sablon • *Rue de Regence 3B; Mon.–Fri. 7 a.m.–6:30 p.m., Sat., Sun., hol. 9 a.m.–7 p.m., guided tour Sun. 4 p.m.; 511.57.41* • A lovely example of late flamboyant Gothic style, the church developed from a 1304 chapel built by the Guild of Crossbowmen. In 1615, Archduchess Isabella, using a crossbow, shot down the guild's target bird atop the church, which garnered her much admiration. The interior has some fine detail, including gothic carvings on the cornerstones, but the church also is much admired simply for its overall harmony with the setting. The fine stained-glass windows are illuminated wonderfully from within at night. Rededicated (by American organist James David Christie) in 1990 after its rebuilding, the organ is often used for concerts.

Place du Petit-Sablon • *across Rue de Regence from Notre-Dame* • is a tranquil Renaissance-style garden with benches well-used by area residents. Elegant effigies of Counts Egmont and Hoorn (who met their death by beheading on the Grand-Place in 1568) have been given a place of honor; the Egmonts were one of the noble families who settled on the Sablon in the 16th century. The pretty park is surrounded by a wrought iron fence, with each of its 48 supporting columns topped with a small bronze statue representing one of Brussels' 16th-century guilds.

Among the greenery of the **Jardin Du Palais d'Egmont** (access from Rue du Grand-Cerf, off Rue aux Laines/Wolstraat at the southeast corner of Petit-Sablon) seek out the statue of **Peter Pan,** a twin casting by Frampton of the whimsical figure with animal friends that's tucked among trees in London's Kensington Gardens. At **Palais d'Egmont** *(not open to the public),* now the property of the Belgian Ministry of Foreign Affairs and used for major conferences, in 1973, the United Kingdom, Ireland, and Denmark signed the documents that made them full members of the European Community (Greece followed suit in 1981, Spain and Portugal in 1986).

At the end of Rue aux Laines, past graceful 19th-century houses, sits the enormous bulk of the **Palais du Justice** (*Law Courts; Place Poelaert*), 17 years in the making to the mid-19th-century-design of **Joseph Poelaert**. He obviously was moved to create a monumental work, since the 2.5 acre-structure is larger by half again than St. Peter's in Rome. Perhaps appropriately, the Palais du Justice sits on the former site of Brussels' gallows; it was the hoi polloi, not those worth bringing to the Grand-Place to be executed publicly, who were hanged here. The Nazis set the buildings on fire on September 3, 1944, and the huge 345-foot-high dome caved in. It's long since been reconstructed and dominates the skyline and the **Marolles** district, located at the base of its plateau.

The Marolles, famous for its ancient Brussels dialect and flea market, is well-stocked with faces familiar from Flemish paintings created four centuries ago. So it may not be surprising to learn that **Pieter Breugel the Elder** lived here. In the **Breugel House** (*rue Haute 132; plans to open the authentically restored house as a museum remain uncertain, inquire at the T.I.B.*) Pieter Breugel the Elder (1525–1569) was born in the North Brabant province in Holland and lived there for the last six years of his life. Most likely apprenticed to master painter Peter Coeck in Antwerp from about 1545 to 1550, in 1551 he created a Freemaster in the Guild of St. Luke there. Breugel traveled in Italy in the early 1550s and from 1559 began producing signed and dated paintings with regularity. In 1563 he married the daughter of his former master and settled in Brussels. Two sons (Pieter "Hellfire," the Younger and Jan "Velvet") were born in the house in 1564 and 1568, but sadly Pieter the Elder died here in September 1569. He was buried in the partly 13th-century **Eglise Notre Dame de la Chapelle** (*at the end of the road, corner of Rue Haute and Rue Blaes*) where he had been married only six years earlier. Breugel's memorial, in the third chapel off the south aisle, was erected by his son Pieter and once was adorned with a painting (now in a private collection) by Pieter Paul Rubens, with whom son Jan Breugel later studied and worked. Undoubtedly, the elder artist strolled these working-class streets searching for faces and figures to put into his well-peopled paintings and, today, Breugelian characters still serve or sit over steins of beer in the cafes.

Attractions Elsewhere in Brussels

Palais du Berlaymont • *Rue de la Loi, Rond-Pont Robert Schuman; 235.11.11; Metro station Schuman* • The rather too-grandly-named building, never noted other than for its shape (the best description of which I've heard is a four-armed starfish), has, since its opening in 1969, been Brussels' symbol of the European Community, serving as office space for some 5,000 Eurocrats. But, now, the building's been found to be full of asbestos and may, in fact, have come down by the time you read this. Construction on other EC complexes already has brought most other activity in the district to a halt; the next building to come on-line will be large enough to house the whole European Parliament (much expanded with 12 member countries, compared with the original six).

Musées Royaux d'Art et d'Histoire • Royal Art and History Museums; *Parc du Cinquantenaire; year-round Tues.–Fri. 9:30 a.m.–5 p.m.; Sat., Sun. 10 a.am.–5 p.m., closed Mon.; however, some sections of this enormous institution are staffed only on certain days, with some collections open solely on odd, or even, days; it's best to call ahead if you are interested in a particular exhibit; 741.72.11; Metro station Schuman; color-coded museum plan, exhibit notes in French/ Flemish only* • The monumental museum wings, surrounded by the 90-acre/36 hectare **Parc du Cinquantenaire,** were built for a national exhibition held in 1880 to celebrate 50 years of Belgian independence; the triple triumphal arch that connects the two colonnaded buildings was built in 1904–05 by architect Charles Girault. The *Museums of Art and History* are in the wing on the right. Among the extensive collections that cross all eras and areas (a fine model/maquette of ancient Rome, for example) are a number of excellent Belgium-related exhibits: the remarkable Flemish Renaissance *Story of Jacob* tapestry set (see *Tapestries* under *Decoration Arts and Traditional Crafts* in front of this book); art nouveau and art deco vases, stained-glass, and jewelry; Belgian lace and furniture; and porcelain from Tournai.

The wing to the left houses the Museums of the Army and Military History, which provide a general impression of the major military and historical events that have taken place on Belgian soil since 1789. Of perhaps more interest to non-Belgians, and not as dependent on non-existent English exhibit notes, are the *armored car* and *aviation* sections that focus mostly on the first and second World Wars. One huge room offers an exceptional collection of World War I fighter planes and *Battle of Britain* (1940) spitfires; gondolas from balloons and airships also are on display.

Atomium • *Blvd. du Centenaire, Laeken; daily year-round 9:45 a.m.–6 p.m.; April to mid-Sept. until 6:30 p.m. and panorama only until 10 p.m.; 477.09.77; Heysel Metro station* • This imaginatively conceived, skillfully constructed symbol of the **1958 Brussels' World's Fair** (and, since then, the city) has just received a long-overdue overhaul. The aluminium-covered steel model of an iron crystal molecule, magnified some 200 billion times, represented the Atomic Age at the World's Fair and later offered exhibits on the peaceful uses of nuclear power. Atomium has nine "electrons," large (60 ft./18 m. in diameter), shiny exhibition-space spheres that are connected by elevators and escalators running up inside 10-foot/3 meter-wide supporting pylons. Since renovation, during which the structural integrity was examined and the interior escalator, the longest in Europe, replaced, a new exhibit devoted to the evolution and recent developments of medical research has been installed. Atomium's top sphere, at 335 feet/102 meters much higher than Brussels' Hotel de Ville's spire, has a panoramic observation area and restaurant.

Mini-Europe • *adjacent to Atomium in Bruparck Center; daily April 1–Jan. 6, 9 a.m.–6 p.m., except in July & Aug. until 8 p.m., weekends 9 p.m.; 477.03.77; Heysel Metro station* • featuring a landscaped layout of approximately 70 major 1:25 scale models of landmark buildings in the 12 EC member states. The detail on some (the Louvain Hotel de Ville, London's Parliament Buildings, Paris's Pompidou Center and Sacre-Coeur, Athens' Acropolis) is remarkable. Pricey (combined ticket with Atomium: BF 400), but worth consideration if you enjoy this sort of attraction.

At nearby **Laeken,** you can tell if King Baudouin and Queen Fabiola are home by whether or not Belgium's black, gold, and red standard is sighted over the Royal Palace. The residence is never open to the public, but the **Royal Greenhouses** are, for about ten days during April and May (exact dates and times, including evenings when greenhouses are illuminated, are available after Jan. 1 from the Tourist Office). Located in the 460-acre/185 hectare Royal Park, the greenhouses, themselves six acres under neo-classical glass-domed rotundas and galleries, were ordered built for the royal blooms, including tropical species brought back from the Belgian Congo, by King Leopold II in the 1870s. It's nearly one-mile/1.5 kms. for a round trip through the greenhouses, highlighted by the azalea house, connecting walks filled with climbing geraniums and fuchsias whose bell-like blossoms form a colorful overhead canopy, ferns, songbirds, glades, and grottos. The architectural treasure, 323,000 square feet of glass set in elaborate ironwork, is a translation of royal vision into reality by architect **Alphonse Balat.** That the structure greatly influenced the development of art nouveau in Belgium and elsewhere was credited by **Victor Horta,** Balat's most famous student, who always counted the Royal Greenhouses as a major source of inspiration for his own art nouveau efforts.

Victor Horta House • *Rue Américaine 25, 1060 Saint-Gilles; year-round Tues.–Sat. 2–5:30 p.m., closed Sun., Mon., hols; 537.16.92; tram 81, 92, bus, 54, 60* • From the moment you reach for the door handle, your fun has begun. Art nouveau, a style determined to do away with straight lines, puts arabesques in iron, curls in wood, and whirls and whiplashes in many materials that normally defy such shapes; its inventive practicality delights. Victor Horta (1861–1947), Belgium's leading exponent of art nouveau, trained under Alphonse Balat and, receiving commissions for houses by 1890, the earliest days of the style, in 1898 bought two plots of land on Rue Americaine and began designing his house and studio. One of the few art nouveau interiors on view to the public, the whole house exudes Horta's sense of creative exhilaration, and reflects the purest realization of his mature artistic concepts. Applied arts flourished in the art nouveau period and Horta, who always aspired to full unity between architecture and interior design, wrote, "in every house, I designed and created the models for each piece of furniture, for every single hinge and door handle, the carpets, and the wall decorations." Horta's art nouveau elements are organic and use a proliferation of vegetable forms, such as flower petal and leaf shapes; a ceiling may be shaped like a calla lily. Throughout the house, banisters curl up staircases like ribbons; cabinets seem to grow out of corners.

Horta based his art nouveau designs on the concept that structural elements could become artistic ones. He showed that iron and stone and bricks and wood could work together in a "human" architecture, and materials formerly used only for industrial buildings could make extra height and light possible in homes. Art nouveau sought to bring light and air into the dark and stuffy decor of the Victorian era. For light, Horta created revolutionary winter gardens by putting open stairwells in the core of a building, topped by a skylight. He often made use of the contoured opalescent glass developed by Americans **La Farge** and **Tiffany** in the 1870s for its soft effect. The pale-colored walls we take for granted are a legacy from the progressive properties of art nouveau.

Horta houses that have survived and can be viewed from the exterior include: the **Tassel House** *(Rue Paul Emile Janson 6; 1893);* the **Solvay Mansion** *(Avenue Louise 224; 1894);* and the **Van Eetvelde Mansion** *(Ave. Palmerston 4; 1895).* Tours through **ARAU** (see *Tours* under *Guideposts*), may get you inside the astonishing, delightful, art nouveau-detailed Van Eetvelde mansion (originally ordered and owned by a baron who was Secretary General of the Belgian Congo in Brussels), which now serves as the offices of the **Federation de l'Industrie du Gaz**. It's located not far from EC headquarters at Rond-Point Schuman, an area worth exploring on foot for the art nouveau exteriors.

In 1916 Horta went to America, where he lectured in architecture and remained until 1919. When he returned to Brussels he began to work in *art deco*. (One of the reasons art nouveau died out as quickly as it did was that it had become so expensive.) Horta drew up the first plans for the Palais des Beaux-Arts in 1919 (undertaken in 1928) and finished final plans for Brussels Gare Centrale (Central Station) in 1937.

David and Alice Van Buuren House • *Avenue Leo Errera 41, 1180 Uccle; guided tour, open only on Mon. 2–4 p.m., groups of 10 or more at other times by appointment; 343.48.51, 344.28.30; from Montgomery Metro station take tram 23, 90 to Churchill stop; booklet in English* • Though its location (a time-consuming, confusing trip on public transportation; you may want to consider a cab) and restrictive opening hours will limit those able to include it in their itinerary, even those relatively uninitiated (as was I) in the linear (particularly when compared with art nouveau) *art deco* style will be intrigued by this highly original house of the 1930s. In fact, the art deco decor occasionally strays from the 1930s, with an original version of "The Fall of Icarus" by Pieter Breugel the Elder and a regal collection of 18th-century blue Delftware.

The house was built in 1929 by Dutchman David van Buuren, who became a private financier and was an experienced collector with reliable, eclectic taste, and his wife Alice, who, after her husband died in 1955, conceived the idea of turning the house (whose every detail had been specially created) into a museum. The house was built and decorated during the "high" art deco period (1925–1939), and the exotic materials typical of the style are much in evidence: black marble from Labrador; furniture made of rosewood from Brazil; brown horsehair upholstery and black horsehair wall covering; white sycamore wood; and black wax polish on oak floors. The talents of **Rene Lalique,** the best glass designer of the times, were used for chandeliers, and **Raoul Dufy** designed bold, brightly colored carpets for the dining room and Van Buuren's office, and the favored Oriental and linear influences are felt throughout.

A substantial part of the pleasure of a visit to the Van Buuren house comes from the garden, divided into several distinct parts. Created from irregularly-shaped and uneven landscape are the ½ mi./¼ mt. *labyrinth* in yew with a cedar tree at its center, the *garden of the heart* planted in pink and red dwarf and old fashioned roses, and the *picturesque garden,* sloped and with an open pavilion.

Erasmus House • *Rue du Chapitre 31, 1070 Anderlecht; 10 a.m.–noon, 2–5 p.m., closed Tues. & Fri.; 521.13.83; Metro Saint-Guidon, tram 103, bus 47, 49; booklet in English* • The great Netherlands humanist **Desiderius Erasmus** lived here only five months in the year 1521, invited as a guest by Canon Wychman to get away from the stench of Brussels to the clean air of the country (the setting was then rural). Erasmus wrote of the comfort, relaxation, and renewed health he enjoyed during his stay in this charming mid-15th-century Burgundian-style brick house, during which he worked on translations of his works. Knowing his feelings for this environment, visitors can get a feel for the life of the remarkable author of *In Praise of Folly* (see also under

The Muse in *The Benelux Cultural Legacy* at front of book), and see the exceptional collection of documents, manuscripts, and mementos contained here. The house was authentically restored and opened to the public in 1932. It has been decorated with a harmonious blend of period furnishings and art, and copies of his own work that bring Erasmus to life. We can see Erasmus in portraits by Quinten Metsys, Albert Durer, and Hans Holbein, as well as in a self-portrait cartoon. And almost sense him sitting—quill pen at the ready—at the desk looking out to the garden through windows of old glass that "wobble" views through it. In the display cases in the library are ancient and modern editions of the scholar's works; of particular impact are those that, in his troubled times, were censored, here seen with great hand-inked Xs across many of the words. When Erasmus left this house, he went to Basel, Switzerland, because the Reformation was making it too dangerous to stay. While Erasmus supported reformation of the Catholic Church, he came to oppose Martin Luther's violent Reformation methods (as he wrote in *Discourse on Freewill*, 1524).

Eglise Saint Pierre et Saint Guidon • *Place de la Vaillance; 9 a.m.–noon, 2:30–7 p.m., Sun. 9 a.m.–noon, 4–7 p.m., closed hols., during services; 521.84.15* • located in the center of this Brussels commune of Anderlecht, a superb 14th- and 15th-century Gothic church with wall paintings. The 11th-century Romanesque crypt, one of the most interesting in Belgium, contains the 12th-century tomb of St. Guidon. Just north of the church is a small, recently restored, **Beguinage** (*rue du Chapelain 8; 10 a.m.–noon, 2–5 p.m., closed Tues. & Fri., New Year's; 521.20.87*), dating from 1252; though the nuns left 200 years ago, their presence is still felt.

SHOPPING..

Belgium's Val Saint Lambert hand-cut crystal is on display at **Art & Selection** (*Rue Marché-aux-Herbes 83*). Belgian lace (covered with a focus on Bruges in the *Decorative Arts and Traditional Crafts* section at the front of this book) is also a Brussels's business of long-standing. Lace shops (with machine as well as handmade items) are concentrated in the small streets off the Grand-Place, particularly **Rue de l'Etuve** in the direction of **Manneken Pis;** you'll also see shops selling machine-made tapestries. At Rue de l'Etuve 26 and 43 are *Semal* shops, which, despite being located in Brussels most touristic street, actually sell some good-quality Belgian souvenirs. If you're looking for EC flag-bearing gear (T-shirts, carry-alls, umbrellas, and smaller items), shops here are worth checking out. Nearby **Picard** *(Rue de Lombard 71),* which deals in Carnival masks and other party paraphernalia, makes an amusing stop.

Its open-air markets are among Brussels's most mentioned attractions. The daily **flower market** carries on a tradition in the **Grand-Place,** which for centuries was the center of market activity in the town. The square's Sunday **bird market** *(7 a.m.–2 p.m.)* has its roots in the exploration of the 15th and 16th centuries, when previously unknown exotic and tropical species were brought to the old world from the far corners of the new, and displayed here to the amazement of all. More diverse items tempt at the **antique and book market** held on the **Grand Sablon** Saturdays from 9 a.m.–6 p.m. and Sundays from 9 a.m.–2 p.m. Casual and avid collectors will find much to catch their attention on the canvas-awninged tables covered with antiques and almost-antiques. The genteel Sablon square, surrounded by well-kept townhouses, is a chic showplace of antique shops and art galleries, with an elegant air unbroken since the 16th century, when it became a residential neighborhood for nobility.

Less pretentious but as much a microcosm of its milieu, the **Marolles** quarter, which it has operated since the 17th century, is the **Vieux Marché** (old market). The flea market takes place on the **Place du Jeu de Balle** daily 7 a.m.–2 p.m., though Saturdays and Sundays are the best days; there's direct access on buses 20, 21, 48, within walking distance of tram stops at **Porte de Hal.** It's situated just off **Rue Blaes,** which parallels **Rue Haute** running through the center of the Marollies. For those seeking a "find," who like to bargain, and are as interested in people-watching as picking through the *brol* (acknowledged junk) and *brocante* (a better class of junk), this is the place. Many of the 200 stallholders come from the working-class and immigrant-occupied Marolles surroundings, which gives the Vieux Marche the feeling of a neighborhood affair, even though dealers from as far away as Britain and Germany may be among the early-bird buyers doing business off the backs of trucks at 7 a.m.

ACCOMMODATIONS.........................

Because the city is dominated by the EC, NATO, trade congresses, and multi-nationals, Brussels' hotels in all price categories have a large business-traveler clientele. With the Monday-to-Friday corporate crowd providing their bread and butter, many hotels, particularly the more expensive ones, offer reduced rates on weekends year-round, and daily during July and August; always ask about special rates.

Deluxe

★★★★★ **Brussels Hilton** • *Blvd. de Waterloo 38; 504.11.11, in U.S. 1-800-HILTONS, Canada 1-800-268-9275, U.K. 0800-289-303, fax 513.72.33* • Located in the exclusive Upper Town, the 24-story, 454-room Hilton, opened in 1967, overlooks the Jardin d'Egmont and the mammoth domed Palais du Justice (floodlit at night). With an elegant international atmosphere, the recently renovated leather-upholstered, flower and art-adorned lobby is a gathering spot for the Bruxellois as well as hotel guests for light meals, tea, and drinks. Tasteful, quiet-colored standard guestrooms have minibar, cable TV with CNN, hair dryers, overnight shoeshine; executive floors offer private lounge, breakfast. The Hilton has three fine restaurants: lighthearted **Café d'Egmont** overlooks that garden's greenery; the formal gourmet **Maison du Boeuf;** and the fashionable **En Plein Ciel** (also a supper club with live music and dancing) on the 27th floor with panoramic view. Health club with sauna, solarium, weights.

★★★★ **Jolly Hotel Sablon** • *Place du Grand-Sablon; 512.88.00, fax 512.67.66, in U.S. 1-800-221-2626, in Canada 1-800-237-0319* • Opened in July 1991, in a uniquely interesting location on the Grand Sablon (at the "top," by the weekend antique market and Eglise Notre Dame du Grand Sablon), the 197-room Italian-operated hotel includes a buffet breakfast in its price. The tasteful period-decorated guestrooms in the highest of the three price categories have jacuzzis. Restaurant, piano bar, hotel garage; 24-hour room service; shuttle service to/from airport.

★★★★★ **SAS Royal** • *Rue du Fosse-aux-Loups 47; 219.28.28, fax 219.62.62.* • Opened in 1990 behind the Place de la Monnaie, the SAS features a dramatic seven-floor glass elevator-served atrium lobby that is decorated with black and white marble, bamboo furniture, greenery, and a waterfall, all set against the backdrop of an original 12th-century city wall. The 281 rooms follow SAS's choose-your-own-decor concept: Scandinavian, Italian, Japanese, or Royal Club executive; all rooms have personal answering machines, telephone in bath, mini-bar, massage showerhead, with shoeshine machine on each floor. There are some nonsmoking and handicap-accessible rooms. In-house eateries include a gourmet fish restaurant, an American 1950s-theme casual bar & grill, an 8th-floor restaurant which serves *smorrebrod* and Belgian specialties, and a lobby bar. Covered parking; fitness center (weights, treadmill, cycles, whirlpool and sauna).

★★★★★ **Brussels Sheraton Hotel & Towers** • *Place Rogier 3, 1210 Brussels; 224.31.11, U.S. & Can. 1-800-325-3535, UK 0800-353535, fax 218.66.18* • Anchoring Place Rogier (Metro stop), not far from the North Station (*Gare Nord*), and at the end of Boulevard Adolphe Max with its department stores and entertainment, the 600-room, 39-story Brussels Sheraton is a modern, self-contained living complex. In addition to superior category rooms (on the smallish side), the Sheraton Towers ("a small VIP hotel within a hotel") has larger rooms, separate sit-down check-in, breakfast (included) in its lounge, turndown service, and special amenities. For all guests, there's a top floor fitness club, with sauna, solarium, gym, and the city's only hotel indoor swimming pool. In the lobby is the gourmet **Les Comtes de Flandre** restaurant and a popular bar. Lobby shops; 24-hour room service; underground parking. Note: There's a small "red light" district beyond the Sheraton in the direction of North Station.

★★★★★ **Royal Windsor** • *Rue Duquesnoy 5; 511.42.15, fax 511.60.04, in U.S. and Canada 1-800-223-6800* • This modern 300-room hotel with smart marble lobby is several blocks from the Grand-Place and an equal distance from the Central Station (Gare Centrale). The attractive, wood-accented guestrooms are small, as are the marble baths. The hotel's gourmet restaurant **Les 4 Saisons** offers fine French cuisine; the Edwardian-style **Duke of Wellington** pub, with polished mahogany, leather upholstery, and etched glass, is a popular local rendezvous; the **Crocodile Club** has late-night live music. Continental breakfast included; 24-hour room service; underground parking at hotel.

First Class

★★★★★ **Amigo** • *Rue de l'Amigo 1; 511.59.10, fax 513.52.77* • A block from the Grote Markt, the Amigo offers Brussels' most central accommodations. The oldest part of the six-floor Spanish Renaissance-style hotel building was formerly a prison: a popular contemporary saying was that a one-night stay here made one a true citizen of Brussels. Although the most visible half of the well-blended building dates only from 1956, the Amigo feels as much like an old country home as a well-serviced hotel. The flagstone lobby features wall tapestries, oriental carpets, antiques, lots of carved wood detail, and a clubby bar. Most of the 200 traditionally-furnished rooms have hair dryers, heated towel racks, alarm cords in bathrooms. Continental breakfast included; restaurant; 24-hour room service; under-hotel parking. When the present-day Duke of Wellington returns to the victory scene of his ancestor, he uses the Amigo's Spanish-style suite.

★★★★ **Metropole** • *Place de Brouckere 31; 217.23.00, in U.S. 1-800-THE OMNI, fax 218.02.20* • Brussels' only remaining grand 19th-century hotel, the 410-room Metropole, opened in 1895, still is situated near the center of things, a block from the Monnaie Opera House, and an easy walk to the Grand-Place. The public rooms, worth a look even if you're not staying, are wonderful: a French Renaissance entrance hall; a reception hall with chandeliers, decorated ceilings, gilted molding details, stained glass, and polished wood; lounge/bar in the style of a gentlemen's club with deep leather sofas, marble columns, mirrors, piano and potted palms. The ground floor restaurant and cafe (whose sidewalk section is one of Brussels' premier people-watching places) offer more amazement. Rooms, on five floors, served by three elevators and located along sprawling corridors (bellhop service), come in many shapes, sizes, and degrees of modernity (older rooms may have more atmospheric appeal). All have minibar, private bath, color TV, 24-hour room service, 24-hour drycleaning, turndown service. The setting is lovely, but I did find front-desk service lackadaisical on a recent visit.

★★★★ **Pullman Astoria** • *Rue Royale 103; 217.62.90, in U.S. 1-800-223-9862, fax 217.11.50* • Built in 1908, during the *Belle Epoque*, and completely redone in 1987, the Astoria once was *the* hotel of Brussels with its *art nouveau* decor. The spacious lobby with Louis XV furnishings, marble pillars with gold leaf Corinthian capitals, mirrors, sconces, standing chandeliers, palms, grand stairway up to the stained-glass ceiling mezzanine, and plush lobby bar (with live music nightly except Sun.) remain most impressive, and popular with the Bruxellois. All guestrooms (standard and larger) have minibar, hair dryer, color cable TV, room service until 10 p.m., modern tile bath, coffee/tea maker; larger rooms add a trouser press, double basins and piped-in music in the bath. Restaurant; no parking; on bus route, within walking distance of Metro.

★★★★ **Sofitel Brussels** • *Ave. de la Toison d'Or, 1060 Brussels; 514.22.00, fax 514.57.44* • Thoroughly modern, the Sofitel is imaginatively tucked into a shopping complex of 80 elegant shops in the upper town; the sleek hotel lobby is up a long escalator from street-level (where there is a bellhop). The 171 well-upholstered, light wood-furnished rooms have twin or king beds, marble baths with glass-stall showers and tubs, minibars, three telephones, and double-glazing on front windows to reduce traffic noise (quieter rooms in back overlook the garden). The off-lobby restaurant with back garden terrace and bar has a very agreeable atmosphere. Nonsmoking rooms available; 24-hour room service; same-day dry cleaning, pressing.

★★★★ **Le Dome** • *Blvd. du Jardin Botanique 12; 218.06.80, fax 218.41.12* • Reopened in 1989 after a complete renovation, the hospitable 77-room Le Dome was built in 1902 and has details of the art nouveau style in vogue then, particularly in the **Bar 1902**. The comfortably upholstered lobby and off-lobby restaurant **Cafe du Dome** feature **Gustav Klimt** prints, greenery, smoked-glass mirrors, and a pleasing light turquoise trim/pink wall color scheme. All guestrooms have minibar, coffee maker, trouser press, remote control color TV, hair dryer. A breakfast buffet is included. Located on the in-town side of Place Rogier (Metro), a 15-minute walk along the shoplined Boulevard Adolphe Max to the edge of the **Ilot Sacre.**

★★★ **New Hotel Siru** • *Place Rogier, 1210 Brussels; 217.75.80, fax 218.33.03* • If, among other things, you are coming to Brussels to enjoy its contemporary art, you could do no better than to bed down here, where many (eventually all) of the 101 rooms have been individually decorated by Belgian artists or sculptors. The contemporary furniture often fits into the scheme of the whole design: in Room 704, for example, a 3-dimensional sculptured couple is stretched over the headboard reading travel brochures and maps. The owners never asked for changes in an artist's concept, though they did reject an entire design if they believed that the resulting room might produce bad dreams; that certainly wouldn't be the case with Room 108: the ceiling fresco by painter Roger Raveel above the bed is entitled "Valium" and is a field of sheep made easy to count. Back to basics. The hotel is located at the corner of Place Rogier (Metro, near North Station), and was remodeled in 1988. There's friendly desk service, breakfast (continental included) served in the attached corner cafe (continue beyond the breakfast room); elevators.

★★★★ **Archimede** • *Rue Archimede 22; 231.09.09, fax 230.33.71* • The hotel is situated on a tree and restaurant-lined residential street a block from the European Community's Berlaymont building, and is popular with visiting EC staffers. The fully-renovated modern interior is eclectically-decorated with faux marble in the elevators and hallways, fine woodwork and formally-dressed mannequins that greet guests in the lobby. The basement breakfast (only; extensive buffet included) room is decorated as an ocean liner, with deck chairs, ship railings, and portholes with views on to a garden. All 56 rooms have remote cable TV, radio, telephone with message system, hair dryer, trouser press.

Moderate

★★★★ **Manos** • *Chaussée de Charleroi 100, 1060 Brussels; 537.96.82, fax 539.36.55* • Built in the 1930s, this hotel features high ceilings and plaster molding details in many rooms. Off the small elegant marble reception area is a lounge decorated with bamboo furniture, paintings, wall panels, marble fireplace, and chandelier; there's also a small library with leather chairs, a pleasant ground floor bar, breakfast (only) room, and walled patio with painted-white iron furniture, and resident white rabbit. All 38 guestrooms have tasteful contemporary furnishings, cable TV, small fridge, modern tile bath, hair dryer. Located on a busy street (tram to Place Royale) off fashionable Avenue Louise, three blocks from the Victor Horta Museum.

★★★★ **Chambord** • *Rue de Namur 82; 513.41.19, fax 514.08.47* • Located at the edge of the fashionable upper town at Porte Namur (Metro stop), the 64-room Chambord also is just a walk down the hill to the Place Royale. There's light-hearted, light-colored decor in the reasonably-sized rooms, which have small marble baths, minibar, color cable TV; front rooms have small balconies. The pleasant, partially skylighted, piano bar (light food service) also serves for breakfast (only, continental, included). Clientele is a mix of business and leisure travelers from several nations. Safe-deposit boxes at hospitable, helpful front desk.

★★★ **Arcade Saint-Catherine** • *Rue Joseph Plateau 2; 513.76.20, fax 514.22.14* • A modern 234-room hotel in an interesting, old section of central Brussels worth exploring, well-situated for the Metro, within walking distance of the Grand-Place. Rooms, in cheerful soft colors, all have compact stall shower/toilet, remote control TV, telephone, individual heat control. Open closet rack, with built-in bench below for suitcase. Inside courtyard rooms are quieter. Buffet breakfast (only, included) served in lobby lounge/bar with nonsmoking section. Credit cards; elevator.

★★★ **Ibis Brussels Center** • *Rue du Marche aux Herbes 100; 514.40.40, fax 514.50.667* • New in 1989, in the Ilot Sacre between the Grand-Place and Central Station (Metro), the Ibis is a cheerful, convenient, value-priced basic property. The 170 average-size rooms include bath/shower, color cable TV, telephone, carpeting (thin). There are luggage carts in lobby for self-porterage in the elevators. The large light lobby with greenery and upholstered furniture includes a restaurant (also used for breakfast, included), and bar. Four accessible rooms; public parking nearby.

★★★ **Hotel Vendome** • *Boulevard Adolphe Max 98; 218.00.70, fax 218.06.83* • This remodeled 19th-century townhouse-turned-hotel is located on a main boulevard near good shopping and transportation, a slightly lengthy but reasonable walk from the Grand-Place. The 100 rooms are basic but cheerful and comfy, with mini-bars and color cable TV. Breakfast (only, included) is served in the skylighted, greenery-filled winter garden; there's also a hotel bar, and front desk service is helpful and friendly.

Inexpensive

★★★ **Arlequin** • *Rue de la Fourche 17; 514.16.15, fax 514.18.25* • New in the late 80s, this 60-room hotel has an extraordinarily central location near the Grand-Place, tucked away in a commercial center in the **Ilot Sacre**. All rooms with a tidy modern decor have tiled bath (tub and hand shower), remote cable TV, decent mattresses, and built-in desk which can double as a suitcase rack. Several business suites are available, and some of the more quiet rooms at the back have views of the **Hôtel de Ville**'s handsome tower. There's a small lobby with chairs by reception (friendly), a bar, and breakfast (only) room. Major credit cards; elevator.

★★★ **Hotel La Madeleine** • *Rue de la Montagne 22; 513.29.73, fax 502.13.50* • Steps from the Grand-Place, Galleries Saint Hubert, and Gare Centrale, there's a real local feeling behind the 15th-century facade of this hotel for budget-conscious guests. All 55 clean and basic bedrooms should have been upgraded by the end of 1991: rooms have folding doors to private baths, hand-held shower heads in tubs, and overhead and beside bed lights; some larger rooms available for a supplement. There's no lobby to speak of, and no room service, but you're welcome to bring in your own treats to the ground-floor lounge; the breakfast (only, continental, included) room is decorated in a pleasant garden style. Central heating; major credit cards; elevator; helpful manager.

★★★ **Opera** • *Rue Grétry 53; 219.43.43* • Located in the heart of Brussels' ancient **L'Ilot Sacre,** this medium-size (52 rooms) clean and utilitarian property has the feel of—and is—a thoroughly European budget hotel. But it's tasteful in its way: restful tones in the decor; halls carpeted and walls papered; functional front desk with youthful English-speakers. Windows of front rooms open on to pedestrian street scenes; back rooms are quieter. Rooms include small built-in desk (can be used as luggage rack), two chairs, wardrobe closet, small curtain-enclosed shower stall. There's a button by each bedroom door to turn on hall lights. Elevator, major credit cards.

★★ **Mirabeau** • *Place Fontainas 18; 511.19.72, fax 514.18.25* • All 30 bedrooms, of which 18 are doubles, are basic but recently renovated, with toilet and shower, TV and telephone. Breakfast (only, included) is served in the family-style lobby lounge with TV. The agreeable English-speaking reception manager reports that the hotel is almost always full from Mon.–Fri. with mostly EC staffers; reservations in advance (*at least* two weeks) a must. Located on a neighborhood square midway between the Bourse and Midi Stations. Elevator, major credit cards.

RESTAURANTS

Culinary connoisseurs frequently rate Brussels as one of the top three restaurant cities—along with Paris and Hong Kong—in the world. The chapter on *Food and Drink* at the front of this book describes traditional Belgian dishes, which are a part of the Brussels' food scene as much as classic French *haute cuisine*. The background on *Belgian Beer* may prove helpful as you sample Brussels' cafes, some of the most interesting of which are included at the end of this section. Except at "name" restaurants, where high prices are sustained by the plethora of expense-account business travelers, restaurant costs in Brussels should not seem steep to those familiar with major cities in northeast North America, and should seem reasonable to visitors from London. Virtually all Brussels' (and Belgian) restaurants pride themselves on providing value for money, and tax and service are always included in the price. Remember that selecting a *menu* (several courses for one fixed price; be sure to inquire if you don't see it listed) will always save over multi-course *a la carte* ordering. Many Brussels restaurants that are priced in the *expensive* category in the evening can be brought down to *moderate* by going there at lunch and/or ordering the *plat du jour* (daily special). Many eateries in central Brussels cater to workers at midday with three-course *menus* in the BF 250–400 range.

Hotel restaurants (some of which are among Brussels' best) have not been included below, but have been mentioned under the hotel's listing. They will be open on Sundays when many independent restaurants close. For any but the most casual establishments, it's wise to at least inquire about reservations if you hope to dine at a particular place. Reservations (as far ahead as possible) are *essential* for any of the top restaurants.

Many opinions (almost as many as there are diners) exist as to which is Brussels' best restaurant. The Bruxellois discuss the topic among themselves as heatedly as they do sports or bicultural politics. You can count on the following selection, presented in no particular order, to include the restaurants that most experts variously purport to be the best. Unless otherwise indicated, all serve classic French cuisine in an elegant atmosphere; some are located outside the metropolitan city. To begin with a flourish, **Comme Chez Soi** *(Place Rouppe 23; closed Sun. & Mon., and July; 512.29.21, fax 511.80.52; expensive/very expensive),* whose proprietor and **Chef Pierre Wynants** is nothing short of a celebrity, both in his 14-table home territory and in culinary circles around the world, remains an institution in the rarified Brussels' culinary realm where dining is an *event*. To dine amid the renovated Victor Horta-style art nouveau decor, however, visitors need to be foresighted and/or favored by the gods: knowledgeable friends tell me that reservations should be made a *minimum* of two months ahead.

It's also wise to plan as far ahead as possible for the following: **Bruneau** (*Avenue Broustin 73; closed Tues. for dinner, Wed., hol., mid-June–mid-July; 427.69.78; very expensive*) serves seasonal fare with a flair in the Uccle area; **Romeyer** (*Chaussee de Groenendaal 109; closed Sun. evening, Mon., Feb., first half of Aug.; 657.05.81; very expensive*) offers innovative culinary creations in an old country house in the *Forêt de Soignes;* **Villa Lorraine** (*Avenue du Vivier d'Oie 75; closed Sun., and August; 374.31.63; expensive*) delights diners with its garden-like indoor and outdoor setting in a renovated chateau on the fringe of *Bois de la Cambre* forest; **Ecailler du Palais Royal** (*Rue Bodenbroek 18; closed Sun., hols. and August; 512.87.51; expensive, plat du jour moderate*), where seafood is the speciality, is located at the top of the Grand Sablon; and **La Maison du Cygne** (*Rue Charles Buls 2, off Grand-Place; closed Sat. lunch, Sun., and August, between Christmas and New Years; 511.82.44; expensive*) has a dream location fronting the Grand-Place.

While the above "best" restaurants are all on the expensive side, I repeat the point that it is *not* necessary to pay dearly to dine divinely in Brussels. And apart from money, for many, the reservation requirements of Brussels' stellar establishments don't leave sufficient room for spontaneous dining decisions. The ordinary mortals among us who are seeking memorable morsels *can* be more spur-of-the-moment about our meals: Brussels surely is one place where if the *carte* posted in the window and the view from the door both strike your fancy, you should feel free to follow your instincts, since almost certainly good, and perhaps great, food awaits.

Traditional Belgian fare first. In a restored, former 16th-century nobleman's world with lots of Flemish details such as the cooper-hooded fireplaces, wood-paneling, and tiles is **Ravenstein** (*Rue Ravenstein 1; closed Sat. lunch, Sun., and August; 512.77.68; inexpensive/moderate*), which, in addition to local fare, specializes in seafood and continental cuisine. **Au Duc d'Arenberg** (*Petit Sablon 9; daily noon–2:30 p.m., 7–10:30 p.m., closed Sun., hol., last week of Dec.; 511.14.75; moderate*) offers rustic decor and traditional food in its tavern/restaurant. Although eateries serving *moules* (mussels) abound in the **Ilot Sacre**, **Au Vieux Bruxelles** (*Rue Saint-Boniface 35; closed Sun., Mon., hols., June and July; 513.01.81; inexpensive*), near Avenue Louise, is *the* place for them as far as the Bruxellois are concerned. **Aux Armes de Bruxelles** (*Rue des Bouchers 13; noon to 11:15 p.m., closed Mon., month of June; 511.55.98; moderate, plat du jour inexpensive*), located on Brussels' "street of restaurants" is an excellent introduction to Belgian specialities, and *moules* prepared in many ways, *waterzooi de hom-*

ard (lobster stew), and *croquettes aux crevettes* (North Sea shrimp croquettes) to *carbonnades flamandes a la biere* (beef stewed in beer), in a pleasant setting. At **'t Kelderke** *(Grand-Place 15; daily noon 0 2 a.m.; 513.73.44; inexpensive)* typical Belgian dishes such as *lapin* (rabbit) cooked with Brussels' *queuze* beer are offered—as well as helpful counsel about the dishes and drink—in an atmospheric 16th-century cellar. **La Roue D'Or** *(Rue des Chaplies 26; until 12:30 a.m., closed mid. July–mid Aug.; 514.25.54; inexpensive)* is a brasserie near the Grand-Place with a varied menu of traditional fare and daily specials.

A search for seafood in Brussels will take you to the Sainte-Catherine district to what used to be the banks of the river Senne, still referred to as the *Marché aux Poisson* (Fish Market). Virtually all the restaurants in the region feature fish, but special among them is **La Sirene d'Or** *(Place Sainte-Catherine 1A; open lunch and dinner, closed Sun., Mon., mid-July to mid-Aug.; 513.51.98; fax 502.13.05; plat du jour inexpensive, menu moderate)*, small, and quite elegant with touches of velvet, lace, and old beams in the decor, and serving dishes such as *bouillabaisse Grand-Marius, fricassee de homard aux asperges*. Thoroughly atmospheric is the **La Truite d'Argent** *(Quai au Bois à Brûler 23; noon–2:30 p.m., 7–11:30 p.m., closed Sat. lunch, Sun., late July–mid. Aug.; 218.95.46; moderate)*, one of whose specialties is lobster and scallops with wild mushrooms. **Jacques** *(Quai aux Briques; 513.27.62; inexpensive)* is small, quite plain, and apparently the perfect choice for the many Bruxellois who call it their favorite bargain fish brasserie in the Marché aux Poissons district. **Scheltema** *(Rue des Dominicains 7; 11:30 a.m.–3 p.m., 6:30 p.m.–12:30 a.m., closed Sun. 512.20.84; moderate, lunch inexpensive)*, with specialties like *saumon grillé à l'orange* and *jardiniere de sole*, is where locals come for seafood (although the menu has other offerings), and to seriously eat, not chat.

When your tastebuds want to travel beyond Belgian borders, the enormous variety of cuisines available in Brussels will be obvious. Among the most numerous are Italian, Spanish, and Chinese. And with some of the other ethnic choices (Turkish, North African, Central African—Zaire) available, it can sometimes seem as if the Third World is feeding the *First* in Brussels. Belgium's lingering occupation by the Spanish may be one of the reasons for the interest in that country's cuisine. In any case, Brussels' seems to have a thriving taste for *paella valenciane*, the specialty at **Casa Manuel** *(Grand-Place 34; daily noon until 1 a.m.; 511.47.47; inexpensive; musicians)*. Also highly popular among the many Spanish restaurants in the Marolles neighborhood is **Alicante** *(Rue Haute 411; daily 11 a.m.–5 p.m., 6 p.m.–midnight; 538.25.54; inexpensive)*. A popular choice for Italian is **Al Piccolo Mondo** *(Rue Jourdan 19; daily until midnight; 538.87.94; inexpensive)*, just off trendy Avenue Louise near Waterloo Blvd. It has a cozy, if non-Italian, environment of brick walls and arches, wood-burning fireplaces, oil paintings, in which dishes such as *saltimbocca alla romana, veal cutlets Milanaise,* and *pastas* are served.

You'll come across pleasant places to pause for liquid refreshment or light cafe fare at every stop of your way around Brussels. On the Grand Sablon, try **Au Vieux Saint Martin** *(Grand Sablon 38; daily 10 a.m.–midnight; 512.64.76; inexpensive)* for sandwiches, omelets, salads, and some heartier fare on the square, and **Les Jardins du Sablon** *(Grand Sablon 30; moderate)* inside the skylighted upmarket complex of art galleries, bookshops, and antiques shops just off it. On the Grand-Place, a favorite with the Bruxellois is **La Brouette** *(Grand-Place 2; lunch to late evening; 511.54.94; inexpensive)* for sandwiches and salads, and special plates served on the cafe's terrace in the shadow of the Hôtel de Ville and full view of the glorious square or inside.

When dining out becomes a drag, as it sometimes does—*temporarily*—during travels, head to Brussels' huge supermarket in the basement of the **City 2** shopping complex at *Place de la Monnaie* for ingredients for an exceptional picnic. To satisfy your sweet tooth in traditional Belgian style, you can start simply, following the smell of vanilla in the air to any of the street-front waffle *(gaufre)* shops on and off the appropriately-named **Rue au Beurre** (Butter Street) off Grand-Place. While on the street, at least visit **Biscuiterie Dandoy** *(Rue au Beurre 31, daily 8:30 a.m.–6:30 p.m., Sun. 10:30 a.m.–6:30 p.m.)* to see its large wooden *speculoos* (spiced cookie) molds, and sample the marvelous (smaller) cookies available by 100-gram servings. **Le pain à la Grecque** (despite its name, a Belgian specialty) is another famed sweet treat at this 1829 institution. For the height of self-indulgence, head to fashionable **Wittamer** *(Place du Grand Sablon 12; daily 8 a.m.–7 p.m., Sun. 7:30 a.m.–6 p.m., closed Monday)* for Brussels' most outrageous *pralines* (handmade, filled chocolates), *manons* (fresh cream-filled chocolates), Viennoise and French pastries, and caramelized fruits.

Although they usually also serve traditional, informal Belgian dishes (and great *frites* with almost anything), **cafes** offer the opportunity to sample Belgium's amazing beers, especially Brussels' own *queuze, kriek,* and *faro.* There could be no better place to begin than at **Falstaff** *(Rue Henri Maus 25; 511.87.89; daily 7 a.m. til 4 a.m.),* with its art nouveau interior, and large open, overhead-heated outdoor terrace facing the Bourse. Close to the Grand-Place in the opposite direction is **La Mort Subite** *(Rue Montagne-aux-Herbes-Potageres 7; 513.13.18);* its name means *sudden death,* but the place is life to many regulars for the large selection of Belgian beers. Featuring another memorable name is **De Ultieme Hallucinatie** *(Koningsstraat/Rue Royale 316; 217.06.14; open until 3 a.m.),* a former house, with three rooms front to back, each with a different character, each a treasure trove of rational-style *art nouveau* detail, each serving cafe or restaurant fare. And, under another great name, **Le Jugement Dernier** *(The Last Judgment; Chaussee de Haecht 165)* is said to serve Brussels largest selection of beers, up to 300, including "seasonal" specials. **La Becasse** *(Rue Tabora 11; 511.00.06)*, down an alley near the Bourse, is known for its jugs of beer served by stiff-aproned waiters. **La Fleur En Papier Dore** *(Rue des Alexiens 53; 511.16.59)* has been called a temple of surrealism, though it's also a favorite quiet tavern. Offering a typical Brussels evening of cafe theater and music (mostly jazz) is **Chez LaGaffe** *(Rue de l'Epee 4; 511.76.39; music from 9 p.m.),* located in the Marolles neighborhood.

Note: To insure that your cafe hopping is entirely pleasant, here's a reminder—valid for cities everywhere—*not* to hang your purse or camera on the back of your chair or to put them on the ground, especially when outside on a terrace.

ENTERTAINMENT AND EVENTS..

The **Palais des Beaux-Arts** *(Rue Ravenstein 23 and Rue Royale 10; Mon.–Sat. 10 a.m.–10 p.m., Sun. 10 a.m.–6 p.m.; program information 513.41.55),* built between 1922 and 1929 to the design of art nouveau architect Victor Horta, is one of Brussels' most important cultural complexes, with concerts halls, art galleries, cinema, and cafes. It is highly regarded for the organ and acoustics in the 2,200-seat main hall. Both it and the **Brussels Conservatory of Music** are settings for the prestigious **Queen Elizabeth of Belgium International Music Competition.** Organized by the late monarch in 1951 for violinists (Queen Elizabeth herself was an accomplished one), the competition was later expanded to include piano, composition, and, in 1988, voice. All concerts of the competition, which welcomes contestants from around the world and takes place before an international jury of musicians, are open to the public (from elimination rounds to finals, and special Laureate performances). The competition, which begins in early May and lasts until mid-June, features violin in 1993, nothing in 1994, piano in 1995, composition/voice in 1996 (the sequence repeats in 1997).

Note: Near the beginning of the 1980 American film *The Competition,* about competing pianists in a fictional, San-Francisco-based situation not unlike the Queen Elizabeth Competition, the character Heidi (Amy Irving) asks Paul (Richard Dreyfuss) if he had gone to compete at Brussels as planned.

The **Palais des Beaux-Arts,** the **Conservatory,** and the **Cathédrale Saint-Michel** are all used as venues for Brussels' performances in the annual September–October **Festival of Wallonia** concerts. The

Cathédrale has *Musical Sundays* from late June through September, with special music (Gregorian Chant, Scarlatti, Haydn, Mozart, Palestrina, Britten, Faure) at the 10 a.m. Mass (information: 217.83.45). Check with the Tourist Office about scheduled concerts on the superb and newly-restored organ of the **Eglise Notre-Dame du Sablon** (see *Organs* under *Music* section of *Benelux Cultural Legacy* chapter at front of this book).

The **Theatre Royal de la Monnaie** *(Place de la Monnaie; 218.12.02)* is notable for its acoustics and recent lavish renovation. Designated the National Opera House in 1963, it is home to the opera company that bears its name; during the late September–April season, artistic director Anne-Theresa Dekeersmaeker stages widely-acclaimed original-language productions with international casts. Brussels' **Twentieth Century Ballet** also is on the bill of fare at the Monnaie.

One of Brussels's entertainment *institutions* is Toone **VII Puppet Theater** *(Impasse Schuddeveld 6, off Petite rue des Bouchers 21; performances at 8:30 p.m., puppet museum open free during intervals between sketches, closed Sun., cafe on premises open noon–midnight; reservations recommended: 511.71.37, 513.54.86)*. It began with Toone I, who, from 1835 to 1880, performed with puppets in a cellar in the Marolles district, and introduced the character **Woltje,** a Brussels' street urchin in a checked jacket and jaunty-angled cap who speaks the Marolle-Brussels dialect. Toone, the VIIth of the tradition, opened in the present theater in 1966, and continues the use of the Brussels' dialect, which makes it unlikely you'll understand much of the dialogue (and piquant asides) in the *Cyrano, Faust, The Three Musketeers, Nativity,* or *Massacre of the Innocents* fare on the program, though that may not matter if you want to see something true to Brussels. The tradition of puppet plays here actually goes back long before Toone, to Spanish times. When the occupying Spanish had heard all they cared to of the criticism and insults hurled at them from the legitimate stage, they closed the theaters. But imaginative minds came up with the idea of using highly portable (and easily hidden) puppets as a means of reaching the population with revilements for the foreign forces. Puppet theater in Brussels is still a place for provocative political and social commentary.

Events from Brussels' annual calendar include the late-April, early-May openings of the **Royal Greenhouses** at Laeken, and a mid-June reenactment of the **Battle at Waterloo.** The twice-in-early-July **Ommegang** (which comes from a Flemish word meaning "walkabout") is a splendidly-costumed reenactment of the festivities staged in 1549 for the entrnace into Brussels of Charles V, his son Philip II (then Duke of Brabant), and his sisters held on the floodlit Grand-Place that is a source of wonderment even for those blasé bureaucrats inclined to call Brussels boring. From June–Sept. there are free nightly **sound and light** shows after dark on the Grand-Place, where, in August in even years, a fabulous **Flower Carpet** is laid. From late July to late August the annual

Brussels Fair is held in the Midi, and September brings **Bruegel festivities**. In December there's a traditional **Christmas market** on the Sablon and nativity scene and Christmas tree on the Grand-Place.

IN THE AREA..

Musée Royal de l'Afrique Centrale • *Royal Museum of Central Africa; Leuvensesteenweg 13; Tervuren; daily mid-Mar.–mid Oct. 9 a.m.–5:30 p.m., mid Oct.–mid Mar. 10 a.m.–4:30 p.m.; 767.54.01; Brussels' metro to* **Montgomery,** *then* Tram 44 *through the lovely 10,000-acre ancient beech tree* **Forest de Soignes;** *museum plan but no exhibit descriptions in English* • Begun in 1898, as the *Musée du Congo,* this museum was an important scientific institute where the information of the Congo could be collected and synthesized. In 1960, the year of the Belgian Congo's independence, its scope was extended to cover all of Africa. Exhibits are arranged in sections covering anthropology, history, and economy. There are zoological dioramas, ethnic sculpture, and souvenirs of the great explorers; of particular interest are those on mineralogy and art, including jewelry and tribal ornaments. The museum—housed in a Charles Girault-designed Louis XVI-style palace built for Leopold II and surrounded by exceptional French gardens—is located in **Tervuren Park,** which also features scenic lakes, the picturesque **Moulin de Gordeal** (windmill), an Arboretum, a Renaissance chapel to Saint Hubert (patron saint of hunters), and stables remaining from the 17th-century castle of Austrian-Hapsburg ruler Charles of Lorraine.

Waterloo • *town of 25,000, 12 mi./20 km. south of Brussels on Charleroi Road; public bus* W *from Brussels'* **Place Rouppe** *twice hourly, takes about an hour* • Today a pleasant Brussels suburb where many resident-alien Americans live, *Waterloo* is also a household word for *defeat* that joined our vocabulary after the retreat of Napoleon Bonaparte from the 1815 battle fought there to decide the future of Europe. No one who has seen the magnificent gifts (on display at **Apsley House** in London) presented to Wellington by European leaders after he defeated Napoleon's armies can doubt their relief at the fall of the charismatic Corsican.

To set the stage: After taking over the leadership of the French forces that had occupied the Netherlands, north and south, in the late 18th century (and showing himself to be a well-rounded genius by introducing such modern measures as the metric system and house numbers for addresses), Napoleon arranged to have himself pronounced Emperor of France in the presence of the Pope in 1804. He continued to turn Europe inside-out with a series of successful military campaigns, before overextending himself in 1812. From the Royal Palace at Laeken outside Brussels, Napoleon signed the order for the advance of his 600,000-troop army into Russia, where climate, unorthodox opponents, and sheer distance defeated him. Back in Central Europe in 1814, Napoleon again met more than his match, and was exiled to the isle of Elba off Italy by the allied powers of Austria, Prussia, Russia, and England, who then convened the **Congress of Vienna** to restructure the political entities of Europe. It was settled that the Belgian territory would be bonded to Holland, but before the details had been dealt with, word came to the diplomats in Vienna that Napoleon had escaped from Elba. Bonaparte made his way to Paris without a shot being fired, easily and quickly rallying the French forces still faithful to him; newly-installed King Louis XVIII fled to Belgium's Ghent. Of the European armies quickly regrouped to confront the Corsican, it was the troops of England's **Duke of Wellington,** Prussia's 73-year-old **General Marshal Blucher,** and Holland's **Prince Willem of Orange** gathered in central Belgium, who would fight the inevitable battle.

Ironically, only a year before, the Duke of Wellington had passed through Waterloo and made the statement that if he were ever to fight in the Netherlands, he would choose the fields at Waterloo for the battle. Yet, it was Napoleon, beating a path to Brussels, which he hoped to recapture (believing, as, indeed, even many of his political opponents did, that Belgium rightfully belonged to France), whose actions largely established the farming village of Waterloo as the site where scores of thousands of soldiers would meet history head-on.

The opposing forces that squared off at Waterloo on Sunday, June 18, were headed by two men of great stature but slight height: Napoleon stood at 5 foot 3 inches; Wellington measured in at 5 feet even. Napoleon commanded 72,000 men and had more heavy hardware than Wellington, who, as supreme commander for the British, Dutch, Belgian, and German forces, had 60,000 (though the Prussian reinforcements who arrived progressively during the day numbered nearly another 45,000). But, as in many battles, Waterloo's outcome was as much the result of weather and the health of its leaders as it was other elements. Through the night before the battle it rained heavily, and Napoleon postponed the beginning of battle until late the following morning to give the ground some time to dry (maneuvering heavy artillery through mud was unwieldy). But those elapsed morning hours later in the battle day added enough time for Marshal Blucher to get to the battlefront with fresh Prussian troops for Wellington. Although the two generals were the same age (45) at Waterloo, Wellington was well, and Napoleon was not, suffering so badly from piles that he spent most of the battle day outside the house **(Caillou)** he used as headquarters in a chair from which the seat had been removed for his comfort. Wellington spent it on his horse, Copenhagen, constantly traversing the undulating terrain that hid battlefield hollows and allowed no single good vantage points for the action, and encouraging his troops. (So close to the action did Wellington stay that day that many of his soldiers were amazed that he survived.)

An account from the diary of a Waterloo resident that cloudy Sunday of June 18, 1815, reads: "The whole morning, soldiers pass in mass formation. Towards 10 o'clock a heavy silence reigns around us. Everyone is struck dumb with the approach of the events which are due to take place." At about 11:30 a.m., Napoleon's forces opened battle against the more-securely positioned Wellington forces (Napoleon later said of Wellington, "In the management of an army he is full equal to myself with the advantage of possessing more prudence." Napoleon, uncharacteristically, tried to apply head-to-head brute force while waiting for reinforcements from a division he had previously sent after the Prussian Blucher; Wellington, having to endure the full force of the French attack alone for far longer than expected was waiting for Blucher himself, who had met with him at 2 a.m. that morning and promised troops. Movement on the distant horizon at about 1 p.m. raised hopes on both sides, but it turned out to be Blucher, progressing very slowly because of the mud.

From that time on, Napoleon, who hadn't expected Blucher to be a factor in the fight, was in a race against time. At 4 p.m., he launched a massive cavalry charge, but Wellington's "squares" held. Later, however, a breakthrough for the French seemed possible, and the Duke of Wellington worried, "Night or the Prussians must come," and, afterwards, an officer said, "I never heard yet of a battle in which every one was killed; but this seemed likely to be an exception." The French marshal who was trying to effect the turnaround requested reinforcements, but Napoleon, thinking of the Prussians marching ever closer, delayed an hour before finally sending the marshal his final reserve, the impressive Imperial Guard. By then, however, they were tactically too late; Wellington had had a chance to regroup and, after the Prussians arrived about 7:30 p.m., what was considered Napoleon's finest force was routed during the general charge mounted against it at 8:15 p.m.

Taking less than 10 hours, Waterloo was a short battle that was long and decisive enough to produce something like peace—at a great cost, however, and only for a short time. The toll for both sides was more than 50,000 casualties. Some 7,000 in Wellington's army were killed or wounded, and the Prussians lost nearly the same number. An accurate count of French army losses was impossible to come by after the final rout, during which many of the men simply slipped away, but a minimum of 30,000 were killed, wounded, or captured. Ten days after the battle, the wounded were still being brought into Brussels.

Tourists sought out Waterloo from the start. That very year, the King of England came to view the battlefield, and on the first anniversary a crowd from many countries gathered in commemoration. **Lord Byron** wrote of Waterloo in his poem *Childe Harold,* and **Victor Hugo** walked the battleground 40 years later seeking inspiration for the Waterloo scenes in *Les Miserables.* Today, from atop the **Butte du Lion** *(Lion Mound; 3 miles south of Waterloo center; 226 steps; daily, same hours as Waterloo Visitor's Center, below),* visitors have a panoramic view of the Waterloo terrain that neither commander nor any combatant on the battle day had. The vast circular Lion Mound was built as a Dutch memorial between 1823–1826 on the site along Wellington's line where the Dutch **Willem of Orange** (who would be crowned King of the less-than-pleased Belgians only three months after Waterloo) was wounded in the shoulder. At the base of Lion Mound is the recently opened (1990) **Waterloo Visitor's Center** *(Route du Lion 252; daily April 1–Oct. 31, 9:30 a.m.–6:30 p.m.; Nov.1–March 31, 10:30 p.m.– 4 p.m.; 02/385.19.12; English language materials and exhibits),* a well-executed and welcome addition to the site. The 40-minute program includes a sound and light model that retraces the main phases of the fighting, and a 200-slide show that—with its imaginative script and extracts from Columbia's Bondartchouk-directed film *Waterloo*—involves viewers in the experience of the battle. The center has maps and illustrations that give visitors a better grasp of where and how the fighting took place. Interactive computerized information terminals have a database that enables you to ask questions (in English) about the battle. Items in the gift/book shop featuring the losing leader vastly outnumber those concerned with the winner at Waterloo.

Next door is the hard-to-miss round building that houses the **Panorama,** which dates back to 1912. Definitely old-fashioned (though restored), this nostalgic in-the-round art work is a 360-degree, 360-foot/110-meter, 40-foot/12-meter painting by Frenchman Louis Dumoulin, his art assistants, and military consultant that places you literally in the center of Waterloo's French Calvary charge. Standing on the viewing platform at the center you can't help but be involved, from the cloudy sky from the recent rain, clouds of smoke from the cannon, and foreground of three-dimensional figures (a wounded horse, soldiers, fences, dirt) that all lend verisimilitude to the scene. Unless you're addicted to such attractions, the **Wax Museum** across the road isn't a necessary stop, though the cafe **Bivodac de L'Empereur** next to it might be.

An alternative site at which to begin your visit to Waterloo is in the town at the **Wellington Museum** *(Chaussée de Bruxelles 147; daily April 1–Nov. 15 9:30 a.m.–6:30 p.m., Nov. 16–Mar. 31 10:10 a.m.– 5 p.m., closed Christmas and New Years; 02/354.59.54; booklet, exhibit notes, and other items in English).* Of the many items of interest in the several rooms of this old coaching inn (at which Wellington spent the night before and the night after the battle), none is more meaningful that the Duke's own bedroom. In it, in the pre-dawn hours of the 18th, he received confirmation that the Prussians would join him in battle against Napoleon later that day, at which point he definitely decided on undertaking the task at Waterloo. And it was to this room that he returned after battle to write the report that was published in *The Times* in London on June 22. In the wing to the rear of the museum are illuminated battle-phase maps that show the relative positions of units at each stage of the struggle.

Next door is the **Tourist Information** office for Waterloo *(Chaussee de Bruxelles 149; 02/354.99.10)*, which can provide specific information about rental bicycles, the sightseeing train which during July and August links up with Waterloo train station, the mid-June authentically-uniformed reenactment, and hours/details about other Waterloo sights. Across the street is the domed 17th-century **Royal Chapel/St. Joseph's Church** (restored). The only object in its large rotunda is a white marble bust of the Duke of Wellington; many burial plaques and other memorials are exhibited on the side walls of the church.

If you are traveling by car to Waterloo and want to see every sight, there's **Caillou**, a farm where Napoleon spent the night before the battle. *La Belle Alliance* is where Napoleon spent much of the day of the battle, and Wellington and Blucher met in happy victory at the end of the battle. From it you can realize how little Napoleon can have known of what was happening on the actual battle front. Various division monuments are located along the sides of roads in the region.

ACCOMMODATIONS/RESTAURANT IN THE AREA

★★★★ **Chateau du Lac** • *Ave. du Lac 87, Genval; 02/654.11.22, fax 02/653.62.00; expensive* • is a lakeside castle hotel 20 minutes south of Brussels, not far cross-country from Waterloo. Fine contemporary decor in an elegant setting, with a good selection of recreational facilities (tennis, golf, riding, watersports). The hotel's restaurant **Le Trefle** *(closed Mon., Tues., early Jan.–early Feb.; expensive)* is considered one of nearby Brussels' best.

FLANDERS: AN INTRODUCTION

Belgium's 5.7 million Flemish *(de Vlamingen* to themselves, *les Flamands* to the French-speaking Walloons) comprise nearly 60% of the country's total population, living in the northern provinces of **West** and **East Flanders, Antwerp, Limburg,** and the northern section of **Brabant.** With the exception of Brabant, each province borders on Holland, with whom Flanders shares the Dutch language.

Despite an attractive beach-bound North Sea coastline (all of Belgium's seashore is located in the province of West Flanders), Flanders' main appeal to overseas visitors is its medieval mercantile towns. Flanders' **Ghent, Bruges, Antwerp,** and **Brussels**—all cloth manufacturing and trading centers with a prosperous burgher class—formed the early core of Low Countries' (Netherlands') culture. Noted for their wealth, Flemish towns attracted artisans and became treasure-troves of 14th-, 15th-, and 16th-century architecture and painting. If you've provided yourself with an appropriately generous amount of time for touring Belgium, you'll find additional examples of sacred and secular structures in Flanders' fascinating Flamboyant Gothic style—exuberant evidence of an opulent past—in **Ypres, Louvain, Mechelen,** and **Oudenaarde.**

While Flanders' early urbanized areas virtually *demand* the attention of travelers, the region also has a variety of rural landscape: moor and heath in the *Kempen,* modest height in the *Flemish Ardennes,* and rich flat *polderland* just behind the *coastal dunes.* Farming has long been a prime livelihood in Flanders, on both its rich and poor land. (The open-air museum of **Bokrijk** *[in the Domain of Bokrijk, northeast of Hasselt, the capital of Limburg province; open daily Easter–Oct. 10 a.m.–6 p.m.; 011/22.27.11]* pays homage to Flanders' farming heritage).

Urban Flanders can trace its beginnings to a gradual shift (following the Frankish period) in the region's transportation routes, from the inland highways that had crossed the Roman Empire to the increasingly important continental waterways and their outlets at the sea. Medieval Flemish settlements along rivers developed as trading sites, eventually evolving into powerful commercial urban entities.

During the **Crusade era,** the **Counts of Flanders** (the countship had come into being in 864) became the "Latin" emperors of Constantinople from 1204–1261. The opening up of sea trade routes to the East during earlier crusades (the First Crusade was in 1099) brought new commercial development to Flanders. The region as a whole flourished over several centuries, particularly in the **cloth and wool trades** with England, in which Flanders had a virtual monopoly.

All of Flanders was affected by the **Reformation,** which began in the early 16th century. The earliest confrontations resulting from its introduction into the Netherlands were in Flanders. In the southern Netherlands (Belgium), Philip embarked on a punishing course of action; when the Spanish inquisition forces became completely unrestrained, many Protestants fled from what had been a flourishing Flanders north to Holland. Such were the numbers of multi-talented Flemish Protestants who left that it constituted a broad-based "brain drain." The flight of talent from Flanders to Holland in the late 16th century (Flemish Antwerp's Golden Age) was so great that there's no doubt it nourished Holland's 17th-century Golden Age. In the early 17th century, the population of Middelburg in Zeeland (southern Holland) was 60% Flemish. The decrease in Flanders' population during the period was so dramatic that not until after the turn of the 19th century did Flemings once again equal, and then overtake, the number of Walloons.

Flanders' decline in population was accompanied by a falling off of prosperity. Under the 1648 *Treaty of Munster,* which ended Holland's *Eighty Years' War* with Spain, the southern Netherlands remained under the Spanish, who agreed to the anti-competitive Dutch demand to close the Scheldt (the Dutch controlled the land on both banks of the river estuary). This action effectively closed the port of Antwerp, leading to a prolonged period of economic ruin for the city, and adversely affecting the economy of all Flanders. Not until the end of the 18th century, under the rule of Napoleon, were the Scheldt and the port of Antwerp reopened, and revitalized.

With their population once again a majority in Belgium by the early 19th century, the Flemings had an impetus to push for the equality of the Flemish language with the French. But numbers alone wouldn't work a realization of their goal.

The use of French in the Walloon (southern) section of Belgium went back almost to the end of Roman rule in the area, and for centuries had been deeply ensconced in European use. The business, and pleasure, of most royal courts was conducted in French; quite simply, the French language was the standard for European statecraft. So widespread was the fashion that even the English court effused in French during various reigns, although England itself often had a less than fond relationship with France. The international fashion for French remained strong for a long period, and still has vestiges: to this day French claims a cultural advantage in the Belgian capital of Brussels. The situation has certainly exacerbated Belgium's complicated internal language controversy, making it hard for the Flemish to get their language claims across.

Even before the Burgundian days in the late 14th century, Flemings of a certain status were forced to conduct their schooling, government, and legal affairs in French. Those who couldn't comprehend French couldn't make sense of the socio-political system. Only peasants used Flemish, which was considered a course, countrified tongue. Once the Dutch in Holland established an "authorized" version of their language, Flemish was considered by many to be a mere dialect (though it is identical in writing) of Dutch.

When the new Belgian State came into being in 1830, though the Flemish by then outnumbered the Walloons, a favoritism for French in all administrative matters was firmly established at the onset. This was the result not only of tradition, but also of a not-entirely unpopular period of French Napoleonic rule from 1799 to 1814, followed (after the fall of Napoleon at Waterloo) by the truly unpopular rule of Dutch King Willem I from 1815–1830. Although he faced a near-impossible situation from the start, Willem's autocratic manner managed to offend both of Belgium's communities even more. Finally, in 1830, the European powers gave recognition to Belgium's insistence on independence. But, while the constitution adopted by the temporary congress was the most liberal charter on the continent, the "new" Belgium clung to old ways: the French language was the sole one for the business of education, law, and government.

A **Flemish Movement** wasn't long in coming. While under Dutch rule, the Flemish language had come into much wider use. After Belgian independence and the reestablishment of the French standard, Flemish writer **Hendrik Conscience** (see *The Muse* under *The Benelux Cultural Legacy*) spoke to fellow Flemings through his book *The Lion of Flanders* (1838). The romantic novel was meant to incite a national awakening of pride in the Flemish culture and language by linking the 14th-century struggle of Flanders against France (in the 1302 *Battle of the Golden Spurs;* see *Belgium: An Historical Perspective*) to the need for 19th-century Flemish Belgians to stand up to their French-speaking countrymen. Conscience could be very explicit in his aims, as he was when he wrote in 1839: "There are twice as many Flemings as there are Walloons. We pay twice as much in taxes as they do. And they want to make Walloons out of us, to sacrifice us, our old race, our language, our splendid history, and all that we have inherited." Some Flemings would find that statement still speaking to their situation today.

Ultimately, Conscience's work and works (his monument is marked with the words: "He taught his people to read") raised the consciousness of some officials, who convened an investigation into the complaints by the Flemish in 1856. The commission found many of the grievances to have merit and recommendations were made. But there were few practical results; political power in the hands of unempathic Liberals prevented implementation of any measures. Only in the periods when the Catholic party predominated (1871–1879 and 1884–1914) was progress made on the issue of Flemish equal language rights.

In the last decades of the 19th century, Flemish nationalism rose alongside the workers' movement, a natural alignment since Belgium's propertied class was French-speaking, and social mobility depended largely on use of that language. Flemish demands focused on gaining an administration and judiciary in Dutch, and having a Dutch-speaking university so that a knowledge of French wouldn't be the only means of entry into the professions. In 1890, it finally became possible to submit doctoral theses in Dutch to the University of Ghent, and, by the beginning of World War I, a number of courses at Ghent (which is, after all, in Flanders) were being offered in Flemish.

During World War I, extreme Flemish nationalists were encouraged by the occupying Germans, who had more concern for the Germanic-rooted Dutch-speaking Flemish than the French Walloons, and were not unaware of the benefits of keeping the level of tension high between Belgium's two communities. Extremist Flemings formed the *Activist Party,* which more or less collaborated with the Germans, who, in turn, rewarded them by making the University of Ghent an all Dutch-language institution. The Germans also enforced the Flemish language laws which had been passed but were largely ignored by Belgian politicians. Flemish nationalists who supported the Activists' aims but could not bring themselves to work with the Germans were called *Passivists*.

After the war, the language reforms granted by the Germans to the Flemish were revoked. Forty-five of the most flagrant Activists were condemned to death in trials for collaboration (though none of the sentences was carried out). Flemish nationalists as a group were publicly judged "traitors to the Belgian motherland," making the mainstream Flemish Movement ineffective. Some war-era Flemish Passivists, however, surfaced as *Maximalists,* wanting to work toward their aims within the existing political structure. They had the support of King Albert I, who addressed the Belgian Parliament directly after the armistice and promised: "In the domain of languages the strictest equality and the most absolute justice will characterize bills which the government will submit."

The Flemish Movement revived in the 1930s under the economic pressures produced in the Great Depression, and some results were finally forthcoming. Laws were passed that permitted the use of Dutch in administration, education, the courts, and the military, in the areas where it was the mother tongue. In 1930, the University of Ghent was officially declared Dutch-speaking. Nevertheless, French speakers still retained the economic base of power in Belgium.

With the invasion and occupation of Belgium by the Nazis in World War II, extreme Flemish nationalists, still smarting from a perceived continued political subjugation of the state by French-speakers' during the period between the wars, again had a certain favor from the Germans (Hitler was said to have found the Flemings "sympathetic" since their language was closer to German and ordered less harsh treatment for them). Some extremists, convinced that the Nazis would win the war and advance the Flemish cause after it was over, collaborated with the occupiers.

Following World War II, retribution for such behavior was demanded. In the many trials held in Belgium, more than three times the number of Flemings as Walloons were sentenced. Since then, the most despicable name a Walloon could call a Fleming has been "collaborator," although enough Walloons had faced similar charges to make the name-calling hypocritical.

Belgium's **King Leopold III** (who had come to the throne following his father Albert's tragic death in a climbing accident in 1934) himself was suspected of collaboration, many of his subjects believed that he should not have remained in Belgium after the Nazi invasion, thereby presenting an appearance of cooperation with the occupiers. After the war, this issue boiled over into demonstrations and riots, which eventually found resolution in the so-called **Royal Question** referendum. Leopold won the March 1950 plebiscite as to whether he should resume the throne by 57%, but the vote was split along lines that directly reflected the country's cultural communities (he was supported by the Catholic vote, which was mostly Flemish, and opposed by the anticlerics, who were largely Walloon). Knowing the Walloons would have considered him only "The King of the Flemings," Leopold decided to hand the crown to his son Baudouin.

The intense emotions stirred by events during and following World War II hardly helped the Flemish cause. It took a mid-century economic evolution to even partially unparalyze the politics. In the 1960s, with its industrious but comparatively unprosperous agricultural business largely ignored and neglected, Flanders finally found its way to the economic forefront. As Wallonia's coal mines were being closed in the 1960s, Flanders' economy finally was addressed, with a conscious effort at encouraging light industry: chemicals, pharmaceuticals, and electrical goods. Flanders forged ahead, and its energetic economy increased its importance politically. It became Flanders' turn at favored financial region status. Today, its agricultural production benefits from generous Common Market subsidies. Port expansion in Zeebrugge, Ostend, and Antwerp (now the world's 5th largest), has made Flanders the most active stretch of shipping anywhere on the North Sea.

Increasing financial success made it easier for Flemings to insist on exercising greater political power in the Flemish mother tongue, to insist on proving Flemish could be just as competent a voice of government as French. The changes in relative economic strength challenged the political relationship between Belgium's two communities. In 1962, the language boundary was officially fixed, and the reciprocal rights on both sides of the "border" spelled out.

In the 1960s, all of the traditional nationwide political parties—Socialists, Catholics, and Conservatives—separated into two sections, one for the Flemish and one for the Walloons. This increased the number of component parts needed to make political compromises. With the language concerns coming ahead of all others, it was ever more difficult to deal with Belgium's national issues. On lesser questions, language matters in Belgium run from the serious to the stupefying: one widely reported situation had Flemish and French-speaking farmers at a standoff over whether or not artificial insemination of their cows should be by bulls from the same language area.

After a period of increasingly strident bi-cultural battle cries, during which it was presumed that a strong central government was necessary to keep the Dutch-speaking Flemish and the French-speaking Walloons away from each other's throats, a new concept emerged that allowed the two communities to function while keeping at a comfortable arm's length from each other. In 1980, the federalization of Belgium process began, with a revision of the Constitution. Gradually throughout the 1980s, Flanders and Wallonia (and Brussels, which forms a third autonomous federal region) assumed strong separate-but-equal grips on their own matters, and, since 1988, each community has had full decision-making powers in such fields as economy, education, energy, environment, housing, health, cultural affairs, and public works. The national budget has been regionalized, and political stability is setting a new tone for the 1990s.

It's unlikely that federalism is the last word on Belgium's language issue. Many Flemish still feel they make more concessions on their side of bilingualism, finding themselves in the uniquely uncomfortable posture of a majority unable to escape from the mentality of a minority.

Commentary on the losses incurred when a country allows itself to be divided in the name of bilingualism comes in connection with **Louvain University**. Located in Flanders (not far northeast of Brussels), Louvain was founded in 1425 by Pope Martin V and Duke John IV of Brabant. Within a century it had become one of the leading universities in Europe, with 6,000 students and 52 colleges, one of which was founded in 1517 by Rotterdam-born Desiderius Erasmus. Erasmus had a dream of offering liberal Catholic education at Louvain, but was caught up in the times of Luther and the Reformation, in response to which strict Catholic orthodoxy was enforced under an official inquisition. This drove Erasmus to Switzerland in 1521, and he was never to return to the Netherlands). Cartographer Gerhard Mercator (1512–1594) learned his geography at Louvain, where he later founded and ran an institute of cartography until he was chased from the Spanish Netherlands in 1544 for his heretical views of the world. Ghent-born Charles V was tutored by some of its leading lecturers.

In many ways, Louvain University's history reflects Flanders'. Once the *lingua franca* for European university instruction was no longer Latin, Louvain adopted the culturally correct French language (hence our easier recognition of the historic institution under its French name *Louvain*, despite its location in Dutch-speaking Flanders and correct Flemish name *Leuven*).

Flanders made a breakthrough in 1930 when the University at Ghent finally was authorized to give its classes in Flemish. Eventually, the

Flemish Movement made enough show of force to make it mandatory that every course offered to the then more than 15,000 students at Louvain be available in Dutch as well as French. In 1962, the policy of duplication of curriculum in both languages, though placing great stress on the university's resources, was reaffirmed. Violent disputes, however, led to the French section being expelled in 1968, the Flemings insisting that classes conducted in French on Flemish soil were no longer acceptable. The historic Louvain officially became Dutch-speaking Leuven University and, in 1970, the decision was made to establish a new French-speaking university at **Louvain-la-Neuve** (New Louvain), 28 km/17 mi. south in the Walloon area of Brabant province.

The **library** of Louvain University had been famous in Europe for centuries for its many fine manuscripts. Among these were a collection of Irish literature, 500 illuminated manuscripts, and 1,000 incunabula (books printed before 1500 in the earliest years of moveable type, many of which had been printed at Louvain). In 1914, at the beginning of the First World War, the central section of the town of Leuven was badly burned by the German army; the Cloth Hall, which the university had occupied since 1432, was demolished and the University Library virtually so. (So, too, were many of the Flemish city's other fine old buildings, in particular the lavish 15th-century Flamboyant Gothic Stadhuis, whose remarkable facade—fortunately rebuilt in its original exterior splendor—is almost as high as it is long). At the end of the war, the *Treaty of Versailles* decreed that Germany must furnish library materials to Louvain of equal value to those destroyed. Other generous contributions of books to restock the Louvain library were made by many institutions, especially ones in Great Britain and the United States, all of whose names are inscribed on the new library's walls. The library, rebuilt in Flemish Renaissance style by architect Whitney Warren, reopened in 1928. (Its soaring steeple contained a carillon contributed by American engineers in commemoration of their compatriots who died during the First World War that has recently been replaced with new donations). The library again suffered damage, though not as extensive, in World War II from Nazi bombs.

While acknowledging the library's tragic losses due to wars, a case can be made that the greatest devastation to the integrity of the Louvain University collection came at the hands of the Belgians themselves. No one can fail to be saddened by the disposition of the historic library as a result of the opening of the French-speaking Louvain-la-Neuve University, a solution that speaks volumes about Belgium's bi-cultural struggle. The contents of the original Louvain University library were split between the old and the new, the Flemish and the French institutions, respectively, strictly by the number: books whose call number ended in an even digit went to one, those ending in odd to the other.

ANTWERP

Guidelines For Antwerp

SIGHTS Three "must-see" sights in Antwerp (Antwerpen, Anvers) are baroque painter **Pieter Paul Rubens' House,** the **Plantin-Moretus House,** and the **Royal Museum of Fine Arts,** but there are other major attractions, among them the Gothic **Cathedral** (Belgium's largest), **Diamond Museum,** and **port.** One of the remarkable aspects about art in Antwerp is that so much of it remains in the specific spaces for which it originally was created: city churches and the patrician townhouses (several now furnished museums) of contemporaries of Rubens. Old Antwerp, around the grand **Grote Markt,** is linked by appealing streets (many pedestrian-only), quaint cobbled alleys, and quiet old squares. Belgium's proud port city is inextricably tied to the **River Scheldt,** the riverfront of interest for its ancient fortress/prison **Steen** (now the **Maritime Museum**), the **Flandria** cruise boat pier, riverbank promenades, and a pedestrian tunnel under the water that leads to a fine view of Antwerp from the far bank. There's striking **after-dark illumination** of the Cathedral, Stadhuis on the Grote Markt, and other buildings and monuments.

GETTING AROUND Antwerp (with a core city population of 250,000, greater city 500,000) sprawls, but several important sights are within a few blocks of the central **Grote Markt,** on which is located the main **City Tourist Office.** Most others are within walking distance either north or south of **Meir** (pronounced *mare,* as in horse), Antwerp's confusingly multiple-named, but essentially straight, main mid-city street, running from **Centraal Station** to the **Scheldt.** The city's public transport network includes trams, metro, and buses (system map at Tourist Office); tickets are sold by 8-ride strip, 24-hour pass, or single ride. Near the Cathedral and Grote Markt, several tram and bus lines converge at **Groenplaats** (identifiable by its statue of *Rubens*), beneath which is a stop on the metro line, which runs under Meir to the Centraal Station. Groenplaats, and **Koning Astridplein** in front of Centraal Station, have taxi stands. Antwerp has a reasonable number of paid parking lots; those in cars should avoid the area around the Grote Markt, which has the most pedestrian-only and congested streets.

BELGIUM · · 435

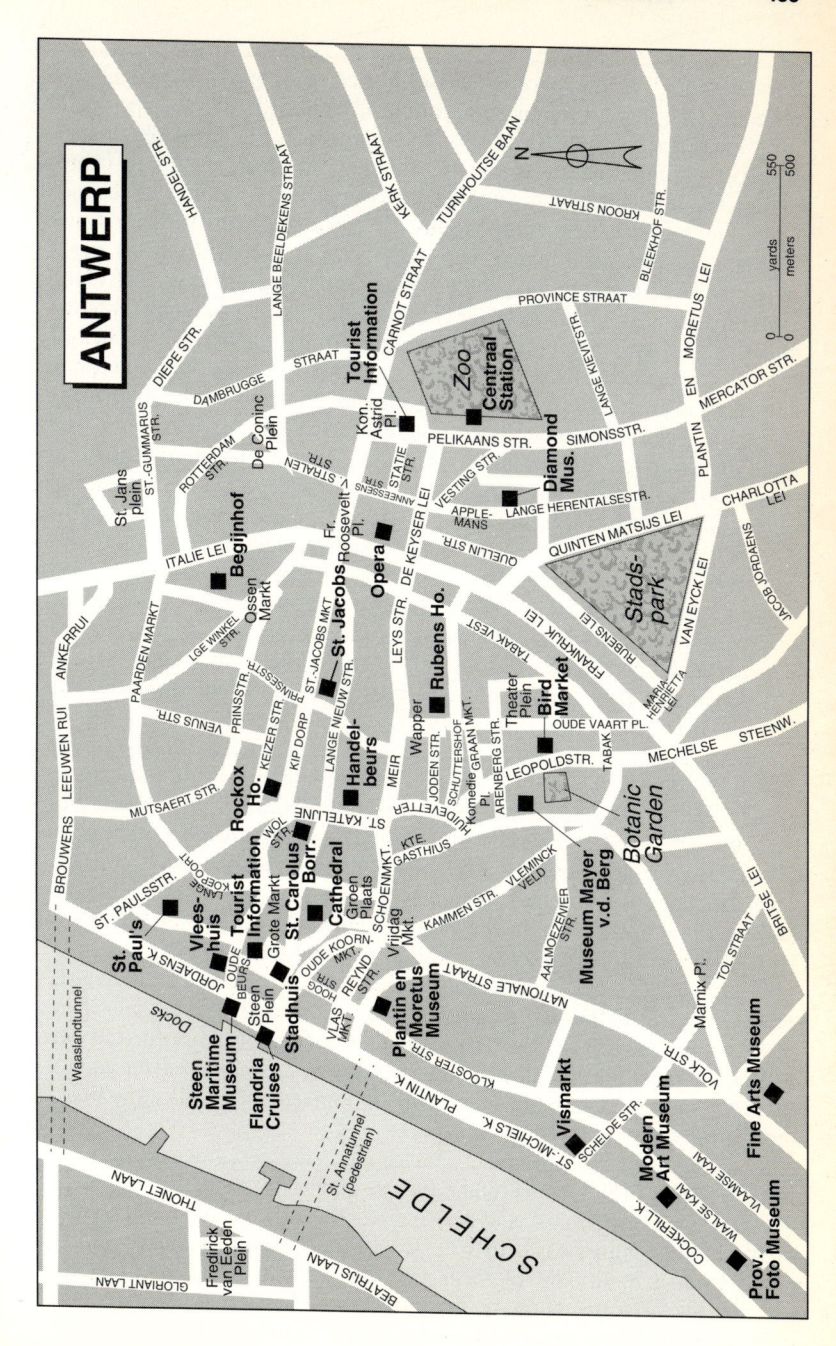

SHOPPING Antwerp provides sophisticated shopping, with all the expected Belgian and European department, clothing, and specialty stores, most located along Meir (Fridays until 9 p.m., other nights until 6 p.m.). The city is noted as an innovative international fashion design center thanks to the styles of the so-called **Antwerp Six**. Antique and secondhand shops are scattered throughout the city and, with Antwerp's history as an international trading hub, one never knows what objects might turn up. The 16th-century cobbled **Vlaeykensgang** alleyway off Oude Koornmarkt is as much worth seeking out for its picturesqueness as its antiques. Art galleries continue to open in Antwerp, many branches of ones in Brussels. Antwerp's brilliantly cut diamonds are sold wholesale and retail in nondescript shops along the side of Centraal Station; prices for unset stones are some 40% off those in the U.S. If you're looking for a gem, though not necessarily a jewel, save Sunday mornings (8:30 a.m.–1 p.m.) for the **Vogelmarkt,** or bird market, a 600-year tradition on the site (near the City Theater); originally, solely geese and chickens were sold, hence its name, but today it's also a flea market. Saturdays from Easter through Sept. (10 a.m.–6 p.m.) there's an antiques market on Lijnwaadmarkt, north of the Cathedral; during the same season, also on Saturdays, artists display their work in the open air on the Wapper outside Rubens' House. Wednesday and Friday mornings at the **Vrijdaymarkt** there are public auctions of secondhand furniture and household goods.

ENTERTAINMENT AND EVENTS A remarkably cosmopolitan and cultured city, Antwerp offers its citizens and visitors a wide variety of regularly scheduled and special events. The monthly *Kalender Antwerpen* (available from the Tourist Office) lists programs for the city's concert, opera, ballet, and theater companies, as well as the 50-odd cinemas (where films are shown in the original language—many in English—with Dutch sub-titles), cabaret, exhibitions, and other events.

ACCOMMODATIONS In addition to modern international chain business hotels outside the city center, Antwerp offers a limited but interesting selection of pleasant in-town properties. Since even central Antwerp is spread out, no hotel will be convenient to all attractions, though most are near public transport.

RESTAURANTS Antwerpians like to dine with wine. An estimated 800 cafes and restaurants, and perhaps 2,000 pubs, mean there's no lack of places for visitors to fit in with local food fashion. Tasters' choices range from a traditional Flemish stew pot to a melting pot of ethnic eateries to meet the culinary preferences of Antwerp's cosmopolitan population. You can satisfy a sweet tooth for Antwerp's *pralines* (filled, handmade chocolates) least expensively at small sidewalk shops, and most imaginatively at **H. Burie** (where white chocolate is molded in *stalks* resembling Belgium's famed white asparagus). Traditional Antwerpse *handjes* ("little hands") are rich butter and almond cookies that honor the *Brabo* legend (see *Antwerp in Context* below).

ARRIVING There is frequent half-hour train service between Antwerp's Centraal Station and all three Brussels' stations. Belgium's dense rail network also makes Antwerp easily accessible from elsewhere in the country, and from most anywhere in Europe (connections through Brussels). Antwerp is under three hours from Amsterdam on numerous direct trains. Belgium's SABENA World Airlines runs regularly scheduled buses between Antwerp (from SABENA's office on De Keyserlei, across from Centraal Station) and Brussels' Zaventem Airport. Those arriving from England by North Sea ferry at Ostend or Zeebrugge can reach Antwerp by rail with a transfer either at Ghent or Brussels (Gare du Nord). Antwerp is well served on the Belgium/European motorway system.

IN THE AREA A short bus ride from Centraal Station to a southern Antwerp neighborhood brings you to the **Middelheim Open-Air Museum,** one of the world's finest sculpture gardens. Also accessible by bus, the streets **Cogels-Osylei** in the city's southeast district of *Berchem* offer a turn-of-the-century architectural free-for-all, with plenty of *jugendstil* (*art nouveau*). Less than 15 minutes by frequent train from Antwerp is attractive **Mechelen,** city of carillon concerts, tapestry tradition, and once an historic Hapsburg Court.

TRAVEL TRIPS The EC has designated Antwerp as **European Cultural Capital** for 1993. Focusing on a rotating basis on worthy cities in community-member countries, the European Cultural Capital spotlight gives the selected destination a special incentive to shine. Citywide, Antwerp has been polishing itself as carefully as it would one of its own fine diamonds for the occasion, with a stepped-up schedule of restoration of historic buildings. The scaffolding that had covered the Cathedral spire for 25 years has now been dismantled. An especially full year of special events is planned (see *Entertainment and Events* section below).

Antwerp in Context

Antwerp's most famous son, artist Pieter Paul Rubens, once observed: "It is not a question of living long, but of living well." He may not have been referring to cities, but his historic and handsome home town has, nevertheless, seen fit to follow the suggestion. Antwerp, which dates from Roman days, not only lives graciously with its long and prestigious past, but enjoys an enviably lively and prosperous present.

Although it is, by Belgian standards, a populous city, with a half million inhabitants, Antwerp retains the feeling and friendliness of a small town. And, though one of the world's premier ports and the world diamond capital, the ambiance of Antwerp is akin to a cosmopolitan village. Antwerpians have devised a life-style of their own design, and seem to identify more with their city than with the rest of Flanders, let alone Belgium. Some residents claim that a lingering influence from the days of Spanish occupation accounts for Antwerpians' being more intuitive and emotional than most northern Europeans. One man told me, "In Antwerp we have our own way of life, but we are xenophiles, not xenophobes."

Antwerp's agreeably integrated population proves it: some 117 nationalities make up the mix. The inevitable influence of its port (the fifth largest in the world, and a regular port-of-call or home port for approximately 300 shipping lines from more than 100 countries) adds more foreign flavor. Some who first came to Antwerp to discuss international trade found the city so well-suited to living well that they returned to stay. Those fortunate enough to be native Antwerpians, though healthily chauvinistic, also are an outlooking lot, having grown up with the tradition of the seven seas on their doorstep. But of the many who leave to see something else of the world, most return to Antwerp's exceptional environment.

Antwerp calls the 16th century its **Golden Age** (Amsterdam had to wait in the wings until the 17th century for its gilded era). The period was the most prosperous of any in Antwerp's history—though the present could come to rival it: currently, the city of Antwerp provides the country of Belgium with close to half the Gross National Product (GNP).

Antwerp's prosperity has always been linked to its port on the Scheldt. More than one Antwerpian may quote the old saying: "The town owes its river to God, but everything else it owes to its river." The Scheldt features in a favorite fable about the city's Roman days. The river at Antwerp, so it is told, was ruled by a giant who demanded tolls from passing ships. Sailors who didn't pay had their hands cut off. Finally, a Roman soldier named **Brabo** decided to defy the giant. In a struggle reminiscent of David and Goliath's, Brabo defeated the giant, whose huge hand he cut off and threw into the river (the very action captured in the *Brabo Fountain* sculpture on the Grote Markt). From this tale, the source of the name Antwerp, from the Flemish *handwerpen* ("throwing the hand") has been suggested. But the more prosaic, and probable, derivation is *aanwerp* ("a promotory in the river"), which describes the present site of **The Steen**, where Antwerp's earliest settlement was founded.

Battered even earlier by Norsemen and Normans, Antwerp was

noted as a seaport by A.D. 1031. In the 12th century, the city gained municipal rights from the Dukes of Brabant. The Hanseatic League set up an establishment here in 1313 and Antwerp acquired the important right of staple for English wool; both brought foreign merchants to the town on the Scheldt in increasing numbers. Residence in Antwerp by the Counts of Flanders (who became unified with Brabant under the Burgundians in 1406) marked the beginning of a period of even greater commercial recognition. While benefitting from association with Brabant's economic progress, Antwerp also gained at the expense of Bruges: as that town lost its access to the sea while the Zwin silted up, during the same period Antwerp's access increased as the mouth of the Scheldt was considerably widened by flooding in Zeeland.

By the end of the 15th century Antwerp became the chief port in all the Netherlands. Major sources of trade were sugar, soap, beer, diamonds, and textiles (the city had gained control of *alum,* a substance indispensable to the cloth industry, by imposing a stage tax for it on the Scheldt). In 1454, Philip the Good established the Antwerp Guild of St. Luke for the encouragement of painting, an act which served as a foundation for the Flemish School. The guild played host to Albrecht Durer during his stay in Antwerp in 1520–1521.

In the 16th century, Antwerp continued to grow as an important trading center for spices and staples, and by then, Antwerp's diamond industry had been in business for a century. Merchants from many cultures—English, German, Italian, Spanish, and Portuguese—met and mingled in the port city. The city's financial establishments lent money to kings and emperors dealing at Europe's first international exchange building, which opened in Antwerp in 1460 (and served as a model for subsequent exchanges in London and Europe). Antwerp became the continent's foremost center of commerce, navigation, finance, and art. Up to 300 vessels put in and out of Antwerp's port daily, and more than 1,000 foreign trading concerns had offices here. Even a Venetian, an ambassador to Antwerp, called the city "the first trading center of the world." Another dubbed the city "the most noble warehouse of the whole world." Finally there was enough money to finish Antwerp's cathedral, whose construction, begun in 1352, had frequently floundered thereafter for lack of funds; the magnificent tower (400 feet/123 meters), added in 1518, marked the completion of the largest Gothic church in the Netherlands. In 1514, Antwerp had a population of 40,000 (which, even then, made it as large as London, and three times the size of any town in Holland), and, by 1560, the city had exploded in size to 100,000. Truly, it was a Golden Age.

But Emperor Charles V, who had ruled the Netherlands through the opening phases of the rapidly spreading **Reformation,** abdicated in 1555 to his son Philip II of Spain. Philip's response to the Protestants practically decreed that prosperous times in Antwerp, by then rent with religious dissent, would not survive his reign. Antwerp's cathedral and other churches were pillaged by Protestant Calvinists in the 1566 *Iconoclast,* which took a great toll on the city's Golden Age artist achievements. The 1576 *Spanish Fury*'s toll was in lives, when the city was sacked and 7,000 citizens killed in an attack by angry Spanish soldiers, mutinous from not having received their pay from the Duke of Alva. (The Spanish Fury caused many Protestants to flee from their lives, including one Jan **Rubens,** a Lutheran lawyer, whose son Pieter Paul was born the next year in exile in Westphalia, Germany). In 1577, with help from Prince Willem (the Silent) of Orange whose rebel forces were for a while headquartered in Flanders, Antwerp stood up to the Spanish, so successfully that for the next eight years the open practice of Catholicism in the city was forbidden. (The Rubens' family weren't able to return from Germany, however, because Pieter Paul's mother was Catholic).

In 1585, after a two-year seige, the Duke of Parma recaptured Antwerp for Spain. This turn of fortune established that Antwerp's future would be with the Spanish or Southern Netherlands (the future Belgium) rather than the Northern Netherlands (Holland). The firm establishment of Antwerp as a Catholic city under Spanish rule drove thousands more Protestants away: diamond cutters went to Amsterdam, tile workers found employment in Delft, and the family of five-year-old Frans Hals left for Haarlem. (Finally, his Protestant father having died, Rubens and his mother returned to Antwerp). The many Antwerp artisans and artists who emigrated north to Holland can truly be said to have had a hand in Amsterdam's upcoming shining century.

The relatively peaceful reign of the equally entitled Archdukes (Isabella, daughter of Philip II and her husband Albert) from 1598–1621 was a period of economic recovery for Antwerp and its port. Baroque art blossomed under Rubens, whose students, studio helpers, and collaborators included Jacob Jordaens, Anthony van Dyck, Adriaen Brouwer, and David Teniers Elder and Younger. At the same time an intellectual coterie, which included Rubens, arose around the brilliant **Balthasar Moretus** of the printing house Plantin-Moretus. The period left a physical imprint upon Antwerp that visitors can see today: writing in 1620 in almost touristic terms, Jan Woverius, humanist, town-clerk, and one-time learned counsellor to the Archdukes, said: "Our City of Antwerp is happy to possess two such great citizens as Rubens and Moretus . . . their houses will evoke the astonishment and admiration of visitors."

No end to an era could be more definitive than that which came to Antwerp with the signing of the 1648 *Peace of Westphalia.* In the agreement that officially ended the 80-year Spanish/Netherlands war, the Spanish accepted the Dutch terms that demanded the closing of the Scheldt to ships (the banks on both sides of the river estuary were in

Dutch territory). The Dutch move to do away with competition for the port of Amsterdam by closing the Scheldt effectively closed the port at Antwerp; as history happened, it would not be reopened for a century and a half. Cut off from sea trade, Antwerp foundered. Its population plummeted: by 1790, it was back to the size it had been in 1514—40,000.

The port of Antwerp owes its revival to Napoleon, who in 1799 took over the reins of the French Revolutionary Army, which earlier in the 1790s had conquered both the Southern and Northern Netherlands. Napoleon reopened the Scheldt with an ulterior motive: to have a naval "pistol pointed at the heart of England." No matter; between 1800 and 1803, dock basins and river quays were built; the Bonaparte Lock was inaugurated in 1811 (and is still in operation). With its port once again open to commerce, Antwerp experienced an astonishing revival.

When Napoleon was defeated at Waterloo in 1815, Antwerp came under Dutch rule in the United Kingdom of the Netherlands partnership enforced upon Belgium by outside European powers. With Antwerp port then doing business under the same flag as the Dutch, its port's revitalization was encouraged. With the improvements, Antwerp developed into the largest port in the United Kingdom of the Netherlands. Dutch trade with its colonies in Indonesia and the Caribbean provided steady traffic in and out of all Netherlands ports, but Antwerp's share of the shipping stopped with Belgium's revolt against Dutch rule in 1830. Whatever Dutch King Willem I felt about being thus "divested" of Belgium, he had no intention of giving up Antwerp harbor without a fight. The Dutch dug in, and great damage was done to the port by bombardment and sieges in 1830 and 1832 before they were dislodged (the new Belgian King Leopold I eventually called in the French for help).

In the 1839 peace that finally established the present Benelux country borders, Holland was granted the the right of levying navigation dues on shipping in the Scheldt. In 1863, Antwerp, with the help of the Belgian government, bought out Holland's right to the levies for a considerable compensation in 1863. At the turn-of-the-century, Antwerp became important as the port for the *Kongobootes* that sailed the seas to and from **Belgium's Congo** colony (now Zaire). When the big ships steamed into Antwerp from Africa they always caused a stir and raised a crowd, and often attracted brass bands onto the piers.

Wartime destruction was heaviest toward the end of World War II, when, retaken by the Allies, the port suffered Nazi V-1 and V-2 attacks in late 1944 and early 1945. Antwerp was the goal of Hitler's last-gasp across-Belgium campaign in the winter of 1944–45, but the *Battle of the Bulge* became bogged down where it began, in the Ardennes. That Hitler had even thought of Antwerp so late in the war was a testament to the port's strategic value. Its location remained important when peace came, and the world wars proved to be only an interruption of the port's 20th-century progress.

Today, Antwerp on the Scheldt, situated some 50 mi./85 km. from the North Sea, is becoming ever more significant as an international crossroads for maritime and continental shipping and distribution. In tonnage and traffic, the city is the fifth largest port in the world and, by most accounts, Europe's most efficient in turnaround time. Port pilots are taken aboard incoming ships at Holland's Vlissengen (Flushing), and in Antwerp proper on out-sailing vessels; their navigational knowledge is vital because of the Scheldt's shifting sandbars and waters (tidal well above Antwerp), which rise and fall about 13 feet between tides. The 37,000-acre/15,000-hectare state-of-the-art port has a control tower with a computerized system to plan and control shipping, and, as of 1991, the world's longest radar chain (78 mi./130 km.), stretching down the Scheldt to the North Sea.

The relative quiet along the waterfront in the center of Antwerp, where old warehouses with stylish iron pediments lie abandoned except for scenery-seeking riverbank pedestrians, belies the port's actual activity. Increasingly after World War II, Antwerp's port spread downstream (nearer to the North Sea) to accommodate larger ocean-going vessels; it now has some 100 kilometers of wet and dry docks, extending north to the Dutch border. Along the Scheldt are five sea-locks, of which the newest, Berendrecht Lock (opened in 1989), is the largest in the world. Major port industries at Antwerp include oil-refineries, petrochemical and automobile assembly plants, grain companies, trans-shipment yards, and multi-national firms such as Bayer and Montsanto. Even segments of Antwerp's old sailors' quarter have moved on down the river, and some of the brothels and rooming houses in the city's waterfront district have been converted into apartments and artists' lofts.

Dockers' pride in their port has helped make Antwerp a highly efficient installation. Four shifts are needed to keep the river-born business moving during the port's 24-hour day. Antwerp's actual dock worker's ways are still traditional, but unions, management, supervisors, and stevedores in the hiring hall haven't come up with anything they like better, and there hasn't been a strike since 1963. Being strike-free has played a big part in Antwerp's having won business over from the ports of Rotterdam and London since World War II.

There are two possibilities for visitors to see something of Antwerp's port. The boats of **Flandria** (berthed on the Scheldt near the Steenplein in central Antwerp), in addition to 50-minute cruises which don't get far enough downstream to show much of the port, also offer day or evening 2.5-3-hour port excursions. For those traveling by car, the 40-mi./65-km. self-guiding *Havenroute* (map available from the Tourist Office), best undertaken when there's a passenger who can serve as navigator, provides insight into the workings of the port.

As visitors discover, Antwerp is a destination with many dimensions, one that integrates new ideas with older ones. The intellectual environment that blossomed as an accompaniment to the art of Antwerp's Baroque period at the end of the 16th century had its birth at the beginning of that century. It was at that time that **Thomas More** (1477–1535), an English humanist and *Man for All Seasons,* used Antwerp as the setting for his book *Utopia.* Considered one of the most influential books in Western philosophy, *Utopia* described a mythical island off South America where wealth was divided equally and all lived in happy cooperation free of war and want. Thomas More was an intimate of Rotterdam-born fellow humanist **Erasmus** (with whom he founded a college at Louvain University, where *Utopia* was first published in 1516).

Book One of *Utopia* opens with More recounting: "The most invincible King of England, Henry the Eighth of that name, sent me into Flanders as his spokesman. . . . (and) since my business required it, I went to Antwerp." More lived in Antwerp from May to October in 1515, and in *Utopia* speaks of his Antwerpian friend Peter Giles, whose house on Oude Beurs he visited many times since it was a prominent meeting place for Humanists, including Erasmus. (The house, *De Spieghel* "the mirror," and its monumental 17th-century gate decorated with a woman looking at herself in a mirror, is located at 16 Oude Beurs just behind the Grote Markt). Humanism was an intellectual and cultural movement concerned with the interest and ideals of people rather than the natural world or religion. In the pages of *Utopia,* it is Peter Giles who introduces More to Raphael, who tells them both of the wonders of the world that he—Raphael—had heard recounted by explorer Amerigo Vespucci (1451–1512). At this time, in accordance with their individual beliefs, most Europeans were either entranced or alarmed by tales about overseas expeditions, but the philosophers of the day saw in the broadened horizons a fresh chance for men to create a better way of life. Hence, More, inspired by Vespucci's voyages, conceived in *Utopia* how an idealistic society might be set up in an unspoiled new world.

During his stay in Antwerp, early on in the city's Golden Age, Thomas More would have observed a metropolis that mixed material success with humanism. More than 450 years later, an antiques dealer has this to say about his city: "We are at a very similar point in history: the humanism of the Renaissance is a philosophy that suits our times." He believes that Antwerpians are open, seeking, and creative, and may well be in the midst of a renaissance that will rival the city's 16th-century glory.

GUIDEPOSTS
Telephone Code 03

Tourist Information — City Tourist Office: Head Office: Grote Markt 15; B-2000 Antwerp; Mon.–Fri., 8:30 a.m.–6 p.m., Sat., Sun., hols. 9 a.m.–5 p.m.; 232.01.03. Information pavilion: Koningin Astridplein in front of Centraal Station: same hours as head office except Mon.–Fri., until 8 p.m., Sat. to 7 p.m; 232.05.70.; both offices closed Christmas and New Year's Day. Accommodations booking assistance.

City Transport — M.I.V.A. Head Office: Grotehondstraat 58; Mon.–Fri. 8:30 a.m.–4 p.m.; 218.14.20

Trains — Centraal Station inquiries: Mon.–Sat. 8 a.m.–10 p.m., Sun. & hols. 9 a.m.–5 p.m.

Airport Bus Service — SABENA office: De Keyserlei 74; 231.68.25. Regularly scheduled coaches to Brussels Zaventem Airport.

Port Cruises — *Flandria*: Steenplein, 233.74.22

City Tours — *Sightseeing Line*: 13-passenger 50-minute narrated (head sets, 7 languages) mini-van tours from Grote Markt: schedule and reservations at Tourist Office.

Consulates — U.S.A.: Nationalestraat 5; 225.00.71
Great Britain: Korte Klarenstraat 7; 232.69.40
Ireland: Rudolfstraat 16; 237.69.94

Emergency — Police: 101; accident: 100; a list of doctors and pharmacists/chemists on night and weekend duty is published in the weekend editions of local newspapers, and available from the Tourist Office or at hotel.

Automobile Aid — Royal Automobile Club of Belgium: 232.16.93

Lost Property — Police headquarters: 231.68.80; Centraal Railway Station: 231.76.90; City tram/bus office: 218.14.11

Post Office — Main Post Office: Groenplaats 42; Mon.–Fri., 9 a.m.–6 p.m., Sat. 9 a.m.–noon; 231.06.70

Telephone/ Head Office: Jezusstraat 1; daily 8 a.m.–8 p.m.;
Telegraph 232.58.10

WHAT TO SEE AND DO......................

Central Antwerp's attractions are grouped below in three general areas, each of which can be covered fairly easily on foot. The most distant site is the Fine Arts Museum (more than a mile from the Grote Markt), to which most visitors take a tram or taxi. Sights start with those within walking distance of the Grote Markt (the Tourist Office there has maps and printed English commentary on eight suggested walking tours), and riverfront, following which are descriptions of sites south, and then north, of Meir. Local custom calls for time out at cafes along the way. Many museums in Antwerp are *open* on Monday; holidays on which they are commonly *closed* are Jan. 1 & 2, May 1, Ascension Day, Nov. 1 & 2, Dec. 25 & 26.

Around the Grote Markt and Riverfront

Grote Markt • *The heart of Antwerp is the Grote Markt, and at that square's center, replacing the former tree of liberty, is the* **Brabo Fountain** (1887, sculpted by Jef Lambeaux). Rimming it are dignified 16th-century guild houses, each topped with a gilt-adorned patron saint appropriate to the particular craft or trade (drapers, haberdashers, coopers, and crossbows) once headquartered therein. The guild houses (some original, such as numbers 38 and 40, others reconstructions of those which once stood elsewhere, such as 15 and 25) are in Renaissance-style, which gives Antwerp's Grote Markt a less ornate appearance than Brussels' Baroque-era main square. Though not used for weekly general markets, Antwerp's Grote Markt is the setting for special festival markets.

Southwest off the Grote Markt is the statue of the **Dock Worker** (by Constantin Meunier). Out the northeast corner across Oude Beurs, at 15 Hofstraat, is Antwerp's old **Stock Exchange,** a beautiful Gothic building from 1515 that now serves as the city's education office (the lovely inner courtyard can be viewed during office hours). Behind Grote Markt to the right of the **Stadhuis,** and between it and the not-distant **Vleeshuis,** one finds exemplary urban renewal in one of the city's most historic sections. An extensive housing project (following the clearance deemed necessary of ancient buildings that had become slum-like) has been built to blend in scale and building materials with original old city buildings.

Stadhuis • *Grote Markt; Mon.–Sat. 9 a.m.–3 p.m., except Mon. 9 a.m.–noon, Fri. noon–3 p.m., Sat. til 4 p.m., closed Sun. and holidays; 220.82.11* • The Grote Markt is dominated by the Stadhuis (Town Hall), whose 247-foot facade has a coat of many colors of marble. Built from 1561–1565 by Antwerp architect Cornelis Floris, it is one of Flanders' earliest and finest buildings in the Renaissance style. During the summer months, the Stadhuis festively flaunts some of the flags of the more than 100 countries whose ships put into Antwerp's port. The impressive interior decoration dates mostly from the city's prosperous 19th century, many earlier works of art having been destroyed or stolen during the French occupation at the end of the 18th century. The former Lords' Chamber, now the **Leys Room,** is decorated with four historical paintings by **Henri Leys** representing the main privileges of Antwerp. Murals on the staircase walls and the Marriage Chamber are also notable.

The statue in the center niche in the front of the Stadhuis is of the Virgin Mary, patron saint of the city, and it recalls the other Madonnas you'll see by the dozen in street corner niches. Two reasons account for their great number. During the days of the St. Luke's Guild, in order to become a *master* member an artist had to create a *masterpiece*; often, Antwerp sculptors selected the Madonna as their subject, and later presented the completed work to the district in which they lived. Secondly, when these statuettes of the Virgin, displayed on street corners, were lighted by votives, they avoided the taxes that otherwise were levied on private street lights.

Onze Lieve Vrouw/Notre Dame Cathedral • *Groenplaats 21; Mon.–Fri. 10 a.m.–5 p.m., Sat. 10 a.m.–3 p.m., Sun. and church festivals 1–4 p.m., not accessible during church services; 231.30.33* • Both because of its position on the ground and the prominence of its steeple in the sky, Antwerp's Cathedral is *the* landmark of the city. Hemmed in by buildings, the Cathedral body cannot be seen as a whole, but the structure nevertheless is an omnipresence in the old center. The largest Gothic church in Belgium, the Cathedral was begun in 1352 under a general design by Jan Appelmans (see the imaginative **Appelmans Monument** by Jef Lambeaux, 1935, to the right of the main door on Handschotenmarkt). With construction spread out until 1521 due to erratic funding, the nave, originally Romanesque, was demolished in about 1425 and begun again in Gothic. The seven-aisle interior is of startling size, even with the choir currently closed off as part of a long-term fundamental $70 million-plus restoration. At 400 feet/122 meters, the Cathedral's soaring spire, completed in 1521, is the highest in the Netherlands and resembles Belgian lace in its delicacy; recently (1990) unwrapped from scaffolding that had contained it since 1965, it brings fresh meaning to the word *inspiring*. The view from its inside out, if you aspire to climb the tower, is pure panorama. Cathedral treasures include three of Rubens' most famous paintings: "Raising of the Cross" (triptych, 1610), "Descent from the Cross" (triptych, 1611–1614), and "Assumption" (1626); Rubens' "Resurrection" is in the Treasury. The central panel of "Descent from the Cross," with its strong diagonal line that draws viewers into the action and emotion of the moment, is the essence of Rubens' best Baroque work. Concerts are occasionally performed on the 5625-pipe organ. Many flat tombstones can be seen in the cathedral floor; people paid a lot to be buried there in the belief that if, on Judgment Day, they are raised to their feet inside a church, they fare better than if in a cemetery.

Handschoenmarkt • This lovely square in front of the Cathedral's main door has retained its historic Frankish triangle shape, which facilitated the protective containment of cattle. At No. 13 is the house (with plaque) in which the artist **David Teniers the Younger** was born in 1610. Cafe-rimmed, the square is a delightful locale for concerts on the Cathedral's 47-bell carillon (Fridays from 11:30 a.m.–12:30 p.m. year-round, and Mondays from 9–10 p.m. from mid-June to mid-September).

In the square is a stone well with a lovely ironwork canopy (c. 1495). The canopy is ascribed to **Quinten Metsys** (or Matsys and Massys, c. 1460–1530), a favorite adopted son of Antwerp, who arrived from Louvain trained as a blacksmith and with a talent for intricate ironwork. But an *artisan* wasn't good enough for the *artist* whose daughter Metsys fell in love with in his new city. As the story of the courtship usually is recounted, Metsys continued to visit the young lady at her home and, one day, speaking with her in her father's studio, he picked up a brush and painted a fly on a canvas that her father had left to dry. A few days later when the father had occasion to look at the painting again, he tried to brush off the fly. When he realized that it was painted and inquired of his daughter who the artist was, he was persuaded to give permission for her to marry Metsys. The Latin phrase inscribed on a tablet to Quinten Metsys that is on the facade of the Cathedral to the left of the door near the well translates to: "Twas love connubial taught the smith to paint." Metsys, who today is considered the first major artist of the Antwerp School, is represented by "The Lamentation of Christ Triptych," and five other paintings in Antwerp's Fine Arts Museum (which has none by his "artist" father-in-law).

Steenplein and Riverfront • The Scheldt is nearly a third of a mile (500 meters) wide in front of the Steenplein, where a statue of **Minerva,** the Roman goddess of wisdom and industry, reflects upon the river. Though the shipping that makes the Port of Antwerp statistics so staggering must now be accommodated downstream by facilities fit to handle it, you'll still have the flavor of river traffic in the center of the city, from the barges heading upstream on the waterway into the heart of the European continent. The entrance to the under-river pedestrian **St. Annatunnel** (built in 1933, about ⅓ mile long) is located west of the Vrijdaymarkt at St. Jansvliet.

The Steen (National Maritime Museum) • *Steenplein 1; daily 10 a.m.–5 p.m.; 232.08.50; exhibits with English explanation* • On the waterfront is Antwerp's oldest (12th century) edifice, the Steen, situated on the site of the city's earliest development. Built as a fortress, and for centuries used as a prison, the Steen was restored (by architects De Waghemakere and Keldermans, who had just completed work on the Cathedral) about 1520 by order of Charles V, whose coat of arms can still be seen on the lovely loggia over the entrance gate. Under Charles' son Spanish King Philip II and the dread Duke of Alva, however, the Steen deteriorated into a torture chamber. Today, no longer fusty or frightening, it is the fascinating setting for the National Maritime Museum. Within the wonderful building are nautical exhibits that include a copy of the state barge built in Antwerp for the Emperor Napoleon on his visit in 1810, sailors' old tatoo paraphenalia, an elaborate tile panel showing a 17th-century sea battle between the Dutch and the English, and a model of Antwerp harbor c. 1515. The widely varied exhibits are shown in 12 sections in a series of mostly small rooms separated by narrow passageways and some steep stairs. There's a cafe in the basement. Beyond the Steen on the promenade along the Scheldt are ships and sailors from around the world, and a waterfront cafe (see *Noorderterras* under *Eating Out*) from which to watch.

Vleeshuis (Butchers' Hall Museum) • *Vleeshouwersstraat 38–40; daily 10 a.m.–5 p.m., closed Mondays except Easter Monday, Whit Monday, and the Monday after the 2nd Sunday in August; 233.64.04* • This large and impressive building was commissioned by De Waghemakere, one of Antwerp Cathedral's architects, for the Butchers' Guild for use as its market and meeting hall. Perhaps Antwerp's finest secular Gothic style building, the Vleeshuis is, appropriately for butchers, an excellent example of a so-called "bacon" construction: horizontal layers of red brick are interspersed with white limestone, which gives the impression of pink meat layered with lard. The exterior view is particularly recommended, but if you have plenty of time in Antwerp, the museum within offers exhibits of local history and crafts, furniture, old musical instruments, and the room on the top floor has a unique wooden ceiling.

South of Meir

Rubenshuis • *Wapper 9; daily 10 a.m.–5 p.m., closed major hols.; 232.47.47; English language guidebook available* • The best place to appreciate Pieter Paul Rubens' personality, if not his works, is in the house he began building in 1610 and lived in from 1616 until his death there in 1640. The mansion, with its restrained Flemish Renaissance street-front facade, makes way for the family living quarters and the artist's exuberant statue-studded studio, linked together by an imposing portico topped with Roman gods Mercury and Minerva that appear in several of his paintings. With stature as "the prince of painters, and the painter of princes," Rubens dominated the Baroque Age in Antwerp.

Rubens was the son of a Lutheran lawyer who had had to flee Antwerp for religious reasons. Thus Rubens was born in Westphalia, Germany, in 1577, returning to Antwerp about 1585 with his Catholic mother (who converted her son to her religion). He was apprenticed successively to three Flemish artists and, in 1598, became a master in Antwerp's Guild of St. Luke, of which he was later dean. In the corner bedroom of his house is the actual chair (with the gilt lettering "PET. PAUL. RUBENS 1633" on the back) that was reserved for him in the painters' room of the Guild's headquarters.

In 1600, Rubens went to Italy, staying in Rome, Venice, and Genoa and studying with masters there. During his eight years in Italy, he went to Spain on diplomatic business for Vincenzo Gonzaga of Mantua, a patron in whose service he worked. Rubens returned to Antwerp in 1608 because of the ill health of his mother (she died while he was enroute), ripe for a full life. The next year, 1609, he became court painter to the Archdukes Isabella and Albert and married Isabella Brant. In 1610, he made an immense investment in land on what is now the Wapper and began designing and building a house and studio (into which he moved five years later though the buildings were not yet finished). By 1611 he was at work on two monumental works for Antwerp Cathedral where they can be seen today: the triptychs "Raising of the Cross" and "Descent from the Cross."

The fleshy flamboyance of Rubens' figures may not be fashionable today, but the flourishing of the Baroque period when and where it did is thoroughly comprehensible in the context of the times. The Baroque style, with its massive forms and near-excessive ornamentation was embraced by the Roman Catholic church in Europe during the Counter-Reformation, undoubtedly the more so for its being in such complete contrast to the unadorned style decreed by Calvinist Protestantism.

But though he breathed Baroque with every brush stroke, Rubens himself was something of a renaissance man. Having studied the classics until the age of 12, and used his eight years in Italy to study archaelogy and to begin a collection of classical statuary, Rubens revealed his close identification with the ancients in the statemen and gods whose likenesses grace his home, inside and out. Within the house, off the painting gallery where he displayed the favorites of his excellent and extensive personal collection, a marble half-pantheon or apsidal gallery served as a display case for his treasured antique busts and statues. In 1618 Rubens exchanged some of his paintings for Greek and Roman statues and other antiquities from the collection of Anwerp's English ambassador Sir Dudley Carlton. "Art above gold for investment," he believed. Rubens' carefully acquired collection of classical art was admired by all who saw it and he was praised as an archaeologist by learned men of his time. One wrote, "Especially with regard to antiquities, Rubens has the most universal and remarkable knowledge I ever met with. He is very well-grounded in all the branches of archaelology." A bust of the Roman Seneca rests above the door to his Great Studio, and stoicism and humanism were guiding philosophies for Rubens. In a cartouche in the portico, Rubens had inscribed in the stone a line from the Roman poet Juvenal: "Leave it to the gods to give what is fit and useful for us; man is dearer to them than to himself."

Although attempts had been made to buy the house for the city of Antwerp as early as 1762, the Rubens House became a museum only in 1946, following a major reconstruction that returned it to its original state. The furniture visitors see today did not, with rare and noted exception, belong to Rubens, but is authentic in re-creating the atmosphere of a patrician house in Antwerp of the 17th century. In the house are some ten paintings by Rubens, perhaps the most interesting being one of his few self-portraits (in the dining room). The art gallery in the house was hung with the artist's favorites in a collection that numbered about 300 at the time of his death. The wide-ranging collection included many Flemish primatives, and it is a sad loss that it was scattered after the artist's death. In the collection were 17 paintings by **Adriaen Brouwer,** whose work Rubens obviously much admired. Brouwer, notorious for a dissolute life, is said to have once been released from imprisonment in the Steen due to Rubens' intercession.

Rubens is said to have loved his work and worked hard at it. But the estimated 1,500–2,000 paintings in his *oeuvre* could not possibly have been realized without his studio staff of students and collaborators. Often, Rubens would create the design for a painting, leave the intermediate execution of it to his pupils, and then add the finishing flourishes that gave it his touch. Such a division of work was quite common in the times, if one had sufficent commissions to warrant supporting a studio. It was in the Great Studio, where several Rubens' paintings are displayed, that several pupils would have worked on a cluster of canvases and panels. In order to assess or show to guests and clients his largest works, those destined to decorate palaces or church altars and meant to be viewed from a distance, Rubens used the *bel-etage* or first floor that looked into the Great Studio. Rubens also had a private studio where he sketched, and had models sit for him. His pupils also had their own studio. In the so-called large bedroom, though not now furnished as a bedroom, Rubens would have seen his son Nicolaas born and his first wife die (probably of the plague), and shared it with his second wife (Helene Fourmont) who he brought here when she was 16 and he was 53. Rubens himself stayed in this bedroom when he was sick—he suffered from gout—near the end of his life, and it was here he died in May 1640.

Plantin-Moretus House • *Vrijdagmarkt 22; daily 10 a.m.–5 p.m.; 233.02.94; English guidebook for sale* • In the elegant 16th-century Plantin-Moretus House, nine generations of the same family lived and ran a printing plant and shop between 1555 and 1876. The first three generations were the most forward-looking and contributed substantially to the intellectual environment of Antwerp, Europe, and well beyond. The founding *Plantin,* French-born Christophe (1520–1589), having been apprenticed to a bookbinder, arrived in Antwerp in 1548, during the city's gilded days. He choose Antwerp over all other cities because "no other town in the world could offer me more facilities for carrying on the trade I intend," and further cited the city's accessibility to skilled craftsmen, raw materials, and international buyers and sellers. Also, Antwerp's place in printing was already well-established. In the pre-1500 incunabula period, Antwerp had been an important center, but when the prosperous early 16th-century era arrived, the city initiated a golden age for the art of mechanical printing. Between 1500 and 1540, half of all the works published in the Netherlands were produced on Antwerp presses.

Plantin turned from binding to printing, and one of his first books, published in 1559, was a volume on the funeral ceremonies of Charles V (who died in 1558) that was nearly as magnificent in its execution as the actual funeral had been. Between 1563 and 67, Plantin's presses turned out the unheard-of average of 50 quality books a year. Probably Plantin's most outstanding undertaking was the *Biblia Polyglotta,* a reliable edition of the Bible-texts in five languages (Latin, Greek, Hebrew, Syriac, and Chaldaic or Aramaean) with appendices on grammar, vocabulary, and culture of remarkable detail. Begun in 1568, the colossal task was finished in 1572, bound up in eight big folios, the most important work ever produced in the Benelux.

In 1572, Christophe Plantin received a monopoly from Philip II for the sale of certain liturgical works in Spain and its colonies (a monopoly which supported what became a rather stagnant printing house under the fourth generation for nearly two full centuries until it was finally ter-minated). Production slowed but was not devastated by the 1576 *Spanish Fury* in Antwerp, and Plantin, himself a devout Catholic, managed to walk a fine line between religious factions during the Reformation/Counter-Reformation. Although he never denied the King of Spain, Plantin managed to print several anti-Spanish works and retain the favor of Dutch Protestant Willem of Orange, who, based in Antwerp for awhile, visited the printing house. When he died in 1589, having published more than 1,500 important works—his first and foremost concern always was the *content* of the books—of humanists, classical authors, and scientific dissertation in 34 years, Christophe Plantin was buried in the high choir of Antwerp's Cathedral.

Plantin bequeathed the printing house and shop to his favorite son-in-law, **Jan Moretus,** who had entered the workshop at the age of 14. Jan's son **Balthasar** (1574–1641), who headed the printing concern from 1610 to 1641, was a man of exceptional intelligence and knowledge, the greatest of the Moretuses. During Antwerp's blossoming in the Baroque era, Balthasar, an intimate of Rubens, encouraged and fostered the work of scholars and artists (he induced Rubens to design and illustrate frontispieces for many volumes). The books published under Balthasar were the firm's most splendid.

The Plantin-Moretus house, which became a museum in 1877, more or less reached its present form under building changes begun by Plantin and continued by Balthasar Moretus, who designed the appealing inner courtyard. Behind the characteristic 18th-century Louis XV–style facade is hidden one of Belgium's finest civic Renaissance constructions. Many rooms have their original character and, with period furniture, offer a clear picture of a rich Antwerp patrician house over the 16th–18th centuries.

What makes the Plantin-Moretus Museum unique is that its working role is emphasized under the same roof: many of the original furnishings of the printing plant, the foundry and fonts, the composers' and correctors' rooms, and shop are in evidence. The house's three richly filled libraries contain about 30,000 volumes, including copies of all the publications by Plantin and the Moretuses and choice works by foreign typographers (including 150 *incunabula* among which is a two-volume Bible c. 1401 of the Czech miniature school that belonged to King Wenceslas of Bohemia, and a priceless copy of the 36-line Gutenberg Bible, the only one in Belgium). Old sheet music, printed with square notes, is also on display. Antique furniture, art (about 150 paintings and family portraits by Flemish masters, including 18 by Rubens), some 650 drawings, a wall map of Flanders by Mercator, tapestries, and walls covered with gilt leather from Mechelen and tall tiled fireplaces round out the charm of the building. Throughout the darkwood-decorated house, the pendants of the large Liege (Belgium) crystal chandeliers house were cut as carefully as diamonds so as to reflect as much light as possible.

Koninklijk Museum voor Schone Kunsten (Royal Fine Arts Museum) • *Leopole de Waelplaats; daily 10 a.m.–5 p.m., closed Mondays; 238.78.09; English language catalogues* • Trade brought riches to Antwerp; riches brought art; and the Museum of Fine Arts eventually reaped much of the reward. It houses an exceptional collection of works by the essentially 15th-century **Flemish "Primatives"**: Jan Van Eyck, Rogier van der Weyden, Hans Memling, Dirk Bouts, and Gerard David. From the Antwerp School, founded by Quinten Metsys (1466–1530) and the Bruegel family, to the Baroque Age, of which Pieter Paul Rubens was the towering talent, the Belgian masters are superbly well-covered. Antwerp's Fine Arts Museum has the world's finest collection of Rubens (17 paintings), and many works by his contemporaries Anthony van Dyck and Jacob Jordaens. Not only the artists of Southern but also of Northern Netherlands (Holland) are well represented: Hals, Rembrandt, Ter Borch.

Antwerp's nationally owned Museum of Fine Arts celebrated the centennial of its residence in its neo-gothic, neo-classic home in 1990, but the nucleus of the collection had its origins with the Antwerp Guild of St. Luke to which city artists belonged between 1454 and 1773. When guilds were disbanded, the paintings that St. Luke's had displayed in the "kunstkamer" (art room or gallery) of its guild house were turned over to Antwerp's Academy of Fine Arts, which established a museum. During the French occupations of the city in 1794 and 1796, many paintings—a total of 70, including 30 well-known works by Rubens, according to an official contemporary report—were confiscated from churches, monasteries, and public buildings, and sent to Paris. After the Battle of Waterloo in 1815, 40 were returned, of which 26 went to the museum.

During the period of the United Netherlands (1815–1830), Dutch King Willem donated several paintings to the Academy, including its first work by a living artist ("The Death of Rubens" by Matthijs van Bree, who was director of the Fine Arts Academy). Willem also granted the museum a substantial subsidy for the purchase of contemporary art from the salons of Amsterdam, Brussels, Antwerp, and Ghent (though the 1830 Belgian revolution naturally nullified the grant, and it was not until 1873 that the museum began buying contemporary works). The museum's limited collection was boosted in 1840 by a bequest of 141 works by Florent van Ertborn, a former burgomaster of Antwerp, who had with flawless taste built an exceptional collection of 15th-century paintings at a time when Flemish "primatives" were not appreciated. In 1859, a gift of 41 works consisting of primarily 17th-century Flemish and Dutch works was received. Together, these donations assured the museum's reputation. Today the collection consists of more than 3,200 paintings, 3,600 drawings, and 400 sculptures.

In the Department of Old Art, displayed on the upper story, the Museum owns some 1,200 paintings that give a survey of Flemish art from c. 1360 until the end of the 18th century, as well as covering most aspects of Dutch, Italian, German, and French art. On the ground floor is displayed a fraction of the Fine Arts' considerable 19th- and 20th-century collection, principally Belgian, beginning with the *Romantic Movement,* whose leading exponent was **Gustaf Wappers** (1803–1874). **Henri De Braekeleer** (1840–1888), represented in the Fine Arts by 33 paintings and 45 drawings, is considered by many to be Belgium's first significant 19th-century figure. **Realism** came into being in Belgium between 1850 and 1860, and the museum is particularly well-represented in realistic landscapes. Antwerp-born sculptor **Jef Lambeaux** (1852–1908), exhibited on the streets of Antwerp as well as in the museum, shows the 19th-century move to *Naturalism.* Of course, no discussion of modern Belgian art can neglect **Surrealism.** Here you find 35 paintings and 606 drawings by **James Ensor** (1860–1949), the reclusive Ostender who held society up to ridicule with his "mask people." Also shown are **Rene Margritte** (1898–1967), who influenced 20th-century art internationally, and **Paul Delvaux** (b. 1897). The museum has an excellent shop.

Museum Mayer van den Bergh • *Lange Gasthuisstraat 19; daily 10 a.m.–5 p.m., closed Mondays except Easter Monday, White Monday, and Monday after 2nd Sunday in August; 232.42.37* • It's been called a connoisseur's collection and, in the medieval, late Gothic, and Renaissance art included, it shows the refined taste of its assembler **Fritz Mayer van den Bergh** (1858–1901), who devoted his life, cut short by an accident, to it. His mother, who had encouraged her son's passion for art, subsequently had built a 16th- century-style house with a late Gothic/Renaissance facade in which to show her son's substantial accumulated treasure. Van den Bergh was one of the first collectors to be interested in **Pieter Breugel the Elder** (1525–1569); in 1897 at an auction in Cologne he was able to buy for a trifle what many consider the centerpiece of his museum. Breugel's "Dulle Griet" (Mad Meg) fascinates visitors with its strangeness, and its having been created under the influence of Hieronymous Bosch is obvious. Among many notables in the museum are a copy of his father's "Census at Bethlehem" by Pieter Breugel the Younger; a "Calvary" triptych by **Quinten Metsys**; a breviary that is a masterpiece of Southern Netherlands miniature art; and "John Reclining on Jesus' Bosom," a life-size sculpture of gilt and polychromed walnut by Master Heinrich of Constance (c. 1300), an art form that's relatively rare in the Netherlands because wood was particularly vulnerable to destruction during the *Iconoclast*. Fine furniture and chimneypieces are found in rooms throughout the museum, and some windows have 15th- and 16th-century stained glass panels inserts.

Provincial Diamond Museum • *Lange Herentalsestraat 31; daily from 10 a.m.–5 p.m.; 324.02.07; good guidebook in English* • A gem on Antwerp's list of attractions is the Provincial Diamond Museum where visitors get to see the whole sparkling history of the stones that have engaged the attention of cutters, polishers, brokers, and buyers in Antwerp for five centuries. Once a symbol of virtue and virility, diamonds today represent value. They are a compact treasure: one ounce of high-quality diamonds is equal to 400 pounds of pure gold. With four of the world's twenty diamond bourses, Antwerp can be considered the capital for the world's diamond dealings: at least 60% of all diamonds traded worldwide pass through Antwerp, and the diamond business by itself represents 7% of Belgium's GNP. The Diamond Museum, opened in 1988, offers an introductory 20-minute video (English version) on Antwerp's historic association with diamonds, and can arrange for you to see a diamond-grinding demonstration. (For more information, see *Diamonds* in *Decorative Arts and Traditional Crafts* under *The Benelux Cultural Legacy*).

Zoo/Dierentuin • *Koningin Astridplein 26; daily 8:30 a.m.–5 p.m., 6:30 p.m. in summer; 231.16.40* • For those who enjoy zoos, Antwerp offers one of the best in Europe (7,000 animals, 900 species, few cages, several special exhibits such as the *nocturama, dolphinarium, aquarium,* and *reptile house* with tropical thunderstorm, and a self-service restaurant) at a surprising location: downtown, directly behind Centraal Station.

North of Meir

Rockox House • *Keizerstraat 12; daily 10 a.m.–5 p.m., closed Mondays; 231.47.10; English guidebook* • Also holding up a mirror to Antwerp's gilded age is the Rockox House, an opulent, splendidly restored, and period-furnished early 17th-century house owned by a former burgomaster and friend of Rubens. The Rockox house was purchased in 1970 by *Kredietbank*—banks in Antwerp make a point of supporting museums—which created a non-profit foundation for it. **Nicolaas Rockox** (1560–1640), member of Antwerp's Civic Guard, seven times alderman, and nine times mayor of Antwerp, humanist, was also a benefactor and patron of Rubens, with whom he shared a belief in the Counter-Reformation and a great knowledge of classical antiquity. Among Rockox's commissions to Rubens was the 1612 "Descent from the Cross" triptych for the chapel in the Cathedral of the Arquebusiers' Guild (of which he was captain); "Christ on the Cross" (now in Antwerp's Fine Arts Museum), and "Christ and St. Thomas," with portraits of himself and his wife on the side panels. "The Adoration of the Magi," commissioned from Rubens as soon as the artist had returned from eight years in Italy for the Chamber of State in the Antwerp Stadhuis, is now in the **Prado Museum** in Madrid.

In 1603, when Rockox became burgomaster for the first time, he bought this and an adjacent property, combining the two into a fine Flemish Renaissance-style patrician dwelling. The house and its original contents were sold at auction in 1715 (in accordance with Rockox's will, which distributed the proceeds to the benefit of the poor), but contemporary documents have made it possible to recreate an appropriate degree of wealth in the Rockox interior. Among the many paintings, one of the most moving is Rubens' "The Virgin in Adoration Before the Sleeping Christ Child," in which the Virgin has the features of Rubens' first wife Isabella Brant, and the Infant Jesus those of his second son Nicolaas. Teniers the Younger, Jordaens, Van Dyck, Jan "Velvet" Breugel, and Pieter Breugel the Younger (whose "Proverbs" is a copy of his father's fascinating original) are all represented among the marvelous pieces of furniture and decorative art that make the house seem so "lived in." The very special atmosphere of the inner courtyard will make you want to linger even longer.

A Note: Normally it's only shown to groups, but inquire in any case about the possibility of seeing the excellent audio-visual presentation *Nicolaas Rockox and His Time,* which beautifully communicates a feeling for Antwerp, its art, and its architecture during the period 1560–1640.

Sint Jacobskerk (St. James) • *Lange Nieuwstraat 73; April 1– Oct. 31 2–5 p.m., no visitors Suns. and during services; 232.10.32; brochure with church layout* • Begun in 1491, though not entirely completed until 1656, and having a late Gothic/Brabant style with some Renaissance influence, St. James is, after the Cathedral, the most important church in Antwerp, and surpassing it in its rich Baroque adornment. St. James was Rubens' parish church and his second marriage took place there in 1630. In Rubens' day, all Antwerp's leading families had their burial vaults and private chapels there. Visitors may seek out Rubens' own chapel and tomb (he died in 1640), which is situated in the ambulatory directly behind the high altar. The centerpiece of the chapel is the painting "Our Lady Surrounded by the Saints," executed by Rubens in 1634 specifically for his sepulchral monument, and generally considered one of his finest works; it is generally accepted that in the painting the figure of St. George is a self-portrait, Mary has the features of Rubens' first wife, the infant Jesus those of his son, Mary

Magdalene his second wife's face, and St. Jerome the features of his father.

Although St. James has known damaging times, in the Calvinist *Iconoclast,* the French Revolution, both world wars, and from arson in 1967, many of its treasures have been saved, and extensive exterior and interior restoration has been completed. Carved-wood confessionals by Artus Quellin the Elder, a majestic marble altar topped with trumpeting angels by Artus Quellin the Younger, and paintings by Jacob Jordaens are among the artistic treasures in the church. There are two organs: the 1727 instrument was once played upon by a nine-year-old Mozart; and an 1884 organ with sculptures set in a handsome carved organ-loft of 1723 was rebuilt into a concert-organ in 1956.

Hendrik Conscienceplein • This charming Antwerp square is made more so by its location in front of the elaborate Rubens-designed Carrolus Borromeo church facade. Dedicated to the writer who helped raise Flemish consciousness in the 19th century (particularly with his book *The Lion in Flanders,* see *Benelux Bibliography* at the back of book), Hendrik Conscienceplein thus is the appropriate site of Antwerp's public library, which is housed in the 17th-century buildings of the former college of the Jesuits who built the church. The square draws lots of readers, at the tables of cafes that line one side, or seats beside the statue (by Frans Joris, 1883) of the square's namesake.

Carrolus Borromeo • *Hendrik Conscienceplein 12; Mon., Wed., Thurs., Fri. 9:30 a.m.–1 p.m., Sat. 9:30 a.m.–noon & 3–6 p.m.; 233.84.33* • The superb Baroque West Front facade of the 17th-century Church of St. Charles Borromeo is thought to have been designed by Rubens, who also was deeply involved with the interior decor, including 39 ceiling paintings from his workshop. The entire original church with its lavish ornamentation was completed in a mere five years (1615–21) thanks to the Jesuits who had heaps of money to throw at the project. But a fire after the church was struck by lightning in 1718 did widespread damage; all that survived from the original was the tower, the West front, three Rubens altarpieces (taken by the Austrians in 1776 and now in Vienna), the choir (dome drawings by Rubens), and two chapels. One, the Chapel of the Virgin, with a ceiling in the style of Rubens, uses 30 types of rare and colored marble; the paintings directly on the marble are by H. van Balen. The surviving 190-foot/58-meter tower, making the transition as it rises in three tiers from square to round, is regarded as a masterpiece. The fine carved confessional stalls of the 1719 rebuilt church are by Van Baurscheit.

Handelbeurs • *at the end of Twaalfmaandenstraat, off Meir* • An 1872 reconstruction in the style of the fire-destroyed 1531 Stock Exchange (which served as a model for many other Western European exchanges), the Handelbeurs is now used as a venue for special exhibits or events. With entrances on all four sides, allowing people to walk through the recently restored skylighted, galleried central hall, thereby short-cutting the outside walk around the exterior of city buildings, the Handelbeurs is a fascinating example of how medieval buildings functioned as public passageways in dense, dead-end alley-constricted centers of old cities. Signs posted at each entrance read: *"honden, fietsen, skateboards verboten"* (dogs, bikes, and skateboards forbidden).

St. Paul's • *Sint-Paulusstraat 20; May–Sept. 9, a.m.–noon, 2–5 p.m., closed Sun. & Mon., daily Oct.–April 9 a.m.–noon; 232.32.67* • Begun in 1517, and finally completed in 1639 after a long break following severe damage in the 1570s by the Calvinists, St. Paul's has Antwerp's last—and, by the time it was finished, well out-of-fashion—Gothic exterior. As a result of the lingering construction, the St. Paul's interior missed an entire subsequent architectural style (Renaissance) and went on to Baroque. "Mysteries of the Rosary" is the theme of a remarkable series of 15 paintings that line the left wall of the soaring nave, above a no less amazing row of wood-carved confessional stalls and life-size statues; painters include Rubens, Jordaens, Van Dyck, Teniers the Elder, the carvers Verbruggen the Elder, Artus Quellin Elder and Younger, and Van Baurscheit the Elder. Rubens' painting (c. 1609) "The Dispute on the Subject of the Holy Sacrament" ornaments an altar in the right forward area of the church.

To the right of the entry of St. Paul's is the **Calvary Garden,** with no less than three dozen full-size white stone figures by various sculptors in the theme of the Jerusalem crusaders. The statues are spread about the small garden plot across which a path leads to a grotto set into the side of the church; within it is a carved figure representing Christ lying in his tomb.

ACCOMMODATIONS............................

Deluxe

★★★★ **De Rosier** • *Rosier 21, 2000; 225.01.40, fax 231.41.11* • On an ordinary old street in central Antwerp is a most extraordinary hotel: a remarkable antique-filled, interior designer-owner-decorated mansion that is an oasis where attentive personal service prevails. Modern art and sculpture are integrated into the richly comfortable, tastefully original guest and public rooms that feature marble, crystal chandeliers, tapestries, track-lighting, paintings, and plants. The ten individually decorated guestrooms each have private bath, TV, and telephone. Breakfast (only, extra charge), formal afternoon tea, and drinks are served in the enchanting glass-enclosed, garden-surrounded Summerpatio Room. No restaurant. Cozy bar, elevator. Advance reservations essential.

First Class

★★★★ **Hotel Carlton** • *Quinten Matsijslei 25, 2018; 231.15.15, fax 225.30.90* • Located across from the city park, a short walk to De Keyserlei, the attractive 9-story glass-fronted Carlton has an appealing marble lobby, off which are a relaxing bar and tasteful restaurant (where continental breakfast, included, is also served). The front desk staff is friendly and helpful. A pleasant mix of international business clients predominates, but leisure travelers also will be happy here (and will have reduced rates on Fri. & Sat. nights). The 95 rooms and suites have bath/shower, mini-bars, remote control cable TV, hair dryers, in-room safes, and turndown service with Godiva pralines on the pillow. An extension with 30 additional rooms recently opened.

★★★★ **Villa Mozart** • *Handschoenmarkt 3, 2000; 231.30.31, fax 231.56.85* • Opened in 1990, this hotel is Antwerp's first in the Grote Markt vicinity, and is located on the delightful Handschoenmarkt across from the Cathedral (light sleepers take note of the carillon that strikes the hours all night long). Behind a restored 5-story period facade 24 guestrooms and 4 suites are tastefully decorated with cane and bamboo furniture upholstered in rich materials. Amenities include extra wide beds, luxury bath, mini-bar, AC, room service. The hotel's **Vivaldi** restaurant serves fine French and international cuisine based on fresh seasonal produce; there's indoor or terrace cafe seating. Buffet breakfast included; year-round discounted weekend rates; public parking garages within two blocks.

★★★★ **Alfa Theater** • *Arenbergstraat 30; 231.17.20, fax 233.88.58* • Located, as the name suggests, in Antwerp's conveniently central theater district, 3 blocks from the Meir, 3 blocks from the Rubens House, and a reasonable walk to the Grote Markt, the hotel has a very friendly staff and good range of in-room amenities: shower and bidet, sitting area, pants press, hair dryers, in-room safe and, in many cases, a mini-kitchenette with fridge and hot plate. Included among the 83 guestrooms is a non-smoking floor (15 rooms), and new and nice executive-style rooms (without kitchenette). There's a modern lobby with leather chairs, restaurant (continental breakfast, included), and bar. Advance booking suggested; parking garages nearby.

★★★★ **Alfa de Keyser** • *De Keyserlei 66, 2018; 234.01.35, fax 232.39.70* • Situated across from the Centraal Station at the head of De

Keyserlei (that leads to the Meir through the center of the city to the Grote Markt) and near public transport, restaurants, and entertainment, the 117-room, 7-story modern hotel with large marble lobby puts a self-conscious emphasis on appearance (uniformed doorman) and service (24-hour). Rooms are contemporary and comfortable, though not particularly distinguished. Some are renovated, some not; a few are non-smoking, all have hair dryers and cable TV with CNN. There's a popular bar in the lobby, and the gourmet restaurant **Chagall** is noted for its nouvelle cuisine. Continental breakfast is included, buffet breakfast is extra; security boxes at front desk; parking garages nearby. A sidewalk escalator outside the hotel delivers you to the underground passage to Centraal Station; SABENA's Brussels' airport bus is next door.

★★★ **Hotel Firean** • *Karel Oomsstraat 6, B-2018; 237.02.60, fax 238.11.68* • Though beyond walking distance from any of central Antwerp's attractions (but convenient to tram lines to both the Cathedral and Centraal Station), this restored, owner-operated 12-room 1921 house is so pleasant that it should be included. The hospitable homelike househotel, with intriguing Art Deco details and all Belgian furnishings, features original Tiffany windows, antique tapestries, back-lighted glass panels, and the additional charm of a flood-lighted rear garden (with bar service for guests). Guestrooms are uniquely furnished in soft colors, with pants press, hair dryer, mini-bar, toiletries, double-glazed windows (for quiet) cable TV, and extra evening housekeeping of rooms. Breakfast (included) is served indoors or on the garden patio; international morning newspapers in lobby. Room service (light food dishes) til midnight, 24-hour laundry, parking, major credit cards. Reservations well-ahead recommended.

★★★★ **Alfa Empire** • *Appelmansstraat 31, 2018; 231.47.55, fax 233.40.60* • Located in the diamond district and just doors from the Diamond Museum, the 70-room Alfa Empire is used heavily by business travelers so there's good service from the front desk in the functional lobby. The comfortable contemporary guestrooms (some with king beds) are extremely spacious, with large desk, hair dryer, pants press, mini-bar, cable TV. Parking garage next door.

Moderate

★★★ **Arcade** • *Meistraat 39, 2000; 231.88.30, fax 234.29.21* • The 150-room, cheerfully decorated, utilitarian modern hotel is located on the Theaterplein (site of general market Sat., bird market Sun.), not far from the Rubens House. Bedrooms have basic contemporary decor: choice of twin or king (small supplement) beds, direct-dial telephone, radio clock alarm, private showers/toilet, an open clothes rack with a wooden bench beneath for suitcases, 2 chairs, and desk. A self-service breakfast (included) is provided in the lobby bar (no restaurant). Major credit cards; front desk staffed 24 hours; disabled-accessible rooms on all floors; public parking in front of hotel.

RESTAURANTS

Prices in Antwerp's better restaurants are generally less than in Brussels. Reservations are essential at the best restaurants, and a call to book if you have a specific place in mind is always a good bet except for the most casual eateries. A number of restaurants are closed on Sundays and holidays, and some close for personal holiday periods, particularly in August.

Consistently ranked as one of the Antwerp's most appetizing restaurants is **La Perouse** *(Steenplein; noon–2:30 p.m., 7–9:30 p.m., closed Sun., Mon., hols., and June through mid-Sept. when it is a Scheldt-cruising restaurant for* **Flandia;** *232.35.28; expensive).* When it isn't floating, La Perouse sits moored on the Scheldt at the foot of Suikkerui. In its ship-shape polished brass and steel atmosphere, seafood is the specialty, especially *waterzooi de poussin,* a creamy fish stew/soup and traditional Flemish dish that doesn't get any better than it is here. **Sir Anthony van Dijck** *(Oude Koornmarkt 16; Mon.–Fri. noon–2:30 p.m., 7–9:30 p.m., closed Sat. & Sun.; 231.61.70; expensive/very expensive),* located in a former burgomeester's home in the charming 16th-century cobbled alley of antique shops called *Vlaeykensgang,* is another regular on the rolls of the city's best restaurants. Though the staff can seem rather too self-important, service takes place in a beautiful setting of antiques, tapestries, candlelight, polished stone tile floors, dark beams, fireplaces, and ivy-draped enclosed courtyard with the sound of dripping water from a fountain. Four and five-course *menus* are offered in addition to wide-ranging *à la carte* choices of inventive French cuisine. **Neuze Neuze** *(Wijngaardstraat 19; noon–2:15 p.m., 7–9:30 p.m., closed Sat. for lunch, Sun., hols., and first half of August; 232.57.83; moderate/expensive)* reveals Antwerp's love of juxtaposing the old and new with smart modern decor under ancient beamed ceilings and arches. The cuisine is French with the flair of its four chefs, who provide a two-course *menu* that's always worth consideration.

De Peerdestal *(Wijngaardstraat 8; noon–2:30 p.m., 6–11 p.m., closed Sun.; 231.95.03; inexpensive),* located in a 400-year-old building in a small pedestrian street that runs into the Hendrik Conscience Plein, offers excellent atmosphere along with its tasty traditional dishes. Good choices include *tomate aux crevettes* (tomato stuffed with small North Sea shrimp), *fondue au fromage* (melted cheese croquette), and *moules* (mussels) in myriad ways; also served at red-check covered candle-lighted tables, beneath old teams and beside brick walls are chicken, steak, fish, soups, and salads. There's a long friendly bar at which to eat in somewhat speedier style, or sit over a drink while reading the *International Herald-Tribune*. **In de Schaduw van de Kathedraal** *(Handschoenmarkt 17; 232.40.14; inexpensive)*, whose name means "in the shadow of the cathedral," sometimes is in the sun; either way, there's always a wonderful view from the base of the lace-like steeple. In addition to the terrace cafe, inside dining is in a pleasant room amid mirrors and banquettes. Not only the setting but the cuisine is traditional Antwerp, from mussels and eel prepared in several ways to meat and potatoes *(frites,* of course). A very different typical Antwerp atmosphere is found at **'t Hofke** *(Oude Koornmarkt 16; daily noon–1 a.m.; 233.86.06; inexpensive)*, a tiny lunchroom- tearoom-bistro tucked into the ancient Vlaeykensgang. At the few tables at the garden—open to the sky—along the alleyway, or the several inside, salads, quiches, and larger meals are served to the sound of classical music and a caged songbird. **De Groote Witte Arend** *(Reyndersstraat 16; daily 11 a.m.–1:30 a.m.; inexpensive)*, most suitable for outdoor weather, is found through an old courtyard just doors from the house of artist Jacob Jordaens (1593–1678) at Reyndersstraat 6. Salads, pasta of the day, lasagna, waterzooi, and sandwiches are brought out to the tables and benches in the courtyard that is draped with plants, studded with statuary, and lifted by the strains of classical music. Antwerpians often sit here over a drink on Monday nights in summer to hear the carillon concert from the nearby cathedral.

De Foyer *(Komedieplaats 18; Mon.–Fri. noon to midnight, Sat. & Sun. 11 a.m.–6 p.m.; 233.55.17; inexpensive)* is upstairs at the curve-fronted *Komedie Theater,* a concert hall closed for ten years that has just reopened after restoration. Occasional classical concerts held in the restaurant's neo-classic room accompany the light fare (quiche, soups, sandwiches) and salad buffet bar. Close by, located in a house just past the pleasant *Botanic Garden,* and one street over from the *Mayer van den Bergh Museum,* is **Botanica** *(Leopoldstraat 24; daily 10 a.m.–11 p.m., Fri. & Sat. 1 a.m.; 225.10.04; inexpensive).* The cozy 49-seat interior, from which there are views of the garden, has an eclectic decor with Japanese prints, Venetian glass chandeliers, and track lighting on the art work. There's a daily three-course *menu* and limited *à la carte* offerings.

Noorderterras *(Jordaenskaai 27; daily 10 a.m.–midnight; 213.15.81; inexpensive/moderate)* is an institution. Situated overlooking the Scheldt, this terrace cafe/taverne provides views that are almost as good as those from a river cruise. Locals come here for big mounds of small *North Sea prawns* with mayonnaise, or *mussels* and *baked Belgium witloof,* all served outside behind glass partitions that shelter from the wind but allow unobstructed views of the river traffic. Inside, there's a restaurant with cloth-covered tables, and a cafe with booths. Only a block from the Scheldt, and with a great view of the handsome historic *Vleeshuis,* is **Jan Zonder Vrees** *(Krabbenstraat 2; daily 9 a.m.–2 a.m.; 232.90.80; inexpensive/moderate),* located in four former 400-year-old houses. Offerings at the outside tables, at the bar, or in the fashionably-decorated restaurant under brick arches, run from snacks, soup, and sandwiches to steak and daily specials.

A well-known delicatessen/restaurant near the Centraal Station is **Panache** *(17 Statiestraat 17; daily noon–1:30 a.m., closed August; 232.69.05; inexpensive),* which will provide you with almost anything edible from picnic makings to a particular dish you've been craving. For take-out fare, stop at the *charcuterie* section in front; for sitdown service, walk through to the large busy dining room with its huge menu. Whenever you're looking for something to eat at late-hours, or on Sundays when many restaurants are closed, you'll find plenty of places near Panache, in the movie/entertainment streets around the *Franklin Roosevelt Plaats* such as *Anneessensstraat, Breidelstraat,* and *Van Ertbornstraat;* most are inexpensive, and offer ethnic fare that reflects Antwerp's cosmopolitan population.

Whether one drinks a pint of pils or a "bowl" of specialty beer, spending time at an atmospheric pub with one or another of Belgium's hundreds of brands of beer is an Antwerp way of life. The oldest pub in Antwerp is **Quinten Matsys** *(Oude Koornmarkt 21; closed Thurs.; 231.45.41),* dating from 1565. Also in existence since Antwerp's 16th-century golden age is **Pelgrom** *(Pelgrimstraat 15; daily from 11 a.m.; 234.08.09),* which serves bar snacks and beer in marvelous brick-vaulted, candlelit cellars well beneath its handsome stepped-gabled facade. **Bierland** *(Korte Nieuwstraat 28)* claims it sells 1,250 kinds of beer (some 840 are Belgian), more than anywhere else in Antwerp, and possibly the world. **In Den Engel** *(3 Grote Markt)* supposedly never closes its doors, and some say it hasn't since it opened them in 1579. With the city's predisposition for creating new beers for special occasions (such as in 1977, the 400th anniversary of Rubens' birth), one can anticipate that 1993, which is not only Antwerp's year as *European Cultural Capital,* but also the 400th anniversary of the birth of local artist Jacob Jordaens, will bring new tastes to test.

ENTERTAINMENT AND EVENTS..

From March to December of 1993, Antwerp will offer a wide-ranging calendar of special events, from nearly all artistic disciplines, in celebration of its selection as **Cultural Capital of Europe 1993.** The program will cover Antwerp's contemporary cultural achievements as well as paying prideful attention to the city's past; historic buildings (many restored) will host many of the myriad performances and exhibits. Among the highlights of ANTWERPEN 93 (opening festival the weekend of March 26–28) is the March 27–June 27 first-ever survey of the entire scope of the work of popular Flemish baroque painter **Jacob Jordaens**, born in Antwerp 400 years ago. It will be on exhibit at Antwerp's *Royal Museum of Fine Arts,* which will also host an international contemporary art show July 25–Oct. 10.

Scheduled muscial events include a festival of contemporary opera (May); spring concerts of polyphonic music—which was an important Flemish contribution to musical history—of the medieval and renaissance periods, and chamber music in private residences; and organ concerts in the cathedral (July and Aug.). Fifteen new sculptures will be added to the **Middelheim Open-air Sculpture Park** (see *In the Area* below). Other special exhibits will take place in the Rubens House, at the Diamond Museum, and on the history of Antwerp in its 16th century Golden Age. A detailed program is available from the Belgian Tourist Office, New York.

As the unofficial capital of Flanders, Antwerp is home to several performing arts companies. The **Royal Flemish Opera,** the **Flemish Chamber Opera,** the **Royal Flanders Ballet,** and the **Royal Flemish Conservatory** provide a full program. The works of the **Royal Flemish Theater** head a theater bill that is the most extensive in Belgium, although most productions are in Flemish.

Year-round, hour-long concerts are played on the Cathedral's 47-bell carillon at 11:30 p.m. Fridays. The weekly mid-June to mid-Sept. Monday night **carillon concerts** at 8 p.m. are a highlight for Antwerpians and visitors alike. Mid-August Antwerp celebrates summer with a week-long list of events, highlighted with the **Rubens Market** and **Ommegangpageant.** Other annual events include the July **Steen Festival,** the August **Middelheim Jazz Festival,** and the November **Antwerp Diamond Awards.** The multi-faceted cultural events of the **Festival van Vlaanderen** (Festival of Flanders) are held each Sept./Oct. Check with the City Tourist Office about the location for the Sept.–May Fri. 12:30 p.m. hour-long **Midday Concerts. Early Music** concerts are held from Oct.–March in the Grand Studio at the Rubenhuis and in the Vleeshuis (Butchers' Hall Museum).

There are several entertainment centers in Antwerp. The **Grote Markt/Groenplaats** area is known for its cafe terraces (also refer to the end of the *Eating Out* above). The so-called **High Town** (along Hoogstraat or High Street, Pelgrimstraat, Pieter Potstraat, and surroundings) has some of the most interesting and cozy of Antwerp's supposedly 2,500 cafes and bars; "brown" pubs, bistros, and jazz clubs can be found in this area. **De Keyserlei** is visited for its boulevard-cafes, taverns, and terraces, and the adjoining neighborhood around Centraal Station has night clubs and cinemas. The **Quartier Latin,** near the City Theater, has artists' cafes and bars.

IN THE AREA..................................

Middelheim Open-Air Museum of Sculpture • *Middelheimlaan 61, outside the Kleine Ringweg/Small Ring Road, south of center city in lovely Nachtegalen Park; daily from 10 a.m., closing hours range from 9 p.m. in June & July to 5 p.m. in winter; 827.15.34* • Art in Antwerp is not limited to Old Masters. At the Middelheim-Open Air Museum of Sculpture, founded in 1950, almost every important sculptor from **Rodin** to the present is represented by major works; prominent among the Belgian sculptors is **Rik Wouters** (1882–1916) and **Constantin Meunier** (1831–1905). In the early years of the museum's development, many foreign specialists and sculptors—among them Russian-born **Ossip Zadkine** (1890–1976), whose works are well-represented in the Benelux, and England's **Henry Moore**—served as consultants to the museum. The collection currently consists of more than 300 works, which are exhibited in a natural outdoor park setting, to be enjoyed in the changing seasons and weather. The Middelheim **Biennials** of modern sculpture (held during odd-numbered years) are highly regarded both in Belgium and abroad.

Cogels-Oyslei • *Berchem District, southeast of city center, bus #16 from De Keyserlei*. These two and the surrounding streets of Antwerp's Zurenborg Quarter have been given historic monument neighborhood status for their eclectic styles of turn-of-the-century architecture, the foremost influence being *Jugendstil* (art nouveau). When the tram lines were extended to this new district, development proceeded as a challenge to the architects of the day to realize their dream concepts; the result is an encyclopaedia of late 19th-century romanticism. Along with the intricate wrought-iron whirls, tiles, glass, and mosaic work details of art nouveau are facades inspired by Arthurian legend, Florentine palazzi, Venetian Gothic, Loire Valley chateaus, and Louis XVI. Many are so amazing you may be tempted to record the street numbers of the most remarkable (On Osylei, I got as far as noting #42–46, 50–52, 60–62, and 80 before I stopped the exercise). **Melloney's** *(Oyslei 16; 10 a.m.–8 p.m., closed Wed.; 230.95.45)* is a tea salon that serves pastries, waffles, tea, and drinks in a house with some of the neighborhood's typical detail and decor.

Mechelen • *Municipal Tourist Office, Stadhuis, Grote Markt; Mon.–Fri. 8 a.m.–6 p.m., except 5 p.m. Oct. 1–Mar. 31, Sat. & Sun. 9:30 a.m.–5 p.m.; 015/21.18.73, fax. 015/20.02.76* • Located midway between Antwerp and Brussels (15 minutes by train from either), Mechelen (pop. 80,000), though overshadowed by both of its bigger neighbors today, once was the capital of the Netherlands. Upon the death of Louis de Male, Count of Flanders, who had acquired Mechelen in 1357, it and the rest of Flanders passed to the dukes of Burgundy in 1384. In Mechelen, the 13th and 14th centuries was a period of flourishing cloth trade. In 1473, Burgundian **Charles the Bold** made Mechelen the seat of his Grand Council, the sovereign tribunal for the Netherlands. Following Charles' death, his widow **Margaret of York,** sister of England's Edward IV, settled in Mechelan in a palace that today is the Schouwburg (municipal theater).

In 1506 Mechelen's apogee of influence came under a second Margaret, of the Austrian Hapsburgs, who was appointed governor of the Netherlands to serve as regent for her nephew, the then six-year-old **Charles V.** From her fine palace (today's Mechelen Law Courts), built in 1507 and considered to be the first building in the Netherlands in the Renaissance style, **Margaret of Austria** oversaw the upbringing and education of Ghent-born Charles, and formed a brilliant court attended by scholars and artists. Visiting luminaries included Erasmus, Sir Thomas More, Albrecht Durer, painters Jan Mostaert, Jan Gossaert, and Bernard van Orley, as well as Mechelan architect Rombout Keldermans, whose family members would make major contributions to many landmark buildings in the Netherlands. In his home **Hof van Busleyden** (today Mechelen's Municipal Museum, Humanists Hieronymus van Busleyden, Erasmus, and Thomas More laid the foundations of Louvain (Leuven) University's College of the Three Languages. After Margaret's death in 1530, the Netherlands capital was transferred by Charles V to Brussels. Although its glory faded rapidly thereafter, Mechelen was compensated by being made an archbishopric in 1559 and to this day is the ecclesiastical capital of Belgium.

Mechelen mirrors the grandeur of its Burgundian-Hapsburg days in many fine buildings. **St. Rombout's Cathedral** tower, a symbol of the city, was begun in 1452 and, under the direction of the local Keldermans's family, reached it present height of 318 feet/97 meters in 1546. It contains two complete 49-bell carillons, which are another symbol of Mechelen (see below). St. Rombout's contains the *Crucifixion* (1627) by **Anthony van Dyck** (one of the artist's most emotive works) and a fine carved Baroque communion bench by Artus Quellin the Younger. The **Stadhuis** (Town Hall) on the Grote Markt, though not obviously unwhole, is composed of finished and unfinished parts. The oldest (14th-century) section, the **Cloth Hall** (on the right), begun in 1320 and modelled on that in Bruges, was never completed because Mechelen's once-illustrious textile industry declined faster than the work on the building progressed. In 1526, the north wing of the Stadhuis was demolished to make way for a new Keldermans-designed Grand Council meeting hall, but work ceased in 1534, a casualty of the death of Margaret of Austria and subsequent move of the court to Brussels. Finally, in 1911, using Keldermans' original plans, the Town Hall was completed.

Besides its architecture, visitors to Mechelen note the carillon school, and concerts on the city's four (with a total of 197 bells) instruments (see chapter on *Carillons* at front of book). Mechelen's centuries-old tapestry weaving (see section on *Decorative Arts and Traditional Crafts* at front of book) continues at the **De Wit** factory. De Wit not only works to preserve antique tapestries, it also carries on the craft as a contemporary art form by creating modern masterpieces. One huge work designed and executed at De Wit was a present from Belgium to the United Nations Headquarters in New York. The excellent woodwork for which Mechelen was famous in the Baroque era is reflected in the fine furniture for which the city is known today.

BRUGES

Guidelines for Bruges

SIGHTS Bruges (Brugge), having become impressively important in commerce and, consequently, in culture between the 12th and 15th centuries, was then all but forgotten as circumstances combined to turn the tide of its fortune. As a result, Bruges (population 35,000 within the historic double encirclement of **canals**) is delightfully stuck visually and atmospherically back in medieval days; many consider it the *best preserved medieval city in Europe,* though it's far too actively engaged in the present to be considered a "museum town." Bruges is small enough to manage all major sights on foot, but so densely packed with enchanting places that you'd never get bored wandering aimlessly. Bruges' **architecture** may be even more outstanding than its art, which features **Flemish "primitive" painters** Van der Weyden, Van Eyck, Memling, Van der Goes, and Gerard David, often displayed in historic settings. There's also a Michelangelo sculpture and exhibits of the traditional town crafts of lace and tapestry. Sounds spill out over the town during the plentiful concerts played on the town carillon, high in Belgium's most beautiful **Belfry,** but reassuring silence can be found in the peaceful precincts of the **Begijnhof.** A night walk around the intimate town, turned to magic by the tasteful illumination of monument buildings, ivy-covered brick facades, canals, and humpback bridges, is mesmerizing, and each season has special appeal. The prime season for **night illuminations** is traditionally May 1 to Sept. 30, but many buildings now are lit year-round.

GETTING AROUND Many travelers arrive in Bruges by train; the **station,** just outside the old city to the south, near the **Minnewater** and **Begijnhof,** is about 1 mi./1.5 km. from the **Markt,** considered the center of Bruges. Close to the Markt is the **Burg** where the **Tourist Office** is located. In this town of lace shops, you'll want to lace up walking shoes to enjoy the cobbled streets in comfort. Supplemental ways to see the town begin with a half-hour **canal cruise** (there are several central departure piers) with multi-lingual commentary; the open boats afford wonderful photographic angles, and umbrellas when it's misting. A **rental bike,** though a bit bumpy on the cobbles, is a great way to see the outer corners of Bruges. **Horse-drawn carriages** congregate on the Burg if you want to see the town to the sound of horse hooves clopping on cobblestones. A far more modern means is by **minibus tour** (English commentary on headsets) with **Sightseeing Line** (departure point in the center of the Markt). Taxi ranks are found at the station and on the Markt, and otherwise should be ordered by telephone; tip included in fare. There's a public bus system (several routes have stops on the Markt), but it's unlikely you'll use it within old Bruges itself.

SHOPPING As capital of West Flanders province, Bruges is well stocked with department stores, boutiques, gift and art galleries. The visitor-season canalside weekend outdoor antiques market on the Dijver is popular. In Breidelstraat, which runs from the Markt to the Burg, and near the Begijnhof, lace shops abound.

ENTERTAINMENT AND EVENTS The periodically published *Agenda Brugge* (free from the Tourist Office) gives a multi-lingual listing of scheduled programs and events. The scope of Bruges' entertainment options runs from several *carillon concerts* weekly, to musical events staged on canals and in churches, to grand costumed historic pageant processions.

ACCOMMODATIONS Bruges, with 100-plus hotels, offers more rooms than any city in Belgium except Brussels; most are in the historic town, at prices in all categories lower than those in Brussels. Reservations at any time of year are recommended, since Bruges is a popular place year-round for weekend getaways for Europeans; particularly heavily booked are the three- and four-day Europe-wide spring holiday week-

BELGIUM · · · 469

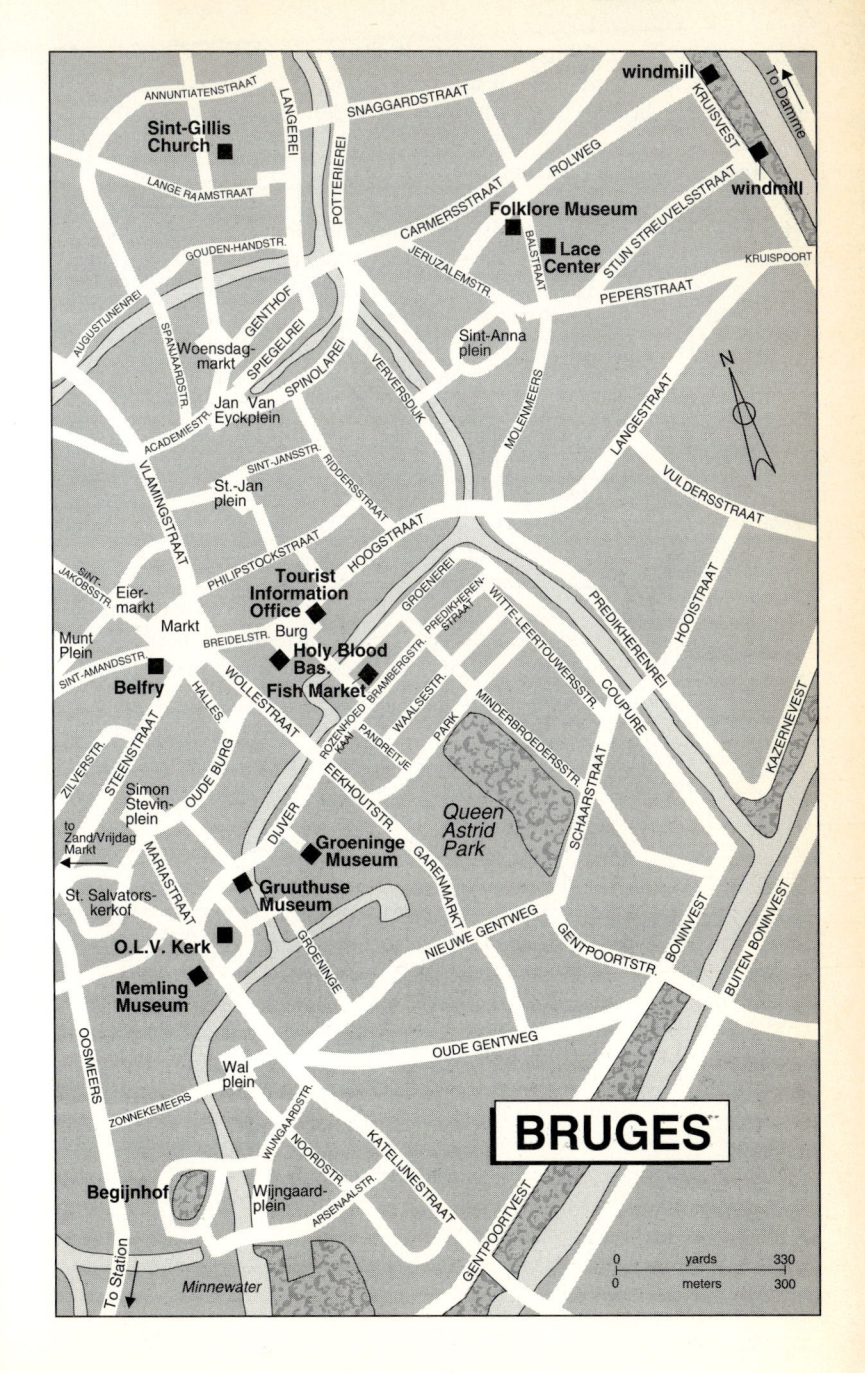

ends at Easter and Whitsun. Bruges is also busy with visitors in July and August, but many come just for the day (a great mistake) and, once the bus-borne hoards of day-trippers have left, Bruges generally has space available for overnighters. If you haven't booked ahead, the Tourist Office provides an accommodations service.

RESTAURANTS Bruges also has more restaurants than anywhere in Belgium other than Brussels. Fine food and pleasurable settings are found in all price ranges. The traditional Flemish, fresh seafood, and French *haute cuisine* choices will satisfy most palettes. If you want something a little lighter, you're in the right place: the English word "snack" was derived from the Dutch/Flemish *snakken* ("to yearn for") and Bruges has plenty of informal eateries that serve both indoors and outside. Bruges is chock full of **chocolate** shops, one of which, **Sukerbuyc** *(Katelijnestraat 5; 33.08.87),* offers not only 65 kinds of handmade chocolates including *pralines* (filled chocolates), but from May–Dec. makes *marzipan* in many fancy and unexpected forms. The delicate sweet biscuits called *dentelles de Brugge* are an edible version of local lace.

ARRIVING **Train** is the choice of many travelers to Bruges; the direct twice-hourly service from Brussels takes just over an hour. If you arrive by **North Sea ferry** from England at either Ostend or Zeebrugge, the first stop on the **boat train** for Brussels (or beyond) is Bruges. Historic Bruges, which has lots of winding one-way streets, was not made for cars. Should you arrive in one, plan to park and forget it until you leave. However, when "disposing" of it, be sure to do so correctly so you won't be towed; there's an underground garage at **'t Zand,** inside the old city via **Koning Albertlaan** from the station, which is close to major roads.

IN THE AREA Some 4 mi./7 km. from Bruges, along a canal lined with wind-bend poplars in polderland so flat that it takes the fertile farm fields forever to meet the huge cloud-besprinkled sky at the horizon, is **Damme.** You can travel by boat, bike, foot, or car to Damme, today a hamlet noted for its restaurants, but whose few fine buildings are vestiges of the days centuries ago when it served as Bruges' outer port on the ill-fated Zwin and had a population of 60,000.

TRAVEL TIPS Bruges is a little over an hour from Brussels by train, easy to do on an individual or commercial motorcoach day trip. But just because that's the way the vast majority of travelers see Bruges doesn't mean that you should. Bruges is one of Europe's most exceptional destinations—even in the Middle Ages, everyone who could came to see it. And that truism, evident during the day, becomes inescapable in the evening when, no matter what the season, you have the city largely to yourself. It's when the crowds have gone that Bruges will bewitch you with its medieval mystique. After dark, the reflections in its canals will capture you in a reflective mood, and, anywhere, it's safe to slow from a stride to a stroll, to stop and stare.

Bruges in Context

In 1896, English writer Arnold Bennett noted in his *Journal:* "The difference between Bruges and other cities is that in the latter you look around for the picturesque, while in Bruges, assailed on every side by the picturesque, you look curiously for the unpicturesque, and don't find it easily." The foresight of Bruges' city fathers in the century since must be lauded; by 1904, they had established a *Commission of Urban Beauty* and imposed strictures to preserve Bruges' Middle Age aspect (even in the Middle Ages, Bruges was considered one of Europe's most beautiful cities). Although in the 20th century, commercialism has reached its tentacles into many of the most remote corners tourists can travel to, Bennett's words about Bruges remain remarkably true.

Bruges is not undiscovered as a place of touristic charm. In the late 19th century, the town awoke from a nearly four-century sleeping-beauty scenario during which relative poverty had preserved its unique architectural heritage. In the century since, Bruges has grown in popularity to the point where it has more pleasure visitors than any other place in Belgium. It was paid holidays for workers (a result of the *Industrial Revolution*) and improved public transportation (particularly the train) in the 19th century that woke Bruges (and other areas, see *Ostend* under *The Belgian Coast*) to its tourism possibilities. Turn-of-the-century revitilization came, too, as the government made plans for the long ago silted-up city to have a port again, developing **Zeebrugge** (meaning "Bruges-on-the-sea") and constructing a cross-country canal from the town to it.

Bruges often is categorized as the "Venice of the North," the canals for which each is noted inviting inevitable comparison. *Bruggelingen* (residents of Bruges) quite reasonably respond that it would make just as much sense to call Venice the *"Bruges of the South."* In fact, the cities have much more in common than watery ways and byways. At their respective apexes of power, Bruges with an earlier start but their successful 13th to early 15th centuries overlapping, both independent, wealthy city states exerted far-reaching commercial and artistic influences. Bruges traded wool, fine cloth, lace, and tapestries to Italy in exchange for commissioned paintings. Venitians maintained important consular and trade offices in Bruges, and also commissioned paintings, from the Flemish "primitive" masters. Eventually, both cities suffered change from circumstances beyond their control.

To speak again of canals, in the 1970s, when Bruges' inner city waterways had become offensive-smelling due to 20th-century industrial waste, a pipeline was constructed to bring fresh lake water into the dredged and cleaned canals, and the waste water from industry (all of which operates beyond the borders of historic Bruges) was diverted away. Today, the bad odor in Bruges' canals is over, a situation that can't now be said of Venice.

The history of Bruges began in the 9th century, when **Boudewijn** (also known as **Baldwin Iron Arm**) boldly eloped with the daughter of French King Charles the Bald. Though less than pleased, in order to provide a united family front against invading Vikings, Charles gifted his impetuous new son-in-law with the misty lands in the extreme north of Gaul (modern Flanders). To withstand the frequent Viking invasions, Boudewijn built a solid fort on the site of today's **Burg.** Soon a village arose around it, taking its name from the bridge (*brug*) he built over the Reie river. From these beginnings in Bruges, Boudewijn went on to become founder of the powerful dynasty of the counts of Flanders (see also *Ghent in Context*). At about the time of Boudewijn, Bruges' future was, for the short term, favorably influenced by a great North Sea inundation of the coast that greatly deepened an arm of water, the **Zwin,** that reached inland to the Reie.

By the 10th century, Norsemen were no longer a nuisance and Bruges was becoming a significant business center. Old annals record the first annual trade fair—it would become the most important in Flanders—in 958, for which merchants arrived in vessels in Bruges' harbor, located where the **Minnewater** is today. During the 11th century, Bruges laid the foundations for its future commercial greatness, fortifying itself physically, and, in 1089, becoming the administrative capital of the County of Flanders. Churches, hospitals, and monasteries began to be built.

Bruges established important economic relations with Germany, England, France, the Baltic, Russia, and the East, and, by the 12th century, had become one of Europe's most prosperous market towns. The cloth trade was becoming highly important—also in the fellow Flemish cities of Ypres and Ghent—and the import and storage of English wool was making a fortune for Fleming nobility and merchants.

On March 2, 1127, Count of Flanders Charles the Good was assassinated in the Burg's **St. Donatian church** (built in the 9th century, consecrated as a cathedral in 1559, and demolished by post-revolution, anti-religious French fanatics in 1799). A heated dispute over Charles' successor arose, and Bruges' wealthy shopkeepers took advantage of the situation to claim the right to participate in governing the flourishing city. From that time, the *meliores civium* ("the best citizens"), in addition to the nobility, could do so, but the manual workers, weavers, and other crafts people were still excluded from the power process.

While Bruges continued to burgeon in business, by late in the 12th century the Zwin, which tidal forces had earlier favored by deepening, began to be threatened with silt, and dredging was done on it between 1175 and 1200. In 1180, Count of Flanders Philip of Alsace, granted town rights to the nearby (4 mi./7 km.) fishing village of **Damme,** on the Zwin. Damme, its harbor created by embanking the Reie in Bruges and damming it (hence its name) where it joined the Zwin, henceforth served as the foreport for Bruges. The **Spielgelrei,** today dead-ended at Jan van Eyckplein, once brought the waters of the Reie from Damme right to Bruges' Markt; there, barges, loaded with wool from ships too large to sail inland beyond Damme, unloaded it into the Cloth Hall.

An indication of the size of the new port in Damme (see *In the Area*) comes from the fact that, in 1213, Philip II of France used it for his fleet, said to number some 1,000 vessels, while he pillaged the town during his war against Count Ferdinand of Flanders. However, Ferdinand's English allies burned most of Philip's fleet as it lay in Damme harbor (thereby creating a new need to dredge). Damme recovered, growing in a few years from virtual non-existence to a population of 10,000, and gaining its own maritime law *(Zeerecht van Damme)* and valuable staple rights on wine and herring.

The early 13th century saw many foreign merchants making themselves at home in Bruges. Nobles built mansions, merchants built town houses. To proclaim its fame, fortune, and freedom, Bruges constructed an exceptionally fine **Belfry** (the first edition of the edifice was built in the early 13th century, destroyed by fire in 1280, and reconstructed in 1282-1296). Bruges founded the **Flemish Hanseatic League of London,** through which it practically monopolized trade with England, whose wool was vital for the Flemish cloth workers. Bruges also obtained a *kontor* from the *Tuetonic Hanseatic League* and was a member of the *Hanseatic League of the Seventeen Cities,* associations which protected members' commercial links. The protection the Bruges-Hansa tie implied led many countries to set up substantial trade missions in the city. Bruges became the transit warehouse for Hansa members from the Baltic to Italy and overflowed with imports: carpets from the East, furs from Russia, velvet from Italy, metals from Poland, exotic fruits from Egypt, and spices from Arabia. The Italian cities of Venice, Florence, Genoa, and Pisa built trade houses in Bruges, which was mentioned by Italian poet **Dante Alighieri** (1265-1321) in *The Divine Comedy*'s *Inferno.*

The growing opulence of Bruges' merchants, who monopolized all trade, contrasted sharply with the poverty of the tens of thousands of exploited workers in the city's 52 guilds. In 1280, the "blue nails" (as textile workers were known due to their dye-stained nails) led a revolt against the more privileged citizens. During this period, Count of Flanders Guy de Dampierre, who had been instrumental in developing Bruges' trade fairs, and sought to maintain Flanders' autonomy from the French crown, met strong resistance from Philip the Fair. Eventually, Philip found an excuse to imprison the rebellious Count in Paris, and annexed Flanders. Burgundian **Philip the Fair** came in triumph from France in 1301 to visit Bruges, then Europe's most important commercial city. Most Bruggelingen turned out to see Philip, many so luxuriously turned-out that his Queen, Joanne of Navarre, is said to have reacted to the sumptuous display of dress and jewels by pronouncing, "I thought that I alone was queen, but I see hundreds around me here."

Under the Burgundians, the unequally favored citizens of Bruges soon squared off into camps: the patricians, who preferred French dominion *(Leliaerts),* against the discontented common people *(Klauwaerts),* who took their name, "lion's paw," from the Lion of Flanders, the count's emblem. Klauwaert **Pieter de Coninck,** a weaver, became leader of their rebellion. Philip's appointee as governor of Flanders, his uncle Jacques de Chantillon, treated the guildsmen of Bruges with such oppressive intolerance that the citizens, under Pieter de Coninck and **Jan Breydel,** revolted against Bruges' French garrison within a year. At dawn on May 18, 1302, as the bells rang for matins (the incident became known as the **Bruges Matins**), some 2,000 French soldiers, and patricians who collaborated with the French, none of whom could, when it was demanded of them, properly pronounce the gutteral sounds of the Flemish words *Schilt ende vriendt* (shield and friend), were slaughtered on the spot.

Six weeks later, the two Bruges guild leaders (remembered in a statue on the Markt) led Flemish burghers against French nobility, achieving victory at the *Battle of the Golden Spurs* at Kortrijk (see *Belgium: An Historical Perspective*). This battle broke the control of trade by the rich merchants and patricians, and put more power in the hands of the guilds.

In 1369, the last Count of Flanders, Louis de Malle, gave his only daughter's hand in marriage to Duke of Burgundy, **Philip the Bold,** and the couple made Bruges their favorite residence in the Netherlands. In 1376, work began on a Stadhuis (town hall) worthy of Bruges (today, the oldest in Belgium and one of most splendid). Philip fostered the Flemish school of painting, giving commissions to many members of the *Guild of St. Luke*. Burgundian Bruges was the meeting place of Europe's North and South, where intellectual ideas intermingled amid the easy exchange of material goods. These, unloaded on the quays at Damme, where the seagoing ships anchored, and transferred to barges, made a continuous procession up the canalized Reie to Bruges. Some 150 ships entered the Bruges/Damme ports in a single day, and the population, which included the consuls from 20 nations and city-states, reached 150,000. But even as Bruges was at its best, Damme, too, was becoming afflicted by sand, the insidious silting preventing the deepest-draft ships from sailing to it up the Zwin, from the North Sea.

In 1429, Isabella of Portugal, whose portrait was painted by Jan van Eyck, sailed into Damme to become the bride of **Philip the Good.** The week-long wedding celebrations were the talk of the West. That same year in Bruges, Philip founded the famed *Order of the Golden Fleece,* both to highlight the splendor and stature of his House of Burgundy and in recognition of the skill of Flemish wool weavers. The Order's insignia, a limp lamb's fleece worn on a substantial gold chain around the neck of its knights—as seen in period portraits such as that of "Anthony of Burgundy" by **Rogier van der Weyden** in Brussels' **Museum of Ancient Art**—took its name from the ancient Greek myth of Jason and his Argonauts' search for the Golden Fleece. Membership in the medieval order of chivalry (limited to 24) was a great honor. Members were chosen by Philip, and subsequent rulers, who would congregate the knights for consultation at chapter meetings. It was an honor, too, to be the venue for such a meeting: the carved choir stalls in Bruges' St. Saviour's Cathedral were commissioned in 1430 for the occasion of the founding of the Order, which returned there in 1478 for the Thirteenth Chapter meeting. In 1464, Philip named Bruges the meeting place for the first *States General of the Netherlands.*

Bruges' cultural high point came with the long reign of Philip the Good (1419–1467). Flemish art flowered, and music played an important part in Bruges life, as shown by the numerous instruments that appear in Flemish paintings. Memling painted *The Last Judgment* as a commission for Tomasso Portunari, who was the director of the Medicis' bank at Bruges, and the same connection may have been the route by which **Hugo van der Goes**'s *Nativity* found its way to Florence's Uffizzi Gallery.

By the 15th century, Bruges was a central clearing house for all European trade, as well as the warehouse for the Hanseatic League. At Vlamingstraat 35 (today a business district not far from the Markt), in a 13th-century family mansion **Huis ter Beurze,** the entreprenurial Brugean innkeeper Joris van der Beurze served the merchants and bankers who met, dined, drank, and negotiated business deals there an assortment of business services that amounted to the world's first currency and commodities exchange (his name *Beurze* in the forms *bourse* and *beurs,* is still in use for stock exchanges worldwide). For his 15th-century clients, Van der Beurze arranged money exchanges, since each of the states and cities that traded in Bruges coined its own currency; he also coordinated weights, since many dominions also maintained their own measurement systems. Eventually, Van der Beurze began a form of *letters of credit,* which, given the weight of the all-metal money in those days, was not only safer from robbery but much easier to manage. On the former site of Huis ter Buerze is a modern bank where you can conduct your financial business.

By Philip's death in 1467, Bruges fortunes had begun to decline, though the pomp and circumstance of civic life under the Dukes of Burgundy concealed the fading glory. In 1468, Damme hosted the wedding, and Bruges the month-long celebrations after, for **Charles the Bold** and the English princess Margaret of York, sister of English King Edward IV. By then, silting on the Zwin made even Damme unreachable by water, and, arriving from England, Margaret could sail only as far as Sluis in Holland, to which the foreport for Damme and Bruges had been moved. Nevertheless, the wedding was a grandiose occasion, the knights of the Golden Fleece gathering for a tournament which they called the **Pageant of the Golden Tree** (re-created every five years in Bruges, next in 1996). But two too-short Burgundian reigns (Charles the Bold died in battle at Nancy in 1477, and his daughter and heir Mary of Burgundy only five years later from a fall incurred while falconing on horseback—both have grand mausoleums in Bruges' Onze Lieve Vrouwekerk), led to the transfer of Flemish power from the French Burgundians to the Austrian Hapsburgs through Mary's husband **Archduke Maximilian.**

Hapsburg rule was not a success for Bruges. In 1488, for a period of 11 weeks, Bruggelingen held Maximilian prisoner at the **Craenenburg** (corner of Markt and Sint-Amandsstraat). The extreme, and ultimately unwise, action was in response to what they considered unjustified infringements upon their freedom (the garrisoning of German soldiers, etc). Having thrown Maximilian in jail to stress how strongly they felt, the citizens also summarily tried and condemned to death the Archduke's local right-hand counsellor, **Pieter Lanchals,** whose execution Maximilian was made to witness. A popular local story is that Maximilian, finally released from jail on the basis of promises (later, largely unkept), ordered Bruggelingen to forever keep swans on their canals in remembrance of Lanchals, whose name is derived from *lange hals* meaning "long neck" and whose coat of arms bore a swan (Lanchals is buried in a chapel in Onze Lieve Vrouwekerk). Though swans (with a B for Bruges and the year of birth marked on their beaks) remain plentiful to this today, the Maximilian incident proved to be Bruges' swan song. The uprising against him had caused political instability, a serious detriment to trade; many foreign merchants, and Maximilian himself, made a permanent move to Antwerp.

The Zwin, continuing to sink under sand, most certainly was a deciding factor in the death blow to Bruges, but there were others. Bruges, among other places in Flanders, had practiced over-restrictive commercial policies in the cloth industry, its merchants and guild members refusing to handle any cloth made by competitive weavers (particularly those in England). As the English industry grew and the country kept more of its own wool, the lack of the raw material led to ruin throughout the Flemish cloth industry. Many Flemish weavers out of work left for England to find new jobs.

Maximilian's grandson, Charles V made a triumphant entry into Bruges in 1515, the year he became ruler of the Netherlands at the age of 15. But any hopes Bruggelingen had that Charles could, or would, change their downhill course ended that year when he selected Brussels as his principal residence. When Bruges at last perceived the full threat to her very existence, it was too late. Native-son **Lancelot Blondeel** (1496–1561), primarily a painter, but also a Renaissance man with an interest in the sciences, was called in by municipal officers to plan a canal to give Bruges renewed access to the sea. Blondeel threw himself into the task, and eventually proposed a massive project. But such was the extent of work required that it was not implemented.

Religious struggles of the second half of the 16th century completed the process of ruin for Bruges as a commercial center. But, after *Iconoclasts* had pillaged, killed priests, and disfigured sacred statues, with the coming of the Counter-Reformation in Flanders Bruges became a safe haven for Catholic nuns, priests, and monks, many of whose institutions survive today. Wealthy burghers built almshouses *(godshuizen)* for the increasingly impoverished city's poor. Business improved somewhat in the 17th century, and a number of houses date from that period. But, basically, Bruges became a backwater.

Finally, in 1811, Napoleon Bonaparte employed Spanish prisoners-of-war to dig a canal between Bruges and the Scheldt—for his own purposes. He wanted to connect Bruges, via Damme, with Breskens in Holland on the Westerscheldt estuary so that his ships could sail from Antwerp to Dunkirk without having to use the North Sea, thereby avoiding the English coast—and the English Navy. But Napoleon's canal plan was interrupted by other events in 1814 and 1815. And the Industrial Revolution continued to pass Bruges by.

Between 1895–1907 the Belgian government under Leopold II built—very much along the lines of Lancelot Blondeel's 16th-century proposal—the **Boudewijn Kanaal** (230 ft/70 m. wide, 26 ft/8 m. deep, and 6.5 mi./10 km. long) to a place on the coast that was named **Zeebrugge.** Subsequent development of the port provided a fishing harbor, an inner harbor, and an outer harbor with 245 acres of water sheltered by a crescent-shaped *mole* or jetty (with *promenade*) that reaches more than 1.5 miles/2.5 km. into the North Sea. The once-open mouth of the Zwin today is but a salt-water marsh nature reserve (see *Het Zoute* under *The Belgian Coast*).

Five centuries after its fall from greater glory, though the Zeebrugge port is important for regional business, tourism has placed Bruges back on the map. But Bruges is again playing a part in the history of Europe, through its *College of Europe,* founded in 1949. Today the multi-lingual international students of the prestigious postgraduate institution (located on the Dijver), well grounded in cultural and scientific studies of contemporary Europe, are much in demand, and serving in positions of importance as the integration process towards a single European marketplace continues.

GUIDEPOSTS
Telephone Code 050

Tourist Info	**Dienst voor Toerisme,** Burg 11, 44.86.86, fax 44.86.00. Mon.–Fri. April–Sept. 9:30 a.m.–7 p.m., Sat., Sun., hols. 10 a.m.–12:30 p.m. and 2–7 p.m.; Oct.–Mar. Mon.–Sat. 9:30 a.m.–1 p.m. and 2–6 p.m., closed Sun., hols.; hotel booking assistance. Guided city walking tours daily July–Aug. 3 p.m., meeting point Tourist Office.
Transportation Information	**Rail:** station office open Mon.–Fri. 7 a.m.–7 p.m., Sat. & Sun. 9:30 a.m.–5:30 p.m., 38.23.82; **bus:** daily 6 a.m.–9 p.m. 35.21.43.
Taxis	Taxi ranks at Station and Markt; to book 33.44.44 and 38.46.60.
Post Office	Markt 5, 33.14.11
Police	Hauwerstraat 7, 33.77.33
Emergency	100; weekend doctors on duty (Fri. 8 p.m.–Mon. 8 a.m.) 81.38.99
Rental Bikes	Railway station: 38.58.71; **'T Koffieboontje,** Hallestraat 4 (by Belfry), 33.80.27; bicycle tour brochure in English available.
Canal Cruises	Five departure points, several on **Dijver** and **Rozenhoedkaai;** Mar.–Nov. 10 a.m.–6 p.m., Dec., Feb. weekends, hols., closed Jan.; duration 1/2 hour.
Horse-drawn Cab Tours	Mar.–Nov. on Burg, 10 a.m.–8 p.m. **Sightseeing Line,** bus stop in center of Markt, schedule, reser. 31.13.55.
Cruises to Damme	*Rederij Benelux Damme,* Noorweegse Kaai 31, Dampoort (Bruges City bus 4); April 1–Sept. 30, departures on the hour 9 a.m.–6 p.m. Info from Damme Tourist Office, 050/35.33.19.

WHAT TO SEE AND DO.....................

What you most want to do in Bruges is look at the delightful details of this lovely little city in gothic garb: the texture of century-smoothed cobblestones, the mellow colors of aged building bricks, lacy wrought-iron lanterns, lace curtains at the windows, flower boxes strung along the canals. Shadings in the changeable sky and reflection creations in canal waters produce natural "special effects" that will leave you looking wonderingly (and wishing, perhaps, for the skill to capture them on film). In a city whose name means "bridges" it's not surprising to find one, **Rozenhoedkaaibrug,** on which stands a statue of the patron saint of bridges (**Jean Nepomucene of Prague** was declared a saint after being thrown from a bridge into the Moldau River for refusing to reveal secrets divulged during a queen's confession). As rewarding as the insides of Bruges' museums are (the Tourist Office sells combination tickets to four major museums (BF 250), a savings for visitors who intend to see them all), it may be that by stopping on bridges to gaze down a canal, you'll discover an image of Bruges that lingers in your mind. So *don't,* however little time you have in this atmospheric city, spend it all indoors—whatever the weather.

Markt • This has been the commercial heart of Bruges for more than a millenium (when the merchants moved the short distance from the town's fortified Burg to set up a permanent main market square). It's unusual for a Markt in the Benelux not to be home to the stadhuis/town hall; Bruges' Markt used to be, but the building burned, and an all important Cloth Hall was built on the site (where the ornate 19th-century West Flanders Provincial House now stands). A new Stadhuis was built on the **Burg** (see below). The dominating monument on the Markt is the Belfry. Around the square are the gabled facades of guildhouses and former dwellings of dukes and foreign dignitaries, many of which at street-level now support terrace cafes that burst with imbibers in pleasant weather. In the center of the Markt is a statue (1887) of **Pieter De Coninck** and **Jan Breydel,** leaders in the *Bruges Matins* and 1302 *Battle of the Golden Spurs.* To have the full impact of the activity on the Markt during Bruges' bustling 13th and 14th centuries you must keep in mind that the **Reie,** the waterway that connected Bruges to Damme and the sea, came right up to the east side of the Markt, to and under the Cloth Hall for all-weather unloading.

Belfry • *Entrance in courtyard of Halle; visits to tower mean climbing 366 mostly stone steps, no elevator; April 1–Sept. 30. daily 9:30 a.m.–12:30 p.m., 1:30–6 p.m.; Oct. 1–Mar. 31, 9:30 a.m.–noon, and 2–5 p.m.; English-language guide and printed booklet about* *tower* • The Bruges Belfry (265 feet/88 meters) is acknowledged to be Belgium's most beautiful. "Thrice consumed and thrice rebuilded," (noted no less a poet than Longfellow [1807–1882] in *The Belfry of Bruges*), its present post-fires square base, which rises from the roof of the *Halle* (market hall), dates from 1296. Used as a storage depot and market, the front dates from 1248, the sides from 1363–1365, and the back, 1561–1566. The graceful octagonal top of the Belfry was added in 1487. The *view* from its top, well-worth the effort of those up to the climb, inspired Longfellow, who climbed it one winter morning and, gazing down, imagined "pageants splendid that adorned those days of old" and "knights who bore the Golden Fleece, Lombard and Venetian merchants, with deep laden argosies" transversing the Markt. At the 55th step is the former treasure chamber, normally on view only through a wrought-iron railing dating from 1300, a typical early example of this Flemish art form; the railing has six locks. In chests in wall niches were stored the town's precious *Charter of Liberty* and *Great Seal*, both destroyed in the Belfry's fire of 1280. (The written evidence of rights awarded to citizens was important; since the Count of Flanders at the time was annoyed by the amount of freedom the Bruggelingen had gained, it has always been suspected that he was responsible for the fire.) At the Belfry's 333rd step you come to the automatic mechanism for the tower clock. At the 352nd is the chamber with the carillon keyboard, above which, behind the uppermost arched openings, are Bruges' 47 mighty bronze carillon bells. The carillon is attended to artistically and maintained mechanically by the present holder of the full-time paid position of *stadbeiaardier*/town carilloneur, the amiable **Aime Lombaert**, whose talents have taken him on carillon-playing tours in the U.S., Canada, and Europe. Perhaps surprisingly, standing by the bells when the carillon is being played won't drive you mad, or make you deaf, but you actually hear the music better from below. From above, however, there's a splendid view across Bruges and the Flemish countryside. Blind visitors to Bruges can get an appreciation of the building from the Belfry "in braille" in front of the Halle; the "hands on" model of the Belfry of which Bruggelingen are so proud also has a description of it in braille.

Burg • This, the most handsome square in Bruges, is the site of the city's founding, where Boudewijn, first Count of Flanders, put up a first, fortified, building in the 9th century. It should be any traveler's first stop, too, for the well-supplied and helpful Tourist Information office is located here. On the site where the Holiday Inn Crown Plaza is now once sat the 9th-century St. Donatian church, broken down brick by brick by religion-hating French Revolutionary zealots in 1799. A smaller version the statue of Jan van Eyck that stands on the nearby Jan van Eyckplein was placed here to commemorate the fact that the artist had been buried in St. Donatian. Remnants of the foundations of the church were discovered in 1955, and have been preserved in a cellar "museum" in the hotel. Several important stops face the square.

Stadhuis • *April 1–Sept. 30, daily 9:30 a.m.–noon, 2–6 p.m., Oct. 1–Mar. 31 closes at 5 p.m.* • Bruges' Late Gothic-style Stadhuis was begun in 1376, making it the oldest in Belgium, and one of the finest. The ornate facade, which took 45 years to finish, is today once again studded with statues, most of its 48 niches only recently refilled with copies of the figures of counts and countesses of Flanders that were removed and ruined by the French in their devastation of the city in 1799. The entrance hall is decorated with colorful guild banners and historic paintings. Also on display are fine antique maps of Bruges, which show that the city is so little changed in 400 years that you could tour from a copy. Be sure to head upstairs to the spacious **Gothic Hall**, with its superb wooden rib-arched and vaulted, vividly painted ceiling (1385–1402), altogether a worthy setting for the first council of the States General of the Netherlands, seated here by Burgundian Philip the Good in 1464. Town authorities met here for centuries, but now the space is reserved for civil wedding ceremonies and official receptions. The circular vaultkeys in the ceiling show scenes from the New Testament and scenes depicting the 12 months and 4 natural elements. Restoration of the room at the turn of the century resulted in the addition of romantic wall paintings by the Flemish artists **Albert and Juliaan de Vriendt** of events in the history of Bruges. Among these are the triumphal return of Bruges warriors from the Battle of the Golden Spurs in 1302, the founding of the Order of the Golden Fleece by Philip the Good in 1429, Bruges renewing its privileges in the Hanseatic League, and the opening of the new Zwin canal in 1404.

Brugse Vrije/The Liberty of Bruges • *daily year-round 10 a.m.–noon, 1:30–5 p.m.* • Its seat established on the Burg in a palace built between 1520 and 1525, the Liberty of Bruges was a feudal territorial subdivision of Flanders, with its own administrative, judicial, and financial authority, which in the course of the 14th century became the fourth most important member of Flanders after Ghent, Bruges, and Ypres. The Liberty of Bruges existed until 1795 when it was abolished by the French. Its Aldermen's Room is visited for the magnificent 1528 **Renaissance chimneypiece** designed by Brugean artist **Lanceloot Blondeel** (1498–1561) that honors Charles V. Charles, portrayed as the worldly prince and Emperor of the Holy Roman Empire, stands in the center, carved in wood with a glowing patina, surrounded by black marble with white alabaster friezes. On either side of Charles are the paired statues of his grandparents, paternal (Emperor Maximilian of Austria and Mary of Burgundy) and maternal (Ferdinand of Aragon and Isabella of Castille); his parents, Philip the Fair and Johanna the Mad, are represented only on medallions, barely visible behind him. On the walls hang copies of two paintings (originals in the Groeninge Museum, see below) on the theme of justice that were commissioned for the Aldermen's Room: "The Last Judgement" (1551) by **Pieter Pourbus,** and the horrifying "Judgement of Cambyses" (1498) by **Gerard David.**

Basilique du Saint-Sang/Basilica of the Holy Blood • *daily April 1–Sept. 30 9:30 a.m.–noon, 2–6 p.m., Oct. 1–Mar. 31. 10 a.m.–noon, 2–4 p.m., year-round closed Wed. p.m.* • The relic, to house and honor which the basilica was built, is a phial said to contain a mixture of blood and water washed from Christ's side as he hung on the cross. The traditional accounting for the relic's arrival in Bruges is that because Count of Flanders, Dierick of Alsace, had executed his duties in the Second Crusade in an exemplary manner, he was given the relic. However, historians have now determined that the Holy Blood didn't arrive in Bruges until the beginning of the 13th century, via Constantinople. In any case, the **Holy Blood Relic** is on view in the **Upper Chapel** every Fri. 8:30–11:45 a.m., 3–4 p.m., and daily for two weeks in the Ascension period (see also *Procession of the Holy Blood* under *Events*) from 8:30–11:45 a.m., 3:00–4:00 p.m. The dimly lit, thick-walled, semi-circular vaulted **Lower Chapel** is worth a look for being one of the purest examples of Romanesque construction in Flanders.

Off the Burg, down **Blind Ezelstraat,** identifiable by its arcade to 15th-century former Palace of Justice, and over a 14th-century bridge is the **Vismarkt,** a beamed open market, neo-classical columned building dating from 1826, a busy scene on mornings (except Sun. and Mon.). Among the buildings surrounding the charming cobbled nearby **Huidevettersplein** (Tanners' Square) are the tanners guild house (1630) and next to it a facade with bas-reliefs representing the different processes of working leather. Leaving the square on the far side, you will be on one of Bruges' most beautiful canals, **Rozenhoedkaai,** with picturesque sights in every direction, and just down from the **Dijver,** Bruges' *museum row.*

Groeninge Museum • *Dijver 12; April 1–Sept. 30 daily 9:30 a.m.–6 p.m., Oct. 1–Mar. 31 9:30 a.m.–noon, 2–5 p.m., closed Tues.; booklet with English translations of the captions by the museum's works of art* • Even though they broke new artistic ground as a group, the leading Flemish "primitive" painters can be appreciated for their individual qualities: **Jan van Eyck** (1390–1441) for realism; **Rogier van der Weyden** (1399–1464) for passionate emotion; **Hans Memling** (1435–1494) for delicacy and purity; and **Hugo van der Goes** (1440–1482) for striking dramatism, a trait duplicated by his student **Gerard David** (1460–1523), the last great master of the *Bruges School.* Its primitive paintings of the Bruges School are the museum's greatest treasure, although the pleasantly human-scale Groeninge collection shows the whole evolution of Flemish art, from the *surrealism* of **Hieronymous Bosch** (1450–1516) to that of **James Ensor** (1860–1949).

Among the more outstanding paintings are Van Eyck's *Madonna with St. Donatian and St. George* with its superb portrait of the donor **Canon van der Paele,** and *Portrait of Margarete van Eyck,* the artist's wife painted in his most realistic mode; Memling's *Triptych* with donors Willem Moreel, burgomaster of Bruges, and his wife; Van der Goes' *Death of a Virgin;* David's *Triptych* including the *Baptism of Christ;* and *Last Judgment* by the intensely individual master Hieronymous Bosch, whose contemporaries could make nothing of his spirit and technique, although Breugel, a century later, seemed able to. The horrifying painting *The Judgment of Cambyses* (1498) by **Gerard David** of a man being skinned alive uses the story from Herodotus of the skin of a corrupt judge being stripped from him and used to make a cushion for the chair on which his son would sit as successor. This painting is said to have been commissioned by the Magistrates of Bruges in atonement for the town's execution of Maximilian's adviser *Pieter Lanchals* (see *History,* above) to hang (as a copy does today) in the **Brugse Vrije** Alderman's Room of the Court of Justice.

At the Groeninge, you'll see many works attributed with the word *"naar"* (meaning "after" or "in the school of"), some of which may be copies (usually contemporary and often excellent—recall Pieter Bruegel the Younger's many copies of his father's works, some of the originals of which no longer exist). The number of works noted "naar" also is an indication, in a world without other methods of artistic reproduction—no art posters—of the popularity of the work in its day. The number of anonymous works *("anoniem")* is a sign of the substantial artistic activity in Bruges during the 14th–16th-century period, during which the painter's names of some unsigned works were lost.

Gruuthuse Museum • *Dijver 17; year-round daily 9:30 a.m.–noon, 2–6 p.m., closed Tues.; numbered room plan)* • This was the luxurious mansion of the **Heren van Gruuthuse** (Lords of Gruuthouse), whose fortune came from their right to impose a tax on the import of "gruut," a mixture of dried plants and flowers used by brewers to flavor beer. Louis de Gruuthuse (a representation of whom is above the door) was a counsellor to Philip the Good and Charles the Bold. Decorative art lovers will rarely have had such a wonderful place to wander around, with room after numbered room (19 in all) of tapestries, porcelain, paintings, brass, musical instruments, furniture, and lace. Plus, it's all displayed in a fine 15th-century noble family's architecturally homogeneous ivy-covered mansion that alone is worth the walk inside. Among the built-in treasures are chimneypieces, tiled hearths, carved ceilings and moldings, and curious corners such as the one found through Room 16. It's a small windowed oratory built into the wall of Onze Lieve Vrouwekerk (see below) directly above the choir of the church. While the Gruut family obviously used the room as a means of "attending" mass without leaving home (a different variation of a private chapel), we spectators get a strange feeling looking down on the tourists in the church. Also worth seeking out are the 16th-century Flemish kitchen (Room 3) and Rooms 18–20, in the height of the house, have an excellent exhibit of antique Flemish lace, which includes a lace altar cover that belonged to Charles V. After examining the lace, visit the outside balcony for views, dominated by the tower of Onze Lieve Vrouw, of the attractive garden, canal, and St. Bonifacebrug behind the house (the garden extends to the *Groeninge Museum* and displays a recent sculpture "The Four Horsemen of the Apocalypse" by **Rik Poot**). One of the many oddities in the multi-faceted Gruuthuse collection is an 18th-century *guillotine,* for some reason left in Bruges by the French after they were defeated in the Battle of Waterloo. In 1989, on the occasion of the 200th anniversary of the French Revolution, this guillotine was loaned to the Bicentennial Committee in Paris because it was unable to find a real one in France, since, after the revolution, they had all been ordered destroyed.

Onze Lieve Vrouwekerk/Church of Our Lady • *April 1–Sept. 30, daily 10–11:30 a.m., 2:30–5 p.m., Oct. 1–Mar. 31, 10–11:30 a.m., 3–4:30 p.m., year-round closed Sun. and hol. mornings, open 2:30–4:30 p.m.* • The Church of Our Lady is predominantly 13th-century Scheldt Gothic. Its 400-foot/122-meter belfry is one of the tallest brick structures in Europe. What draws many here is the "Madonna and Child" by **Michelangelo** (1475–1564). One of the few works by the master to have left Italy during his lifetime, the Bruges Madonna was one of 15 statues Michelangelo was commissioned to sculpt for the Piccolomini altar in the Duomo of Siena. For various reasons, only four statues of the series were completed, of which this is one. The Brugean merchant Jan van Moeskroen is generally credited with bringing the statue to Bruges in 1506 and donating it to this, his own, parish church. (He is buried beneath the altar by the statue). The chubby Christ child and his mother, favorite subjects of Michelangelo, are made of glowing white Carrara marble and sit in a black marble niche. The half-turned pose of the child demonstrates the sculptor at his best and most typical. Though twice stolen (by the French in 1794 and the Nazis in 1944), both times the piece was recovered in good condition.

The untimely death of Mary of Burgundy, wife of Maximilian of Austria, at age 25 in a horseback riding fall, meant the end of Burgundian rule for Bruges and all Flanders, the Hapsburgs of Austria taking over through her widower Maximilian. Mary was buried here in Bruges' most important church, where her father Charles the Bold also lay. Their life-size recumbent effigies atop *mausoleums* are among the art treasures here executed by Brussels goldsmith **Pieter de Beckere** in 1495–1502. Over the altar which the mausoleums face is the large 16th-century "Crucifixion" triptych by **Barend van Orley.** Other paintings in church are by **Anthony van Dyck, Gerard David, Pieter Pourbus.** In the North Ambulatory you can see the gothic 1474 oratory of the Gruuthuse. The ornate north portal (1465), one of the oldest preserved parts of Our Lady, known as **Paradise Porch,** has been restored and used as a baptismal chapel. Weekend church services Sat. 5 & 7 p.m., Sun. 9 & 11 a.m., 6:30 p.m.

Memling Museum/Sint-Jans Hospitaal • *Mariastraat 38; April 1– Sept. 30, daily, 9:30 a.m.–noon, 2–6 p.m., Oct. 1–Mar. 31. 10 a.m.– noon p.m., 2–5 p.m., closed Wed.* • Across the street from the Church of Our Lady is Sint-Jans Hospitaal, founded in 1118, one of the oldest hospitals in Europe, and longest operating at one site until it was relocated outside the town in 1965. The beautiful, spacious old hospital ward brick buildings, largely from the 13th and 14th centuries, are expected to be used as an art exhibition center, with studio, shop, and cafeteria, in the future. The hospital, which welcomed pilgrims, orphans, soldiers, and the sick over the centuries, has many early medical instruments, fascinating pieces of early furniture such as an 18th-century "carrying chair" with handles, a pedestrian ambulance. You'll be rewarded for spending time with the apothecary to the paintings.

But set apart, in the former chapel of the hospital, are the six sole but exceptional works of German-born but Bruges-developed Flemish primitive artist Hans Memling (c. 1435–1494) that make up his museum. One of the six, the "Ursala Shrine," actually is a series of six magnificent paintings itself, set in an intricate small Gothic Church-shaped reliquary. More like the miniatures in "The Book of Hours," they are scenes from Ursala's martyred life. The large triptych of the "Mystical Marriage of Saint Catherine," its wings extended fully for front and back views, is free-standing in the center of the chapel, with chairs for visitors who want to take advantage of the unique opportunity to be able to concentrate on so few wonderful works at one time. "The Lamentation over Christ Triptych" was commissioned by St. Jan's hospital brother Adrian Reyns. After the multi-panels pieces, it's a relief to study the single image in the "Portrait of a Woman Sibylla Sambetha," thought to be the daughter of Moreel, one of Memling's patrons. It is fascinating for its delicacy, and mere whisper of lace for the headpiece.

When you exit, turn right on **Mariastraat** and walk the short distance to the canal for a view of a wonderful exterior view of St. Jan's (this location has great photograph potential from cruise boats). If you continue straight on, you'll shortly see Wijngaardstraat on the right leading to the Begijnhof.

Begijnhof/Beguinage • *Wijngaardstraat, to Minnewater bridge and entrance gate* • is one of Bruges' most memorable spots. **Winston Churchill** was so captivated by the sight of the Begijnhof with spring daffodils in bloom that he recorded it in a watercolor (reprinted on postcards for sale in town). Since the last Begijn died here in 1930 (the first came in 1245), the Begijnhof has been in the loving care of Benedictine nuns, which you may see strolling in traditional black-robed, flowing white-headclothed 15th-century style vestments. They are quietly impressive figures as they walk across the paths to the white-washed buildings of their lovely private world. Part of the Begijnhof's charm is its peacefulness, and, though thousands of tourists may be milling around just beyond the gate on a sunny weekend day in summer, within its precincts the request for quiet usually is respected. The central lawn is dotted with tall trees and parted here and there by paths, all open to the elements; the light and sky seem always to make a fresh, frequently dramatic, impression. The **Begijnhof church**, a triple-nave 13th-century gothic structure (though in rebuilding after a 1584 fire, it took on more Baroque lines), has multiple services most days: 6:15 a.m., 7:15 a.m.; noon, 5 p.m.; five services on Sun., one on Sat. at 5 p.m. (some have chanting and/or organ music; confirm times).

Beguine's House • *daily April 1–Sept. 30, Mon.–Sat., 9:30 a.m.–noon, 1:45–5:30 p.m., Sun. 10:45 a.m.–noon, 1:45–6 p.m.; Oct. 1–Mar. 31., Mon.–Sat. 10:30 a.m.–noon, 1:45–5 p.m., same Sun. hours as summer* • to the immediate left as you enter the Begijnhof via the bridge and gate off the Wijngaardplein, is a reconstruction of a 17th-century beguinal residence. The furnishings (among which is a fine oak Renaissance cupboard) and household effects provide a picture of the daily life of the Beguines. The typical Flemish kitchen has Dutch tiles (c. 1500) around the hearth and a biblical-scene tile tableux over the fireplace. Just beyond the Begijnhof is the *Minnewater* (Lake of Love), Bruges' former commercial dock, now turned poetic corner.

Sint Salvator Cathedral • *Sint Salvators Kerkhof; April 1–Sept. 30. Mon.–Sat. except closed Wed. 10 a.m.–noon, 2–5 p.m., Sun. & hol., 3–5 p.m.; Oct. 1–Mar. 31, Mon.–Sat., 2–5 p.m.* • This, the oldest parish church in Bruges, is essentially 13th-century Gothic, though the base of the West tower is c. 1200, with brickwork among the oldest in Belgium, and the nave from the 14th century, having been rebuilt after a fire. It became Bruges' cathedral in 1834, thus restoring the bishopric of Bruges, which had been abolished by Napoleon in 1802. The French, in fact, had demolished Bruges' previous cathedral, St.

Donatian, in 1799; of the surviving art treasures many were given to its successor. Sint Salvator is notable for its priceless 18th-century *Gobelin* and series of six *tapestries* from Brussels. The Baroque bronze, wood, and marble rood-screen features the "Creator" by **A. Quellin** (1682). Above the choir stalls, commissioned in 1430 on the occasion of the founding of the *Order of the Golden Fleece* in Bruges, are the escutcheons of the Knights of the Order which met here for the 13th Chapter in 1478. The **Cathedral Museum** *(April 1–Sept. 30, Mon.–Sat., 10 a.m.–noon, 2–5 p.m., Sun. & hols., 2–5 p.m.; Oct. 1–Mar. 31, Mon.–Sat., 2–5 p.m.; closed Wed. year-round, Sun. in winter)* was added as an annex in 1912. Of particular note among the paintings, carvings, and metalwork in the seven rooms is the triptych the "Martyrdom of St. Hippolytus" by **Dirk Bouts** and **Hugo van der Goes.** Cathedral services on the weekend are Sat. 4 & 6 p.m., Sun. 11:30 a.m. & 6 p.m.

Lace Museum/Kantcentrum • *Peperstraat 3, by Jeruzalem Church; year-round Mon.–Fri, 10 a.m.–noon, 2–6 p.m., Sat. 2–5 p.m., closed Sun., hols.* • Lace-making is a tradition in Bruges (see *Lace* section of *Decorative Arts and Traditional Crafts* at front of book). The fashion of trimming garments with lace (originally as collar protectors) meant that gold and silver threads were sometimes used in lace-making for the wealthy. The use of lace in fashion began in the 15th century and reached its height under the hands of Bruges women in the 17th century. On display is bobbin lace made as long ago as the 17th century (a copy of **Vermeer**'s "Kantwerkster" (Lacemaker) from that period is on the wall, as well as copies of other 16th- and 17th-century Flemish and Dutch paintings that show fine lace fashion details). Visitors see many lace patterns, the most complicated of which required 250 bobbins. Fully as interesting as the antique pieces is the modern lace in creative new patterns. The museum is located in the tastefully restored 15th-century almshouses of the Jeruzalem Church, still privately owned by the Adornes family. Since the lace museum here has less extensive displays than those at the **Gruuthuse Museum,** perhaps the major reason for seeking out the center is to observe the women learning and working at bobbin lace-making on their lap cushions. The interesting, interactive experience is available afternoons only. The center has a small shop with lace-making supplies and small framed pieces for sale.

Folklore Museum/Museum voor Volkskunde • *Rolweg 40; April 1–Sept. 30, daily, 10 a.m.–noon, 2–5:30 p.m., Oct. 1–Mar., 10 a.m.–noon, 2–4:30 p.m., closed Tues. and early Jan.–early Feb.; descriptive details in Dutch only* • Local folklore museums, as you probably know by now, are popular in the Benelux, but, among the many, Bruges' ranks as one of the best. The attractive museum is in a row of cottage-like buildings surrounding a garden that are set up as a series of old shops: a Flemish version of a general store; pipe, hat, and bootmakers shops; a chocolatier with marvelous old chocolate and cookies molds; and a schoolroom. An authentic old cafe (**De Zwarte Kat/The Black Cat**) serves drinks during opening hours.

Not far from the Lace and Folk museums are three windmills perched picturesquely on Bruges' grassy ramparts (with walking/cycling paths) where, in the 13th and 14th centuries, medieval fortifications encircled the city. The 1770 **Sint-Janshuysmolen** *(Rolweg; May 1–Sept. 30, 10 a.m.–noon, 2–5:30 p.m., closed rest of year),* a so-called stilt-windmill, is in working order and in summer when there's sufficient wind, the vanes turn at full speed. Also standing beside the canal which nearly encloses the old central city is the **Kruispoort** (1402), a fortified gate built in unusual white sand-lime bricks. Nearby, you can pick up the canal-side path to Damme.

SHOPPING

Though a small piece of light-weight lace commands a heavy price (handmade, a four-inch square is a full day's production), it's big business in Bruges. Many shop windows are filled with lace for sale, and the product is pretty enough to counter the commercialism. If you're a potential buyer, you'll want to know where you can get what you're paying for, especially if you decide to splurge on handmade lace, as opposed to the Hong Kong machine-made variety sold in many shops. Pieces range from postcard-size scenes to bridal veils to huge tablecloths, and some shops also sell antique lace (about the only way today to get a piece of Bruges' famed Fairy Stitch). Look for shops posting the yellow **Quality Control** shield; they sell government-tested and inspected lace, thereby offering consumer protection and knowledgeable advice. Among Bruges' **Quality Control** shops are **Bobbin Lace Palace** *(Breidelstraat 20; 33.08.93),* **Duchesse** *(Breidelstraat 4),* **Melissa** *(Katelijnestraat 38; 33.45.32),* and **Het Zwanenspel** *(Jozef Suveestraat 29; 34.04.17).* Family-operated **Rococo** *(Wollestraat 9)* is the largest lace shop in Bruges, in a two-story 1892 building with a beautiful *art nouveau/jugendstil* interior. Most of these shops are open seven days a week in the tourist season, accept major credit cards, and advise on tax-free export purchases; at one or more you may be able to see a demonstration of lace-making (otherwise, visit the **Lace Museum/Kantcentrum,** see under *What to See and Do).* Note: Brugean Quality is *not* the same quality-control government organization.

In a different tradition, visit **Classics Kunstatelier** *(Oude Burgstraat 32),* in a 15th-century building near Simon Stevinplein, which has a huge display (up to 250 pieces) of Flemish and Brugean tapestries and other wall hangings, and other decorative art. Bruges **carillon recordings** are for sale at the information desk at the base of the Belfry.

ACCOMMODATIONS..........................

All hotels included below are located within canal-enclosed historic Bruges. The Tourist Office has a list of bed-and-breakfast establishments and can make recommendations. Although restaurants are not a rule in Bruges hotels, those in several are among the finest dining establishments in the city; for simplicity's sake, I have included details with the hotel listing.

Deluxe
★★★★★ **Holiday Inn Crowne Plaza** • *Burg 10; 34.58.34, in U.S. and Canada 800-465-4329, fax 31.23.93* • This recently opened 96-room hotel, located on Bruges' most architecturally outstanding square, has an essentially modern brick facade of controversial but carefully-overseen design meant to match neighboring buildings in scale and materials. All guestrooms have TV, telephone, individually controlled AC, double-glazing on windows, minibar, hair dryer, trouser press; some non-smoking rooms are available. There's a restaurant, coffeeshop with outside terrace, lobby bar, and 16-hour room service. Some space in the cellar has been set aside to show the foundations of the 9th-century St. Donatian church that once existed on the site before it was destroyed by the French in the later 1700s.

★★★★ **De Tuilerieen** • *Dijver 7; 34.36.91, fax 34.04.00* • Located on the canaled Dijver, this luxurious hotel was created several years ago in an elegant townhouse whose dignity has been preserved but updated. The black and white marble-floored entry hall and stately chandeliered lobby with delicious plasterwork detail prepare one for the comfort found in the 25 country home style guestrooms, all with bath, TV, telephone, minibar. Under a glass shell behind the hotel are a swimming pool, Jacuzzi, sauna, solarium. Breakfast buffet included; bar; parking.

First Class
★★★★ **Oud Huis Amsterdam** • *Spiegelrei 3; 34.18.10, fax 33.88.91* • These two restored 16th-century former "gentlemen's houses" with full canal frontage offer an owner-overseen oasis just a short walk from the Markt. Each of the 22 antique and old print-decorated guestrooms is furnished individually, all have remote-control TV (placed pleasantly out of view in wardrobe cupboards), telephone, modern bath (some with whirlpool), hand-held shower; there's turn-down service with

a praline on your pillow. Breakfast (only, included) is served overlooking Spiegelrei canal, drinks in the warm wood-panelled bar with fireplace and Cordoba-leather covered walls. There's a terrace with tables in the quiet back courtyard, and a garden (which back bedrooms look on to) with a surprising sculpture. Friendly, superior service from reception, including free horse-drawn carriage ride from/to dinner at the family's excellent **'t Bourgoensche Cruyce** restaurant/hotel (listed under *Accommodations*) from April–Sept. Some rooms at moderate rate. Elevator; limited on-street parking.

★★★★ **Die Swaene** • *Steenhouwersdijk 1; 34.27.98, fax 33.66.74* • There's a home-like atmosphere to this fastidiously operated family hotel, created from three adjoining 15–17th-century houses on a particularly picturesque stretch of canal. The hotel is so central that by day cruise boats and horse-drawn carriages pass the front door, but by night its quaint corner of old Bruges is as quiet as you could want. There's a garden for pre-dinner drinks and a tapestry-hung lounge upstairs for after-dinner coffee. Hallways are filled with an eclectic collection of paintings and statues, and the cozy front lobby has English-language newspapers. The 24 guestrooms are comfortably and individually furnished, most with antiques; many face the canal, all have bath/shower, TV, telephone, minibar. Buffet breakfast included; elevator; major credit cards. The in-house **Die Swaene Restaurant** *(closed Wed., Thurs. night; expensive,* menus *moderate)* sets a table fit for its superb service and celebrated continental cuisine. Specialties include fresh fish, its in-house foie gras, and homemade sorbet, served between courses, served on Belle Epoque china, with soft classical music and candlelight.

★★★ **De Orangerie** • *Karthuizerinnenstraat 10; 34.16.49, fax 33.30.16* • Situated in a 1680s former monastery and mansion, De Orangerie is filled with fine old details such as plasterwork, stained-glass windows, stone floors, but, most of all, it's garden-like, from the rattan furniture, greenery-covered trellises, and skylighted green-and-white painted halls. The lovely public rooms, with a surprising mix of old Flemish furniture with good copies of contemporary paintings by Belgian artist Paul Delvaux, face on to a canal. Only guests can enjoy the hotel's canalside terrace cafe. All 19 comfortable guestrooms have TV, telephone, bath, minibar, hair dryer; some have windows that open over the canal, others face the interior garden courtyard. Breakfast (only) included; bar; elevator; major credit cards.

Moderate

★★★★ **Pandhotel** • *Pandreitje 16; 34.06.66, fax 34.05.56* • This owner-run 18th-century mansion-hotel, in the plane-tree shaded Pandreitje at the end of which is Bruges' most famous Belfry/canal view, has an intimate, tasteful interior with plenty of personal touches in the service. The classic decor in the entry/reception hall features crystal chandeliers, marble, oriental rugs, oil paintings, plants, and lots of architectural detail. The 24 uniquely decorated rooms have TV, telephone, clock-radio, minibar, bath, and hairdryer; six are specially designed luxury rooms. The comfortable lounge has newspapers, drink service during the day; a buffet (included) is served in the garden-like breakfast drawing-room. Elevator.

★★★ **Duc de Bourgoyne** • *Huidenvettersplein 12; 33.20.38, fax 34.40.37* • Long revered for its fine food, the guestrooms at the Duc de Bourgoyne shouldn't be ignored, especially since they share the same unsurpassed canalside setting in the center of Bruges for which the restaurant is noted. Of the 10 bedrooms in the 1648 building, 6 have water views; all are different in shape, size, and price. Guestroom decor, like the restaurant's, is dark wood and traditional; all rooms have bath with fixed shower head, telephone, TV; breakfast is included. No elevator; major credit cards accepted. The **Duc de Bourgoyne Restaurant** *(closed Sun. evening, Mon.; expensive,* menu *moderate)* has a lengthy listing of classic choices. Its large-windowed Rubenesque-decorated formal dining room overlooks one of Bruges' loveliest converging of canals, a setting that's illuminated at night, with the Belfry in view. Both the hotel and restaurant are closed for the months of Jan. and July.

★★★★ **Biskajer** • *Biskajerplein 4; 34.15.06, fax 34.39.11* • This quiet, modern-but-snug hotel is located on the lovely old Jan van Eyckplein which has a statue of the artist at the end of the Spiegelrei canal. Centrally located, just beyond city congestion, the 17 rooms in the three-story hotel are spacious and contemporary, with TV, telephone, radio, bath/shower. Buffet breakfast included. The hotel's restaurant (**Biskaje;** *Jan van Eyckplein 13; daily 9 a.m.–11 p.m. 33.01.40; inexpensive*), whose kitchen is open all day, specializes in spare ribs and *fish Biskaje;* there's a pleasant beam-ceiling interior and outside cafe with pleasant views.

★★ **Ter Brughe** • *Oost Gistelhof 2; 34.03.24* • This 20-double-room hotel is a 500-year-old restored protected monument building, once a patrician mansion and canalside warehouse. A friendly staff, which makes it more a house than a hotel, welcomes guests to the traditionally decorated lobby that features large paintings of the history of Bruges. All the modernly furnished rooms have tile bath, TV, telephone, mini-fridge; some on the top floor have ceiling beams. The handsome vaulted brick cellar where breakfast (only, included) is served has huge water-level warehouse doors that swing open to greet the swans that await their breakfast. No elevator; bar; major credit cards.

★★★★ **Academie** • *Wijngaardstraat 7; 33.22.66, fax 33.21.66* • Located near Bruges' peaceful Begijnhof, this imaginative modern hotel, created from an old brick-walled maltery, comes with high-tech details such as a personal hotel card that turns on the electricity in your room. Public rooms, restaurant, and bar, are situated around a central glass-domed courtyard. The 34 good-size rooms have basic, contemporary decor, with desk, small table, and chairs, TV, telephone, shower. There's a tavern in the old vaulted cellar. Breakfast and parking included.

Inexpensive

★★★ **Adornes** • *St.-Annarei 26; 34.13.36, fax 34.20.85* • With a three-canal-junction location in a residential area of old Bruges, away from but within walking distance of the Markt, this 20-room hotel is situated in three restored 17th-century gabled houses. The big-windowed, small lobby is decorated comfortably with leather couches and an antique-tapestry on the wall. Rooms (some on the small side; higher-priced ones on the top floor are larger and have exposed ceiling beams) have basic modern furniture, TV, telephone, clock-radio, desk, and small but cozy bathrooms with bath/hand-held shower, hair dryer. A buffet breakfast (only, included) is served in a cozy dining room. Elevator.

★★ **'t Bourgoensche Cruyce** • *Wollenstraat 41; 33.79.26, fax 33.88.91* • Although better known as a restaurant than a hotel, the 6 attractive (though not luxurious) antique-decorated rooms upstairs all have TV, telephone, bath/shower, and breakfast (included). The hotel is situated on a quiet courtyard a short distance from the Markt, and most rooms face a picturesque canal. The family-run hotel is *not* closed on the days its restaurant is. No parking; no elevator (but help with luggage); major credit cards. **Restaurant 't Bourgoensche Cruyce** *(open lunch and dinner, closed Tues., April–Sept., closed Sun. & Mon. lunch Oct.–Mar.; 33.79.26; expensive,* menu *moderate)* has a small ground floor canal-view dining room, with a few tables on a canalside courtyard terrace. It features gastronomic versions of regional specialties, with fresh in-season fare. Reserve as far ahead as possible.

★★ **Egmond** • *Minnewater 15; 34.14.45* • A bit basic and old-fashioned, this family-run hotel, in a 300-year-old former manor house in a quiet park setting a short distance from the bustle of the shops by the Begijnhof, offers details such as antique reproduction furniture and tiled fireplaces in some of the 9 rooms (all of which have views on the park, TV, telephone, bath). The breakfast (only, included) room also looks onto the park, a section of the grassy former ramparts that ring Bruges. Next door in the park is **Kasteel Minnewater,** a terrace cafe/restaurant that overlooks the Lake of Love. Free parking; major credit cards; no elevator, but most rooms are on the ground floor.

RESTAURANTS................................

In a country celebrated for its food, Bruges is second only to Brussels for pride of palate. Reservations are recommended for Bruges's better restaurants, a category that certainly includes **Vasquez** *(Zilverstraat 38; daily lunch, dinner, closed Wed. and Thurs. lunch; 34.08.45; expensive),* whose adventurously classical gastronomic cuisine (not *nouvelle,* but unusual pairings and seasoning of traditional fresh local foods) is served in the elegant surroundings of a 15th-century emmissary of Isabella of Portugal. **De Zilveren Pauw** *(Zilverstraat 41; closed Tues. evening, Wed.; 33.55.66; moderate),* a small 13th-century house originally used by traveling monks now with an art nouveau decor including a stunning 20-foot stained-glass ceiling, and garden terrace, offers finely prepared regional specialties that should be lingered over. Located in the delightful sun-filtered leafy square just back from the Rozenhoedkaai is **Den Braamberg** *(Pandreitje 11; lunch and dinner, closed Sun. night, Thurs.; 33.73.70; moderate),* which serves fish and lamb specialties. In a discussion of some of Bruges' best restaurants (which includes those mentioned under the **Die Swaene, Duc de Bourgoyne,** and **'t Bourgoensche Cruyce** hotel listings), one must mention **De Snippe** *(Nieuwe Gentweg 53; closed Sun., Mon. lunch; 33.70.70; expensive)* even though it is located outside the old city. Here, *haute cuisine* (caviar mousse, scallops with truffles, wild duck) is offered in an 18th-century townhouse.

Since **De Visscherie** *(Vismarkt 8; closed Tues.; 33.02.12; moderate)* faces the fish market, you could hardly expect it to specialize in anything else, and it does it well, with a wide choice of fresh fare. Equally central, in a casual setting just off the Burg, **Breydel-De Coninck** *(Breidelstraat 24; open noon–9 p.m., closed Tues. dinner, Wed.; 33.97.46; inexpensive)* is *the* place in Bruges for mussels, served in enormous enameled pots until you "say when."

With its charming olde world interior, and canalside view similar to the expensive **Duc de Bourgoyne** next door, **'t Dreveken,** also known as **'t Huidevettershuis,** *(Huidenvettersplein 10–11; kitchen open noon–9:30 p.m., closed Tues.; 33.95.06; moderate)* is a great choice for regional specialties. With a less historic atmosphere, but certainly in the center of things is **Den Gouden Cop** *(Steenstraat 1; inexpensive),* one of about a dozen brasseries/terrace cafes that line two sides of the **Markt.**

It, and most of the others, offer a continuous service of soups, sandwiches, and snacks to a full meal during the day and evening. There's both outside and glassed-in dining with a view of town activity. **Restaurant Belfort** *(32 Markt; inexpensive)* is another pleasant, convenient cafe, with varied dishes that include such typical local fare as asparagus soup and Dutch herring.

Tea rooms, a name *Bruggelingen* employ, serve lighter dishes such as pancakes, snacks, and pastry, especially in the afternoon, though many also serve more substantial fare for lunch and dinner. In one of the most picturesque corners of Bruges, where the Groenerei crosses other canals, you can sit on the bricked terrace at **Uilenspiegel** *(Langestraat 2; inexpensive)* and sample a wide range of tasty snacks with a drink. At **Belle Epoque** *(Zuidzandstraat 43; daily from noon through dinner; 33.18.72; inexpensive to moderate)* there's a cozy yet chic feel to the *art nouveau* decor that accompanies the friendly service and imaginative menu (paté maison, croque monsieur, salads, waterzooi, scampi). **Bistrot De Serre** *(Simon Stevinplein 15; kitchen open daily 11 a.m.–9:15 p.m., closed Tues. year-round, Sun. Sept.–June; 34.22.31; inexpensive)* is tucked into a garden behind an attractive square halfway between the Begijnhof and the Markt. Dine indoors or at a marble-top table in the small garden on tasty casual fare—omelettes, salads, toast Hawaii (open-face toasted cheese and pineapple sandwich), soups—or rest from nearby shopping over a beer, wine, or coffee and a dessert crepe. Not far away is **'t Keteltje** *(Oude Burg 20; daily 11 a.m.–11 p.m., closed Thurs.; 33.29.79; inexpensive)*, where Belgian waffles and pancakes (25 varieties of sweet and savory) are a specialty.

If you're looking for a place for a drink with a view, you can't do better than **'t Klein Venetie** *(Braambergstraat 1; 10:30 a.m.–2 a.m., closed Tues. from 5:30 p.m., Wed.; 34.01.75; inexpensive)*, which offers one of the most pleasant views in Europe, across a confluence of canals, and along a converging line of gables, to the Belfry. For those who want to become better acquainted with *Belgium beer*, the helpful bar attendants at tiny **De Garre** *(tucked away at the end of the alley located between 12 and 14 Breidelstraat; 11 a.m.–1 a.m., last call accompanied by the playing of Bolero; closed Wed.)* can certainly begin your education. Courses in beer bartending are taught by the friendly owner of **'t Brugs Beertje** *(Kemelstraat 5; 4 p.m.–1 a.m.; closed Wed.)*, which serves the largest selection of beer in Bruges, more than 300 kinds. Under such conditions, the bartenders obviously have to be prepared to help you choose your Belgian brew.

ENTERTAINMENT AND EVENTS

Bruges offers one of the most extensive programs of **carillon concerts** in the Benelux. Thanks to the talent, energy, and enthusiasm of *stadsbeiaardier* (town carilloneur) **Aimé Lombaert,** more people get to hear a carillon here than perhaps anywhere else in the world. From June 15 to Sept. 30, hour-long concerts are played at 9 p.m. on Mon., Wed., and Sat.; from Oct. 1–June 14, afternoon concerts are played at 2:15 p.m. on Wed. and Sat. Sundays concerts are played at 2:15 p.m. year-round. For Bruggelingen, high points of the year are the 11 p.m. concerts played by Lomaert on Christmas Eve and New Year's Eve. The annual **Festival of Flanders** (July 25–Aug. 8, 1992) brings some of the continent's best classical music to Bruges in nightly competitions; the main event of the 1992 program is the 10th harpsichord competition. Booking is strongly recommended because of local popularity. In August 1992 Bruges will stage a **Festival on the Canals** on six different nights. Historic scenes and periods are recreated in costume, music, by over 500 performers in several squares, all illuminated, continuously from 9 p.m.–midnight. It's a spectacular show for spectators, but be forewarned of crowds.

The **Procession of the Holy Blood** (May 28 in 1992, May 20, 1993), held annually on Ascension Day, is the veneration of what is believed to be a drop or two of Christ's blood mixed with water washed from his crucified body, a relic brought to Bruges in the mid-13th century. The blood is in a rock-crystal phial which rests in a silver reliquary, presented to Bruges in 1611 by Archdukes of the Spanish Netherlands Isabella and Albert. After religious services in the morning in the **Basilica of the Holy Blood,** and a leisurely lunch break, the relic is carried through the streets accompanied by a costumed cast of thousands. The centuries-old tradition arose from the annual gathering of feudal lords and burghers 'round the relic to offer oaths of loyalty, and gradually evolved into a procession, with the magistrates and guilds of the city in full dress for the affair. The present religious-historical affair through the decorated streets of ancient Bruges includes tableaux (groups which perform episodes from the Bible), floats, and authentically-dressed groups recalling old city guilds, foreign merchants from Bruges 14th-century golden age, the entry into Bruges of the "Count of Flanders" and his richly-dressed retinue of courtesans, with cortege of choirs, banners, and musical instruments. Reserved grandstand tickets on procession route available from Tourist Office from Feb. 1.

IN THE AREA..................................

Damme • *Tourist information, Huis De Grote Sterre, Jacob van Maerlantstraat 3; Mon.–Fri. 9 a.m.–noon, 2–5 p.m., Sat. & Sun. 2–6 p.m.; 050/35.33.19; pop. 1,000)* • From its founding, Damme's history was inextricably linked with Bruges, both the flourishing and the fall. Damme's picturesque **Marktplein** shows typical Flemish gables, and a statue of 13th-century poet Jacob van Maerlant who was born here and would have witnessed his city's great growth. The elegant **Stadhuis** *(July 1– Sept. 15 daily 10 a.m.–noon, 4–6 p.m.)* whose elegant 15th-century Gothic facade is studded with statues of counts of Flanders; on the right are the figures of Duke of Burgundy Charles the Bold and English princess Margaret of York, who were married in 1468 in Damme (at St. John House, Kerkstraat 4). The original tower clock of the Stadhuis dates from 1459. Several spacious, impressive rooms usually are open inside.

RESTAURANTS **Die Drie Zilverren Kannen** *(Markt 9, Damme; 35.56.77; moderate)* offers fine Flemish dishes in a decor to match; it's wise to reserve. **Ter Kloeffe Bretoens Pannekoekhuis** *(Hoogstraat 1; closed Mon. evenings, Tues.; 050/35.41.24; inexpensive)* a less formal typical old beamed and tiled choice, serves savory and sweet Brittany crepes.

GHENT

Guidelines for Ghent

SIGHTS A first, and lasting, impression of Ghent (*Gent* in Flemish, *Gand* in French) is of marvelous medieval structures, whose sturdy stone facades reflect well in canal waters. Considering the monuments are mostly in shades of gray, city street scenes are amazingly vibrant. Prime sights are central, particularly the towers of **St. Bavo's Cathedral** (which contains the famed Van Eyck brothers' *The Adoration of the Mystique Lamb*), the **Belfry**, and **St. Nicolaas church**—the three almost aligned in the famous view of them from **St. Michiel's bridge**. The bridge spans Ghent's former harbor, from the **Graslei**, with its magnificent row of early 13th- to 16th-century buildings, to the **Korenlei**, from which it's a short scenic walk to the c. 1180 **Castle of the Counts**.

GETTING AROUND If you arrive by train at **St. Pieter's Station,** Tram 1 take 1.5 mi./2.5 km. from it to **Korenmarkt** in the center of historic Ghent (population 150,000). **Tourist Information** is in the close-by **Stadhuis**/Town Hall crypt. The bus, tram, trolley system (map available) covers the city well but, since Ghent's major sights are compactly located and its streets and squares warrant walking-speed appreciation, you're unlikely to make much use of it once you're in the center. **Sightseeing Line** offers a minibus tour (commentary in English on headset), and horse-drawn carriages are available in season. Canal cruises, while affording some attractive perspectives, are limited in their course; much of the route must be retraced since many canals no longer connect with each other due to early 20th-century filling in of some sections.

SHOPPING As the capital of East Flanders province, Ghent has long been the main market town for a large area. Major commercial streets include **Veldstraat,** which has department and larger stores, **Volderstraat** with smaller and smarter shops, and the surrounding Kouter, Nederkouter, Zonnestraat, and Brabantdam, which all attract their share of business. Ghent has many markets, the main ones being **Groentenmarkt** (food and general wares) Mon.–Sat. a.m., with artists' works Sun. a.m.; **Vrijdagmarkt** (new wares) Fri. 7 a.m.–1 p.m., Sat. 1 p.m.–6 p.m.; **Kouter** (flowers) daily 7 a.m.–1 p.m.; and **St. Michielsplein** (food) Sun. mornings.

ENTERTAINMENT AND EVENTS From late June–end of August, **carillon concerts** are played Saturdays 9–10 p.m. on the **Belfry**'s 53-bell (some Hemony-cast) instrument by town carilloneur Jos D'Hollander. In July and August, St. Bavo's offers **organ concerts** Thursdays at 8 p.m. Concerts are Ghent's main events in the annual Aug.–Oct. **Festival of Flanders;** St. Bavo's, the Stadhuis, and the old abbeys provide memorable settings (schedule available from the middle of May, call 25.77.80). Although staged only once every five years (next in 1995), *Floralia* is an internationally attended flower show that celebrates the beauty of the blooms that annually produce good business for Ghent. Northwest of the city, *begonias* (Belgium's national flower), *azaleas,* and *roses* are cultivated by colorful fields-full around **Lochristi** (6 mi./9 km.), the heart of the flower district, where at the end of every August there's a **Begonia Festival.**

ACCOMMODATIONS With the opening in the last few years of new properties in the center, Ghent now has a better selection of hotels handy for tourists. However, major trade fairs and exhibitions held several times yearly at the *Palace of the Floralia/Congressgebouw* can fill them with business travelers.

RESTAURANTS Ghent restaurants tend toward the traditional rather than the trendy, and you won't have trouble finding historic settings in which to sup and sip.

ARRIVING **St. Pieter's Station** has twice hourly service to/from Brussels and Bruges, more or less midway between which is Ghent. There's hourly service to Antwerp, to the northeast. Boat trains meeting North Sea ferries from England at either Ostend or Zeebrugge pass through Ghent on the way to Brussels. Ghent is served by regional/international motorways (the E17 and E40), and is approximately equidistant (36 mi./60 km.) from Antwerp, Brussels, Ostend, Tournai, and Lille (France).

TRAVEL TIPS Not that you wouldn't begin your visit at the tourist office anyway, but in Ghent it's particularly helpful since several city sights (the Cathedral, Stadhuis, and Cloth Hall with the multi-media *The Ghent Experience*) offer tours/screenings in English at set times, and it's worth knowing when in order to plan your touring.

Ghent in Context

Many travelers will be more interested in Ghent's prosperous past than in its prosperous present, particularly the *appearance* of that past. The 12th century is conjured up in the sight of the moated **Castle of the Counts,** which passes into the realm of fairy tales when floodlit at night. A castle probably was first built on the site by **Boudewijn (Baldwin, the Iron Arm),** who visited Ghent from Bruges about 867. (Settlement in the area began in the 7th century with two abbeys, *St. Bavo* and *St. Pieter,* the later buildings of both surviving today). Boudewijn's castle at the confluence of the *Lieve* and *Lys* rivers was originally built for defense against raids by Norsemen, who continued on up the *Scheldt* to Ghent after dropping in on Antwerp. But enlargements to this seat of the Counts of Flanders (of whom Boudewijn was the first) in the 11th and 12th centuries increasingly were made with an eye on managing the independently minded people in Ghent's cloth industry, which had come to prominence during the 12th century. The basic structure of the castle we see today was completed about 1180.

Ghent's river port was a necessity from the start of its cloth industry, due to the need to import wool from England. The **Graslei,** on the right bank of the Lys, and **Korenlei** on the left, formed the central harbor; the oldest building on the Graslei, the **Staple House** *(Spijker),* dates from c. 1200. Early in the 13th century Ghent supplemented its natural inland waterways with canals, one being dug to Bruges, from which, by way of the Zwin, there was access to the North Sea.

In the 13th century, with the cloth business flourishing, Ghent experienced continued expansion—at the end of the 13th century Ghent had a larger population than Paris—but also increased political unrest, a situation that would continue to shape the city's history. Difficulties arose between the increasingly ambitious textile citizen workers and the town's rich patricians (who generally remained loyal to their suzerain, the French king). Although the Counts of Flanders had granted a charter to Ghent in 1180, and added citizens' rights, such as in 1212 the election of town magistrates, heretofore appointed, since, the economic success generated by the burghers led to an even greater demand for independence. In 1302, a Ghent contingent of workers led by **Jan Borluut** joined other Flemish workers (mostly weavers, particularly from Bruges) in the *Battle of the Golden Spurs* (see *Belgium: An Historical Perspective*), a confrontation with French nobility which the workers won.

In 1338, when the Count of Flanders at the beginning of the Anglo-French *Hundred Years' War* sided with France (thereby threatening Ghent's cloth trade, which depended heavily upon English wool), **Jacob van Artevelde** (1287–1345), a patrician who supported the merchants, took over the leadership of Ghent to protect business, and made an independent alliance with English **King Edward III**. (Edward, at the beginning of the Hundred Years' War with the French, had declared *himself* king of France, a position Van Artevelde supported). In the course of the alliance, Edward visited Ghent and his third son, **John of Gaunt** (a form of *Ghent*), was born there to Queen Philippa (of Hainaut, in Wallonia) in St. Bavo Abbey in 1340. Both Ghent merchants and England's wool-growers prospered under the arrangement, but guildsmen, unsure of Van Artevelde's ambitions, murdered him in 1345. The Hundred Years' War continued with various players, including pro-French **Count of Flanders Louis de Malle** and Van Artevelde's son Philip, who lost his life when the French won the battle at Westrozebeke. Upon De Malle's death in 1384, because his daughter and only heir had married **Philip of Burgundy** (in Ghent's St. Bavo's Abbey), Ghent became a part of the duchy of Burgundy, and Flanders as a separate county ceased to exist.

From the middle of the 14th century, the cloth industry in Ghent (and elsewhere in Flanders) began to decline, mainly due to competition from the English, who themselves had begun making cloth from their wool. But the excellent reputation of the luxurious Ghent/Flemish cloth, which was exported throughout Europe and as far afield as North Africa and the Middle East, remained a reference point: **Geoffrey Chaucer** (c.1340–1400) in his *Canterbury Tales* spoke of the skill of the wife of Bath as surpassing that of the weavers of "Ipres and Gaunt." And, a century later, **Jan Van Eyck,** using the new oil paint medium, finally could show the texture of the brilliantly colored heavy cloth well enough in art works such as the *Ghent Altarpiece* that we can appreciate the quality of the famed Flemish product.

Throughout its existence Ghent has been a "fighting" town, striving for city and civilian rights; as a result, construction on buildings often was interrupted by unrest. Thus, though the city center is a veritable textbook of architectural styles from the 12th to the 20th century, several important structures begun centuries ago were completed only relatively recently. The **Cloth Hall,** started early in the 15th century, was not completed in its original design until the beginning of the 20th. In the case of the **Stadhuis,** construction, begun in the late 15th century, stretched into the 18th, with exterior statues added in the 19th; the result is one Renaissance facade, one late-Gothic, and assorted-era outside ornamentation.

Under the Burgundians, who took over rule near the end of the 14th century, Ghent workers didn't alter their fighting ways. In 1453, after a five-year revolt, a humiliating loss of privileges was imposed upon them by **Philip the Good.** In 1477, however, Gentenaars rebounded by holding Philip's granddaughter, **Mary of Burgundy,** captive until she signed the *Great Privilege* which conferred many rights back to the people. But Mary was killed in an accident soon after, and back came her widower, **Maximilian of Austria,** who as the first of the region's Hapsburg line of rulers, subdued Ghent again. The Netherlands-born Humanist **Erasmus** (c. 1466–1536), covered both positive and negative points about Gentenaars in his words: "I do not think that one could find in the whole of Christendom a town which could compare with Ghent as for its political organization or the nature of its people."

Because of their particularly impassioned positions on civil rights, Gentenaars, even more than in other medieval towns, treasured their **Belfry** (1321–1380), historically, a town's most important building since it served as a safe-deposit box for its charter and rights, as well as a bell tower from which to ring warnings of danger or celebration. In Ghent's Belfry hung a huge bell, around whose rim appeared the words: "My name is Roeland. When I clap there is fire. When I toll there is a storm in Flanders." Roeland itself became a player in the stormy year of 1540. By then, Emperor **Charles V,** Maximilian's grandson, who was born in Ghent in 1500, had become tired of his birthtown's belligerence. Angered at the disorder and defiance of the Gentenaars, Charles ordered the great 12,000-pound/6,000 kg. *Roeland* removed from the Belfry, a move of great symbolic significance. Then he dismantled the entire early defensive works of city (the 1491 medieval tower *Rabot* is all that survives). As a result, though he was the most famous person ever born in Ghent, Charles V was disliked there for much of his lifetime.

Although by the end of the 14th century, the cloth industry had been ruined in Flanders by English competition, Ghent shipping got a new source of revenue after 1500—partly as a result of the increasing prominence of Antwerp, with whom Ghent shared the Scheldt river—from the export of grain from France. Boatmen (whose guildhalls stand on the Graslei and Korenlei) replaced cloth makers as Ghent's most important workers. The addition of the 16th-century **Corn Merchant's House** and the **Free Boatmen's Guild Hall** (1500–1531) on the Graslei reflected the new times; the forwarding and carrying trade in grain enabled Ghent to weather the loss of the cloth industry (which the Flemish cloth towns of Ypres and Bruges did not do). By 1547, Ghent had cut a new canal (18.5 mi./30 km.) directly north to **Terneuzen** (now in Holland), on the *Westerscheldt,* the wide Scheldt estuary that leads into the North Sea. All was well until Ghent's port was effectively closed by Dutch demands for sole control of the Scheldt estuary in the 1648 agreement with the Spanish that settled the *Eighty Years' War.* Following the fate of Antwerp, whose port also was closed, Ghent remained in decline until 1795, when the French under **Napoleon Bonaparte,** then in control of the Netherlands north and south, reopened the Scheldt.

In 1814, during the six months of negotiations that preceded the signing of the **Treaty of Ghent** (see *Stadhuis* under *What To See and Do*) that ended the American-English War of 1812, U.S. participant **John Quincy Adams** lived in the city. It is said that Ghent was chosen as the site of the negotiations because of the luxury of its amenities. Which could be one reason why, the next year, **Louis XVIII** moved to Ghent in refuge during the *Hundred Days* from Napoleon's return to France following his escape from Elba until his final abdication after defeat in the Battle of Waterloo (March 15–June 28, 1815).

Under the *United Kingdom of the Netherlands,* which put Belgium and Holland together as a single country in the European realignment that followed Waterloo, Ghent fully regained the use of its port, and expanded her sea trade. With the encouragement of Dutch King Willem I, Ghent's Terneuzen canal was expanded in 1827 to handle seagoing vessels, an important development in the city's maritime history. Because of trade with the Dutch overseas colonies, Ghent remained faithful to the *House of Orange* during the *Belgian Revolution* of 1830, though it lost the business after Belgium achieved independence that year.

Although its impressive 12th-century textile trade had become history during the 14th century, in the early 19th century Ghent entrepreneurs, freed from the framework of guilds (Napoleon had disbanded them), turned again to textiles. The leaders of the thriving cotton mill business became known as "cotton barons." They became enamored of an aristocratic life style, buying titles, marrying into old families, beginning art collections, and building sumptuous town mansions. Fine French-style facades from the era still line **Jan Breydelstraat, Koningstraat, Kouter,** and **Veldstraat.**

An interesting tale of industrial espionage plays a prominent part in

Ghent's second textile success story. **Lieven Bauwens** (1769–1822), a tanner's son, and later burgomaster, single-handedly revolutionized the cotton industry in Ghent. In the year 1789, while living in Manchester, England, Bauwens managed to "come by" a copy of the plan for the **spinning jenny** power-loom, which, together with parts for an entire machine, he smuggled out of England hidden in sacks of coffee, as well as enticing two technicians to join him in Ghent. (The spinning jenny, consisting of a number of spindles turned by a common wheel worked by hand—the first machine on which a number of threads could be spun at once—was invented c. 1767 by **James Hargreaves,** a Lancashire, England, weaver). Back in Ghent, Bauwens immediately set up a factory featuring his new acquisition. Such was the spinning jenny's impact that in the single subsequent decade, Ghent employees in the cotton-spinning industry jumped from next-to-none to 10,000, many having to be housed in makeshift workers' camps. In England, Lieven Bauwens was sentenced to death in absentia and buried in effigy; in Ghent, he's honored with a statue on a square named for him near St. Bavo cathedral. Belgian historians gave some slight recompense to England by dubbing Ghent the "Manchester of the Continent." A sample of the smuggled spinning jenny is on exhibit at the **Castle of the Counts,** an appropriate location since the venerable structure was enlisted for duty as a cotton factory in the 19th century.

Ghent boomed in the industrial revolution, its population trebling from 1801 to 1900 (from 55,000 to 160,000). As the number of factories expanded, so did the squalid conditions of the workers. Historic buildings, as well as workers, were sacrificed to the industrial system. So was the Scheldt river, parts of which were covered, its main course diverted out of the center of Ghent. With the city sublimated to industry, its mass of workers pulled from the surrounding countryside and herded into squalid living conditions in back streets, it's little wonder that the socialist movement in Flanders began and became centered in Ghent. With the workers' movement related to the **Flemish Movement,** it was an achievement when, in 1930, the *University of Ghent* (which Willem, King of the United Netherlands had ordered established in 1817) finally became a Flemish-speaking institution.

After 1960, Ghent's economic future focused beyond textiles, on the chemical and steel industries, and, particularly, its port. In 1968 a new lock at Terneuzen made it possible for vessels as large as 60,000 tons to use the canal, and Ghent's tonnage has increased nearly ten times in the intervening years. The port is to be further expanded so that by the turn of the century ships of 125,000 tons will be able to discharge goods at its inland terminals. Ghent, Belgium's second port, has a different focus from the international outlook of its first, Antwerp, concentrating instead on incoming vessels that discharge cargoes to be channelled to the European hinterland by barge, road, and rail. Ghent's port provides 50,000 jobs (directly and indirectly) for its greater city population of 250,000.

While patently respecting their past, Gentenaars know that the city and its citizens have always been at their best when industry is doing well, which it is today. But never again, as in the 19th century, will Ghent neglect its historic gables at the expense of business. The medieval **Castle of the Counts** will never again have to house industry within its walls: the **Dienst Monumentenzorg en Stadsarcheologie** (city department for the care of buildings) will see to it.

GUIDEPOSTS
Telephone Code 091

Tourist Information	Crypt of Stadhuis (Town Hall; April 1–Oct. 31, Sun.–Thurs. 9 a.m.–8 p.m., Fri. & Sat., 9 a.m.–7 p.m.; Nov.–Mar., daily, 9 a.m.–5 p.m.; 24.15.55.
Trains	Main station **St. Pieter's** in SW of city, 1.5 mi./2.5 km from center.
Bus/Tram Info	30.41.95
Minibus Tours	**Sightseeing Line** minibus tours, departure from Belfry; schedule, reser. from Bruges office: 050/31.13.55.
Canal Cruises	**Bootjes van Gent,** open boats, Korenlei, 23.17.23; **Benelux,** open and covered boats, Graslei, 21.84.51; Easter to end Oct.
Post Office	Main office: Korenmarkt

WHAT TO SEE AND DO ....

Ghent's major sights are covered below more or less in order of their significance. Conveniently, the most important also are the most centrally located. From the end of April through Oct., and Fri. & Sat. the rest of the year, Ghent's historic buildings are illuminated nightly from 8 p.m. (or dark, which can be as late as 10 p.m. in June, July, and Aug., 9 p.m. in May, Sept.). This makes it difficult to see the impressively flood lit **Castle of the Counts, Graslei,** etc. unless you overnight in the city.

St. Bavo's Cathedral • *St. Baafs Plein; April 1–Sept. 30, Mon.–Sat., 9:30 a.m.–noon, 2–6 p.m., Sun. 1–6 p.m.; Oct. 1–Mar. 31, Mon.–Sat., 10:30 a.m.–noon, 2:30–4 p.m., Sun., 2–5 p.m.; admission fee of BF 30 includes crypt* • Relatively ordinary on the outside, St. Bavo's is anything but inside, with its admirable proportions and rich ornamentation. The Ghent-born future Emperor **Charles V** was christened here on March 7, 1500. Claiming first attention for most visitors to St. Bavo's, whose choir dates from the 13th century, nave and transepts from the 15th, is the world-famous medieval masterpiece by **Jan** and **Hubert van Eyck,** *The Adoration of the Mystical Lamb* (1432), a 24-panel polyptych also referred to as *The Ghent Altarpiece*. Recently, it has been restored and relocated within the church (a controversial move, many believing the naturally lighted Donors' Chapel where the altarpiece had been displayed for most of its more than five and a half centuries preferable to the artificial lighting at the new position). An improvement for viewers is that now, unlike in the past, they can walk at their own pace completely *around* the work, whose side panels are now extended out flat. Perhaps the profit from some of *your* travelers' checks helped American Express pay the bill for cleaning the 24 panels (12 paintings each on the front and back), and framing them under protective glass.

Famed in part because it represents a breakthrough in northern European painting style and technique (see *Art* under *The Benelux Cultural Legacy* at front of book) with its Flemish "primitive" realism, and very early use of oil mixed with pigments (which greatly heightened the color and texture possible), the *Altarpiece* generally is thought to have been designed by Hubert, the elder Van Eyck brother, in 1420. Hubert died in 1426 before he could contribute much to the execution of the altarretable; his brother Jan, considered the superior painter, completed the 24 panels by 1432. The wealthy childless donors of the work, Joos Vijd and his wife Elizabeth Borluut, appear in rich red robes on a panel beneath the "Annunciation." Jan van Eyck was honored in his lifetime for this and other paintings, being made both court painter and a member of the *Order of the Golden Fleece* by Duke of Burgundy Philip the Good.

The Adoration of the Mystical Lamb is a compilation of Christian, cultural, social, and physical science beliefs about the world at the time of its creation, and was conceived to assist the faithful by depicting graphically the hidden meaning of the Holy Mass. The center panel shows the slaughtered Lamb on the altar dripping blood into a cup; the panel above shows Christ sitting enthroned. Other panels show people from all walks in the world forming a community of praise and thanksgiving. The Van Eycks created over 300 distinct individual faces on the 24 panels, and more than 200 species of flowers, trees, and shrubs are readily identifiable due to their realistic detail. Panels showing music in the making recall the centuries-old sentiment that "singing is twice praying, playing is thrice praying."

If an intriguing past adds to a painting's allure, it's little wonder *The Mystical Lamb* is renowned. The 15th-century work had a first brush with destruction in the 1500s, when ultraconservative Calvinists came to St. Bavo's during the **Reformation's** *Iconoclasm* with the mutilation of art works and "graven images" on their mind; the altarpiece survived by being hidden high in the cathedral tower. During the Counter-Reformation, art collector Philip II wanted to acquire the painting for his collection, but in the end it was spared shipment to Spain. Hapsburg Holy Roman Emperor Joseph II, while ruler of the Austrian Netherlands (1765–1790), carried his modesty to the ridiculous degree of ordering the side-panel nude figures of *Adam* and *Eve* replaced with ones in which the parties were clothed in animal skins. (Adam and Eve were "unclothed" again after his death, and Joseph II's versions now hang near the west entrance). In 1795, French forces shipped all 24 panels to Paris; fortunately, after the 1815 defeat of Napoleon at Waterloo, they were returned to St. Bavo's. The Cathedral itself, having had copies made, sold the original side panels in 1816 to pay for church restoration. A British antique dealer acquired them, subsequently selling several to **Kaiser Willem I,** who spliced the double-sided panels so they could be displayed along a wall in **Berlin's Imperial Museum.** The nude Adam and Eve panels eventually were purchased in 1861 by **Brussels' Museum of Ancient Art,** which later returned them to St. Bavo's as part of a multi-national plan to reconstruct the masterpiece under its home roof. The 1919 *Treaty of Versailles* at the end of World War I ordered the panels that remained in Germany returned to Ghent, and in 1920 the whole work was once again set up in the cathedral.

Perhaps the strangest episode in the legend of the "Lamb" began the night of April 10, 1934, when the *Righteous Judges* and *John the Baptist* panels disappeared. Eventually, a ransom note for BF 1 million arrived, and "John" was recovered from a luggage locker in Brussels' Gare du Nord. But, to this day, the original "Judges" is missing, the only reference to it since being an inaudible whisper from a man on his death bed to his priest. The man, a once-wealthy Ghent burgher and former canon at St. Bavo's, admitted stealing the panels for ransom. But the priest could not make out the words of his final confession about the fate of the "Judges." In 1941, the panel was replaced by a copy made by artist **Jef Vanderveken,** who was so good at his job that, never wanting the copy to be mistaken for the original, included the features of the then Belgian king, Leopold III, in the piece.

After Belgium was occupied in 1940 in World War II, Nazi officer **Gehring** came to Ghent specifically to see *The Adoration of the Mystical Lamb.* He showed so much interest in the altarpiece that, after his visit, the Bishop had it hidden, and then smuggled out of Belgium to the town of Pau in unoccupied France. However, when the Nazis reached that region of France in 1942, they took possession and shipped it to a castle in German Bavaria. Near the end of the war, Hitler ordered it, and other religious art works, taken to a salt mine near Salzburg, Austria, on the pretense of protecting them from the approaching "atheistic" Russians who "would have blown them up." American Army soldiers in Austria at the end of the war stumbled across the stolen art. *The Mystic Lamb,* after restoration in Brussels, was joyously welcomed back to St. Bavo's, which proclaimed the occasion a feast day.

St. Bavo's has other important pieces, among which are four pillar-shaped *copper candlesticks* (at the tomb of Bishop Allamont, d. 1673) that bear the arms of England's Henry VIII, by whose order, and for whose tomb at St. George's Chapel at Windsor, they originally were created in 1530. They came into the hands of Oliver Cromwell, who sold them to a Bishop Triest, who presented them to St. Bavo's. In the *Rubens' Chapel* is Pieter Paul's monumental *Conversion of St. Bavo* (the saint's face is said to be a self-portrait of the artist), commissioned directly by the Cathedral in 1624. The striking mid-nave white-marble-entwined-with-dark-oak *pulpit* (**Laurent Delvaux,** 1741–1745) is a sculptural testament to old man Time, who is being awakened by a trumpet-tooting angel. The *Triptych of the Calvary* (1464) by **Justus van Gent** in the 12th-century Romanesque crypt is considered one of the church's finest treasures. St. Bavo's organ sports a sumptuous 1653 Baroque-style case. Outside, in a small square behind the Cathedral, is a bronze sculpture honoring the brothers Van Eyck, shown seated on a bench, their heads wreathed in laurel.

Gravensteen/Castle of the Counts • *Sint-Veerleplein; daily April 1–Sept. 30, 9 a.m.–5:15 p.m., from Oct. 1–Mar. 31 same hours but closed Mon.; 25.93.06; important elements identified in English* • This magnificent, almost unrivalled example of a feudal fortress of the Counts of Flanders, its massive medieval shape rising from the reflective waters of its moat, was built about 1180 by **Philip of Alsace,** following the style of crusaders' fortified castles in Syria. The counts' need for a castle was less for the protection of the town, and more for control over demanding citizen-workers in Ghent's rapidly expanding cloth industry. Gravensteen was, in fact, stormed by such individuals in 1302, during the period of the *Battle of the Golden Spurs,* and again in 1338 by weavers led by Jacob van Artevelde. In 1349, after occupation by 14 of his fellows, the Count of Flanders abandoned the undoubtedly dark and dreary Gravensteen for the airier gothic **Prinsenhof** (which no longer stands); from that time, the castle ended its military role, though retaining ceremonial functions. In subsequent centuries, it served as Mint and High Court of Justice (from which days as a prison date the extensive collection of painful-even-in-appearance torture instruments displayed in rooms throughout), before becoming in 1797 (until 1887) a cotton-spinning factory. Between 1894 and 1913 the Castle of the Counts was restored, and thereafter opened to the public. Although it's possible to find them closed due to more recent restoration, several rooms in the count's residence tower *(donjon)* usually are open. They include the vaulted *Audience Chamber* where for 300 years the Council of Flanders sat. From the *Upper Hall,* winding stairs lead to the roof, from which there's a fine view across Ghent. The *Great Hall* was the setting for a huge banquet for the seventh chapter meeting of the *Order of the Golden Fleece* given by Philip the Good in 1445. Parts of the 9th-century castle formerly on the site survive and can be seen in the *cellars* of the keep. When leaving the Gravensteen, go beyond its moat to the corner of Gewad and Burgstraat (across the street from **Hotel Gravensteen**) to see the 1559 Renaissance facade off the **House of the Crowned Heads,** which has portraits of all the Counts of Flanders from Boudewijn to Philip II.

Graslei • The Graslei is the site of the old port of Ghent (today, the departure point for cruises of the city's remaining canals). Easily identifiable midway (No. 15) along the row of impressive quayside buildings is **Spijker** or **Koornstapelhuis** (public grain warehouse), the oldest (c. 1200), also the plainest, in Romanesque style, where grain was held as customs duty payment in kind. Also a standout is the 1682 tiny **Tolhuisje** (little customs house). On **Korenlei,** opposite and from which there is a fine view of the Graslei with its buildings reflected in the water, the most elegant facade is No. 9, the former 16th-century brewery **De Zwaene** (the swan), on which medallions show swans swimming away from each other.

Vleeshuis/Meat Hall • *Groetenmarkt* • Built in 1406–1410, and restored in 1912, this long attractive structure of local sandstone included an indoor market for the sale of meat, butchers' guildhall and chapel, and small houses against the south facade where the poor could collect the bowels of slaughtered animals. Lying opposite on the Lys is the **Vishall/Fish Hall** *(Sint-Veerleplein 5),* the present a reconstruction after an 1872 fire. The monumental Baroque entrance gate has a sculpture of Neptune and allegorical figures representing the rivers Lys and Scheldt. Past the Vishall and Gravensteen is the lovely **Lievekaai,** a once-busy quay on the large turning-basin of the 13th-century canal (whose waters enclose the castle) that connected Ghent to the sea; today, its waters are a quiet romantic spot, lined with step-gabled houses and weeping willows.

Belfroi/Belfry • *Sint-Baafsplein; daily mid-March to mid-Nov. 10 a.m.–noon, 2–5:30 p.m.; elevator* • Begun in 1313, Ghent's medieval municipal tower, city symbol of power and autonomy, was finished in 1380, and topped off with a dragon-shaped weathercock. One of the purposes of a belfry was to safeguard town privileges or charters: Ghent's were secured in the *Secret* room under triple lock and key in a solid oak chest. The belfry was named for the bells hung there, which city watchmen would sound in appropriate alarm. In 1315, **Roeland** was cast as Ghent's stormbell; weighing 12,000 pounds, it is said to have taken seven strong men to swing Roeland enough to make it ring. Charles V, displeased with Ghent citizens' rebelliousness, had Roeland removed from the Belfry in 1540, though eventually it took up its position in the tower again. In 1659, town fathers melted Roeland down; the vast amount of metal thus produced enabled the famed Hemony brothers to cast a complete 37-bell carillon (those bells cast from the original Roeland still form the heart of Ghent's now-expanded carillon, considered one of the best in Belgium). The largest of the bells cast in 1659, Roeland's heir, rang the hour for Ghent's Belfry clock in its G-pitch. Today, it is exhibited on **Emile Braunplein** at the foot of the Belfry, having cracked in 1914 when the tower bells were being switched to electric power. The third **Roeland** to hang high in the tower was cast in 1984.

Adjoining the Belfry is the **Lakenhal/Cloth Hall,** where the 30-minute multi-media *The Ghent Experience* is shown (English language showings 10:50 a.m. & 3:20 p.m., but confirm times at Tourist Information next door). The artistic slide-show triptych, presented in a plush-seat theater, reveals the city's pleasing face while at the same time offering an historical perspective. The **Cloth Hall,** itself a symbol of Ghent's substantial success in the earliest days of Europe's textile industry, was begun in 1425, though, with fortunes changed, not completed until this century. Once serving as a place of assembly for wool and cloth merchants, the restored Gothic underground hall, divided into three aisles by 20 pillars, today is a restaurant (see *Restaurants, Raadskelder*).

Stadhuis/Town Hall • *corner of Botermarkt and Hoogpoort; guided visits in English Mon. to Fri. 4 p.m., meet at Tourist Information, Stadhuis crypt* • The Stadhuis facade shows several architectural styles: Flamboyant Gothic (by **Waghemakere** and **R. Keldermans**) fronts the Hoogpoort, a sober Renaissance style employed during the Calvinist period faces Botermarkt, with Baroque and Empire finally finishing the job in the 17th and 18th centuries. The spread-out construction, from 1321 to 1750, resulted in part from issue-oriented city conflicts. The interior, on view only on guided tours, is best noted for the **Pacificatiezaal,** the room in which the *Pacification of Ghent*—meant to restore order after the Reformation outrages between the Catholics and Protestants—was signed on December 8, 1576. The event is noted by a wall plaque; another announces that here for six months in 1814 meetings took place between England and the United States (represented by **John Quincy Adams**) to arrive at the terms for the *Treaty of Ghent* to end the War of 1812. A second name for the great wood-beamed, stained-glass-windowed room is the **Tribunal Hall,** since the **Court of Justice** sat here. The immense floor of 2,401 polished light-and-dark-toned stones is laid out in a *maze.* One of the punishments meted by the Court was "humiliation," which meant that in front of the 13 aldermen and other representatives, the guilty person had to make his way on his knees from one end of the room to the other, retracing his route if he wound up at a "dead-end" in the maze (the shortest successful route is 500 meters/0.3 mile). In the **Hall of Honors** hangs an impressive portrait of Vienna's Maria-Theresa in a gown made all of lace. The dress, made by orphan girls of Ghent, was a present to the Hapsburg Empress, who in turn presented Ghent with this painting of her wearing the impressive attire. The **Troonzaal** or Throne Room, a Gothic hall in which the Ghent City Council now meets, is hung with huge historic paintings.

Sint Niklaaskerk • The third of Ghent's trio of towers (the others being the Belfry and St. Bavo's) is atop **St. Niklaas** church (Korenmarkt), next to the Belfry. Built beginning in the 13th century, it is Belgium's best example of the Scheldt Gothic style. Since 1960 it has been undergoing extensive exterior restoration, and you may still find it closed to the public.

St. Niklaas is steps from one end of **St. Michiel's Bridge,** whose fixed version, though only dating from 1909, is Ghent's most monumental bridge, with a fine lantern and sculpture of St. Michiel midway across. On the far side of the bridge, which crosses the old harbor from the Graslei to the Korenlei, is the sober Brabantine Gothic **St. Michiel's Church.** Its tower cannot be included in Ghent's skyline lineup since it never was finished. The church, begun in 1440 from which date the church gets its spacious late-Gothic style, was officially completed otherwise in 1648. Among many paintings inside, the most noted is **Anthony van Dyck**'s "Crucifixion."

Vrijdagmarkt • This square still hosts the Friday market its name suggests, but from medieval times it also has been the center of political life in the city, serving as the setting for forums and foment for the tradesmen whose former guild houses front it. The dramatic bronze figure (1863) in the center is **Jacob van Artevelde,** who became a martyr in civilian confrontations in 1345. The turreted **Toreken** (1460) at the southeast corner was the Tanners Guild Hall, today a municipal building. A bell in the tower used to be rung to announce the opening of the market. Standing out among older facades is the monumental **Ons Huis,**

Socialistische Werkersvereneigingen (Our House, Socialist Workers Unions), built c. 1900 in the *art nouveau* style.

Just off the Vrijdagmarkt is **Mad Meg/Dulle Griet** (Groot Kanonplein). This 16-foot/5-meter 15th-century cannon of wrought iron, weighing 35,000 pounds/16,000 kg., used to shoot heavy stone balls with an ear-shattering sound. Today, Meg is silent, aimed across the peaceful, picturesque **Kraanlei**, whose canalfront houses, dating as far back as the Renaissance and featuring many ornamental details, drop straight into the water. At Kraanlei 63, in 18 beautifully restored 14th-century former almshouses is the **Museum of Folklore** (*daily April 1–Oct. 31, 9 a.m.–12:30 p.m., 1:30–5:30 p.m.; Nov. 1–Mar. 31, 10 a.m.–noon, 1–5 p.m., closed Mon.; condensed guide in English*). The series of rooms in the museum show how life was lived by typical Gentenaars, particularly craftspeople in the 19th century. Worth a look at from the outside even if you don't have time to delve around inside.

Museum voor Schoen Kunsten/Fine Arts Museum • *Nicolaas de Liemaeckereplein 3; daily, except Mon., 9 a.m.–12:30 p.m., 1:30–5:30 p.m.* • Many major Belgian and Dutch artists are represented in the broad-ranging collection that goes back to the Flemish primitives. Highlights include two works by **Hieronymus Bosch** (1474–1516), his name saint "St. Hieronymus" and the "Bearing of the Cross"; the "Stigmata of St. Francis of Assisi" by **Rubens;** and "The Village Lawyer" by **Pieter Breugel the Younger.** Also of interest are paintings from the 20th-century **School of St. Martens-Latem** (Latem is a suburb of Ghent), whose members include **Gustave De Smet** and **Jan Brusselsmans,** as well as several works by **James Ensor.**

Another museum which, like the Fine Arts Museum, is outside the old center of Ghent (in the region of St. Pieter's Station) but worth a visit if you have time is the **Bijlokemuseum** (*Godshuizenlaan 2; daily, except Mon., 9 a.m.–12:30 p.m., 1:30–5:30 p.m.*). One of Ghent's several ancient abbeys, this of the Cistercian sisters, it is notable especially for the beautiful brick Gothic facades of the 14th-century dormitory and refectory (with molded brick ornamentation). The interior of the house of the abbess has been reconstructed in authentic Ghent style. Its other name, the **Museum of Antiquities,** is rather a misnomer for its collections of every day items, weapons, porcelain, and Chinese art collection. The nearby **Abbey of St. Bavo** (*Gandastraat; daily, except Mon., 9 a.m.–12:30 p.m., 1:30–5:30 p.m.*) is most interesting for the building, a 12th-century Romanesque refectory and lavatory and ancient cloister, though a **Lapidary Museum** (with precious stones, mosaics, ornamental pavings and ancient architectural ornaments) has been located there since 1882. The Abbey was the site selected by Charles V for a citadel to be built to check the rebellious city after an insurrection against him in 1540; he destroyed the abbey church and used the domestic buildings as barracks. The fortress remained in use until the end of the 18th century, after which much of it was dismantled. The Abbey oversees the **Museum voor Sierkunst/Museum of Decorative Arts** *(Jan Breydelstraat 5; same days, hours as St. Bavo)* which occupies a 1754 former mansion of the De Coninck family, with fine period woodcarving, furniture, ceramics, etc.

ACCOMMODATIONS............................

All the properties included below are located in the center of historic Ghent. Since the *usual* overnight traveler to Ghent is business-oriented, inquire about special hotel rates and packages at weekends.

First Class
★★★★ **St. Jorishof (Cour Saint-Georges)** • *Botermarkt 2, B-9000; 24.24.24, fax 24.26.40* • A hostelry from its beginnings in 1228 (making it, some say, Europe's oldest hotel), St. Jorishof today sports a more modern, 16th-century, stepped-gable facade. Used as a guildhall by Ghent's *Crossbows* and by the *States-General of Flanders* for its meetings in the 15th-century, here on Feb. 11, 1477, **Mary of Burgundy** was forced to sign Ghent's *Great Privilege,* on which occasion the Lion of Flanders symbol was carved into the monumental mantlepiece of the balconied **Gothic Hall,** today one of Ghent's most popular restaurants (gastronomic fare, decor of stained-glass, dark wood). **Emperor Charles V,** born in Ghent in 1500, was a frequent guest at the hotel later in his life, and **Emperor Napoleon** stayed here in 1805. All 36 rooms, most of which are in a modern annex in the hotel's inner courtyard, have pleasant traditional decor, bath and/or shower and toilet, TV, telephone, automatic wake-up, and most have a minibar. Elevator; parking; major credit cards. Hotel closed last 3 weeks of July, 2 weeks beginning Christmas Day.

Moderate
★★★ **Hotel Gravensteen** • *Jan Breydelstraat 35, B-9000; 25.11.50, fax 25.18.50* • A friendly welcome awaits at the elegant marble entryway of this well-restored 1865 Second Empire–style mansion that once belonged to one of Ghent's textile merchants. It's located across from The Castle of the Counts, doors from the Decorative Arts museum, and a single attractive block from the Graslei. The 17 comfortable, contemporarily furnished rooms all have bath/shower, toilet, TV, telephone, minibar, and individual heat control; buffet breakfast (included) is served in a room facing the back garden. Ask for access to the hotel's topfloor *belvedere* that overlooks the Castle of the Counts, magically illu-

minated at night. Elevator; parking; major credit cards; year-round weekend rates, discounts during week Dec./Jan. & July/Aug.

★★★★ **Novotel Gent Centrum** • *Goudenleeuwplein 5; 24.22.30, fax 24.32.95* • This modern 117-room chain hotel, located by the Belfry, has been created behind a preserved 14th-century facade. The basic bedrooms have bath, TV, telephone, individually controlled heat. The hotel's public rooms are light and airy, and include a restaurant, garden terrace, and bar that's become a popular local meeting place. There's also a swimming pool, sauna. Parking; wheelchair access; night reception staff.

★★★ **Hotel Ibis** • *Limburgstraat 2, B-9000; 33.00.00, in U.S. & Can. 800-221-4542, fax 33.10.00* • This recent modern addition to Ghent's old center hotel stock is almost inexpensive and wonderfully situated a half-block from the cathedral, and an equal distance from a small canal. All 120 contemporary rooms come with bathroom, toilet, TV, telephone; a few are wheelchair-accessible. In the lobby are a restaurant (continental breakfast, included), bar, and flower-shop. Parking; major credit cards.

RESTAURANTS......................................

Waterzooi, a chicken or fish soup/stew with vegetables, is Ghent's foremost specialty, with *Gentse hutsepot*, a meat stew, and *stoverij*, steak and kidney flavored with beer, also readily available. *Rabbit* comes young and older: the first with prunes, the later as jugged hare. *Mokken*, a small round cake made of flour and syrup, is a local treat, as is almond-bread and rye bread with currants. A spicy Ghent tradition is *Tierenteyn*, a locally made (for 200 years) dijon-style mustard that's sold in a shop on Groetenmarkt.

Jan Breydel *(Jan Breydelstraat 10; 25.62.87; moderate),* just steps from the *Castle of the Counts,* offers relaxed garden-greenery elegance, showing good taste and a delicate touch in the decor as well as the cuisine. There's a priority on fresh ingredients, seafood, and regional specialties. At **Graaf van Egmond** *(St. Michielsplein 21; open daily; 25.07.27; moderate downstairs, inexpensive upstairs),* if you're lucky and get a table by the window, you'll enjoy a wonderful view of Ghent's famed towers and the *Graslei.* Downstairs in the delightful c. 1200 townhouse such Flemish dishes as *carbonnade flamande* (beef stew with beer) and, in season, sensational *asparagus à la flamande* are served. The grill upstairs—same view—offers simpler fare. **Het Coorn-

metershuys *(Graslei 12; open lunch through evening; 23.49.71; moderate; light lunch inexpensive)*, tucked upstairs behind a 14th-century facade on Ghent's gorgeous *Graslei,* serves Flemish specialties as well as other daily choices to the strains of classical music (music selections are also listed in the menu) in a room whose walls are decorated with musical instruments; in addition to full dinners and light lunches, pancakes, snacks, and pastries are served, so it makes a good refreshment stop even for coffee. With the name **Waterzooi** *(Sint-Veerleplein 2; closed Tues. evening, Wed.; 25.05.63; inexpensive)* this could be where you decide to try Ghent's celebrated fish (the original ingredient) or chicken (today, a well-established alternative) stew with vegetables; portions will please your palate and your purse. The **Raadskelder** *(Sint-Baafsplein; open daily 9:30 a.m.–1 a.m.; 25.43.34; inexpensive)* is the 15th-century vaulted cellar of the *Cloth Hall* that adjoins the Belfry; you can sit in church pews and pause over a cup of coffee or four-course tourist menu. It's large and caters to crowds (you could get caught with a busload of tourists), but the fare is fine and, since you're bound to pass it in your sightseeing, at least stick your head in and see the setting.

The **Patershol quarter,** located near the Castle of the Counts, as well as being an interesting district that retains a medieval street pattern and after long neglect now is being restored, also is a neighborhood known for its restaurants. Since many of the buildings in the area were small to begin with, so are the restaurants, and thus reservations are in order. **By der Wyzer er der Xot** *(Hertogstraat 8; noon–2:30 p.m., dinner from 6:30 p.m., closed Sun., Mon.; 23.42.30; moderate)* serves up its fish and meat dishes in three beamed rooms in this 17th century gabled brick corner house. **Valentijn** *(Rode Koningstraat 1; open noon–2:30 p.m., 7–9:30p.m., closed Sat. lunch, Sun., Mon.; 25.04.29; inexpensive, special seasonal monthly menu moderate)* includes traditional dishes (*waterzooi,* eels in green sauce) among its offerings to guests seated in the attractive brick-walled space. **Amadeus** *(Plotersgracht 8; daily 6 p.m.–midnight, Sun. from noon; 33.27.74; inexpensive),* which bills itself as a spare rib restaurant, is darkish and cozy, with lots of beveled glass, wood, and old tiles; tables are covered with red and white oilskin, but the napkins are cloth.

Ghent cafes with character include **Oud Middelhuis** *(Graslei 6),* which gives you a chance to step behind one of the Graslei's famous facades, this one from the 17th-century; some 300 beers (8 on tap) are listed as being available. In the c. 1439 setting of **De Dulle Griet** *(Vrijdagmarkt 50; daily noon–1 a.m.; 24.24.55; inexpensive)* only 250 sorts of beer are served, but that includes all of Belgium's Trappist and Abbey-produced brews, in a genuine pub setting: mugs hanging above the bar, kegs for tables. If you decide to dine (reservations suggested) there's a restaurant upstairs, with scenes of old Ghent on the walls, dark beams, and a view onto historic Vrijdagmarkt.

THE BELGIAN COAST

Belgium's 40-mile/65-km. North Sea coast, slanting northeast to southwest from Holland to France, lies entirely within the province of West Flanders. In the 12th and 13th centuries, much of it lay under water at high tide, and only in the 14th and 15th centuries did the Belgian coast take its current shape. The wide beaches (up to 2,000 ft/600 meters in some spots) at low tide attest to the flatness of the land, much of which is polder, kept dry by the extensive use of dikes. Perhaps surprisingly, Belgium's seaside towns are sunnier than those inland, even as nearby as Bruges. Many Belgians take summer holidays on their own beaches, but Germans, French, and the British join them; the Dutch are less likely to because of their own fine sandy shores in Zeeland, just up the coast. Despite its limited length, Belgium's North Sea coast has an unbroken string of resorts with piers, promenades, and seaside recreational opportunities, each with a different character that tends to pull in a compatible socio-economic crowd. Most summer visitors do not come to the Belgian coast for culture, but overseas travelers may be interested in the area's isolated but interesting artistic attractions. Of course, if you're suffering from a surfeit of fine art, you can find solace by putting sand between your toes during solitary walks on Belgium's firm beaches or soft dunes, knowing all the while that you're never far from a cool drink or fine meal along any of the shop and restaurant-lined seaside promenades.

Guidelines for the Belgian Coast

SIGHTS Many area attractions are scenic: sand dunes, broad beaches, nature reserves, sea, and, of course, the hoped-for accompaniment of sun. **De Panne,** southwest of which the beach stretches into France to **Dunkirk**/Dunkerque, is renowned for restaurants. Just north at **St. Idesbald** is the home and museum with the life-long works of Belgian Surrealist painter **Paul Delvaux.** Shrimp are big in **Oostduinkerke-aan-Zee,** where the now-only-for-tourists horseback fishermen work. The mid-coast *Queen of the Coast* **Ostend** retains something of its grand-dame air, still welcoming the passenger and car ferries from England that in the 19th century made it the most British beachhead in Belgium. Ostend fishermen maintain a fleet, fish auction, and market which adds color to the hotel and restaurant-lined waterfront; Ostend artist **James Ensor** left a studio in his house and works in the local museum. Continuing up the coast, **Da Haan** has an especially broad and safe swimming beach that's sought out by families with children, while **Blankenburge,** once a small fishing village, has become the liveliest location, especially popular with holiday makers who enjoy dancing and other night life. **Knokke-Heist** at the northeast end is by far the most fashionable resort on Belgium's coast, for its shops, galleries, and casino. Gambling's technically against Belgian law, but four casinos flourish on the coast: in addition to Knokke, at Ostend, Blankenburge, and Middelkerke; all have restaurants.

GETTING AROUND Knokke-Heist, Blankenburge, Zeebrugge, and Ostend are served by trains from Brussels through Bruges; otherwise, a car is necessary to explore the coast. Modern coastal trams are convenient if you have the time; there's half-hourly service in summer from Knokke via Zeebrugge to Ostend, and from Ostend to De Panne (approximately 70 minutes from Ostend to either end of the coast). As at beach resorts everywhere, the coastal road (not always in sight of the sea) can be crowded in summer. Cycle paths in dunes and walking paths in nature reserves are well-signposted.

SHOPPING Ostend is the main town on the Belgian coast, with the largest selection of stores. Upmarket boutiques and art galleries are found in **Knokke.** Shops in both Ostend and Knokke are open year-round, and many open on Sundays. Elsewhere one finds the usual resort and souvenir shops in-season, when they're often open seven days a week and closed completely out-of-season.

ENTERTAINMENT AND EVENTS Carrying on the tradition for the tourists, the **horseback shrimp fishers** appear about low tide in the morning (check exact time locally) at **Oostduinkerke-aan-Zee** in July and August on sturdy Brabant farm horses. (The tradition, it's said, began as early as the late 1400s, when farmers, needing to supplement meager earnings, put their horsepower to work dragging nets through the sea). At the **Knokke Casino,** concerts performed by internationally known entertainers and musical ensembles and exhibitions are frequent fare; in summer the **World Press Photo** exhibit and **Art Exhibition** featuring well-known and new talent make an annual appearance. **Ostend's casino** has varied entertainers and entertainment throughout the year.

ACCOMMODATIONS The most plentiful choice of better quality hotels is found in Knokke-Heist. Elsewhere along the coast are plenty of three-star properties, a sprinkling of two- and four-star hotels, and a number of *pensions;* many close out of season. In season, especially from late July to early September, when making a reservation be sure to establish whether accommodations are *en pension* (including payment for dinner in the hotel restaurant), and whether there's a minimum-length stay.

RESTAURANTS You can choose an eatery with confidence anywhere on the coast. In this resort area for food-loving Belgians, an establishment that didn't deliver much-better-than-decent dishes wouldn't be in business long. Naturally, fresh fish and seafood (especially the small North Sea "gray" shrimp and mussels) are specialties.

ARRIVING Passenger/car ferries and the speedier hovercraft sail a number of times daily around-the-clock and year-round between England's Channel port of Dover and Belgium's Ostend and Zeebrugge; somewhat less regular service sails from Folkestone, Felixstowe, and Hull.

IN THE AREA Inland from the southwest end of Belgium's coast, from De Panne via Veurne, is **Ypres/Ieper** (pronounced EE'pe) most remembered since World War I as the center of the muddy, bloody *battlefields of the Ieper Salient.* But, centuries earlier, Ypres (together with Bruges and Ghent) was famous as one of Flanders' fine cloth-making towns; its magnificent Flamboyant Gothic **Cloth Hall** (rebuilt to the original exterior design after being destroyed in the war) serves as a memorable reminder of the period.

TRAVEL TIPS Coastal towns are popular with Belgian and European summer holidaymakers and well-ahead reservations for the better hotel or pension properties in July and August are essential. Tourism information for the whole West Flanders coastal region can be had in Bruges from **Westtoerisme** (Kasteel Tillegem, 8200 Brugge, 050/38.02.96). Otherwise, visit the tourist centers in individual towns.

ON THE ROAD ....

By beginning a tour of Belgium's coast at its northern or "upper" end, you'll also be starting with the top socio-economic stretch of shore. **Knokke-Heist** is sign-posted on good roads from **Bruges,** the nearest major inland destination (10 mi./16 kms.). En route, take in the villages of **Damme** (see *In the Area* under *Bruges*) and **Oostkerke** if you want to see the picturesque character of white farmhouses and windmills, tree-lined canals, and big sky in this flat corner of the country.

Knokke-Heist

Tourist Information, Zeedijk, Lichttorenplein, Knokke; 050/60.16.16 • is part of a five-town community, the cultural and social centerpiece of which is the **Casino** *(Zeedijk 509).* Knokke—pronounced kuh-nock-kuh—Heist. Built in 1930 with touches of art deco, the Casino is wonderfully decorated with **Rene Magritte**'s *Le Domaine Enchante* murals (eight paintings reproduced in enormous enlargements) in the *Salle Magritte* dining room (weekly *gastronomic dinners*). Among the art exhibited elsewhere in the building are paintings by **Paul Delvaux** and a sculpture by **Niki de Saint-Phalle** in the lobby, where hangs a 2,000-light Venetian crystal chandelier, reputed to be the largest in Europe; just outside is the sculpture *Poet* by **Zadkine**. Though you needn't, if you'd like an occasion to dress to-the-hilt, an evening at Knokke's cosmopolitan casino can provide it. Knokke has 50-plus **art galleries** (in the latter part of the 19th century many painters settled here, the best known being Felicien Rops and Claude Lemonnier, which began to lend Knokke its aesthetic air), and branches of many of Brussels' most exclusive clothing and jewelry boutiques. Somewhere between self-conscious Knokke's fashionable beach-front promenade and its best shopping streets (**Lippenslaan, Kunstlaan,** and **Dumortierlaan,** is **Place m'as tu vu?** ("Did You See Me? Square").

       ACCOMMODATIONS ★★★★★ **La Reserve** • *Elizabethlaan 160, Knokke; 050/61.06.06; First Class* • The only five-star property on the coast, located directly across from the casino, a short walk to the seafront, La Reserve's 110 guestrooms share quarters in a large comfortable complex with the **Thalassa Center** *(050/60.06.12),* a health spa offering hot sea-mud baths and other saltwater treatments. The generous-size modern rooms with balconies and minibars have all the amenities associated with a luxury property, including free use of the health spa's fitness center (exercise equipment, sauna, seawater pool), a good restaurant, lounge bar, and tennis.

Het Zoute

The upper most of Knokke-Heist's five towns is Het Zoute, so exclusive that it borders only on the Het Zwin salt marsh nature reserve that extends to the Dutch border. (Over the border a car ferry at nearby Breskens quickly crosses the **Westerschelde** to **Vlissingen/Flushing** seaport in Dutch Zeeland). The *Zwin* marshes—all that's left of the waterway to the sea that centuries ago was Bruges' route to success—bloom in sea lavender in July and August (*reserve open daily April–Sept. 9 a.m.– 7 p.m., closed Oct.–March;* restaurant *Chalet du Zwin* at entrance; inquire about guided walks). You can climb high dunes for far-sighted views of the North Sea, or of flat polderland far across which steeples reveal unseen towns. Het Zoute actually is called *Le Zoute* by the nobility and ultra upperwardly mobile who frequent it (the French version of its name being far more fashionable, even among Flemings). Le Zoute, an enclave begun at the turn of the century under the design of German urbanist M. Stubben, remains a residential region where exterior building style (even of the petrol/gas station) is strictly overseen. The winding streets of Le Zoute are adorned with dazzling low-rise white-walled, red-roofed villas that offer obvious evidence of the taste, as well as the wealth, of the European jet-setters who reside within.

Ostend/Oostende

Tourist Information at Wapenplein 3; Easter period and late June–mid-Sept., daily, 9 a.m.–1 p.m., 2–8 p.m.; rest of year Mon.–Fri., 8 a.m.–noon, 1:45–5:45 p.m., Sat. 9 a.m.–noon, 2–5 p.m., closed Sun; 059/ 70.11.99; year-round pop. 80,000 • A fishing village from its founding in the 11th century, Ostend was granted approval to build a port in 1445 by Burgundian Philip the Good. During a three-year siege (1601–1604) by the Spanish, the dunes east of the town were pierced to flood the hinterland, the gully thereby created eventually being enlarged as a new harbor. The first passenger ferry sailed between Ostend and Dover in the English Channel in 1846, and Ostend remains Belgium's most important passenger port, with up to 16 daily crossings to/from Dover by ferry and jet foil in summer, at least eight in winter. Ostend still is "the most British resort" in the Benelux, and many come over the sea from England for a day of intensive shopping and eating. Their leading position in the Industrial Revolution is what first began to bring the British to Ostend in large numbers in the 19th century; workers in England were among the first "average people" to be given a paid annual holiday, and many took advantage of the Belgian/England ferry crossing to travel to the continent, at least as far as Ostend. (General tourism didn't develop for the Belgians themselves until the 1930s, when the government voted paid annual holidays for workers, and they could head to their own North Sea shore.)

Ostend's greatest glory came with its distinction as a **royal residence.** Leopold I first came to Ostend in 1834, and had a *rail line* built from Brussels to Ostend in 1838. The first *casino/kurzaal* opened in 1852. When Leopold II made the resort his summer home, and nobility and other royalty followed him there, Ostend became known as one of

Europe's most fashionable places. The turn-of-the-century *Belle Epoque* was its golden age; then classical buildings covered with rococo detail decorated the seafront, as did the elegantly outfitted ladies parading under parasols along the promenade. The *Wellington Race Course* and *thermal baths* added more allure. Ostend's climate in winter is milder than in much of northern Europe so the resort had year-round life, as it does today.

Heavily bombed in World War II, and rebuilt by short-sighted developers, Ostend today has few grand facades facing its promenade; modern buildings, some of controversial height, do so instead. Nevertheless, it's still grand to stroll the elevated **Albert I Promenade** that runs the 4 mi./6 km. length along Ostend's beaches, the most central of which is the **Grootstrand** (large beach), which lies between the **Thermae Palace Hotel** (next to the **Palais des Thermes** with its mineral and Turkish baths and other "cures") and **Ostend's Casino.** As well as gaming rooms (one with murals by **Paul Delvaux**), the Casino offers top live entertainers, opera, ballet, and concerts in a 1,700-seat hall and one of the city's best restaurants, **Fortuna** *(Kurzaal; 6:30 p.m.–1 a.m.; moderate; reservations 059/70.51.11)*, set on the upper floor near the action at the tables. The Albert Promenade continues southeast around a bend onto the **Visserskaai,** a favorite with seaside strollers for its atmosphere of fishing ships, fish stalls, and fish restaurants. Highly regarded locally is **Lusitania** *(Visserskaai 35; daily noon–3 p.m., 6–10 p.m.; 70.17.65; inexpensive/moderate)* where the tiny "gray" *North Sea shrimp* will be at their freshest. Moored in the old harbor is *Mercator,* a three-masted former training ship of the Belgian merchant fleet, now a museum.

James Ensorhuis • *June–Sept., daily, 10–noon, 2–5 p.m., closed Tues. and month of Oct.; from Nov. to May Sat. & Sun. only, 2–5 p.m.)* • Artist **James Ensor** (1860–1949), the son of an English father and Ostend mother, was born in this house and rarely traveled far from it during his lengthy life. Ensor's art left behind the *Impressionist* style he'd grown up with and settled on *Symbolism*. He became known for putting masks of the sort used in *Carnival* celebrations on the faces of his canvas-bound people, to indicate both the inner worlds of human fears and fantasies, and the falseness and hypocrisy of bourgeois society. For all his reclusiveness, rarely leaving Ostend for a single day, Ensor was an individual, a socialist, a blasphemer of religious doctrines; his 14-foot *Entry of Christ into Brussels* (1888) is a prime expression of his ideas. The "bad boy" of Ostend was a founder of (and surely must have named) the masked **Ball of the Dead Rat,** which remains one of the social Belgian carnival season's most social affairs. On the ground floor of Ensor's house is the reconstructed shop for shells and souvenirs previously kept by his aunt and uncle; the next floor has memorabilia connected with the artist and his times. The top story contains the studio where Ensor produced virtually all his works; the furniture, and views from the windows, are recognizable in many of his paintings.

None of Ensor's original art is on display at his house (though some of his favorite masks are), but his paintings, as well as drawings, can be seen at Ostend's **Museum voor Schone Kunsten/Fine Arts Museum** *(Wapenplein; daily 10 a.m.–noon, 2–5 p.m., closed Tues., Jan. 1, May 1, Dec. 25; 059/80.53.35)*. The collection concentrates on Flemish and international paintings of the 19th and 20th centuries. Another eminent Ostend artist, **Leon Spillaert** (1881–1946), also is well represented. The museum is part of the **Feest en Kultuur Paleis** (1958), which also contains the *Tourist Information office*. The building features a large clock with the signs of the zodiac, and a 49-bell carillon on which concerts are regularly given (inquire about schedule).

ACCOMMODATIONS ★★★★ **Andromeda** • *Albert I Promenade 60; 059/80.66.11; moderate* • Located right on the sea, next to the Casino, this 10-story, modern balconied building is Ostend's top hotel property, with a marble lobby, 90 comfortably furnished guestrooms, and breakfast included.

St.-Idesbald

Not far down the coast you can meet another Belgian artist at the **Paul Delvaux Museum** *(Kabouterweg 42, St. Idesbald; daily Easter–Sept. 10:30 a.m.–6:30 p.m., closed Mon., except open Mon. in July and Aug; open only weekends, hols. Oct.–Dec. 10:30 a.m.–4:30 p.m., closed Jan 1 to Easter; 058/51.29.71)*. Paul Delvaux (born in 1897), who feels the light is better by the sea, painted *surrealistic* canvases in this region for more than 40 years before putting up his brushes at about the age of 90. The museum, opened in 1985 and expanded in 1988, displays by far the largest number (perhaps 100) of the artist's works in the world. The earliest painting in the collection (which covers all of Delvaux's artistic periods) is the 1922 *Vue de la Gare du Quartier Leopold* (View of Leopold Quarter's Station), which shows he was already on the track of one of his recurring themes. Growing up in Brussels near that station, Delvaux always was highly interested in trains, and has used rail cars and stations in many paintings as a metaphor for life: are the trains arriving or leaving? Are stations lighted or dark? Are they empty? Cool, distant, white-skinned nude women people Delvaux's pictures, sometimes seated in trains, at other times in classical architectural settings where they stand showing as little emotion as a statue. Located in a residential neighborhood, the well-arranged museum also has a small shop with posters and catalogues, and a garden cafe.

De Panne

Tourist Information Gemeentehuis, Zeelaan • Situated in a dune "valley" or "pan" on a broad white beach that's a favored summer holiday resort for working and middle class families with children, De Panne seems an unlikely spot for visitors to discover close connections with both the world wars that scarred the 20th century. During **World War I,** Belgium's **King Albert I** and **Queen Elizabeth** lived in De Panne, serving along with the thousands of Allied soldiers stuck in the trenches around nearby **Ypres/Ieper** (see below) who clung, at a horrendously high cost, to this small, still-free, slice of land in western Belgium from 1914 to 1918. In De Panne, the "capital" of this unconquered corner of Belgium, King Albert and Queen Elizabeth lived for the duration at *Villa Maskens;* the queen tended wounded front-line soldiers in the seafront hotel *L'Ocean,* which was used as a field hospital.

Inland 4 mi./6 km. from De Panne is **Veurne/Furnes** *(Tourist Information, Grote Markt 29; 058/31.21.54),* in whose **Gerechtshof** (1613–1618), one of many 16th- and 17th-century Flemish Spanish-style buildings that rim the town's outstandingly attractive main square, the Belgian military maintained its headquarters during World War I. Just north of De Panne, in **Nieuwpoort,** a statue of King Albert commemorates the occasion in October 1914 when, via a network of locks, water-control expert **Hendrik Geeraert** (remembered by a sculpted bust) was able to flood the entire Yser river plain; this effectively halted the German offensive and, for better or worse, the Belgian and Allied army was able to entrench itself behind the Yser for the following four years.

A monument on De Panne's **Leopold I Esplanade**—which commemorates where, in 1831, newly independent Belgium's new King Leopold I first set foot on his subjects' soil—marks one of the spots where a retreating British Army in late May 1940 reached the beach. Most of it also eventually reached Britain, during the subsequently successful evacuation operation best-known by the name of the nearby French coastal town, **Dunkirk/Dunkerque.** Though many know Dunkirk's place in early World War II history, far fewer know that Belgium's **De Panne,** just 1 mi./2 kms. from the eastern French border on the North Sea, was just as much involved in the massive rescue operation. After the May 10, 1940, invasion of all three Benelux countries by the Nazis, a 340,000-soldier-strong British and Allied (largely French) army was landed on the continent, but soon it was overwhelmed. On May 28, Belgium's King Leopold III surrendered near Bruges, which meant that the Allies' northern flank was gone. Faced with the danger of being surrounded and cut off from the sea, and the knowledge that the Allied cause would be seriously, if not fatally, impaired if it were captured, the British Army ordered a retreat to the coast at Dunkirk, from which it hoped soldiers could get back to England. The Nazis quickly made Dunkirk harbor unusable to large ships through massive bombardment. A sea evacuation began as best it could, with soldiers wading out from the beaches to reach the smaller military ships that lay as close as possible off-shore.

A desperate appeal was sounded in England, with requests going out to every port, marina, and yacht club to send any boat available to the beaches between Dunkirk and De Panne. Hundreds of craft, tugboats, sailboats, motorboats, and lifeboats, many with Sunday sailors at the helm, came out of the English Channel and across the North Sea, converging on the French/Belgian border. Though the *Luftwaffe* did its worst, by June 3, the "Mosquito Armada," as it was dubbed, had evacuated 233,000 British and 112,500 other Allied troops—in an operation that British strategists once had hoped would save 50,000. **Winston Churchill** appeared before Parliament on June 4, 1940, to tell the amazing story; elated, he nevertheless warned, "We must be very careful not to assign to this deliverance the attributes of a victory. Wars are not won by evacuations."

IN THE AREA..............................

Ypres/Ieper/Wipers • *Tourist Information Stadhuis, Grote Markt; April 1–Sept. 30 Mon.–Fri. 9:00 a.m.–5:30 p.m., Sat., Sun., hols. 9:30 a.m.–5:30 p.m.; Oct. 1–March 31 Mon.–Sat. 9 a.m.–4:30 p.m., Sun. & hols. 11 a.m.–4:30 p.m.; 057/20.26.23; pop. 35,000* • "Hardly a man is now alive/Who remembers . . ." wrote Henry Wadsworth Longfellow, more than 80 years after Paul Revere's historic horseback ride on the eve of the beginning battle of the American Revolution. And so it is in Belgium nearly 80 years after World War I. Hardly a man is now alive who actually partook of the mud and the blood of battle around Ypres between 1914 and 1918, but the country, and the countryside itself, can't help remembering. Remembrance of soldiers past comes at one, or some, of the 170 military cemeteries that lie thickly around Ypres. It was a place that had the misfortune in October 1914 of being situated between the rivers Lys and Yser, a position that both the Allies and the Germans believed offered a last chance to break out of siege warfare.

As early as 1915, in the 1914–1918 "war to end war" in which he would die, **John McCrea** (1872–1918), an officer with the Royal *Canadian Medical Corps,* wrote in a poem published in *Punch* magazine on December 8:

"In Flanders fields the poppies blow
Between the crosses, row on row,

That mark our place; and in the sky
The larks, still bravely singing, fly
Scarce heard amid the guns below.

We are the dead. Short days ago
We lived, felt dawn, saw sunset glow,
Loved and were loved, and now we lie
In Flanders fields."

No countries know better than the Benelux that World War I was *not* the war to end war. Rather, it deteriorated into "The Great War and the Petty Peace," so-called in *The Outline of History* by H. G. Wells (1866–1946), who also wrote in that 1920 volume: "Human history becomes more and more a race between education and catastrophe."

A scorched tree-stump-strewn landscape, military divisions mired in mud, soldiers in sodden clothes, and four years of a physical and mental health-threatening routine of daily bombardment: This was the truth of trench warfare along the **Ypres Salient.** The water table on this part of Flanders lies only a few feet below ground level even in dry times, and, after rain, the bomb craters and trenches wound up with standing-water; survivors said that it always seemed to be raining. Men drowned in mud. **German General Erich Ludendorff** later wrote, "It was no longer life at all. It was mere unspeakable suffering."

The Salient was the name given to the arc-shaped Allied front rounding Ypres; it was an arena of battle that took the maximum toll and returned the minimal result of any in World War I. Once the Salient was established, it became a symbol that the Allies felt they must not lose: The British felt compelled to keep fighting because they'd paid so dearly so far; the French were forbidden by their military doctrine from any action other than fighting to the death; and the Belgians, of course, desperately desired to hold on to the tiny bit of free national territory that remained to them. On three occasions amid the endless months of entrapment in trenches actual battles broke out; at enormous cost, the Allies managed never to let their line break. During the first battle of Ypres (Oct. 19–Nov. 22, 1914), the Salient position was established. During the second battle (April 22–May 25, 1915), the Germans, on the defensive on the Western Front at the time, brought out their new gas weapon, which, on meteorological advice, was introduced on the Ypres Salient. Still widely known by the name *Ieperiet,* the **chlorine gas** came out of cylinders in a yellowish cloud; those it didn't kill often were impaired for life. The third battle (June 7–Nov. 4) involved valiant Allied marches through quagmires, but to no definitive end.

Located on the Grote Markt at Ypres is the **Cloth Hall,** on the first floor of which is the **Ypres Salient 1914–1918 Remembrance Museum** *(April 1–Nov. 15, 9:30 a.m.–noon, 1:30–5:30 p.m., open to groups* *on request rest of year; 057/20.26.26).* Comprehensive and professional—compared with the many small, more commercial ventures scattered around the Salient—the museum includes dioramas of the battlefront, a collection of trench signs, trench art, a mock-up of a section of trench, displays showing all aspects of action along the Salient, and a large model of the devastated town of Ypres as it lay after the war. A large collection of photographs taken before, during, and after the war do more than many exhibits to convey the terror and tedium of the trench warfare. They do little to glamorize the grim events of the four years that left half a million dead.

Ypres' **Cloth Hall,** originally built in 1260–1304, is one of the largest (the facade is 432 feet/132 meters long) and most beautiful civil Gothic buildings in Europe. Its enormous area, used for storing and selling cloth, testifies to the success of the town's trade in the 13th and 14th centuries (when it competed with Bruges and Ghent); the strong square **Belfry,** rising 230 feet/70 meters from the center of the hall, dominates the region. This splendid structure, situated on Ypres' attractive cobbled main square that's garnished with cafes, itself is an example of the mind-boggling expenditure of energy and resources that war demands. By 1918, historic, elegant Ypres had been reduced to *rubble,* a word that describes a level of destruction that most of us have never seen (and which the world did not see again until Dresden in World War II). At the end of World War I, it was said that a man on horseback could see straight across the city of Ypres. Some British proposed leaving post-war Ypres as a relic to the war there, building instead, a whole new city for its displaced populace somewhere else. But Ypres rebuilt its Cloth Hall, and Cathedral, and many other buildings, to their original design, stone by stone.

The stones of the reconstructed Cloth Hall at Ypres are monuments to the waste of war, as are the gravestones that fill silent fields in the surrounding countryside. Cemeteries are as much a part of the landscape as any natural feature in this area of Flanders. **Tyne Cot Cemetery,** at **Passendale/Paschendaele,** with 11,908 graves, mainly of British, Australians, and New Zealanders, and a long wall that bears the names of 34,957 British soldiers who were reported dead or missing after August 15, 1917, is the largest British war cemetery in the world—though it's only one of some 170 here in Flanders. **Vladslo,** a German military cemetery in the Praatbos, contains the gray, flush with the ground, gravestones of 25,638 men. One buried here is Peter Kollwitz, killed at the age of 17 on October 23, 1914. His mother, Berlin artist Kathe Kollwitz-Schmidt, produced a deeply touching two-piece sculpture of mourning parents for the carefully kept cemetery. Stones in many cemeteries in Flanders are marked only with the words: *A Soldier of the Great War.*

You can walk Ypres' main street to the **Menen Gate** (designed by

Sir Reginald Blomfield, 1927) at the end. Covering the huge stone arch are the chiselled names of Britain's 54,896 missing soldiers with no known grave. Every evening since the Gate was dedicated (except for the years of World War II), the **Last Post** has been played by two town buglers at 8:00 p.m., while police briefly halt the flow of traffic. The continued playing of the Last Post reinforces what a local man told me, "The War is still close here, still a sort of trauma." And how could it not be? One in three of the shells fired during World War I didn't explode at the time. In the decades since, more than a few unfortunate farmers have plowed up shells in their fields that turned out to be live; even today, one or two people a year die from ammunition fired in 1914–1918.

It's a surrealist switch from war to another event for which Ypres is known, the **Kattestoet/Cat Procession,** whose history may hark back to worries about witchcraft. It is said that, long ago, in the belief that black cats held the souls of witches, live black cats were periodically flung from the top of the **Ypres Cloth Hall** tower; since 1870, stuffed cloth cats have been substituted and the second Sunday each May occasion has added a parade and festivities. Another theory about the origin of the cat throwing, which is deeply rooted in Ypres history, is that it began with the early (13th century) days of the Cloth Hall, when woolen cloth ready for sale was stored in the upper story. In order to keep the damage from rats in the storehouse down, cats were brought in in the fall. In the spring, when the wool cloth had all been sold, the felines—which many people did believe represented evil spirits—were simply tossed out.

WALLONIA: AN INTRODUCTION

The southern, slightly larger half of Belgium is French-speaking Wallonia. Its 5,800 square miles comprise the provinces of Hainaut, Namur, Liege, and Luxembourg in their entirety. Wallonia also includes a good chunk of centrally located Brabant, Belgium's only province split by the *Language Frontier*. The name Wallonia derives from the *Wala,* romanized early Celtic inhabitants of the region—the northern reaches of Caesar's Gaul—whose development of the French language began in the days of the Roman occupation. Thus was established the beginnings of Belgium's linguistic/cultural border (to the north of which, in what became Flanders, there developed a Frankish influence and Germanic language base). Today's inhabitants refer to themselves as *les Wallons,* and the Flemish call them *de Walen.*

The preeminence of French in *both* regions that make up present-day Belgium dates from the 14th century, when the French Burgundians fought the Counts of Flanders and won supremacy in law and language. From that time until late in the 20th century in Belgium (and for many centuries in the courts of most European rulers, including the English), French was *the* language of politics, law, and culture. The status of the French language conferred what amounted to special treatment for Belgium's Walloons over the Flemish. The government of both populations was conducted solely *en français.* In the law courts it was the same, which meant that Flemings frequently were unable to understand the charges being brought against them. Perhaps most important of all, schools taught classes only in French, which tended to keep the Flemish uneducated and down on their small farms. Only as the Flemish Movement gathered strength in the late 19th century and into the 20th, has Belgium changed from an essentially single-language country to a bilingual one.

Long first in language, Wallonia takes a back seat to Flanders in terms of the interests of most foreign travelers. However, for visitors with time to see more of Belgium than its unfailingly fine Flemish art cities, Wallonia offers a number of choices. The French-speaking community has two historic, artistically and architecturally significant cities: **Tournai,** a Roman-era town and former Frankish capital at the western end of Wallonia, and **Liège,** a once esteemed and influential prince-bishopric, to the east. To a great extent, however, southern Belgium's charms are scenic, clustered in the wooded forests and rushing river gorges of the **Ardennes.**

The *Meuse, Sambre, Ourthe, and Semois* river valleys claim picturesque fortress towns: **Namur, Dinant, Huy,** and **Durbuy.** In the healthy outdoor surroundings it isn't surprising to find a spa, but Belgium's **Spa** was Europe's prototype. Castles (as old as **Bouillon,** whose owner mortgaged it to outfit a company for the *First Crusade* in A.D. 1096, and as elegant as the still-occupied **Beloeil,** seat of the princes of Ligne), abbeys (Orval's earliest ruins date from the 12th century), grand gardens (such as the many-fountained **Annevoie**), and gaping natural caves (as at **Han-sur-Lesse**) punctuate a rural driving route with interesting focal points.

Unlike Flanders's World War I sites around Ypres, Wallonia's battlefields shed light on World War II, especially at **Bastogne,** near the Luxembourg border. Bastogne was the center of the once-strategic, now primarily scenic, "bulge" of land in the Ardennes that gave name to Hitler's last desperate, doomed but destructive, campaign.

Steel and coal have given Wallonia prosperity in the past two centuries. Belgium's coal-field band extends into Flanders, but its south central region to the east of Charleroi in Wallonia is the **Pays Noir** (black country), where conical slag heaps are a lingering aspect of the countryside which, until the 1960s, was one of the world's premier coal-mining areas. Coal fired the Walloon economy, and also gave it iron and steel industries. The greatest development of the Belgian coal seams took place in the first half of the 19th century—the *Industrial Revolution* reached Wallonia before it arrived in either northern France or Germany's Ruhr valley, and well before the rest of continental Europe. Belgium led the way in Europe with its coal-pits, iron foundries, and rolling mills (such as the *Cockerill* works at Seraing). The technical advances and economic results achieved in Wallonia affected the development of the industry on the entire continent. Since it was an entrepreneur in an industry that admittedly produced pits of human misery in the 19th century, sociologists studied the social conditions of Wallonia's mining districts with considerable interest. Many artists were moved to put human faces to the industry, and only recently, the sculptor **Zadkine** created a monument to miners for the town of **Wasmes**.

Though he hadn't come to draw and paint its people, an as yet unself-defined Dutchman, **Vincent van Gogh,** arrived in 1878 at the age of 25 at the village of Wasmes in Belgium's **Borinage** region to work as a pastor-on-probation among the miners. Vincent, the son of a Protestant preacher, hadn't done well in two previous attempts (the second in Brussels) at formal training for the clergy, and thus went unsponsored on a small stipend from his father to the grim coal mining district, hoping to succeed there in the dispensation of care and compassion so that he might have the work assignment made formal. Van Gogh's letters from that period describe the immense heaps of coal at the entrance to the mines, the dunghills and ash heaps that made up the dreary landscape, and the miners: "thin and pale from fever, tired and emaciated, weatherbeaten and prematurely aged, the women as a whole faded and worn." He went underground to observe miners working in little cubicles "like the partitions in a crypt," and watched too-heavily laden children loading coal on horse-drawn carts. Vincent cared for the casualties of mine cave-ins and explosions, nursed victims of typhus and other diseases, and preached from the Bible.

Van Gogh thought he had found his life's work, and the Brussels missionary society also began to think so. He began to take the words of the New Testament literally: "Sell that thou hast, and give it to the poor." Vincent, turned evangelist, moved out of his comfortable rented room into a shack where he slept on the floor, gave away much of his clothing, used his undergarments as bandages for the injured, and let coal dust accumulate on his face to signify his identification with the begrimed miners. Some called him the "Christ of the Coal Mine." But his excessive zeal and hounding of local authorities and mine owners to improve the workers' conditions led to Vincent's dismissal.

Shortly thereafter, Vincent "disappeared" in the Borinage for about nine months; he never revealed how he fed and clothed himself during this period of emotional crisis, although he later referred to it as a "molting time." During it he made the decision to become an artist. At 27 years of age, beginning with sketches of the Belgian coal miners and their surroundings, Van Gogh plunged himself into the art work to which he would devote himself for the remaining ten years of his life.

Vincent's first studio was in the cottage of a Borinage coal miner, in a bedroom he shared with the miner's children. Commencing his self-education in what he described as a "rage of work," with art materials and prints to copy sent from Paris by his brother **Theo,** Van Gogh found his quarters so crowded and dark that he did most of his work outside, until the onset of autumn made that impossible. Finally leaving the Borinage in the fall of 1880, Vincent went to Brussels, where he spent the winter working at drawing until finances forced him to return to Holland. Van Gogh's time in the Borinage was seminal, though it should not be confused with his later period (1883–1885) of drawing and painting in the Dutch village of Nuenen (see *Nuenen* under *North Brabant* in *Southern Holland*), during which he also painted peasants and produced his first masterpiece, *The Potato Eaters.* His work in the Borinage led Vincent to write five years later (1885) in a letter to Theo: "Painting peasant life is a serious thing and I should reproach myself if I did not try to make pictures which will arouse serious thoughts." Clearly, something of his missionary spirit remained.

In the town of Wasmes where Van Gogh had lived was the *Marcasse mine,* the scene of so many disasters that scarcely a family in that Walloon community was unscathed by contact with it. After the most recent mining disaster, in 1960, tons of concrete were used to seal the shaft of Marcasse, closing what in some ways was a black chapter in Belgium's history. When, by the end of the 1960s, all the mines in Wallonia had been shut down due to the exhaustion of their earthy riches, the move threatened one of the *Black Country*'s major monuments. An industrial architectural triumph is celebrated in somewhat surreal fashion at the remarkable restored ruin known as **Grand Hornu.** *(rue Sainte–Louise 82; Mon.–Sat. March 1–Sept. 30 10 a.m.–noon, 2–6 p.m., Oct. 1–Feb. 28 10 a.m.–noon, 2–4 p.m.; closed Mon.; 065/77.07.12 or 065/38.23.95).* Built between 1820–1832, Hornu was designed by Bruno Renard and Henri de Gorge as a city where work and living space were to complement each other in one complex. This 19th-century urban "utopia" provided miners and their families with housing, schools, library, hospital, and theater, all situated around a great central square. Once the mines were closed, a wrecker's hammer awaited Hornu, since the government couldn't decide upon a future use for the site. But Borinage architect **Henri Guchez,** well known beyond the borders of Belgium, bought it and has saved Grand Hornu for posterity, describing it as not only a gem of industrial architecture, but a page of Walloon history. Today, restored and listed as an industrial archaeological site, the roofless main structure with its arches and columns is a temple to its time.

Wallonia, with its last coal mine closed, still remains a leader in steel, an industry centered largely around Liège. Though the steel industry passes through periodic slumps in the international marketplace, in 1991 Belgium's *Arbed SA* and *Cockerill Sambre SA* metal/steel companies placed 267th and 276th in the U.S. magazine *Forbes*'s list of the world's 500 largest non-American corporations. Nevertheless, there has been an overall turn in Belgium's industrial tide in favor of Flanders's preeminent North Sea ports, and the transportation infrastructure of connections from them deep into the continent.

There are compensations for the Walloons: Despite a considerably smaller population and a much weaker economy than Flanders, they can take pleasure in knowing that they pay much less than half of the national tax revenue that equally funds the country's two cultural communities. And it's a feather in Wallonia's hat that French-speakers continue to have an upper hand in cultural influence in Belgium's bilingual capital.

TOURNAI

Guidelines for Tournai

SIGHTS Tournai (Doornik in Flemish), with an urban population of 35,000, is dominated by its unique five-towered **Cathedral,** a 12th and 13th-century Romanesque/Gothic masterpiece that's the centerpiece for city orientation. Once Roman, and by the 5th century the capital for the Franks, Tournai's numerous historic sights are mostly situated in its southwest quarter, near the **Escaut (Scheldt)** river, crossed by the picturesque 13th-century **Pont des Trous,** from which there's a superb view of the city and cathedral towers. Tournai has Belgium's oldest **belfry** (c. 1200) and Europe's oldest **burgher houses** (12th century). Victor Horta's *art nouveau* art museum has paintings by Tournai-born, Flemish "primitive" school founding father **Robert Campin** *(The Mas-*

ter of Flemalle) and his pupil **Rogier de la Pasture/Rogier van der Weyden;** other museums show off fine old examples of the city's locally-produced sculpture, tapestries, and porcelain. Skillfully illuminated, the Cathedral seems to dominate the town center at night even more than during the day.

GETTING AROUND Tournai's rail station is at the northeast edge of the center city. It's more or less a straight line, and a bit over one mile/two kilometers, from the train station up Rue Royale and across the river to the Cathedral; if you have luggage or prefer to begin walking in the center (Cathedral/Belfry/Grand Place), from which other important sights are accessible by foot, take a taxi from the station. For a 45-minute overview of the city, the Tourist Office (across from the Belfry) has established a taxi route with English commentary cassette tape that the driver keeps in sync with sites; book at tourist office.

SHOPPING A principal city of the Belgian Walloon province of Hainaut, Tournai is a major shopping center, with outlets located principally in the pedestrian precinct around and to the southeast of **Place St-Pierre.** Open-air produce and general markets are held Saturdays on the Grand Place and Place St-Pierre 8 a.m.–1 p.m.; at that time there's also a flower market on Place Emile Janson, which abuts the Cathedral. A flea market takes place on Place St-Pierre Sun. 8 a.m.–1 p.m. The **Quai du Marché Poisson** along the river has assorted antique shops.

ENTERTAINMENT AND EVENTS **Carillon concerts** are played at 11:30 a.m. Sats. from June through Aug. in the Belfry; there are outside cafes at its base, but because of traffic you might hear the bells better from a bit farther away. Ask at the Tourist Office about Sunday afternoon concerts in the Cathedral in July & Aug., and Sunday morning concerts by Conservatory students from Nov.–March. Each second Sunday in June is Tournai's **Day of Four Processions,** which features just that. On the second Sunday in Sept. at 3 p.m. is the historic **Procession of the Plague,** which commemorates the deadly epidemic in the year 1090, and displays some of the Cathedral's priceless art treasures.

ACCOMMODATIONS Hotels in the old city with good standards of comfort and service are limited. Plan ahead if you anticipate overlapping with Tournai's trade fairs in April/May and Sept/Oct.

RESTAURANTS Tournai offers a reasonable selection of in-town restaurants serving appetizing food in appealing settings. Cuisine generally is French-influenced, with an emphasis on fresh Belgium ingredients such as endive, Ardennes ham, rabbit, and asparagus. Local sweets include plum tarts and *faluches* (butter and brown sugar cakes).

ARRIVING Direct trains from Brussels to Tournai (79 km./48 mi.) take about an hour. The city also has direct rail service from Liège and Lille (France, 26 km./16 mi.). Motorway access is via A 27.

IN THE AREA Some 16 mi./27 km. southeast of Tournai is **Chateau de Beloeil,** the largest of Belgium's 30-odd privately-owned castles (of which Belgium has one of Europe's richest legacies). The residence of the *princes de Ligne* since the 14th century, Beloeil's contents of 15th–19th-century furniture, portraits, tapestries, and objets d'art are on view to the public. The park is one of the finest in Belgium, attributed to **Le Notre,** who designed the gardens at Versailles.

Tournai in Context

Tournai's story spans two thousand years, covering periods as a Roman crossroads, capital of the Frankish empire, and an 11th and 12th-century bishopric that presided spiritually over a population of more than one million, including all of Flanders. Thereafter, Tournai was more closely tied to France, whose influence and flavor are felt today in this Walloon city noted for its art and architecture. The history of Tournai Cathedral, which always has been at the heart of the town both physically and philosophically, in many ways mirrors the history of the city itself.

A rustic Roman settlement a century before the birth of Christ, **Tornacum** became, in the course of Emperor Claudius's organization of Gaul between A.D. 41–54, a post on the road from Boulogne to Cologne. That road, in the Tournai countryside, cut through limestone hills, whose quarries would make Tournai wealthy. In A.D. 432, the Romans routed, Tournai was chosen as their residence by the Merovingian kings of the embryonic Frankish empire. **Clovis** is believed to have been born in Tournai c. 465, and his father Childeric died here in 482. Taking rule that year, Clovis remained in Tournai until near the end of the 5th century, when he moved the royal seat to Paris. Before his death in 511, Clovis compensated Tournai by making it an ecclesiastical capital of great authority, encompassing what would become Flanders (including Bruges, Ghent, and Ypres), and a great deal of France. Important civil powers were ceded to the citizens of Tournai (later to be vassals of the kings of France), which made the town virtually independent as ruled by its Bishop. About A.D. 501 Tournai native-son and bishop, **Eleutherus,** built the first of several churches on the site of the present Cathedral. Outside the early sacred structure Eluetherus was beaten to death by heretics c. 532; raised to sainthood, he was named patron saint of Tournai in 1064.

An enlarged cathedral replaced the early one about 850, but it was burned in 881 by Norsemen, who had sailed inland from the North Sea up the Scheldt. The cathedral was rebuilt with the resources of the Bishop, in whom were vested vast powers, including the coining of money, gathering of fines and taxes, functioning as the town's judicial and policing authority, the head in every way of Tournai's economic, social, intellectual, and political life. A fire in 1060 caused great damage to the cathedral but it was restored by the time Tournai, and all of Flanders and Brabant, was ravaged by a devasting plague.

The sick poured into the cathedral to pray for an end to the awful outbreak. After several seemingly miraculous cures, their numbers increased, and the statue of the Virgin before which they prayed became known as **Our Lady of the Sick.** On September 14, 1090, Tournai's bishop organized a procession, a sort of demonstration against the plague, to which crowds from Flanders and districts south of the Scheldt came, jostling their way through the old city and the cathedral for a whole week. (The week-long event immediately became annual, and one of the great pilgrimages of northern European Christendom. The procession itself, often led by a luminary, such as the Count of Flanders, is observed in Tournai to this day). The popularity of the Procession of the Plague led to the construction of the great cathedral we see in Tournai today.

The nave of a new and magnificent Romanesque cathedral was raised by 1171, with the transcept completed by the end of the 12th century. The building of a grand cathedral couldn't have happened at a better time. The 11th and 12th centuries were Tournai's golden age (a goldsmith, **Nicolas of Verdun,** produced what is widely considered to be the city's single most outstanding piece of art; see the *Shrine of Notre Dame* under the *Cathedral Treasury*). In addition to being excellent goldsmiths, craftsmen in Tournai were also known throughout Europe for their work in wood, ivory, and Tournai's famous "blue" stone. The blue stone is actually slate-colored, locally quarried limestone (and also called "Tournai marble"). When left rough for exterior work, it is gray, but when used for ornamental works and polished, it is black and shiny. It was well-known for both its building and carving qualities. Examples of the quality carving can be seen in the Cathedral today, but a large part of the work of its golden age *Tournaisienne*-style sculptors was mutilated during the religious troubles of the 16th century. In architecture, not only does the Cathedral, considered by many the most remarkable Romanesque basilica in Europe, show the heights achieved in 12th-century Tournai, but so do the Romanesque burghers' houses, the oldest, c. 1175, surviving in Europe.

During the 11th and 12th centuries, Tournai benefited from the economic expansion of Flanders, in part because of the Scheldt, which linked it to Ghent and the interior of France. Along the river, Tournai traded in Flemish wool and cloth, and in its own local stone. Power struggles arose with the kings of France, who wanted to bring Tournai under their rule in order to gain more direct control in Flanders and to strengthen their military position by holding the strategic crossing of the Scheldt at Tournai directly. In 1187, the French got their way, taking over rule of Tournai. With the French firmly established as the masters in Tournai, French styles and fashion became popular. In 1243, Bishop Walter de Marvis, under the influence of his frequent journeys in France, began to find the Romanesque style old-fashioned, and decided upon a makeover for his Cathedral in the more *a la mode* Gothic style being fostered in France. The Gothic conversion began with the Choir (modeled upon Amiens Cathedral), which was completed in 1255. Financial problems prevented re-styling the rest of the Cathedral, and the nave remained Romanesque, with Belgium's largest collection of 13th-century mural paintings.

Being under the rule of the French kings, to whom it remained loyal, Tournai supported France against England during the Hundred Years' War (1337–1453). The city gave early proof of its stance, withstanding a seige in 1340 by English King Edward III (who had declared himself King of France in 1337, a claim which Ghent and other places in Flanders supported because of their dependence upon English wool for the cloth trade). Its continued support of France during the succeeding 100 years led **Jeanne D'Arc** (1412–1431), the fervent French maiden who died at the stake, to refer to "the gentle, loyal Franks of Tournai" in 1429.

The Hundred Years' War didn't deter an awakening in art in the Netherlands in the late 14th and early 15th century, and Tournai produced an important pair of painters for the formative Flemish "primitive" style: **Robert Campin** (the "Master of Flemalle") and his pupil **Rogier van der Weyden.** The city's stone sculptors continued to be active in the 15th century, producing beautiful carved fonts in Tournai "marble" which remain revered art works in churches as far afield as England and Spain. During the 14th century, services in the Cathedral, served by 42 canons, 12 vicars, and some 50 chaplains, were sung continuously throughout the day from Matin to Compline, from which a remarkable school of singing developed. The manuscript still exists for the **Tournai Mass** (c. 1330), the oldest mass for three voices in existence.

Though the Hundred Years' War had ended, France and England seemed unable to keep uninvolved. England's recently crowned (1509) young King **Henry VIII,** still a Catholic at this point, agreed with the Pope and Maximilian in the 1513 *Treaty of Mechelen* to invade France. That year, Henry seized Tournai, and remained in the city for three weeks, during which he attended services in the Cathedral, and gave

Thomas Wolsey (later Cardinal Archbishop of York) the bishopric. Henry's forces used Tournai as a base, during which time the town was fortified (see *Tour Henry VIII* in *What to See and Do* below). With a treaty signed, Wolsey, in order to gain favor with them, sold Tournai back to the French in 1518. A mere three years later, Tournai fell under seige from the army of young Emperor Charles V, and was thus wrested from France within a month, thereafter becoming a province of the Spanish Netherlands.

The religious clashes of the Reformation left lasting scars on Tournai's stones. In an attempt to stop the spread of Calvinism, Charles V's son, Philip II, divided several large bishoprics into smaller ones. As a result, Tournai lost its dominion over Ghent, Bruges, and Ypres, which became independent bishoprics in 1559. The Calvinist rebellion made headway anyway, and, on August 24, 1566, extremists among the local Protestant population forced entry into the Cathedral and laid waste to its medieval art treasures. The iconoclastic struggle lasted until September 16 and, for the first year in nearly five centuries, Tournai's **Procession of the Plague** did not take place. Catholic Philip II contributed further to the devastation by confiscating goods from Protestant churches, burning many of the heretics along the way. With civil order restored, the repair of the Cathedral was undertaken. A commission was given to Cornelis Floris of Antwerp for a rood-screen to replace the Gothic one destroyed by the religious rioters. The impressive red marble and alabaster arch bridges the Cathedral's Romanesque nave and the Gothic Choir with the Renaissance style.

In 1653, works by unknown artists were unearthed in Tournai by a worker digging in the garden of the Church of St-Brice. His spade having accidentally broken into a tomb, the worker was astonished to find what contemporary reports indicate was a treasure not unlike King Tut's, located centuries later. What had been uncovered—the inscription *482 Childerici Regis* inside left no doubt—was the coffin of 5th-century Frankish King Childeric, founder of the Merovingian dynasty and the father of Clovis. His skeleton was wrapped in a robe decorated with hundreds of figures of bees—a symbol for royalty—in gold. In addition, countless coins of gold and silver bearing the image of Childeric, jewelry, and ornate weapons were found. Unfortunately, the items, sent out of the country by various foreign rulers, do not survive, having been subsequently stolen and/or melted down. But there's a better ending to the discovery in the late 1980s of an even earlier, 4th century, tomb near what had been a Roman necropolis in Tournai. The sarcophagus, on view in Tournai's **Museum of History and Archeology,** is adorned with unusually elaborate lateral carvings, which leads experts to believe it belonged to a person of importance. Because of its fragility, archeologists have not opened it for fear of damaging some of the exquisite decoration.

Though several times trying to throw off the Spanish yoke, Tournai remained part of the Southern Netherlands until French King **Louis XIV** captured it in 1667. Louis's influence is still felt in the town in domestic and military architecture, the latter in the form of fortifications built by Vauban. Under the *Treaty of Utrecht* (1713), Tournai was made a part of the Austrian Netherlands, which it remained until the 1792–1794 conquest of the Netherlands by post-Revolution French soldiers who wreaked devastation throughout Belgium. In Tournai, they destroyed art both in and outside the Cathedral, with the French government organizing an auction of all contents that could be carried away. The French army dismantled the five towers of the Cathedral, the symbol of the city, and spoke of demolishing the whole structure. Fortunately, they didn't follow through and Tournai's Bishop Francois-Joseph Hirn (1802–1819) committed himself to restoring and re-equipping the Cathedral. He successfully recovered **Nicolas of Verdun's golden reliquary** and that of St. Eluetherus, as well as tapestries and pieces of metal-work that had escaped destruction. Large-scale restoration of Tournai's sacred centerpiece was carried out in the 1840s.

Until 1940, Tournai was one of the best preserved towns in Belgium, with thousands of old houses dating mostly from the 17th and 18th centuries. But, in 1940, Nazi air raids flattened an estimated 60% of the city, including most of the Grand' Place (a model showing the devastation is in the **Musee de Folklore**), but not the city's c. 1200 **Belfry.** The Cathedral was hit by an incendiary bomb, which turned some art treasures into ashes before prisoners released from the local jail could put out the blaze. Fortunately, the five-towered Tournai landmark escaped serious structural damage. In a happier ending to the war, Tournai was the first Belgium town to be liberated by British troops, in September 1944. Today, the many remaining ancient monuments, and those that have been carefully restored, are plentiful enough by far to give travelers visiting Tournai the look and feeling of its distinguished history.

GUIDEPOSTS
Telephone code 069

Tourist Office   Vieux Marché-aux-Poteries 14; 22.20.45; Mon.–Fri. 9 a.m.–7 p.m., Sat. & Sun. 10 a.m.–1 p.m., 3–6 p.m.

River cruises   Landing stage near Pont Des Trous; May 1–Aug. 31, daily except Mon., one hour duration; departures 11 a.m., 2:30 and 4:15 p.m. (confirm times with Tourist Office).

WHAT TO SEE AND DO......................

You'll certainly get visual variety in Tournai, in the array of outstanding examples of architecture from the *Romanesque* (12th century), *Gothic* (13–15th century), and *Renaissance* (16–17th century) periods. Sections of city ramparts from the 11th and 13th centuries remain, as centrally located as the **Tower of the Six** in Place Reine Astrid, near the **Belfry**. Buildings around Tournai's *Grand' Place,* badly damaged by Nazi air raids in 1940, have been reconstructed and colorful banners are flown from *guildhouse* facades from Easter through September. The originally 1611 **Renaissance Cloth Hall,** rather than the **Hôtel de Ville** (located in the Parc Communal in an 18th-century building that incorporates part of the ancient Saint Martin Abbey), has pride of place on the Grand' Place. All museums and sights in Tournai (except the Cathedral, see below) are open daily except Tues., for the same hours year-round *(10 a.m.–noon and 2–5:30 p.m., closed Tuesday, in the month of Sept., and on 1/1, 11/11, 12/25);* most are free.

Cathedral of Notre Dame • *Treasury open 10 a.m.–noon, 2–4:30 p.m. daily, the cathedral itself is open earlier* • Exhibiting the strength and simplicity of the *Romanesque* style, the vaulted energy and upreaching of the *Gothic,* and a beyond-value *Treasury,* Tournai's cruciform cathedral is considered Belgium's best, one of Europe's finest. The Romanesque nave, of gray Tournai limestone quarried just outside the town, was completed in 1171. The choir, originally completed in 1200, was rebuilt in the Gothic style by 1255. And to this day, the low Romanesque arches in the large nave (440 feet/132 mt. long, 215 ft/65 mt. wide, 80–110 feet/24–33 mt. high), stand in stark contrast to the soaring Gothic choir beyond, somehow successful aesthetically. Typical of Scheldian architecture are the capitals of the columns carved with flowers, animals, and plants. Alas, the support the columns lend has been slipping; some of the ceiling has fallen in and various columns list to port or starboard. Tournai's burgomaster has formed a committee to oversee the preservation of this amazing example of early Belgian architecture endeavor. The stained-glass windows in the apse are copies of ones in Sainte-Chapelle in Paris; those in the transcept masterpieces are from c. 1500 by Dutch artist **Arnold van der Spits** from Nijmegen. In the **St. Louis Chapel** (1299) are the paintings "Crucifixion" by Jacob Jordaens and "Deliverance of Souls from Purgatory" by Pieter Paul Rubens.

The standout in Tournai's well-laden **Treasury** is **Nicolas of Verdun**'s golden reliquary to the Flemish Notre Dame, which dates from 1205. A second reliquary, by an unknown goldsmith, is the 1247 **Shrine to St. Eleutherus.** A documented **Arras tapestry** from 1402, a gift to the Cathedral, shows Tournai's Belfry, houses and city walls, and scenes in still-vivid red and blue hues of its history, including the 1090 plague. Duquesnoy's fine 17th-century calvary in ivory is quite a contrast to the artist's **Mannequin Pis** in Brussels. Also on display is Archbishop of Canterbury **Thomas à Becket's chasuble,** worn when he said mass here in 1170, still in exile from England in the Abbey of Pontigny, France. Only weeks later, having returned to Canterbury, he was murdered in his cathedral. (The chasuble was given to the Bishop of Tournai in 1838 by the last monk at Pontigny). **Charles V's mantle** was worn by the Emperor when he presided at the December 1531 meeting of the Twentieth Chapter of the Order of the Golden Fleece held in the Cathedral.

The most outstanding characteristic of the Cathedral is its **five towers,** virtually the city's symbol. The massive central tower, wider than the others (though its pyramid-shaped peak is not as high in stone), is topped by a taller cross making it the same height (272 ft./72 mt.) as the four four-storied square corner towers that surround it. The porch of the Main Portal (west side) displays many beautiful figures carved in relief in Tournai stone. In the center under a canopy is a statue of the Virgin, prayed to as **Our Lady of the Sick** since the Cathedral's construction not long after the 1090 plague. A statue near the Cathedral on the south side was created by Tournai-born artist **Rogier de la Pasture** (who changed his name from its French form to the Flemish **Rogier van der Weyden** after he moved to Flanders's Brabant and Brussels). Rogier, born c. 1399 to a knife-maker in Tournai, studied under Robert Campin (now believed to be the Master of Flemalle, who was once thought to have been van der Weyden). The Tournai painters' guild register shows that Rogier worked with Campin from 1427–1432. By 1435, he was settled in Brussels, where he worked until he died in 1464. The *Port Mantilus* door on the north side of the Cathedral has exceptional 12th-century sculptures. The door is named for the blind man Mantilus whom St. Eleutherus, the Cathedral's first bishop, is said to have cured, and is alluded to in the nearby sculpture **The Parable of the Blind** (Guillaume Charlier, 1908). Also on the north side of the Cathedral is **Janson Square,** from which you have the best view of the Cathedral nave and flying buttresses.

Belfry • *SE end of the Grand' Place* • Tournai's Belfry is the oldest in northern Europe, c. 1200. Its 236 ft./72 meter height can be mastered on 256 stone steps for a wonderful view of the Cathedral, which seems so close you feel you ought to be able to touch it. The Belfry carillon (concerts, see *Events*) has 43 bells.

Musée des Beaux-Arts • *Parc Communal, enclos Saint-Martin* • Opened in 1928, its exhibit space enlightened by Victor Horta's art nouveau architectural genius with skylights, the museum has an exceptional collection (left to the city in 1904 by a local business man) that spans the periods from the early Flemish to the present, with an emphasis on Belgian and French artists. Among the Old Masters you'll find **Robert Campin, Rogier van der Weyden, Pieter Breughel the Younger, Jan Breughel,** and **Pieter Paul Rubens.** One of the rooms off the museum's central hall (in which there is a displayed sculpture by **Guillaume Charlier**) is devoted to the huge historical works of Tournai's 19th century master **Louis Gallait.** One of the most effective and interesting is the "Plague in Tournai;" others of note are "The Abdication of Charles Quint" and the "Last Rites over Counts Egmond and Hoorn." You certainly won't mind seeing non-Belgian works by **Manet, Monet, Seurat,** and **Van Gogh.**

Tapestry Museum • *in Hotel de Ville, Parc Communal, next to Musee des Beaux Arts* • A new addition on the Tournai scene, the Tapestry Museum displays the city's wonderful collection of 15th-century tapestries, which includes many smaller masterpieces (all formerly at the **Museum of History and Archeology**). At the museum, you can observe weavers at work, continuing an artistic tradition for which Tournai for centuries was renowned. Fine examples of another historic Tournai craft, sumptuously colored and decorated porcelain, can also be found here.

Musée du Folklore • *Reduit des Sion, alley off Grand' Place; little English documentation, although some exhibits can still be enjoyed* • Housed in a typical 1677 house with a double gable and arches on the upper story, the museum illustrates local lifestyles and traditions. Exhibits cover interesting tidbits of city history: items from Belgium's first newspaper, the Tournai-published *Courier de L'Escaut,* which began in 1829; a copy of the original city relief plan/model made for Louis XIV in 1707, from which Vauban worked to fortify the city with walls and 68 towers and canalize the Scheldt; and a model of the condition of Tournai's Grand' Place after the 1940 air raids.

Pont des Trous/Bridge of Gaps • *Across the Scheldt in the northwest of the old center* • Helping Tournai develop astride the Scheldt, this bridge (towers from 1281, the three gothic-style arches took an additional 25 years) is medieval military architecture at its best. Built to guard the entrance to the city by river, it was defended by a series of portcullises. Restored after World War II, the arches (the "gaps" in the frame) were raised 7 feet/2 meters to facilitate river navigation. From the bridge (cafe on top, eateries inside, see *Restaurants*) is a great view of the Cathedral's five towers, but if you back up a bridge to the **Pont Delwart,** you get a view that includes this very picturesque restored ancient arched Tournai-stone bridge.

Romanesque Houses • *Rue Barre Saint-Brice* • On a continuation of Rue de Derasse off Rue Royale (which follows a straight and pleasant route across the river between the Cathedral and the station) are found the strongly-horizontal Romanesque facades of what are believed to be western Europe's oldest (1175–1200) burghers' homes. The facades, right up to their gables, are built of the blue/gray Tournai Scheldt valley stone. Also on the same street are Gothic houses, dating from the 14th and 15th centuries.

Continue to the nearby end of Rue Barre Saint-Brice to **Eglise Saint Brice,** begun in the 13th century, most noteworthy for having been built alongside the cemetery where the tomb of **Frankish King Childeric** (father of Clovis), buried in 482, was found in 1653 (plaque on Place Clovis 8). From here, it's a short walk SE across the *Rue de Pont* and the river back into the center.

Tour Henri VIII • *Place Verte, Rue du Rempart* • All that remains of the citadel built here under the orders of Henry VIII, who stationed an army of 5,000 in Tournai while making war against France from 1513–1515, is this tower (the rest demolished by Louis XIV). Squat and cylindrical and 20 ft/6 mt. thick at the base of its walls (probably an imitation of the Tower of London), the massive keep was built in 1515, two years after Tournai was occupied by the King of England. The two brick-vault ceilinged halls, one above the other, house displays of weapons and armory and a small World War II resistance museum.

ACCOMMODATIONS

Inexpensive

★★★ **Le Parc** • *Place Reine Astrid 7; 21.28.93, fax 21.46.82* • Centrally located on an attractive square steps from the Belfry, this 19th-century former villa has 13 tastefully and individually furnished guestrooms, all with bath/toilet, TV/video, telephone, minibar/fridge. Rooms are generous-sized, those on the top floor shaped by the eaves; front rooms have views of Cathedral towers. Public rooms in this personable property feature architectural details, an antique-accented decor, and include an attractive bar, winter-garden lounge, and oasis terrace in back. No elevator; parking; breakfast included; major credit cards. The hotel's **Le Parc Restaurant** *(daily noon–3 p.m., dinner from 7 p.m.; moderate; six-course* menu *with wines expensive)* is popular locally and concentrates on French cuisine and regional specialties (warm foie gras, sweetbreads, rabbit, duck, fish, rhubarb mousse).

★★★★ **Condor Hotel** • *Place St-Pierre; 21.50.77, fax 21.50.78* • This modern hotel, with helpful front desk service, is physically light and bright but corridor noises carry through the thin walls. If your plans call for a weekend sleep-in, ask for a back room, since the morning markets in the square begin setting up before 7 a.m. All 38 rooms have tile bath/showers, TV with remote control, telephone; some have views of the Cathedral that looms just up the street. There's a garden, terrace tables, hotel restaurant (with view of the Cathedral), and lobby bar (open until midnight), all locally popular. Breakfast included; elevator; major credit cards.

RESTAURANTS..................................

While Tournai may not be on the beaten tourist path, local residents enjoy dining out and it's wise to inquire at the better restaurants about the need for reservations and which credit cards are accepted. Together with **Le Parc** (see under *Accommodations*), **Charles Quint** *(Grand-'Place 3; noon–2 p.m., 7–10 p.m., closed Wed. evening, Thurs., 3 weeks late July–mid Aug., a week at Carnival; 22.14.41; moderate to expensive)* is considered near the top of Tournai's in-town choices. Preparation is classical Belgian cuisine, with a focus on fish. The **Pont des Trous** *(Quai Staline; kitchen open from noon for lunch, 6:30 p.m. for dinner, closed Mon.; 21.16.16; moderate)* is an atmospheric eatery actually located in Tournai's handsome triple-arched 1304 bridge.

A la carte choices in the more formal **Rotisserie** *(11:30 a.m. for lunch, 7:30 p.m. for dinner)* are limited, but the **Taverne** *(open from 10 a.m.)* offers choices in its casual fare; or simply have a drink on the terrace atop the Scheldt. **Le Pressoir** *(Vieux Marché-aux-Poteries 2; lunch from noon, dinner; 22.35.13; moderate)* serves its specialties of foie gras, lobster, and turbot in a 17th-century house with cathedral view; allow enough time for the leisurely, even slow, service. Across the street from the Cathedral is the **Bistro de la Cathédrale** *(Vieux Marché-aux-Poteries 15; daily noon–2:30 p.m., 7–11 p.m.; 21.03.79; inexpensive)*, which can provide informal fare or a more complete meal featuring *Lapin (rabbit) a la Tournaisienne, Magret de canard* (duck), fish. The house specialties at **Le Carillon** *(Grand' Place 64; noon–3 p.m., 7–10:30 p.m., closed Sat. noon, Mon., month of Sept.; 21.33.79; moderate,* plat du jour *inexpensive)* are foie gras and fish. Down by the riverside is **O Pere au Quai** *(Quai Notre-Dame 18; noon–2:30 p.m., 7–11 p.m., closed Wed., month of Aug.; 23.29.22; inexpensive)* serving simply prepared food (grilled fish and meat, salad bar) in a pleasing setting.

IN THE AREA..

Beloeil Castle • *Rue du Chateau, Beloeil; daily April 1–Oct. 31 10 a.m.–6 p.m.; 069/68.94.26, 68.96.55; self-guided visits; printed history of family and chateau in English; parking* • For six centuries Beloeil has been the residence of the 1000-year-old **de Ligne dynasty**. The present Prince de Ligne Antoine is married to Alix of Luxembourg, sister of the Grand Duke of Luxembourg. The distinguished de Lignes have included knights who fought in the crusades, a knight of the *Order of the Golden Fleece*, and Eugene, who, in 1830, was offered the crown of newly-independent Belgium but declined. Fire broke out in Beloeil in 1900, and the chateau had to be rebuilt under Louis, ninth prince of de Ligne. The great marble entrance hall and central staircase create a stately setting, but much of the house, with its valuable and attractive contents (furniture, portraits of family and foreign royalty, master paintings, 17th-century tapestries, silverware, Chinese porcelain, and library with 20,000 leather-bound volumes) is much more intimate. A past president of the *European Historic Houses Association*, Prince Antoine has said of himself, "I am by birth a lifetime caretaker." Among other on-going maintenance, Beloeil has 240 windows to clean and 6.3 miles/ 10 km. of hedge to clip: Following the example of many English stately homes, Antoine de Ligne decided to open his chateau to the public to cover the high cost of everyday upkeep.

A recent additional attraction on the grounds—included in Beloeil's hefty entrance fee of BF 330—is **Minibel,** where many of Belgium's architectural treasures have been carefully recreated on a scale of 1:25. A small train-on-wheels transports visitors from the chateau, through the 63-acre park with woods and waters, bowers and flowers, and formal French-style gardens (which you may also enjoy on foot) to Minibel, and nearby cafeteria and restaurant (069/68.96.53).

LIEGE

Guidelines For Liège

SIGHTS At the heart of Liège are the **Prince-Bishops Palace** on Place St-Lambert and **Perron** monument on the adjacent Place du Marche, both attesting to the city's history of independence. Several restored **mansion-museums,** and the **Museum of Walloon Life** in a former convent, shed light on Liège life. The city's selection of churches with Romanesque foundations includes St. Barthelemy's with its famed 12th-century **baptismal font** by Renier du Huy. Readers of works by native son **Georges Simenon** will find that the atmosphere of his books, though often set in Paris, is thickly in Liège. Adding flavor to Belgium's Walloon bastion is the river **Meuse** (the *Maas* in nearby Holland), which flows through the city, separating the old town from the colorful workers' quarter of **Outremeuse**.

GETTING AROUND Although Liège is a large city, many of its important sights and museums are located within walking distance of each other, not far from the main **Tourist Office** *(Feronstree 92)*. Staff there can arrange for a guided (English) set-price **city taxi tour.** Taxi ranks are located at Gare Guillemins, Place du Marche, Place St-Lambert, Place Foch, Place de la Cathédrale, Place de la Republique Française, and Blvd. d'Avroy. Liège has a good **bus network;** maps of the system are posted at stops, and available at the tourist office. Main terminals are Place Saint-Lambert, Place du Theatre, Place Cathédrale, and Place des Guillemins. There are **boat cruises** on the **Meuse** (schedule at tourist office), though the scenery doesn't justify the full-day river trip to nearby Maastricht in Holland; take a train instead.

SHOPPING Liège is famed for its Sunday morning (9 a.m.–2 p.m.) market **La Batte** (a Walloon word that means *embankment*), held along the Meuse between Place Cockerill and Pont Maghin. The amazing range of foodstuffs, household items, clothing, small animals, and cosmetic merchandise, combined with thousands of browsers and buyers (many from neighboring Holland and Germany), give this flea market something of the flavor of a medieval fair. Shoppers from near and far also come weekdays to Liège, a major regional market town with one of Europe's largest center-city pedestrian precincts. It has some 5,000 retail outlets, from large department stores and fashion boutiques, to antiques shops; (prime streets include Rue de la Cathedrale, Rue St.-Paul, Rue de la Regence, Blvd. de la Sauveniere, Place du Marche, Feronstree, Pont d'Avroy, and, across the river, Rue Jean d'Outre-Meuse). Antiques shops are clustered around Rue St. Thomas, Rue des Mineurs, and Rue du Palais. Liège's **Val Saint Lambert** handcut crystal has been produced since 1826 at the factory south of Liège in Seraing *(Crystalworks Val-Saint-Lambert; Rue du Val 245; 041/37.09.60; exhibits of glassblowing; items by apprentices, students, and other articles for sale in* Studio Crystal, *April 1–Oct. 31 Tues.–Sun. 10 a.m.–5 p.m., closed Mon., rest of year Sat., Sun., hols. only, same hrs.; accessible by bus from* Jemeppe Gare Routiere *in Liège).*

ENTERTAINMENT AND EVENTS Born in Liège, composer **Cesar Franck** (1822–1890) attended the **Conservatoire** *(Rue Forgeur 14; 22.03.06),* which still offers concerts of his and other works, as does the **Orchestre Philharmonique** *(Rue Forgeur 11; 23.67.74).* The active **Opera Royal de Wallonie** *(Place de la République Francaise; 23.59.10)* occasionally pays honor to Liege-born **Andre Ernest Gretry** (1741–1813), a composer particularly noted for his comic operas. For performance schedules of these, midday and Sunday morning concerts, and others inquire at the tourist office. **Jazz** can be heard in Rue Roture in Outremeuse at **Le Lions'Envoile** and **Le Cirque Divers,** and at **Les Caves de Porto** in Feronstree in the old town. Music clubs and cafes also are centered in the **Carre** (Old Town) which is bordered by Blvd. Sauveniere, Pont d'Avroy, Vinave d'Ile, and rue des Dominicaines. August 15 is Liège's **Free Republic of Outremeuse**'s feast day, celebrated in the streets with spirited traditional events and a fun fair. The 4th weekend in June is observed in the **Commune of Saint-Pholien** with morning concerts, open air Mass, festive lights and fireworks, and a meeting of the "giants." **September Nights** is an annual Liège music festival; at the end of September, the **Fetes de Wallonie** is held in the court of the Prince-Bishops Palace.

ACCOMMODATIONS Comfortable, convenient hotels in Liège are limited, so plan ahead with reservations when possible. The tourist office will assist.

RESTAURANTS Many of Liège's typical dishes are pork specialties (such as *boudin blanc,* a white sausage). City restaurants serve fare from French *haute* cuisine to *potee,* the Walloon word for *stew. Boulets frites* are large firm balls of bread stuffing flavored with meat and doused in gravy. Local street-stand favorites include *bouketes* (thick buckwheat pancakes). The farmstead-studded **Herve** region, to the northeast of Liège, is famous for its odorous cheese; it's served locally spread on toast and topped with syrup. Pubs (Liège's 10,000 student population helps support them, and the city's many terrace cafes and taverns) can't legally, but often do, pour *peket,* a powerful local gin.

ARRIVING Liège is an international rail crossroads, with direct trains from Brussels and Luxembourg City, and many connections. The principal rail station is *Gare des Guillemins* (with taxis), about 1.5 mi./2 kms. from the **Place St-Lambert.** The city also is linked to major European cities by motorway, and to regional cities from its airport. If you arrive in Liège by car, there's a car park beside the main tourist office *(Feronstreet 90),* and others at Place Cathédrale, Place du Marché, Place

Saint-Lambert; center city driving is hampered around Place Saint-Lambert because of traffic overload, coupled with construction.

TRAVEL TIPS Municipal financial difficulties have interrupted the building of Liège's Metro, leaving an unsightly construction site in front of the **Bishop's Palace** at **Place St-Lambert** in the center of the city. The unfortunate fiscal situation also means that museum hours have been reduced because of cutbacks in personnel; confirm the opening hours given below when you arrive.

Liege in Context

Liège (Luik), *la cite ardente,* despite Namur's official position as capital of Belgium's French-speaking Wallonia, acts as if *it* possesses that status. Certainly Liège, a fiercely independent municipality for far more than a millennium, is an ardent caretaker of the Walloon language. (*Walloon* is an ancient Latin dialect—as French itself was a Latin dialect, originally spoken solely in the *Ile de France* region. Walloon, the most northern of the Latin languages, didn't gain the same cultural and social status that the French dialect did (by being the language of the Ile de France state which gained wide-ranging political power in the Middle Ages). Instead, Walloon remained an essentially rural tongue; under the status consciousness that came with the affluence of the 19th-century Industrial Revolution, it suffered such a popular decline that it actually was forbidden in schools. Today, though, the right to teach Walloon has been restored, its use continues to slide. Liège's support includes Walloon theater, and a language exhibit in the excellent **Museum of Walloon Life** (possibly Belgium's best institute of local culture and folklore).

Liège marks its beginning from the building of a chapel in 558 by St. Monulphus, Bishop of Tongeren-Maastricht (two nearby Roman-era towns, considered to be the oldest in Belgium and Holland, respectively). A later Bishop of Tongeren-Maastricht, **St. Lambert,** was murdered in Liège (supposedly for having accused nobleman Pepin of Herstal of incest) in 705. His successor **St. Hubert** (see *Saint-Hubert* village in *The Ardennes* section) erected a church in Lambert's honor, which rapidly became a place of pilgrimage, no doubt influencing Hubert's decision to move the see to Liège. The Liège bishopric was established in 721, with a residence for the bishop built next to St-Lambert's church. First Holy Roman Emperor **Charlemagne** (742–814) is said to have granted Liège its first city privileges (a fact commemorated by an equestrian statue of the Frankish ruler at the north end of the **Parc d'Avroy**).

Under **Notger,** who, after his coronation as bishop in 980, made sage territorial moves that gained him temporal powers and made him the first to hold the title of *Prince-Bishop of Liège,* the city became the capital of an ecclesiastical/political principality whose rulers would hold power for more than 800 years, until the end of the 18th century, holding sway over parts of Germany (the Holy Roman Empire) and today's Belgium, Holland, and France, with a total area equivalent to 2/3s of present-day Wallonia. Administrative and judiciary bodies were created and Liège became an intellectual and artistic center. (Among other cultural developments, Liège became famous for its school of song, fostered by the collegiate churches there and, in the 14th century, supplied many of the singers for the Sistene Chapel at the Vatican, which had been reestablished in 1376.) Bishop Notger also expanded trade and fortified the city, several sturdy churches being incorporated into the city walls. Under Notger and his successor, the foundations for the churches of **St. Denis, St. Martin, St. Paul, St. Jean, St. Jacques,** and **St. Barthelemy** were laid, giving the episcopal town a skyline of steeples. At the end of the 12th century, Bishop Albert de Cuyck recognized the liberties of Liège, and from then on its citizens lived with the then unheard of concept that "a poor man is king in his castle."

Perhaps inevitably, the powerful, often secular, Prince-Bishops (many "bishops" in name only and enjoying a worldly lifestyle far from Liège) became a dynasty, nephews being elected by the cathedral-chapter in the footsteps of their uncles (even as titular Catholic bishops, the fathers were not supposed to have sons). The authority of the Prince-Bishops often became a source of conflict for the Liègeois, who sought more power for ordinary citizens. Many dissensions in the 13th and 14th centuries ended with concessions made by the Prince-Bishops to the guilds and workers. In the 15th century, the Dukes of Burgundy, who had already obtained possession of the rest of what is now Belgium, sought to add the principality of Liège to their sphere.

The independent and unsupportive attitude of the Liègeois finally brought Duke of Burgundy **Charles the Bold** to the boiling point. He and his army marched on the city, arriving at the end of October, 1468. They camped on the heights above the city, near the present Citadel, and prepared to storm the city. On the night of October 29/30, some 600 daring Liège men, led by **Vincent de Bueren,** made their way up the steep slope to the camp (the 373 steps of the **Montagne de Bueren** commemorate the deed) with the thought of assassinating Charles. But they attacked the wrong tent, were caught, and were killed to the last man. Charles set to the task of leveling Liège, pillaging it first, then setting it afire. The city is said to have burned for seven weeks; across it, only churches and monasteries—Charles being a devout Catholic—were spared (and eight houses as lodging for the religious). Thus, most of Liège's medieval heritage went up in smoke, leaving it with, by Belgium standards, a surprisingly recent Old Town. Before he left to return to Bruges, taking with him Liège's symbol of its liberties, the **Perron** (a smaller, and alas portable, form of the Flemish Belfries which symbolized civil freedoms), Charles annulled the city's rights. Such was this last Duke of Burgundy's power that, until his premature death in 1477 at the Battle of Nancy, the Liègeois couldn't even rebuild their homes. Charles's daughter, **Mary of Burgundy**, restored Liège's rights and returned the precious *Perron*.

Under Prince-Bishop **Erard de la Marck** (1505–1538), Liège regained status as a political/religious center, beginning another period of prosperity, and one of relative peace for three centuries. The principality's purposeful policy of neutrality in foreign affairs managed to keep it out of the religious wars of the 16th century. The rebuilding necessitated by the devastation delivered by Charles the Bold continued, first in the old familiar Gothic style, but soon succumbing to the newer Italian Renaissance style. The imposing new Prince-Bishops palace built by Erard de la Marck led the way, and the Italian, and therefore Catholic-sanctioned-style, then spread rapidly during the Counter Reformation; more than 100 churches were built across the principality of Liège in the following century. Also popular was a simpler architectural style which became known as the "Meuse Renaissance." During the 16th century, without the upheaval of the religious wars that embroiled much of northern Europe, the principality of Liège became the first place on the Continent to open and exploit its coal mines (it had done so to some degree since the 12th century), developing the iron ore, coal mining, and munitions industries that continued to serve as a base for its economy in later centuries. (Though remaining politically neutral, Liège felt free to supply arms and ammunition to others, even to those foreign leaders who were fighting wars on its own doorstep.)

In the 17th century, unwise alliances made by the prince-bishopric without the consent of the Liègeois resulted in the principality declaring war on French King Louis XIV. French bombing of Liège in 1691 destroyed the **Hôtel de Ville** and many other buildings and monuments around the Place du Marché, including the **Perron**. A new Perron, created in 1697 and mounted firmly on a large fountain, was one of the first of a wave of replacement structures, including the Hôtel de Ville, built in Liège in the 17th and 18th centuries.

Peace and prosperity returned to Liège, but it was accompanied by great social inequalities. On August 18, 1789, a month after the storming of the **Bastille** in Paris (the beginning of the French Revolution), the Liègeois arose in their own revolution. Among the actions taken by Liègeois "patriots" (encouraged by the Revolutionary French Army whose soldiers headed north with their extremist anti-religious fervor) was the tearing down of **Cathedrale St-Lambert**, to them a symbol of social injustice as strong as the Bastille had been for the French. The participating Liègeois, unlike the French Revolutionary forces that destroyed so many churches in the Benelux, were not against religion, but against the prince-bishop and his 60 canons who had grown rich and contemptuous of the privileges of the people. In 1794, Dumouriez captured Liège for revolutionary France and expelled Antoine de Mean, the last prince-bishop.

After the Napoleonic era, Liège, no longer an independent principality, became (along with the rest of Belgium) united with Holland. Despite the economic benefits realized by the city under that union (a university in 1817 and the founding of the steel industry at Seraing to the south of the city, as well as expansion of its coal, arms, and glass production), the Liègeois supported the establishment of a free Belgium. Many, under the leadership of Charles Rogier, went to Brussels in the summer of 1830 to support the armed rise against Dutch rule.

With a free Belgian nation finally realized, Liège—one of the earliest cities in Europe to have entered the new Industrial Revolution—continued to move ahead full steam. Installations for modern steel production were built upstream on the Meuse between 1835 and 1850, and docks were expanded downstream. After train tracks were laid to Liège (1842), the mainstream Meuse was straightened in its path through the city, while the side streams were filled in to form fine wide avenues for the flourishing city: rue de la Régence, Rue d'Avroy, and Boulevard de la Sauveniere, which shows its former river oxbow shape.

Outremeuse, on an island in the Meuse in the center of Liège, long a workers' quarter of the city known for its independent, rebellious working class character, love of tradition, and devotion to the Liege dialect, had few riches to be content with. Although well established—two ancient crafts had long been localized here, weavers in Saint-Nicolas Outremeuse and tanners in the adjoining commune of Saint-Pholien—much of Outremeuse was little more than a swamp until built up in the 19th century as a workers' residential neighborhood. It was in Outremeuse, at the core of *la cite ardente,* that Liège-born author **Georges Simenon** (1903–1989; see also *The Muse* in *The Benelux Cultural Legacy* chapter) was raised. Simenon, perhaps the world's most widely translated 20th-century writer, though he often set his stories in Paris (to which he moved after beginning his career as a reporter for the *Gazette de Liège*), constantly drew on the scenes and experiences of his youth in Liege for the character and characters in his books. In 1973 he wrote: "Most of us owe our experience to our childhood and adolescence. Though I am seventy, I act, think and live like a child from Outremeuse."

Visitors interested in exploring *Simenon's Liège,* which though being restored here and there is not so very different in many ways today from when the writer lived there in the early 20th century, can do so in depth with the help of a guide (arranged through the tourist office), but there are many sites associated with Simenon that you can see on your own (the tourist office pamphlet *Itineraire Simenon* is in French only, but of some use for addresses). The Outremeuse Simenon grew up in, though only just across the Meuse from the old center of Liège, was such a separate world that when those on the "island" needed to cross the **Pont des Arches** they changed out of their working clothes (though crossing via the **Passerelle** footbridge they didn't feel the need to do so). Simenon's grandfather, as owner of a hat shop (then at **Rue Puits-en-sock 58**), was an important member of Outremeuse's **St-Nicolas** parish, and had a pew with his name and took collections on Sundays. Simenon's mother ran a boarding house on the street that today has been renamed **Rue Georges Simenon**. The writer-to-be joined other rebellious youth in the **Impasse de la Houpe** behind **St.-Pholien**'s church to drink and do dope. Slightly older, he met other artist friends who considered themselves above the rules and prejudices of the conventional world at **La Cague (The Keg)**. Across the Passerelle foot bridge, he enjoyed the typical **Cafe Lequet** *(Quai dur Meuse 17)*, at one time owned by his aunt, and still rich with the atmosphere that Simenon wrote into his books. Simenon was intimately connected with many inhabitants of the nearby narrow **Rue du Champion** (running between the Rue de la Cathédrale and the Quai sur Meuse), which continues to be a street of prostitute-rented rooms. (Simenon claimed to have "known" some 10,000 women in his life). He frequented **Le Carré**, in his youth a decent entertainment district with cabarets, though it turned into a dangerous "Little Chicago" from pre-World War II until the 1960s, after which it gradually returned to the pleasant student cafe and upmarket bistro neighborhood it is now. Today, Simenon would hardly recognize **Rue Roture,** in his day badly run down, but now a typical Outremeuse street that is atypical for its restored buildings filled with restaurants and cafes. You may (though many others do not) find it a coincidence that the name *Maigret*—Simenon's famous fictional detective—appears on a memorial at the **Hôtel de Ville** honoring Liege policemen who died in the First World War. Retaining his ties with Liège, Simenon made a personal gift of a fountain to the university campus.

During World War I, Liège's economic progress, as in the rest of German-occupied Belgium, slowed. Throughout that conflict, workers in Liège's famous small arms factories stood up to the enemy by refusing to produce weapons. Developments after the war included the opening in 1939 of the **Albert Canal,** which connected Liège on the Meuse to Antwerp on the Scheldt, and to the North Sea. When the Second World War was over, the importance of the canal became doubled. Today the third largest inland port in Europe (after Paris, France and Duisburg, Germany), Liège has port installations up and downstream on the Meuse from the center of the city, the center downstream at Monsin, at the entrance to the Albert Canal, marked by a monument topped with a 40-foot/12-meter high figure of King Albert.

Many Liègeois feel that more damage was done to the face of their city during "urban planning" than in either world war. With coal still being mined in the 1950s and early 1960s, Liège had the wherewithal to wrap itself in modern trappings. The demolition of grand 19th-century mansions and older, rundown, buildings that no one then had a thought to preserve, has left many an ordinary office highrise in Liège. Today a much greater awareness of Liège's architectural legacy exists, the restored building that houses the tourist office on Feronstree being an example. The coal mines are all closed now, and Liège's future is structured in steel and its excellent mid-continent position in Europe's evolving single-market.

GUIDEPOSTS
Telephone code 041

Tourist Information	Feronstree 92; Mon.–Fri., 9 a.m.–6 p.m. (5 p.m. from Nov. 1–Mar. 31), Sat. 10 a.m.–4 p.m., Sun. & hols. 10 a.m.–2 p.m.; 22.24.56. There's a smaller tourist office at **Guillemins** station (52.44.19).
Bus	24-hour information: 67.00.64
Trains	Information: 52.98.50
Police	101
Post Office	Main office: Rue de la Regence 51, Place du Marche
Telephone/ telegraph	Rue de l'Universite 32, daily 8 a.m. to 7 p.m.

WHAT TO SEE AND DO......................

The center of Liège, **Place St-Lambert,** is currently an eyesore rather than a elegant open space due to the presently discontinued construction of a city Metro and other road works. Two centuries ago, the square probably looked even worse, after the demolishment by French and local revolutionaries of the site's Cathédrale St.-Lambert, first begun by Bishop Hubert (c. A.D. 705). Liège's **Palais des Princes-Eveques** (Palace of the Prince-Bishops), which faces Place St-Lambert, also has origins dating back to Hubert (later St-Hubert, patron of hunters), who transferred the see here in 720 and built a modest "bishop's house." The palace it became was destroyed by fire in 1505 and replaced by the one we see today in Renaissance style (except for the classic facade by the Brussels architect Jean-Andre Anneessens built following a 1734 fire).

Notable are the two inner courtyards, the first with 60 surrounding columns, the capital of each sculpted with different fantastic faces and figures, inspired by discoveries just then being made in the New World, and by *The Praise of Folly* by **Erasmus** (1466–1536), of whom the builder, Bishop Erard de la Marck, was a devotee. The second courtyard is a particularly peaceful setting. Since the end of the rule of the bishops in 1794, the palace has served as the seat of the Law Courts and, since the birth of the Belgian nation, as home of the provincial government. The **Perron** on the adjoining **Place du Marché** is the symbol of Liege's communal freedoms, the present one crafted and topped by the **Three Graces** by Liege sculptor **Jean del Cour** in 1697. Attractively surrounded by 17th and 18th century buildings, the square hosts a daily flower, fruit, and vegetable market, a function it has performed from the city's earliest days. Although the classical style Hôtel de Ville (town hall) which overlooks Place du Marché dates only from the early 18th century (Louis XIV style), town business has been conducted on the site since the 13th century in a house called **La Violette,** a term still used locally to refer to the town hall. Inquire in the impressive waiting hall about viewing the richly decorated ceremonial rooms.

Behind and rising above these Liege landmarks is the **Citadel,** located some 400 steps up the so-called **Montagne de Bueren** (built in 1875 and named for Vincent de Bueren, a fierce defender of Liège against Duke of Burgundy Charles the Bold's attack in 1468). Though there's a view of the city from the Citadel, it's no longer as panoramic as advertised, being somewhat blocked by vegetation. An interesting alternative to climbing all 400 stairs is to head from the **Hors-Chateau** (a street built in the 11th century outside the city walls, today lined with 17th- and 18th-century houses amid 20th-century structures) to the base of the Montagne de Bueren, and take a left into the **Impasse des Ursulines.** Here is Liège's **Museum of Architecture,** a block of 17th-century buildings preserved *in situ* or rebuilt here amid terraced landscaping (the museum is essentially a documentation and cultural center, so the view from the outside is almost as good as going inside). Beyond the museum, further up the Impasse, a door opens in the high wall on the left hand side and leads to a large park reaching up the hillside, and a footpath, *Sentier des Coteaux,* which followed to the left offers fine views down the slope, over the old convent buildings housing the Museum of Walloon Life, the Prince-Bishops Palace, and the roofs of the area's 17th and 18th century houses. Past the quiet chestnut-shaded yard of the former convent **Cour des Minimes,** you come out on Rue du Peri, which turns downhill into picturesque **Rue Pierreuse,** and back to the **Prince-Bishops Palace** and Place du Marché.

From Place du Marché, a relatively short, roughly circular route, on and off the three parallel streets of **Feronstree, Hors-Chateau,** and Meuse riverside **La Batte/Quai de Maestricht** (all of which have some interesting 17th and 18th-century facades) will bring you to most of Liège's major sights. As an aid to those with limited time, they are discussed below in order of relative importance/interest.

Église St-Barthélemy • *Place St-Barthelemy; Tues.–Sat., 10 a.m.– 1 p.m., 2–5 p.m., Sun., 2–5 p.m., closed Mon.; 22.08.00* • Although it dates back to the 11th century (the Romanesque narthex is being restored), with many typical local Mosan architectural characteristics and twin Rhenan towers in evidence, St-Barthelemy is visited primarily for its early 12th-century brass **baptismal font,** one of Belgium's most famed art treasures, attributed to goldsmith **Renier de Huy.** The font was originally ordered by Abbot Hellin at the beginning of the 12th century for **Notre-Dame-aux-Fonts,** the parish church which stood next to **Cathédrale St-Lambert.** Serving as its baptistry, for centuries it was the only church in Liège where the sacrament of baptism could be celebrated. Like St-Lambert's, Notre Dame was destroyed during the French period at the end of the 18th century, but the font was hidden and escaped harm (except for the lid, which was lost), being presented to St-Barthelemy in 1804. Today, it stands in that church to the left of the altar in a glassed-in space that you can enter to examine the art work at close range. The beautiful bronze tub seems to be carried by ten oxen (originally 12, symbolizing the apostles) set in a stone base. Five scenes of baptism, including the main scene in which Christ is being baptized by John the Baptist, are arranged around the tub, the whole design showing the influence of classical, Byzantine, and Mosan art traditions. The small glowing faces of the figures are remarkably expressive. Although not operating during my most recent visit, inquire about the 30-minute multilingual audiovisual program that describes the creation of this wonderful work.

Musée de la Vie Wallonne • *Museum of Walloon Life; Cours des Mineurs 1; Tues.–Sat. 10 a.m.–5 p.m., Sun. & hols. 10 a.m.–4 p.m., closed Mon.; 23.60.94; exhibit notes in French only, limited multi-lingual information given at some points, worth a visit in any case* • This exceptionally well-displayed collection on Wallonia's social and economic history is handsomely housed in the restored Mosan Renaissance brick-and-limestone 17th-century former Minorites convent. It's an appropriate location for such a museum, since, during its active days, the convent was a Liègeois gathering spot for guild meetings and other important civic occasions, as explained in the recorded multi-lingual commentary to which one can listen while seated on a bench on a balcony overlooking the peaceful interior courtyard. From food (a typical Ardennes kitchen and *salle d'alimentation* with cookie molds from Dinant, festive breads, cheese and butter preparation) to local festivals, the important local industries of coal mining and crystal-cutting, workers' places (pewtermaker's, pipemaker's, coppersmith's and cooper's), and the geographic and linguistic features of the region, the whole panoply of Wallonia and its traditions from the late-18th to early-20th centuries are presented. Also on hand is an amusing collection of puppets (puppet theater is still active in Liège), including favorite folklore characters and typical Liegeois *Tchantches*. Other popular puppets from the cast of characters in the city's history include Charlemagne, Charles the Bold, and Christ, who hangs on a cross for his part in Passion Plays. The puppets' respective sizes reveals much about them, since "good" characters are always larger. In the basement of the museum (ask at the reception desk), a coalmine gallery has been reconstructed.

Musée Curtius • *Quai de Maestricht 13; Mon., Thurs., Sat. 2–5 p.m., Wed. and Fri. 10 a.m.–1 p.m., closed Tues., major hols., guided tours 1st and 3rd Sun. each month 10 and 11:30 a.m.; 23.20.68* • Housed in the Mosan Renaissance mansion built on the river bank between 1600 and 1610 by Liège Commissary Jean Curtius, this museum of archeology and decorative arts documents life in the Meuse valley since Roman times. The archeological items displayed in the period interior cover the region's prehistory to early Middle Ages, while the art work is from the medieval period until the end of Liège's *Ancien Regime* (prince-bishopric). Highlights include the *Gospel Book* of Notger, Liège's first prince-bishop (972–1008), beautifully bound and decorated with an ivory sculpture on the cover (to which enamels were added in the 12th century), the "Dom Rupert Virgin," a masterpiece of 12th-century Mosan sculpture, and two polychrome chimney-pieces from 1604. Sharing the building is the **Glass Museum,** with a rich collection of ancient pieces of glass from the Islamic world and Venice, as well as contemporary creations. Belgian glass, which has a prestigious history in Liège through the local **Val-St-Lambert Crystal Manufacturers** founded in 1826, is particularly well represented.

Musée d'Ansembourg • *Feronstree 114; Tues.–Sun. tours at 1, 2, 3, 4, and 5 p.m.; closed Mon., major hols.; 23.20.68* • Another mansion museum (18th century) is devoted to the decorative arts and furniture of Liège's golden age. The sumptuous interior, which remains authentic to its original design of 1738–1741 and includes the Cordoba leather-lined dining room with remarkable local Regency-style dresser, delft-tiled kitchen hung with copper utensils, and drawing room with tapestries from the Belgian town of Oudenaarde, can be enjoyed at your own pace. Other rooms are filled with fine plasterwork and painted ceilings, carved wainscoting and panelling, monumental fireplaces and mantelpieces, and fine furniture (Liège was famous for cabinet-making in the 16th–18th centuries), all executed by Liege craftspeople.

Musée d'Armes • *Museum of Arms; Quai de Maestricht 8; Mon., Thurs., Sat. 10 a.m.–1 p.m., Wed., Fri. 2–5 p.m., 1st and 3rd Suns. of month only; closed Tues., major hols. and first half Feb.; 23.15.62* • Liège has held an important place is the history of firearms manufacturing since the 14th century, and still enjoys international fame from its School of Arms Manufacture and the Fabrique Nationale in nearby Herstal. At this museum, which shows the history and evolution of sporting and defense weapons, Liège offers one of the world's foremost collections of firearms. On display are some 12,500 pieces dating from the 14th to the 20th centuries, many exceptional for their beautiful decorative inlaid and engraved work (a hallmark of Liege weapons), others for their rarity (such as the unique 7-barrelled flint-lock machine gun, c. 1810, made in the U.S.). All are housed in the neo-classical mansion built in 1814 by Liège architect Barthelemy Digneffe for weapons-builder Pierre-Joseph Lemille. Also to be seen is a portrait by **Ingres** of then Major Consul **Napoleon Bonaparte,** who visited Liège in 1803 to sign a decree granting money to reconstruct a city district that had been destroyed in 1794 in French/Austrian conflict.

It is necessary to leave Liège's "museum circuit" to see the most important of the many churches (Catholic) which, as an episcopal see, the city has long supported. Liège's churches sometimes were spared the devastation wreaked on other city structures (as was the case under Burgundian Charles the Bold's 1468 attack, see *Liège in Context* above), though the situation was the very opposite for the unfortunate **Cathédrale St-Lambert,** that historic structure in the center of the city razed by anti-religious revolutionaries at the end of the 18th century. Most Liège churches show a mixed architectural heritage due to their great age and subsequent events such as fire, feuds, and fashion. A wonderful example is **Eglise St-Jacques** *(Place St-Jacques; Mon.–Fri. 8 a.m.–noon, Sat., Sun. and July & Aug. 8 a.m.–5 p.m.; English booklet).* Built beginning in Romanesque style in the early 11th century (the narthex remains, though the rest of the chancel collapsed on June 30, 1513), the nave and eastern chancel were rebuilt in Flamboyant Gothic, and the porch (in 1558) in Italian Renaissance. During the French Revolution at the end of the 18th century, St-Jacques managed to escape destruction, and King Leopold I intervened for its restoration in the mid-19th century (another long-term restoration was begun in 1962). From the rear of the nave the view of the lace-like, carved-stone ceiling vaulting is remarkable. The large, impressive white statues (most by 17th-century Liège sculptor **Jean del Cour**) hanging on pillars in the nave were carved in lime wood and painted white, since marble was so expensive. Other notable interior details include the 16th-century stained glass windows in the chancel; carved 14th-century stalls dating from the Romanesque church; and beautiful Renaissance-style organ case dated

1600 by Andre Severin of Maastricht, who is buried beneath his creation.

Cathédrale St-Paul • *Place Cathédrale* • Promoted from church to cathedral in 1801 following the demolishment by revolutionaries of St-Lambert's, St-Paul's was founded in 971. Itself demolished in the 13th century, the rebuilding of the present structure spans the centuries from the 14th to the 19th, when stones from dismantled St-Lambert's were used to complete St-Paul's with a spire similar to the one toppled from the former cathedral. Restoration in the 19th century left St-Paul's with little original detail, and the cathedral is visited for its **Tresor/Treasury** *(entry from the south transept or apply at the Sacristan at 2A Rue St-Paul at the side of the church; closed from 12:30–2 p.m., and for the day at 5 p.m.).* The most outstanding articles, saved from the rich collections of St-Lambert's, are the imposing life-size silver reliquary-bust of St-Lambert containing his skull (1505), a 10th-century icon of the Virgin, and 9th-century book of the Gospels. Best known is the embossed gold reliquary offered to St-Lambert's by Charles the Bold in 1471 as expiation for having leveled Liège, save for the churches, in 1468. The golden statue, created by his own court jeweler, shows a repentant-faced Charles on his kneel in front of a standing St. George; Charles holds a box containing skin from a hand of St-Lambert.

ACCOMMODATIONS..........................

First Class
★★★★ **Ramada Hotel Liége** • *Blvd de la Sauveniere 100; 22.49.10, fax 22.39.83* • With 105 rooms on six floors, the well-located, service-oriented 1960s-built Ramada is Liège's leading hotel. Used most by business travelers, the Ramada, while not elegant, functions well and is comfortable. Its location is more convenient than most hotels in the city, about a three blocks' walk to Place St-Lambert, as near to shopping and entertainment. In-room amenities include TV, telephone, mini-fridge. The hotel's elegant French restaurant, **Rotisserie de la Sauveniere** (moderate), is very well regarded locally. Lobby bar; breakfast extra; parking available.

Inexpensive
★★★ **Cygne d'Argent** • *Rue Beekman 49; 23.70.01* • This 23-room hotel, located in a residential neighborhood just a block outside Blvd. Sauveniere, is a longish but possible walk to sights, and served by bus routes. Front desk staff is helpful with questions. The front lobby has couches, TV, bar service, and a small restaurant. The standard bed-

rooms include good mattresses, TV, telephone, private bath with stall showers, hairdryer, and individually controlled heat. Noise from the hall can carry into rooms. A basic continental breakfast is included, additional charge for cooked one. Elevator; major credit cards; short taxi ride to Guillemins station; parking available.

RESTAURANTS..................................

The height of Liège haute cuisine can be enjoyed at **Au Vieux Liège** *(Quai de la Goffe 41; closed Sun., Wed. evening, month of August; 23.77.48, reservations suggested; moderate)*, where the setting also is superb, in a 16th-century national monument townhouse with period furnishings. The menu, served in dining rooms upstairs where formally-dressed waiters await in candlelight, features finely-prepared fish, but includes other offerings. The best of several eateries situated around the **Place du Marché** is **Brasserie As Ouhes** *(Place du Marché 21; noon–2:20 p.m., 6 p.m.–midnight, closed Sun., Sat. for lunch, and second half of July; 23.32.25, reservations suggested; moderate)*, which offers a broad selection of regional and French fare in an attractive atmosphere.

For *cuisine Liègeoise* head for **Mame Vi Cou** *(Rue de la Wache 9; daily 12:30–3 p.m., 7:30–10 p.m.; 23.71.81, reservations recommended; moderate,* menu *inexpensive)*. Located in a small street beside **Inno** department store, Mame Vi Cou provides an atmosphere of country inn in a city alley, with cozy brick walls and beamed ceiling, a saint's niche on the wall, and live piano music and candlelight, to accompany its reasonably-priced regional dishes. This is the place to sample *boudin blanc* (white sausage). *jambon d'Ardennes* with caramelized onions, vegetable soup, pig's feet, and *pan perdu* as a dessert. **Cafe Lequet** *(Quai sur Meuse 17; 22.21.34; inexpensive)* is a typical Liège tavern, with a limited selection of tasty regional fare and daily specials. Once owned by the aunt of author Georges Simenon, it's a great place to mix with the Liègeois he wrote about.

If you're looking for a change of fare, the **Carré**, a pub and cafe-filled quarter in central Liège, will give you plenty of alternatives. One is **Ristorante i Giardini Pizzeria** *(Rue d'Amay 10; 22.03.64; inexpensive)*, whose renovated, skylighted garden also offers a change of scenery. **Rue Roture,** across the Passerelle footbridge from old Liège in **Outremeuse,** is that distinctive district's destination for generally inexpensive restaurants. Although the street has been getting a face lift, don't limit your choices just because a facade seems a bit rough or plain: if the menu and atmosphere inside seem inviting, you can be sure the food and service that follow will be too—as the local clientele indicates. **Cirque Divers** *(Rue Roture 14; 41.02.44)* is a brasserie, restaurant, gallery, and theater.

THE MEUSE VALLEY

Introduction

Upstream and southwest of Liège, the Meuse arches around the western edge of the Ardennes, passing through **Huy, Namur,** and **Dinant,** south of which it enters France. Signs of industry and commercial river traffic are few south of Namur, which leaves Dinant favorably situated for the recreational use of the river. Most of the region's other waterways—the **Semois, Lesse, Sambre, Samson,** and **Ourthe**—flow into the **Meuse,** which is Wallonia's watery highway of history. From pre-historic days, the Meuse has served as the most convenient means of transportation through the region: It was the route used by Roman legions policing this far northern corner of their Empire; the river road taken by invading Vikings; and a respite river-borne stretch of the long pathway west for central European pilgrims making their way mostly on foot in medieval days from monastery to chapel to Spain's Santiago de Compostela St. James's shrine.

The upper valley of the Meuse, which begins south of Namur, has a particular charm, with wooded hillsides, strange rock formations and near vertical escarpments that plunge to the river, and picturesque villages built of the local blue/gray stone and roofed with local slate. Today its scenic towns are touted as peaceful sites for tourists, but for many centuries the strategic significance of the Meuse meant that its towns, squeezed onto narrow banks beneath rocky cliffs, were spared few of the sieges and bombardments that extended well into the present century. Most Meuse towns are dominated still by their citadels, whose first foundations may have been built more than a thousand years ago.

Although largely vanished as an industry in the upper Meuse valley, the iron ore in its hills, in combination with plentiful timber to feed furnaces, and rushing rivers to power water-wheels, produced a flourishing iron empire in the area early on. Many of today's Mosan titled families can trace their fine castles, a number open to the public, and family fortunes back to the forges. The 18th-century gardens that complement the castle at **Annevoie** were funded by ironmaster Charles-Alexis de Montpellier in the 18th century and, at **Jehay Castle,** present resident Count Guy van den Steen carries on the iron tradition as an artist, creating great iron gates and handsome hearthplates for his home.

Guidelines For The Meuse Valley

SIGHTS Anchored by the slate-roofed towns of **Huy** and **Dinant,** and city of **Namur** (the administrative capital of Wallonia), the Meuse Valley is dotted with idyllic villages—such as **Celles**—fortified farms, owner-occupied museum castles (some with wonderful gardens), and—above all—citadels that crown their towns. Many examples of Mosan-style architecture (a mix of Romanesque and Gothic), are to be seen. The Meuse Valley offers the opportunity for cruising from one town to another to keep up the region's tradition of river travel, and white-water kayaking. Rock climbers can train on sheer cliff faces fronting the Meuse.

GETTING AROUND You can travel by train to Namur, and from that major junction to Huy and Dinant, the tracks (and the roads) hugging the river banks in many places. However, the Meuse valley, even with the aid of the cruise boats that ply between Namur and Dinant and some of the smaller towns in season, cannot be seen in all its scenic beauty without a car.

SHOPPING As a provincial capital, **Namur** is the primary urban center for a wide area; its main shopping street is **Rue de L'Ange. Dinant** has long produced engraved yellow copper *(Dinanderie)* articles for religious or domestic use. Fashioned since well before the 14th century—by which time some 7,500 of Dinant's population of 50,000 were employed in dinanderie—copperware in Dinant today has experienced a revival as a cottage industry; hand-beaten items can be found in several shops locally. In **Huy,** which has an ancient tradition of metalworking (12th-century goldsmith **Renier de Huy** created Liège's celebrated baptismal font), craftsmen eventually turned to pewter, many products in which can be found in shops.

ENTERTAINMENT AND EVENTS Among the many **Wallonia Festival** activities in Namur in September are the historic *stilt-walkers* (see *Namur* below). Namur and Dinant both have **casinos,** which host many cultural events.

ACCOMMODATIONS Hotels in the region are limited in number and inclined to be very small (the exception being the modern **Novotel,** south of Namur in **Wepion**). Country hotels focus on their kitchens as much, and often more, than guestrooms, which can number as few as a half dozen.

RESTAURANTS The Meuse Valley offers Belgian countryside tourism at its best, so you can feel certain of reaping rewarding meals. In towns, restaurants at hotels always make good, often the best, choices. In the country, restaurants and hotels usually come coupled, and will be your best, maybe only, bet for dining. Their kitchens will feature regional specialties such as the fish dish *Escaveche de la Meuse,* as well as river trout and crayfish, and *flamiche,* a bubbling, warm cheese and butter tart. Dinant is well-known for its *couque,* hard pastry and honey cookies baked in molds in many forms, sometimes of considerable size. The *fraises* (strawberries) of Wepion are famous.

ON THE ROAD

From Liège, follow the Meuse upstream (southwest) enroute to **Huy,** and detour north of the river to **Jehay Castle** *(Jahey-Amay; Easter to mid-Sept. Sat., Sun., hols. 2–6 p.m.; 085/31.17.16; printed guide in English).* A moated Meuse Renaissance castle of the 16th century, Jehay, begun as a fortified manor in the 15th century, achieved its present general form by 1680, when Francois van den Steen acquired the property, which is still in the family. The outer walls and towers have a unique checkerboard effect created by the use of alternating dark and light square stones. During his long lifetime, present owner **Comte Guy van den Steen** has entirely refurbished the house and filled it with historic furnishings. A respected artist, van den Steen has added to the castle's *objets d'art* with his chief talents as sculptor and ironwright. Among his works that adorn Jehay are the fine *iron* entry gate, iron railings and chimney pieces, the important *bronze* work *Marsyas tortured by the Nymphes,* which shows the 3-dimensional relief perspective developed by the artist, a sensitive sculpture of the "floating" figure in *Ophelia's Death,* and other sculpted works in the tradition of Rodin. Elsewhere in the rooms on display (tours are self-guided, on the ground floor only) are magnificent 17th and 18th century European *silver,* fine *tapestries* (16th-century Brussels, and 17th-century Flemish from a cartoon by **Teniers** and **Aubusson**). The large dining room has Renaissance and Gothic *furniture,* while the small dining room an 18th-century Liège crystal chandelier, English furniture, portrait of Nell Gwynn, one of several by Charles II's court painter **Pieter Lely** (1618–1680), and self-portrait by **"Velvet" Brueghel** (1568–1625). A circular tower room displays collections of *porcelain*—Delft, Limoges, English, and Chinese. The living room and library are handsome and homey rooms which you could live in, which the Van den Steens do. Across the moat from the castle are the **gardens,** remodeled in the French style by the current owner, who also added Italian touches: fountains, urns, and sculpture. In the castle's 12th-century vaulted cellars, the Count, also devoted to *archeology,* has assembled an extraordinary private collection of finds from digs across Europe and on the grounds of Jehay, a site which he has proven has been occupied for 30,000 years.

Huy

Tourist Office Quai de Namur 1; 085/21.29.15; pop. 20,000 • Huy (pronounced *hwee*), which sits on both banks of the Meuse, is thought to have received the first parish charter in Europe (1066). Its south bank is dominated by the **Citadel,** the site's first fortifications, built in the 11th century. Two of Huy's historic "four wonders" survive: the **Bassinia** fountain on the Grand' Place, and the **Rondia,** a large radiant rose window in the **Collegiate Church of Notre-Dame** *(Quai de Namur, next to the Tourist Office, inquire about opening hours, due to restoration).* Above the church's former entrance to the canons' cloister are the so-called "Bethelehem" bas-reliefs, with various scenes of the nativity, including a highly unusual reclining Mary, recovering from childbirth. Notre-Dame, whose first stone was laid in 1311, also has a carillon with Hemony bells.

Near the church is Huy's **old town,** an area of ancient merchant and craftsmen shop-lined streets, centered by the Grand' Place, on which sits the classic brick and bluestone 1766 **Hôtel de Ville,** and a cluster of cafes. The square is anchored with the **Bassinia fountain,** a bronze basin that dates from 1406, to the top of which was later added a tiny town crier. Adjacent is **Place Verte,** with its market, and 15th-century **Maison Nokin.** Huy's oldest house, the **Maison de la Tour,** an example of Gothic civil architecture from the second half of the 12th century, is at the corner of Rue de la Cloche and Rue des Freres-Mineurs. The latter street leads to the **Municipal Museum** *(the former Freres-Mineurs Monastery, Rue Vankeerberghen; April 1–Oct. 20 Mon.–Sat. 2–6 p.m., Sun. and hols. 10 a.m.–noon, and 2–6 p.m.; 085/23.03.77).* The monastery buildings and columned cloister, originally dating from the 13th century, were completely transformed following the secularization of church property by the French throughout Belgium in 1796, but many of the Meuse Renaissance features remain. Collections inside contain artifacts reflecting the history of the town and region. Of interest is the *Huy pewter* (made with tin from Cornish mines in England), which local artisans crafted as early as the 7th century and until the 19th. Some contemporary pieces, made in historical designs, are on display here, and on sale in shops in town.

Hôtel de la Cloche *(Quai de la Batte on the Meuse; lunch and dinner; inexpensive/moderate),* a 1406 building that is a marvelous example of the region's medieval architecture, is an atmospheric restaurant on the Meuse bank opposite the citadel (used by the Nazis as a prison for Belgian resistors).

Namur

Tourist Office Place Leopold, near the station; Mon. to Fri. 9 a.m.–noon, 2–5 p.m., Sat. and Sun. to 3 p.m.; 081/22.28.59; pop. 102,000
• Namur is the capital of Wallonia (as well as of the province that shares its name), centrally situated on the Meuse, between Belgium's industrial southwest and its scenic southeast Ardennes. Citizens of Namur have a national reputation for being slow, not in the sense of being unintelligent, but in speech and pace of life; the snail is a sort of symbol for their easy-going city.

Namur's outstanding sight is its **Citadel** *(daily June 1–Sept. 30 11 a.m.–7 p.m., and late April–end May and Oct. Sat., Sun., hols.; 081/22.68.29; car park at top of a winding road, or cable car; illuminated at night year-round; cafeteria; multilingual brochure and plan)*, which has a premier panoramic view of the city. Namur had to pay a price for its superior strategic situation, in sieges over the centuries. During the most famous siege, by the French in 1692, **Louis XIV** looked on while his soldiers eventually captured the city (Racine, on hand as a war correspondent, did double duty as a writer by producing an ode in honor of the victory). After the victory Louis let loose his military architect **Vauban,** who modified the citadel to withstand modern fire power. Though the site seems to have been fortified since Celtic times, much of what is seen today dates from the Dutch era of the United Kingdom in the early 19th century; it was used as a military compound until 1975, when it was turned over to the city to be used as a museum. A tourist train-on-wheels takes visitors around the pretty hill-crest 16-acre wooded site, pausing at marvelous viewpoints, and stopping at underground galleries, early 19th-century barracks used by the Dutch, and a museum of old tools. A cassette tape (in English and French) is played on the train during the tour, and there's also a 20-minute video that traces the history of the citadel.

The **Cathédrale de St-Aubain** *(daily 10 a.m.–6 p.m., closed Mon., hols., from Nov. 1–Easter 2–5 p.m.)* is one of Belgium's finest Baroque churches. In addition to the paintings (a **Jordaens,** possible **Van Dyck,** and several from **Rubens's** studio) is a small black marble cenotaph behind the high altar. It contains the heart of **Don Juan of Austria,** illegitimate son of Emperor Charles V and half-brother to Philip II of Spain, who died in Namur in 1578 under mysterious circumstances. In 1577, Don Juan, hero of the **Lepanto** naval battle in which Christians won against the Turks, successfully took Namur by siege, thereafter praising the well-situated citadel by saying, "When Namur falls, Europe falls." In 1578, while camping northeast of Namur at Bourge, Don Juan, aged 31, died. One story suggests that Don Juan was sent a pair of poisoned gloves by a lady jealous of his other amorous adventures. Another tale tells of him dying from wearing a pair of poisoned boots, the plot of his jealous half-brother Philip II.

The Convent of the Sisters of Notre-Dame *(Rue Julie-Billiart 17; 10 a.m.–noon, 2–5 p.m., closed Tues.)* holds Namur's most prized treasures, the works of 12th-century master goldsmith **Hugo of Oignies**. Some of the jeweled crosses and reliquaries show Wallonia customs from the artist's era. One reliquary shows a scene of men jousting on *stilts,* a popular pastime that remained so in Namur until relatively recent times. The activity is said to have begun after citizens rebelled against a siege upon their city started by Count Jehay, ruler of the Province of Namur. Several citizens tried for an audience at which to discuss the situation, but the Count apparently retorted he would receive no supplicants, whether they arrived "by foot, carriage, horse, or boat." Someone devised the idea of sending a delegation on stilts, which so dumbfounded and delighted the Count that he agreed to lift the seige.

The **Felicien Rops Museum** *(Rue Fumal 12; 10 a.m.–noon, 2–5 p.m., closed Sun.)* is a complete change—not to everyone's taste, even in the artist's own home town, and nearly a century after his death (1898). Rops, a painter and illustrator, was admired by many for his explicit and irreverent works, which caused indignation in the 19th century and can still raise an eyebrow. In season, there are **boat trips on the Meuse** *(for information call 082/22.23.15).*

RESTAURANTS **Le Petit Bedon** *(Rue Armee Grouchy 3; inexpensive/moderate)* is locally acclaimed in Namur for its meals of the plenty of the region, including *potée Liègeois* (ragout of red cabbage, sausage, potatoes, and pears), cheeses including Namur *chevre,* and oxtail soup. A number of restaurants *(inexpensive)* are located along *Rue des Brasseurs,* on the city's oldest street, near the Sambre river. There also are cafes, inside and out, in the squares that open up within the network of crooked stone pedestrian streets in the old town.

ACCOMMODATIONS IN THE AREA

★★★★ **Novotel Namur** • *Chaussée de Dinant 1149, Wepion; 081/46.08.11, fax 081/46.19.90; moderate* • With 110 rooms, this sprawling modern hotel, 3 mi/5 km south of Namur, is anything but typical of rural Belgium. It's also atypical in its range of amenities, from indoor and outdoor swimming pool, elevators, TV in every room, many in-room refrigerators, and hotel bar. Breakfast extra (BF 375 per person).

Annevoie Gardens

Chateau d'Annevoie, 5181 Annevoie; gardens open daily April 1–Oct. 31 9 a.m.–7 p.m.; castle open daily in July and Aug. 9:30 a.m.–1 p.m., 1:30–6:30 p.m., May and June weekends and hols., mid to late-April and Sept. Sun. and hols.; 082/61.15.55) • Lying slightly inland west of the Meuse, midway between Namur and Dinant, **Annevoie** is one of the treasures of Belgium for its gardens, in which water is the element that provides the wonder. Landscaped in the mid-18th century by Charles-Alexis Montpellier, whose family seven generations later still remain the caretakers, the gardens incorporate the formal, symmetrical French, the unruly and romantic English, and the classical statuary Italian styles. Annevoie is considered most unusual for its **fountains.** And *they* are unusual for operating entirely by gravity, with water brought by oak wood pipe from four nearby natural springs. The fountains, that splash, spout, and spring from cascades, geysers, reflecting pools, and descending steps, have flowed 365 days each of its nearly 240 years. Silver waters, green trees and plantings, statues, and surprising, secluded corners—not flowers—remain the concept of the older sections of the garden (as at Versailles, with which it is often compared, though Annevoie has more variety of mood). Flowers, which were not in fashion when the garden was constructed, were added in the 1950s to accommodate 20th-century tastes.

Annevoie's **chateau,** a manor house enlarged in the 18th century by the founding father of the Montpellier family, is gently curved to match the shape of the valley in which it sits. A highlight is the *white ballroom,* magnificently decorated 200 years ago with Rococo bas-reliefs by the Italian Moretti brothers. Though tours of the garden are guided in July and August, visitors are free to wander thereafter (tours of the chateau are always guided). Near Annevoie's entrance are a restaurant, a cafeteria, and a gift shop. Some summer evenings, the gardens are illuminated and the settings are used for concerts.

Dinant

Tourist Office Rue Grande 37; Mon.–Fri. 8:30 a.m.–5 p.m., and on Sat. & Sun. in July & Aug; 082/22.28.70, pop. 12,000 • There's no mistaking Dinant, with the bulbous black steeple of its **Eglise Notre-Dame** set against the sheer stone face that rises behind it. A surprising appearance on the late 13th-century church, the steeple was built for another building—the Hotel de Ville—but was later considered too large for it. It's just as well the tower wasn't attached to the church in 1228, when stones from the cliff above fell on the Romanesque church, killing 36 people. Its Gothic successor incorporated the original carved sandstone arch on the north portal, and the three carved Romanesque arches in the bapistry.

The shape of Dinant is long and narrow, the main street running a block above, and parallel to, the right bank of the river. From **Place Reine Astrid,** by Eglise de Notre-Dame and at the base of the 408 steps (and *téléférique*) up to the Citadel, the street is named for **Adolphe Sax** (1814–1894), who was born on this street and invented the saxophone (although he had to go to court many times to defend his invention, it finally was patented in 1846). The extension of the street south of Place Reine Astrid is **Rue Grande,** on which are located the **Hôtel de Ville** (which was the summer palace of the prince-bishops of Liege) and the **casino,** next to which is the **cultural center** (and tourist office). Rue Grande becomes **Rue Leopold,** which runs to the northern edge of Dinant where it passes between a spiny outcrop of stone running down the steep cliff and the single rocky pinnacle (130 ft./60 mt.) on the riverbank known as **Rocher Bayard.** *Bayard* was the name of the magical horse of the legendary *Four Sons of Aymon,* who waged a lengthy war with *Charlemagne,* their deeds and valor the stuff of Meuse valley folklore. It was, according to local legend, when the Frankish Emperor was in pursuit that Bayard, with the four brothers astride him, is said to have struck a hoof and splintered the rock as he jumped across the Meuse. The truth is that the rock spike was formed when Louis XIV blew up the cut to create a wider path for his soldiers to walk in and seize the town in 1675. A plaque on Rocher Bayard notes that Belgium's **King Albert** climbed the detached needle-shaped stone in 1933 (see also *Freyr* below).

No one can ignore Dinant's **Citadel** *(open daily year-round, except closed Fri. in Nov., Dec. Jan., Feb., Christmas, and New Year's; 9:30 a.m.–6 p.m. July and Aug., 10 a.m.–4 p.m. rest of year; 082/22.21.19; teleferique/cable car from base station near Eglise Notre-Dame; car park at top).* Dating from 1530, and set 330 feet/100 meters above the Meuse, up 408 steps, pre-9th century fortifications were destroyed by the Vikings, with replacement defenses built by the Bishop of Liège in 1051. Among the history retold in the exhibits at the top is the siege in 1466 by Burgundian **Charles the Bold,** who was often at odds with the powerful prince-bishops of Liège, for whom Dinant was a stronghold and summer residence. During the encounter, Charles reputedly ordered some 800 residents of Dinant, bound in pairs back-to-back, thrown into the Meuse. The Citadel today, as at Namur, is basically Dutch in design; guided tours (only) include the Dutch-era (early 19th century) forge, kitchen, bakery, and prison cells; a museum with weapons, historical dioramas, the carriage used by **Madame de Maintenon** (who stayed at Dinant in 1692 while Louis XIV seiged Namur), casements, and the galleries in which French soldiers held out (unsuccessfully) against the Germans in 1914. A rather effective gimmick near the end of the visit is the "Abri Effondre" (ruined shelter) during which visitors by special effect get the impression that the stone floor is shaking, in a simulation of the force of the devastating bombing unleashed by the Allies on Dinant to unseat the Nazis from the Citadel near the end of World War II. From the terrace of the Citadel are wonderful views; panoramic perspectives of Dinant and the Meuse also are possible from the **Montfort tower,** accessible by chairlift; the amusement park attractions beyond the tower may be of less interest.

RESTAURANTS **Hostellerie Thermidor** *(Rue de la Station 3; 082/22.31.35; moderate),* operated by its owner/chef, is one of the best choices for a relaxing lunch or dinner. For more informal fare, **Le Duc de Bourgogne** *(Place de Reine Astrid 7; closed Tues.; 082/22.22.29; inexpensive)* is well-located in the center of Dinant, its daily two-course *menu* that feature items such as *omelets, waterzooi, croquettes, fondu,* and *fish soup* popular with residents. The square on which it sits has several other restaurant/cafes, and, in good weather, terrace tables from which there's a wonderful view straight up to the Citadel and down to the Meuse.

In The Area

Vèves • *Celles-Houyet; Easter to Oct. 31 10 a.m.–6 p.m., guided tours, in English, available July and Aug.; 082/66.63.93; notes on exhibits in French and Dutch only, but detailed printed notes in English on loan from attendant* • looks just the way visitors would wish a castle to, solid yet romantic, with five round towers in a wooded, hilltop setting. The courtyard has a half-timbered 16th-century wall, but most of the castle today dates from the 18th century. Although the **Counts de Liedekerke Beaufort** who own it live in **Noisy,** a chateau visible on the hill across the valley, Veves has a pleasantly lived-in look, with fine 18th-century furniture, tapestries, paintings, and portraits. These include a portrait of Napoleon on his death bed engraved from an original life drawing by a family member. There also are portraits of England's Charles II and his mistress Barbara Villiers; the child of that liaison, Charlotte Fitz Roy, is a direct ancestor of the current countess of Vèves. The subject of another painting is close to home: the *Siege of Dinant* by Louis XIV. The dining room table, is surrounded with 12 rare Louis XV chairs, is set with silver, crystal, and Sevres; the old kitchen adds to the feeling that someone is going to cook tonight's dinner there.

Celles • This picturesque hamlet in the vicinity of Vèves, 6 miles/ 10 kms. from Dinant, is well worth a stop. The only specific sight in this typical blue-gray stone village (with stone barns, as well as homes) is the partially fortified, Romanesque **Eglise Saint Hadelin,** an outstanding example of the Mosan style that dates from c. 1035. Its 13th-century choir stalls are among the oldest in Belgium.

Foy-Notre-Dame • The church (1622–1626) in this village, located between Celles and Dinant, was on a pilgrimage route. It is noted for its coffered oak ceiling, 21 sections of 7 squares, each painted with a scene or a saint from the Gospels; its ornamentation was in reaction to Protestant disdain for all decoration.

Bouvignes • *1 mi./2 km. north on the Meuse from Dinant* • is a medieval town which had a running competition with Dinant for centuries. Its 16th-century **Maison Espagnole** in the center houses an interesting **Museum of Lights** *(Place du Baillage; mid-May to late Sept. daily 1–6 p.m., closed Mon.; 082/22.49.10)*, but the building is just as worthy of a visit. There's a far-reaching viewpoint over the Meuse above Bouvignes at ruined **Crevecoeur** castle (accessible by car, then some walking). The tale is told that when the French sacked and burned both Dinant and Bouvignes in 1554, three widows of the castle's defenders took over the heroic stance until ammunition ran out, whereupon they leapt, hand-in-hand, to their death.

ACCOMMODATIONS/RESTAURANTS IN THE AREA

★★★★ **Moulin de Lisognes** • *Rue de la Lisonnette, Lisogne; 082/22.63.80, fax 082/22.21.47; inexpensive* • This attractive stone 9-room hotel/restaurant in a former water mill, a short distance northeast of Dinant, offers telephone, minibar, private bath in each of the comfortable rooms; although the prices for all rooms are the same, some have balconies, ceiling beams, the pleasant sound of a rushing stream and garden view out back. There's a terrace with tables, free use of a clay tennis court, and pleasing public rooms. The good restaurant (where breakfast, included, also is served) offers three-course *menus* daily, as well as *a la carte* choices that feature local specialties.

★★ **L'Auberge de Bouvignes** • *Rue Fetis 112, Route de Namur; 082/61.16.00; inexpensive* • This rustic brick inn in a rural location on the banks of the Meuse (2 mi./3 km. north of Dinant) has six guestrooms, several with private bath, but is renowned locally for its kitchen (*a la carte* expensive, *menu dégustation* moderate), open for lunch and dinner.

★★★ **Hostellerie Val Joli** • *Rue Saint Hadelin 2, Celles; closed Wed. evenings, Thurs., and Dec. 15–Jan. 15; 082/66.67.68; inexpensive* • The establishment has seven bedrooms (most with bath and TV), but the real pride of the place is its kitchen, which serves gourmet fare worthy of the Belgians from afar who seek it out. The place is cozily small, so be sure to book (major credit cards accepted).

Freyr

Despite a tragic fall from the sheer sheet of limestone near **Marché-les-Dames** (on the Meuse north of Namur) that killed Belgian climber and beloved soldier-king **Albert** on February 17, 1934, members of the *Royal Belgian Alpine Club* still use the steep rock faces at Freyr, slightly south of Dinant, for practice. Those who make it to the top of the rock wall are rewarded with a far-sweeping view of the Meuse, across to another fine castle—this by French architect **Andre Le Nôtre**—featuring extensive formal gardens with orange groves and waterfalls. At **Freyr castle**, French King Louis XIV, in Dinant in 1675 on otherwise unsociable business, is said to have tasted his first cup of coffee.

THE ARDENNES

Introduction

The **Ardennes**—possibly the inspiration for Shakespeare's *Forest of Arden* in *As You Like It*—covers nearly one-third of southeast Belgium. The definition of what strictly is, and isn't, the Ardennes—many non-Belgians hold the inaccurate idea that everything south and east of the Meuse river is a single undifferentiated area—matters most to those who live there. Visitors consulting a map will note the large green forested stretches that indicate the ruralness of the region. The highest reaches of the Belgian Ardennes (the Ardennes extend well into the Grand Duchy of Luxembourg) are farthest east, in the German-speaking **Cantons de l'Est**, where fine winter skiing exists. The most visited sections of the Ardennes are more central, sought out for sport by hunters (the wild boar is a virtual symbol of the region, and stags and roe deer also are plentiful) and fishers, and by almost everyone for the gastronomic preparation of the fresh catch in the region's renowned restaurant retreats.

Rivers run through the Ardennes. The **Ourthe** heads roughly south to north, finishing its course by flowing into the Meuse at Liège. The **Semois** cuts the southern Ardennes laterally, snaking east (its headwaters are near Arlon) to west, where it disappears into France under the name Semoy. The **Lesse**, rushing through the mid-Ardennes for centuries, has created limestone caverns so vast that the smallest Ardennes village could be set inside the subterranean space. These rivers and their tributaries have sculpted the scenery on exhibit in the Ardennes.

Guidelines for the Ardennes

SIGHTS Belgium's forested, river-fed Ardennes region is essentially scenic. The virgin vistas above ground are complemented by an underground landscape of **limestone caves (Han-sur-Lesse**'s water-carved caves are an exceptional subterranean sight). Attractions include castles of noble lineage and monasteries from the Middle Ages (such as the picturesque ruins of the 9th-century feudal castle [illuminated on summer nights] above **La-Roche**) and small stone-built villages of the Ardennes (like **Redu,** written up as the "village du livre" for its bookshops). **Spa**'s natural spring waters, and the list of those who have "taken the cure" there since the 16th century, made the town's name synonymous with health resorts since. **Bouillon,** on the *points-de-vue*-studded **Semois** river, is dominated by a castle which its owner Godfrey mortgaged to the prince-bishops of Liège for money to raise an army to fight in the First Crusade (1096). At **Bastogne,** which put the Ardennes on the map on Christmas of 1944, there's a fine memorial and historical center that brings the Second World War's *Battle of the Bulge* into focus.

GETTING AROUND A car is essential for visiting the Ardennes. Roads are in reasonable-to-better repair, but don't estimate driving time solely on kilometers to be covered, since the switchbacks in and out of river valleys will slow you down—appropriately. The sights described below are highlights of the region, covered roughly north to south, with no suggested route. The *Belgium Tourist Map* (available from tourist offices) designates the particularly attractive stretches of road in green; you may want to supplement it with a more detailed driving map that shows smaller roads if you plan a real exploration of the Ardennes.

SHOPPING Other than regional souvenirs that tempt you along the way, the Ardennes is not the place for serious shopping, its village stores being, by-and-large, too small to supply much more than basic needs.

ENTERTAINMENT AND EVENTS Hunting season is celebrated the first Sunday of September with an **International Hunting Day** afternoon pageant at **Saint Hubert.** On Nov. 3rd, at the **Feast of St. Hubert** (patron saint of hunters), the sound of hunting horns reverberates in the Basilica during the Huntsmen's Mass and Blessing of the Animals. Torchlight visits to **Bouillon Castle** take place on many evenings in July and August. Bouillon and other hilltop castles, ruins, and citadels in the Ardennes are illuminated at night in July and August, and at holiday periods the rest of the year.

ACCOMMODATIONS The most interesting and atmospheric choices in the Ardennes—some of which are renowned—are located in the country, or near to but outside of towns—another reason you need a car in the region. Wherever you overnight in the Ardennes, it is expected that you will take dinner there; since most country hotel/restaurants take pride in their kitchen (owners often are the chef), you'll undoubtedly enjoy the experience.

RESTAURANTS The Ardennes plays a leading role in Belgium's reputation as a culinary capital. Small family-run hotels may be famed for their restaurant fare, and even casual eateries chanced upon are likely to impress visitors with their food standards. *Jambon d'Ardennes* (ham, thinly sliced) is a specialty offered everywhere, as are other high-quality pork products. *Goose* appears frequently on menus, and *goose paté* is a popular starter. *Wild boar,* sometimes marinated, *marcassin,* young wild boar, and *venison* are served during the fall game season, as is *hare ragout.* *Trout* come fresh from the rivers that rush through the Ardennes, and local *crayfish* may be fried or boiled in hot *bouillon* (named for the region's feudal-age town). Belgian *white and blue cattle* produce tasty low-fat beef. If you're not already replete, *tarte au riz* (rice tart) can end an Ardennes repast.

ARRIVING Though not themselves part of it, Namur and Liège are the towns that serve as gateways to the Ardennes. Except for the towns of **Spa** (via Liège) and **Bastogne** (via Namur), the Ardennes scenery and finest gastronomic fare are virtually unreachable by rail. A car is required for discovering the delights of the region.

TRAVEL TIPS The Ardennes is highly popular with Belgians and other Europeans for weekends (many country inns and hotels feature all-inclusive *gastronomique weekends*). During the fall game season, inns with a reputation for fine food are even more in demand. For greater schedule flexibility (though by all means book ahead), you might try to arrange your country travel during the week.

ON THE ROAD ....

Since much of the rural region's charm comes to light by exploring for favorite viewpoints, villages, and restaurants, the attractions below should be considered only an outline upon which to base your Ardennes adventure.

Spa

(Office du Tourisme, Pavillon des Petits Jeux, Place Royale 41; 087/ 77.25.10, 77.25.19; pop. 10,000), in the northern Ardennes, in well-wooded hills 22 mi./35 km. SE of Liège is **Spa** which served as the archetype for Europe's health resorts which initially grew up around mineral springs whose waters had assorted health-giving minerals and properties. The name *Spa* continues in wide use today, even for establishments (especially in North America) where "the waters" and serious health-care "cures" have been replaced with more beauty-conscious treatments. Spa's springs were known in Roman days (historian **Pliny the Elder** recorded them as located in northern Gaul at a place called Spa in his *Historia Naturalis*), but rediscovered by local citizens c. 1300. By the 1500s, its waters had made such a name for themselves—for the relief of anemia, gout, rheumatism, and digestive disorders—that people from all over Europe began seeking out Spa. Spa's reputation grew to such an extent that, by the 18th century, people of power and influence summered in Spa whether they needed the "cure" or not. The tables at the casino became equally fashionable as a gambling outing, and Spa was dubbed "the cafe of Europe" by no less a personage than **Joseph II**. Russia's **Czar Peter the Great,** who suffered badly from indigestion which produced highly embarrassing burps, came for the cure in 1717 and Spa didn't disappoint him.

Belgian King Leopold II had the neo-classical **Establissement Thermal** (also know simply as the **Therme** or baths) built in the center of Spa between 1868–1875. The attractive building of wrought iron and glass that today houses the tourist office was built in 1860 as the **Pavillon des Petits Jeux,** a games pavilion for rainy days, or rendezvous point after concerts in the park. The arrival of the railroad in Spa, which brought the genteel middle class, eventually spelled doom for the resort. It became too egalitarian to serve as an exclusive social preserve. The curative properties of its waters, however, continued to attract people to Spa—as they still do today.

Some of the closing matters of the First World War took place at Spa. In March 1918, it became German General Headquarters (established at the **Hotel Britannique,** today a school). At Spa, on November 9, **Kaiser Wilhelm,** who had been living at a residence just outside the town, learned of the unauthorized abdication announced in Berlin by his chancellor Prince Max von Baden. Early the next day, the Kaiser left Spa by train for Holland (see *Kasteel Huis Doorn,* page 317). During the Second World War, Spa was taken over by the Nazis. As an important base in occupied Belgium, however, it was physically well treated.

Though no longer a grand resort today, Spa's waters still are big business. Some 350 people, mostly Belgians, undergo nearly 500 treatments daily at the Therme (see below). Belgian national health care covers the thermal treatments ordered by the many doctors who are scientifically convinced of the health-giving attributes with which the waters are endowed. **Spa Monopole,** which has run the Therme for more than 50 years, also bottles the beneficial waters (also see below).

The most accessible place to "take the waters" in Spa is at **Pouhon Pierre-le-Grand** *(Place Pierre-le-Grand; daily Easter holidays, April–Oct. 10 a.m.–noon, 2–5:30 p.m.; Jan., Feb., Mar., Nov. and Dec. weekdays 2–5 p.m., weekends and hols. 10 a.m.–noon, 2–5 p.m., 087/77.25.10, 77.25.19),* named for Spa's most famous patron, Russian Czar Peter the Great. Here, at the fountain that for many years was simply an open spigot in a niche, then put under a colonnaded shelter in 1822, and finally in 1880 encased in a setting of glass and wrought iron in its present octagonal stone building, is the most potent of Spa's *pouhons* (mineral springs, these tasting strongly of iron). The water costs BF 7 per glass, a bargain BF 10 for a liter, though you may not desire that much once you inbibe. In the winter garden section of Pouhon Pierre-le-Grand, decorated with a medal showing the arms of Russia that is a gift from Peter the Great in gratitude for his cure here in 1717, is an immense fresco "The Golden Book." Finished in 1894 by painter **Antoine Fontaine,** who spent 12 years on it, this monumental work depicts the main characters in Spa's historical pageant as a fashionable health resort. Among them are Pliny the Elder, shown as a Roman statue, philosophers Montaigne and Descartes; composers Meyerbeer, Offenbach, and Gounod; writers Hugo and Dumas; and royalty including Cosimo III de Medici, England's King Charles II, Prime Minister Disraeli, and Duke of Wellington (who visited Spa three years after his victory at Waterloo). Occasionally, the artist has employed whimsy in his grouping of the figures, having Pauline Bonaparte, in Spa in 1812, being listened to attentively by Charles II, here in 1654, or Meyerbeer (1859) rubbing shoulders with Czar Peter (1717). The tourist office has a copy on which the nearly 100 figures are identified by number. Outside the building a monument lists distinguished visitors to Spa from the 16th to the 19th centuries, and there's a memorial to the US 1st Army, which liberated Spa on September 10, 1944.

A more formal "taking the cure" occurs at **Establissement Thermal** *(Place Royale; Mon.–Fri., 8 a.m.–noon, 1:30–3:30 p.m., Sat., 8 a.m.–noon; 087/77.25.60),* which offers a careful medically supervised program of *balneotherapy* (the treatment of diseases by baths and water cures). The Baths, which came into being in 1875 under the encouragement of Leopold II, who wished Spa's facilities aggrandized, are housed in great marble halls and tiled *Salon de Repos* (resting room). Private treatment rooms have great copper tubs and pails for the prescribed peat baths. The waters that gush from the bronze sculpted spigot in a marble fountain in the reception lobby are the extremely low-saline waters of the **Reine** spring, with very different qualities—and taste!—from Spa's pouhons. Be sure to step inside to see the fountain and great painted-ceilinged hall, even if just on the excuse of picking up an English brochure at the reception desk.

Therapy practiced at the Therme employs a mix of three natural elements: the low metal-bearing, extremely low sodium-content cold waters of **Spa Reine** (Queen's spring) piped directly to the center; the gaseous carbonaceous waters of the "pouhon" iron-rich waters of the Marie-Henriette and Wellington springs that directly feed the carbonated baths; and peat baths. The nearly salt-free Spa Reine, with the lowest salt content of any mineral water marketed in Belgium, is the basis for all salt-free diets, and aids in reducing the body's sodium balance through its effectiveness as a diuretic. Because other thermal treatments often induce sweating, the salt-free replacement of fluid in the body with Spa Reine is encouraged. The naturally carbonated pouhon iron-rich waters, given only upon medical recommendation (a medical examination by a staff doctor is required before treatment) have a sedative and vasodepressive effect on the cardiovascular system. The compression (according to Archimedes's principle) of blood-vessels and veins that results from the immersion of the body in copper tubs in body-temperature water eventually increases cardiac flow and decreases cardiac activity; with water temperature regulated and fixed at body temperature, the patient is in thermal equilibrium, which enables the cardiovascular apparatus to function at its lowest level. Peat baths began with materials from Belgium's **Hautes Fagnes plateau** to the east of Spa. The biological transformation process of that peat bog (the slow rotting of sphagnum, a sort of saturated moss that can grow several feet deep, the first stage of the transformation of vegetable matter into coal) produces an acidic medium. When the finely-sieved dried peat is ground and mixed with Spa's carbonated waters, the temperature of the therapeutic mud bath created is 40 C./104 F., and a whole-body mud bath produces muscular relaxation and reduced pain for rheumatic disorders, including gout. Following the peat bath, a washing-off shower is given progressively along the limbs and trunk, followed by a carbonated bath in the same treatment room, for a full relaxation effect. Auxiliary treatments at the Therme include hydrotherapy (various showers and messages at varying temperatures and pressures), mechanotherapy (with exercise machines), and "inhalations." The Thermal Institute has an X-ray and clinical biology laboratory; an independent institute maintains a hydrology laboratory that meticulously tests and regulates the Spa Reine water and all treatments. A medically-prescribed cure, a combination program of the above treatments, usually lasts 3 to 4 weeks, but you can make reservations for individual treatments: peat and following carbonated bath about BF 1,000, underwater massage BF 700, or one-day session BF 1,600.

Even if you don't care to indulge in a treatment, you can get an idea of the life-style of those who did during Spa's heyday at the **Musée de la Ville d'Eau/Spa Museum** *(Avenue Reine Astrid 77; open daily mid June–mid Sept. 2:30–5:30 p.m., Sat., Sun., hols. same hrs. April 15–June 14 and Sept. 16–Dec. 31, closed Jan. 1–April 14.; 087/77.13.06; no English description on exhibits, but the museum will lend you notes in English).* In the villa that was the residence of Belgium's **Queen Marie-Henrietta** (who lived here, apart from her husband Leopold II, for ten years until her death in 1902) is an assortment of articles showing Spa's history as a resort. It also features old posters (postcard-size copies on sale) that advertised Spa's attractions in Britain and across the continent, old bottles once used for its waters, and the local handicrafts created for visitors who came to take the waters (who were called *Bobelins* by the residents of Spa). The items, which date back to early visitors in the 17th century, often relate directly to the matter of "taking the cure." Walking sticks and canes (*bordons*) were popular with those making the steep climbing tour to the **Sauveniere** and **Geronstere** springs outside the town. Gradually, the sticks became embellished, painted, and varnished, and the artisans, accomplished in design, embarked upon other decorated trinkets. These included *orangettes*, small sweetmeat boxes, that held *carminatives* (aniseed, ginger, fennel, and preserved fruits) taken to correct the hardness of Spa's ferruginous pouhon waters on the stomach. Other items were small dials made of ivory, with which Bobelins could keep count of the number of glasses of water they had taken (prescribed treatments often meant drinking a dozen or more a day). Ladies wore the dial at their waist, gentlemen in their buttonhole.

The most successful Spa creations were small decorated toiletry boxes called *jolities*, whose decoration changed with the fashion, the full range of designs on display in the museum. In the 17th century, inlaid mother-of-pearl and turtoise shell were popular. The brilliantly-colored ornamentation of the boxes evolved into exquisite miniature works of art. Lacquer-ware boxes were so well done that it took an authority to tell them from articles imported from China and Japan. Tastes and techniques kept changing over the centuries, from India ink interpretations, to classical mythological motifs, landscapes, and adaptation to any art vogue that came along: Louis XVI, Napoleonic, Romantic. During the 19th century, the idea of soaking the wood for the boxes in the pouhon waters produced a gray background for the decoration. The peak of production for Spa's jolities came in the late 1800s, when the town supported 15 manufacturers. By 1900, when art deco designs were being produced, however, the number had fallen to four. Today, in addition to looking for Spa boxes in shops, you can visit **La Manufacture des Jolities et Bois de Spa** *(Rue de Renesse 28; Mon.–Fri. 8:30 a.m.–*

noon, 1:30–5 p.m., Sat. 2–5 p.m., closed Sun., *guided tours with advance reservation from May 15–Sept. 15; 087/77.03.40).*

Established in 1577, Spa's **Casino** *(Rue Royale 4; daily from 3 p.m., closed Dec. 24; 087/77.20.52)* is the oldest in the world. Though the present impressive center-of-town neo-classical building with gardens that houses the casino dates only from 1921 (rebuilt following a fire), its Hall, used for balls and theater, survives from the fine 1763 building built under the orders of Prince-Eveque de Liege. Sharing the gaming room, where Black Jack, and European and American roulette are played, are a bar and the enjoyable restaurant **La Rotonde** *(moderate).*

Spa Monopole S.A *(Rue Auguste Laporte 34, near the station; multilingual bottling plant hour-plus tours and free water-tasting Mon.– Fri. 9:30–11 a.m., 1:30–3 p.m.; 087/87.73.11; reservations preferred)* features Spa's water. *Spa Reine* (non sparkling) and *Spa Gazeuse* (carbonated) is bottled locally by Spa Monopole and sold throughout Belgium. Beyond town borders, however, you need to order *Spa* water by name; asking simply for "mineral water" may produce France's *Perrier* for its snob appeal.

Spa Promenades/open sightseeing trains or baladeuses *(Rue Pre Jonas 26; daily June, July, Aug., and in May, Sept., Oct. in good weather; 087/77.37.51)* offers several itineraries (approximately 45 mins. each) of the town and its surroundings, including Spa's pouhons, other mineral springs in the forest just outside the town. Promenades to these springs under individual foot power is a centuries-old part of the "cure" at Spa. The tourist office has maps of many waymarked walks from the town, but the classic **Tour des Fontaines**/seven springs tour (signposted, reaching an altitude of 1345 feet/410 meters), which can be made by car, takes in the springs on the periphery of Spa (Wellington, Marie-Henriette, Tonnelet, Sauveniere, Groesbeck, Geronstere, and Barisart). The waters of each (classified as "ferruginous, carbogaseous, and cold") have varying amounts of iron and are free. The waters flow from small fountains, protected by small shelters or niches; the **Groesbeek** is named after a baron by that name who built the marble niche over that spring in 1651. The **Sauveniere** spring, thought to have been the first discovered, was by the 14th century believed to provide a cure for sterility. The sulfureous **Geronstere** was the preferred spring of Peter the Great during the cure for indigestion that he meticulously followed. There's a good taverne and restaurant with terrace at Geronstere *(087/77.03.72);* refreshments are also available at Barisart and Tonnelet springs. Inquire at the tourist office about daily guided walks to the springs in July and Aug, and on Fri., Sat., & Sun. out of season.

ACCOMMODATIONS are surprisingly limited and modest in Spa itself. In town is ★★ **L'Auberge** • *Place du Monument 3; 087/87.74.10,* *fax 087/87.78.40; moderate* • has 27 rooms with bath and down-home decor and comfort; front rooms overlooking a small square. Breakfast is served in the hotel restaurant which occupies the ground floor. Some 2 mi./3 km. outside Spa is the much more interesting. ★★★★ **Manoir de Lebioles** • *in Creppe; 087/77.10.20; First Class* • an 18th-century turreted castle with terraced gardens, great baronial entrance hall, pretty lounge with period furnishings and open fire for afternoon tea, and six fine guestrooms the size of suites, all with far-reaching views from the windows. The restaurant (expensive, reservations recommended), formal in setting and service, serves haute cuisine. The specialty is the seven-course *Menu Gastronomique* featuring seasonal fare, but there's a four-course *Menu Traditional* (moderate).

RESTAURANTS In Spa, **Le Grand Maur** *(Rue Xhrouet 41; closed Mon. and in Feb.; 087/77.36.16; moderate)* serves classic French and Belgian cuisine in elegant surroundings. Advance booking is suggested. **La Rotonde** *(Rue Royale 4; 087/77.39.29; moderate)* restaurant at Spa's Casino is popular, price-conscious, and tasty in a setting that's good fun.

ACCOMMODATIONS/RESTAURANTS IN THE AREA

★★★★ **Hostellerie Saint-Roch** • *Rue du Parc 1, Comblain-au-Pont; 041/69.13.33; moderate* • Located some 30 kms south of Liège, and about the same distance west of Spa, this delightful luxury country inn with gourmet restaurant (*menus* moderate) makes for a thoroughly enjoyable visit for any reason, and it's a good point from which to explore many of the sights in the Meuse valley and northern Ardennes, as well as Liège and Spa. The 12 guestrooms, with a refined country decor, all have private baths. Dining is elegant in taste and service, and drinks are served on a terrace overlooking the Ourthe river and lovely rural scenery beforehand by the gracious owner/hosts. The venison and fish from the Ardennes are succulently supplemented by vegetables from the inn's own garden.

★★★ **Ferme Libert** • *Beverce 26; Malmedy; 080/33.02.47, fax 080/33.98.85; inexpensive* • Southeast of Spa is a more rustic experience in a half-timbered, family-style farm house, with a sweeping view over the hills of the northern Ardennes and newly-constructed guestrooms in a complementary Tudor-style lodge next door. The restaurant (moderate, some *menus* inexpensive) is the real attraction here, with diners dropping in from far afield for the substantial and satisfying Belgian country cooking.

Durbuy

Tourist Information **Corn Market/Spanish House,** *Rue Halle aux Bles; daily in July and Aug. 10 a.m.–6 p.m., 10 a.m.–noon, and 1–5 p.m. rest of year; 086/21.24.28; population 321* • Durbuy (pronounced *door BWEE'*) is the quintessential Ardennes *village,* although it has rights granted in 1331 upon which it stakes its claim to be the smallest *town* in the world. Durbuy is more delightful seen without the in-season day-visitor crowds that come by coach and carload, but leave at night. Even though Durbuy has some 20 hotel/restaurants, most are 20 rooms or less which limits overnight guests (and those out walking in the early morning mountain mists). In a few minutes you can traverse the tiny old town, built mostly of local gray stone, and there are no "must see" sights. That leaves you free to breathe the air, enjoy the rush of the Ourthe river through the village, and maybe take a waymarked walk, which is what the Belgians do to build up an appetite for the much-anticipated meals that are a gastronomic magnet. The **castle** of the Counts of Ursel *(turret 11th century, though mostly 19th reconstruction, open to the public)* hangs high above the banks of the Ourthe; the buildings along Durbuy's two or three streets in the old town (which, with an essentially unaltered ground-plan from the 14th century, is vehicle-free—of necessity!—on weekends in July and August) are mostly 16th century. The most unusual structure, housing the tourist office, is the **Spanish House,** parts of whose timber-framed facade date from the 14th century.

ACCOMMODATIONS/RESTAURANTS

★★★★ **Le Sanglier des Ardennes** • *Rue Comte d'Ursel 99; 086/21.32.62, fax 086/21.24.65; hotel moderate, restaurant moderate, except menu gastronomique expensive; hotel closed in Jan., restaurant closed Thurs. as well as in January* • This friendly family-run hotel is comfortable and charming, but the focal point of the establishment is its kitchen. Owner and master chef Maurice and son Frederic, the renowned **Caerdinals,** are known well beyond the borders of Belgium for their inspired classic cuisine, served in the dining room overlooking the rushing Ourthe river, whose soothing sound carries to the rooms at the rear of the hotel. Fish come straight from the river, grilled and flavored with lemon; perhaps roast pigeon will be enhanced with a subtle sauce, and sweetbreads with herbs. In season, *venison* and *marcassin* are featured. There are 19 rooms at Le Sanglier des Ardennes, all with TV, telephone, and bath, several with exceptional contemporary decor and skylights; back rooms have the sound of the river. (The owners also have three other properties in tiny Durbuy, including the 7 all-suite **Hôtel Cardinal,** in a corner of the village sheltered by the 14th-century ramparts, which provide a total of 45 rooms.)

The restaurant/hotel does not take its name *Le Sanglier des Ar-*

dennes from the wild beast of which it makes a feast. The "Wild Boar of the Ardennes" was the name given to the historical character **William de la Marck** (1446–1485), a nobleman who was banished from Liège for murdering the secretary of a prince-bishop of Liège (William's family supplied several prince-bishops). Thereafter, he led the life of a robber baron, with strongholds throughout the Ardennes. In 1482, William returned to Liège and captured it, slaying the bishop. He escaped, but later, after accepting an invitation to a feast, was captured by the subsequent bishop Jean de Hornes, who sent William off to Maastricht where the saga of *Le Sanglier des Ardennes* (who is referred to by **Sir Walter Scott** in his 1823 novel *Quentin Durward* in which a boar hunt figures prominently) ended with his execution.

ACCOMMODATIONS/RESTAURANTS IN THE AREA

★★★★ Chateau d'Hassonville • *5406 Marche-en-Famenne (Aye); 084/31.10.25, fax 084/31.60.27; First Class for park view, Moderate for courtyard-facing rooms* • This castle-hotel south of Durbuy, en route for the caves of Han-sur-Lesse (see below) This turreted 50-room 1687 castle, surrounded by a forest preserve, was built as a hunting lodge for Louis XIV of France during his belligerent stay in Belgium. Guestrooms are generally spacious, with a mix of antique and contemporary furnishings, all with private bath; resident owners extend gracious and helpful service. Public rooms are charming, and breakfast is served in a winter garden overlooking the lawns outside. There's a restaurant (closed Mon. evening and Tues.), so you can settle in for a delicious stay (or gastronomique weekend). Recreation opportunities include wooded walks, use of bicycles, golf putting green, and in-house snooker.

Han-sur-Lesse

From Mar. 1–Nov. 30 and Christmas hols. the nearly 2 hr. tours depart every 30 min. from 10 a.m.–4:30 p.m., except 9:30 a.m.–5 p.m. May and June, 6 p.m. July and Aug.; closed Jan. & Feb.; 084/37.72.12; wear flat walking shoes fit for damp surfaces, frequent stairs, and a sweater for the year-round 54 F/12 C temperature; guides are multilingual, booklet in English • In a region where world-class caves are not uncommon, those of Han-sur-Lesse stand out above others. The small central Ardennes town from which the caves take their name is almost entirely given over to visitors headed underground. The first account of an excursion to Han's enormous network of caves, carved from limestone by rushing river water and decorated by drippings that have formed stalactites, stalagmite floors, and other crystallizations over 300 million years, was made in 1771. As early as 1800, scientists and adventurers came knocking at the doors of local guides seeking a look for themselves. After hours, these same guides gradually explored the caves and expanded their tours (the most recent rooms you see were discovered in 1962). The earliest guides led the way with a flickering torch made from rags soaked in kerosine. In the 19th century, oil lamps were employed, but since 1905, electricity has lighted the caves—safely *and* tastefully. The extraordinary caves at Han could have been ruined by touristy technology, but, instead, a marvelous sense of wonderment has been preserved. Stalactites, growing at the rate of 1.5 inches/4 centimeters per century, some hanging several *meters* from the ceiling, help put into perspective the great age of the earth. The tour begins with a steam tram ride from the center of the village (ticket office opposite the church) to the entrance. The path inside the caves (roughly 1.4 miles/2 km., with a total of about 500 stairs) passes through great galleries, some hung with "draperies" (a kind of stalactite) among other formations, sometimes in sight of the River Lesse (whose circuitous underground course, only recently charted by speleologists, takes water up to 12 hours to travel through the caves), which earlier explorers dubbed the Styx, after the river of the dead in Greek mythology. The largest of Han's caves is called the *Dome,* its ceiling reaching higher than the spire of Brussels's **Hôtel de Ville.** Safely seated in the cavernous *Salle des Armes,* visitors are treated to a short *son-et-lumiere* program that highlights various formations to the accompaniment of music, but, while enjoyable, it doesn't outdo the natural grandeur of the setting. More interesting is the experience when the lights are shut off, plunging the huge cave into subterranean darkness, before a spot of flickering light appears near the roof and gradually descends, eventually revealing itself to be a torch carried by a runner in imitation of the pre-electric lighting of the caves. Exit is by punt, which glides on the Lesse to the cave mouth, from which it's a short walk back to the center of town, and to cafes and restaurants for refreshments.

In town, the **Museum of the Underground World** *(Place Theo Lannoy 3; April 1–Nov. 11 daily from 10 a.m.–6 p.m., except 8 p.m. weekends in May, June, every day in July, Aug.; 084/37.70.07)* displays the finds from underwater and river bed research in the caves. These include tools of flint and bone, ornaments of bone and animal teeth, and pottery made by Neolithic Stone Age cave dwellers (2,000 B.C.). Brilliant Bronze Age (1200–700 B.C.) findings include weapons and jewels, brooches, and five plates of a gold necklace. There are also findings from the second *Iron Age* (Gallic Period, the last century B.C.), as well as evidence of the use of the caves during the Middle Ages and during the 16th-century religious wars.

Han-sur-Lesse also has a **safari park** (reduced combination ticket with caves) where animals wander freely and are seen from a motorized safari car. The tour takes about 1.5 hours, same opening times as caves.

Saint-Hubert

Tourist Office Place de l'Abbaye • In the forest of the Ardennes, **Hubert,** son of a noble family, is said to have been converted. On Good Friday in the year 683, his hounds having cornered a stag, Hubert suddenly saw between its antlers a lighted cross, and heard a voice reproaching him for hunting on a holy day. Whereupon, he renounced the world and entered the abbey at Stavelot. While in Rome in 705, Hubert learned of the murder in Liège of Lambert, Bishop of Tongeren-Maastricht. Offered the bishopric, he at first refused, considering himself unworthy, but later accepted after having a vision of an angel holding the robes of investiture. Taking office and moving the bishopric to Liège, Hubert eventually became a saint, the *patron of hunters*. His feast day, November 3, is celebrated throughout the Ardennes, though nowhere more colorfully than at the Mass attended by the red-jacketed huntsmen in the **Basilica of Saint-Hubert** *(center of town, daily 9:30 a.m.–5 p.m., except from Nov. 4–Easter weekends only; 061/61.23.88).* The church has a baroque facade but exceptional flamboyant Gothic interior with lofty brick vaulting. Of great beauty is the retable with 24 *Limoges* enamels (1560) based upon **Albrecht Durer's** engravings. The ancient tomb of the saint (who died in 727) is now empty (his relics were buried in the forest during the French invasions and never relocated thereafter), the cenotaph atop it a gift in 1847 from King Leopold who loved to hunt.

Those particularly interested in the hunting tradition of the Ardennes can visit **Chateau Lavaux-Sainte-Anne** *(Lavaux-Sainte-Anne, 7 km. west of Han-sur-Lesse; daily, except Jan. 1, 9 a.m.–6 p.m., except 5 p.m. Dec.–Feb; 084/38.88.83; information sheet, some exhibit descriptions in English),* a moated castle with massive squat round towers (15th and 16th century) that houses a **museum of hunting and nature.** Amid fine oak furniture and chandeliers from Liege, the old kitchen and a well-decorated dining room, are chairs and sconces made of antlers, stuffed and mounted wild boar heads, paintings of pink-jacketed hunters on horseback, and a room with copies of the Stone Age hunting scenes painted on the Lascaux caves in France. The museum's extensive displays of area wildlife do not especially seek to defend hunting, but rather to show the part that hunting plays in biological balance. The castle, grounds with grazing deer, and hills on the horizon provide a pleasing view for diners in the **Restaurant du Chateau de La Vaux Sainte Anne** *(luncheon from noon, dinner from 7:30 p.m., closed Mon., Tues., and Jan.; 084/38.88.83; moderate, three-course menus inexpensive),* located in the adjoining 17th-century fortified feudal farm buildings.

Bouillon

Pavillon du Tourisme, Porte de France in July & Aug., 061/46.62.89; tourist office at castle open all year, 061/46.62.57; pop. 6,000 • Bouillon, the most important town in the Ardennes's scenic Semois valley, is dominated by its castle that crowns a rocky knoll encircled by the Semois. **Bouillon Castle** *(open March, Oct., Nov. 10 a.m.–5 p.m., until 6 p.m. in April, May, June, Sept.; July and Aug. 9:30 a.m.–7 p.m.; Dec. 10 a.m.–5 p.m., closed Mon. & Tues.; Jan. & Feb. open weekends only; in summer guided tours in English if requested; in July & Aug. evening tours at 10 p.m. by torchlight daily except Mon., Thurs., and when other special events are scheduled; castle illuminated from outside year-round at night; 0661/46.62.57; guide book in English; wear footwear appropriate for uneven and rough stone surfaces)*, whose foundations date from the 11th century, is Belgium's oldest and one of its finest and most interesting feudal remains. It was the property of **Godfrey** (Godefroid) of Bouillon (c. 1060–1100), presented to him, along with the duchy to which it was attached, by a childless uncle. Godfrey de Bouillon, having proved himself a strategist and committed Christian early in life, not surprisingly responded to the call of charismatic Pope Urban II for Knights of Christ to recover the Sacred City of Jerusalem, then held by the Seljuk Turks. The pope set a date when the march to Jerusalem should begin, August 15, 1096. With no heirs of his own, Godfrey made the decision to sell the entirety of his duchy, with castle, to Prince-Bishop of Liège Otbert for funds to raise and support an army for the undertaking. He made an agreement with Otbert for the possibility of buying back his possessions within three years, counting on bringing back riches from the Middle East, but Godfrey was never to return from the *First Crusade* (fewer than 50,000 of the original crusaders' army of 600,000 survived). Having raised further money by selling civic rights to the city of Metz, which was a part of his duchy, Godfrey set off well-manned and well-supplied. When he eventually reached the Holy Land, he distinguished himself in battle, first at Antioch (where he is said to have cut a Muslim in two at the waist with a strong swipe of his sword), and then at Jerusalem, which was taken by the Christians on July 25, 1099. As a result of his conduct in the First Crusade, Godfrey de Bouillon was offered the title "King of Jerusalem," which he refused on the grounds that he would be unable to wear a golden crown in the city where Christ had worn a crown of thorns. He did accept the title "Protector of the Holy Sepulchre," though he held it for less than a year before dying from poisoned cider in Syria. Godfrey is buried in Jerusalem in a marked grave at the **Church of the Holy Sepulchre.**

Back in Bouillon, his castle remained in the possession of the prince-bishops of Liege for a subsequent six centuries, until usurped by the de la Marck family, which had running battles over its possession with the de la Tours. Under Louis XIV, the castle and town were taken by the French and fortified by military architect Vauban. Today it is the property of the state.

Bouillon castle, which spreads massively along a rocky ridge (the facade is 375 yards/343 meters in length), as we see it today dates mainly from the 16th and 17th century, particularly because of Vauban's many modifications at the end of the 17th century, which were adaptations due to the advent of artillery. Near the entry (admission, tourist information) you can look down upon the moat which could be filled at will from the castle's excellent wells. There are commanding views of the town from the terrace, and of the castle itself from the top of the so-called **Tower of Austria,** and the watch-turret. At many places, the castle is highly evocative in its unfluffy simple feudal stone strength. There are few furnishings or decoration to speak of. One room, perhaps Godfrey's rock-hewn bedroom, contains a statue of the crusader, armor and some weapons, and an ancient wooden cross flat in the floor, discovered in 1962 and remaining of unknown age and origin. Another room holds Godfrey's Chair, a two-directional lookout, again hewn from bedrock. Rampart walks, semi-circular flanking towers, unusual double-storied, three-slitted loop holes, and dungeons all lend authenticity to this fascinating feudal fortress—a great place to visit, but you wouldn't want to live there.

There's parking at the castle and on its grounds the **Cafe d'Ardenne** *(closed Wed., inexpensive)* has tasty, non time-consuming snacks and meals.

Ducal Museum and Godfrey of Bouillon Museum • *below castle, on road to it; daily April 1 to June 30 10 a.m.–6 p.m., July 1– Aug. 30 9:30 a.m.–7 p.m., Sept. 1–Oct. 31 10 a.m.–5 p.m., Sat. and Sun. in Nov. and Dec. 10 a.m.–5 p.m.; 061/46.68.39; some exhibit notes in English, taped commentary in English played upon request* • Located in an 18th-century building, beneath the castle on the road leading up to it, the museum is divided into two major sections. History and folklore exhibits include a model of Bouillon in 1690, but the section on Godefroid de Bouillon, on the upper floors, is much the more interesting. It focuses largely upon the Crusades, the march through Europe to the Middle East, the weapons such as catapults, crossbows, and battering rams used in the capture of Jerusalem, life-size models of armored knights, Templars armaments used in their 13th-century fights against the Moslem infidels, and maps of the regions involved in the crusades. A case with small figures shows the dress worn by the various groups of people who went to the crusades. Among the Eastern and ecclesiastical art from the era is a rare 14th-century carved ivory Virgin.

For rental pedal boats and canoes (kayaks, single or two-seater) in Bouillon, see **Les Triton-Semois** *(Quai des Saul 2; Easter to end Sept. 9 a.m., last departure 3 p.m.; 061/46.63.91).* For reservations for a descent of stretches of the Semois by kayak, contact Recreation Center **Moulin de la Falize** *(061/46.62.00, fax 061/46.72.75; March 1–Oct. 31).* In the summer season, wheeled **tourist trains** *(061/46.70.04; weekends mid-Lent to Nov. 11, except daily in July, Aug., from approximately 10 a.m.–5 p.m.; 45 minutes, 5 miles/8 kms.)* depart regularly from the Pont de Liège and Pont de France in town for rides up to the Castle.

Tombeau de Geant/Giant's Tomb

For a striking sample of the scenery in the Semois valley, turn west about 2 mi./3 km. north of Bouillon, at signs for *Sensenruth* and *Ucimont*. Shortly, just through the hamlet of **Botassart,** you will come upon the rural setting of the beautiful, unspoilt, far-reaching view across to the forested mound of land, almost completely surrounded by an oxbow in the Semois, known locally as the *Tombeau de Geant*. There's a bench or two from which to survey and savor the splendid sight, and a picnic table. Before leaving Botassart, visit the village chapel (1625), with its distinctive old Ardennes-style slate-tiled steeple. Note particularly the interesting wooden ceiling, from which the rope connected to the village bell hangs accessibly from the center aisle in case there's a need to ring out an alarm.

ACCOMMODATIONS/RESTAURANTS IN THE AREA

★★★★ Auberge du Moulin Hideux • *Rt. de Dohan 1; 6831 Noirefountaine; 061/46.70.15; moderate* • Its name (the hideous windmill) doesn't seem to fit (though it does sit across from an old water mill) this pretty country inn, situated 2 miles/4 km. north of Bouillon. A fire on the hearth, greenery in the glassed-in bar, and soft, leather lounge furniture express the smart but warm welcome extended to guests. The 10 charming bedrooms all have private bath and the same comfortable contemporary coziness as found downstairs. The restaurant (*a la carte* expensive, *menus* moderate) is considered one of Belgium's best, with classic French Belgian cuisine featuring, not unexpectedly, wild fresh game from the surrounding forests, saddle of pork, and river fish, with wonderful soups and *mousse de paté* for starters.

★★★★ **Hostellerie Sainte-Cecile** • *Rue Neuve 81; 6819 Sainte-Cecile-sur-Semois; closed Wed. except in July and Aug.; 061/31.31.67; moderate* • Situated between Bouillon and Orval, this pleasing country hotel/restaurant requires that you take dinner; *menus* (a choice of three, all moderate) are varied and enticing. All bedrooms have comfortable furnishings, telephone, and modern bath, those in back overlook a stream, garden, and terrace with tables. There's a TV-lounge and bar.

Abbaye Notre-Dame d'Orval

If you've followed the Semois valley as far as Florenville, head a bit farther south to the Abbey of Orval *(signposted; daily 9:30 a.m.–6 p.m.; 061/31.10.60; ground plan in English).* The monastery (the first monks arrived at Orval in 1070) had a resurrection in 1948, when the Cistercian Order was resettled in buildings designed by architect **Henri Vaes,** rising from the foundations of the previous one, laid waste by the French at the end of the 18th century. The new, working, buildings cannot be visited by outsiders (except those who have arranged with the Father porter to stay for a contemplative period), but the ruins of the monastery built here in the 12th and 13th centuries can be. Among the most evocative of the mellow-colored stones that remain standing are those of the north wall of the transept, with the empty tracery of a one-time rose window. The ancient porch, former refectory, and garden of medicinal plants offer an atmosphere for contemplation. The ruins are in startling contrast to the new church with its gigantic madonna and child, so large you can ponder it from the grounds of the old abbey. A 20-minute audio-visual program (ask to see the English version) not only discusses the history of Orval but describes the life style of a present day monk. In the shop near the entrance, the Trappist monks, known for their silence with each other, are more than willing talk to you as you survey the religious souvenirs, and give in to the temptation of the Abbey's delicious homemade cheeses and breads and home-brewed Trappist beer (Orval produces one of only six authentic Trappist beers in the world, five of which are produced in Belgium, the remaining one in Holland). Many visitors come to buy bottles of this noblest of beers directly from Orval, but you can't drink it on the premises; for that, there's a cafe across the street.

Bastogne

Tourist Information, Place McAuliffe 24; daily year-round 8:30 a.m.– noon, 1–5:30 p.m., closed Mon.; 062/21.27.11; pop. 12,000 today, 4,000 in 1944 • Many people are familiar with the Ardennes because of Bastogne, which held center stage during the *Battle of the Bulge* late in World War II. Since Roman days, the location has been at the intersection of main roads through the Belgian/Luxembourg Ardennes; in 1944 that crossroads became key in the U.S. Army and Allied resistance that made *Bastogne* for Hitler comparable to what *Waterloo* was for Napoleon. That snowy December, Bastogne was the gift the Nazis couldn't wrap up for Hitler's Christmas. The ghost of that Christmas past is given substance at Bastogne's **Historical Center** and **Mardasson Monument.**

Today, Bastogne, once again a modest market town, well-endowed with shops that serve the surrounding Ardennes countryside, is mostly recovered from the shattering results of the Nazi surge of Panzer divisions towards the Meuse that stagnated and "bulged" around the town. One day before the beginning of the Allies' Arnhem operation (see page 308), two days before the ending of the Nazi Falaise Gap debacle in Normandy, and three months to the day before the campaign was finally launched on December 16, 1944, Hitler declared, "I have just made a momentous decision. I shall go over to the counter-attack out of the Ardennes with *the objective—Antwerp."* Hitler's aim was to trap the British and Canadian armies north of Antwerp, forcing them to surrender, and separating them from the U.S. Army, which he believed would then lack the skill and will to continue fighting alone. Though his own leaders seriously questioned the campaign, Hitler pursued it. **Field Marshal von Rundstedt,** who is unfairly credited with developing it, was quoted as saying, "All, absolutely all, conditions for the possible success of such an offensive are lacking." Nevertheless, Hitler issued handwritten orders stating rigidly "No alterations permitted" in the codenamed *WACHT AM RHEIN*/*Watch on the Rhine* (the code was later changed to *HERBSTNEBEL*/*Autumn Mist*—though *Winter Snow* would have proved more appropriate, for the battles were fought in what would be the coldest winter to date in the 20th century). Hitler's push was to be east to west along a 60-mile north/south front between Monschau (Germany) and Echternach (Luxembourg) by Panzer and infantry divisions, which would quickly reach the *Meuse,* cross it south of Liege and Namur, and then turn northwest for Brussels and Antwerp.

What indications of action Allied intelligence heard didn't seem to warrant interrupting the planning for upcoming Christmas festivities; most of the forces were already convinced that the Nazis were too weak to mount a broad attack. And the Ardennes, except for the Nazis' easy breakthrough into the Benelux there in September 1940, was thought to be terrain too troublesome for a ground attack, especially in winter. (As a result of that reasoning, both sides had been regarding the eastern Ardennes as a place for tired troops to rest and untested ones to get their front line bearings.) Supreme Commander Eisenhower expressed concern about the lack of Allied coverage in the area, but allowed Omar Bradley to reassure him.

December 16 dawned gray, making Allied air attack impossible, and eight Panzer armored divisions rolled forward from their position on the Germany/Luxembourg border to begin their advance to Antwerp. Within a day they were already well behind in their scheduled crossing of the Meuse. They never would make it; one jeep on Dec. 17 bringing the Nazis as close as they would come to crossing the Meuse. Moving ahead of their Panzer divisions, in one of seven confiscated American jeeps (the other six were all captured) that hoped to seize bridges over the Meuse, were four Nazis, disguised in American overcoats. Their jeep was bound for Dinant, whose Meuse bridge was under the guard of a British Royal Tank Regiment. Reaching the east side of the Dinant bridge, the four American-cloaked Nazis in the American jeep sped through the British guard, who were thus unable to warn the occupants that the west end of the bridge had been set with anti-tank mines. The jeep occupants were killed instantly, and the British were relieved to find that under their American overcoats were Nazi uniforms.

One reason that their campaign fell behind schedule so soon is that from the second day, the Nazis were already feeling a shortage of fuel, having failed to find the stores of hidden Allied petrol that their plan had depended upon. And the U.S. Army resistance was more resolute than expected, especially in Luxembourg: German General **von Manteuffel** said later, "The courageous resistance of the 28th at Clervaux and Wiltz made possible the installation of the (Allied) defence of Bastogne." The closed-in weather, though it did hamper Allied air strikes, also made cross-country travel far more difficult. The roads themselves, too few and too small for the Panzer divisions, "bulged" from the traffic. Both sides were confused in their movements, particularly when fog settled over the landscape, but there was one clear fact: all roads ran through one of two points, Bastogne and St. Vith. Once the latter fell on December 21, the focus was all on the former.

In fact, Bastogne had been surrounded by Nazi Panzer infantry since December 20, but their commanders' freedom to act was frozen by the plan foisted on them by Hitler: press on to the Meuse, regardless. Those inflexible orders, which even Manteuffel would not risk straying from for fear of Hitler's wrath, saved Bastogne. Manteuffel ordered the 2nd Panzer tanks to head for the Meuse, and left only an infantry division to attack Bastogne, which though it could surround the town couldn't break into it.

On Dec. 21, there were few U.S. airborne troops holding out in Bastogne and they were running low on artillery ammunition and supplies. Fearing Allied reinforcements (said to be on the way from *Patton's Third Army*, headquarters then in Luxemburg City), von Rundstedt had to temper the orders to his own outnumbered troops that they take Bastogne, but only in such a way as to not hinder the Nazi advance to the Meuse.

On Dec. 22, under siege by the surrounding Nazis, the American perimeter was approached at midday by four Nazis carrying a white flag. The one who could speak limited English requested to see the American commander. He was blindfolded and led to **Brigadier-General McAuliffe,** to whom he handed a note from Nazi General von Luttwitz of the Panzer corps. The message demanded the surrender of the American garrison on honorable terms, stating that otherwise the town and all military and civilians in it would be annihilated. Upon reading it, McAuliffe's immediate reaction was *"Aw, Nuts!"* (many suggest that he used a stronger term, but, during one of many post-war visits back to Bastogne, McAuliffe confirmed his response). Hard pressed to find the words for a formal refusal, McAuliffe finally followed the suggestion of a staff member, and simply wrote down his first words (now in the notebooks of Americana). Handed the note by an American lieutenant, the Nazi spokesman found the slang beyond his comprehension and responded, "I do not understand. Is your commander's reply favorable?" To which the lieutenant replied, "It is certainly not affirmative. In plain English it means the same as 'Go to hell'. You understand that, don't you." The German saluted, was blindfolded, and driven back to the outpost.

On Dec. 23 the skies cleared, and huge Allied C47 transport planes dropped in 144 tons of ammunition, medical and other supplies by parachute. Now the Americans could pick off the Nazis, sitting ducks in their dark uniforms against the snow that had begun to fall, any natural camouflage in the woods burned away with napalm.

On Christmas Day, just before dawn, the Nazis in 18 tanks broke through into Bastogne, but the Americans met them with such firepower that all 18 were put out of operation. Thus, even before the first three Sherman tanks of the 4th Armored finally arrived on Dec. 26, it was clear that the Nazi effort was lost, but that day General von Manteuffel wrote in his journal, "Despite my advice, Hitler remains stubborn about Bastogne."

On Dec. 30, snow fell thicker. On Dec. 31, the Germans attacked Bastogne 17 times, with heavy losses all around. Of the situation in the ebbing hours of 1944, von Manteuffel would write, "The ultimate defeat of the *Wehrmacht* was only a question of time, for the men and equipment to carry on the war were lacking." Still, the Nazis mounted further attacks on January 3 and 4, the toll of these last encounters in the Battle of Bastogne the heaviest of all. In the Battle of the Bulge as a whole, between its opening on December 16, 1944, and closing during the final week of January 1945 (by which time the Nazis had been forced back to the approximate line that they had held when Hitler had begun his push to Antwerp), casualties, including wounded, missing in action, and those taken prisoner, for both sides amounted to well over 150,000, with more than 21,000 dead.

If you're arriving in Bastogne by car, follow signs to **Mardasson,** 1 mi./2 km. north of the center. There, it's best to begin your visit at the **Bastogne Historical Center** *(Colline de Mardasson; Mar. 1 to April 30 and Oct. 1–Nov. 15 10 a.m.–4 p.m., May 1–June 30 and Sept. 9:30 a.m.–5 p.m., July and Aug. 9 a.m.–6 p.m.; 061/21.14.13; all* *displays multilingual, gift/bookshop with English literature),* which is unique among military museums in that many of the details were authenticated, exhibits created, and commentary scripted with the collaborative help of both **U.S. Army General McAuliffe** and **Nazi General von Manteuffel,** who worked together here at the center after having fought each other on opposing sides. The museum has several elements, the first being an illuminated model showing the phases of the **Battle of the Bulge** around Bastogne while simultaneously projecting actual still photographs of the confrontation onto a circle of screens around the amphitheater. Written and spoken commentary throughout is in English (and other languages). Another of the center's ingredients is its exceptional collection of authentic uniforms for both sides (General Baron von Manteuffel donated the leather greatcoat he wore during the campaign), as well as items brought by returning veterans, and those found on the actual battlefield. Several well-done dioramas are peopled with wax mannequins of the major players: generals McAuliffe, von Manteuffel, Patton, Bradley, and Eisenhower, and show battle gear and lighter equipment of the parachute division, vehicles, and weapons. Finally, the cinema shows clips of film shot by Americans and Germans during the battle days, beginning with Panzer divisions on the move towards Belgium through Wiltz and Clervaux in Luxembourg. We see not only shelling, but the actual taking of prisoners, troops on both sides walking out with their wounded, and scenes showing the snow-camouflage overcoats and tank covers (many for the Allies from bed sheets donated by the Belgians). Also on display is a copy of the Christmas message of McAuliffe to his cold, weary soldiers. Of the 200,000 or so annual visitors to the center, approximately 15% are Americans, 50% Dutch, 20% Belgian. Allow *at least* an hour for a visit, and additional time for the Mardasson Monument near it.

A visit to the Historical Center will give you a deeper appreciation for Battle of the Bulge whose casualties are commemorated at the close-by **Mardasson Monument** (free access at all times), erected in 1950 under the initiative of the Belgo-American Association. The tall star-shaped memorial, with the names of the U.S. states inlaid around the upper edges and the sides inscribed with the military companies that participated in the Battle of the Bulge, also includes, on ten large stone slabs, a detailed account of the battle written by U.S. military historian S.L.M. Marshall. In the crypt beneath the monument, the 76,890 Americans killed, wounded, and marked missing at Bastogne and the other battles in the Bulge theater are remembered with three chapels (Protestant, Catholic, and Jewish), decorated with mosaic murals by **Fernand Leger.** Via interior spiral stairway, you can reach the viewing platform atop the monument. At each of the star's five points is a description of the battle action that took place in that direction, today all rolling pastureland.

Elsewhere in the town of Bastogne are monuments of the events of the chilling winter of '44/45. A Sherman tank and a bust of McAuliffe are on the square that bears the Brigadier-General's name. An area driving route brochure, available from the tourist office or Historical Center, enables you to follow the signposted main stages of the campaign in your car or, in summer, a tourist train takes visitors to many of the sites. There are several choices for food on **Place McAuliffe** and just off it is Bastogne's leading plain-but-pleasant 27-room hotel/restaurant **Hotel Lebrun** *(Rue du Marché 8; 062/21.11.93; hotel inexpensive, restaurant moderate,* menus *inexpensive).*

THE GRAND DUCHY OF LUXEMBOURG

Introduction

"Of all nations on earth, Luxembourg is one of the most stable and prosperous, where nature is preserved and foreigners—whether residents or tourists—are welcomed. In all, one of the world's happiest."
.... Former United Nations Secretary-General Xavier Perez de Cuellar, 1989

The above statement may not quicken the senses, but it's surely reassuring about a country few people know much about. Most are surprised to learn what a wealth of treasure and pleasure await in this condensed dose of Europe.

The Luxembourg Landscape

The smallest member state of the European Community, surrounded by Belgium to the north and west, France to the south, and Germany to the east, the Grand Duchy of Luxembourg measures a mere 999 square miles. Which makes it smaller than America's smallest state, Rhode Island, and only 1/16th the size of Switzerland, itself a very small nation. In travel terms, Luxembourg is 50 miles/80 km. north to south, 32 miles/52 km. east to west. You could drive up or down its length in one and a half hours, entirely across it in one.

Geologically, Luxembourg falls into two regions: the hilly slate Ardennes known as the **Oesling** in the north; and the larger, more populated fertile farmland appropriately called **Gutland** (Good Land). Even the poorly endowed land in Luxembourg has been brought to a high level of agricultural return. The southern part of the Ardennes plateau, across the country from Vianden to Wiltz, is cut with deep valleys. Gutland has a more extensive river system. The differences in altitude

BELGIUM
GERMANY
FRANCE
N
0 miles 6
0 kilometers 10
Lieler
Troisvierges
Our River
Clervaux
Wiltz
Vianden
Esch-sur-Sûre
Bourscheid
Sûre R.
Eschdorf
Diekirch
Ettlebruck
Beaufort
Berdorf
Sûre River
Echternach
Grosbous
Colmar-Berg
Mullerthal
Larochette
Consdorf
Useldange
Mersch
Hollenfels
Wasserbillig
Septfontaines
Gaichel
Eischen
Eisch River
Alzette River
Grevenmacher
Moselle River
Dommeldange
Luxembourg
Arlon
Findel
Ahn
Koepchen
Wormeldange
Ehnen
Hamm
Remich
Petange
Rodange
Mondorf-les-Bains
Alzette River
Moselle R.
Esch/Alzette
Schengen
GRAND DUCHY OF LUXEMBOURG

from north to south affect the climate; the high Ardennes in the north have far more rainfall, a cold snowy winter, and a late spring (mid-May), while the south has a milder climate, warmer summer, and long growing season. More than one third of the Grand Duchy is forest. Much is preserved, either by the government, or maintained as private hunting reserves—such as the extensive lands owned by Grand Duke Jean.

Geographically, Luxembourg has several distinct tourism regions. Just outside of Luxembourg City to the northwest is the **Eisch River Valley,** more memorably known as the Valley of the Seven Castles. Most of the famed castles are now picturesque ruins perched above their villages. A short distance directly north, having crossed into the Ardennes, is the scenic **Sûre River valley.** In the forests and towns to the north and south of it much of the *Battle of the Bulge* action in Luxembourg took place in the winter of 1944/45. Mid-country, near the eastern boundary, is the region known as **Little Switzerland,** which is characterized by large, unusual rock formations. Virtually all of Luxembourg's shared eastern border with Germany is created by three rivers, the **Our** in the north, the **Sûre** in the midregion, and **Moselle** to the south. The Moselle Valley is the vineyard of Luxembourg, and has been since Roman days. The south and southeast sections of the Grand Duchy are the most heavily agricultural, with outcrops that reach into France's Lorraine plateau.

Luxembourg lies in the heart of industrial Europe, and is itself a highly industrialized nation. Most heavy industry lies in the **terre rouge** in the southwest, where the earth is red from its iron ore content. However, despite its industry (mostly steel) and minuscule size, Luxembourg gives the impression of being full of wide-open, unpopulated spaces. And even in the industrial southwest, development is controlled and green space preserved. In the north, the **Sûre River,** which crosses Luxembourg from the Belgian to the German border, has no industry on it at all, its reaches carefully kept clean for their beauty and recreational use. The Grand Duchy has an excellent record of compliance with European Community environmental regulations, ranking second only to Denmark among the 12 member states. According to the World Resources Institute in Washington, D.C., 21.1% of Luxembourg's total land area is protected, as compared with 8.6% in the United States and 10.6% in the United Kingdom.

Tourism, one of the Grand Duchy's five most important revenue sources, is one reason why Luxembourgers work to keep their land pristene. The offer of rambling and hiking in unspoilt countryside is one of its strongest selling points to European travelers; Luxembourg's network of marked walking paths is the densest in the world. But an even more important factor behind the preservation of the Grand Duchy's naturally scenic landscape is that it is an essential element in the quality of life that Luxembourgers seek for themselves.

The Luxembourg People

"Of all the countries I have visited, the Grand Duchy of Luxembourg is the smallest, but it is the one that has charmed me most and where hospitality has been most simple and cordial."

. . . . Sir Winston Churchill

One of the wonders of Luxembourg is that, despite being overrun, occupied, ruled, and even incorporated, by many mainland European powers, over the centuries, up to and including the 20th, its people have maintained a national character entirely their own. Surrounded by Germany, Belgium, and France, Luxembourg is not a mixture of the three, but a distinct social and political entity. Despite the inevitable legacy of linguistic, artistic, and social influences from foreign occupiers, the Grand Duchy's own cultural values have the deepest roots.

Lately, there has been a peaceful, productive "invasion" of foreigners. They now account for 25% of the Grand Duchy's total resident population. These foreigners, who hold 40% of the jobs in the Grand Duchy's banking industry—and include more than 10,000 individuals, with families, who work for one of the European Community institutions based here—provide what Luxembourg, with one of the lowest birth rates in the world, does not: a sufficient supply of workers at all skill levels, to keep its prosperous economy on course.

Luxembourg's commerce is of necessity international. Since it was partitioned in 1839, the country has recognized that it was not large enough to be economically self-supporting. This knowledge creates a cosmopolitan streak in the solid core of traditional family and community values in the Luxembourgers' life. As the humorous self-description—"one Luxembourger, a rose garden; two Luxembourgers, a koffeeklatsch; three Luxembourgers, a band"—shows, they are a people who make time for life's basic pleasures.

Amid its international diversity, Luxembourg society retains one element of homogeneity: religion. Some 95% of Luxembourgers are Catholic (down from 99.5% in 1871, and 96.9% in 1970). Although they do not hesitate to differentiate themselves as practicing or nonpracticing, a basic acceptance of the Church and its sacraments is taken for granted. Ever since foreign workers were needed in the country in the last quarter of the 19th century, Luxembourg has drawn mostly Catholic migrants (especially Portuguese, who make up 9% of the current population), thus perserving the singular religious character of the country.

Luxembourgers have managed to fashion a very high standard of living for themselves. According to the recent Larousse-published *Euroscopie* (which contains vast collections of statistics of living and working conditions in the 12 EC countries), Luxembourgers, on the surface of things, as well as in less material ways, are the most satisfied with their lot. In addition to having the highest disposable incomes and longest holidays of their European neighbors, they have the greatest number of houses equipped with central heating, washing machines, dish washers, and electronic gadgets. (Other surveys show that Luxembourgers are the EC's highest domestic consumers of electricity, but with all their rivers they can produce it themselves). The Grand Duchy also has the most automobiles and hospital beds. Some 60% of house occupiers own the lodgings they live in. And, even though the country has the most telephones per capita in Europe, the country is small enough to make do with one code for the whole country.

A complex history has brought Luxembourg to the position that one hears the maxim "To be a Luxembourger is by necessity to be a European" expressed in one form or another almost every day in conversations with local people. The lingual pluralism that plays an important part in Luxembourgers' social and professional lives, opening them up to other cultures, begins at an early age. German is taught from the age of six, French from the age of seven. Most students learn English.

One of the founding fathers of the European Community concept, **Robert Schuman** (1886–1963), was born and raised in Luxembourg City. Born of a Luxembourg mother and French father (from Lorraine, which like Luxembourg, has a multi-culture history as a pawn between Germany and France), Robert Schuman lived his formative years, from birth until the age of 18, in Luxembourg City, in the suburb of **Clausen** in the Alzette Valley. The house in which he grew up, at Rue Jules Wilhelm 4, today sits just beneath the **Kirchberg Plateau** where the buildings of the European Center rise; in 1990, following restoration, it opened as the **European Study and Research Centre Robert Schuman,** with the mission of promoting knowledge of the history, and encouraging the further exploration, of European unification. Raised in Luxembourg, a student at several German universities, later a French citizen (as a result of the 1919 Treaty of Versailles which gave Lorraine back to France), and in the French government from 1919 to 1962, Schuman was well-prepared and well-positioned for his European role. Later in his life, at the pinnacle of his political career, Schuman said his early life in Luxembourg gave him "a sense of life I never had to change in the years to follow." He also referred to his formative education in Luxembourg in these words: "We had the window wide open beyond the political borders, towards East and towards West." Luxembourg is glad to be able to cite Schuman as one of its own; May 9, observed annually as the "birthday" of the European Community, is, in this Catholic country, sometimes referred to as *St. Schuman's Day*.

Luxembourgers have a motto, a line from their national anthem, *"Mir woelle bleiwe wat mir sin,"* which translates as, "We want to remain what we are." Among the many things Luxembourgers are is a people who have proven they can cope. (Henry Miller once observed: "In Luxembourg there are no neurotic people and no lunatic asylums.") They have avoided the complexes that could come with trying to feel at home in a world in which their homeland is seemingly insignificant, and have confidence in and ease with the times that is enviable.

Luxembourg: An Historical Perspective

Luxembourg's geographic position in Europe has been perceived as central and strategic since its settlement by Romans. Throughout most of its history, Luxembourg has been fortified to protect it from foreign armies. Unfortunately those very fortifications often invited invaders, and, later, European power brokers who felt free to arbitrarily cut Luxembourg down in size and install soldiers in its capital.

Given its diminutive dimensions, the name "The Grand Duchy of Luxembourg" could be considered too much of a mouthful. At the peak of its political power in the 14th and 15th centuries, when it provided four rulers who served as Holy Roman Emperors, Luxembourg was much larger physically, but the Grand Duchy has never played as important a part on the international stage as it does today. Its petite proportions allow Luxembourg to help solve sensitive international situations by eliminating any feeling of competition from larger countries.

The Luxembourg land spent long centuries in international entanglement before it finally achieved the status of independent state. Foreign occupiers since the Middle Ages left their footprints upon the soil, and more ancient antecedents left artifacts beneath it. Evidence of *Neolithic* man (after 10,000 B.C.) can be seen in the countryside and in the collections of the Musée de l'Etat in Luxembourg City. In the millennium before Christ the region was occupied by *Celts*. The most significant of the prehistoric tribes in Luxembourg were the *Treveri* (Trier) and *Mediomatrici* (Metz), both of which followed the faith of their priests, the *Druids*. Remains of Celtic fortified compounds can be seen on the **Titelberg** and around **Mullerthal** ("Little Switzerland").

Caesar's conquest of Gaul (58–51 BC) resulted in the incorporation of the Luxembourg area into the Roman Empire. Three major Roman roads connected it to what is now Germany; the most important to Trier, an administrative center second only to Rome. There followed in the Luxembourg region a rapid process of Latinization, with increased order and security, as well as flourishing trade and agriculture, in particular, *viniculture* along the Moselle. Gallo-Roman villas with baths, mosaic floors, and murals were built both in towns and in the countryside (remnants can be viewed in museums in Luxembourg City and Diekirch). Despite its domination, the Roman influence did not eradicate the region's Celtic culture. The officially forbidden Druidism remained, but Christianity also became established in Luxembourg by the 4th century. As Roman power weakened, Luxembourg faced attacks from the Vandals, Visigoths, and Huns (their leader **Attila** recalled in the town name **Ettelbruck,** meaning "Attila's bridge"). In 450 AD, the Franks crossed the Rhine, bringing the Roman rule of the region to a close. The Franks settled large areas of Luxembourg, especially around the Moselle, establishing their Germanic language throughout.

In 496, Frankish King **Clovis** converted to Christianity. As a result, the religion spread throughout the population. Monastic orders brought their enlightenment into the Dark Ages all across Europe. In Luxembourg, the era was highlighted in 698, when Anglo-Saxon Benedictine **St. Willibrord** founded the **Echternach Abbey,** which became famous for the **Echternach School of Book Illumination.**

The Frankish Empire, of which Luxembourg remained a part, reached its climax under Emperor **Charlemagne,** who sent some one thousand Saxon families to settle the sparsely populated Ardennes during the 9th century. The Frankish empire faced grave territorial divisions under Charlemagne's weak successors. Under the *Treaty of Verdun* (843), Luxembourg became part of Lorraine, which subsequently was divided between France and Germany by the 870 Treaty of Mersen. This marked the beginning of a conflict that would last over a thousand years, as Luxembourg was perpetually bounced between the powers of France and Germany.

On April 12, 963, the Abbey of St. Maximin in Trier, which had been established in the same era as Luxembourg's Echternach Abbey, granted to **Sigefroi, Count of Ardennes,** a deed to a rocky promontory on which stood the ruins of a Roman fort known as **Castellum Lucilinburhuc** or "Little Castle." (A copy of the deed can be seen in Luxembourg's *National Library,* the original remains in Trier.) At *Lucilinburhuc*—a name that evolved to *Lutzelburg* and eventually Luxembourg—Sigefroi built a fortified castle. The House of Luxembourg thus born at Sigefroi's fortress remained independent as part of the Frankish Empire for nearly five centuries, though its fortunes rose and fell under the combined influences of family land holdings, adeptness at arms, oaths of loyalty, and well-made marriages.

Knights from Luxembourg accompanied Godfrey de Bouillon on the first crusade, and served in Asia Minor on subsequent ones. They had left their Luxembourg castles **(Bourscheid, Esch-sur-Sûre, Hollenfels),** whose ruined turrets look so romantic today, though the reality of life within the walls of the feudal fortresses must have been anything but. Some of Luxembourg's absentee landlords fell in battle. Those who returned often were debt-ridden, their lands in disarray; some found their castles confiscated by strong arms and swords that had stayed home.

One leader of Luxembourg, **Henry the Blind,** Count of Namur set in motion events that were to improve the situation immeasurably. Late in the 12th century, Henry, having no direct heir, was preparing to bequeath his immense possessions to his nephew Baldwin of Hainault when, at the age of 65, love played a hand; he married Agnes of Gelderland, who gave him a daughter. Baldwin revealed his displeasure by pillaging Namur and breaking the power of the aged Henry. But Henry's late-in-life daughter, **Ermesinde** (1196–1247), through resourceful marriages and far-reaching ideas of leadership and reform, re-established Luxembourg's prestige and extending its frontiers from the Moselle to the Meuse. After the death of her second husband, Ermesinde herself took over the reins of rule, by bringing together feuding noblemen into a kind of council of state, and granting burghers rights which loosened the hold of feudal lords over them. In 1244, she granted a charter of freedom to the City of Luxembourg. Realizing that education was the key to the continuation of these reforms, Ermesinde also founded schools, convents, monasteries, and cultural institutions. Her legacy to Luxembourg was a secure, well-administered country with long-lasting social institutions. Her heirs continued the family line that would prove one of the most illustrious of the Middle Ages.

In the 14th century, the House of Luxembourg became one of the dominant forces in Europe. In 1308, Ermesinde's great grandson **Henry VII,** count of Luxembourg, was crowned head of the Holy Roman Empire in Rome. In 1312, **Dante** hailed him as the "Restorer of Justice, Peace, and Liberty." Upon his untimely death in 1313 (of malaria in Pisa, where he is buried in the cathedral), his son **John,** who had added Bohemia to the House of Luxembourg by marriage at the age of 14, took over. So popular was John as an ideal of knighthood that he remains Luxembourg's national hero to this day. For the first 30 years of his rule, John set out almost every spring on military campaigns from the North Sea to the Vistula to increase, or keep intact, his holdings. Despite failing eyesight that gave him the epithet *"The Blind,"* John answered the appeal of French King Philip VI when England's **Edward II, the Black Prince,** invaded France. All but sightless, he lead his army into the *Battle of Crecy* (1346), in which he was slain. In tribute, the victorious Edward said of Luxembourg's John the Blind, "The battle was not worth the death of this man." Edward took the three ostrich feathers from John's helmut, and the motto *Ich dien* ("I serve") in tribute to John's loyalty, and adopted them as the crest and motto for the **Prince of Wales** (currently Prince Charles).

Charles IV, son of John the Blind, through his own and family marriages, and treaties, brought Luxembourg to the size and status his father had sought by the sword. As Holy Roman Emperor, Charles maintained a court at Prague that dazzled all of Europe. When Charles's younger brother **Wenceslas** married **Jeanne, Duchess of Brabant,** thereby acquiring Brabant and Limburg, and much of what is Belgium's Luxembourg province today, he brought the House of Luxembourg to its greatest expanse. Charles honored Wenceslas by making Luxembourg a duchy in 1354. In 1356, Duke Charles and Duchess Jeanne of Brabant issued one of the most important written municipal charters of merchants' rights, the *Joyeuse Entree* (Joyous Entry), which was of equivalent significance for Belgium and Luxembourg as the *Magna Carta* was for England. In it, the Duke and Duchess promised that they would impose no restriction on trade, except legal taxes; gave subjects the right to revolt if the Duke exceeded his legal powers; and pledged not to declare offensive war "except at the advice, will and consent of our good cities and land."

But, **Wenceslas II,** who became Emperor and Duke of Luxembourg in 1383, used his holdings almost exclusively as a source of revenue and troops for armies, and created a series of civil wars between sovereigns that plagued the House of Luxembourg. The last male of the line, Holy Roman Emperor **Sigismund,** through marriage also the King of Hungary, and thus foretelling the region's future ties with the Hapsburgs, died in 1437. In 1443, the Duchy of Luxembourg was bought by **Philip the Good of Burgundy,** thereby losing its autonomy and dynasty and becoming a province (linked under Philip to the Netherlands). Philip established French as Luxembourg's language of government and administration, which it remains today. The Burgundian Netherlands passed to the Hapsburgs in 1477, and among the titles **Charles V** received at his birth in Ghent in 1500 was Duke of Luxembourg. From that time, Luxembourg essentially shared the history of the Netherlands.

Staunchly and overwhelmingly Catholic (which it remains today), Luxembourg sided with the Belgians in support of Catholic, Spanish Hapsburg King **Philip II,** rather than Protestant Holland, during the Reformation and subsequent religious unheavals in the 16th century. Luxembourg, often a stake in the battles waged between the European powers, was annexed in 1684 by France's **Louis XIV,** who held the duchy until 1697 when it was returned to Spain. During the French occupation Louis's military architect **Vauban** fortified the site of Luxembourg City so fully that it became known as the *"Gibraltar of the North."* In 1714, at the end of the war of the Spanish Succession, Luxembourg, along with Belgium, passed to Austria, and remained a part of the Austrian Netherlands until 1795. From that year until the fall of Napoleon in 1814, Luxembourg, with its Benelux neighbors, was incorporated into revolutionary France.

In 1815, the European powers meeting at the *Congress of Vienna* to balance the forces on the continent, dared not leave Luxembourg to itself. They felt its strategic position and fortifications made it too strong to ignore, yet its size left it exposed to takeover from others. They "settled" the situation by raising the status of Luxembourg to *Grand Duchy* and giving it as a personal property to the Dutch King. This made House of Nassau **Willem I** and his heirs the hereditary *Grand Dukes of Luxembourg,* a situation which lasted until 1890 (see *The Grand Ducal Family* under *Keys to the Grand Duchy* below). There was more to the arrangement: the Congress of Vienna also called for the territory of Luxembourg lying east of the **Moselle** and **Our** rivers to be joined to Prussia, giving in compensation to the dismembered Grand Duchy the greater part of the duchy of Bouillon and part of the former prince-bishopric of Liège (territory that conforms today to Belgium's province of Luxembourg). Although linked by the same sovereign, Luxembourg was designated politically independent of Holland and the United Kingdom of the Netherlands, so the ruling powers meddled further by deciding that the Grand Duchy must be a part of the *Germanic Confederation,* and that Luxembourg City should be a Confederation fortress with a garrison of *Prussians.*

In 1830, the Grand Duchy, with the exception of Luxembourg City, which, with its Prussian garrison, was not allowed to join and thus remained under Dutch King Willem I, joined with Belgium in a revolt against the United Kingdom of the Netherlands. Upon Belgium achieving its independence, the Grand Duchy (again, with the exception of Luxembourg City), put itself under Belgian rule. In 1839, a date of mixed blessings for Luxembourgers—since it marks both its first true independence and the date of its partition—the *Treaty of London* divided the Grand Duchy in two. The larger, French-speaking western part went to Belgium, becoming that country's Luxembourg province, its largest. The eastern portion remained with the Dutch, and Willem, persuaded by the logistical difficulties entailed in maintaining a fiefdom separated from Holland by a still hostile Belgium, granted Luxembourg a measure of autonomy. Thus, the Grand Duchy assumed its present frontiers, and a date from which to date its independence.

In 1842, at Prussia's insistence, Luxembourg joined the German *Zollverein* (customs union). That association, in which Luxembourg remained until the First World War, laid the foundation for the Grand Duchy's development during the Industrial Revolution; German capital, manpower, and markets were the base upon which Luxembourg created its great *steel* economy in the last quarter of the 19th century. In 1848, **King Willem II** (1792–1849), by far the preferred of the Grand Duchy's Dutch rulers, gave Luxembourg its *constitution.* (Willem II is honored in Luxembourg City with an equestrian statue on **Place Guillaume,** named for him. (The statue, cast in 1884 by sculptor Antonin Mercie, was such a good likeness of Willem II that the Dutch ordered a copy in 1924). In 1859, with Dutch help, Luxembourg got its first railroad, an event of such surpassing importance to the Grand Duchy that the poem "Feierwon" written to commemorate the occasion ranks in importance with the national anthem "Our Homeland." In 1867, upon the dissolution of the Germanic Confederation, and with many nations uneasy about the fortress-capital at the fulcrum of Europe, the European powers, met again in London. They certified Luxembourg's freedom, guaranteeing the Grand Duchy's neutrality, setting up a program for the dismantling of its fortresses, an arranging for the withdrawal of the Prussian garrison. Luxembourgers, not noted for excess, are said to have danced in the streets as the Prussians departed. They then went about the business of reaffirming their constitution. In a single century since, Luxembourg has progressed from feudal fortress to full-scale modern nation.

In order to maintain its economic independence, Luxembourg was compelled to call in foreign workers from the time of its steel industrial expansion beginning in the 1870s (from that period, a high percentage of foreigners has remained a characteristic of the country). Luxembourg's own work force was particularly small because many residents had emigrated at the end of the 18th and early in the 19th century, when the country had been impoverished and barely unable to feed its people. (The people of Luxembourg heritage living in the United States today number more than the entire population of the Grand Duchy).

In 1914, despite its neutrality, which had been dictated by the European leaders in 1867, Luxembourg was occupied by Germany on August 2. During the First World War, more than 3,000 Luxembourgers lost their lives fighting for the Allied cause, a substantial sacrifice for so small a nation. At the end of the war in 1918, Grand Duchess Marie-Adelaide was accused of alleged pro-German sympathies. From Nov. 1918 to Jan. 1919 Luxembourg went through a *Grand Crise* (great crisis) that ended with Marie-Adelaide's abdication. Then began a popular process to determine whether Luxembourg should become a republic and elect a president, or place **Charlotte,** sister of Marie-Adelaide, on the throne. In the plebiscite held in the fall of 1919, more than 50% of the people chose Charlotte to be Grand Duchess, and her popularity rose much higher during her 45-year reign, during which she enjoyed undiminished affection.

In 1921, to replace the German Zollverein trade union, Luxembourg signed a customs and economic treaty with Belgium *(BLEU, the Belgium-Luxembourg Economic Union),* which pegged their currencies to each other. The internationally outlooking Grand Duchy also joined the *League of Nations.* Despite the depression, Luxembourg's steel industry grew to the point of being ranked seventh in the world in productivity by the end of the 1930s. In 1939, with rumblings of large-scale war again being heard in Europe, Luxembourg reasserted its neutrality. The Grand Duchy also threw a particularly strenuous centenary celebration of its independence, as a message to Hitler to respect its freedom.

But it was to no avail. On May 10, 1940, Hitler's Nazis marched in and occupied all three Benelux countries. However, since Luxembourg City had been home to a Prussian garrison in the 19th century, Hitler used an *"absorption" policy* on the Grand Duchy. Unlike Holland, Belgium and other countries "occupied" by the Fuhrer's forces, Luxembourg was *incorporated into the Third Reich,* meaning that its citizens were liable for conscription into the *Wehrmacht.*

In 1941, the Nazis undertook a census in the countries they occupied. On the printed form under the question "What is your nationality?" was the notation that Luxembourgers, as well as Alsatians, should write "German." On the day before it was due, the Nazis recalled the census in the Grand Duchy, having learned that the population was planning wholesale defiance and would write "Luxembourg." This resistance was a precurser to the general strike in 1942, staged in response to the call for military service in the *Wehrmacht* (women also were conscripted, for labor). Luxembourgers walked out of their factories, first nailing the country's flag to their masts. More extreme reprisals followed. A number of Luxembourgers managed to escape, enlisting with British, Canadian, U.S., Free French, and Free Belgian forces. Many who were inducted into the *Wehrmacht,* under the threat that otherwise their families would be deported to Prussia, were sent to fight for the Nazis' on the Russian front. Between 1943–1945, many Luxembourgers wound up as "irregular" German troops at the Russian POW camp at Tambow (a model of which can be seen at the **Diekirch Historical Museum** of the Battle of the Bulge, see *Diekirch* under *Grand Tour of the Grand Duchy* chapter). Luxembourgers at Tambow banded together for support and many survived more than two years of incarceration there.

On September 9, 1944, **Petange,** near the Belgian border in southwest Luxembourg, became the first town in the Grand Duchy to be liberated, by soldiers of the *First U.S. Army, 5th Armored Division*. It is impossible for us to fully understand what the liberation meant to Luxembourgers, except to note that these many years later September 9 is still observed annually in Petange. Every five years since 1944, a large ceremony has been staged at night, with a torchlight parade from Petange's town hall to its town monument. Erected in 1947, its inscription in French reads "In memory of the first American soldier who fell in the liberation of Luxembourg," followed in Letzebuergesch with "Monument to an Unknown Soldier—We Will Never Forget." But, thanks to the Luxembourg group CEBA that researches aspects about the war, in 1987 the American soldier was identified. At the following five-year observance, in 1989, family members of the man who had died in the first armored car across the border were on hand on September 9th for ceremonies that unveiled a plaque to, and renamed the square for, **Hyman Josephson,** 2nd Lieutenant, U.S. Army.

On September 10, 1944, the U.S. Army had pushed through to liberate Luxembourg City; their progress was made so quickly that the rapidly retreating Nazis did not have time to destroy much of the capital. All of the Grand Duchy was quickly freed by the Allies, mostly American, who were joyously welcomed.

Although almost no one on either side believed the Nazis could—or would—mount another large-scale attack, Hitler conceived and implemented a counter-offensive that, although Antwerp was the object, got bogged down and was waged largely in the Luxembourg and Belgian Ardennes. On December 16, with the opening of what became known as the *Battle of the Bulge* (see *Bastogne* under *Ardennes, Belgium*), Hitler's *Wehrmacht* once again occupied Luxembourg soil. In the snow and cold of the winter of 1944/45, particularly around **Wiltz** and **Clervaux,** Luxembourg suffered its worst damage, and the Allies some of their greatest casualties, of the Second World War. By the time the last town in Luxembourg was freed for a second time (**Vianden** on February 12, 1945), one third of Luxembourg's farmland was unusable; 60,000 people were homeless; and half the country's roads, bridges, tunnels, and train tracks had been destroyed. Also, many of Luxembourg's steel plants were burnt out from forced overproduction.

From the late 19th century until the shift away from its industrial base in the late 20th century, Luxembourg's prosperity rested mainly on steel. The prime company, *Arbed,* at its peak before the widespread steel crisis began in 1975, was Europe's fourth largest producer, a multinational with 100,000 employees in plants in Europe, America, and Asia. Arbed also provided more than steel to Luxembourg's economy, since, as was discovered in the 19th century, the waste from the smelting process proved an effective fertilizer for the Grand Duchy's northern and central farmlands. After the Second World War, Luxembourg put its steel industry back in shape so swiftly that by the mid-1950s, the country had one of the highest GNPs per capita in Europe, but it had learned not to put all its economic aspirations in a single industry. When the steel industry crisis of the 1970s hit, the "Luxembourg Model"—scaling back the number of hours per worker to avoid lay-offs—was widely imitated. By then, banking had replaced steel as Luxembourg's number one industry.

Post-war economic planning began in the Benelux even before the end came. By September 5, 1944, Antwerp and Brussels had been liberated, and on that day in London, representatives in exile of the governments of Luxembourg, Holland, and Belgium (which coined the acronym BENELUX) signed a document entitled *Customs Convention,* roughly based on the 1921 BLEU agreement between Belgium and Luxembourg that had proved extremely successful. The intent of the three governments was to form a complete and durable economic union and to restore economic activity by establishing a common tariff of import duties. Not until 1948 did the convention become operational, and not until 1958 was a Benelux *Treaty of Economic Union* finalized. But despite rough edges the Benelux survived, primarily because the leaders in all three countries never abandoned the conviction that the idea of union was essentially sound. In 1949, Luxembourg became a founding member of the North Atlantic Treaty Organization (NATO), having abandoned its traditional policy of neutrality (it having proved inadequate to guarantee its liberty and independence). The Grand Duchy has a volunteer army of 450 people.

Even while the kinks in the Benelux were being worked out, Luxembourg was being linked to an expanded European economic union. In 1950 **Jean Monnet,** a far-sighted Frenchman who preferred to remain in the background, proposed a plan to **Robert Schuman,** the Luxembourg-born-and-raised French foreign minister, for the formation of a supranational *European Coal and Steel Community (ECSC)*. Working enthusiastically on the initiative, Schuman suggested that "the pooling of coal and steel production will immediately provide for the establishment of common bases for economic development as a first step in the federation of Europe, and will change the destinies of those regions which have long been devoted to the manufacture of munitions of war, of which they have been the most constant victims." A treaty between the three Benelux countries, plus Germany, France, and Italy, was signed in 1951, with Monnet serving as president, and Luxembourg established as the seat of High Authority.

The ECSC proved such a success that, in 1955, the foreign ministers of its members solicited suggestions for extended cooperation in economic spheres. The most important message came from the Benelux, which by then was seeing palpable benefits from integration. The Benelux statement said, "The moment has come to pass into a new state of European integration. . . . this must be achieved first in the economic field." In 1957, a treaty was signed in Rome between the six ECSC members to form the *European Economic Community (or Common Market)*. Luxembourg City was designated the headquarters for several of its permanent institutions: the Secretariat of the European Parliament; the Court of Justice (which is similar in many ways to the Supreme Court in the United States); the Court of Auditors; and, appropriately, the European Investment Bank.

Today, with more than 160 banks, and a total of more than 200 financial institutions that include substantial securities and reinsurance markets, sleek **Boulevard Royal** is Luxembourg City's answer to "Wall Street." The Grand Duchy's financial services sector employs about

15,000 people (one in six working Luxembourgers is employed in some facet of the business), and accounts for roughly 15% of GNP. Private investments in Luxembourg banks are estimated at $160 billion.

The Grand Duchy of Luxembourg had its most recent six-month turn in the rotating presidency of the European Community during the first half of 1991 (Holland took over for the latter half of 1991). The country holding the presidency, among other Community business, can put forth ideas of particular interest to it, and, during its previous presidency in 1985, Luxembourg brought to the signature stage the *Single Europe Act ("1992"),* the treaty being signed onboard the *Marie-Astrid* Moselle River cruise ship out of Luxembourg's wine-growing village of **Schentgen.** During its 1991 presidency of the EC, while furthering the implementation of numerous single-market initiatives, Luxembourg also was called upon to mediate in follow-up meetings to the Iraq/Kuwait Persian Gulf war, and to serve on the three-member EC team that sought to find a non-violent solution to the ethnic strife in Yugoslavia. Among the modern buildings of the **European Center** that rise above Luxembourg City from the **Kirchberg Plateau** is the **European School.** It was the first of its kind when it was conceived in 1953: an educational system for the children of ECSC-employee families that provided for students speaking totally different mother tongues, an immersion in varied cultural milieus, and stressing the principle of European unity. Today, teachers originating in all the countries of the EC give lessons to 3,000 students from all the EC nations, and more, nursery school through high school (the diploma is accepted at any university in the EC). Now having been copied by nine other European schools, Luxembourg's continues to set the pace, helping the children sitting on the school benches to leave their national mentality behind them, providing an education that vouchsafes that the European citizen of tomorrow is open-minded.

Keys To The Grand Duchy

TOURIST OFFICES   Travel and attraction information for the Grand Duchy is available in Luxembourg City at *Syndicat d'Initiatives et de Tourisme* at Place d'Armes (which also is the City Tourist Office; 2.28.09, fax 47. 48.18); at the Air Terminus at the rail station (Place de la Gare; 48.11.99); and at Findel Airport (40.08.08). Local tourist office information is given under individual towns (see *Grand Tour of the Grand Duchy*).

WEATHER   Luxembourg has a temperate climate, with no extremes. Although the Ardennes shelter the country from some of the wind and rain that are more of a constant in Holland and Belgium, an umbrella and raincoat still are suggested. The following chart shows the *average* of the daily high and low temperatures (in Fahrenheit) by month for **Luxembourg City,** as well as the average number of days each month with no measurable rainfall.

Average Daily Temperature (in Fahrenheit)

Weather in Luxembourg City—Lat. 49°37′—Alt. 1,025′

	JAN.	FEB.	MAR.	APR.	MAY	JUNE	JULY	AUG.	SEPT.	OCT.	NOV.	DEC.
	35°	38°	42°	49°	55°	61°	64°	64°	60°	50°	43°	38°
Days with No Rain	16	13	16	14	15	13	15	15	14	14	12	15

NATIONAL HOLIDAYS New Year's Day; Easter Monday (date varies); Labor Day (May 1); Ascension Day (date varies); Whit Monday (date varies); National Day (June 23); Assumption (date varies); All Saints' Day (Nov. 1); Christmas Day; St. Etienne (Dec. 26). Days that are not national holidays but on which administrative and public offices, schools, and similar institutions are closed are Carnival (including Shrove Tuesday, date varies); Octave (May/June, date varies); Whit Tuesday (date varies); All Souls' Day (Nov. 2); Christmas Eve; New Year's Eve.

LUXEMBOURG LANGUAGE No one else speaks **Letzebuergesch:** Luxembourgers know that no one learns it unless at a mother's knee. In fact, the language has been almost entirely an oral tradition over the centuries, and only recently was given concrete written form (see also *Language,* under *Practical Travel Information* at front of book). Here's a sample to make us appreciate the fact that Luxembourgers have been considerate enough to learn other languages. *Wei geet et lech?* (How are you?), *Kennt Dir mir hellefen?* (Can you help me?) *Vill Gleck!* (Good luck!).

TOURIST SEASON Officially, the tourist season in Luxembourg runs from Easter to late October. However, some attractions, even in Luxembourg City, and especially in more rural areas of the Grand Duchy where the focus is on outdoor tourism, some close by mid-September until the following Easter, or later. It is wise to confirm opening hours if you are making travel plans to include specific attractions or museums. There are plenty of reasons (scenery, fine dining, walking, little worry about full hotels) to travel out of season, although keep in mind that a number of small rural hotels close entirely out of season. After September, the weather is more inclined to gray and wind, though Luxembourg can have an "Indian Summer." In the spring give the trees time to grow new leaves if you want to see this *Green Heart of Europe* at its best.

TRAVEL DISTANCES Luxembourg City is centrally located in Europe, posting the following distances to other major cities and transportation hubs:

City	Miles	Kilometers
Amsterdam	223	360
Brussels	127	205
Frankfurt	160	258
Ostend	206	332
Paris	206	332
Zurich	246	396

TRAINS While the train is an excellent way to get to/from **Luxembourg City,** it is *not* the ideal mode of transportation for touring the Grand Duchy. The rail network, although serving the major towns of Ettelbruck, Diekirch, Wiltz, and Clervaux, neglects the best scenery and some of the most special countryside towns. While trains do operate in tandem with the national bus system, and thus afford access to most places, for travelers with limited time (not to mention energy and initiative), they are not the best way to see how exceptionally scenic the Grand Duchy is.

DRIVING If it is at all possible, I recommend you explore the remarkably varied and rural Grand Duchy of Luxembourg by car. When working out a realistic itinerary, it's important to keep in mind the *scale* of your Luxembourg map (the tourist office offers a free one of the Grand Duchy that is as detailed a road map as you'll need). Even allowing for frequent car-stopping scenery and wandering at will in the most interesting towns, you can cover quite a patch of the country on a day's drive. Add an overnight, better two, and you can be a master traveler in this lovely little land.

Although Luxembourg City now faces the same traffic jams at the beginning and end of the business day that have come to plague all European cities, the situation in the countryside of the Grand Duchy is completely different. Never have I driven on such untrammeled roads, almost all unbusy byways. Often when traveling alone by car and navigating for myself, I opt to collect a rented car at the airport, or other location outside a major city, in order to avoid congestion while I'm becoming familiar with unfamiliar traffic patterns. But there's no need for that in Luxembourg. And, ten minutes after departing downtown, you'll be completely in the country, and nearly to your first destination, no matter in what direction you're heading. You don't need to know route numbers, only the name of the town you're headed to, and an interim village or two. as you'll see from the scenic roads that are highlighted in green. There are so many around the country that you'd be unable to avoid them if you tried to, and I've even found myself spellbound by stretches not specially marked for their scenic appeal.

Throughout Luxembourg road signage is extremely well-done, with indicators for upcoming villages and towns appearing at every crossroad where needed. Many of the well-paved roads are two-lane, and you will occasionally come upon a farm vehicle or truck; be cautious about passing because of the possibility of oncoming traffic around a road bend. On any roads you'll hardly see a car from one quarter hour to another, though you must drive prepared to come across an oncoming car, traveling speedily. If one approaches from behind, just pull over when it's safe to let it pass, and go on with your leisurely appreciation of the scenery.

Because its *V*alue *A*dded *T*ax rate is lower than other European countries (an advantage that could eventually disappear with the implementation of 1992), car-rental rates in Luxembourg are among the least expensive on the continent. Round-trip *Icelandair* transatlantic passengers flying from JFK Airport in New York via Reykjavik, Iceland, are entitled to that airline's extremely favorable rental cars rates with unlimited mileage (toll-free U.S. inquiries to Icelandair 1-800-223-5500).

THE FLAG   After you've been in Holland, Luxembourg's flag will seem familiar, since until 1890, the hereditary ruler of the Netherlands' House of Nassau were also the grand dukes of Luxembourg. Today, the Grand Duchy's horizontally striped red, white, and blue standard is the same as Holland's except for a slightly lighter shade of blue. Since, however, that change was only made official in 1981, many older flags with the darker blue remain in use. The historic flag of Luxembourg, an upright red lion on a background of white and blue stripes, is sometimes used within Luxembourg.

THE GRAND DUCAL FAMILY   The Grand Duchy of Luxembourg is a hereditary constitutional monarchy. Although it finally was granted independence by a conference of European nations in 1867, Luxembourg remained under the rule of **Dutch King Willem III,** who was Grand Duke of Luxembourg in his own right through the **House of Orange-Nassau** (whose ancestral home is **Vianden Castle,** see *Vianden* under *Grand Tour of the Grand Duchy*). In 1890, Willem III died without a male heir, and the Dutch crown passed to his daughter **Wilhelmina.** However, in Luxembourg, because of the *Salic Law* which applied at the time making women ineligible to succeed to the throne, there was a discontinuation of dynastic links with the Orange-Nassaus, and its rule passed to **Duke Adolphe of Nassau-Weilburg,** who became founder of Luxembourg's Royal House. When Adolphe's son, **Guillaume I** (William), who had abolished the Salic Law, died in 1912, his eldest daughter **Marie-Adelaide** became Grand Duchess. When Luxembourg was occupied by the Germans in World War I, Marie-Adelaide remained in the country; afterwards, she was faced with charges of alleged pro-German sympathies, which forced her to abdicate. A referendum put to the people in 1919 confirmed the ruling house and called for her sister Charlotte to assume the throne.

Grand Duchess Charlotte, married to Prince Felix of Bourbon-Parma, healed Luxembourg's monarchy, becoming a much loved leader. When the Nazis invaded Luxembourg in May 1940, Charlotte escaped the country with her family and ministers and formed a government in exile. Her work on behalf of Luxembourg and the Allies during the war in England, Portugal, and Canada (where her son Jean went to university), was a source of pride to her people. On her return to Luxembourg in 1945, Charlotte was greeted by the premier with words of regard from her nation that were often repeated thereafter: *"Madame, we love you"* (they are inscribed in Letzebuergesch on the sculpture of the former Grand Duchess paid for by public subscription and erected on Luxembourg's **Place Clairefontaine** after her death in 1985). In 1964, after 45 years on the throne, Charlotte abdicated in favor of her son Jean.

Still monarch of Luxembourg today, **Grand Duke Jean,** who was born in 1921 and served as a lieutenant with the *Irish Guards* from 1942 to 1945, married Princess **Josephine-Charlotte** of Belgium, sister of King Baudouin. The Ducal Palace in Luxembourg City serves as the royal couple's in-town residence and office; their country castle is north of the capital at Colmar-Berg. Grand Duke Jean, who celebrated the 25th anniversary of his reign in 1989, and Grand Duchess Josephine-Charlotte have five children (and 14 grandchildren). Their eldest son, H.R.H. **Prince Henri,** born in 1955, is heir to the throne. He received his graduate education in France, Switzerland, and England, and holds a masters degree in political science and a Staff College Certificate from the *Royal Military Academy* at Sandhurst, England. The Crown Prince is highly effective in his job as chairman of the *Board of Economic Development of Luxembourg.* In 1981, he married **Maria Teresa** (now Princess), who was born in Cuba in 1956, her parents moving to New York in 1959 at the time of the revolution. Eventually her family moved to and became citizens of Switzerland, where Maria Teresa met Prince Henri while he was studying at the *University of Geneva.* The popular couple has four children, the eldest a son, **Guillaume.**

LUXEMBOURG CITY

Guidelines For Luxembourg City

SIGHTS One of the world's most picturesquely situated capitals, Luxembourg City should be enjoyed as much for its visually engaging setting (with mid-city ravine, walled by former fortifications and romantically illuminated at night) as for any other specific attractions. From the pedestrian **Promenade de la Corniche** are panoramic vistas that have given it the name "the most beautiful balcony in Europe." The city's *upper town* is set on plateaux, above the winding green valley of lower town, the site of several suburbs with cafes, and walking paths with superb views up at the bastions. Centers of activity are in upper town, at the **Place d'Armes** (tourist office), **Marché-aux-Poissons** (the original hub of the ancient city, with the **National Museum** and **Bock casemates**), and **Place de la Constitution** (overlooking the *Petrusse Valley*). The **European Center** on Kirchberg Plateau houses the offices of the Luxembourg-based European Community institutions; its modern buildings provide an intriguing contrast to the city's fairy-tale turrets.

GETTING AROUND Although the city is not large, Luxembourg's layout is complex, set on several levels and cut by two rivers, the *Alzette* and *Petrusse,* with their rock-walled, wooded valleys. Virtually all sights, shopping, and much of the charm are in the old *upper town,* as distinguished from the modern *European Center* on the Kirchberg Plateau across the dramatic **Grand Duchess Charlotte ("Red") Bridge** (1966), and the 19th-century sections of the city, across the arched **Pont Adolphe** (1903) in the direction of the *Gare* (station). Since the views from points in the upper and lower city are so much a part of Luxembourg's beauty, sightseeing on foot will prove the most memorable. The upper city is quite compact, with several sections pedestrianized. The tourist office provides an excellent leaflet *(A Walk through the Green Heart of Europe)* that outlines two 3 mi./5 km. walking tours covering the highlights in both the upper and lower city. The *elevator* (free, 6:30 a.m.–2 a.m.) on **Place du Saint Espirit** connects the upper town with the lower's **Grund** suburb (cafes and restaurants). Travel by foot can be supplemented as needed by city buses and taxis. Bus terminals and taxi ranks are located at the station, **Place Aldringen,** and **Place de**

Paris; taxis, although tip is included in the fare, are expensive, with surcharges for luggage, travel at night (10%), and on Sundays (20%). For interesting, and easy, views from the paved pathways through the Petrusse and Alzette valleys, take **Luxembourg Live,** a tourist train on wheels *(April 1–to Oct. 31, daily departures from 10 a.m.–6 p.m. from the Adolphe Bridge at Place de Bruxelles, tickets (220 Flux) from Kiosk Luxembourg Live. The 45-minute tours include an audio dramatization; English language on headset of the city's turbulent history).* Although its audio show is gimmicky, if you're not planning to take independent walks in the center-city valleys, the perspectives of the former fortifications offered during the tour are highly recommended. Because of pedestrian and one-way roads, restricted on-street parking, and the challenge of Luxembourg City's upper and lower city topography, it's preferrable to have a car *only* when you need one to explore the countryside; **Kemwel** is a reputable, budget-priced local car-rental firm. If you arrived by car, leave it in a center city car park. Two-hour motorcoach tours with a drive-by of major city sights and a stop at the **US Cemetery at Hamm** are offered by **Voyages H. Sales** *(26 Rue du Cure; mornings daily April 1–October 31, several days weekly the rest of the year; 46.18.18; bookings also at tourist office, hotels).* The company also offers diverse day tours in the Grand Duchy on Wed., Sats., and Suns. from spring to Sept. 30.

SHOPPING Though Luxembourg is not inexpensive, the quality of goods sold is very high, and the range of items for a city its size surprisingly broad, due to the demands of its cosmopolitan population. Choices range from boutiques along the chic pedestrian **Grande Rue,** to fresh produce and general wares at the Wednesday and Saturday morning open-air markets held on **Place Guillaume** in front of the Hôtel de Ville. Luxembourg's own **Villeroy & Boch** provides desirable souvenirs. Note that many shops do not open Mondays until 2 p.m.

ENTERTAINMENT AND EVENTS In warmer months through September, almost **nightly concerts** in the bandstand entertain *al fresco* diners around **Place D'Armes.** After-dark illumination produces a setting for fairy tales at the former fortifications (year-round in Petrusse Valley). Other city buildings and monuments are floodlighted from late spring through Sept., and a walk about town to view them is memorable evening entertainment, although the tourist office can provide a listing of concerts and other events. You can also check the "What's On" page in *Luxembourg News Digest,* the country's weekly (Thurs.) English-language newspaper. It will give you an idea of the activities of the U.S., British, Canadian, and other English-speaking nationals who live in the Grand Duchy.

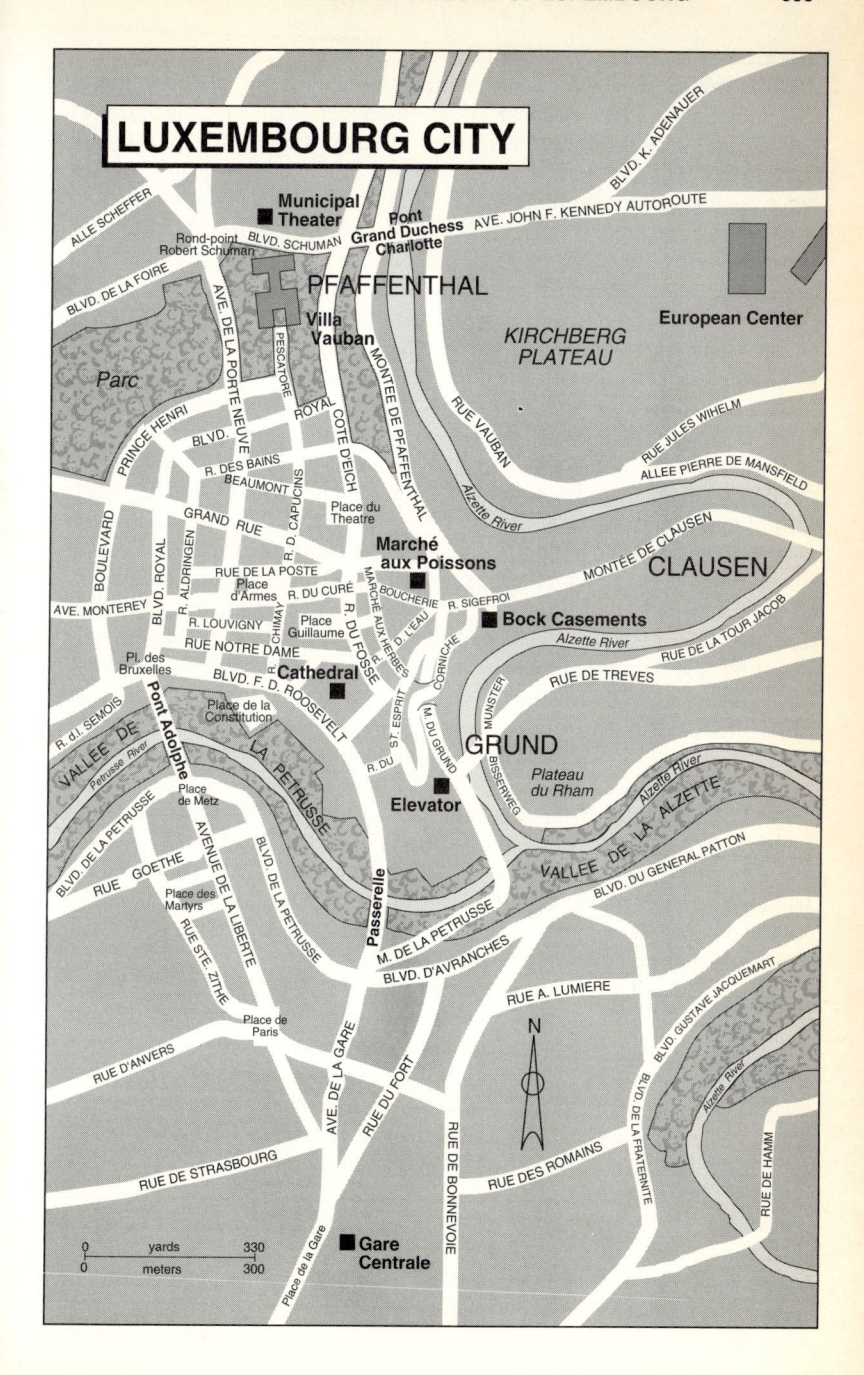

THE GRAND DUCHY OF LUXEMBOURG · · · 609

ACCOMMODATIONS There's adequate choice for pleasant rooms in Luxembourg City. Because of its relatively small size, location of hotel makes less difference here than in larger European capitals. Fall start-up sessions for the European Community Council of Ministers and other congresses/conventions make rooms in the better hotels harder to come by in September and October, and again in April and June; plan ahead if you're travelling in those periods.

RESTAURANTS French/Belgian preparation and German portions is an apt characterization for Luxembourg cuisine. Foods are generally rich, and many regional specialties are similar to those in the Belgian Ardennes: jambon d'Ardennes, pate, charcuterie, venison, hare, sausage, and river fish: pike, trout, and crawfish. The beginning of the *moules* (mussels) season in September (until April) is as much on the minds of inland Luxembourgers as their Benelux cohorts on the coast. Entirely of local origin is the smoked pork and broad bean dish (*Jud mat gardebo'nen*), *Thuringen sausage,* and a strong local cheese *kachkes* (mysteriously described as "cooked in the making" and served on buttered black bread with mustard). In September, *quetsch* (small plums) tarts are a treat. *Filet Americaine* appears on many a menu, but you won't be asked how you want it cooked; it's *steak tartare.*

ARRIVING Luxembourg's national passenger airline is **Luxair** *(43.61.61)*, with one-class service connecting many major European airports with **Findel Airport,** 3.5 miles/6 km. northeast of Luxembourg City. **Public bus #9** runs between the airport and the train station in Luxembourg City; Luxair also operates a full schedule of buses between the airport and the station, and will accept payment in foreign currency. **Icelandair** has flights to Luxembourg, via Reykjavik, Iceland, from JFK/New York and Baltimore/Washington. **Sabena World Airlines** *(70 Grand Rue; 2.12.12)* has service to/from Brussels.

IN THE AREA The **Luxembourg American Cemetery and Memorial at Hamm** (included on most city coach tours), several miles outside Luxembourg City, is the dignified resting place for 5,067 Americans, including **U.S. Army General George (Blood and Guts) Patton Jr.,** who was headquartered in Luxembourg City during the *Battle of the Bulge,* which produced most of the casualties.

TRAVEL TIPS Despite their cosmopolitan climate, Luxembourgers maintain a civilized pace of life. Even many professionals hold to the tradition of a two-hour lunch (noon–2 p.m.), which is a standard for most offices, shops, and museums. Many workers go home to have lunch with their families. Even the city's parking meters take a noon–2 p.m. lunch break.

Luxembourg City in Context

Although a small city, its greater population approximately 120,000, Luxembourg is home to a substantial percent of the 377,000 people who live in the Grand Duchy. Atypical of the historic, even romantic, appearance of much of the old capital is **Boulevard Royal,** frequently referred to as "Wall Street." But the gleaming glass towers of the modern monetary institutions housed along it do not rise so high that they hide the sky; center city structures cannot surpass in height the **Gella Fra** (gilded woman) atop the **War Memorial** on **Constitution Plaza.** In Luxembourg, buildings are kept in proportion, and business, though prospering, is kept in perspective. Rarely are transactions allowed to encroach on after work socializing with friends or family over food and drink at one of the cafes on **Place d'Armes** or elsewhere.

Which is not to say that business is not held in high regard in Luxembourg City. Luxembourg's annual **Schueberfouer sheep fair,** founded in 1340 by **John the Blind,** attracted traders of all varieties from all over Europe (on **Grande Rue** a charming sculptured fountain with sheep and musical instruments commemorates the historic fair), and shows an early commitment to commerce. Today, some 85% of the country's GNP comes from exports and imports, so there remains a recognition of the country's dependence on foreign trade. Nevertheless, one can hardly argue with Luxembourg's semi-laid-back life-style, since the country has one of the highest standards of living in the world.

From its beginnings, Luxembourg City had a market, **Marché-aux-Poissons** (fish market), situated only a short distance from the castle acquired by Sigefroi in 963. The site may have been one of commercial dealings even earlier, since it was the actual intersection of two important Roman roads: the grand consular road from Paris via Reims and Arlon to Trier, and the one linking Metz via St. Vith and Liège to Aachen. As early as the 4th century, the clifftop site above the Alzette Valley had an observation tower that formed part of the Roman defense system against the Franks, and probably came in useful during invasions in the first half of the 5th century led by the dreaded Hungarian **Attila.** By about 450, the Romans gave up on the region. That early fortress, which had became known as **Castellum Lucilinburhuc,** was probably in ruins when **Sigefroi, Count of Ardennes,** acquired it on Palm Sunday in 963, in exchange for the Abbey of St. Maximin in Trier. On a neighboring rock, **The Bock,** Sigefroi set about building a new castle (fortress), using his own workmen and employing the farmers and craftsmen who were already living in the valley on the banks of the

Alzette, in what today are the suburbs of **Grund** and **Pfaffenthal.** Around the nearby Marche-aux-Poissons market place, Sigefroi's servants and retainers established their homes, thus making it the true center of the rapidly growing village. Between the market and the Bock, Sigefroi began building a court chapel in 987, naming it for **St. Michel.** Expansion was so rapid that by the year 1050 it was necessary to build a second wall to contain the town (which then reached to the present **Rue du Fosse** and meant the addition of a new market, on the site of today's **Rue du Marche-aux-Herbes**).

The town continued to prosper, receiving its charter from **Countess Ermesinde** in 1244. A third wall became necessary for the upper town and was begun under **John the Blind** in about 1320, taking most of the century to complete. Between 1387 to 1395, the lower town of **Grund** also was surrounded by fortifications, and **Pfaffenthal** was protected by a wall built across the bottom of the Alzette valley and given three gates. Such security measures were considered essential because of the economic and strategic importance of the mills, tanneries, and, above all, the water supplies in the lower town.

Though Luxembourg was elevated to a duchy (from a county) in 1354, and the House of Luxembourg produced rulers of power and prestige in the 14th and 15th centuries, their additional titles, such as Holy Roman Emperor, meant that its leaders often were absentee landlords. And Luxembourg's fortifications alone couldn't fend off the Burgundians, who, under **Philip the Good,** took the town by force one night in 1443, thus confirming the acquisition of the Duchy of Luxembourg by the **House of Burgundy.** From this time, for five hundred years, the strongly fortified town frequently found itself a pawn in the military policies of foreign powers. The Austrians, Spanish, French, Dutch, Prussians, and Germans all have laid claim to Luxembourg.

The French under **King Louis XIV** did the most to change the face of the city. Having seiged the town in 1683, claiming it in 1684, Louis set his great military engineer, **Maréchal de Vauban,** to the task of addressing the changes in defensive fortifications required by more modern weaponry. Luxembourg's high walls and massive towers, built in the Middle Ages, could not stand up to the bombardment by the contemporary artillery, and so Vauban transformed the walls into ramparts and fortifications beneath the ground. Vauban recruited 3,000 laborers and, within the four years from 1684 and 1688, created an impregnable fortress out of the natural advantages of the Luxembourg City setting.

Austrian Hapsburg engineers further strengthened and extended the casemates and forts during their occupation of Luxembourg in the 18th century. By the time they were through, in addition to visible fortified girdles, watchtowers, and bastions, Luxembourg had a virtual underground city in its sandstone rockbed. The **Bock Casemates** alone had a

14 miles/23 km. network of tunnels, and down huge staircases some 120 feet beneath the surface were great galleries to shelter thousands of soldiers as well as their horses, plus barracks, and kitchens, bakeries, and slaughterhouses to sustain, and workshops of maintain, the troops.

Again, however, fortifications proved not to be the sole factor for defense. On June 7, 1795, after a seven-month blockade and four-month siege by the *Army of the French Republic,* the fortress city was starved into submission. Reporting the news to the French National Assembly, General Carnot claimed, "This fortress is second only to Gibraltar." After Napoleon's fall in 1814, leaders meeting at the *Congress of Vienna* took over the future course of both the city and the duchy of Luxembourg, though their fates would not, for a while, be the same. Luxembourg City was ordered to accept a Prussian garrison. **Dutch King Willem I** was named hereditary Grand Duke when he was presented with an upgraded Grand Duchy, which he governed as a province in his kingdom. The marking of the boundaries of the Luxembourg City fortress as federal territory (the fortress city, under Prussian insistence, had become a part of the *German Confederation*) took until 1829. From 1835–1838, Willem undertook extensive repairs and modernization on the fortifications.

Late in the 1850s, the Dutch laid the first railway lines in Luxembourg, and by 1861 the fortress city was connected by train to Trier, and by 1866 to Liège. Ironically, while providing a terrific boost economically, the international rail routes simply enhanced the strategic value of the fortress of Luxembourg, and, as a result, even more extensive work on the fortifications followed. Finally, in 1866, Luxembourg became freed of the need to quarter Prussian troops by the dissolution of the German Confederacy. But it became the object of a complicated conflict between the French Napoleon III and German Bismarck over the use of the famous fortress, leading to a Franco-Prussian crisis that could have degenerated into war. The idea of "neutralizing" Luxembourg, launched by Holland's Prince Henry, took hold with the Dutch King-Grand Duke. In 1867, the *Treaty of London* was signed between Great Britain, Russia, France, Prussia, the Netherlands, Austria, Belgium, Italy, and Luxembourg, guaranteeing perpetual neutrality of the Grand Duchy, and the evacuation and eventual razing of the city's fortress. On September 9, the last Prussian soldier left.

On that day in 1867, before dismantling began, the fortifications of Luxembourg City covered nearly 445 acres/180 hectares, the town itself being only 296 acres/120 hectares in area. The dismantling took 16 years, costing over one and a half million gold-currency francs, a staggering sum for the time. The land freed from fortifications was put to good use, picturesque promenades, fine parks, and new residential and business districts. From 1933, the casemates of the Petrusse, with their monumental staircase and five-story height, were restored, and in 1936 work began on the Bock casemates. In 1938, all the old fortifications were converted to civil defense shelters for thousands.

Nazis, having incorporated the Grand Duchy into the Third Reich, felt free to change the street signs after they invaded Luxembourg in May 1940. The prominent street that today is *Avenue de la Liberté* from 1940 to 1944 bore the name *Adolphe Hitler Strasse*. From 1940 until Sept. 10, 1944, the headquarters of the *Gestapo* was located in a villa at 57 Blvd. de la Petrusse (today, it's the Ministry of Public Health). Worse, the Nazis tore down the **War Monument** on Place de la Constitution that had been built to honor the dead from the First World War. On 10 September 1944, the Nazis were chased out of Luxembourg City for good by the Allies, primarily by U.S. Army forces. General Omar Bradley immediately set up headquarters for the 12th Army Group at 2 Place de Metz, and, across that square, in the turreted State Savings Bank, was General H.S. Vandenberg's of the 9th US Air Force. From December 21, 1944, during the *Battle of the Bulge* (and until March 27, 1945), **General George Patton** established his H.Q. for the 3rd Army in the Pescatore Foundation (today, a senior citizens' home). It was in the chapel of the Foundation on December 23rd that Patton delivered the prayer for fair weather for his troops and air forces, that began: *"Sir, this is Patton talking. The last fourteen days have been straight hell. Rain, snow, more rain, more snow—and I'm beginning to wonder what's going on in Your headquarters. Whose side are You on, anyway?"*

Emerging from the war, Luxembourg soon became a center for activities meant to design a Europe that would not again put itself through such armed conflagrations. In 1952, Luxembourg was chosen as headquarters for the High Authority of the supra-national **European Coal and Steel Community** (ECSC), brought into existence with the essential support of Robert Schuman, who had been born and educated in the city. The ECSC led directly to the creation of the **European Community** (EC) which also chose Luxembourg as the site for several of its permanent institutions. Luxembourg City's prosperous and peaceful present, its development now under the direction of its own people, is a situation in sharp contrast to its heavily fortified past, perpetuated for centuries by fearful foreigners. Today, disarmed and delightful, Luxembourg is setting an example for the world.

Guideposts
Country-wide telephone code 352

City Tourist Office Place D'Armes; June 15–Sept. 15 Mon.–Fri. 9 a.m.–7 p.m., Sat. 9 a.m.–1 p.m., 2–7 p.m., Sun. 10 a.m.–noon, 2–6 p.m.; remainder of year

	Mon.–Fri. 9 a.m.–1 p.m., 2–6 p.m., closed Sat., Sun.
Auto. Assoc.	*Automobile Club de Luxembourg,* 13 Rue de Longwy, Bertrange, Open Mon.–Fri. 8:30 a.m.–noon; 1:30–6 p.m.; Reciprocal service with other auto clubs, and 24-hour breakdown service. Tel: 45.00.45
Emergencies	Medical, police, fire: 012
Post Offices	25 Rue Aldringen Mon.–Sat. 7 a.m.–8:30 p.m., also fax services, 4.76.51; daily at Place de la Gare 6 a.m.–10 p.m., and Findel Airport daily 7 a.m.–10 p.m. available.
Telephone	38 Place de la Gare; 4.99.11
Trains	Chemins de Fer Luxembourgeois, Gare Centrale, info., res.: 6 a.m.–8 p.m., Tel: 49.24.24
Embassies	U.S.A.: 22 Blvd. Emmanuel Servais, 46.01.23; United Kingdom: 28 Blvd. Royal, 2.98.64.

WHAT TO SEE AND DO......................

The city's weathered sandstone walls, great viaducts, plateaus set with steeples and turrets, and river valleys filled with suburb towns and terraced gardens, provide scenes of exceptional interest. The views are equally outstanding whether seen from above, along the **Promenade de la Corniche,** or from below, looking up at the solid stone bastions built into the walls from paths in the green parks in the center of the valley floor. Its setting is what makes Luxembourg delightfully unique, so experience that above all else during your stay. Luxembourg is blessed with many parks, built on the land circling the inner city that became available after the fortifications were dismantled. Other squares, many with statues and monuments, add interest to walks around town. Sights are described below in two groupings, the first radiating out from the **Marché-aux-Poissons,** followed by those near the **Place de la Constitution.**

Musée de l'Etat/National Museum • *Marché-aux-Poissons (fish market), entrance from Rue Wiltheim; Tues.–Fri. 10 a.m.–4:45 p.m., Sat. 2–5:45 p.m., Sun. 10–11:45 a.m. & 2–5:45 p.m., closed Mon.* • The museum, located in a former governor's house, has an extensive collection of art and artifacts from all periods of Luxembourg's history.

The archaeological department has fine *prehistoric, Gallo-Roman,* and *Frankish items,* the Gallo-Roman material being outstanding. Something of the history of the city is depicted through maps, weapons, and a bronze model of the fortress before it was dismantled. The art department includes a collection of works by modern *Luxembourg artists,* in particular **Joseph Kutter** and **Dominique Lang.**

The **Industrial and Popular Arts** section of the National Museum *(Rue Wiltheim; open Tues.–Fri. from 1–5 p.m., Sat. & Sun. 2–6 p.m., closed Mon.; 47.93.30; no English documentation but well worth a visit)* is located across the road in two restored 17th and 18th century burghers' houses. Worth a visit for themselves, the handsome houses, which retain their original interior design, have high beamed ceilings, old wooden floors, and stone casement windows (out which are wonderful views of the Alzette Valley). The decorations, from the mid-15th to the end of the 18th century, include tapestries, porcelain, paintings, free-standing and build-in (wall cupboards) furniture. The museum seems to get more wonderful as you wander, especially on the lower floors, which have fully-furnished rooms with leather wall-coverings, painted panels, and tiled fireplaces. Down in the vaulted cellars, which made me wonder if I had somehow stumbled into the underground network of casemates at the nearby Bock (see below), was an unusual and fascinating display of dozens of 16th–19th century intricately-designed cast-iron fireplace pieces and ornamental stoves.

From the museum, walk a few doors down Rue Wiltheim to **"Zum Welle Mann"** tavern (closed Mon.), a part of the museum. Only light snacks and beverages are served, but the atmosphere and views out the rear windows over the Alzette valley are superb. At the foot of Rue Wiltheim are the 11th-century **Trois Towers,** from which you can connect with other roads down to the **Pfaffenthal** suburb.

The National Museum is on the site that became the market and hub of the early town which grew around Sigefroi's castle on the nearby Bock. In this oldest part of the city is Luxembourg's oldest house **Um Bock,** on Rue Loge, now a restaurant. Across the road is **St. Michel's Church** *(Rue Sigefroi).* Originally founded by Sigefroi as his castle chapel in 987, St. Michel's was extended in the mid-14th century, but was damaged and rebuilt several times until taking its present appearance in 1688. The Renaissance doorway dates from 1689, a gift from Louis XIV, hence the French *fleur de lys.* The facade contains the remains of Roman window vents, while the interior is a typical example of late Gothic vault style.

Bock Casemates • *entrance at Bock/Promenade de la Corniche; April 1–September 30 daily 10 a.m.–5 p.m.; self-guided tour; brochure in English; wear flat shoes for several flights of steep narrow stone stairs with handrails, uneven ground* • During the dismantling of the fortifications beginning in 1867 (the process took 16 years), most of the city's fortifications were blown up. But it was impossible to destroy the underground casemates without damaging the city above them. The main connections and entrances were closed, but about 11 miles/17 km., on several levels connected by staircases, remain. The garrison of the Bock Casemate was 1,200 men, and the main gallery held 50 cannon in loopholes which were enlarged during the dismantling and now afford remarkable views over the city. During this century's wars, the casemates, which have space for 35,000 people, were used as bomb shelters. *Note:* The Bock Casemates should be your first choice if you're not planning to visit both the city's casemate attractions; they give a far better idea of Luxembourg's former underground fortifications and allow you to explore at your own pace.

In 1963, just opposite the Bock, important remains of Sigefroi's ancient 963 **Luxembourg Castle** *(open at all times)* were discovered. They are preserved as the **Monument of the Millennium** of the city. Beyond the castle, on the **Montée de Clausen** road that leads across the Alzette valley and down into the suburb of **Clausen,** is the "**Hollow Tooth,**" a watchtower built by Vauban that got that name from its appearance after being blown up during the dismantlement of Luxembourg's fortifications.

Promenade de la Corniche • Sure-footed, properly shod visitors with stamina for steep stone stairs will find the casemates fascinating from the inside, but if for any reason that excursion isn't possible, a stroll along the pedestrian Promenade de la Corniche, which runs downhill from the Bock will give you a good sense of the city's former fortifications and scenic setting. Bridges, here the high arched railway viaduct and the low-lying one across the reflective waters of the Alzette, frame many of Luxembourg's views. From the Corniche you see the 22-story tower (tallest in the Grand Duchy) that indicates the **European Center** on the **Kirchberg Plateau.** It plays a significant part in contemporary Luxembourg life but, unless you have a special interest, there's no real reason for tourists to go there. Walk the Corniche as far as the **Place du St-Espirit,** if you want to remain in the upper town, or continue heading steeply down **Montée du Grund** to the bridge at the bottom across the Alzette in the suburb of **Grund** (cafes, restaurants). The free **public elevator** (lift) built into the valley wall will whisk you back up to Place du St-Espirit. From there walk to **Blvd. Franklin Roosevelt** and past the Cathédrale to Place de la Constitution.

Place de la Constitution is a major orientation point in Luxembourg, which spreads out in odd patterns due to its topography. Crowning the **Bastion Beck,** built to this amazing level above the Petrusse Valley in the course of the fortification of Luxembourg, Place de la

Constitution is instantly recognizable by the **War Memorial** obelisk. It was erected in 1923 to commemorate Luxembourgers who gave their lives in the First World War (although the Grand Duchy had to comply with its **Statue of Unarmed Neutrality,** a number of its citizens volunteered to serve with the Allied armies, particularly the French). Atop the slim obelisk was placed the golden statue of a woman (a Victory figure), who soon gained the name **Gelle Fra** (gilded woman), which became commonly used for the whole Constitution Square area. Not appreciating the sentiments it instilled in Luxembourgers, the Nazis pulled the monument down on October 21st, six months after their invasion of the Grand Duchy in May 1940. Most of the pieces were recovered and hidden by Luxembourgers, but the action came to symbolize Nazi oppression, and, when the war was over, it became important to re-erect the monument. But it could not be completed because for the golden statue remained missing. Finally, it was found in the early 1980s, restored, and, on Luxembourg's National Day, June 23, in 1985, the monument was officially reinaugurated in the presence of His Royal Highness Grand Duke Jean.

If you are facing the Petrusse Valley, to the far left of the square is a long stairway that leads down to paths beneath the walls of the upper town. Other stairs lead to the green valley floor itself, where you'll find yourself amid some pretty surprising mid-city scenery.

Petrusse or Constitution Casemates • *Place de la Constitution; Easter & Whitsun weekends, July & Aug., approx. 11 a.m.–4 p.m., but hours posted at entrance; guided tours only, 40 mins* • The Petrusse casemates date from the first half of 17th century, the Spanish era of modernization of the fortifications, although the French Vauban, and, in the 19th century the Austrians, also implemented their ideas. The Spanish added many bastions, including the formidable **Bastion Beck,** named for the Spanish governor under whose rule it was begun. Its "platform," after the work was finished by Vauban, reached the level of the present Place de la Constitution. The casemate tour, which covers lots of stairways, includes a visit to one of the outside terraces that overlooks the Petrusse Valley.

Cathédrale Notre-Dame • *North entrance, Rue Notre Dame* • is almost across from Constitution Square. The south side of the cathedral faces across the Blvd. Franklin Roosevelt to the Petrusse Valley, but entry is usually made on the north, through the masterful Renaissance portal **Daniel Muller,** 1613–1615) of the mainly Gothic style church built between 1613–1618 by Jean du Blocq. The three naves of equal height are typical of the hall-style church of the late Gothic period. The rood-screen also is Muller's work, with a rich, exuberant treatment that shows the transition from the Renaissance to the Baroque. The Cathedral's **triple towers,** today a landmark on the Luxembourg's skyline, were only completed in 1937, added at the time of an extension to the structure. The **crypt** (open to the public) is a national monument for the country, in it the remains of **John the Blind,** Count of Luxembourg and casualty of Crecy (1346), and the burial vaults of the Grand-Ducal family.

Place Guillaume is located upstairs opposite the cathedral on Rue Notre Dame. It is the setting for the **Hôtel de Ville** *(not open for tours),* which was built during the 1830s to replace the former one, now the Ducal Palace. In the main council hall was signed the *European Coal and Steel Community Agreement* in 1952. General markets are held in the square on Wed. and Sat., their activity then taking center stage instead of the equestrian statue of Dutch King/Grand Duke of Luxembourg **Willem II** (for whom the square is named), which usually dominates. Willem faces down the short *Rue de la Reine* to the **Grand Ducal Palace** *(Corner Rue de Marché aux Herbes & Rue de la Reine; usually open to the public most days from mid-July to end Aug., during the Grand Duke's vacation, but due to major restoration, it is not expected to be open until summer 1994).* The palace, whose attractive 1572 facade in Renaissance style has an interesting Spanish-Moorish strapwork decoration (at the time it was built, the Spanish ruled), was originally the town hall, built to replace the previous one on the site destroyed in 1554 in a gunpowder blast that caused extensive damage in the town. (This site very likely has been the setting for Luxembourg's various town halls since the city received its charter in 1244). The civil guard met here, and, while a town hall, it housed a prison and the municipal weighing scales. The balustrade, originally in stone, was replaced with one in wrought iron in 1741, when the building was enlarged. From the time Luxembourg was taken by the French in 1795, the building has served as a building for national government, and, since 1890, it has been the residential palace of the Grand-Ducal family. Various fine buildings that house other government offices are located between the palace and the cathedral.

From the other end of Place Guillaume, at which there is a statue to **Michel Rodange** (1827–1876), the Luxembourg poet who wrote a *Letzebuergesch* version of the epic poem "Reynard the Fox" (see also *The Muse* under *Benelux Cultural Legacy*), a covered passage leads to Rue du Cure and Place d'Armes.

Place d'Armes takes its name from the days when it served as a parade ground for the French stationed in the city in 1685. The Place d'Armes today is the social center of the city, the congenial Luxembourgers' favorite **cafe congregating spot,** with a bandstand that keeps a busy schedule in summer. At one end of the square is a statue of

Michel Lentz, author of the national anthem, with its famous line *"We want to remain what we are."* At the other, with the **Tourist Office** tucked into offices there, is the 1906 **Cercle** municipal cultural building, whose pediment is decorated with a frieze depicting the granting of the town charter to Luxembourg by Countess Ermesinde in 1244. The European Coal and Steel Community were given the use of the building from 1953 to 1969.

Marquette/Model • *Rathskeller of the Cercle Theater, entrance on Rue de la Cure; daily except Tues. Easter to Oct. 14. 10 a.m.–12:20 p.m., 2–6 p.m. in July and Aug.; Oct. 15–Easter, apply at City Tourist Office, Place d'Armes; 50-min. A-V show and commentary at Model is presented in English several times daily, at last check at 11 a.m., 3 and 5 p.m., but confirm times at tourist office* • The Model, located around the corner from Place d'Armes, a copy of that made under French King Louis XIV (the original is in the Hotel des Invalides in Paris), shows the full development of the **Luxembourg City fortress,** as envisioned by Vauban near the end of the 17th century. The **audio-visual presentation** takes you through the highpoints of the city's history. A careful study of the Model helps you appreciate what nine centuries of evolution as a fortress meant to the layout of Luxembourg in terms of walls, gates, towers, turrets, bastions, and barriers built on the site.

Pescatore Museum • *Municipal Park; Ave. E. Reuter* • Built on municipal parkland on the site of razed Vauban fortifications, the mansion houses a fine art collection that normally is open to the public during July and August. However, with restoration under way at the Ducal Palace (see above), Grand-Duc Jean will be using this building as his temporary office, and it will probably not reopen to the public until the summer of 1994. Perhaps the Grand Duke will enjoy working while being surrounded by the works of likes of **Jan Steen, Pieter Breughel the Younger, Jan Breughel the Younger, Teniers the Younger, Dou, Canaletto, and Courbet.**

Radio-Tele Luxembourg, a powerful component of the Grand Duchy's important telecommunications industry, is located on an adjoining portion of the Municipal Park, where once Fort Louvigny stood. To the north, at the edge of the Municipal park, is **Rond-Point Robert Schuman.** This founding father of the European Community is honored by a monument located near the modern **Municipal Theater,** the city's main performance center. The focal point of the Schuman Monument are several steel girders, signifying Schuman's role in the establishment of the European Coal and Steel Community, which was a precursor to the Common Market. From the monument, Blvd. Robert Schuman leads across the vivid red **Grand Duchess Charlotte Bridge** to the **European**

Center, passing practically over the house in which he grew up that sits in the Alzette valley suburb of Clausen beneath it.

SHOPPING

Luxembourg's 12% VAT (Value-Added Tax) is one of lowest in Europe. Although that situation could change as a result of Europe's economic union, it shouldn't happen at least until 1993, meaning savings for shoppers on the high-quality international items on sale on and near the pedestrian **Grand Rue.** Luxembourg's shops are small and personalized; there are no department stores in the city. Though many of the fine **Villeroy & Boch** (2 Rue de Fosse) products are made in factories in Germany, the company maintains its Luxembourg roots (there's a large tableware factory in **Septfontaines** in the Eisch River valley) that go back to the 18th century. Several of its china patterns are produced in Luxembourg, the 1989 **Mon Jardin** design, **Petite Fleur, Naif** (Naive), and **Botanic.** These lines are somewhat less expensive in the Luxembourg store than they would be elsewhere. A number of private **art galleries** featuring the works of Luxembourgers have opened in the city. If you enjoyed the cast-iron fireback pieces at the Industrial Arts section of the National Museum, look for the miniature items, called "Tak," made in the shape of castles and other subjects by Luxembourg's **Fonderie de Mersch.** There's a flea market on the 2nd and 4th Saturdays each month.

ACCOMMODATIONS

Most of the hotels in Luxembourg City itself are independent properties, many family-run, some multi-generational. Several international chain hotels, particularly popular with business travelers, are located just outside the city. Near Findel Airport is the **Aerogolf-Sheraton,** and in a wooded suburb several kilometers from the city center is the **Inter-Continental,** popular as quiet conference site. The **Pullman** property (the newly renovated former Holiday Inn) is presently the only hotel at the European Center on Kirchberg plateau. Most hotels included here have their own restaurants, of a more than acceptable standard. The tradition of hotel-restaurants is strong in this region, and you'll rarely go wrong by dining "in-house," since a hotel's restaurant also must satisfy discriminating local customers in order to survive outside of the tourist season. All prices are inclusive of taxes and service.

Deluxe

★★★★ **Grand Hotel Cravat** • *29 Blvd. F.D. Roosevelt; 22.19.75; fax 22.67.11* • Facing the Place de la Constitution, overlooking the Petrusse Valley, the Grand Hotel Cravat sits at the very core of the city's sightseeing, shopping, business. A fourth-generation family hotel of a superior standard, it offers a traditional European atmosphere and personal Luxembourg service to its international clientele. The renovated rooms on the front facing the Petrusse Valley have the finest hotel room views in the city. The traditional but welcoming marble-floored lobby has a bar that is a popular community convening place, as is the **Taverne**, which serves local informal fare. The 60 guestrooms (most recently renovated) on 6 floors, have bath with bidet, hair dryers, makeup mirrors, good lighting, turn-down services, French slatted-shades for complete darkness, TV, telephone. Continental breakfast, served in the **Cravat** formal restaurant, is included. Although the Cravat family is more than able to serve diplomats, it can still employ cozy touches such as changing the carpets in the elevator to tell you what day of the week it is. Parking lot.

★★★★★ **Le Royal** • *12 Blvd. Royal; 4.16.16, Fax 22.59.48, in U.S. 1-800-223-5652* • Located on Luxembourg's "Wall Street," the attractive modern, 170-room air-conditioned property is the only one in center city to offer business and communications services, fitness center (pool, sauna, weight machines, solarium, massages), Royal Club executive floors, free airport shuttle, make it popular with business travelers. Guestrooms have modern decor in quality materials, marble baths, bidet, hair dryers, pant press, minibar, terry robe, desk, sitting area; buffet breakfast is included. Tennis in season. Both formal and informal restaurants, with summer terrace. Parking.

★★★★ **President Hotel** • *32 Place de la Gare; 48.61.61, fax 48.61.80* • Located across the street from the train station/air terminal, convenient to buses and taxis, this 7-story 40-room hotel has a stylish marble lobby and a professional and helpful front desk staff. In the lobby is an attractive leather chair and wood panel bar, in the basement a restaurant created in a old railway car. All rooms have basic modern furniture, private bath, TV, telephone, minibar, trouser press, hair dryer, French-style window slats that absolutely keep out the light, and double-glazed windows to keep out traffic noise.

★★★★ **Hotel Central Molitor** • *28 Avenue de la Liberté; 48.99.11, fax 48.33.82* • This 1913 3rd-generation refurbished family-run hotel, located midway between the station and Place de la Constitution, has a traditional atmosphere in its public rooms, which include a respected restaurant and bar. Behind the stately old facade, the 36-rooms of the

4-story hotel all have modern furniture, private bath, telephone, TV, light and doorlock control panel at bedside, wall safe, sound-proofed doors and windows, and many have mini fridges. Underground parking nearby; multiple bus lines just outside hotel.

First Class

★★★ **Hotel Français** • *14 Place d'Armes; 47.45.34, fax 46.42.74* • Situated right in the heart of Luxembourg, on the lively Place d'Armes, this 20-room (6 suites), 5-story hotel has attractive hallways decorated with art works and sitting areas. All the modern rooms have TV, telephone, private bath; twins are larger than doubles. Front rooms face the square, where the hotel has a popular terrace cafe and brasserie. Major credit cards; breakfast included; elevator; car parks nearby; guests allowed to drive to hotel (in pedestrian area) to unload luggage.

Moderate

★★★ **Auberge Du Coin** • *2 Blvd. de la Petrusse; 40.21.01, fax 40.36.66* • This recently renovated, turn-of-the-century home is located in a quiet residential area near the Petrusse valley, three blocks from Ave. de la Liberte. All 25 rooms have lightwood furniture, private bath, TV and telephone. There's a pleasant lobby and an elegant restaurant and a brasserie, where breakfast, included, is served.

★★ **Hotel Italia** • *15 rue d'Anvers; 48.66.26, fax 48.08.07* • As one enters this hotel, located just off Place de Paris, halfway between the rail station and the old city, one can't ignore that it's also a restaurant, since that's where the reception desk is. The larger of the 20 rooms (only slightly higher in price and worth it) are the twins; rooms in the back of the building are quieter. All have bath, shower, bidet, TV, and telephone. Rooms and hallway decor is basic (indoor/outdoor carpet) but clean. There's a garden terrace with tables for use by diners (and hotel guests at breakfast, included) at the very popular locally *Italia Restaurant* (noon–2:30 p.m., 6–10:30 p.m.; moderate, *menus* inexpensive), noted for its Italian and classic dishes.

★★ **Hotel Schintgen** • *6 Rue Notre-Dame; 22.28.44, fax 46.57.19* • Located just behind Grand Hotel Cravat, one block from Place de la Constitution, two from Place d'Armes, this 35-room, no-lobby hotel is basic but well-placed. Rooms, all with telephone, have small, old-fashioned tiled bathrooms with shower stalls, toilet, and basin behind a sliding door, are clean, four of the rooms are larger. Food service, other than breakfast (included), consists of bottled beverages sold at the front desk. Elevator; major credit cards.

RESTAURANTS..

The fact that Luxembourg cuisine can be described as substantial and nourishing doesn't mean it's not refined. French touches feature at many restaurants, although, with a large number of resident non-nationals, many foreign cuisines are represented, Italian and Chinese being particularly popular. Though Eurocrats on expense accounts cause the best restaurants to be pricey, Luxembourgers' own love of good food encourages value for money in all price ranges. Menu prices generally include both VAT and service charges, though it's still customary locally to tip (about 10%) if service is good. Because it is a diplomatic and international business center, Luxembourg City tends toward the more formal in dress, especially outside the summer tourist season; at the best restaurants, men will be most comfortable in suits, women in appropriate dresses. Menus, always posted, in the larger restaurants generally give an English translation of the French. Except for the most casual places, it's a good idea to inquire about reservations, essential at the top spots. Most of the hotels listed above have restaurants, all worthy of your consideration.

Considered one of the finest restaurants in the city is **Clairefontaine** *(9 Place de Clairefountaine; closed Sat. lunch, Sun., hols., and three weeks from mid-July; 46.22.11, fax 47.08.21; expensive),* located on the expansive square surrounded by elegant old buildings that now house government departments, it's French cuisine was described by one Luxembourger as simply *"extraordinary."* **Saint-Michel** *(32 Rue de l'Eau; closed Sat., Sun., and Aug.; 22.32.15, fax 46.25.93; expensive/very expensive),* also serving classic French cuisine, has an elegant setting and service in Luxembourg's oldest and quaintest quarter. For seasonal and French gourmet fare at a more reasonable price, Luxembourgers have taken themselves to **Speltz** *(8 Rue Chimay; closed Sat., Sun.; 47.49.50; moderate/expensive)* since it opened in 1989 in a cozy, candlelit 17th-century house.

On at least one night you'll want to dine on the **Place d'Armes** to savor its special local atmosphere. It will be evident that the many Luxembourgers there, who love nothing more than getting together with friends over food and drinks, are among those most enjoying the music coming from the bandstand, the evening air and atmosphere. Cafes rim the square, all have menus posted, so take your pick.

On many local lists the best places for a bottomless bowl of steamed mussels (moules) is **Ems** *(30 Place de la Gare; daily 11 a.m.–1 a.m.; 48.77.99; inexpensive).* It's across from the station, a friendly brasserie that often gets full, in which case you could find yourself in a great conversation with Luxembourgers sharing your booth. The menu includes a number of regional dishes and local beer and wine. Also informal, with wooden tables and chairs, but well regarded for its typical Luxembourg fare, *choucroute, pate,* etc. is **Maison des Brasseurs** *(48 Grande Rue; 7 a.m.–7 p.m., closed Suns., hols.; 47.13.71; inexpensive).* In addition to four-course menus in the inexpensive range, it also serves soups, salads, and omelets. For a complete change of scene and cuisine, but not price, if you've a taste for Italian, a good bet is **Bacchus** *(32 Rue du Marché-aux-Herbes; noon–2:30 p.m., 6 p.m.–midnight, closed Mon; 47.13.97; inexpensive/moderate).* There's an upmarket atmosphere: peach-colored rattan furniture, lovely Villeroy & Boch pink-marbled ware, and international music piped in for the largely local crowd. The pasta is exceptional (served in starter or main course portions), and there's pizza and calzone.

Fashionable atmospheres are becoming common in the lower town suburb of **Grund,** a delightful excursion via the *elevator* from Place du St. Espirit from the upper town. **Scott's Restaurant** *(4 Bisserweg; noon–2 p.m., 7 p.m.–10:15 p.m., closed Mon.; 47.53.52; inexpensive/moderate; reservations taken, ask for table with view of upper city)* was the first eatery to open in the Grund, in 1986, in a restored 1790 building by the Alzette river. Particularly popular with the English, Irish, and Americans living in Luxembourg, the well-presented meals range from fish, meat, to salads; decor is fashionable yet fanciful. The pub downstairs is open daily from noon to 1 a.m., serving bar snacks and 25 kinds of beer, inside and on the riverside terrace. Across the way is **Cafe Am/haffchen** *(9 Bisserweg; 5 p.m.–1 a.m. daily, closed Mon.; inexpensive),* with delightful outdoor garden seating amid lime trees, or indoors in a living room/library setting that's cozy, contemporary (the works of Luxembourg artists hang on the walls), and can be crowded. Drinks, sandwiches, and tempting toasties. In the suburb of **Clausen,** two cafes with authentic local atmosphere and fare are **Mansfield** *(3 Rue de la Tour Jacob; 43.34.86; inexpensive/moderate)* and **Mousel's Cantine** *(46 Montée de Clausen; closed Sun.; 47.01.98; inexpensive/moderate),* which actually looks into the **Mousel** beer brewery.

The pastries of Luxembourg are renowned. Two shops traditionally compete as the source of the city's best pastries: **Namur** *(Rue des Capucins, more than 125 years in business)* and **Oberweis** *(Grande Rue, over 25 years old).* Better try them both. The popularity of cake, and coffee, are a holdover tradition from the Austrian-era here. Luxembourgers' love for coffee is shown by the fact that there is no word in Letzebuergesch for breakfast: the word "coffee" stands in for it. For superior picnic supplies, plus pastries, pay a visit to **Kaempf-Kohler** on Rue du Cure.

ENTERTAINMENT AND EVENTS..

Luxembourg's late-Aug.-early-Sept. **Schueberfouer,** a large itinerant fair held on the vast Glacis Square near Rondponit Robert Schuman, is a direct continuation of the annual trade fair founded in 1340 by **John the Blind.** Luxembourg's **National Day** is June 23, but the festivities begin the night before with a torchlight parade through town to the Ducal Palace, and fireworks. In December, the Place d'Armes hosts the **Christmas Market,** with its decorated stalls and large central Christmas tree, and food stands selling warm mulled wine. On Easter Monday, Luxembourgers gather on Marché-aux-Poissons for a traditional celebration of **Emais'chen,** often attended by the Grand-Ducal Family, that includes the buying of small whistling porcelain birds, sold only on the day. This Catholic country's main religious ceremony is the **Octave** or Pilgrimage of Our Lady of Luxembourg, the city's patron saint, with processions through the streets, decorated with altars of flowers, between the 3rd and 5th Sundays after Easter. Luxembourgers love music, and stage a full and varied program of guest performances in symphony, opera, and ballet by Europe's finest companies at the modernistic **Municipal Theater** (near Rond-Point Robert Schuman); the prime season is fall through spring. Annually in spring, Luxembourg hosts **Printemps Musical,** a festival of international artists catering to all musical tastes. Inquire at the tourist office about possible concerts in the National Library.

IN THE AREA..

Luxembourg American Cemetery and Memorial • *in suburb of Hamm, 3 mi./5 km. west of Luxembourg City, signposted* • At the end of the Second World War, 83 temporary U.S. military cemeteries existed in North Africa, the Middle East, Italy, Great Britain, and Western Europe, and a decision was taken after study to consolidate them into 13 permanent U.S. cemeteries in Europe, of which the **Luxembourg American Cemetery** is one. The people of Luxembourg, in gratitude for the liberation by the *First U.S. Army,* particularly the *Fifth Armored Division,* of their country in September 1944, and again in the *Battle of the Bulge* in February 1945 by the *U.S. Third Army* commanded by **General George S. Patton Jr.,** purchased this 50 acre/20 hectare site for perpetual use by the American Government, the agreement being ratified in 1951.

Most of those buried in the cemetery at Hamm died in the Battle of the Bulge, which opened on 16 December 1944, with a lightning counter-attack under **Field Marchal von Rundstedt** swept across the northern half of Luxembourg and into Belgium. Northern Luxembourg suffered twice in the Battle of the Bulge, first during the advancing attacking by the Nazis, and again during their retreat, forced foot by foot back across the **Siegfried Line** in Germany by the Allies, mostly Americans of the U.S. Third Army. During the heavy fighting in the winter of 1945 the American Burial Service recovered the bodies of victims burying them in a provisional cemetery at Hamm, which was opened on 29 Dec. 1944. At the end of the war there were 8,411 graves. The cemetery was closed from March 1948 to December 1949, during which time the remains of the dead were either returned to the U.S. or permanently interred in Luxembourg, according to the wishes of the next-of-kin. When the cemetery opened on 16 Dec. 1949, on the 5th anniversary of the beginning of the battle, 5,076 servicepeople lay buried by name beneath white stone Roman crosses or Stars of David, buried without distinction to rank, race, or religion, an exception being made for the 22 pairs of brothers who are buried side by side. The headstones of the 101 graves of unknown soldiers or airmen read "Here lies in honored glory a comrade in arms known but to God." The grave of General Patton, who wished to be buried with his men, is set slightly aside, due to the great numbers of people who visit his grave.

Each of America's war cemeteries in Europe was designed individually by an American architect or firm to complement the specific setting, though all have the common elements of a non-denomination chapel, a permanent inscription of the names of those missing in action, and display of the military campaign in the region where the memorial is located. At Luxembourg, the chapel at the woods encircled cemetery has inscribed above the Blue Belge (Belgian) marble altar the words: "I give unto them eternal life and they shall never perish." The West Pylon on the cemetery terrace that overlooks the field of markers bears a map that shows the military operations in northwest Europe from the landing in Normandy until the end of the war; the East Pylon has a map illustrating movements of the Battle of the Bulge.

One mile/1.5 km. away is the **German Cemetery at Sandweiler;** 5,599 German victims were brought to this temporary cemetery by the American Burial Service during the final months of battle in the Ardennes. In 1952, an agreement was signed between the government of the Grand Duchy of Luxembourg and the Federal Republic of Germany which made this the first cemetery of the 1939/45 war which the German Association for the Provision of War Graves had been able to build outside its country. Also brought here were the 5,286 dead, mostly from mass graves, of German soldiers from some 150 other Luxembourg municipalities. The German cemetery at Sandweiler was dedicated in June 1955. Of the 10,913 buried there, there is a common grave for 4,829

German soldiers (4,014 of whom are identified by name on bronze plaques); the others lie beneath stone crosses inscribed with their names, and dates of birth and death.

GRAND TOUR OF THE GRAND DUCHY

Introduction

Luxembourg can claim, with justification, that its historic capital city is also its most picturesque town. This means that visitors whose only time in the Grand Duchy will be spent in Luxembourg City can rest assured that they're seeing sights that are the country's highlights. However, if you can linger longer, you'll be well rewarded for further exploration in the Grand Duchy. As in Luxembourg City, the picturesque and the spectacular combine in the countryside, and, though small in scale, the Grand Duchy offers sights and scenery that are remarkable for their variety.

Guidelines for the Grand Duchy

SIGHTS   Specific attractions include **Celtic earth forts** at Aleburg near Larochette; **Roman mosaics** in Diekirch; Luxembourg-born photographer Edward Steichen's just-restored **The Family of Man** exhibit in Clervaux Castle, which also houses a collection of **models of the finest castles** in the Grand Duchy; the attractive historic Abbey town of Echternach; **Battle of the Bulge** monuments and museums; and **Vianden Castle,** Luxembourg's finest and best restored feudal fortification (the ancestral home of the House of Orange-Nassau, a heritage shared by the Dutch Royal Family and the Grand-Ducal family). Even without these, the Grand Duchy is memorable for its splendid scenery, which varies from lush vineyards that run down sunny slopes to the Moselle, to fantastic rock formations in "Little Switzerland," to river-carved valleys and high plateaus with far-reaching vistas of fertile farming fields.

GETTING AROUND   **Car** is by far the best way to get the full impact of the Grand Duchy's appeal. Second-best is to take one of the several sightseeing **day motorcoach tours** offered by **Voyages H. Sales**

(26 Rue du Cure; April 1 to Sept. 30, every Sat., Sun., or Wed., depending upon the itinerary; departures from Luxembourg City, station and Place de la Constitution; telephone information and reservations 50.10.50). Among the places visited in different tours are Vianden, Echternach, Clervaux, Little Switzerland, Larochette, and the Moselle Valley, each tour giving a fairly good cross section of Duchy scenery. Luxembourg's **train/bus transportation network** covers the country, but with too time-consuming connections for most visitors. Those who want to give it a try should purchase a bargain one-day *Network Ticket* (FLux 120, valid until 8 a.m. the following day), good for all trains and buses in the Grand Duchy and on municipal buses in Luxembourg City. **Bicycles,** if you can take the hilly terrain, can be rented in Luxembourg City, Diekirch, and Vianden (details at local tourist offices).

SHOPPING For serious shopping, even Luxembourgers go to the capital, the only city in the Grand Duchy. For basic items, and souvenirs, the towns with the largest selection of shops are Diekirch, Wiltz, and Echternach.

ENTERTAINMENT AND EVENTS The summer season is filled with special concerts and activities, staged for and enjoyed by tourists and Luxembourgers both during July and August. Among the annual events is **Echternach's Dancing Procession** (Whitsun Tuesday at 9 a.m.) and in June, Echternach hosts the **International Music Festival. Remembrance Day** (1st weekend in July) is held annually in Ettelbruck in honor of U.S. Army General George S. **Patton,** commander in Luxembourg during the battle of the Bulge. **Grevenmacher** on the Moselle River holds the largest **Wine and Grape Festival** with procession (2nd weekend each September) of the several celebrations of the gathering of the grapes from the vineyards. Beer doesn't take a backseat to Luxembourg's wine, at least in the case of celebrating. **Diekirch's Beer Festival** *(3rd Sunday in July)* honors that town's home brewery, one of five in the Grand Duchy.

ACCOMMODATIONS While hotel choices are limited in number in the Grand Duchy (a greater selection exists in the tourism centers of Vianden and Echternach), very pleasant properties are scattered throughout the countryside. All are spotless, run with pleasant personal attention, almost invariably have restaurants, and offer value-for-FLux. In July and August, the highs summer tourist season in the countryside, although many Europeans come on camping holidays, reservations at hotels should be made as far ahead as possible. In June and Sept. you should be able to "drop in" and find rooms available, but later than that you may begin to run into hotels in the tourist areas that have closed for the season. Local tourist offices can provide help with accommodations, and are the best source if you are seeking bed-and-breakfast or pension-style accommodations.

RESTAURANTS As has been pointed out before, country hotels, whether rural or in towns, are always a solid choice for a meal.

TRAVEL TIPS Remember, when driving on the remarkably traffic-free roads in the Grand Duchy, that you must keep in mind the *possibility* of vehicles coming at a good clip around every corner—not always easy to do when, with the possible exception of July and August, you'll often have the roads largely to yourself for miles on end.

THE ROUTE.................................

Because the country's so small, it's possible to take a spontaneous sort of trip in Luxembourg, if that's the type of travel you prefer (keeping in mind only finding a bed for the night in the busy tourism months of July and August). Below is a description of the most worthwhile places and sites to consider seeing in the course of your tour. Coverage follows in a roughly clockwise route, leaving from Luxembourg City northwest to the Eisch Valley **(Valley of the Seven Castles)**, and then looping up the left (west) side of the Luxembourg map, taking in **Esch-sur-Sûre, Wiltz,** and **Clervaux** in the north. The route then drops southeast to **Vianden,** which, if you intended to see but one country town in the Grand Duchy, should be the one. South of Vianden is **Diekirch,** to the southeast of which are **Mullerthal/Little Switzerland** and **Echternach.** South from there the road follows along the **Moselle River,** which forms Luxembourg's border with Germany, past the vineyards to **Mondorf-les-Bains,** from which it's a short dash back to Luxembourg City.

ON THE ROAD ....

Valley of the Seven Castles

Within 10 minutes of leaving the center of Luxembourg, you'll be entering the forests of the **Eisch Valley.** Most of the castles from which the valley takes its name are now in ruins, but no less picturesque for that. Take the road through **Kopstal** and, with a possible detour to see the hill-top and valley castles at **Ansembourg,** and perhaps another to see **Hollenfels,** now a youth hostel but still with its handsome Knights'

Hall, then on to **Septfontaines** (for a stop at its small 13th-century church). From there head to **Gaichel**.

ACCOMMODATIONS/RESTAURANTS ★★★★ **Hotel-Restaurant de la Gaichel** • *Gaichel-Eischen; 3.91.29, fax 3.90.37; deluxe* • Located "at the very end" of Luxembourg—a walk on the gardened grounds could take you over the border into Belgium—this gracious and elegant small hotel, a former country home, has 15 rooms. All have private bath, are comfortably decorated and have balconies. The excellent restaurant (moderate-expensive), which has outdoor terrace dining overlooking the garden in appropriate weather, specializes in seafood, but also offers imaginative meat preparations.

Esch-sur-Sûre

Tourist office in Townhall, open daily except Mon. July 1–mid-Sept. 10 a.m.–noon, 2–6 p.m.; Pop. 204 • This typical Ardennes village, with narrow winding stone streets, sits on a chunk of land that's almost entirely encircled by the Sûre. As seen from the road on the hills above it, Esch has one of the most photogenic settings in the Grand Duchy. The ruins of its probably 10th-century castle, demolished by the French revolutionary army, hang above it (site open at all times, floodlighted at night in season). If you arrive out of season, after Aug., you'll find many places already closed, though seeing it solitary is not without its charm, and you're sure to find food at a hotel or two. There are scenic stretches of road on both sides of the Sûre west from Esch, and north of the river to the east. If you are heading east at this point, **Bourscheid Castle** is worth a look.

ACCOMMODATIONS/RESTAURANTS ★★★ **Beau-Site** • *2 Rue de Kaundorf; 8.91.34; moderate* • This genial family-maintained 25-room hotel fronts the Sure River (terrace with tables), by the stone bridge that crosses it into the town. All of the rustic decor bedrooms have bath/shower and toilet, some have private balcony. Some rooms have telephone, none TV. There's a restaurant, where breakfast (included) is also served. Parking. Reservations in July and August strongly suggested.

Wiltz

Tourist office at Castle; open June 15 to Sept. 15, 10 a.m.–noon, 1:30–5:30 p.m.; 95.74.44; pop. 4,000 • Wiltz sits on a steep hillside, divided into an upper and lower town. At the castle in the upper town, in addition to the tourist office is a small museum of the *Battle of the Bulge*. The castle grounds in July host an **International Open-Air Festival** of music and theater. Near the Hôtel de Ville is a monument dedicated to **General Dwight D. Eisenhower,** who spent the night here when supreme commander of the allied armies on Nov. 8, 1944, and another to the *28th U.S. Infantry Division,* which was headquartered here on 19 Dec. 1944 when Wiltz was taken by the 5th German Parachute Division. The **National Strike Monument** in the center of town recalls the heroic resistance here in 1942 against the German introduction of military service, six people being shot for their participation.

Clervaux

Tourist office in Castle, April 1–June 30 Mon.–Fri. 2–5 p.m.. July 1– Oct. 31 Mon.–Sat. 10 a.m.–noon & 2–6 p.m., also on Sun. in July & Aug.; 9.20.72; pop. 1,000 • The first sight as you approach Clervaux is of the neo-Romanesque (1910) **Benedictine Abbey of St. Maurice,** whose extensive red roof rises in pleasing contrast above the green forest that surrounds it. But once you've wound your way over curving Ardennes' roads into the steep town, it's **Clervaux Castle,** rising on a rocky spur, that takes your attention. Its origins go back to the 12th century, but since that time the stolid feudal fortress has undergone numerous additions and alterations, particularly while serving as the seat of the powerful counts who were overlords of extended territories. In 1762, then owner **Count Adrian-John-Baptist of Lannoy** had the splendid **Loreto Chapel** built in the park of the castle; the castle and chapel were spared destruction by the French Revolutionary Army in the 1790s because the people of Clervaux declared them to be the property of a "Citizen Lannoy." Following inheritance quarrels in the 19th century, the legal victor in 1887 had the administrative buildings in the first courtyard demolished, using the stones to build a luxurious villa (today the **Hotel Parc,** see below) in the adjacent park. Clervaux experienced devastating destruction during the *Battle of the Bulge,* including the castle which, defended by the soldiers of the 110th Regiment of the 28th Infantry Division, fell in flames when the town was take on 17 December 1944 by the 2nd German Armored Division. Clervaux finally was retaken by the 26th U.S. Infantry on 26 Jan. 1945. Clervaux without its castle was unthinkable, so shortly after the Second World War ended, restoration was begun. Today, the castle is not only the heart of the town's history, but of its present life. The town hall *(Mairie)* and the tourist office are located within its walls. The castle also houses several exhibits.

In the summer of 1992, for the first time, **Clervaux Castle** will display the complete set of photographic images (503, assembled from 68 countries) from the original attendance-breaking **The Family of Man** show conceived by *Luxembourg-born* **Edward Steichen** (1879–1973) when he was director of photography of New York's *Museum of Mod-*

ern Art (MOMA). Working on the exhibit, for which his vision was to show a time-span that included birth, the world at work, family life, friendship, leisure, disease, war, and death, at the age of 73, Steichen, from scanning some 2 million photographs, and then a short list of 10,000, eventually narrowed the number to 503. It ranged from the works of the world's most famous photographers (though Steichen modestly selected only two of his own images) to simple family snapshots. The Family of Man opened at MOMA in New York in 1955, and eventually travelled to 69 countries where it was viewed by over 9 million people. Having kept close ties with Luxembourg all his life, even though he had left the country as a two-year-old, in 1966 Steichen arranged for the most complete version of The Family of Man, minus only a dozen images from the original, to be donated to the Luxembourg government. Steichen himself came to Luxembourg in 1966 to help settle the question of where such a large show could be permanently displayed, since many of the pictures are mounted on large boards. The castle at Clervaux was settled upon. But for many years since, only a limited number of the pictures were displayed, the others, in storage, became moldy and yellow. Fortunately, provisions were made in time for them all to be fully restored, and displayed. The problem of space, which is why some of the images were in storage in the first place, has been addressed by the renovation of space within Clervaux Castle.

Elsewhere in Clervaux Castle is an extremely interesting permanent display of *models* of the Grand Duchy's most important **castles** (notes on history of each castle in English). Since so many of the castles are now in ruins, the models furnish us with a better idea of the original, and how the fortification was placed on its site. The largest of the more than a dozen models is for Vianden Castle, and, in this one case, is a model of the whole town.

Across the courtyard, still in Clervaux Castle, is a museum of memorabilia from the **Battle of the Bulge.**

On *Maria Theresa Square* in the pedestrianized center of Clervaux stands the **Monument to the GI 1944–45,** a statue of a typical soldier to honor the sacrifice of the common GI for the liberation of Luxembourg. Don't miss the charming other memorial, *"To our Liberators"* a modern frieze mounted on the wall of the bank building facing the standing monument that depicts a heartwarming scene of citizens greeting the GI.

ACCOMMODATIONS/RESTAURANTS ★★★ Hotel du Parc • *2 Rue du Parc; 9.10.68; moderate* • This 110-year-old elegant mansion, surrounded by century-old trees, sits on a rise across from, and eye-level with Clervaux Castle, some of whose stones went into its construction. The 8 attractive guestrooms all have private bath, telephone, and radio. The public rooms have an old-world charm, with plaster work, wood paneling, monumental fireplaces (with fires laid when the weather warrants) in the dining room and lounge. The kitchen is well-regarded, and the place is particularly popular on weekends. Parking; sauna and solarium in cellar.

Vianden

Tourist office in Victor Hugo House, Grand Rue; April 1–Oct. 31 daily 9:30 a.m.–noon, 2–6 p.m., closed Wed. except in July and Aug.; 8.42.57, fax 84.90.81; inquire about special summer concerts, events; pop. 1,600 • For many, Vianden is the favorite destination in the Grand Duchy. A medieval town, spreading down a single steep stone street from its craggy heights with fine views to the river **Our** at the bottom, Vianden is defined mostly by its **castle,** which dominates the entire area. A **chairlift** *(Rue du Sanatorium; daily April 1–Sept.; 8.43.23)* provides a silent and steep sweep up and over trees to a height (1,444 feet/440 meters) from which one actually looks *down* at Vianden Castle. At the top there's a terrace cafe, *of course,* from which to enjoy the surpassing view of the river, town, and grandeur of the forests and grassy plateaus.

Vianden Castle • *daily in April 10 a.m.–5 p.m.; May 1–Aug. 31 9 a.m.–7 p.m.; in Sept. 9 a.m.–6 p.m.; in Oct. 10 a.m.–4:30 p.m.; Nov. Mon.–Fri. 11 a.m.–4 p.m., Sat. & Sun. 10 a.m.–4:30 p.m.; Dec. 1–Mar. 31; Sat., Sun., hols. only 10 a.m.–noon, 1–4 p.m.; English brochure and floor plan for self-guided tour; majestically illuminated at night April 1–Sept. 30* • The Grand Duchy's most historic, best restored, and most frequently photographed castle, Vianden is the ancestral home of *Orange-Nassau, Holland's Royal House,* which has ties to Luxembourg's Grand Ducal family through another Nassau branch. One of the largest feudal fortresses in the area, and certainly the one in the best shape today, the spectacularly situated castle was begun in the 12th century, and enlarged in the 13th century, Vianden's peak of power, when it used the **Count's Hall** and could accommodate 500 knights-at-arms. By late in the 13th century, the counts of the *House of Vianden* controlled lands that included 211 villages, hamlets, and mills, and produced **Count Henry II,** who became bishop of Utrecht. That was Vianden's apex. Its nadir came after then owner, King Willem I of Holland/Grand Duke of Luxembourg put the castle up for public auction in 1820. The buyer sold the castle's roof and other parts as building materials and, in 1827, once-proud Vianden was declared a ruin. Ownership eventually evolved back to the Nassaus and the Grand Ducal family; and in 1978, Grand Duke Jean ceded the castle, then but a shell of its former self, to the state. Since then, Vianden Castle has been painstakingly restored, the process only recently completed. You'll have a great sense of discovery exploring the castle. The "upper" chapel, 13th century, is a jewel, elegant and light, modelled after Charlemagne's palace chapels at Aachen and Nijmegan. It was used by the lords and ladies of the court, while the "lower" chapel was for the lower classes and servants, who could hear but not see the services in which the upper classes participated. The main section of the castle, built about 1210, has two huge halls. The Count's Hall, lined with wardrobes and wall cabinets, and hung with a *16th-century Flemish tapestry* "The Trojan War" and 17th-century tapestries from Amiens and Brussels, is now the sometimes site of **concerts.** The *Banqueting Hall,* where recorded classical music plays faintly, is also finely furnished, and has portraits, a 17th-century Aubusson tapestry "The Wedding at Cana," and an impressive fireplace. Elsewhere in the castle is an *Orange-Nassau geneology* painted on the wall. The counts of Vianden and counts of Nassau first merged in the 14th century, and **Rene de Chalon,** who died in 1544, was the first count of the Orange-Nassau dynasty. In the same way the castle is a magnificent sight from other terraces in the town, so are the views of the town from the castle terraces.

Other proper attractions in Vianden include the **Victor Hugo House** *which shares quarters and opening hours with the ground floor tourist office; all exhibit material in French only).* French author Victor Hugo lived here in 1871, having been to Vianden before (in 1862, 1863, and 1865). During those visits he produced a series of drawings of the Grand Duchy's castles, and later published a book of sketches entitled "Les Ardennes." The house, in which he stayed only from 6 June–22 Aug. 1871, contains photocopies of some of Hugo's drawings, letters, photographs, and other memorabilia. Across the street from the house is a bust of Hugo by **Rodin,** mounted on the corner of the bridge over the Our. The cafe outside the simple **Hotel Victor Hugo** provides great views to accompany a drink. **The Museum of Rustic Arts** *(98 Grand Rue; April 1–Sept. 30 10 a.m.–noon, 2:30–6 p.m. daily; 8.45.91; no English documentation)* is a former bourgmestre's house with several ground floor rooms of fine furnishings. Almost across the street from the museum is the ancient twin-naved **Trinitarian church,** built in the gothic style in 1248, and one of the oldest religious buildings in Luxembourg. The restored cloister behind it holds the tombstones of the Counts of Vianden. The **pumping station** (tours) and the **Barrage de Lohmuhle,** which forms the lower reservoir north of Vianden on the Our, are masterpieces of technology, among the best power generators in Europe, and popular local tourist attractions.

ACCOMMODATIONS/RESTAURANTS ★★★ **Hotel Heintz**
● *55 Grand Rue; 8.41.55, 8.45.59; moderate; closed mid-Nov. until Easter* ● The Heintz is famous for its hospitable air and congenial family atmosphere that instill a feeling of being well-cared for. Guests to Luxembourg from afar invariably find their way here: **Beatrice Patton,**

widow of General George; **Margaret Truman; Perla Mesta,** former U.S. Ambassador to Luxembourg, the "Hostess with the Mostest." But the Heintz isn't grand, it's simply gracious. The 30 guestrooms (8 with balconies and view of hills behind hotel) have basic traditional furnishings, all with private bath room, telephone. The hallways and public rooms in the centuries-old building are appropriately and delightfully decorated in antiques, oil paintings, orientals, with wonderful wooden chests and clocks. The restaurant is renowned, every detail overseen by owner **Magda Hansen** herself, the fourth generation to provide personalized attention to guests of the homey Heintz. Elevator; parking; private gardens.

Diekirch

Tourist office Place Guillaume; Mon.–Fri. 9 a.m.–noon, 2–5 p.m., from July 1–Aug. 15 also on Sat. & Sun.; 80.30.23; pop. 5,600 • Located in the center of the Grand Duchy, where the Oesling (Ardennes) and the fertile Gutland (Good Land) regions meet, Diekirch, today a popular tourism center for continental campers and hikers, has interesting attractions from both its ancient and relatively recent history. The pedestrian shopping core of Diekirch is cozy and companionable, dotted with outdoor cafes in season, a community bulletin board on a central square, and several fountains, the best being a delightful donkey with movable parts, across from the tourist office. Diekirch was a prehistoric Celtic center, the **"Devil's Altar" dolmen** outside town a relic from the period. The town's Roman era also is evident, most especially at the **Municipal Museum** (see below). But the Second World War put the strongest stamp on Diekirch attractions.

Diekirch Historical/Battle of the Bulge Museum • *10 Bamertal; May 1–October 31, and week before, week after Easter, 10 a.m.–noon, 2–6 p.m.; 80.89.08; guided tours on request; multi-lingual brochure, exhibit notes* • In large part, the museum commemorates aspects of the *Battle of the Bulge* around Diekirch in the winter of 1944–45 (although the scope of the museum may be enlarged). The details offered here about what *"absorption"* into the Third Reich, as opposed to "merely" being *occupied,* meant to the lives of Luxembourgers makes us appreciate their uniquely difficult experience during the war. Particularly poignant are the exhibits relating to the compulsory conscription of young Luxembourg men into the *Wehrmacht* from August 1942. This act was considered one of the worst of the Nazis war crimes, since it sent Luxembourgers to the German Front (mostly to Russia) to wage armed war against the Allied forces they supported, those Allies, not realizing they were firing on Luxembourgers, forced to wear Nazi uniforms. From 1941, all Luxembourg young men and women were obliged to provide the Nazis with labor in war industry factories and to live apart in work camps.

The Diekirch Museum is not political. It's purpose is to show what happened. The exhibits explain facts such as that by the time of the Battle of the Bulge, most of the German soldiers who were doing the fighting were but 16 or 17, following Hitler's orders to fight not Nazi ideologists. Germans and American soldiers who once fought each other have since met here. The museum, which opened in 1984, was conceived by a young Luxembourg man who was not born when the war ended. **Roland Gaul,** who today is the public relations staff person for the U.S. Embassy in Luxembourg City, explains he "just grew up with the Battle of the Bulge," and as he and his friends, out "playing cowboys and Indians" in the woods would find German helmets or pistols, his interest in a museum developed. The effort to open the museum and run it all came from volunteer efforts. Among the highly interesting exhibits is a model of the Russian prison camp at **Tambow** that claimed so many Luxembourgers. There are diaramas of the *"white jungle warfare"* in the snow for which Luxembourg women stitched white clothing together to form camouflage for the soldiers, to examples of the "propaganda pamphlets" used as psychological warfare from both sides. One such piece, written by the Germans in correct American slang that was meant to affect American morale by making them homesick at Christmas, was dropped over the lines in the Ardennes.

Municipal Museum • *Place Guillaume; May 1 to October 10 a.m.–12, 2–6 p.m., closed Thurs* • Highlights of the local relics from Roman culture on display are two large 4th-century mosaics, which give an idea of the decorative detail to be found in the villas of the occupiers of the region in that era. One mosaic, found in 1926 when excavation works were proceeding on Diekirch's Esplanade, with a central figure of a lion surrounded by bright geometrical figures, is well preserved. The other was found in 1950 when a town street was being widened. In it, a stylized flower motive surrounds an intriguing head of a *Medusa,* which shows a different face when viewed from opposite ends of the mosaic floor.

On the Diekirch side of **Ettelbruck** to the southwest, in **Patton Park,** sheltered by an arc of weeping willow trees, is the oft-photographed statue of U.S. Army **General George S. Patton,** portrayed in the act of raising his field glasses to survey the Ardennes. (A casting of the statue also stands at the U.S. Army's West Point Military Academy. Ettelbruck also has a mall museum of Patton paraphernalia.

Little Switzerland

Set in the valley of the **Ernz Noire** river, this area of fantastically shaped sandstone rocks and outcrops set in wooded glens and ravines, sometimes in sight of the road, often offering its sights only to those who "walk in" a bit further. The proximity of impressive viewing can be gauged by the number of cars at the several parking sites provided along the road that leads through **Mullerthal** (*pop. 45, altitude 820 ft./250 meters*). That village, more or less at its center, has given its name to the region, which is full of serious hikers and recreational ramblers in the summer and early fall. The region got its unlikely name "Little Switzerland" (*not* used by Luxembourgers) from the Dutch (who, presumably, were responding over-enthusiastically to the area's altitude; they call the only slightly higher spots in Holland's SE Limburg Province the "Dutch Alps"). In any case, under the Dutch King/Grand Duke **Willem II,** Holland first became connected to Luxembourg by **rail.** The exclamations of Dutch soldiers who had served in Luxembourg over the scenery around Mullerthal brought many Dutch here on holiday, particularly once the train could bring them to nearby Diekirch in comfort. Their name for Mullerthal stuck, as did their interest in the area, the Dutch still being the main holiday makers here. The authentic character of the restored village of **Christnach** and the popular tourist center of **Consdorf** are two of the entry points into the Mullerthal. The village of **Waldbillig** (pop. 275), set on a green plateau surrounded by deep forest, was the birthplace in 1827 of **Michel Rodange,** Luxembourg's most famous poet.

Echternach

Tourist office Porte St. Willibrord at Basilica; Mon.–Fri. 9 a.m.–noon, 2–5 p.m., in July and Aug. also on Sat. & Sun.; 7.22.30; pop. 4,000
• Echternach, known as having the most attractive main square in Luxembourg, is also one of Europe's earliest centers of Christianity. **Willibrord,** an Anglo-Saxon missionary from Northumberland, founded a Benedictine Abbey here in 698, which makes Echternach the oldest settlement in the country. Some Roman remains and medieval ramparts add to its historic interest and atmosphere. Echternach's religious, spiritual, and artistic achievements reached their height with the **Echternach School of Book Illumination** in the 10th and 11th centuries. The Kells-style (from the *Book of Kells* in Ireland) influenced the monks at Echternach and it is thought possible that some of the Kells artist-monks may even have come to St. Willibrord's Abbey, since it became one of the best equipped ateliers in Europe for illuminating manuscripts (there is a museum of illuminations in the abbey). Although the **Basilica of St. Willibrord,** built about 800, over Willibrord's original abbey, today only dates from after the Second World War (the *Ardennes offensive* doing more damage than centuries of pillaging), the crypt, c. 800, from the first building, remains intact. It houses the tomb of St. Willibrord. Echternach's lovely main square lacks symmetry, but that is part of its

charm. A noticeable part of the irregularity of shape is caused by the **Denzelt** (the old courtrooms), one reason the gothic building attracts so much attention. Many of the facades around the square have been restored, which makes it a more pleasant pastime than ever to sit at one of its cafes. The town is known for its unique **Dancing Procession** *(Whitsun Tuesday),* which takes place on the square attracts thousands of pilgrims. Dating from the 13th century, the procession may commemorate St. Willibrord's cure of epilepsy.

   ACCOMMODATIONS/RESTAURANTS ★★★★ **Hotel Bel-Air** • *1 Route de Berdorf; 72.93.83, fax 72.86.94; First Class* • Located less than a mile/1 km. from the center of Echternach, this modern hotel sits in its own park, offering views from its terraces and glass-walled dining rooms of the Sure Valley. The 33 guestrooms in this well-serviced hotel all have private baths, TV, telephones. Tennis; gourmet restaurant; wooded walks begin just steps from the door.

Moselle Valley

Leaving Echternach on a scenic route roughly south, in the direction of Trier, you arrive at the Moselle river, with its attractive tree-shaded and path-lined embankments. It's a lovely ride along the river (and *on* the river, too, if you'd like to cruise on the **Princess Marie-Astrid** boat). The colors of the scenery change with the stage of the grapes growing in the vineyards that cover the banks on both the Luxembourg and German sides of the Moselle. As well as being pretty, the vineyards are important business; Luxembourg's Minister of Agriculture also carries the title of Minister of Viniculture (see *Luxembourg Wines* under *Benelux Food and Drink* chapter at front of book).

  As you approach **Wormeldange** (from the North), look for signs to **Koeppchen,** and follow them up into the vineyards, your destination as you drive through them the **St. Donat Chapel.** There is a bench from which to survey the magnificent panorama that lies before you. Just beyond Wormeldange is **Ehnen,** a delightful village of medieval character, with narrow stone streets and the only round church in the Grand Duchy.

Mondorf-les-Bains

Tourist office 31 Ave. Fr. Clement; Mon.–Fri. 9 a.m.–noon, 2–6 p.m., also from Easter to Aug. 31 Sat. & Sun. 2–6 p.m.; 6.75.75 or 6.81.49; pop. 2,500 • Mondorf-le-Bains had its beginnings, and most "fashionable" years, as a resort during the last part of the 19th century. The discovery of its springs are said to be the result of an unpopular tax on salt imposed by unpopular Dutch King/Grand Duke of Luxembourg

Willem I in the early 19th century, during his rule of the United Kingdom of the Netherlands from 1815 to 1830. Unwilling to pay for the excessively taxed salt, Luxembourgers began digging here and there to see if they could find salt in the ground. What they found were the 28-degree thermal springs that have since been praised for their powers to help those suffering from arthritis, rheumatism, and liver ailments. Today, there is a state-run **health center** with hot springs and the latest medical equipment, located in the center of extensive well-maintained gardens, with flower beds (tulips, roses) and paths that encourage healthy walks. There are also daily concerts in the park in summer by the excellent local brass band. In 1988 **Le Domaine Thermal** *(Mon.–Fri. 9 a.m.–10 p.m., Sat., Sun. 9 a.m.–8 p.m.; 66.12.12., fax 66.10.93)* opened offering a full range of baths, inhalations; while there's a full course of cures, there's also a focus, unusual for European spas, on fitness too, with exercise equipment and classes, plus sauna and whirlpool. A 4-star 10-room hotel (moderate) is in the same complex. In 1983, Mondorf opened its **Casino-2000,** the Grand Duchy's only casino, with roulette, blackjack, and slot machines. It took the conservative country a century to debate the issue as to whether to allow gambling within its borders. The casino is formal, and there's a 34-room first-class hotel (moderate) attached to it.

Not at Mondorf-les-Bains for their good health at the end of the Second World War were 53 notorious war criminals of the Third Reich, including **Reichsmarshal Hermann Goering** and **Fieldmarshal von Rundstedt,** as Mondorf had the doubtful privilege of having its then Palace Hotel turned into "Camp Ashcan" as an incarceration center. They remained here from May to August 1945, during which the first inquiries for the Nuremberg War Crimes Trials took place.

ACCOMMODATIONS/RESTAURANTS ★★★★ **Hotel du Grand Chef** • *36 Avenue des Bains; 6.81.22; First Class* • This gracious hotel which occupies the former 1852 home of a French nobleman, who enjoyed it during Mondorf's height of fashion, is set in its own private park, within walking distance of Casino-2000, which opened in 1983 and has an attached luxury hotel. While thoroughly modernized, the hotel, long a favored destination for Luxembourgers out for a weekend daytrip for its restaurant, retains the elegance of its origins. The 41 rooms all have private bath, TV.

BENELUX BIBLIOGRAPHY: RANDOM READINGS

The Netherlands in Perspective: The Organizations of Society and Environment, by William Z. Shetter, Martinus Nijhoff Publishers, Leiden, Holland, 1987, 333 pages. A wide-ranging contemporary picture of Dutch society presented (in English) for anyone with an interest in Holland beneath the surface. Written by a member of the Department of Germanic Studies of Indiana University who has 40 years of personal experience with Holland.

The Embarrassment of Riches: An Interpretation of Dutch Culture in the Golden Age, by Simon Schama, Alfred A. Knopf, New York, 1987. A wonderfully readable tome, authoritatively documented and well-grounded in art history and appreciation, that brings alive myriad aspects of life as it was in 17th-century Holland.

Orange & Stuart 1641–1672, by Pieter Geyl, Charles Scribner's Sons, New York, 1969. In-depth coverage which communicates the pressures put upon the House of Orange by the more powerful English Stuarts, both when the latter were kings of England and when they were exiled on the continent, in the period prior to the William (Holland's Prince of Orange) and Mary marriage and subsequent reign.

The First Salute, by Barbara W. Tuchman, Knopf, 1988. Includes interesting information about the Dutch trade with, early recognition of, and financial support for the American colonies during their War of Independence against England.

A Bridge Too Far, by Cornelius Ryan. The book, originally published in 1974 and from which the film was made, relates the details of the ill-conceived and unsuccessful World War II *Market-Garden Operation* that hinged upon the taking of the bridge over the Rhine at Arnhem in central Holland in September 1944. Presently out-of-print but available at libraries.

The Diary of Anne Frank (originally entitled in Dutch *The Secret Annex*), by Anne Frank. Covering the period from July 9, 1942, when the Frank family had to go into hiding from the Nazis in Amsterdam, less than a month after Anne had received a diary for her 13th birthday. The Diary covers the two-year period during which Anne had to exist in close quarters with her parents, sister, and four strangers, until August 1944, when the family's whereabouts were betrayed to the Nazis by someone seeking the "head money" given as a reward for such information. Anne subsequently died at the Bergen-Belsen concentration camp. From the pages of this diary of difficulties shines the eternal power of human hope: Despite her unmarked grave, Anne's wish to "live on after my death" is realized on bookshelves around the world that hold her *Diary,* and in hearts that share her ideals. (See also *Anne Frank House* under *Amsterdam, What To See and Do*).

The Hiding Place, by Corrie ten Boom, Viking Press, 1971. The story of the Ten Boom family of Haarlem who risked, some losing, their lives to hide and help to safety Dutch resistance workers and others who were hunted by the Nazis during World War II. Their house can be visited (see also Ten Boom House under *Haarlem, What To See and Do*).

The Hidden Force, by Louis Couperus, Library of the Indies: University of Massachusetts Press, 1990. Couperus was a member of the class of upper-level East Indies civil servants (for the Dutch colony of Indonesia) in The Hague at the turn of the century. In this book, written in 1900, he shows the mysterious Far East through the uncomprehending eyes of a colonial administrator (see also *The Muse,* Dutch Authors, Benelux Cultural Legacy).

The Black Tulip, by Alexandre Dumas (out of print in English). A melodramatic tale which conveys some of the excitement and excess of the *Tulipmania* era in early 17th-century Holland (see also chapter in this book: *The Bulb Field Business*). Look for old editions in libraries.

Hans Brinker: The Silver Skates, by American Mary M. Dodge, many editions still in print; first published in the 1860s. A dated but interesting picture of Dutch life in places such as Broek-in-Waterland, where the story is set, Amsterdam, Haarlem, Leiden, and The Hague. One of the characters in the book relates the fictional tale of a boy who plugged a leaking dike with his pudgy finger and stayed there all night thus saving his village of Spaardam, not far from Haarlem, from inundation. The unlikely deed so captured American tourists' imaginations that the Dutch (who only recently have been raising their children on *Hans Brinker*) decided to satisfy their visitors' expectations by erecting a statue to the brave Dutch boy. (See also *Spaarden, In The Area* under *Haarlem*)

Europe, a Tapestry of Nations, by Flora Lewis, Simon and Schuster, 1987. Series of essays on Europe and European countries by a long-time observer of Europe for *The New York Times.* Includes chapters on *The Low Countries: The Bourgeois Monarchies; Netherlands: Dear Father State; Belgium; Divided by Language; and Luxembourg: A Simple Grand Duchy.*

The Europeans, by Luigi Barzini, Penguin, 1983. Essays by a distinguished Italian journalist on various West European countries, including a chapter on *The Careful Dutch.*

A New Guide to the Battlefields of Northern France and the Low Countries by Michael Glover, Michael Joseph Ltd., 1987. Has in-depth coverage of the Low Country battles of *Waterloo* (1815); *Ypres* (1914 to 1917); *Arnhem* (1944); and the Bastogne/Ardennes campaigns of *The Battle of the Bulge* (1944–45). (See also under appropriate destination in text.)

The Sorrow of Belgium, by Hugo Claus, originally published in 1983; U.S. English edition by Pantheon. When published (in Dutch), the novel became an overnight best seller in Flanders and Holland, since it covered a subject of bitter debate, that of collaboration with the occupying Nazi enemy during World War II. The book recalls the period 1939–1947.

The Continuing Battle: Memoirs of a European (1936–1966) by Paul-Henri Spaak; Little, Brown & Co. 1971. Several times Prime Minister of Belgium between 1938 and 1957, and also foreign minister, president of the United Nations General Assembly, and Secretary-General of NATO in 1957, Spaak had a unique perspective on Europe as a stateman. This volume follows the development of Spaak's two ideals, the Atlantic Alliance and European unity, through the crises and coalitions of the Benelux Plan, the European Coal and Steel Commission, EEC (Common Market), and the Cold War.

Pedigree, by Georges Simenon, Hamish Hamilton, London, 1962. A novel about a Belgian youth, Roger Mamelin, up to the age of 16 which Simenon, while not wishing the book to be called autobiographical, acknowledges comes "very close to reality." Simenon was born and grew in Liège, Belgium (see also under Liège, *What To See and Do,* and *Belgian Authors* under *The Muse* in *The Benelux Cultural Legacy* chapter).

The Life and Times of Hercule Poirot, by Anne Hart, G. P. Putnam's Sons, 1990. The famed detective created by Agatha Christie was Belgian, and many of the "biographical" details about Poirot in this book, reconstructed from the texts of his adventures, shed light on Belgium (see also *The Muse* under *Belgian Authors*).

A BENELUX LEXICON

While you may never *need to know* Dutch/Flemish or French in order to communicate in the Benelux, it may be *nice* to know some basic words. **Language notes:** The only difference in the Dutch alphabet is the "ij" as a single letter that is interchangeable with the letter "y," and pronounced as a "long i." For example, the Dutch word "ijs" (ice cream) is pronounced as the English "ice." Words beginning with "ij" capitalize both letters, as in *IJsselmeer,* and appear in alphabetized lists under *Y*. The letter "g" in Dutch has a gutteral sound, much like the "ch" in the Scottish word "loch." An example is the Dutch cheese *"Gouda,"* which is correctly pronounced *"HOW' da."* A basic in the Dutch language is the diminutive "je," which best translates as "little." While employed to indicate small physical size, it also often connotes affection, as when tacked on to people's names or belongings. When dining out in Holland or Flanders, French cuisine terms often will be understood in restaurants.

English	Dutch/Flemish	French
Numbers		
zero	nul	zero
one	een	un, une
two	twee	deux
three	drie	trois
four	vier	quatre
five	vijf	cinq
six	zes	six
seven	zeven	sept
eight	acht	huit
nine	negen	neuf
ten	tien	dix
eleven	elf	onze
twelve	twaalf	douze
thirteen	dertien	treize
fourteen	veertien	quatorze
fifteen	vijftien	quinze
sixteen	zestien	seize

BENELUX LEXICON

English	Dutch/Flemish	French
seventeen	zeventien	dix-sept
eighteen	achttien	dix-huit
nineteen	negentien	dix-neuf
twenty	twintig	vingt
twenty-one	een en twintig	vingt et un
fifty	vijftig	cinquante
one hundred	honderd	cent
two hundred	tweehonderd	deux cent
one thousand	duizend	mille
1st	eerste	premier (ière)
2nd	tweede	deuxième
3rd	derde	troisième

Days / Dagen / Jours

English	Dutch/Flemish	French
Monday	Maandag	Lundi
Tuesday	Dinsdag	Mardi
Wednesday	Woensdag	Mercredi
Thursday	Donderdag	Jeudi
Friday	Vrijdag	Vendredi
Saturday	Zaterdag	Samedi
Sunday	Zondag	Dimanche

General

English	Dutch/Flemish	French
Please	Alstublieft	S'il vous plaît
Thank you, very much	Dank U, zeer	Merci, beaucoup
Good morning	Dag	Bonjour
Good Evening	Gouden avond	Bonsoir
Good night	Goede nacht	Bonne nuit
Good-bye	Tot ziens	Au revoir
Mr. sir	Mijnheer	Monsieur
Mrs. Ms.	Mevrouw	Madame
Gentlemen	Heren	Messieurs
Ladies	Dames	Mesdames
W.C.	De toilet	La toilette
Excuse me	Pardon	Excusez-moi
Yes, no	Ja, neen	Oui, non
How much?	Hoeveel?	Combien?
Price	Prijs	Prix

BENELUX LEXICON

English	Dutch/Flemish	French
Expensive, cheap	Duur, goedkoop	Cher, bon marché
Old, new	Oud, nieuw	Vieux, nouveau
Where is?	Waar is?	Où est?
To the left	Links	À gauche
To the right	Rechts	À droite
Entrance, exit	Ingang, uitgang	Entrée, sortie
Doctor	Dokter	Médecin
Hospital	Ziekenhuis	Hôpital
Post office	Postkantoor	Bureau de poste
Stamp	Postzegel	Timbre
Airmail	Luchtpost	Par avion
Police station	Politiebureau	Poste de police
No smoking	Verboden te roken	Defense de fumer
Admission free	Vrije toegang	Entrée libre
Open, closed	Geopen, gesloten	Ouvert, ferme

Travel Terms

English	Dutch/Flemish	French
Travel bureau	Reisbureau	Bureau de voyage
The railway station	Het station	La gare
Return ticket	Retour	Billet aller-retour
One-way ticket	Enkele reis	Billet aller
Fare	Prijs van het reiskaartje	Prix du billet
First class	Eerste klas	Première classe
Second class	Tweede klas	Seconde classe
Fast train	Sneltrein	Train rapide
Local train	Stoptrein	Train omnibus
Dining car	Restaurantiewagen	Wagon-restaurant
Weekdays only	Alleen op werkdagen	En semaine seulement
Bus/tram stop	Bushalte	Arrêt l'autobus
Room with bath, shower	Kamer met bad/douche	Chamber avec salle de bain, douche
Gasoline, petrol	Benzine	Essence
Oil	Olie	Huile
Parking place	Parkeerplaats	Stationnement, parking
Key	Sleutel	La clef

Benelux Bill of Fare

English	Dutch/Flemish	French
table d'hôte	menu	prix-fixe
bill of fare, menu	kaart	carte
wine list	wijnkaart	carte des vins

English	Dutch/Flemish	French
bill	de rekening	l'addition
Is the tip included?	Service inclusief?	Service compris?
fried	gebakken	frit
smoked	gerookt	fumé
rare	bleu (almost raw)	saignant (safely rare)
medium	half gaar	à point
well done	goed gaar	bien cuit
soup	soep	soupe
bread, white/brown	brood, witte/bruin	pain, blanc/bis
roll	broodje	petit pain
egg	ei	oeuf
cheese	kaas	fromage
whipped cream	slagroom	crème fouettée

Meat/Fish

English	Dutch/Flemish	French
	vlees/vis	viande/poisson
pork	varkens	porc
sausage	bloedworst	boudin
roast beef	rosbief	rosbif
chicken	kip	poulet
hare	haas	lièvre
rabbit	konijn	lapin
venison	ree	chevreuil
salmon	zalm	saumon
trout	forel	truite
pike	snoek	brochet
sole	tong	sole
monkfish	lotte	lotte
herring	haring	hareng
eel	paling	anguille
lobster	kreeft	homard
oysters	oesters	huitres
shrimp	garnalen	crevettes
mussels	mosselen	moules
snails	slakken	escargots

Vegetables/Fruit

English	Dutch/Flemish	French
	groeten/vruchten	légumes/fruit
asparagus	asperges	asperges
beans	bonen	feves
string beans	snijbonen	haricots verts
chicory	witloof	chicons

English	Dutch/Flemish	French
cauliflower	bloemkool	choux-fleur
Brussels sprouts	Brusselse spruitjes	choux de Bruxelles
cabbage	kool	chou
mushrooms	champignons	champignons
onions	uien	oignons
peas	erwten	petit pois
potatoes	aardapplen	pommes de terre
rice	rijs	riz
salad	sla, salade	salade
apple	appel	pomme
cherries	kersen	cerises
lemon	citroen	citron
orange	sinaasappel	orange
pineapple	ananas	ananas
strawberries	aardbeien	fraises
pear	peer	poire
peach	perzik	pêche

Seasonings

sugar	suiker	sucre
salt	zout	sel
pepper	peper	poivre
mustard	mosterd	moutarde
vinegar	azijn	vinaigre
oil	olie	huile
honey	honig	miel

Beverages / dranken / boissons

a bottle of de . . .	een fles	une bouteille
a glass of, cup of	een glas, kop	un verre, tasse de
coffee, tea	koffie, thee	cafe, the
milk	melk	lait
juice	sap	jus
mineral water	mineraalwater	eau minerale
beer	bier	biere
wine (red, white)	wijn (rode, witte)	vin (rouge, blanc)

HOTEL QUICK-REFERENCE TABLES

Prices given below—for a room for two with private bath, inclusive of tax and service—are in local currencies: Dutch guilders for Holland, Belgian and Luxembourg francs (on a par) in those countries. (Note under prices in front of the book the different categories for individual Benelux countries.) Prices quoted were as accurate as possible at press time, but, as explained on pages 6 and 7 of this guide, they may increase during the life of this guide. **NOTE:** Where hotels have posted a range of rates for double rooms, an *average price* has been given; this means that in many cases rooms will be available at prices **less** than those listed below.

HOLLAND..

RANDSTAD HOLLAND

Amsterdam (Telephone Code 020)	Phone	Rate (in Dutch guilders)	Page
Agora	6272200	160	158
Ambassade	6262333	245	156
American	6245322	480	154
Amstel	6226060	775	153
Amsterdam Wiechmann	6263321	185	157
Apollo	6735922	495	154
Atlas	6766336	180	157
Avenue	6238307	210	157
Borgmann	6735252	195	156
Canal House	6225182	210	156
Doelen Karena	6235632	335	155
De l'Europe	6234836	590	152
Golden Tulip Barbizon Centre	6851351	520	154
Golden Tulip Barbizon Palace	5564564	560	153
Grand Hotel Krasnapolsky	5549111	475	154
Hotel The Bridge	6237068	140	159
Jan Luyken	5730730	290	156

HOTEL QUICK-REFERENCE TABLES

Amsterdam (Telephone Code 020)	Phone	Rate (in Dutch guilders)	Page
Marriott	6075555	400	155
Owl	6189484	155	157
Pulitzer	5235235	495	153
Ramada Renaissance Amsterdam	6212223	525	152
Rho	6207371	130	158
Rokin	6267456	110	159
Scandia Crown Hotel Victoria	6234255	380	156
Schiller Karena	6231660	300	155
Seven Bridges	6231329	140	159
Toro Hotel	6737223	140	158
Vondel	6120120	165	157
Washington	6796754	155	158

Heemskerk (Telephone Code 02510)			
Chateau Marquette	41414	210	168

Haarlem (Telephone Code 023)			
Carillon	310591	99	178
Carlton Square	319091	350	178
Golden Tulip Lion D'Or	321750	210	178

Leiden (Telephone Code 071)			
De Doelen	120527	155	194
Golden Tulip Leiden	221121	300	193
Mayflower	142641	175	194
Nieuw Minera	126358	140	194

The Hague/Scheveningen (Telephone Code 070)			
Aquarius	3543543	130	213
Bel Park	3505000	135	213
Carlton Beach	3541414	260	213
City Hotel	3557966	145	214
Corona	3637930	390	212
Des Indes	3632932	490	211
Esquire	3522341	125	214
ParkHotel	3624371	225	212
Petit	3465500	145	213
Seinduin	3551971	105	214
Steigenberger Kurhaus	3520052	360	212

Voorburg (Telephone Code 070)			
Vreudg & Rust	3872081	360	215

	Phone	Rate (in Dutch guilders)	Page
Wassenaar (Telephone Code 01751)			
Auberge de Kievet	19232	390	216
Delft (Telephone Code 015)			
De Ark	157999	205	229
Leeuwenbrug	147741	155	230
MuseumHotel	140930	220	229
Rotterdam (Telephone Code 010)			
Atlanta	4110420	270	244
Bienvenue	4669394	95	245
Hilton International	4144044	680	243
Inntel	4134139	250	244
Parkhotel	4363611	270	243
Scandic	4134790	195	244
Van Walsum	4363275	160	244
Gouda (Telephone Code 01820)			
Keizerskroon	28096	100	248
Utrecht (Telephone Code 030)			
Malie	316424	150	266
Scandic Crown	925200	315	266
Smits	331232	240	266

NORTHERN HOLLAND

	Phone	Rate	Page
Edam (Telephone Code 02993)			
De Fortuna	71671	140	277
Enkhuizen (Telephone Code 02280)			
Die Port Van Cleve	12510	135	279
Leeuwarden (Telephone Code 058)			
Oranje	126241	220	283
Stavoren (Telephone Code 05149)			
De Vrouw van Stavoren	1202	90	284
Geithoorn (Telephone Code 05216)			
De Jonge	1360	110	286
Blokzijl (Telephone Code 05272)			
Kaatje Bij de Sluis	1833	270	286

	Phone	Rate (in Dutch guilders)	Page
Zwolle (Telephone Code 038)			
Grand Hotel Wientjes	254254	260	289
Elburg (Telephone Code 05250)			
Het Smeede	3877	115	289

CENTRAL HOLLAND

	Phone	Rate	Page
Apeldoorn (Telephone Code 055)			
De Keizerskroon	217744	290	303
Zeist (Telephone Code 03404)			
'T Kerckerbosch	14734	205	308
Baarn (Telephone Code 02154)			
Kasteel De Hooge	12541	310	308
Bosch en Duin (Telephone Code 030)			
Auberge de Hoefslag	251051	370	309

ZEELAND

	Phone	Rate	Page
Middelburg (Telephone Code 01180)			
Beau Rivage	38060	145	316
Du Commerce	36051	135	316
Veere (Telephone Code 01181)			
De Campveerse Toren	1291	130	318
Zierikzee (Telephone Code 01110)			
Mondragon	13051	130	321

NORTH BRABANT

	Phone	Rate	Page
Den Bosch (Telephone Code 073)			
Golden Tulip Central	125151	255	326
Heusden (Telephone Code 04162)			
In Den Verdwaalde Koogel	1933	130	327
Breda (Telephone Code 076)			
De Klok	214082	155	329

LIMBURG

	Phone	Price (in Belgian francs)	Page
Maastricht (Telephone Code 043)			
Beaumont	254433	195	342
Bergere	251651	140	343
Du Casque	214343	220	342
Du Chene	213523	150	343
Derlon	216770	400	342
Maastricht	254171	525	342
Wittem (Telephone Code 04450)			
Kasteel Wittem	1208	240	346
Kerkade (Telephone Code 045)			
Kasteel Erenstein	461333	260	346

BELGIUM ....

	Phone	Price (in Belgian francs)	Page
Brussels (Telephone Code 02)			
Amigo	511.59.10	7,900	411
Arcade Saint-Catherine	513.76.20	3,600	414
Archimede	231.09.09	6,250	413
Arlequin	514.16.15	2,700	415
Chambord	513.41.19	3,900	414
Chateau du Lac	654.11.22	6,900	410
Hilton Brussels	504.11.11	12,400	414
Ibis Brussels Center	514.40.40	4,150	410
Jolly Hotel Sablon	512.88.00	10,000	415
La Madeleine	513.29.73	2,750	412
Le Dome	218.06.80	6,900	413
Manos	537.96.82	4,100	410
Metropole	217.23.00	6,400	415
Mirabeau	511.19.72	2,050	413
New Hotel Siru	217.75.80	5,290	415
Opera	219.43.43	2,150	410
Pullman Astoria	217.62.90	7,900	412
Royal Windsor	511.42.15	13,500	411
SAS Royal	219.28.28	11,700	410
Sheraton Hotel & Towers	224.31.11	10,600	410

HOTEL QUICK-REFERENCE TABLES

Brussels (Telephone Code 02)	*Phone*	*Price (in Belgian francs)*	*Page*
Sofitel Brussels	514.22.00	6,500	412
Vendome	218.00.70	3,250	414

FLANDERS

Antwerp (Telephone Code 03)

Alfa De Keyser	234.01.35	6,700	459
Alfa Empire	231.47.55	5,550	460
Alfa Theater	231.17.20	5,900	459
Arcade	231.88.30	3,000	460
Carlton	231.15.15	5,950	459
De Rosier	225.01.40	8,500	458
Firean	237.02.60	5,600	460
Villa Mozart	231.30.31	7,800	459

Bruges (Telephone Code 050)

Academie	33.22.66	4,200	492
Adornes	34.13.36	2,750	492
Biskajer	34.15.06	3,150	491
't Bourgoensche Cruyce	33.79.26	2,000	492
Die Swaene	34.27.98	6,100	490
Duc de Bourgogne	33.20.38	4,100	491
Egmond	34.14.45	2,650	492
Holiday Inn Crowne Plaza	34.58.34	10,500	489
Orangerie	34.16.49	6,500	490
Oud Huis Amsterdam	34.18.10	5,800	489
Pandhotel	34.06.66	4,650	490
Ter Brughe	34.03.24	3,700	491
Tuilerieen	34.36.91	8,000	489

Ghent (Telephone Code 091)

Gravensteen	25.11.50	4,700	511
Ibis	33.00.00	3,450	512
Novotel Ghent Centrum	24.22.30	4,650	512
St. Jorishof	24.24.24	5,500	511

BELGIUM COAST

Knokke (Telephone Code 050)

La Reserve	61.06.06	6,000	517

Ostend (Telephone Code 059)

Hotel Andromeda	80.66.11	4,500	520

HOTEL QUICK-REFERENCE TABLES · · · 655

	Phone	Price (in Belgian francs)	Page
Tournai **(Telephone Code 069)**			
Condor Hotel	21.50.77	2,800	540
Parc	21.28.93	2,300	539
Liège **(Telephone Code 041)**			
Cygne d'Argent	23.70.01	2,000	554
Ramada Hotel Liège	21.77.11	6,000	554

MEUSE VALLEY

Bouvignes (Telephone Code 082)
L'Auberge de Bouvigne	61.16.00	2,000	565

Celles (Telephone Code 082)
Hostellerie Le Val Joli	66.67.68	2,000	565

Lisogne (Telephone Code 082)
Moulin de Lisogne	22.63.80	2,500	565

ARDENNES

Spa (Telephone Code 087)
L'Auberge	87.74.10	2,300	573
Manoir-de-Lebioles	77.10.20	5,000	574

Beverce (Telephone Code 080)
Ferme Libert	77.72.47	1,100	574

Comblain-au-Pont (Telephone Code 041)
Hostellerie Saint-Roch	69.13.33	4,000	574

Durbuy (Telephone Code 086)
Le Sanglier des Ardennes	21.32.62	2,850	575

Marché-en-Famenne/Aye (Telephone Code 084)
Chateau d'Hassonville	31.10.25	5,000	576

Noirefontaine (Telephone Code 061)
Le Moulin Hideux	46.70.15	4,800	581

Sainte-Cecile-sur-Semois (Telephone Code 061)
Hostellerie Saint-Cecile	31.31.67	2,500	581

GRAND DUCHY OF LUXEMBOURG..................................

Luxembourg City (Telephone Code 352)	Phone	Price (in Luxembourg francs)	Page
Auberge du Coin	40.21.01	2,800	623
Central Molitor	48.99.11	4,200	622
Français	47.45.34	3,600	623
Grand Hotel Cravat	22.19.75	5,900	622
Italia	48.66.27	2,500	623
President	48.61.61	5,700	622
Royal	4.16.16	10,000	622
Schintgen	22.28.44	2,600	623

THE GRAND DUCHY

Gaichel-Eischen (Telephone Code 352)
Hotel-Restaurant de la Gaichel	3.91.29	4,000	631

Esch-sur-Sure (Telephone Code 352)
Beau Site	8.91.34	2,600	631

Clervaux (Telephone Code 352)
Du Parc	9.10.68	2,200	633

Vianden (Telephone Code 352)
Hotel Heintz	8.41.55	2,200	635

Echternach (Telephone Code 352)
Hotel Bel-Air	72.93.83	3,900	639

Mondorf-les Bains (Telephone Code 352)
Hotel du Grand Chef	6.81.22	3,100	640

INDEX

Aalsmeer, Holl., 15
Aalsmeer Flower Auction, 101, 166
Aalst, Belg., 14
Afsluitdijk, Holl., 116, 271, 272, 274, 279, 280–281, 290
Air travel, 31–32; *see also* transportation *under specific locations*
Alkmaar, Holl., 73, 167–168, 277
Amersfoort, Holl., 293, 304–309
  Museum Flehite, 304–305
  Nederlandse Beiaardschool, 109, 305
  Onze Lieve Vrouwetoren, 304
  restaurants, 307, 308–309
Amsterdam, Holl., 128–169
  accommodations, 129, 152–160
  Anne Frank House, 145–146
  architecture, 60–62, 63
  Begijnhof, 60, 144–145
  canals, 128, 140
  Concertgebouworkest, 74–75, 165
  emergencies, 28, 138
  entertainment and events, 129, 132, 165–166
  Floating Flower Market, 100–101, 140
  guidelines, 128–129, 132
  guideposts, 138–139
  Historisch Museum, 144
  history, 127, 133–139
  Jewish Historical Museum, 137, 140, 148–149
  Jordaan, 146–147
  Koninklijk Paleis, 142–143
  map, 130–131
  museums, 50, 53, 60, 61, 137, 140–141, 142–150, 307, 341
  Nederlands Scheepvaart Museum, 149
  Nederlands Theater Museum, 147
  Nieuwe Kerk, 143–144
  Oudekerk, 73, 111, 141–142
  personal security, 27–28, 132–133
  prices, 4–5
  Red Light District, 150
  Rembrandt House, 140, 148
  restaurants, 129, 160–164, 168–169
  Rijksmuseum, 50, 61, 140, 307, 341
  Rijksmuseum Vincent Van Gogh, 53, 140–141
  Schiphol Airport, 30, 31, 116, 132
  shopping, 30, 129, 150–152
  Stadhuis, 148
  Stedelijk Museum, 141
  Telehouse, 29
  transportation, 129, 132, 138
  walking tours, 129, 139
  Westerkerk, 146
  Willet-Holthuysen Museum, 147
  World War II, 136–137
Antwerp, Belg., 434–467
  accommodations, 436, 458–461
  architecture, 57, 58–59, 60
  carillons, 110, 464
  Carrolus Borromeo, 457
  Cogels-Oyslei, 465
  Diamond Museum, 70, 434, 455
  emergencies, 444
  entertainment and events, 436, 437, 463–465
  Grote Markt, 434, 445–446, 464
  guidelines, 434, 436–437
  guideposts, 444–445
  Handelbeurs, 457–458
  Handschoenmarkt, 447
  Hendrik Conscienceplein, 457
  history, 428, 437–443
  Koninklijk Museum voor Schone Kunsten, 434, 453–454
  map, 435
  Middelheim Open-Air Museum, 437, 464, 465
  museums, 58–59, 70, 434, 437, 445, 448, 449–455, 464, 465
  Onze Lieve Vrouwekerk, 58–59, 72, 105, 446–447
  Plantin-Moretus House, 58–59, 434, 451–453
  restaurants, 436–437, 461–463
  Rockox House, 455–456
  Rubenshuis, 434, 449–451
  St. Paul's, 458
  shopping, 436
  Sint Jacobskerk, 456–457
  Steen, 434, 448
  transportation, 434, 437, 444
  Vleeshuis, 448
  Zoo/Dierentuin, 455
Apeldoorn, Holl., 293, 300–304
  Het Loo palace, 295, 300–303
  Royal Park, 293

658 · · · INDEX

Architecture:
  Art Deco, 62–63, 407
  Art Nouveau, 62, 380, 398, 405–406, 437, 537
  Baroque, 60, 560
  Begijnhofs, 59–60
  classical, 60, 61
  Flamboyant Gothic, 427
  Gothic, 57–58, 60, 108, 195, 226, 325–326, 481, 533, 536, 539
  historical legacy, 56–63
  Mosan, 56, 557
  Museum, 550
  neo-classical, 61–62, 231–232
  Reformation, 59
  Renaissance, 58–59, 60, 173, 536, 558
  Rhine-Meuse, 56–57
  Romanesque, 536, 539, 542
  Scaldian, 57
  see also specific buildings
Ardennes region, Belg., 526, 566–587
  Abbaye Notre-Dame d'Orval, 582
  accommodations, 568, 573–574, 575–576, 581–582, 587
  castles, 567–568, 575, 578, 579–580
  gastronomique weekends, 568
  guidelines, 567–568
  hunting, 566, 576, 578
  museums, 572, 577, 578, 580
  restaurants, 568, 573, 574, 575–576, 578, 580, 581–582, 587
  shopping, 567, 572–573
  Tombeau de Geant, 581
  transportation, 567, 568
Arnhem, Holl., 293, 294–300
  accommodations, 295
  Grote Kerk, 296
  guidelines, 294–295
  Kroller-Muller Museum, 294, 295, 298–300
  Openluchtmuseum, 295, 297–298
  restaurants, 295, 303–304
  shopping, 295
  transportation, 294, 295
  World War II, 295, 296–297, 298
Art, 43–56
  Antwerp School, 447
  Baroque, 449–451
  Bruges School, 482–483
  De Stijl, 265
  Dutch, 48–52, 105, 128, 187–189, 195, 203, 220–223, 265
  Flemish, 44–48, 366, 386, 453–454, 467, 482–483
  genre, 50–51
  landscapes, 51, 173, 454
  19th century, 52–54, 454
  portraits, 49, 50, 173
  still life, 51–52
  Surrealist, 454, 483
  20th century, 54–55, 454
  see also specific museums
Artists, *see* Painters; *specific museums*
Arts, decorative, 64–70, 339, 511, 530, 531, 552, 558
Authors, 77–83

Baarle/Nassau-Baarle/Hertog, Holl., 329–330
Bastogne, Belg.:
  Battle of the Bulge, 526, 567, 582–587
  Historical Center, 585–586
  Mardasson Monument, 586
Beer, 89–92, 379, 629
Belgian Coast, 514–525
  accommodations, 516
  casinos, 515
  entertainment and events, 515
  guidelines, 514–516
  horseback shrimp fishers, 515
  museums, 519–520
  restaurants, 516
  shopping, 515
  transportation, 515, 516
Belgium, 356–587
  beer, 89–91, 379
  BTR (Belgium Tourist Reservations), 377–378
  carillons, 104–111, 497, 508, 530, 559
  castles, 526, 531, 541, 556, 557, 558–559, 564, 565, 566, 567–568, 575, 578, 579–580
  driving, 378–379
  emergencies, 23, 28; *see also* guideposts *under specific locations*
  entertainment and events, 14–16, 363–364, 377–378; *see also specific locations*
  federalism, 361–363, 385, 432
  Flemish Movement, 429–431, 502
  history, 364–374
  holidays, 377
  hotel prices, 7
  landscape, 356, 358, 427
  language frontier, 3, 27, 358–360, 362, 373–374, 375–377, 384–385, 428–433, 525–526
  map, 357
  money, 23–24

people, 358–364
pigeon racing, 364
rail travel, 378; *see also* transportation *under specific locations*
restaurants, 7; *see also specific locations*
royal family, 371, 372–373, 380, 405, 431, 518, 521
Sightseeing Line, 379, 391, 468, 497
tourist offices, 19–20, 375; *see also* guideposts *under specific locations*
weather, 12, 377
windmills, 422, 488, 517
World War I, 356, 371–372, 389–390, 433, 521–525
World War II, 372, 373, 390, 430, 431, 433, 505–506, 519, 521–522, 526, 535, 567, 582–587
Beloeil Castle, Belg., 531, 541
Benelux:
  bibliography, 641–643
  cultural legacy, 43–83
  history and overview, 1–4, 373, 390, 600–601
  lexicon, 644–648
  practical travel information, 10–42
Bergen op Zoom, Holl., 323, 324
Bicycles, 33–34, 125, 363
Binche, Belg., 14
Blankenburge, Belg., 15, 515
Blozijl, Holl., 274, 286–287
Bouillon, Belg., 567, 579–582
Bouvignes, Belg., 565
Breda, Holl., 324, 327–329
  carillon, 110, 329
Breukelen, Holl., 270
Broek-in-Waterland, Holl., 275
Brouwershaven, Holl., 322
Bruges, Belg., 467–496
  accommodations, 468, 470, 489–493
  art, 45–46, 467
  Basilique du Saint-Sang, 482, 495
  Begijnhof, 486
  Belfry, 479–480
  Burg, 480–481
  carillons, 104, 110, 111, 467, 468, 480, 495
  emergencies, 478
  entertainment and events, 14, 468, 495
  Folklore Museum, 487–488
  Groeninge Museum, 482–483
  Gruuthuse Museum, 67, 69, 483–484, 487
  guidelines, 467–468, 470–471
  guideposts, 478
  history, 471–478
  Kantcentrum, 68–69, 487, 488
  Liberty of Bruges, 481–482
  map, 469
  Markt, 479
  Memling Museum, 485
  museums, 67, 68–69, 479, 482–488
  Onze Lieve Vrouwekerk, 484–485
  organs, 72
  restaurants, 470, 493–494
  shopping, 468, 488–489
  Sint-Jans Hospitaal, 45, 485
  Sint Salvador Cathedral, 486–487
  Stadhuis, 481
  transportation, 468, 470–471, 478
Brussels, Belg., 380–425
  accommodations, 381, 409–415
  architecture, 61, 62, 380
  Art in the Metro, 394–395
  Atomium, 390, 404–405
  BALCONOP, 378
  Breugel House, 403
  Brewers Guildhall, 91
  Christmas market, 16, 422
  Comic Strip Center, 62, 364, 398
  David and Alice Van Buuren House, 407
  Eglise Notre-Dame du Grand Sablon organ, 72, 402, 421
  emergencies, 391
  entertainment and events, 75, 363–364, 378, 381, 420–422
  Erasmus House, 407–408
  European Community capital, 373, 374, 381, 385, 390, 403–404
  Galleries Saint Hubert, 397–398
  Grand-Place, 380, 392–393, 421, 422
  guidelines, 380–381, 384
  guideposts, 391–392
  history, 384–391
  L'Ilot Sacre, 394
  Mannekin Pis, 390, 393–394, 397
  map, 382–383
  Marolles district, 403
  Mini-Europe, 405
  museums, 62, 67, 69, 380, 384, 393, 394, 397–408, 422
  Ommegang, 15, 421
  Place Royale district, 398–402
  prices, 4–5
  restaurants, 381, 384, 416–420
  Royal Greenhouses, 405, 421
  Sablon district, 380, 402
  Sainte Catherine/Saint Gery district, 396–397
  shopping, 381, 397–398, 408–409

INDEX

Brussels, Belg. (*continued*)
  socio-politics, 361–362, 385, 390
  Theatre de la Monnaie, 396, 421
  Toone Puppet Theater, 363–364, 421
  Transportation, 381, 384, 391
  Victor Horta House, 405–406
  Zaventem Airport, 31–32, 384
Bulbs, 10, 14, 95–101, 119, 170, 176, 181, 183, 274
Business hours, 41

Carillons, 15, 71, 102–111
  Belgium, 104–111, 466, 467, 468, 480, 495, 497, 508, 530, 559
  five-octave, 110
  Hemeny, 105–106, 108, 111, 218, 227, 239, 249, 279, 304, 340, 497, 508, 559
  Holland, 73, 104–111, 168, 218, 227, 276
  keyboards, 104–105
  Magna Campana, 104
  Mechelen, 104–110, 466
  Nederlandse Beiaardschool, 109, 305
  Roeland, 110, 500, 508
  Royal Carillon School, 107–108, 109
  Salvator, 109
  tremolo, 106–107
  Tuning, 105–106, 107
  in U.S., 107–108
  World War II, 109–110
Cars, 34–37; *see also* transportation *under specific locations*
Casinos, 515, 517, 519, 557, 569, 573, 640
Castles:
  Belgium, 526, 531, 541, 556, 557, 558–559, 564, 565, 566, 567–568, 575, 578, 579–580
  Holland, 260, 268–269, 275, 295, 306, 327–328
  Luxembourg, 590, 628, 630–631, 632–635
Caves, 339, 341, 567, 576–577
Celles, Belg., 557, 564–565
Celtic earth forts, 628, 636
Christmas season, 16, 216, 249, 422, 626
Clervaux, Lux., 628, 632–634
Clothes, packing tips, 18
Cloth industry, 498–502, 525, 533
Coal mines, 527–528, 529
COBRA (Copenhagen, Brussels, and Amsterdam), 54
Communications, 29–30; *see also* guideposts *under specific locations*

Composers, 75–77
Consulates, embassies, 28–29
Conversion charts:
  feet/meters, 36
  liters/gallons, 36
  metric weights and measures, 36, 38
  miles/kilometers, 39
  temperature, 12, 13
Crafts, traditional, 64–70
Cruquius, Holl., 116, 170, 180
Currency exchange, 23–24
Customs regulations, 30–31

Da Haan, Belg., 515
Damme, Belg., 470, 478, 496, 517
Decorative arts, 64–70, 225–226, 339, 511, 530, 531, 552, 558
Delft, Holl., 217–231
  accommodations, 218, 229–230
  canals, 217, 218, 219, 224, 225
  carillons, 110, 218, 227
  entertainment and events, 15–16, 218
  Grote Markt, 217, 218, 227, 229
  guidelines, 217–218
  guideposts, 224–225
  Het Wapen van Savoye, 226
  history, 218–224
  museums, 225–228
  Nieuwe Kerk, 227
  Oude Kerk, 226
  Porceleyne Fles, 65, 217, 218, 228–229
  Prinsenhof, 225
  restaurants, 218, 230–231
  shopping, 217, 224, 228–229
  transportation, 217, 218, 224
Delftware, 64–66, 217, 220–221, 228–229
Delta Project, 116–117, 119, 310, 311, 312, 319–321
Denijn, Jef, 106, 107
De Panne, Belg., 521–522
Deventer, Holl., 303
Diamond cutting, 69–70
Diekirch, Lux., 636–637
Dikes, 113, 116, 119, 180, 250, 254, 271, 272, 274, 275, 276, 279, 280–281, 290, 307, 311–312
Dinant, Belg., 556, 557, 558, 562–564
Disabled travelers, 21
Documents, 21–22
Dordrecht, Holl., 233, 247
  carillons, 110
Dreischor, Holl., 322

Drink, 89–94
  beer, 89–92, 379, 629

wine, 92–94, 639
Driving, 34–37; *see also* transportation *under specific locations*
Durbuy, Belg., 575–576
Duty free shopping, 30

Easter, 10, 14, 20, 109
Echternach, Lux., 638–639
 Dancing Procession, 629, 639
 School of Book Illumination, 638
Edam, Holl., 274, 276–277
Eindhoven, Holl., 323, 324
Eisch River Valley, Lux., 590, 630–631
Elburg, Holl., 274, 289–290
Electric current, 39
Embassies, consulates, 28–29
Emergencies, 23, 28; *see also specific locations*
Enkhuizen, Holl., 274, 275, 278–280
 Zuiderzee Museum, 273, 278–279
Esch-sur-Sure, Lux., 631
Etiquette, 41–42
Eupen, Belg., 14, 16
European Community (EC), 2, 4, 362, 373, 374, 375, 385, 390–391, 601–602, 610, 614
European School, 602
European Study and Research Centre Robert Schuman, 592–593, 602

Ferries, 33
Festivals, 14–16; *see also* entertainment and events *under specific locations*
Film, 26
Flanders region, Belg., 356, 426–524
 history, 427–433
 "In Flanders Fields," 522–523
 socio-politics, 361–362, 385, 390
Flevoland province, Holl., 274, 290–291
Flowers, *see* Bulbs
Food, 84–88
 Indonesian, 87–88, 196
 see also restaurants *under specific locations*
Franeker, Holl., 274, 282–283
Freyr, Belg., 566
Friesland province, Holl., 270–272, 274

Ghent, Belg., 496–415
 accommodations, 497, 511–512
 architecture, 57, 496
 Belfry, 496, 500, 508
 Castle of the Counts, 496, 498, 502, 503, 506–507
 Cloth Hall, 500, 508
 entertainment and events, 497
 Graslei, 496, 498, 507
 guidelines, 496–498
 guideposts, 503
 history, 498–503
 Korenlei, 496, 498, 507
 museums, 505–506, 510–511
 restaurants, 498, 512–514
 St. Bavo's Cathedral, 45, 496, 497, 504–506
 shopping, 497
 Sint Niklaaskerk, 509
 Stadhuis, 508–509
 transportation, 497, 498, 503
 University, 429–430, 502
 Vrijdagmarkt, 509–510
Giethoorn, Holl., 274, 285–286
Glossary, 644–648
Goes, Holl., 312, 313, 319
Gouda, Holl., 248–257
 accommodations, 248–249
 cheese market, 250
 Christmas candlelight ceremony, 16, 249
 entertainment and events, 249
 Grote Markt, 248, 251
 guidelines, 248–250
 guideposts, 250–251
 Het Catherina Gasthuis, 250, 252
 history, 250
 De Moriann, 253
 museums, 248, 251–253
 restaurants, 249
 shopping, 248, 253–254
 St. Janskerk, 251–252
 Stadhuis, 252–253
 transportation, 248, 249, 250
 Waag, 249, 253
Groningen, Holl., 73, 271

Haarlem, Holl., 169–181
 accommodations, 178
 architecture, 60
 bulbs, 98, 170, 181
 Corrie ten Boom Huis, 177–178
 Frans Hals Museum, 50, 169, 170, 173, 175–176
 Grote Markt, 169, 171, 173, 175
 guidelines, 169–170
 guideposts, 174
 history, 170–174
 restaurants, 178–179
 shopping, 169
 St. Bavokerk, 72–73, 169, 170, 171, 173, 175, 176–177
 Teylers Museum, 177

Haarlemmermeer, Holl., 116, 170, 180
Haastrecht, Holl., 249
Hague, The, Holl., 195–216
  accommodations, 196, 211–214
  architecture, 61
  Binnenhof, 204
  emergencies, 203
  entertainment and events, 198
  Gemeentemuseum, 54, 62, 195, 208
  Gevangenpoort, 205
  Grote Kerk, 206
  guidelines, 195–196, 198
  guideposts, 202–203
  Historical Museum, 204–205
  history, 198–202
  Lange Voorhout, 204
  Madurodam, 208–209
  map, 197
  Mauritshuis, 49, 61, 195, 203–204, 228
  Mesdag Museum, 53, 206–207
  Museon, 208
  museums, 195, 203–209
  Noordeinde palace garden, 206
  Panorama Mesday, 206–207
  Peace palace, 195, 201, 207–208
  Prinsjesdag, 15
  restaurants, 196, 214–216
  Schilderijenzall, 205–206
  shopping, 196
  transportation, 196
Hamm, Lux., American Cemetery and Memorial, 608, 610, 626–627
Han-sur-Lesse, Belg., 567, 576–577
  Museum of the Underground World, 577
Harderwijk, Holl., 290
Harlingen, Holl., 281
Hasselt, Belg., Bokrijk open-air museum, 427
Health tips, 22–23
Heerlen, Holl., 332
Hemeny brothers, 105–106, 108, 111
Herring season, 14–15, 85
Het Zoute, Belg., 517–518
Heusden, Holl., 326–327
Hiking, 590
Hillegom, Holl., bulb season, 98
Hindeloopen, Holl., 273, 274, 284
Hoge Veluwe National Park, Holl., 53, 293, 294, 295, 298–299
Holland, 112–355
  art, 48–52, 105, 128, 187–189, 195, 203, 220–223, 265
  beer, 91–92
  bicycles, 125
  carillons, 73, 104–111, 168, 218, 227, 276
  castles, 260, 268–269, 275, 295, 306, 327–328
  driving, 125
  Elfstedentocht, 16
  entertainment and events, 14–16, 100, 216
  GWK *(Grenswisselkantoren)*, 24, 25
  health service, 22–23
  history, 119–122, 127
  holidays, 122–123
  hotel prices, 7
  hydro-engineering, 116–117, 119, 170, 310, 311, 312, 319–321
  Informatiecentrum Nieuw Land, 116, 272–273, 290–291
  landscape, 112–113, 116–117
  Leisure Card, 123
  map, 114–115
  money, 23–25
  National Strip Card, 124
  NRC (Netherlands Reservation Center), 123–124
  people, 117–119
  Queen's Birthday, 14, 97–98, 122, 129, 132, 216
  rail travel, 124; *see also* transportation *under specific locations*
  restaurants, 7; *see also specific locations*
  royal family, 121–122, 125–126, 216, 301
  skating, 16
  spirits, 94
  Tourist Menu program, 25
  tourist offices, 19–20, 122, 295–296; *see also* guideposts *under specific locations*
  transportation, 295–296; *see also specific locations*
  VVV (tourist offices), 19–20, 122, 295–296; *see also* guideposts *under specific locations*
  walking tours, 125
  weather, 12, 123
  windmills, 113, 116, 119, 180, 233, 247, 254, 288, 307
Holland, Central, 293–309
Holland, Northern, 270–293
Holland, Southern, 293, 309–347
Hoorn, Holl., 274, 277–278
  West Fries Museum, 273, 278
Hotels, 7–8, 25; *see also* accommoda-

INDEX · · · 663

tions *under specific locations*
Hunting, 566, 567, 578
Huy, Belg., 556, 557, 559

IJmuiden, Holl., 180–181
IJsselmeer, Holl., 116, 137, 272, 275, 279
Illuminated building facades, *see* Nightseeing
Indonesian food, 87–88, 196
Insurance, medical, 22–23
International Student Identity Card, 20–21

Kampen, Holl., 274, 288–289
Kasteel De Haar, Holl., 268–269
Kasteel Huis Doorn, Holl., 306
Kennemerduinen National Park, Holl., 170
Kinderdijk, Holl., 233, 247
Knokke-Heist, Belg., 515, 516–517

Lace, 68–69, 487, 488
Language:
  Belgium's "language frontier," 3, 27, 358–360, 362, 373–374, 375–377, 384–385, 428–433, 525–526
  Benelux lexicon and notes, 644–648
  Dutch, 2, 26, 27, 77, 78, 358, 359, 377, 385, 427, 428, 430, 432–433
  English, 3, 26–27, 77, 358, 375, 376–377, 592
  Flemish, 3, 27, 77, 359, 362, 376–377, 428, 429–430, 41
  French, 3, 26, 27, 77, 78, 358, 359, 362, 376–377, 385, 428–429, 431–433, 592
  Frisian, 78
  German, 26, 27, 77, 78, 358, 377, 592
  Letzebuergesch, 26, 27, 77–78, 603
  Walloon, 544
Leeuwarden, Holl., 282–283
Leiden, Holl., 182–195
  accommodations, 193–194
  bulb season, 98, 183
  emergencies, 190
  Groenpoort, 186
  guidelines, 182–183
  guideposts, 190–191
  history, 183–190
  museums, 191–193
  restaurants, 194–195
  shopping, 182, 191
  Thanksgiving Day Service, 16, 182, 187
Lelystad, Holl., Informatiecentrum Nieuw Land, 116, 272–273, 290–291
Leuven, Belg., *see* Louvain, Belg.

Liege, Belg., 526, 541–546
  accommodations, 543, 554–555
  churches, 551, 553–554
  entertainment and events, 543
  guidelines, 541–544
  guideposts, 549
  history, 544–549
  mansion-museums, 541, 542, 544, 549–554
  Museum of Walloon Life, 541–542, 544, 551–552
  Prince-Bishops Palace, 541, 549
  restaurants, 543, 555–556
  shopping, 542
  transportation, 543–544, 549
Limburg province, Holl., 309, 331–347
Limmen, Holl., Hortus Bulborum, 100
Liqueurs, 94
Lisse, Holl.:
  Keukenhof garden, 14, 98–99, 169, 170
  Museum voor de Bloemboolenstreek, 98
Literature, 77–83, 292, 407–408, 547–548
Little Switzerland region, Lux., 590, 637–638
Loenen, Holl., 270
Lombaert, Aime, 110, 111, 480, 495
Louvain, Belg.:
  carillons, 110
  University, 432–433
Luxembourg, Grand Duchy of, 588–643
  Battle of the Bulge, 600, 610, 626–627, 631, 633, 636–637
  beer, 92, 629
  castles, 590, 628, 630–631, 632–635
  driving, 604–605, 628
  emergencies, 23, 28
  entertainment and events, 14–16, 603
  grand ducal family, 598, 605–606
  history, 593–602
  holidays, 603
  hotel prices, 7
  landscape, 588, 590–591
  language, 592, 603
  map, 589
  money, 23–24
  people, 591–593
  tourist offices, 19–20, 602
  transportation, 604
  VAT, 605, 621
  weather, 12, 602–603
  wine, 92–94, 639
  wine festivals, 15, 93, 629
  World War II, 598–600, 610, 614, 626–627, 631, 633, 636–637

Luxembourg, Grand Duchy of (*cont.*)
  see also Luxembourg City, Lux.; Luxembourg Grand Tour
Luxembourg City, Lux., 607–628
  accommodations, 610, 621–623
  architecture, 57
  Bock Casemates, 612–613, 616–617
  Cathedrale Notre-Dame, 618–619
  Christmas market, 16, 626
  emergencies, 615
  entertainment and events, 15, 608, 626
  Findel Airport, 32, 610
  Gella Fra, 618
  guidelines, 607–609, 610–611
  guideposts, 614–615
  history, 611–614
  map, 609
  Model, 620
  museums, 615–621
  Place d'Armes, 619–620
  restaurants, 610, 624–625
  St. Michel's church organ, 72
  shopping, 608, 621
  transportation, 607–608, 610, 615
Luxembourg Grand Tour, 628–640
  accommodations, 629–630, 631, 633–634, 635–636, 639, 640
  castles, 628, 630–631, 632–635
  driving, 628, 630
  entertainment and events, 629, 631–632
  museums, 631, 633, 635, 636–637, 638
  photography, Family of Man exhibit, 628, 632–633
  restaurants, 630, 631, 633–634, 635–636, 639, 640
  route, 630
  shopping, 629
  transportation, 628–629
  Valley of the Seven Castles, 590, 630–631

Maastricht, Holl., 14, 332–347
  accommodations, 334, 342–343, 346
  entertainment and events, 333
  guidelines, 332–334
  guideposts, 337–338
  history, 335–337
  museums, 339–341
  Onze Lieve Vrouwekerk, 56, 341
  restaurants, 334, 343–345, 346
  St. Pietersberg caves, 339, 341
Makkum, Holl., 274
  Royal Makkum Delftware, 66, 273, 281, 283
Malmedy, Belg., 14

Maps:
  Amsterdam, 130–131
  Antwerp, 435
  Belgium, 357
  Belgium's "language frontier," 359
  Benelux, vi–vii
  Bruges, 469
  Brussels, 382–383
  The Hague, 197
  Holland, 114–115
  Luxembourg, 589
  Luxembourg City, 609
Margraten, Holl., U.S. military cemetery, 334, 345
Marken, Holl., 274, 276
Mechelen, Belg., 437, 466–467
  Royal Carillon School, 107–108, 109
  Royal Manufacturers of Tapestry Gaspard de Wit Ltd, 67–68, 467
  St. Rombout's carillons, 104–110, 466
Menu, use of term, 25
Metric weights and measures, 36, 38–39
Meuse, River, 526, 542, 547
Meuse Valley, Belg., 526, 552, 556–566
  accommodations, 557, 561, 565–566
  Annevoie gardens, 556, 562
  castles, 556, 557, 558–559, 564, 565, 566
  entertainment and events, 557, 561
  gardens, 556, 558, 562, 566
  guidelines, 557
  Jehay Castle, 556, 558–559
  museums, 557, 559, 560, 561
  restaurants, 557–558, 559, 561, 564, 565
  shopping, 557
  transportation, 557, 561
Middelburg, Holl., 312, 313, 314–316
  Lange Jan, 314
  Roosevelt Study Center, 315
  Stadhuis, 314–315
  Zeeland Museum, 315–316
Mondorf-les-Bains, Lux., 639–640
Money, 23–25
Monnickendam, Holl., 274, 276
Moselle River Valley, Lux., 590, 639
Muiden, Holl., 275, 292–293
Museums, 38; *see also specific locations*
Music, 71–77; *see also* entertainment and events *under specific locations*

Naarden, Holl., 275, 292
Namur, Belg., 556, 557, 560–561
Netherlands, *see* Holland
Neunen, Holl., 330–331

INDEX · · · 665

Van Gogh Documentation Center, 330–331
News, newspapers, 41
Nightseeing, 15, 37–38, 381, 396, 421, 468, 498, 503, 530, 560, 567, 568, 608, 631
North Brabant province, Holl., 309, 322–331
  guidelines, 323–324
  history, 322–323
  Noord Brabant Museum, 326

Oirschot, Holl., 323
Oosterbeck, Holl., Airborne Museum, 295, 298
Organs, 71–73, 169, 216, 249, 264, 497
Ostend, Belg., 514, 518–520
  casino, 515, 519
  James Ensorhuis, 519–520
  shopping, 515
Otterlo, Holl., Kroller-Muller Museum, 53, 62, 238
Oudenaard, Belg., carillons, 105
Oudewater, Holl., 250, 254–257
  Heksenwaag and Museum, 256

Packing tips, 17, 18–19
Painters:
  Belgian, 54–55, 380, 538
  Dutch, 44–54, 140–141, 221–223, 227, 238–239, 299, 330–331, 380, 527–528
  Flemish, 44–48, 366, 380, 386, 453–454, 467, 482–483, 504, 533, 538
  French, 538
  Luxembourg, 55, 621
  see also specific locations and museums
Parking, 37; *see also* guideposts *under specific locations*
Passports, 21–22, 24
Petange, Lux., 599–600
Photography exhibits, 141, 628, 632–633
Polder province, Holl., 272–293
  accommodations, 274, 279–280
  entertainment and events, 273–274
  guidelines, 273–274
  restaurants, 274, 280
  shopping, 273
  transportation, 273
Polders, 116, 137, 254, 290–291, 427
Prices, 4–5, 6–7
PTT (post, telefoon, telegraff), 29; *see also* guideposts *under specific locations*

Rail travel, 32–33; *see also* transportation *under specific locations*
Randstad region, Holl., 126–270, 293
Redu, Belg., 567
Restaurants, 7, 25; *see also* Food; restaurants *under specific locations*
Road signs, 35
Rock climbing, 557, 566
Roman baths, 332, 339, 569
Roman mosaics, 628, 637
Rotterdam, Holl., 231–248
  accommodations, 243–245
  Boymans-van Beuningen Museum, 238–239
  Delfshaven, 239–240
  emergencies, 237
  entertainment and events, 233
  Euromast & Spacetower, 242
  guidelines, 231–233
  guideposts, 237
  Havenroute, 247–248
  Historical Museum, 240, 242–243
  history, 234–237
  Kijk-Kubus, 241
  museums, 231, 238–243
  Oudehaven, 63
  Oude Kerk, 239
  Prins Hendrik Maritime Museum, 240
  restaurants, 232, 245–246
  St. Laurenskerk, 73, 240–241
  Schielandshuis Museum of History, 242–243
  shopping, 232
  Spido Cruises, 233, 237, 248
  transportation, 232, 233, 237
  World War II, 63, 73, 234–235, 241
  Zestienhoven Airport, 233

Saint-Hubert, Belg., 578
Sandweiler, Lux., German Cemetery, 627–628
Scheldt, River, 434, 442, 447–448, 502, 529, 532–533, 538
Scheveningen, Holl., 14, 196, 202, 209–210, 212–214, 216
Schoonhoven, Holl., 250
  Nederlands Goud, Zilver, en Klokkenmuseum, 257
Seasons, 10–11, 14–16
Security, personal, 27–28, 132–133, 420
Senior citizens, 20
's Hertogenbosch, Holl., 325–326
Shopping:
  duty free, 30
  hours, 41

666 · · · INDEX

Shopping (*continued*)
  see also specific locations
St.-Idesbald, Belg., Paul Delvaux Museum, 520
Sittard, Holl., 332
Sloten, Holl., 274, 285
Slot Zuylen, Holl., 268
Sluis, Holl., 312
Smoking, 40
Spa, Belg., 526, 567, 569–574
  Musee de la Ville d'Eau, 572
Spaarndam, Holl., 179–181
Spakenburg, Holl., 305, 307–308
  Museum 't Vurhuus, 308
Spinning jenny, 502
Staphorst, Holl., 274, 287
Stavoren, Holl., 284–285
Steel industry, 590, 597, 600
Students, 20–21

Tapestries, 66–68, 306, 315, 340, 487, 538, 558, 635
Temperature, conversion chart, 12–13
The Hague, Holl., *see* Hague, The, Holl.
Tholen, Holl., 312
Thorn, Holl., 332
Time, 13
Tipping, 40
Toilets, public, 40
Tourist offices, 19–20; *see also* guideposts *under specific locations*
Tournai, Belg., 526, 529–541
  accommodations, 530, 539–540
  architecture, 57, 62, 526, 529, 536
  Belfry, 529, 530, 535, 537
  blue stone, 532, 533, 539
  burgher houses, 529
  Cathedral of Notre Dame, 57, 529, 530, 533, 535, 536–537
  entertainment and events, 530, 534
  guidelines, 529–531
  guideposts, 535
  history, 531–535
  Museums, 62, 67, 534, 535, 538–539
  Pont des Trous, 538
  restaurants, 530–531, 540
  shopping, 530
  Tapestry Museum, 66–67, 538
  Tour Henry VIII, 539
  transportation, 530, 531
Transportation, 31–37, 97–99; *see also specific locations*
Tulips, *see* Bulbs

Urk, Holl., 274, 287–288
Utrecht, Holl., 258–270, 293
  accommodations, 259, 266
  Centraal Museum, 265
  Dom, 258, 261, 263–264
  entertainment and events, 259
  guidelines, 258–259
  guideposts, 262
  Het Catharijneconvent, 265
  history, 260–262
  museums, 259, 263–266
  Oudegracht, 259, 262, 267
  restaurants, 267–268
  Rietveld-Schroderhuis, 265
  shopping, 258–259
  transportation, 258, 259, 262, 265
  Van Speelklok tot Pierement, 264

Valkenburg, Holl., 332
VAT (value-added tax), 25, 40, 605, 621
Vecht, River, 269–270
Veere, Holl., 312, 317–318
Vianden, Lux., 628, 634–635
  Barrage de Lohmole, 635
  Castle, 635
  Victor Hugo House, 635
Vlissingen, Holl., 312, 313, 314

Wallonia region, Belg., 356, 358, 525–587
  Grand Hornu, 528–529
  Pays Noir, 527–528, 529
  socio-politics, 361–362, 385, 390
Warner, Sally Slade, 107–108, 110
Wasmes, Belg., 527–528
Waterloo, Belg., 384, 388–389, 421, 422–426
WCs (water closets), 40
Weather, 11–13
Wepion, Belg., 558
Wijk bij Duurstede, Holl., 306
Windmills:
  Belgium, 422, 488, 517
  Holland, 113, 116, 119, 180, 233, 247, 254, 288, 307
Wine, 92–94, 639
Witch hunts, 254–256
Workum, Holl., 283
World War I:
  Belgium, 356, 371–372, 389–390, 433, 521–525
  British war cemetery, 524
  German military cemetery, 524
  Last Post, 525

World War II:
- American Cemetery and Memorial, 608, 610, 626–627
- Amsterdam strike, 136–137
- Battle of the Bulge, 526, 567, 582–587, 600, 610, 626–627, 631, 633, 636–637
- Belgium, 372, 373, 390, 430, 431, 433, 505–506, 519, 521–522, 526, 535, 567, 582–587
- bomb damage, 63, 73, 234–235, 241, 311–312, 314, 433, 535
- carillons, 109–110
- German Cemetery, 627–628
- Holland, 121–122, 136–137, 234–235, 241, 295, 296–297, 298, 311–312, 314
- Luxembourg, 598–600, 610, 614, 626–627, 631, 633, 636–637
- Market-Garden operation, Arnhem, 295, 296–297, 298
- Nazi art acquisitions, 239, 505–506
- U.S. military cemetery, 334, 345

Writers, 77–83, 292, 407–408, 547–548

Ypres, Belg.:
- Cloth Hall, 523–524, 525
- World War I, 521–525

Zaandam, Holl., 73
Zaanse Schans, Holl., 167
Zandvoort, Holl., 181
Zeeland province, Holl., 309, 310–322
- accommodations, 313
- entertainment and events, 313
- guidelines, 312–314
- history, 310–312
- restaurants, 313
- shopping, 313
- transportation, 312, 313, 314
Zierikzee, Holl., 312, 313, 321–322
Zuiderzee, Holl., 116, 137, 271, 272–293; *see also* Polder province, Holl.
Zutphen, Holl., 303
Zwolle, Holl., 289